The
Carolina Reader

2010 Edition

Edited by Lee Bauknight with Kevin Trumpeter

FOUNTAINHEAD
PRESS

As a textbook publisher, we are faced with enormous environmental issues due the large amount of paper contained in our print products. Since our inception in 2002, we have worked diligently to be as eco-friendly as possible.

Our "green" initiatives include:

Electronic Products
We deliver products in non-paper form whenever possible. This includes pdf downloadables, flash drives, & CD's.

Electronic Samples
We use a new electronic sampling system, called Xample. Instructor samples are sent via a personalized web page that links to pdf downloads.

FSC Certified Printers
All of our Printers are certified by the Forest Service Council which promotes environmentally and socially responsible management of the world's forests. This program allows consumer groups, individual consumers and businesses to work together hand in hand to promote responsible use of the world's forests as a renewable and sustainable resource.

Recycled Paper
Almost all of our products are printed on a minimum of 10-30% post consumer waste recycled paper.

Support of Green Causes
When we do print, we donate a portion of our revenue to Green causes. Listed below are a few of the organizations that have received donations from Fountainhead Press. We welcome your feedback and suggestions for contributions, as we are always searching for worthy initiatives.
Rainforest 2 Reef
Environmental Working Group

Cover design: Doris Bruey
Book designer: Ellie Moore

Copyright © 2010

For information, please call or write:
    1-800-586-0330
    Fountainhead Press
    Southlake, TX 76092

Web site: www.fountainheadpress.com
E-mail: customerservice@fountainheadpress.com

First Edition

ISBN: 978-1-59871-240-7

Printed in the United States of America

Contents

CHAPTER

1 | Intellect and Imagination

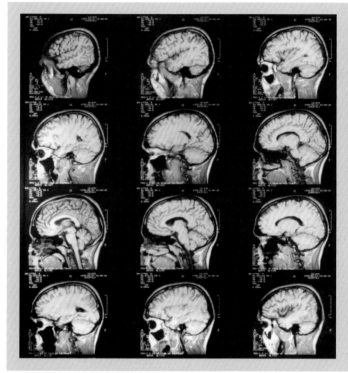

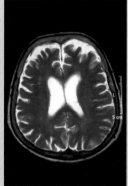

IMAGE 1.1
At left, a magnetic tomography of a human head.

IMAGE 1.2
Above, a computer enhanced MRI of a human brain.

Are you ready for the intelligence-augmented 'You+' that futurist Jamais Cascio argues is already in the works? Or are you more comfortable with 'Classic You,' the You born of Plato's cave and nurtured on education and knowledge, creativity and imagination? Whatever your response, the readings in this chapter will challenge you to think in new ways about how we perceive, imagine, experience, and make sense of the world.

> *Plato, one of the monumental figures in Western thought and philosophy, lived and taught in ancient Greece from about 427–428 B.C. to 347 B.C. In "The Allegory of the Cave" from Book VII of* The Republic, *Plato uses an imaginary dialogue between Socrates (the teacher) and Glaucon (the student) to expound on the nature of perception and reality; on knowledge and truth; on teaching and learning; and on the philosopher's place in society.*

THE ALLEGORY OF THE CAVE Plato

And now, I said, let me show in a figure how far our nature is enlightened or unenlightened:— Behold! human beings living in an underground den, which has a mouth open towards the light and reaching all along the den; here they have been from their childhood, and have their legs and necks chained so that they cannot move, and can only see before them, being prevented by the chains from turning round their heads. Above and behind them a fire is blazing at a distance, and between the fire and the prisoners there is a raised way; and you will see, if you look, a low wall built along the way, like the screen which marionette players have in front of them, over which they show the puppets.

I see.

And do you see, I said, men passing along the wall carrying all sorts of vessels, and statues and figures of animals made of wood and stone and various materials, which appear over the wall? Some of them are talking, others silent.

You have shown me a strange image, and they are strange prisoners.

Like ourselves, I replied; and they see only their own shadows, or the shadows of one another, which the fire throws on the opposite wall of the cave?

True, he said; how could they see anything but the shadows if they were never allowed to move their heads?

And of the objects which are being carried in like manner they would only see the shadows?

Yes, he said.

And if they were able to converse with one another, would they not suppose that they were naming what was actually before them?

Very true.

And suppose further that the prison had an echo which came from the other side, would they not be sure to fancy when one of the passers-by spoke that the voice which they heard came from the passing shadow?

No question, he replied.

To them, I said, the truth would be literally nothing but the shadows of the images.

That is certain.

And now look again, and see what will naturally follow if the prisoners are released and disabused of their error. At first, when any of them is liberated and compelled suddenly to stand up and turn his neck round and walk and look towards the light, he will suffer sharp pains; the glare will distress him, and he will be unable to see the realities of which in his former state he had seen the shadows; and then conceive some one saying to him, that what he saw before was an illusion, but that now, when he is approaching nearer to being and his eye is turned towards more real existence, he has a clearer vision,—what will be his reply? And you may further imagine that his instructor is pointing to the objects as they pass and requiring him to name them,—will he not be perplexed? Will he not fancy that the shadows which he formerly saw are truer than the objects which are now shown to him?

Far truer.

And if he is compelled to look straight at the light, will he not have a pain in his eyes which will make him turn away and take in the objects of vision which he can see, and which he will conceive to be in reality clearer than the things which are now being shown to him?

True, he said.

And suppose once more, that he is reluctantly dragged up a steep and rugged ascent, and held fast until he's forced into the presence of the sun himself, is he not likely to be pained and irritated? When he approaches the light his eyes will be dazzled, and he will not be able to see anything at all of what are now called realities.

Not all in a moment, he said.

He will require to grow accustomed to the sight of the upper world. And first he will see the shadows best, next the reflections of men and other objects in the water, and then the objects themselves; then he will gaze upon the light of the moon and the stars and the spangled heaven; and he will see the sky and the stars by night better than the sun or the light of the sun by day?

Certainly.

Last of all he will be able to see the sun, and not mere reflections of him in the water, but he will see him in his own proper place, and not in another; and he will contemplate him as he is.

Certainly.

He will then proceed to argue that this is he who gives the seasons and the years, and is the guardian of all that is in the visible world, and in a certain way the cause of all things which he and his fellows have been accustomed to behold?

Clearly, he said, he would first see the sun and then reason about him.

And when he remembered his old habitation, and the wisdom of the den and his fellow-prisoners, do you not suppose that he would felicitate himself on the change, and pity them?

Certainly, he would.

And if they were in the habit of conferring honours among themselves on those who were quickest to observe the passing shadows and to remark which of them went before, and which followed after, and which were together; and who were therefore best able to draw conclusions as to the future, do you think that he would care for such honours and glories, or envy the possessors of them? Would he not say with Homer,

'Better to be the poor servant of a poor master,'
and to endure anything, rather than think as they do and live after their manner?

Yes, he said, I think that he would rather suffer anything than entertain these false notions and live in this miserable manner.

Imagine once more, I said, such a one coming suddenly out of the sun to be replaced in his old situation; would he not be certain to have his eyes full of darkness?

To be sure, he said.

And if there were a contest, and he had to compete in measuring the shadows with the prisoners who had never moved out of the den, while his sight was still weak, and before his eyes had become steady (and the time which would be needed to acquire this new habit of sight might be very considerable) would he not be ridiculous? Men would say of him that up he went and down he came without his eyes; and that it was better not even to think of ascending; and if any one tried to loose another and lead him up to the light, let them only catch the offender, and they would put him to death.

No question, he said.

This entire allegory, I said, you may now append, dear Glaucon, to the previous argument; the prison-house is the world of sight, the light of the fire is the sun, and you will not misapprehend me if you interpret the journey upwards to be the ascent of the soul into the intellectual world according to my poor belief, which, at your desire, I have expressed—whether rightly or wrongly God knows. But, whether true or false, my opinion is that in the world of knowledge the idea of good appears last of all, and is seen only with an effort; and, when seen, is also inferred to be the universal author of all things beautiful and right, parent of light and of the lord of light in this visible world, and the immediate source of reason and truth in the intellectual; and that this is the power upon which he who would act rationally, either in public or private life, must have his eye fixed.

I agree, he said, as far as I am able to understand you.

Moreover, I said, you must not wonder that those who attain to this beatific vision are unwilling to descend to human affairs; for their souls are ever hastening into the upper world where they desire to dwell; which desire of theirs is very natural, if our allegory may be trusted.

Yes, very natural.

And is there anything surprising in one who passes from divine contemplations to the evil state of man, misbehaving himself in a ridiculous manner; if, while his eyes are blinking and before he has become accustomed to the surrounding darkness, he is compelled to fight in courts of law, or in other places, about the images or the shadows of images of justice, and is endeavouring to meet the conceptions of those who have never yet seen absolute justice?

Anything but surprising, he replied.

Any one who has common sense will remember that the bewilderments of the eyes are of two kinds, and arise from two causes, either from coming out of the light or from going into the light, which is true of the mind's eye, quite as much as of the bodily eye; and he who remembers this when he sees any one whose vision is perplexed and weak, will not be too ready to laugh; he will first ask whether that soul of man has come out of the brighter light, and is unable to see because unaccustomed to the dark, or having turned from darkness to the day is dazzled by excess of light. And he will count the one happy in his condition and state of being, and he will pity the other; or, if he have a mind to laugh at the soul which comes from below into the light, there will be more reason in this than in the laugh which greets him who returns from above out of the light into the den.

That, he said, is a very just distinction.

But then, if I am right, certain professors of education must be wrong when they say that they can put a knowledge into the soul which was not there before, like sight into blind eyes.

They undoubtedly say this, he replied.

Whereas, our argument shows that the power and capacity of learning exists in the soul already; and that just as the eye was unable to turn from darkness to light without the whole body, so too the instrument of knowledge can only by the movement of the whole soul be turned from the world of becoming into that of being, and learn by degrees to endure the sight of being, and of the brightest and best of being, or in other words, of the good.

Very true.

And must there not be some art which will effect conversion in the easiest and quickest manner; not implanting the faculty of sight, for that exists already, but has been turned in the wrong direction, and is looking away from the truth?

Yes, he said, such an art may be presumed.

And whereas the other so-called virtues of the soul seem to be akin to bodily qualities, for even when they are not originally innate they can be implanted later by habit and exercise, the virtue of wisdom more than anything else contains a divine element which always remains, and by this conversion is rendered useful and profitable; or, on the other hand, hurtful and useless. Did you never observe the narrow intelligence flashing from the keen eye of a clever rogue—how eager he is, how clearly his paltry soul sees the way to his end; he is the reverse of blind, but his keen eyesight is forced into the service of evil, and he is mischievous in proportion to his cleverness.

Very true, he said.

But what if there had been a circumcision of such natures in the days of their youth; and they had been severed from those sensual pleasures, such as eating and drinking, which, like leaden weights, were attached to them at their birth, and which drag them down and turn the vision of their souls upon the things that are below—if, I say, they had been released from these impediments and turned in the opposite direction, the very same faculty in them would have seen the truth as keenly as they see what their eyes are turned to now.

Very likely.

Yes, I said; and there is another thing which is likely, or rather a necessary inference from what has preceded, that neither the uneducated and uninformed of the truth, nor yet those who never make an end of their education, will be able ministers of State; not the former, because they have no single aim of duty which is the rule of all their actions, private as well as public; nor the latter, because they will not act at all except upon compulsion, fancying that they are already dwelling apart in the islands of the blest.

Very true, he replied.

Then, I said, the business of us who are the founders of the State will be to compel the best minds to attain that knowledge which we have already shown to be the greatest of all—they must continue to ascend until they arrive at the good; but when they have ascended and seen enough we must not allow them to do as they do now.

What do you mean?

I mean that they remain in the upper world: but this must not be allowed; they must be made to descend again among the prisoners in the den, and partake of their labours and honours, whether they are worth having or not.

But is not this unjust? he said; ought we to give them a worse life, when they might have a better?

You have again forgotten, my friend, I said, the intention of the legislator, who did not aim at making any one class in the State happy above the rest; the happiness was to be in the whole State, and he held the citizens together by persuasion and necessity, making them benefactors of the State, and therefore benefactors of one another; to this end he created them, not to please themselves, but to be his instruments in binding up the State.

True, he said, I had forgotten.

Observe, Glaucon, that there will be no injustice in compelling our philosophers to have a care and providence of others; we shall explain to them that in other States, men of their class are not obliged to share in the toils of politics: and this is reasonable, for they grow up at their own sweet will, and the government would rather not have them. Being self-taught, they cannot be expected to show any gratitude for a culture which they have never received. But we have brought you into the world to be rulers of the hive, kings of yourselves and of the other citizens, and have educated you far better and more perfectly than they have been educated, and you are better able to share in the double duty. Wherefore each of you, when his turn comes, must go down to the general underground abode, and get the habit of seeing in the dark. When you have acquired the habit, you will see ten thousand times better than the inhabitants of the den, and you will know what the several images are, and what they represent, because you have seen the beautiful and just and good in their truth. And thus our State which is also yours will be a reality, and not a dream only, and will be administered in a spirit unlike that of other States, in which men fight with one another about shadows only and are distracted in the struggle for power, which in their eyes is a great good. Whereas the truth is that the State in which the rulers are most reluctant to govern is always the best and most quietly governed, and the State in which they are most eager, the worst.

Quite true, he replied.

And will our pupils, when they hear this, refuse to take their turn at the toils of State, when they are allowed to spend the greater part of their time with one another in the heavenly light?

Impossible, he answered; for they are just men, and the commands which we impose upon them are just; there can be no doubt that every one of them will take office as a stern necessity, and not after the fashion of our present rulers of State.

Yes, my friend, I said; and there lies the point. You must contrive for your future rulers another and a better life than that of a ruler, and then you may have a well-ordered State; for only in the State which offers this, will they rule who are truly rich, not in silver and gold, but in virtue and wisdom, which are the true blessings of life. Whereas if they go to the administration of public affairs, poor and hungering after their own private advantage, thinking that hence they are to snatch the chief good, order there can never be; for they will be fighting about office, and the civil and domestic broils which thus arise will be the ruin of the rulers themselves and of the whole State.

Most true, he replied.

And the only life which looks down upon the life of political ambition is that of true philosophy. Do you know of any other?

Indeed, I do not, he said.

■ READING AND WRITING

1. Draw the den that Plato describes, its inhabitants, and light source. What does this help you understand about "The Allegory of the Cave"?
2. What are the central points that Plato makes about perception, knowledge, and learning in the "Allegory"?
3. The speaker in this piece is Socrates, and he argues that a liberated prisoner must return to the den after becoming enlightened. Why, according to Socrates, is this difficult? Why is it important?
4. Plato seems to think that only a few individuals can ever leave the cave and become enlightened by understanding the Beautiful, Just, and Good. Has our thinking about this changed since the 4th century B.C.?

■ DEVELOPING LONGER RESPONSES

5. Pretend you are a lawyer tasked with defending Plato's argument that most of us experience life as series of shadows cast on a cave wall. How would you go about making your case? What evidence might you use to prove it?

© AP Photos.

IMAGE 1.3

Examine this image. Can you say for sure who or what the shadows represent? Are they cast by mourners? Grave-diggers? Unconcerned passers-by? Does the "truth" of the image matter to you? Several texts in this chapter explore the tensions between perception and reality (or between what we *think* we know and what we *can* know). Plato opens this discussion in "The Allegory of the Cave" by likening us all to prisoners who spend their lives able to "see only their own shadows, or the shadows of one another." Based on your reading in this chapter, how do you think education, knowledge, and imagination can help us see beyond the shadows, beyond the world of illusion? Do you see any value in trying to expand our familiar—albeit limiting—ways of thinking about the world around us?

John Durham Peters is a professor in the Department of Communication Studies at the University of Iowa and the author of more than 50 articles and books. According to his web page, Peters "is interested in media and cultural history, communication and social theory, and understanding communication in its broad historical, legal, philosophical, religious, and technological context." The following essay was first published in the journal Media, Culture, and Society and later in Peters' book Courting the Abyss (2005) and in the collection Media Witnessing: Testimony in the Age of Mass Communication (2009).

WITNESSING John Durham Peters

Witnessing is a common but rarely examined term in both the professional performance and academic analysis of media events. Media institutions have enthusiastically adopted its rhetoric, especially for nonfiction genres such as news, sports, and documentary. Such titles as *Eyewitness News, See it Now, Live at Five,* or *As it Happens* advertise their program's privileged proximity to events. Media personae such as correspondents and newsreaders can be institutionalized as witnesses. Cameras and microphones are often presented as substitute eyes and ears for audiences who can witness for themselves. Ordinary people can be witnesses *in* media (the vox pop interview, "tell us how it happened"), *of* media, and *via* media (watching history unfold at home in their armchairs). The media claim to provide testimonies for our inspection, thus making us witnesses of the way of the world. As a term of art, witnessing outshines more colorless competitors such as viewing, listening or consuming, reading, interpreting, or decoding, for thinking about the experience of media. What is the significance of this pervasive way of talking?

In this chapter, I propose to untangle the concept of witnessing in order to illuminate basic problems in media studies. Witnessing is an intricately tangled practice. It raises questions of truth and experience, presence and absence, death and pain, seeing and saying, and the trustworthiness of perception—in short, fundamental questions of communication. The long history of puzzlement and prescription about proper witnessing that developed in oral and print cultures is a rich resource for reflection about some of the ambiguities of audiovisual media. Hoary philosophical issues (such as the epistemological status of the senses) often show up in media practices in surprising ways; in turn, media practices can, if seen in the proper lighting, also clarify old philosophical worries.

An important step in this direction has been taken in John Ellis' *Seeing Things* (2000), whose lucid arguments I wish to extend and nuance. Witnessing, for Ellis, is a distinct mode of perception: "We cannot say we do not know" is its motto. To witness an event is to be responsible in some way to it. The stream of data flowing through the unaided senses already exceeds our explanatory schemata. The present moment supplies enough sensory information to outlast a lifetime of analysis. Audiovisual media, however, are able to catch contingent details of events that would previously have been either imperceptible or lost to memory. A camera can reveal the impact of a bullet in an apple; the tape recorder can fix an off-the-record comment. Such mechanical, "dumb" media seem to present images and sounds as they happened, without the embellishments and blind spots that human perception and memory routinely impose. We thus find ourselves endowed with a much amplified and nuanced record of events, a "super-abundance of details" rich with evidentiary value. Though photography, sound-recording, film, and radio have all expanded the realm of sensory evidence, Ellis singles out television in particular. "Separated in space yet united in time, the co-presence of the television image was developing a distinct form of witness. Witnessing became a domestic act .... Television sealed the twentieth century's fate as the century of witness" (Ellis, 2000, p. 32). Liveness is a key characteristic of televisual witnessing, including the morally problematic witnessing of violence and carnage. He advances witnessing as a key term for media analysis that, he believes, is freer of ontological baggage than other more commonly used concepts.

For Ellis, in sum, witnessing has to do with complicity; owes much to modern media of inscription; is an attitude cultivated by live television, particularly nonfiction programming; and a valuable resource for media analysis. I would concur with Ellis in everything with the exception that witnessing actually carries weighty baggage, if not ontological, at least historical. Yet this baggage is not only a burden, but also a potential treasure, at least since it makes explicit the pervasive link between witnessing and suffering and shows the degree to which media problems with witnessing are built upon venerable communication problems that are incoherent in the witness as a kind of signifying act. The "baggage" has three main interrelated sources: law, theology, and atrocity. In law, the notion of the witness as a privileged source of information for judicial decisions is ancient and is part of most known legal systems. In theology, the notion of witness, especially as martyr, developed in early Christianity, though it has resonance for other religious traditions as well. The third, most recent, source dates from the Second World War: the witness as a survivor of hell, prototypically but not exclusively the Holocaust or *Shoah*. These three domains endow "witnessing" with its extraordinary moral and cultural force today, since each ties the act of witnessing, in some deep way, to life and death. The procedures of the courtroom, the pain of the martyr, and the cry of the survivor cast light on basic questions such as what it means to watch, to narrate, or to be present at an event. Witnessing, as an amazingly subtle array of practices for securing truth from the facts of our sensitivity to pain and our inevitable death, increases the stakes of our thinking about media events.

■ Analyzing the term

As a noun, *witness* is intricate. The term involves all three points of a basic communication triangle: (1) the agent who bears witness, (2) the utterance or text itself, (3) the audience who witnesses. It is thus a strange but intelligible sentence to say: the witness (speech-act) of the witness (person) was witnessed (by an audience). A witness can also be the performance itself. Thus we speak of a Holocaust survivor's witness against fascism. In

African-American churches when preachers ask "Can I get a witness?", they invite audience affirmation and participation, the witness as a public gesture of faith. In religious contexts, witness can also have a more private meaning as inward conviction of religious truth, which in turn may motivate the activity of "witnessing" (evangelizing). In law, literature, history, and journalism alike, a witness is an observer or source possessing privileged (raw, authentic) proximity to facts. A witness, in sum, can be an actor (one who bears witness), an act (the making of a special sort of statement), the semiotic residue of that act (the statement as text), or the inward experience that authorizes the statement (the witnessing of an event).

As a verb, to *witness* has a double aspect. To witness can be a sensory experience—the witnessing of an event with one's own eyes and ears. We are all, constantly, witnesses in this sense simply by virtue of finding ourselves in places and times where things happen. Most of what we witness is insignificant in the larger scheme of things and vanishes into oblivion. But witnessing is also the discursive act of stating one's experience for the benefit of an audience that was not present at the event and yet must make some kind of judgment about it. Witnesses serve as the surrogate sense organs of the absent. If what we have witnessed is crucial for a judgment, we may be summoned to a formal institutional setting: a court of law, a church, or a television studio. A witness is the paradigm case of a medium: the means by which experience is supplied to others who lack the original.

To witness thus has two faces: the passive one of *seeing* and the active one of *saying*. In passive witnessing an accidental audience observes the events of the world; in active witnessing one is a privileged possessor and producer of knowledge in an extraordinary, often forensic, setting in which speech and truth are policed in multiple ways. What one has seen authorizes what one says: an active witness first must have been a passive one. Herein lies the fragility of witnessing: the difficult juncture between experience and discourse. The witness is authorized to speak by having been present at an occurrence. A private experience enables a public statement. But the journey from experience (the seen) into words (the said) is precarious. Witnessing presupposes a discrepancy between the ignorance of one person and the knowledge of another: it is an intensification of the problem of communication more generally. It always involves an epistemological gap whose bridging is always fraught with difficulty. No transfusion of consciousness is possible. Words can be exchanged, experiences cannot. Testimony is another's discourse whose universe of reference diverges from one's own. Like somebody else's pain, it always has a twilight status between certainty and doubt. A parent may bear witness to a child that a stove is hot, but getting burnt may be more persuasive. Witnessing is a discourse with a hole in it that awaits filling.

■ The unreliability of witnesses

Witnesses, human or mechanical, are notoriously contradictory and inarticulate. Different people who witness the "same" event can produce remarkably divergent accounts. Though awareness of the poor epistemological quality of witnessing is ancient, twentieth-century social science has explored it in detail. Eyewitness testimony, for instance, has been subject to intense social-psychological scrutiny (for example, Ross *et al.,* 1994). We now know that errors in identifying people and faces are common, with potentially devastating consequences for justice. In reports by different eyewitnesses, moustaches fly on and off faces, blondes morph into brunettes, and clothes change color like chameleons. Hats have major effects on recognition, because of the role of the hairline in identifying faces. Post-event tampering, both from inside and outside, can also alter testimony. From within, the psychological process of dissonance-reduction has the paradoxical effect of increasing confidence in accuracy of recall even while the memory of the event is fading; from without, testimonies can be shaped by the schematic constraints of narrative structure and altered, perhaps even created, by the way they are probed ("refreshed") by others. Social science methodology has noted the dubious evidentiary status of statements about even one's own attitudes and opinions. From polling, we know about acquiescence effects (the tendency of people to agree), the huge effects of phrasing on reported opinions, and the divergence between front-door and back-door measures (Webb *et al.*, 1981). Fabrication seems inherent in the loose coupling between sentences and the world; witnesses are evidently a fallible transmission and storage medium for sensory experience.

The legal theory of evidence is also a compendium of reflections about the (un)reliability of witnesses. There is a long history of excluding people as incompetent witnesses on various grounds. Non-Christians, convicts, interested parties, spouses, children, the insane, or those standing in a relationship of professional privilege with the defendant have all been considered hindered in truth-telling or as possessing special motives to fabrication. As in survey research, the law has an acute awareness about the ways that modes of interrogation (for example, leading questions) can manufacture, rather than elicit, testimony.

Since the transformation from experience to discourse lies at the heart of communication theory, witnessing entails many of the most fundamental issues in the social life of signs, especially how the raw, apparently private, stuff of sensation can have any input into the public world of intelligible words (also a fundamental question in empiricist philosophy since Locke and Hume). The forensics of the trial, the pains of the martyr, and the memoirs of the survivor are all attempts to overpower the melancholy fact that direct sensory experience—from the taste of pineapple to the pains of childbirth—vanishes when put into words and remains inaccessible to others except inasmuch as they claim to share similar experiences. Sensation is encircled into privately personal ontologies. Only words are public.

■ Pain and the veracity gap

A variety of answers have been offered to cope with the fallibility of witnessing. Devices to compensate for its inherent dubiousness are ancient. One can vouch for veracity by an oath promising to trade death or pain for truth, a practice that persists in the children's line, "cross my heart and hope to die." One may appeal to ultimate authority: "God is my witness." According to Aristotle, witnesses in a court of law testify at risk of punishment if they do not tell the truth; he considers dead witnesses more trustworthy, since they cannot be bribed (*Rhetoric*, 1376a). To witness as if you were as dumb and indifferent as the dead is the obvious ideal, since you would be free from interest, interpretation, care, and spin. A signature is a testimony: "in witness hereof …," and like all forms of witnessing, it founders on the reef of forgery. The requirement of swearing on a Bible before testifying in court is yet another device to enforce truth-telling, presumably by instilling the specter of eternal consequences. A reminder of the ancient worry about corrupt testimony is the ninth Mosaic commandment forbidding false witness (not the same thing as simple lying).

From the ancient Greeks to "modern" intelligence-gathering, the effort to assure the transition from sensation to sentences in testimony has involved torture—a perverse but illuminating fact. As Page duBois (1991) argues, the ancient Greek word for torture, *basanos*, originally meant a touchstone, against which you could rub golden artifacts to test if they were genuine; if so, a bit would rub off and leave a mark. From there, *basanos* came to mean any test of truth or authenticity (for example, of friendship or fidelity), and eventually moved specifically into torture, which served as an instrument of proof in ancient Athens. In Greek ideology, torture served as a cultural line dividing slaves, who respect only bodily pain, and citizens, who speak the *logos* in freedom. Since slaves supposedly lie compulsively, torture exposes the truth by extinguishing the power to invent. (Here again we see the snobbery about who can be expected to be a truthful witness.) Torture enforces the claim that slaves are ruled by necessity (*anangkê*). A slave could not appear in court, but a slave's testimony obtained under torture was admissible as evidence. Even so, there were already doubts about the notion that pain produces truth. Aristotle (*Rhetoric*, 1377a) thought testimony obtained under torture "inartistic" and generally distrusted testimony in any case.

The shift toward the confession as a source of legal proof in thirteenth-century Europe reintroduced judicial torture. It was not understood as a kind of punishment, but, cruel as it may sound, as a kind of data-gathering; that innocent people might suffer and even die under interrogation was considered an unfortunate by-product of legal investigation (Langbein, 1977; Peters, 1985). Pain was supposed to be the midwife of authenticity. Judicial torture was an attempt to assure the validity of the confession, a rather nasty way of coping with the veracity gap. In our grisly age, torture is both a method of punishment and of extracting intelligence, a fact signaled in the French term *la question*, which means both torture and interrogation, or the English phrase, "put to the question." Even a polygraph test—a "lie-detector" that circumvents discourse to tap "direct" physiological indicators— shows the retreat to the body as the haven of truth. Deathbed confessions possess special legal status, since the incentive to deceive is thought minimal. As one judge wrote, "they are declarations made in extremity, when the party is at the point of death, and when every hope of this world is gone; when every motive to falsehood has been silenced, and the mind is induced by the most powerful considerations to speak the truth …" (Cross, 1974, p. 472). Here again is the sense that death or pain impels the mind to forego the temptation to embellish.

The bodily basis of testimony is seen in a strange etymological complex. Testimony stems from *testamentum*, covenant (*testis* plus *mentum*), *Testis*, which in Latin means both witness and testicle, itself stems from *tertius*, meaning third (party). In ancient Greek, the word for witness is the word for testicle: *parastatês*, which literally means bystander. In German, *Zeugnis* means testimony, and *zeugen* means to testify as well as to procreate. The explanation of this pervasive and odd system of metaphors is obscure, but one may conjecture that the testicles, as physical bystanders to the act of procreation, were thought witnesses of paternity or virility in Indo-European culture. That knowing first-hand should be associated with the testicles may suggest an ancient preference for the testimony of men over women. This curious web of metaphors, whatever its significance, attests to some deep assumptions about the physicality of witnessing. The body serves as a sort of collateral to justify the loan of our credence. The whole apparatus of trying to assure truthfulness, from torture to martyrdom to courtroom procedure, only testifies to the strange lack at its core. Witnessing is necessary, but not sufficient: if there are no witnesses, there is no trial, but witnesses do not secure a conviction or acquittal. A witness is never conclusive or final despite the most militant attempts of martyrs or torturers to make it so.

Another ancient attempt bodily to bridge the gap between inner conviction and outer persuasion is the tradition of Christian martyrology. As Paul Ricoeur argues:

> The witness is capable of suffering or dying for what he believes. When the test of conviction becomes the price of life, the witness changes his name; he is called a martyr. But is it a change of name?—Martus in Greek means "witness." ... Testimony is both a manifestation and a crisis of appearances (1981, p. 129).

To judge from appearances is the fate of all who have to rely on communication for access to others' experiences. The martyr's death proves nothing for certain, but demonstrates the limit-case of persuasion, the vanishing point at which proof stops and credence begins. Saints Stephen or Sebastian, or their secular equivalents, the many political martyrs whose legacies are so powerful today, may impress bystanders with their composure under the most gruesome abuses, but their deaths alone will not convince anyone of the truth of their faith: one needs internal grounds for believing. To bear witness is to put one's body on the line. Within every witness, perhaps, stands a martyr, the will to corroborate words with something beyond them, pain and death being the last resorts.

Since the Second World War, new kinds of witnessing have been forged in the furnace of suffering. The Holocaust has generated deep thinking about the nature of witnessing (Felman and Laub, 1992). It is striking, by the way, that Ellis (2000), despite his incisive comments on psychoanalytic working-through of trauma and the complicity of the bystander, hardly mentions the Holocaust—perhaps because it is too obvious. In any case, from ashes and hell have emerged witnesses whose task, paradoxically, is to proclaim experiences that cannot be shared and to immortalize events that are uniquely tied to the mortal bodies of those who went through them. Elie Wiesel, for instance, has made his career reflecting on the privilege and loneliness of the survivor. One's responsibility to bear witness, he argues, cannot be delegated: testimony is unique to the survivor. It is important for the witness to remain silent; but it is also impossible for the witness to describe the event. The militancy in the survivor's voice owes to the battle against oblivion and indifference. Such militancy is found no less in the martyr, who likewise uses his or her body as spectacle of pain to convict the conscience of the observer. Already having cheated death, the survivor seeks to save his or her experiences for others who can never have them.

Specifically, the witness has become a literary genre growing out of the Second World War. Primo Levi, Anne Frank, Victor Klemperer, Wiesel, to name a few, have the cultural authority of witnesses of atrocity. As survivors of events, they in turn bear active witness which we, at one remove, can in turn witness passively. There is a strange ethical claim in the voice of the victim. Witnessing in this sense suggests a morally justified individual who speaks out against unjust power. Imagine a Nazi who published his memoirs of the war as a "witness"—it might be accepted as an account of experience; but never as a "witness" in the moral sense: to witness means to be on the right side. Václav Havel, Jacobo Timerman, Rigoberta Menchú, Martin Luther King, Solzhenitsyn, Mandela, Aung San Suu Kyi—those who have languished in jail—all stand as witnesses against inhumanity. (*Testimonlo* is a recent genre of Latin American writing which records the cry against oppression.) The prison (or prison camp) is the house of witness, a maker of moral authority, just as prison literature has turned out to be one of the great forms of twentieth-century writing. The moral privilege of the captive and martyr is a founding narrative in European civilization, as in the case of both Socrates and Jesus. Not surprisingly, there has been something of a scramble to capture the prestige of the victim-witness, and media who speak of their role as witnesses are not immune. (A recent book on the making of *Schindler's List* is pretentiously called *Witness*, confusing the film and what the film was about.) Witnessing places mortal bodies in time. To witness always involves risk, potentially to have your life changed. The Roman poet Ovid bemoaned his banishment to the Black Sea for seeing something in the emperor's court he was not supposed to. You can be marked for life by being the witness of an event. The FBI runs the evocatively named "witness protection program" providing personal security and sometimes new identities for those willing to turn state witness. Abraham Zapruder is famous (and his heirs are now rich) for a few seconds of home-movie footage of a presidential parade in Dallas on November 22, 1963. In Graham Greene's *Brighton Rock*, the gangster Pinky marries the only witness to a murder he committed in order to make her, as a wife, an incompetent witness, but of course, as usual in Greene, a sort of redemption occurs via the corruption. That simply seeing can mark your bodily fate is a suggestive way of getting beyond the idea of mere spectatorship.

In sum, the indisputables of pain and death can serve as a resource to persuade others of the truth of one's words of witness. Witnessing is a mode of communication intimately tied to the mortality of both the one who bears witness and the one who in turn witnesses that act. As Jorge Luís Borges writes:

> Deeds which populate the dimensions of space and which reach their end when someone dies may cause us wonderment, but one thing, or an infinite number of things, dies in every final agony … In time there was a day that extinguished the last eyes to see Christ; the battle of Jenin and the love of Helen died with a man (1964, p. 243).

Witnessing, as we will see, not only turns on the mortality of the witness, but the contingencies of the event.

◼ Objectivity and the veracity gap

A different tradition seeks to secure the validity of statements without the metaphysical and moral conundrums of pain. Very roughly speaking, the effort to put testimony on a sound footing is a project of the Enlightenment, both in the effort to minimize violence and to secure trustworthy knowledge. Indeed, one of the major tasks in the rise of modern science generally, with its need for cumulative observation from many eyes and ears, was to overcome the low repute of testimony. This was first achieved in seventeenth-century England with the creation of a genteel class of scientists, whose shared social status and norms of civility established a basis for trusting each other's reports (Shapin, 1994). As one scholar quips of the epistemology of testimony in early modern English science, gentlemen prefer gentlemen (Lipton, 1998). Without trust in others' statements about sensory experiences, science as we know it would be impossible. Further, the use of scientific instrumentation was motivated in part by the desire to bypass the stains of subjectivity, fallibility, and interest that attach to our sense organs. Scientific instruments such as the microscope or telescope were thought thing-like, and hence credible, in their indifference to human interests. The camera and microphone inherit this tradition of objectivity as passivity.

John Locke exemplifies these transformations. In his *Essay Concerning Human Understanding* (1975, book 4, chapters 13-16), Locke inverts the medieval notion of testimony: he maintains it is not the authority of an ancient text (such as scripture) but the report of the senses. Few things, he argues, in human knowledge are demonstrably certain. As social creatures with limited time to gain knowledge of a world in commotion, we rely on the reports of others but must find ways to test their trustworthiness. Among the various standards he offers, key is a hierarchy of testimony determined by the witness's proximity to the event: "any Testimony, the farther off it is from the original Truth, the less force and proof it has" (1975, pp. 663-664). Eyewitness accounts lose truth (but may gain color) as they pass from mouth to mouth:

> A credible Man vouching his Knowledge of it, is a good proof; But if another equally credible, do witness it from his Report, the Testimony is weaker; and a third that attests the Hear-say of an Hear-say, is yet less considerable (1975, p. 664).

Locke notes already the infinite regress in witnessing: to be an active witness requires another to witness your testimony (a passive witness).

Locke reflects the low legal status of hearsay: the reporting of statements made by someone else outside court without the opportunity for cross-examination. Any statement not made in court under oath is of dubious admissibility. Hearsay is quotation, testimony at secondhand. Each sentence is supposed to be funded by direct sensation, and in reporting another's reports, one is a passive witness of an active witness (instead of the reverse), which is dangerously derivative. The low esteem in which hearsay is held signals not only the hierarchy of the senses (the precedence of eyes over ears) but also the working epistemology of the courtroom: the act of linking experience and discourse must be done in a controlled setting in which speech is subject to cross-examination and penalties for perjury are in force. In this the law still maintains respect for death or pain as truth-serums. Witness is borne under sanction—whether of pain or death or legal charges and dishonor. One testifies quite literally *sub poena*—under threat of punishment. Witnesses can find themselves bodily compelled to appear in court. It does not take a Foucault to see that today witnessing is policed at its boundaries by an apparatus of pain.

Legal rules prefer a mechanical witness. A witness, for instance, may not offer an opinion (about culpability, for instance) but may only describe the facts of what was seen. The blanker the witness the better. Things, after all, can bear witness—the biblical stone of witness, trophies, or other sorts of material evidence (bloodstains). The ideal human witness would behave like a thing: a mere tablet of recording. The structure of address in testimony should be radically open and public, not varying the story for different audiences. ("Estoppel" is the legal principle that prevents altering testimony previously given.) Since a dumb witness does not know what is at stake, there is no motive to lend comfort to one party or the other.

In the preference for the dumb witness lies a distant origin of both scientific and journalistic ideas of objectivity: the observer is a mirror, dull as the microscope to human concerns or consequences. The objective witness is very different from the survivor, whose witness lies in mortal engagement with the story told. The objective witness claims disembodiment and passivity, a cold indifference to the story, offering "just the facts." The hearers have to compose the story for themselves. In one sense, the claim to objectivity is simply passive witnessing idealized, that is, the dream of an unadulterated and public record of events as they "really happened." The cultural authority of mechanical recording lies in the claim to document events without the filter of subjective experience. Since witnesses were supposed to be like machines, machines are also held to be good witnesses. The conventional wisdom about film and photography today, however, is the inescapability of interest in all representation. What most irks the friends of science and reason—Locke's heirs—about this position is not so much the notion that a consensual and objective document of events is impossible, but rather its darker corollary: that pain serves as the default measure of reality and authenticity. We were, they say, supposed to have graduated from all that!

■ Broadcasting and the veracity gap

Distance is a ground of distrust and doubt. We waver about another's testimony because of our distance from the experience they narrate. In the same way, reports from distant personae are more dubious than those from people we know and trust. The communication situation of broadcasting is analogous to that of witnessing: experiences are mediated to an audience which has no first-hand acquaintance with them. The legitimation of the veracity gap in media followed the same path as in witnessing: using pain and the body as a criterion of truth and truthfulness. The body is authenticity's last refuge in situations of structural doubt. Perhaps the best single thing Walter Cronkite ever did for his reputation of credibility, besides the years of steady service, was to shed an unrehearsed tear on camera when reporting the news of President Kennedy's assassination. In the Gospel of Luke, Christ's disciples "were startled and terrified, and thought that they were seeing a ghost" (Luke 24:37). The resurrected Jesus assures them, "Handle me and see, for a ghost does not have flesh and bones as you see that I have" (Luke 24:39). Modern media—which resurrect and transport phantasms in optical and acoustic channels—both place us in the situation of doubting Thomas and attempt a similar reassurance: handle me and see (Peters, 1999).

One of the most daring things in media events theory (Dayan and Katz, 1992) is the question: just when can media be agents of truth or authenticity instead of prevarication and ideology? In other words, can the media sustain the practice of witnessing? The notion that home audiences could be witnesses is one of those apparent category mistakes whose elaboration the media events movement has made its task. It is easy to mock Ronald Reagan for confusing newsreels and his own experience: he claimed to have witnessed the liberation of the concentration camps in the Second World War when he had never left the United States. He believed in false presence: that he had really been there when he had only watched films. But presence-at-a-distance is precisely what witnessing a media event claims to offer. Critical theory has rightly highlighted the veracity gap in mass communication, the hermeneutics of suspicion, but media events studies seek the conditions in which the willing suspension of disbelief is justified. In media events, the borrowed eyes and ears of the media become, however tentatively or dangerously, one's own. Death, distance, and distrust are all suspended, for good and evil.

Singularity is key to the communication economics of witnessing. President Clinton came to my hometown, Iowa City, Iowa, for example, in February 1996, on a campaign stop, and spoke in an indoor arena. The whole event was to be televised locally, but the tickets were snapped up within two hours. Why the excitement to attend when one could get a better view on television at home? Because at home you cannot be a witness to history. If Clinton were to be shot, or make a major announcement, people could say, "I was there." That would be a witness forever thereafter restricted to 14,000 people (if they are honest), whereas we home viewers, a much larger and potentially infinite group, would only be able to say, "I saw it on television." There is no comparison in the authority or cultural capital of the two statements! Clinton's goal after the speech was to touch as many people as possible, to spread the charisma of the king's body by working the crowd, in the apt idiom of "pressing the flesh." A live witness can shake hands with the great man, receive the torch of contagious magic, in the same way that Clinton shook JFK's hand as a teenager (luckily for him on camera). "Handle me and see" said the man we know mostly as a TV persona.

"Being there" matters since it avoids the ontological depreciation of being a copy. The copy, like hearsay, is indefinitely repeatable; the event is singular, and its witnesses are forever irreplaceable in their privileged relation to it. Recordings lose the *hic et nunc* of the event. The live event is open to unscripted happenings, chance, and gaffes. Accidents are a key part of media events—going off script. That so much of live coverage involves some sort of trauma suggests the draw of the unpredictable and of those occurrences that leave a mark in time. Media events are not always the happy social body celebrating its core values, but also the nasty stuff of degradation and disaster (Carey, 1998; Liebes, 1998).

Presence is fragile and mortal; recordings have durability that survives in multiple times and spaces. Billions of dollars in the entertainment industries turn on this apparently minute distinction. Why will people pay high prices for music performed in concert whose quality and polish is often better on the CD-player at home? Obviously extra-musical values shape concert-going: party, spectacle, noise, dance. Even so, live music is different. A concert is an event, not a record. A homemade bootleg tape is a souvenir, a marker of time and place, but a CD made from the tape is a commodity, even if they are musically identical. In a concert, one's mortal time-line on earth is spent. Touch and eye contact with the artist are possible. So is imperfection: in the concert one may hear strains edited out in the studio and witness the labor of the performing body. What post-production adds musically (for example, overdubbing) it subtracts from eventfulness, since those sounds never could have occurred in time as we know it. Recording media can do time-axis manipulation, stopping, slowing, speeding, or reversing time—one reason why audiovisual media, despite aptitude in recording, are dubious witnesses. The body, however, lives only in real time. Singing, dancing, and live performance all engage time's passage. Music can reveal the meaning of, and sometimes even provide a brief escape from, growing older.

■ Why liveness?

The love of liveness also relates to the power of real time. If one sees it live, one can claim status as a witness present in time if not in space; if one sees it on tape, one is no longer a witness, but rather the percipient of a transcription. Sports fans, in the case of big games, will remain glued to the television screen, even though they know that any key plays will be shown ad nauseam in the game's afterlife as reportage and video. They must be there *as it happens*. To see the big moment with even a slight delay is to be placed in a derivative role, a hearer of a report rather than a witness of an event. The fan wants to be involved in history (the happening), not historiography (the recording). The few seconds between occurrence and replay open up a metaphysical gulf in the meaning and quality of what is seen. As far as the electromagnetic tracings are concerned, the live event and its instant replay are identical, but in the psychology of the fan, one is history, the other is television. One is a window to the event, the other is its representation. Liveness serves as an assurance of access to truth and authenticity.

The hard-core sports fan sweating the seconds actually offers a profound lesson about the nature of time. Why should liveness matter? It does matter, to the tune of billions of dollars in bids for live rights, because events only happen in the present—in a word, gambling. As Walter Benjamin noted, gambling is a phantasmagoria of time. No one knows what the future holds, and the gambler infuses the present with the diceyness of the future. There is absolutely no point in betting on a game or a race whose outcome is already known. A classic con-job, as in the film *The Sting*, is to institute a small time lag in publicizing race results so that punters think they are betting on an uncertain future when in fact they are wagering on an already determined past. A few seconds do matter, and profoundly. The past, in some sense, is safe. The present, in contrast, is catastrophic, subject to radical alterations. In a single second a swerve of the steering wheel or a pull of the trigger can change history forever. Possible futures come into being and vanish with every act. In a brief moment the penalty kick is made or missed, a life conceived or taken. All history culminates in the present moment. Of course, the present is rarely so dramatic, but without a live connection its explosive possibility—its danger—is missing. Nothing quite excites like an event about to take place. In Raymond Williams' phrase, one waits for a knock on the door. Fortuna, goddess of history and gamblers, reveals her face only in the present. In the past she veils herself as necessity, in the future as probability.

The contrast between the live and the recorded is a structuring principle of broadcasting. It replays the contrast of fact and notion, so central to modern historiography, a field, like law and theology, whose enterprise rests on the evaluation of resources and documents—testimonies. Though theorists justly remind us of the factuality of fictions and the fictive character of facts, this contrast stubbornly resists total resolution. The division of fact and fiction, so central for historians and sports fans, as well as the structuring principle of media and literary genres, turns on witnessing. An event requires witnesses, a story only needs tellers and listeners. A fiction can be heard or told, but a fact is witnessed. Some kinds of events (baptisms, marriages) legally require witnesses. Testimony assures us, as children often ask about stories, that it really happened.

Historicity (or historical authenticity) has a similar logic to live coverage. If in visiting the Tower of London I am told that a block of wood is the one on which Henry VIII's victims were dispatched, I will act and feel differently than if I learn the block is a replica, even if it is physically identical or equally old. The block hovers in a limbo between reality and fake, its metaphysical status depending on something so slight as a caption. The caption "real" ties it to a tradition of testimony passed across the generations, an accumulation of time that links the block historically to the event. If it has the right label I can ponder edifying lessons about overweening power and look for traces of martyr's blood; I will have to work a lot harder if the caption announces that it is only figurative. Live broadcasting, like objects certified as historical, offers the chance to witness, while recorded material stands at one remove as a representation (replica) of events. It takes about a sixth-grade education in our post-modern age to puncture the idea that history is free of representation, so that is not the point. Rather, it is to read small distinctions about what is real in cultural matters, distinctions too often written off as neurosis or fetishism, as insights into structures of history and experience. Between the historical and the verisimilar lies a small but gigantic gap, that of testimony.

Of four basic types of relations to an event, three can sustain the attitude of a witness. To be there, present at the event in space and time is the paradigm case. To be present in time but removed in space is the condition of liveness, simultaneity across space. To be present in space but removed in time is the condition of historical representation: here is the possibility of a simultaneity across time, a witness that laps the ages. To be absent in both space and time but still have access to an event via its traces is the condition of recording: the profane zone in which the attitude of witnessing is hardest to sustain (see Table 1.1).

TABLE 1.1   SORTS OF WITNESSING AN EVENT

	Presence in time	Absence in time
Presence in space	BEING THERE Assembled audience. For example, concert, game, theater	HISTORICITY (dead not "live") Serial mass audience. For example, shrine, memorial, museum
Absence in space	LIVE TRANSMISSION Broadcast audience. For example, radio, TV, webcast	RECORDING Dispersed, private audience. Profane, witnessing difficult. For example, book, CD, video

■ Fact and fiction, pain and time

Ultimately, the boundary between fact and fiction is an ethical one before it is an epistemological one: it consists in having respect for the pain of victims, in being tied by simultaneity, however loosely, to someone else's story of how they hurt. We may weep in reading of the slaughter of the innocents by King Herod, but we owe them nothing besides remembrance. "Live" pain is different. Simultaneous suffering forms the horizon of responsibility: liveness matters for the living. Facts impose moral and political obligations that fictions do not. This is the ancient ethical problem of tragedy: why people take pleasure in sights that would terrify or disgust them in real life. Aristotle's *Poetics* starts the debate about why we take pleasure in depictions of violence and human suffering. In tragedy, the representation of pain (and pain is definitional for the genre) is not supposed to excite the spectator to humanitarian service but to clarify through representation what is possible in life. The drama offers terror without danger, pity without duty. The awareness of its unreality releases us from moral obligation to the sufferers we behold. Fiction lacks the responsibility or complicity that Ellis makes definitional for witnessing. As David Hume remarked (1987), "it is certain, that the same object of distress, which pleases in a tragedy, were it really set before us, would give the most unfeigned uneasiness." Factual distress calls for our aid, not our appreciation; our duty, not our pleasure. Death is meaningful in fiction: it marks the passage of time, punishes the wicked, gives closure to events. But in fact, death is a blank, completely beyond meaning. "Nothing brings them back, neither love nor hate. They can do nothing to you. They are as nothing" (Conrad, 1921). The contrast of fact and fiction has less to do with different orders of truth than with who is hurting and when. Living people's pain is news; dead people's pain is history.

It is easy to make fun of the obsession to keep up to date with the news. Kierkegaard suggested that if we treated all news as if it had happened 50 years ago we would sound its true importance. He is right about triviality, but misses what he is so lucid about elsewhere: the present moment as the point of decision. We have to keep up with the world because we are, in some complicated way, responsible to act in it, and we can only act in the present. We feel guilty about hurt people in news, not in fiction films. Pain separates facts from fictions. Facts are witnessed, fictions are narrated. Fictions may indeed inspire us to action, but the beholders' responsibility is diffuse. "Live" coverage of global sorrow is ethically recalcitrant: because it is fact, we are not protected by the theater's "teleological suspension of the ethical" (Kierkegaard); because it is spatially remote, our duty to action is unclear. We find ourselves in the position of spectators at a drama without the relief of knowing that the suffering is unreal. Hence the "unfeigned uneasiness" (Hume) we face in watching the news. We feel a gruesome fascination for trauma without the exoneration of knowing it is all an experiment in mimesis. We are witnesses without a tribunal.

Finally, the curious thing about witnessing is its retroactive character, the jealousy the present has for the past. The present may be the point of decision, but it is always underinformed about what will come after. Most observers do not know they are witnesses when the event is happening: they are elected after the fact. A vast quantitative difference separates what we experience and what we are summoned to witness. There is a lot more sensation around than stories. In testifying we must take responsibility for what we once took little responsibility for. We must report an event, the details of which have assumed as massive an importance as they were once trivial. What time did you catch the bus? What color was the car? What kind of shoes was the defendant wearing? In witnessing we look backwards on events we did not realize we were observing, restoring deleted files from memory. We do not know that what we notice or neglect may be the key to prison and liberty for someone. The present is blind to what the future will value. We did not notice the butterfly that started the typhoon.

Hence the notion, found in liberalism, existentialism, and Christian theology alike, that it is the duty of everyone to be vigilant—to be ready to stand as a witness at any time or place. Testifying has the structure of repentance: retroactively caring about what we were once careless of. A later moment revisits an earlier one in which consciousness was not fully awake. The witness's attitude to sensation (radical vigilance) goes together with the future anterior attitude to time (treating the present as if it was being witnessed from the future). To witness is to wish that the record of the past were more whole, and to grasp this lesson now is to live vigilantly, to make the present worthy as we imagine contemplating it from a future point. To cope with our fixity in the present, we can at least be awake. Every act puts one in the witness box, both seeing and saying. In Christian eschatology this attitude is dramatized by the notion of a Last Judgment that calls up the whole history of the world as judge and witness. In Nietzsche's thought it is the notion of the eternal return, acting in the present so that the action could be eternally repeated (and witnessed) without regret. In everyday civic ideology it is the idea that citizens have a duty to be informed about the events of the day. In a phrase all broadcasters would endorse, and with apologies to Matthew 25:13, the motto of witnessing should be: "Watch, therefore, for you know neither the day nor the hour wherein the event will come."

■ References

P. duBois (1991) *Torture and Truth* (London: Routledge).

J.L. Borges (1964) "The Witness," *Labyrinths Selected Stories and Other Writings* (New York: New Directions).

J.W. Carey (1998) "Political Ritual on Television," in T. Liebes and J. Curran (eds) *Media, Ritual, and Identity* (London: Routledge).

J. Conrad (1921) *The Secret Agent* (New York: Doubleday).

R. Cross (1974) *Evidence*, 4th edn (London: Butterworths).

D. Dayan and E. Katz (1992) *Media Events: The Live Broadcasting of History* (Cambridge, MA: Harvard University Press).

J. Ellis (2000) *Seeing Things: Television in the Age of Uncertainty* (London: I.B. Tauris).

S. Felman and D. Laub (1992) *Testimony: Crises of Witnessing in Literature, Psychoanalysis, and History* (New York: Routledge).

D. Hume (1987) "Of Tragedy," *Essays: Moral, Political, and Literary*, rev. edn (Indianapolis: Liberty Fund).

J.H. Langbein (1977) *Torture and the Law of Proof: Europe and England in the Ancient Régime* (Chicago: University of Chicago Press).

T. Liebes (1998) "Television's Disaster Marathon," in T. Liebes and J. Curran (eds) *Media, Ritual, and Identity* (London: Routledge).

P. Lipton (1998) "The Epistemology of Testimony," *Studies in the History and Philosophy of Science*, vol. 29, no. 1, 1-31.

J. Locke (1975/1690) *An Essay Concerning Human Understanding*, ed. P.H. Nidditch (Oxford: Clarendon Press).

E. Peters (1985) *Torture* (New York: Blackwell).

J.D. Peters (1999) *Speaking into the Air* (Chicago: University of Chicago Press).

P. Ricoeur (1981) "The Hermeneutics of Testimony," in *Essays in Biblical Interpretation* (London: SPCK).

D.E. Ross, J.D. Read, and M.P. Toglia (1994) *Adult Eyewitness Testimony: Current Trends and Developments* (Cambridge: Cambridge University Press).

S. Shapin (1994) *A Social History of Truth: Civility and Science in Seventeenth-Century England* (Chicago: University of Chicago Press).

E.J. Webb, D.T. Campbell, R.D. Schwartz, L. Sechrest, and J.B. Grove (1981) *Nonreactive Measures in the Social Sciences* (Boston: Houghton Mifflin).

■ READING AND WRITING

1. According to Peters, what are the four types of witnessing? What are the characteristics of each type?
2. What are the moral and ethical obligations of witnessing? How do media technologies and the ubiquity of information complicate these obligations?
3. Does Peters believe that the camera is objective? Do you? Explain your responses.
4. Early in his essay, Peters writes that witnessing "raises questions of truth and experience, presence and absence, death and pain, seeing and saying, and the trustworthiness of perception. ..." How do Peters' questions and conclusions about these issues compare with Plato's claims in "The Allegory of the Cave?"

■ DEVELOPING LONGER RESPONSES

5. Think of an event for which you decided to become an eyewitness. Explain what took you to that event and how it felt to be a witness in time and space.

■ USING RESEARCH

6. Peters' argument uses evidence from several academic disciplines, including philosophy, science, literature, media studies, jurisprudence and legal theory, and psychology. Using the library's databases, find a source from one of these fields that deals with some of the same issues Peters discusses. How does this source approach the topic differently?

"A single death is a tragedy, a million is a statistic," poet, essayist, and novelist Annie Dillard writes in "The Wreck of Time," quoting Josef Stalin. Later, she asks, "How can an individual count," a question she uses to challenge readers on multiple levels. This essay, first published in Harper's *in 1998, was adapted for her book* For the Time Being *(2000).*

THE WRECK OF TIME: TAKING OUR CENTURY'S MEASURE   Annie Dillard

I

Ted Bundy, the serial killer, after his arrest, could not fathom the fuss. What was the big deal? David Von Drehle quotes an exasperated Bundy in *Among the Lowest of the Dead*: "I mean, there are *so* many people."

One R. Houwink, of Amsterdam, uncovered this unnerving fact: The human population of earth, arranged tidily, would just fit into Lake Windermere, in England's Lake District.

Recently in the Peruvian Amazon a man asked the writer Alex Shoumatoff, "Isn't it true that the whole population of the United States can be fitted into their cars?"

How are we doing in numbers, we who have been alive for this most recent installment of human life? How many people have lived and died?

"The dead outnumber the living, in a ratio that could be as high as 20 to 1," a demographer, Nathan Keyfitz, wrote in a 1991 letter to the historian Justin Kaplan. "Credible estimates of the number of people who have ever lived on the earth run from 70 billion to over 100 billion." Averaging those figures puts the total persons ever born at about 85 billion. We living people now number 5.8 billion. By these moderate figures, the dead outnumber us about fourteen to one. The dead will always outnumber the living.

Dead Americans, however, if all proceeds, will not outnumber living Americans until the year 2030, because the nation is young. Some of us will be among the dead then. Will we know or care, we who once owned the still bones under the quick ones, we who spin inside the planet with our heels in the air? The living might well seem foolishly self-important to us, and overexcited.

We who are here now make up about 6.8 percent of all people who have appeared to date. This is not a meaningful figure. These times are, one might say, ordinary times, a slice of time like any other. Who can bear to hear this, or who will consider it? Are we not especially significant because our century is—our century and its nuclear bombs, its unique and unprecedented Holocaust, its serial exterminations and refugee populations, our century and its warming, its silicon chips, men on the moon, and spliced genes? No, we are not and it is not.

Since about half of all the dead are babies and children, we will be among the longest-boned dead and among the dead who grew the most teeth—for what those distinctions might be worth among beings notoriously indifferent to appearance and all else.

In Juan Rolfo's novel *Pedro Páramo*, a dead woman says to her dead son, "Just think about pleasant things, because we're going to be buried for a long time."

II

On April 30, 1991—on that one day—138,000 people drowned in Bangladesh. At dinner I mentioned to my daughter, who was then seven years old, that it was hard to imagine 138,000 people drowning.

"No, it's easy," she said. "Lots and lots of dots, in blue water."

The paleontologist Pierre Teilhard de Chardin, now dead, sent a dispatch from a dig. "In the middle of the tamarisk bush you find a red-brick town, partially exposed. … More than 3,000 years before our era, people were living there who played with dice like our own, fished with hooks like ours, and wrote in characters we can't yet read."

Who were these individuals who lived under the tamarisk bush? Who were the people Ted Bundy killed? Who was the statistician who reckoned that everybody would fit into Lake Windermere? The Trojans likely thought well of themselves, one by one; their last settlement died out by 1,100 $_{\text{B.C.E.}}$ Who were the people Stalin killed, or any of the 79.2 billion of us now dead, and who are the 5.8 billion of us now alive?

"God speaks succinctly," said the rabbis.

Is it important if you have yet died your death, or I? Your father? Your child? It is only a matter of time, after all. Why do we find it supremely pertinent, during any moment of any century on earth, which among us is topsides? Why do we concern ourselves over which side of the membrane of topsoil our feet poke?

"A single death is a tragedy, a million deaths is a statistic," Joseph Stalin, that connoisseur, gave words to this disquieting and possibly universal sentiment.

How can an individual count? Do we individuals count only to us other suckers, who love and grieve like elephants, bless their hearts? Of Allah, the Koran says, "Not so much as the weight of an ant in earth or heaven escapes from the Lord." That is touching, that Allah, God, and their ilk care when one ant dismembers another, or note when a sparrow falls, but I strain to see the use of it.

Ten years ago we thought there were two galaxies for each of us alive. Lately, since we loosed the Hubble Space Telescope, we have revised our figures. There are nine galaxies for each of us. Each galaxy harbors an average of 100 billion suns. In our galaxy, the Milky Way, there are sixty-nine suns for each person alive. The Hubble shows, says a report, that the universe "is at least 15 billion years old." Two galaxies, nine galaxies … sixty-nine suns, 100 billions suns—

These astronomers are nickel-and-diming us to death.

III

What were you doing on April 30, 1991, when a series of waves drowned 138,000 people? Where were you when you first heard the astounding, heartbreaking news? Who told you? What, seriatim, were your sensations? Who did you tell? Did you weep? Did your anguish last days or weeks?

All my life I have loved this sight: a standing wave in a boat's wake, shaped like a thorn. I have seen it rise from many oceans, and I saw it rise from the Sea of Galilee. It was a peak about a foot high. The standing wave broke at its peak, and foam slid down its glossy hollow. I watched the foaming wave on the port side. At every instant we were bringing this boat's motor, this motion, into new water. The stir, as if of life, impelled each patch of water to pinch and inhabit this same crest. Each crest tumbled upon itself and released a slide of white foam. The foam's bubbles popped and dropped into the general sea while they were still sliding down the dark wave. They trailed away always, and always new waters peaked, broke, foamed, and replenished.

What I saw was the constant intersection of two wave systems. Lord Kelvin first described them. Transverse waves rise abaft the stern and stream away perpendicular to the boat's direction of travel. Diverging waves course out in a V shape behind the boat. Where the waves converge, two lines of standing crests persist at an unchanging angle to the direction of the boat's motion. We think of these as the boat's wake. I was studying the highest standing wave, the one nearest the boat. It rose from the trough behind the stern and spilled foam. The curled wave crested over clear water and tumbled down. All its bubbles broke, thousands a second, unendingly. I could watch the present; I could see time and how it works.

On a shore, 8,000 waves break a day. James Trefil, a professor of physics, provides these facts. At any one time, the foam from breaking waves covers between 3 and 4 percent of the earth's surface. This acreage of foam is equal to the entire continent of North America. By coincidence, the U.S. population, in other words, although it is the third largest population among nations, is as small a portion of the earth's people as breaking waves' white foam is of the sea.

"God rises up out of the sea like a treasure in the waves," wrote Thomas Merton.

We see generations of waves rise from the sea that made them, billions of individuals at a time; we see them dwindle and vanish. If this does not astound you, what will? Or what will move you to pity?

IV

One tenth of the land on earth is tundra. At any time, it is raining on only 5 percent of the planet's surface. Lightning strikes the planet about a hundred times every second. The insects outweigh us. Our chickens outnumber us four to one.One fifth of us are Muslims. One fifth of us live in China. And every seventh person is a Chinese peasant. Almost one tenth of us live within range of an active volcano. More than 2 percent of us are mentally retarded. We humans drink tea—over a billion cups a day. Among us we speak 10,000 languages.

We are civilized generation number 500 or so, counting from 10,000 years ago, when we settled down. We are *Homo sapiens* generation number 7,500, counting from 150,000 years ago, when our species presumably arose; and we are human generation number 125,000 counting from the earliest forms of *Homo.*

Every 110 hours a million more humans arrive on the planet than die into the planet. A hundred million of us are children who live on the streets. Over a hundred million of us live in countries where we hold no citizenship. Twenty-three million of us are refugees. Sixteen million of us live in Cairo. Twelve million fish for a living from small boats. Seven and a half million of us are Uygurs. One million of us crew on freezer trawlers. Nearly a thousand of us a day commit suicide.

Head-spinning numbers cause mind to go slack, the *Hartford Courant* says. But our minds must not go slack. How can we think straight if our minds go slack? We agree that we want to think straight.

Anyone's close world of family and friends composes a group smaller than almost all sampling errors, smaller than almost all rounding errors, a group invisible, at whose loss the world will not blink. Two million children die a year from diarrhea, and 800,000 from measles. Do we blink? Stalin starved 7 million Ukrainians in one year, Pol Pot killed 1 million Cambodians, the flu epidemic of 1918 killed 21 or 22 million people … shall this go on? Or do you suffer, as Teilhard de Chardin did, the sense of being "an atom lost in the universe"? Or do you not suffer this sense? How about what journalists call "compassion fatigue"? Reality fatigue? At what limit for you do other individuals blur? Vanish? How old are you?

V

Los Angeles airport has 25,000 parking spaces. This is about one space for every person who died in 1985 in Colombia when a volcano erupted. This is one space for each of the corpses of more than two years' worth of accidental killings from leftover land mines of recent wars. At five to a car, almost all the Inuit in the world could park at LAX. Similarly, if you propped up or stacked four bodies to a car, you could fit into the airport parking lot all the corpses from the firestream bombing of Tokyo in March 1945, or the corpses of Londoners who died in the plague, or the corpses of Burundians killed in civil war since 1993. But you could not fit America's homeless there, not even at twenty to a car.

Since sand and dirt pile up on everything, why does the world look fresh for each new crowd? As natural and human debris raises the continents, vegetation grows on the piles. It is all a stage—we know this—a temporary stage on top of many layers of stages, but every year a new crop of sand, grass, and tree leaves freshens the set and perfects the illusion that ours is the new and urgent world now. When Keats was in Rome, I read once, he saw pomegranate trees overhead; they bloomed in dirt blown onto the Coliseum's broken walls. How can we doubt our own time, in which each bright instant probes the future? In every arable soil in the world we grow grain over tombs—sure, we know this. But do not the dead generations seem to us dark and still as mummies, and their times always faded like scenes painted on walls at Pompeii?

How can we see ourselves as only a new, temporary cast for a long-running show when a new batch of birds flies around singing and new clouds move? Living things from hyenas to bacteria whisk the dead away like stagehands hustling between scenes. To help a living space last while we live on it, we brush or haul away the blowing sand and hack or burn the greenery. We are mowing the grass at the cutting edge.

VI

In northeast Japan, a seismic sea wave killed 27,000 people on June 15, 1896. Do not fail to distinguish this infamous wave from the April 30, 1991, waves that drowned 138,000 Bangladeshi. You were not tempted to confuse, conflate, forget, or ignore these deaths, were you?

On the dry Laetoli plain of northern Tanzania, Mary Leakey found a trail of hominid footprints. The three barefoot people—likely a short man and woman and child *Australopithecus afarensis*—walked closely together. They walked on moist volcanic tuff and ash. We have a record of those few seconds from a day about 3.6 million years ago—before hominids even chipped stone tools. More ash covered their footprints and hardened. Ash also preserved the pockmarks of the raindrops that fell beside the three who walked; it was a rainy day. We have almost ninety feet of the three's steady footprints intact. We do not know where they were going or why. We do not know why the woman paused and turned left, briefly, before continuing. "A remote ancestor," Leakey said, "experienced a moment of doubt." Possibly they watched the Sadiman volcano erupt, or they took a last look back before they left. We do know we cannot make anything so lasting as these three barefoot ones did.

After archeologists studied this long strip of record for several years, they buried it again to save it. Along one preserved portion, however, new tree roots are already cracking the footprints, and in another place winds threaten to sand them flat; the preservers did not cover them deeply enough. Now they are burying them again.

Jeremiah, walking toward Jerusalem, saw the smoke from the Temple's blaze. He wept; he saw the blood of the slain. "He put his face close to the ground and saw the footprints of sucklings and infants who were walking into captivity: in Babylon. He kissed the footprints.

Who were these individuals? Who were the three who walked together and left footprints in the rain? Who was that eighteenth-century Ukrainian peasant the Baal Shem Tov, the founder of modern Hasidism, who taught, danced, and dug clay? He was among the generations of children of Babylonian exiles whose footprints on the bare earth Jeremiah kissed. Centuries later the Emperor Hadrian destroyed another such son of exile in Rome, Rabbi Akiba. Russian Christians and European Christians tried, and Hitler tried, to wipe all those survivors of children of exile from the ground of the earth as a man wipes a plate— survivors of exiles whose footprints on the ground I kiss, and whose feet.

Who and of what import were the men whose bones bulk the Great Wall, the 30 million Mao starved, or the 11 million children under five who die each year now? Why, they are the insignificant others, of course; living or dead, they are just some of the plentiful others. And you?

Is it not late? A late time to be living? Are not our current generations the important ones? We have changed the world. Are not our heightened times the important ones, the ones since Hiroshima? Perhaps we are the last generation—there is a comfort. Take the bomb threat away and what are we? We are ordinary beads on a never-ending string. Our time is a routine twist of an improbable yarn.

We have no chance of being here when the sun burns out. There must be something ultimately heroic about our time, something that sets it above all those other times. Hitler, Stalin, Mao, and Pol Pot made strides in obliterating whole peoples, but this has been the human effort all along, and we have only enlarged the means, as have people in every century in history. (That genocides recur does not mean that they are similar. Each instance of human evil and each victim's death possesses its unique history and form. To generalize, as Cynthia Ozick points out, is to "befog" evil's specificity.)

Dire things are happening. Plague? Funny weather? Why are we watching the news, reading the news, keeping up with the news? Only to enforce our fancy—probably a necessary lie—that these are crucial times, and we are in on them. Newly revealed, and I am in the know: crazy people, bunches of them! New diseases, sways in power, floods! Can the news from dynastic Egypt have been any different?

As I write this, I am still alive, but of course I might well have died before you read it. Most of the archeologists who reburied hominid footprints have likely not yet died their deaths; the paleontologist Teilhard is pushing up daisies.

Chinese soldiers who breathed air posing for 7,000 individual day portraits—twenty-two centuries ago—must have thought it a wonderful difference that workers buried only their simulacra then so that their sons could bury their flesh a bit later. One wonders what they did in the months or years they gained. One wonders what one is, oneself, up to these days.

VII

Was it wisdom Mao Tse-tung attained when—like Ted Bundy—he awakened to the long view?

"The atom bomb is nothing to be afraid of," Mao told Nehru. "China has many people. … The deaths of ten or twenty million people is nothing to be afraid of." A witness said Nehru showed shock. Later, speaking in Moscow, Mao displayed yet more generosity: he boasted that he was willing to lose 300 million people, half of China's population.

Does Mao's reckoning shock me really? If sanctioning the death of strangers could save my daughter's life, would I do it? Probably. How many others' lives would I be willing to sacrifice? Three? Three hundred million?

An English journalist, observing the Sisters of Charity in Calcutta, reasoned: "Either life is always and in all circumstances sacred, or intrinsically of no account; it is inconceivable that it should be in some cases the one, and in some the other."

One small town's soup kitchen, St. Mary's, serves 115 men a night. Why feed 115 individuals? Surely so few people elude most demographics and achieve statistical insignificance. After all, there are 265 million Americans, 15 million people who live in Mexico City, 16 million in greater New York, 26 million in greater Tokyo. Every day 1.5 million people walk through Times Square in New York; every day almost as many people—1.4 million—board a U.S. passenger plane. And so forth. We who breathe air now will join the already dead layers of us who breathed air once. We arise from dirt and dwindle to dirt, and the might of the universe is arrayed against us.

■ READING AND WRITING

1. What is Dillard's main point in this essay? What is she trying to persuade her audience to think or do?
2. What is the effect of Dillard's quoting so many people? Do all of these voices strengthen her claims? What do these voices say about Dillard's relationship to the topic of death and the randomness of violence?
3. Explain Dillard's critique of the use of numbers and statistics to represent human beings and to quantify human suffering. Do you think there is a better way to talk about human tragedies—and to make distant tragedies seem significant—than by using statistics?
4. Dillard poses a number of questions throughout her essay. How would you respond to this one, from the end of the piece: "One small town's soup kitchen, St. Mary's, serves 115 men a night. *Why feed 115 individuals?*"

■ DEVELOPING LONGER RESPONSES

5. Throughout the essay, Dillard meditates on one central issue (the significance or sacredness of life in a world of random death) mostly by juxtaposing various quotations, anecdotes, and reported conversation. Use a similar quotation/collage method to ponder another issue (some possibilities: happiness, success, commitment, loyalty, virtue, evil, love).

■ USING RESEARCH

6. Like many great writers, Dillard offers a new way of talking about a very old issue: What can we say about the value of life in light of the certainty, and ubiquity, of death? Many philosophers, theologians, and scientists have pondered this issue at length. Your research task is twofold: First, make a list of at least four academic disciplines, other than English or literature, that deal with this question. And, second, find one primary source from one of these disciplines and compare the source's treatment of the issue with Dillard's.

> *Georges Poulet (1902-1991) was a theorist associated with the Geneva school of criticism, which practiced phenomenology, the branch of philosophy that explores how we experience the world. In the following excerpt, Poulet offers an eloquent, if complicated, account of the experience of reading fiction.*

from
PHENOMENOLOGY OF READING Georges Poulet

At the beginning of Mallarme's unfinished story, *Igitur*, there is the description of an empty room, in the middle of which, on a table there is an open book. This seems to me the situation of every book, until someone comes and begins to read it. Books are objects. On a table, on bookshelves, in store windows, they wait for someone to come and deliver them from their materiality, from their immobility. When I see them on display, I look at them as I would at animals for sale, kept in little cages, and so obviously hoping for a buyer. For—there is no doubting it—animals do know that their fate depends on a human intervention, thanks to which they will be delivered from the shame of being treated as objects. Isn't the same true of books? Made of paper and ink, they lie where they are put, until the moment someone shows an interest in them. They wait. Are they aware that an act of man might suddenly transform their existence? They appear to be lit up with that hope. Read me, they seem to say. I find it hard to resist their appeal. No, books are not just objects among others.

This feeling they give me—I sometimes have it with other objects. I have it, for example, with vases and statues. It would never occur to me to walk around a sewing machine or to look at the underside of a plate. I am quite satisfied with the face they present to me. But statues make me want to circle around them, vases make me want to turn them in my hands. I wonder why. Isn't it because they give me the illusion that there is something in them which, from a different angle, I might be able to see? Neither vase nor statue seems fully revealed by the unbroken perimeter of its surfaces. In addition to its surfaces it must have an interior. What this interior might be, that is what intrigues me and makes me circle around them, as though looking for the entrance to a secret chamber. But there is no such entrance (save for the mouth of the vase, which is not a true entrance since it gives only access to a little space to put flowers in). So the vase and the statue are closed. They oblige me to remain outside. We can have no rapport—whence my sense of uneasiness.

So much for statues and vases. I hope books are not like them. Buy a vase, take it home, put it on your table or your mantel, and, after a while, it will allow itself to be made a part of your household. But it will be no less a vase, for that. On the other hand, take a book, and you will find it offering, opening itself. It is this openness of the book which

I find so moving. A book is not shut in by its contours, is not walled-up as in a fortress. It asks nothing better than to exist outside itself, or to let you exist in it. In short, the extraordinary fact in the case of a book is the falling away of the barriers between you and it. You are inside it; it is inside you; there is no longer either outside or inside.

Such is the initial phenomenon produced whenever I take up a book, and begin to read it. At the precise moment that I see, surging out of the object I hold open before me, a quantity of significations which my mind grasps, I *realize* that what I hold in my hands is no longer just an object, or even simply a living thing. I am aware of a rational being, of a consciousness; the consciousness of another, no different from the one I automatically assume in every human being I encounter, except that in this case the consciousness is open to me, welcomes me, lets me look deep inside itself, and even allows me, with unheard-of license, to think what it thinks and feel what it feels.

Unheard-of, I say. Unheard-of, first, is the disappearance of the "object." Where is the book I held in my hands? Is it still there, and at the same time it is there no longer, it is nowhere. That object wholly object, that thing made of paper, as there are things made of metal or porcelain, that object is no more, or at least it is as if it no longer existed, as long as I read the book. For the book is no longer a material reality. It has become a series of words, of images, of ideas which in their turn begin to exist. And where is this new existence? Surely not in the paper object. Nor, surely, in external space. There is only one place left for this new existence: my innermost self.

How has this come about? By what means, through whose intercession? How can I have opened my own mind so completely to what is usually shut out of it? I do not know. I know only that, while reading, I perceived in my mind a number of significations which have made themselves at home here. Doubtless they are still objects: images, ideas, words, objects of my thought. And yet, from this point of view, there is an enormous difference. For the book, like the vase, or like the statue, was an object among others, residing in the external world: the world which objects ordinarily inhabit exclusively in their own society or each on its own, in no need of being through by my thought; whereas in this interior world where, like fish in an aquarium, words, images and ideas disport themselves, these mental entities, in order to exist, need the shelter which I provide; they are dependent on my consciousness.

This dependence is at once a disadvantage and an advantage. As I have just observed, it is the privilege of exterior objects to dispense with any interference from the mind. All they ask is to be let alone. They manage by themselves. But the same is surely not true of interior objects. By definition they are condemned to change their very nature, condemned to lose their materiality. They become images, ideas, words, that is to say purely mental entities. In sum, in order to exist as mental objects, they must relinquish their existence as real objects.

On the one hand, this is cause for regret. As soon as I replace my direct perception of reality by the words of a book, I deliver myself, bound hand and foot to the omnipotence of fiction. I say farewell to what is, in order to feign belief in what is not. I surround myself with fictitious beings; I become the prey of language. There is no escaping this takeover. Language surrounds me with its unreality.

On the other hand, the transmutation through language of reality into a fictional equivalent has undeniable advantages. The universe of fiction is infinitely more elastic than the world of objective reality. It lends itself to any use; it yields with little resistance to the importunities of the mind. Moreover—and of all its benefits I find this the most appealing—this interior universe constituted by the language does not seem radically opposed to the *me* who thinks it. Doubtless what I glimpse through the words are mental forms not divested of an appearance of objectivity. But they do not seem to be of a nature other than my mind which thinks them. They are objects, but subjectified objects. In short, since everything has become part of my mind, thanks to the intervention of language, the opposition between the subject and its objects has been considerably attenuated. And thus the greatest advantage of literature is that I am persuaded by it that I am freed from my usual sense of incompatibility between my consciousness and its objects.

This is the remarkable transformation wrought in me through the act of reading. Not only does it cause the physical objects around me to disappear, including the very book I am reading, but it replaces those external objects with a congeries of mental objects in close *rapport* with my own consciousness. And yet the very intimacy in which I now live with my objects is going to present me with new problems. The most curious of these is the following: I am someone who happens to have as objects of his own thought, thoughts which are part of a book I am reading, and which are therefore the cogitations of another. They are the thoughts of another, and yet it is I who am their subject. The situation is even more astonishing than the one noted above. I am thinking the thoughts of another. Of course, there would be no cause for astonishment if I were thinking it as the thought of another. But I think it as my very own. Ordinarily there is the *I* which thinks, which recognizes itself (when it takes its bearings) in thoughts which may have come from elsewhere but which it takes upon itself as its own in the moment it thinks them. This is how we must take Diderot's declaration "Mes pensées sont *mes* catins" (My thoughts are *my* whores"). That is, they sleep with everybody without ceasing to belong to their author. Now, in the present case things are quite different. Because of the strange invasion of my person by the thoughts of another, I am a self who is granted the experience of thinking thoughts foreign to him. I am the subject of thoughts other than my own. My consciousness behaves as though it were the consciousness of another.

This merits reflection. In a certain sense I must recognize that no idea really belongs to me. Ideas belong to no one. They pass from one mind to another as coins pass from hand to hand. Consequently, nothing could be more misleading than the attempt to define a consciousness by the ideas which it utters or entertains. But whatever these ideas may be, however strong the tie which binds them to their source, however transitory may be their sojourn in my own mind, so long as I entertain them I assert myself as subject of these ideas: I am the subjective principle for whom the ideas serve for the time being as the predications. Furthermore, this subjective principle can in no wise be conceived as a predication, as something which is discussed, referred to. It is I who think, who contemplate, who am engaged in speaking. In short, it is never a *HE* but an *I*.

Now what happens when I read a book? Am I then the subject of a series of predications which are not *my* predications? That is impossible, perhaps even a contradiction in terms. I feel sure that as soon as I think something, that something becomes in some indefinable way my own. Whatever I think is a part of *my* mental world. And yet here I am thinking a thought which manifestly belongs to another mental world, which is being thought in me just as though I did not exist. Already the notion is inconceivable and seems even more so if I reflect that, since every thought must have a subject to think it, this *thought* which is alien to me and yet in me, must also have in me a *subject* which is alien to me. It all happens, then, as though reading were the act by which a thought managed to bestow itself within me with a subject not myself. Whenever I read, I mentally pronounce an *I*, and yet the *I* which I pronounce is not myself. This is true even when the hero of a novel is presented in the third person, and even when there is no hero and nothing but reflections or propositions; for as soon as something is presented as *thought*, there has to be a thinking subject with whom, at least for the time being, I identify, forgetting myself, alienated from myself, "JE est an autre," said Rimbaud. Another *I*, who has replaced my own, and who will continue to do so as long as I read. Reading is just that: a way of giving way not only to a host of alien words, images, ideas, but also to the very alien principle which utters them and shelters them.

The phenomenon is indeed hard to explain, even to conceive, and yet, once admitted, it explains to me what might otherwise seem even more inexplicable. For how could I explain, without such takeover of my innermost subjective being, the astonishing facility with which I not only understand but even *feel* what I read. When I read as I ought, i.e., without mental reservation, without any desire to preserve any independence of judgment, and with the total commitment required of any reader, my comprehension becomes intuitive and any feeling proposed to me is immediately assumed by me. In other words, the kind of comprehension in question here is not a movement from the unknown to the known, from the strange to the familiar, from outside to inside. It might rather be called a phenomenon by which mental objects rise up from the depths of consciousness into the light of recognition. On the other hand—and without contradiction—reading implies something resembling the apperception I have of myself, the action by which I grasp straightaway what I think as being thought by a subject (who, in this case, is not I). Whatever sort of alienation I may endure, reading does not interpret my activity as subject.

Reading, then, is the act in which the subjective principle which I call *I*, is modified in such a way that I no longer have the right, strictly speaking, to consider it as my *I*. I am on loan to another, and this other thinks, feels, suffers, and acts within me. The phenomenon appears in its most obvious and even naivest form in the sort of spell brought about by certain cheap kinds of reading, such as thrillers, of which I say "It gripped me." Now it is important to note that this possession of myself by another takes place not only on the level of objective thought, that is with regard to images, sensations, ideas which reading affords me, but also on the level of my very subjectivity. When I am absorbed in reading, a second self takes over, a self which thinks and feels for me. Withdrawn in some recess of myself, do I then silently witness this dispossession? Do I derive from it some comfort or, on the contrary, a kind of anguish? However that may be, someone else holds the center of the stage, and the question which imposes itself, which I am absolutely obliged to ask myself, is this: "Who is the usurper who occupies the forefront? What is this mind who all alone by myself fills my consciousness and who, when I say *I*, is indeed that *I*?"

There is an immediate answer to this question, perhaps too easy an answer. This *I* who thinks in me when I read a book, is the *I* of the one who writes the book. When I read

Baudelaire or Racine, it is really Baudelaire or Racine who thinks, feels, allows himself to be read within me. Thus a book is not only a book, it is the means by which an author actually preserves his ideas, his feelings, his modes of dreaming and living. It is his means of saving his identity from death. Such an interpretation of reading is not false. It seems to justify what is commonly called the biographical explication of literary texts. Indeed every word of literature is impregnated with the mind of the one who wrote it. As he makes us read it, he awakens in us the analogue of what he thought or felt. To understand a literary work, then, is to let the individual who wrote it reveal himself to us *in* us. It is not the biography which explicates the work, but rather the work which sometimes enables us to understand the biography.But biographical interpretation is in part false and misleading. It is true that there is an analogy between the works of an author and the experiences of his life. The works may be seen as an incomplete translation of the life. And further, there is an even more significant analogy among all the works of a single author. Each of the works, however, while I am reading it, lives in me its own life. The subject who is revealed to me through my reading of it is not the author, either in the disordered totality of his outer experiences, or in the aggregate, better organized and concentrated totality, which is the one of his writings. Yet the subject which presides over the work can exist only in the work. To be sure, nothing is unimportant for understanding the work, and a mass of biographical, bibliographical, textual, and general critical information is indispensable to me. And yet this knowledge does not coincide with the internal knowledge of the work. Whatever may be the sum of the information I acquire on Baudelaire or Racine, in whatever degree of intimacy I may live with their genius, I am aware that this contribution (*apport*) does not suffice to illuminate for me in its own inner meaning, in its formal perfection, and in the subjective principle which animates it, the particular work of Baudelaire or Racine the reading of which now absorbs me. At this moment what matters to me is to live, from the inside, in a certain identity with the work and work alone. It could hardly be otherwise. Nothing external to the work could possibly share the extraordinary claim which the work now exerts on me. It is there within me, not to send me back, outside itself to its author, nor to his other writings, but on the contrary to keep my attention riveted on itself. It is the work which traces in me the very boundaries within which this consciousness will define itself. It is the work which forces on me a series of metal objects and creates in me a network of words, beyond which, for the time being, there will be no room for other mental objects or for other words. And it is the work, finally, which, not satisfied thus with defining the content of my consciousness, takes hold of it; appropriates it, and makes of it that *I* which, from one end of my reading to the other, presides over the unfolding of the work, of the single work which I am reading.

And so the work forms the temporary mental substance which fills my consciousness of what is, revealing itself within the interior of the work. Such is the characteristic condition of every work which I summon back into existence by placing my consciousness at its disposal. I give it not only existence, but awareness of existence. And so I ought not to hesitate to recognize that so long as it is animated by this vital inbreathing inspired by the act of reading, a work of literature becomes (at the expense of the reader whose own life it suspends) a sort of human being, that it is a mind conscious of itself and constituting itself in me as the subject of its own objects.

READING AND WRITING

1. How does Poulet define the act of reading? (In your response, take into account the physical, intellectual, and emotional effects.) Compare his definition with your own thinking about reading.
2. Do you think that digital reading—of online texts or e-books—can produce the transformations that Poulet describes? Explain your response.
3. Poulet writes that, while reading, "I am on loan to another, and this other thinks, feels, suffers, and acts within me." Who is this "other" that Poulet mentions? How does this other come into being?

DEVELOPING LONGER RESPONSES

4. Write a brief essay in which you analyze the physical, intellectual, and/ or emotional effects you experience while reading. To do this well, you will have to pay attention to your reading process and record your experiences as you read.

Jeanette Winterson is a widely acclaimed writer of fiction and essays whose best-known works include Oranges Are Not the Only Fruit *and* Written on the Body. *The following piece is from her 1997 collection* Art Objects: Essays on Ecstasy and Effrontery, *an impassioned defense of the arts. In this essay, Winterson argues forcefully for the primacy of the imagination.*

IMAGINATION AND REALITY   Jeanette Winterson

The reality of art is the reality of the imagination.

What do I mean by reality of art?

What do I mean by reality of imagination?

My statement, and the questions it suggests, are worth considering now that the fashionable approach to the arts is once again through the narrow gate of subjective experience. The charge laid on the artist, and in particular on the writer, is not to bring back visions but to play the Court photographer.

Is this anathema to art? Is it anti-art? I think so. What art presents is much more than the daily life of you and me, and the original role of the artist as visionary is the correct one. "Real" is an old word, is an odd word. It used to mean a Spanish sixpence; a small silver coin, money of account in the days when the value of a coin was the value of its metal. We are used to notional money but "real" is an honest currency.

The honest currency of art is the honest currency of the imagination.

The small silver coin of art cannot be spent; that is, it cannot be exchanged or exhausted. What is lost, what is destroyed, what is tarnished, what is misappropriated, is ceaselessly renewed by the mining, shaping, forging imagination that exists beyond the conjectures of the everyday. Imagination's coin, the infinitely flexible metal of the Muse, metal of the moon, in rounded structure offers new universes, primary worlds, that substantially confront the pretences of notional life.

Notional life is the life encouraged by governments, mass education and the mass media. Each of those powerful agencies couples an assumption of its own importance with a disregard for individuality. Freedom of choice is the catch phrase but streamlined homogeneity is the objective. A people who think for themselves are hard to control and what is worse, in a money culture, they may be skeptical of product advertising. Since our economy is now a consumer economy, we must be credulous and passive. We must believe that we want to earn money to buy things we don't need. The education system is not designed to turn out thoughtful individualists, it is there to get us to work. When we come home exhausted from the inanities of our jobs we can relax in front of the inanities of the TV screen. This pattern, punctuated by birth, death and marriage and a new car, is offered to us as real life.

Children who are born into a tired world as batteries of new energy are plugged into the system as soon as possible and gradually drained away. At the time when they become adult and conscious they are already depleted and prepared to accept a world of shadows. Those who have kept their spirit find it hard to nourish it and between the ages of twenty and thirty, many are successfully emptied of all resistance. I do not think it an exaggeration to say that most of the energy of most of the people is being diverted into a system which destroys them. Money is no antidote. If the imaginative life is to be renewed it needs its own coin.

We have to admit that the arts stimulate and satisfy a part of our nature that would otherwise be left untouched and that the emotions art arouses in us are of a different order to those aroused by experience of any other kind.

We think we live in a world of sense-experience and what we can touch and feel, see and hear, is the sum of our reality. Although neither physics nor philosophy accepts this, neither physics nor philosophy has been as successful as religion used to be at persuading us of the doubtfulness of the seeming-solid world. This is a pity if only because while religion was a matter of course, the awareness of other realities was also a matter of course. To accept God was to accept Otherness, and while this did not make the life of the artist any easier (the life of the artist is never easy), a general agreement that there is more around us than the mundane allows the artist a greater license and a greater authority than he or she can expect in a society that recognizes nothing but itself.

An example of this is the development of the visual arts under Church patronage during the late medieval and Renaissance periods in Europe. This was much more than a patronage of money, it was a warrant to bring back visions. Far from being restricted by Church rhetoric, the artist knew that he and his audience were in tacit agreement; each went in search of the Sublime.

Art is visionary; it sees beyond the view from the window, even though the window is its frame. This is why the arts fare much better alongside religion than alongside either capitalism or communism. The god-instinct and the art-instinct both apprehend more than the physical biological material world. The artist need not believe in God, but the artist does consider reality as multiple and complex. If the audience accepts this premise it is then possible to think about the work itself. As things stand now, too much criticism of the arts concerns itself with attacking any suggestion of arts as Other, as a bringer of realities beyond the commonplace. Dimly, we know we need those other realities and we think we can get them by ransacking different cultures and rhapsodizing work by foreign writers simply because they are foreign writers. We are still back with art as the mirror of life, only it is a more exotic or less democratic life than our own. No doubt this has its interests but if we are honest, they are documentary. Art is not documentary. It may incidentally serve that function in its own way but its true effort is to open to us dimensions of the spirit and of the self that normally lie smothered under the weight of living.

It is in Victorian England that the artist first becomes a rather suspect type who does not bring visions but narcotics and whose relationship to different levels of reality is not authoritative but hallucinatory. In Britain, the nineteenth century recovered from the shock of Romanticism by adopting either a manly Hellenism, with an interest in all things virile and Greek, or a manly philistinism, which had done with sweet Jonney Keats and his band

and demanded of the poet, if he must be a poet, that he is either declamatory or decorative. Art could be rousing or it could be entertaining. If it hinted at deeper mysteries it was effeminate and absurd. The shift in sensibility from early to late Wordsworth is the shift of the age. For Tennyson, who published his first collection in 1830, the shift was a painful one and the compromises he made to his own work are clear to anyone who flicks through the collected poems and finds a visionary poet trying to hide himself in legend in order to hint at sublimities not allowed to his own time. Like Wordsworth before him, Tennyson fails whenever he collapses into the single obsessive reality of the world about him. As a laureate we know he is lying. As a visionary we read him now and find him true.

And what are we but our fathers' sons and daughters? We are the Victorian legacy. Our materialism, our lack of spirituality, our grossness, our mockery of art, our utilitarian attitude to education, even the dull grey suits wrapped around the dull grey lives of our eminent City men, are Victorian hand-me-downs. Many of our ideas of history and society go back no further than Victorian England. We live in a money culture because they did. Control by plutocracy is a nineteenth-century phenomenon that has been sold to us as a blueprint for reality. But what is real about the values of a money culture?

Money culture recognizes no currency but its own. Whatever is not money, whatever is not making money, is useless to it. The entire efforts of our government as directed through our society are efforts towards making more and more money. This favors the survival of the dullest. This favors those who prefer to live in a notional reality where goods are worth more than time and where things are more important than ideas.

For the artist, any artist, poet, painter, musician, time in plenty and an abundance of ideas are the necessary basics of creativity. By dreaming and idleness and then by intense self-discipline does the artist live. The artist cannot perform between 9 and 6, five days a week, or if she sometimes does, she cannot guarantee to do so. Money culture hates that. It must know what it is getting, when it is getting it, and how much it will cost. The most tyrannical of patrons never demanded from their protégées what the market now demands of artists; if you can't sell your work regularly and quickly, you can either starve or do something else. The time that art needs, which may not be a long time, but which has to be its own time, is anathema to a money culture. Money confuses time with itself. That is part of its unreality.

Against this golden calf in the wilderness where all come to buy and sell, the honest currency of art offers quite a different rate of exchange. The artist does not turn time into money, the artist turns time into energy, time into intensity, time into vision. The exchange that art offers is an exchange in kind; energy for energy, intensity for intensity, vision for vision. This is seductive and threatening. Can we make the return? Do we want to? Our increasingly passive diversions do not equip us, mentally, emotionally, for the demands that art makes. We know we are dissatisfied, but the satisfactions that we seek come at a price beyond the resources of a money culture. Can we afford to live imaginatively, contemplatively? Why have we submitted to a society that tries to make imagination a privilege when to each of us it comes as a birthright?

It is not a question of the money in your pocket. Money can buy you the painting or the book or the opera seat but it cannot expose you to the vast energies you will find there. Often it will shield you from them, just as a rich man can buy himself a woman but not her love. Love is reciprocity and so is art. Either you abandon yourself to another world that you say you seek or you find ways to resist it. Most of us are art-resisters because art is a challenge to the notional life. In a money culture, art, by its nature, objects. It fields its own realities, lives by its own currency, aloof to riches and want. Art is dangerous.

FOR SALE: MY LIFE. HIGHEST BIDDER COLLECTS

The honest currency of art is the honest currency of the imagination.

In Middle English, "real" was a variant of "royal."

Can we set aside images of our own dishonored monarchy and think instead about the ancientness and complexity of the word "royal"?

To be royal was to be distinguished in the proper sense; to be singled out, by one's fellows and by God or the gods. In both the Greek and the Hebraic traditions, the one who is royal is the one who has special access to the invisible world. Ulysses can talk to Hera, King David can talk to God. Royalty on earth is expected to take its duties on earth seriously but the King should also be a bridge between the terrestrial and the supernatural.

Perhaps it seems strange to us that in the ancient world the King was more accessible to his people than were the priests. Although King and priests worked together, priesthood, still allied to magic, even by the Hebrews, was fully mysterious. The set-apartness of the priest is one surrounded by ritual and taboo. The priest did not fight in battle, take concubines, hoard treasure, feast and riot, sin out of humanness, or if he did, there were severe penalties. The morality of the priesthood was not the morality of Kingship and whether you read *The Odyssey* or The Bible, the difference is striking. The King is not better behaved than his subjects, essentially he was (or should have been) the nobler man.

In Britain, royalty was not allied to morality until the reign of Queen Victoria. Historically, the role of the King or Queen had been to lead and inspire, this is an imaginative role, and it was most perfectly fulfilled by Elizabeth the First, Gloriana, the approachable face of Godhead. Gloriana is the Queen whose otherness is for the sake of her people, and it is important to remember that the disciplines she laid upon her own life, in particular her chastity, were not for the sake of example but for the sake of expediency. The Divine Right of Kings was not a good conduct award; it was a mark of favor. God's regent upon earth was expected to behave like God and anyone who studies Greek or Hebrew literature will find that God does not behave like a Christian schoolmistress. God is glorious, terrifying, inscrutable, often capricious to human eyes, extravagant, victorious, legislative but not law-abiding, and the supreme imagination. "In the beginning was the Word."

At its simplest and at its best, royalty is an imaginative function; it must embody in its own person, subtle and difficult concepts of Otherness. The priest does not embody these concepts, the priest serves them. The priest is a functionary, the King is a function.

Shakespeare is preoccupied with Kingship as a metaphor for the imaginative life. Leontes and Lear, Macbeth and Richard II, are studies in the failure of the imagination. In *The Winter's Tale*, the redemption of Leontes is made possible through a new capacity in him; the capacity to see outside of his own dead vision into a chance as vibrant as it is unlikely. When Paulina says to him, "It is required you do awake your faith" she does not mean religious faith. If the statue of Hermione is to come to life, Leontes must believe it *can* come to life. This is not common sense. It is imagination.

In the earliest Hebrew creation stories Yahweh makes himself a clay model of a man and breathes on it to give it life. It is this supreme confidence, this translation of forms, the capacity to recognize in one thing the potential of another, and the willingness to let that potential realize itself, that is the stamp of creativity and the birthright that Yahweh gives to humans. Leontes' failure to acknowledge any reality other than his own is a repudiation of that birthright, a neglect of humanness that outworks itself into the fixed immobility of his queen. When Hermione steps down and embraces Leontes it is an imaginative reconciliation.

I hope it is clear that as I talk about King and priest I am dealing in abstracts and not actualities. I do not wish to upset republicans anywhere. What I do want to do is to move the pieces across the chessboard to see if that gives us a different view.

By unraveling the word "real" I hope to show that it contains in itself, and without any wishful thinking on my part, those densities of imaginative experience that belong to us all and that are best communicated through art. I see no conflict between reality and imagination. They are not in fact separate. Our real lives hold within them our royal lives; the inspiration to be more than we are, to find new solutions, to live beyond the moment. Art helps us to do this because it fuses together temporal and perpetual realities.

To see outside of a dead vision is not an optical illusion.

The realist (from the Latin *res* = thing) who thinks he deals in things and not images and who is suspicious of the abstract and of art, is not the practical man but a man caught in a fantasy of his own unmaking.

The realist unmakes the coherent multiple world into a collection of random objects. He thinks of reality as that which has an objective existence, but understands no more about objective existence than that which he can touch and feel, sell and buy. A lover of objects and of objectivity, he is in fact caught in a world of symbols and symbolism, where he is unable to see the thing in itself, as it really is, he sees it only in relation to his own story of the world.

The habit of human beings is to see things subjectively or not to see them at all. The more familiar a thing becomes the less it is seen. In the home, nobody looks at the furniture, they sit on it, eat off it, sleep on it and forget it until they buy something new. When we do look at other people's things, we are usually thinking about their cachet, their value, what they say about their owner. Our minds work to continually label and absorb what we see and to fit it neatly into our own pattern. That done, we turn away. This is a sound survival skill but it makes it very difficult to let anything have an existence independent of ourselves, whether furniture or people. It makes it easier to buy symbols, things that have a particular value to us, than it does to buy objects.

My mother, who was poor, never bought objects, she bought symbols. She used to save up to buy something hideous to put in the best parlor. What she bought was factory made and beyond her purse. If she had ever been able to see it in its own right, she could never have spent money on it. She couldn't see it, and nor could any of the neighbors dragged in to admire it. They admired the effort it had taken to save for it. They admired how much it cost. Above all, they admired my mother; the purchase was a success.

I know that when my mother sat in her kitchen that had only a few pieces of handmade furniture, she felt depressed and conscious of her lowly social status. When she sat in her dreadful parlor with a china cup and a bought biscuit, she felt like a lady. The parlor, full of objects unseen but hard won, was a fantasy chamber, a reflecting mirror. Like Mrs. Joe, in *Great Expectations*, she finally took her apron off.

Money culture depends on symbolic reality. It depends on a confusion between the object and what the object represents. To keep you and my buying and upgrading an overstock of meaningless things depends on those things having an acquisitional value. It is the act of buying that is important. In our society, people who cannot buy things are the underclass.

Symbolic man surrounds himself with objects as tyrants surround themselves with subjects: "These will obey me. Through them I am worshipped. Through them I exercise control." These fraudulent kingdoms, hard-headed and practical, are really the soft-center of fantasy. They are wish fulfillment nightmares where more is piled on more to manufacture the illusion of abundance. They are hands of emptiness and want. Things do not satisfy. In part they fail to satisfy because their symbolic value changes so regularly and what brought whistles of admiration one year is next year's car boot sale bargain. In part they fail to satisfy because much of what we buy is gadgetry and fashion, which makes objects temporary and the need to be able to purchase them, permanent. In part they fail to satisfy because we do not actually want the things we buy. They are illusion, narcotic, hallucination.

To suggest that the writer, the painter, the musician, is the one out of touch with the real world is a doubtful proposition. It is the artist who must apprehend things fully, in their own right, communicating them not as symbols but as living realities with the power to move.

To see outside of a dead vision is not an optical illusion.

According to the science of optics, if an image consists of points through which light actually passes, it is called real. Otherwise it is called virtual.

The work of the artist is to see into the life of things; to discriminate between superficialities and realities; to know what is genuine and what is a make-believe. The artist through the disciplines of her work, is one of the few people who does see things as they really are, stripped of associative value. I do not mean that artists of whatever sort have perfect taste or perfect private lives. I mean that when the imaginative capacity is highly developed, it is made up of invention and discernment. Invention is the shaping spirit that re-forms fragments into new wholes, so that even what has been familiar can be seen fresh. Discernment is to know how to test the true and the false and to reveal objects, emotions, ideas in their own coherence. The artist is a translator; one who has learned how to pass into their own language the languages gathered from stones, from birds, from dreams, from the body, from the material world, from the invisible world, from sex, from death, from love. A different language is a different reality; what is the language, the world, of stones? What is the language, the world, of birds? Of atoms? Of microbes? Of colors? Of air? The material world is closed to those who think of it only as a commodity market.

How do you know but every bird that cuts the airy way
Is an immense world of delight closed by your senses five?
                    William Blake, *The Marriage of Heaven and Hell* (c. 1790)

To those people every object is inanimate. In fact they are the ones who remain unmoved, fixed rigidly within their own reality.

The artist is moved.

The artist is moved through multiple realities. The artist is moved by empty space and points of light. The artist tests the image. Does light pass through it? Is it illuminated? Is it sharp, clear, its own edges, its own form?

The artist is looking for real presences. I suppose what the scientist Rupert Sheldrake would call "morphic resonance;" the inner life of the thing that cannot be explained away biologically, chemically, physically. In the Catholic Church "real presence" is the bread and wine that through transubstantiation becomes the living eucharist; the body and blood of Christ. In the Protestant Church the bread and wine are symbols only, one of the few places where we recognize that we are asking one thing to substitute for another. For the average person, this substitution is happening all the time.

The real presence, the image transformed by light, is not rare but it is easily lost or mistaken under clouds of subjectivity. People who claim to like pictures and books will often only respond to those pictures and books in which they can clearly find themselves. This is ego masquerading as taste. To recognize the worth of a thing is more than recognizing its worth to you. Our responses to art are conditioned by our insistence that it present to us realities we can readily accept, however virtual those realities might be. Nevertheless art has a stubborn way of cutting through the subjective world of symbols and money and offering itself as a steady alternative to the quick change act of daily life.

We are naturally suspicious of faculties that we do not ourselves possess and we do not quite believe that the poet can read the sermons in stones or the painter know the purple that bees love. Still we are drawn to books and pictures and music, finding in ourselves an echo of their song, finding in ourselves an echo of their sensibility, an answering voice through the racket of the day.

Art is for us a reality beyond now. An imaginative reality that we need. The reality of art is the reality of the imagination.

The reality of art is not the reality of experience.

The charge laid on the artist is to bring back visions.

In Shakespeare's *Othello*, we find that the Moor wins Desdemona's heart by first winning her imagination. He tells her tales of cannibals and of the Anthropophagi whose heads grow beneath their shoulders. What he calls his "round unvarnished tale" is a subtle mixture of art and artfulness. When a Shakespearean hero apologies for his lack of wit we should be on our guard. Shakespeare always gives his heroes the best lines, even when the hero is Richard II.

Othello's untutored language is in fact powerful and wrought. He is more than a master of arms, he is a master of art. It is his words that win Desdemona. She says "I saw Othello's visage in his mind." His face, like his deeds, belongs to the world of sense-experience, but it is his wit that makes both dear to her. For Desdemona, the reality of Othello is his imaginative reality.

> OTHELLO   she thank'd me,
> And bade me, if I had a friend that lov'd her,
> I should but teach him how to tell my story,
> And that would woo her.

The clue here is not the story but the telling of it. It is not Othello the action man who has taught Desdemona to love him, it is Othello the poet.

We know that Shakespeare never bothered to think of a plot. As a good dramatist and one who earned his whole living by his work, he had to take care to make his historical ransackings state-satisfactory. The engineering of the plays gives pleasure even to those who are not interested in the words. But the words are the thing. The words are what interested Shakespeare and what should closely interest us. Shakespeare is a dramatic poet. He is not a chronicler of experience.

I have to say something so obvious because of the multitude of so-called realists, many making money out of print, who want art to be as small as they are. For them, art is a copying machine busily coping themselves. They like the documentary version, the "life as it is lived." To support their opinions they will either point to Dickens or Shakespeare. I have never understood why anyone calls Dickens a realist, but I have dealt with that myth elsewhere in these essays. As for Shakespeare, they will happily disregard the pervading spirit behind the later plays, and quote *Hamlet* Act III, Scene II "The purpose of playing … is, to hold, as 'twere, the mirror up to nature."

But what is nature?

From the Latin *Natura*, it is my birth, my characteristics, my condition.

It is my nativity, my astrology, my biology, my physiognomy, my geography, my cartography, my spirituality, my sexuality, my mentality, my corporeal, intellectual, emotional, imaginative self. And not just my self, every self and the Self of the world. There is no mirror I know that can show me all of these singularities, unless it is the strange distorting looking-glass of art where I will not find my reflection not my representation but a nearer truth than I prefer. *Natura* is the whole that I am. The multiple reality of my existence.

The reality of the imagination leaves out nothing. It is the most complete reality that we can know. Imagination takes in the world of sense experience, and rather than trading it for a world of symbols, delights in it for what it is. The artist is physical and it is in the work of true artists in any medium that we find the most moving and the most poignant studies of the world that we can touch and feel. It is the writer, the painter, and not the realist, who is intimate with the material world, who knows its smells and tastes because they are fresh in her nostrils, full in her mouth. What her hand touches, she feels. R.A. Collingwood said that Cézanne painted like a blind man (critics at the time agreed though for different reasons). He meant that the two dimensional flimsy world of what is overlooked by most of us, suddenly reared out of the canvas, massy and tough. Cézanne seems to have hands in his eyes and eyes in his hands. When Cézanne paints a tree or an apple, he does not paint a copy of a tree or an apple, he paints its nature. He paints the whole that it is, the whole that is lost to us as we pass it, eat it, chop it down. It is through the painter, writer, composer, who lives more intensely than the rest of us, that we can rediscover the intensity of the physical world.

And not only the physical world. There is no limit to new territory. The gate is open. Whether or not we go through is up to us, but to stand mockingly on the threshold, claiming that nothing lies beyond, is something of a flat earth theory.

The earth is not flat and neither is reality. Reality is continuous, multiple, simultaneous, complex, abundant and partly invisible. The imagination alone can fathom this and it reveals its fathomings through art.

The reality of art is the reality of the imagination.

◼ READING AND WRITING

1. What arguments is Winterson making about art and imagination in this essay?
2. How does Winterson define "notional life"? What are her objections to this way of living? What does she propose in its place?
3. Is Winterson fair in characterizing contemporary Americans (i.e., you and me) as "credulous and passive" in the face of "notional reality"? Give three reasons why she may be partly right, and three reasons why she may be partly wrong.
4. In her essay, Winterson writes: "At the time when they [children] become adult and conscious they are already depleted and prepared to accept a world of shadows," a subtle allusion to Plato's "Allegory of the Cave." In what ways do you feel this is an accurate description of your situation as a college student? In what ways do you feel it is inaccurate or unfair?

◼ DEVELOPING LONGER RESPONSES

5. Is Winterson's account of art compatible with life in a democracy? Consider especially her discussion of the work of art and her riffing on the word "real," its relationship to "royal," and her discussion of royalness and Otherness.

■ USING RESEARCH

6. "We think we live in a world of sense-experience and what we can touch and feel, see and hear, is the sum of our reality," Winterson writes, adding that "neither physics nor philosophy accepts this." Using resources available through the library, find at least two sources that verify Winterson's claim that "neither physics nor philosophy accepts this" idea.

One of America's foremost poets, Yusef Komunyakaa is also a Vietnam War veteran, an essayist, and a professor of creative writing. In this memoir essay, first published in The Washington Post Magazine in 2000, he reflects on the difficulties he would face in straddling the worlds of his past and his future.

THE BLUE MACHINERY OF SUMMER   Yusef Komunyakaa

"I feel like I'm part of this damn thing," Frank said. He carried himself like a large man even though he was short. A dead cigarette dangled from his half-grin. "I've worked on this machine for twenty-odd years, and now it's almost me."

It was my first day on a summer job at ITT Cannon in Phoenix in 1979. This factory manufactured parts for electronic systems—units that fit into larger, more complex ones. My job was to operate an air-powered punch press. Depending on each item formed, certain dies or templates were used to cut and shape metal plates into designs the engineers wanted.

"I know all the tricks of the trade, big and small, especially when it comes to these punch presses. It seems like I was born riding this hunk of steel."

Frank had a gift for gab, but when the foreman entered, he grew silent and meditative, bent over the machine, lost in his job. The whole day turned into one big, rambunctious dance of raw metal, hiss of steam, and sparks. Foremen strutted about like banty roosters. Women tucked falling curls back into their nets, glancing at themselves in anything chrome.

This job reminded me of the one I'd had in 1971 at McGraw Edison, also in Phoenix, a year after I returned from Vietnam. Back then, I had said to myself, this is the right setting for a soap opera. Muscle and sex changed the rhythm of this place. We'd call the show "The Line."

I'd move up and down the line, shooting screws into metal cabinets of coolers and air conditioners—one hour for Montgomery Ward or Sears, and the next two hours for a long line of cabinets stamped McGraw Edison. The designs differed only slightly, but made a difference in the selling price later on. The days seemed endless, and it got to where I could do the job with my eyes closed.

In retrospect, I believe I was hyper from the war. I couldn't lay back; I was driven to do twice the work expected—sometimes taking on both sides of the line, giving other workers a hand. I worked overtime two hours before 7 a.m. and one hour after 4 p.m. I learned everything about coolers and air conditioners, and rectified problem units that didn't pass inspection.

At lunch, rather than sitting among other workers, I chose a secluded spot near the mountain of boxed-up coolers to eat my homemade sandwiches and sip iced tea or lemonade. I always had a paperback book in my back pocket: Richard Wright's *Black Boy*, Albert Camus' *The Fall*, Frantz Fanon's *The Wretched of the Earth*, or C.W.E. Bigsby's *The Black American Writer*. I wrote notes in the margins with a ballpoint. I was falling in love with language and ideas. All my attention went to reading.

When I left the gaze of Arizona's Superstition Mountain and headed for the Colorado Rockies, I wasn't thinking about higher education. Once I was in college, I vowed never to take another job like this, and yet here I was, eight years later, a first-year graduate student at the University of California at Irvine, and working another factory job in Phoenix, hypnotized by the incessant clang of machinery.

Frank schooled me in the tricks of the trade. He took pride in his job and practiced a work ethic similar to the one that had shaped my life early on even though I had wanted to rebel against it. Frank was from Little Rock: in Phoenix, everyone seemed to be from somewhere else except the indigenous Americans and Mexicans.

"If there's one thing I know, it's this damn machine," Frank said. "Sometimes it wants to act like it has a brain of its own, as if it owns me, but I know better."

"Iron can wear any man out," I said.

"Not this hunk of junk. It was new when I came here."

"But it'll still be here when you're long gone."

"Says who?"

"Says iron against flesh."

"They will scrap this big, ugly bastard when I'm gone."

"They'll bring in a new man."

"Are you the new man, whippersnapper? They better hire two of you to replace one of me."

"Men will be men."

"And boys will be boys."

The hard dance held us in its grip.

I spotted Lily Huong the second day in a corner of the wiring department. The women there moved their hands in practiced synchrony, looping and winding color-coded wires with such graceful dexterity and professionalism. Some chewed gum and blew bubbles, others smiled to themselves as if they were reliving the weekend. And a good number talked about the soap operas, naming off the characters as if they were family members or close friends.

Lily was in her own world. Petite, with long black hair grabbed up, stuffed beneath a net and baseball cap, her body was one fluid motion, as if it knew what it was doing and why.

"Yeah, boys will be boys," Frank said.

"What you mean?"

"You're looking at trouble, my friend."

"Maybe trouble is looking for me. And if it is, I'm not running."

"She is nothing but bona fide trouble."

I wonder if she was thinking of Vietnam while she sat bent over the table, or when she glided across the concrete floor as if she were moving through lush grass. Lily? It made me think of waterlily, lotus—how shoots and blooms were eaten in that faraway land. The lotus grows out of decay, in lagoons dark with sediment and rot.

Mornings arrived with the taste of sweet nighttime still in our mouths, when the factory smelled like the deepest ore, and the syncopation of the great heaving presses fascinated me.

The nylon and leather safety straps fit our hands like fingerless gloves and sometimes seemed as if they'd pull us into the thunderous pneumatic vacuum faster than an eye blink. These beasts pulsed hypnotically; they reminded everyone within earshot of terrifying and sobering accidents. The machinery's dance of smooth heft seemed extraordinary, a masterpiece of give-and-take precision. If a foolhardy novice wrestled with one of these metal contraptions, it would suck up the hapless soul. The trick was to give and pull back with a timing that meant the difference between life and death.

"Always use a safety block, one of these chunks of wood. Don't get careless," Frank said. "Forget the idea you can second-guess this monster. Two months ago we had a guy in here named Leo on that hunk of junk over there, the one that Chico is now riding."

"Yeah, and?"

"I don't believe it. It's crazy. I didn't know Leo was a fool. The machine got stuck, he bent down, looked underneath, and never knew his last breath. That monster flattened his head like a pancake."

One morning, I stood at the checkout counter signing out my tools for the day's work and caught a glimpse of Lily out of the corner of my eye. She stopped. Our eyes locked for a moment, and then she glided on toward her department. Did she know I had been in 'Nam? Had there been a look in my eyes that had given me away?

"You can't be interested in her," Paula said. She pushed her hair away from her face in what seemed like an assured gesture.

"Why not?" I said.

"She's nothing, nothing but trouble."

"Oh?"

"Anyway, you ain't nobody's foreman."

I took my toolbox and walked over to the punch press. The buzzer sounded. The gears kicked in. The day started.

After three weeks, I discovered certain social mechanisms ran the place. The grapevine, long, tangled, and thorny, was merciless. After a month of the job I had been wondering why Frank disappeared at lunchtime but always made it back just minutes before the buzzer.

"I bet Frank tells you why he comes back here with a smile on his mug?" Maria coaxed. She worked as a spot-welder, with most of her day spent behind heavy black goggles as the sparks danced around her.

"No."

"Why don't you ask Paula one of these mornings when you're signing out tools?"

"I don't think so," I said.

"She's the one who puts that grin on his face. They've been tearing up that rooming house over on Sycamore for years."

"Good for them," I said.

"Not if that cop husband of hers comes to his senses."

It would have been cruel irony for Frank to work more than twenty years on the monster and lose his life at the hands of a mere mortal.

The grapevine also revealed that Lily had gotten on the payroll because of Rico, who was a foreman on the swing shift. They had been lovers and he had put in a good word for her. Rico was built like a lightweight boxer, his eyes bright and alert, always able to look over the whole room in a single glance. The next news said Lily was sleeping with Steve, the shipping foreman, who wore western shirts, a silver and turquoise belt buckle, and cowboy boots. His red Chevy pickup had a steer's horn on the hood. He was tall and lanky and had been in the Marines, stationed at Khe Sanh.

I wondered about Lily. What village or city had she come from—Chu Chi or Danang, Saigon or Hue? What was her story? Did she still hear the war during sleepless nights? Maybe she had had an American boyfriend, maybe she was in love with a Vietnamese once, a student, and they had intimate moments besides the Perfume River as boats with green and red lanterns passed at dusk. Or maybe she met him on the edge of a rice paddy, or in some half-lit place in Danang a few doors down from the Blue Dahlia.

She looked like so many who tried to outrun past lovers, history. "*She's nothing but trouble …*" Had she become a scapegoat? Had she tried to play a game that wasn't hers to play? Didn't anyone notice her black eye one week, the corner of her lip split the next?

I told myself I would speak to her. I didn't know when, but I would.

The women were bowed over their piece work.

As a boy I'd make bets with myself, and as a man I was still making bets, and sometimes they left me in some strange situations.

"In New Guinea those Fuzzy Wuzzies saved our asses," Frank said. "They're the smartest people I've ever seen. One moment almost in the Stone Age, and the next they're zooming around in our jeeps and firing automatic weapons like nobody's business. They gave the Japanese hell. They were so outrageously brave it still hurts to think about it."

I wanted to tell him about Vietnam, a few of the things I'd witnessed, but I couldn't. I could've told him about the South Vietnamese soldiers who were opposites of Frank's heroes.

I gazed over toward Lily.

Holding up one of the doodads—we were stamping out hundreds hourly—I said to Frank, "Do you know what this is used for?"

"No. Never crossed my mind."

"You don't know? How many do you think you've made?"

"God only knows."

"And you don't know what they're used for?"

"No."

"How much does each sell for?"

"Your guess is as good as mine. I make 'em. I don't sell 'em."

He's right, I thought. Knowing wouldn't change these workers' lives. This great symphony of sweat, oil, steel, rhythm, it all made a strange kind of sense.

"These are used in the firing mechanisms of grenade launchers," I said as I scooped up a handful. "And each costs the government almost eighty-five dollars."

The buzzer sounded.

In the cafeteria, most everybody sat in their usual clusters. A few of the women read magazines—*True Romance, Tan, TV Guide, Reader's Digest*—as they nibbled at sandwiches and sipped Cokes. One woman was reading her Bible. I felt like the odd man out as I took my paperback from my lunch pail: a Great Books Foundation volume, with blue-white-black cover and a circle around *GB*. My coworkers probably thought I was reading the same book all summer long, or that it was a religious text. I read Voltaire, Hegel, and Darwin.

Voltaire spoke to me about Equality:

All the poor are not unhappy. The greater number are born in that state, and constant labor prevents them from too sensibly feeling their situation; but when they do strongly feel it, then follow wars such as these of the popular party against the Senate at Rome, and those of the peasantry in Germany, England and France. All these wars ended sooner or later in the subjection of the people, because the great have money, and money in a state commands everything: I say in a state, for the case is different between nation and nation. That nation makes the best use of iron will always subjugate another that has more gold but less courage.

Maybe I didn't want to deal with those images of 'Nam still in my psyche, ones that Lily had rekindled.

"You catch on real fast, friend," Frank said. "It is hard to teach a man how to make love to a machine. It's almost got to be in your blood. If you don't watch out, you'll be doing twenty in this sweatbox too. Now mark my word."

I wanted to tell him about school. About some of the ideas filling my head. Lily would smile, but she looked as if she were gazing through me.

One morning in early August, a foreman said they needed me to work on a special unit. I was led through the security doors. The room was huge, and the man working on the big, circular-dome object seemed small and insignificant in the voluminous space. Then I was shaking hands with the guy they called Dave the Lathe. Almost everyone had a nickname here, as in the Deep South, where, it turned out, many of the workers were from. The nicknames came from the almost instinctual impulse to make language a game of insinuation.

Dave was from Paradise, California. He showed me how to polish each part, every fixture and pin. The work led to painstaking tedium. Had I posed too many questions? Was that why I was working this job?

Here everything was done by hand, with patience and silence. The room was air-conditioned. Now the clang of machines and whine of metal being cut retreated into memory. Behind this door Dave the Lathe was a master at shaping metals, alloyed with secrets, a metal that could be smoothed but wouldn't shine, take friction and heat out of this world. In fact, it looked like a fine piece of sculpture designed aeronautically, that approached perfection. Dave the Lathe had been working on this nose cone for a spacecraft for more than five months.

Dave and I seldom talked. Lily's face receded from my thoughts. Now I stood across from Dave the Lathe, thinking about two women in my class back at the University of California with the same first name. One was from New York. She had two reproductions of French nudes over her bed and was in love with Colette, the writer. The other woman was part Okinawan from Honolulu. If we found ourselves in a room alone, she always managed to disengage herself. We had never had a discussion, but here she was undressing in my mind. At that moment, standing a few feet from Dave the Lathe, I felt that she and I were made for each other but she didn't know it yet.

I told Dave that within two weeks, I'd return to graduate school. He wished me luck in a tone that suggested he knew what I'd planned to say before I said it.

"Hey, college boy!" Maria shouted across the cafeteria. "Are you in college or did you do time like Frank says?" I wanted the impossible, to disappear.

Lily's eyes caught mine. I still hadn't told her I felt I'd left part of myself in her country. Maria sat down beside me. I fished out the ham sandwich, but left Darwin in the lunch box. She said, "You gonna just soft-shoe in here and then disappear, right?"

"No. Not really."

"*Not really*, he says," she mocked.

"Well."

"Like a lousy lover who doesn't tell you everything. Doesn't tell the fine print."

"Well."

"Cat got your tongue, college boy?"

"Are you talking to me or somebody else?"

"Yeah, you! Walk into somebody's life and then turn into a ghost. A one-night stand."

"I didn't think anyone needed to know."

"I suppose you're too damn good to tell us the truth."

She stood up, took her lunch over to another table, sat down, and continued to eat. I didn't know what to say. I was still learning.

There's good silence. There's bad silence. Growing up in rural Louisiana, along with four brothers and one sister, I began to cultivate a life of the imagination. I traveled to Mexico, Africa, and the Far East. When I was in elementary school and junior high, sometimes I knew the answers to questions, but I didn't dare raise my hand. Boys and girls danced up and down, waving their arms, with right and wrong answers. It was hard for me to chance being wrong. Also, I found it difficult to share my feelings; but I always broke the silence and stepped in if someone was being mistreated.

Now as I sat alone, looking out the window of a Greyhound bus at 1 a.m., I felt like an initiate who had gotten cold feet and was hightailing it back to some privileged safety zone. I began to count the figures sprawled on the concrete still warm from the sun's weight on the city. There seemed to be an uneasy equality among destitute: indigenous Americans, Mexicans, a few blacks and whites. Eleven. Twelve. I thought, a massacre of the spirit.

The sounds of the machines were still inside my head. The clanging punctuated by Frank's voice: "Are you ready to will your body to this damn beast, my friend?"

"No, Frank. I never told you I am going to college," I heard myself saying. Did education mean moving from one class to the next? My grandmothers told me again and again that one could scale a mountain with a good education. But could I still talk to them, to my parents, my siblings? I would try to live in two worlds—at the very least. That was now my task. I never wanted again to feel that my dreams had betrayed me.

Maybe the reason I hadn't spoken to Lily was I didn't want to talk about the war. I hadn't even acknowledged to my friends that I'd been there.

The bus pulled out, headed for LA. With its headlights sweeping like slow yellow flares across drunken faces, as if images of the dead had followed Lily and me from a distant land only the heart could bridge.

■ READING AND WRITING

1. Throughout his essay, Komunyakaa gives us many subtle clues as to how he feels different from his factory co-workers. One repeated clue is his reading. What does his choice of reading (Darwin, Voltaire) tell us about him? How does his reading—and, by implication, his educational aspirations—position him among the factory workers?
2. Why do you think Komunyakaa is reluctant to talk about his military service in Vietnam with his fellow workers?
3. Near the end of his essay, Komunyakaa writes: "Did education mean moving from one class to the next?" What are the different meanings that "class" could have in this sentence? How are they relevant to the story?
4. What does this essay say about the potential costs of education?

■ DEVELOPING LONGER RESPONSES

5. Do you think the personal essay—specifically, the memoir—is an effective genre for presenting an argument? Point to specific elements of Komunyakaa's essay to support your response.

■ USING RESEARCH

6. Komunyakaa's experience is not unlike that of many contemporary writers with blue-collar backgrounds, including B.H. Fairchild (one of whose poems is called "The Art of the Lathe"), Octavia Butler, Gary Lutz, Jayne Ann Phillips, and Sherman Alexie. Research one of these writers' backgrounds and compare the memories and conclusions he or she presents with Komunyakaa's.

Nicholas Carr, whose most recent book is The Big Switch: Rewiring the World, From Edison to Google *(2008), writes on the social, intellectual, and business implications of technology. He uses his own experience as a starting point in this examination of how digital technologies such as Google's search engines affect intelligence. He wrote this essay for the July/August 2008 issue of* Atlantic Monthly.

IS GOOGLE MAKING US STUPID?   Nicholas Carr

"Dave, stop. Stop, will you? Stop, Dave. Will you stop, Dave?" So the supercomputer HAL pleads with the implacable astronaut Dave Bowman in a famous and weirdly poignant scene toward the end of Stanley Kubrick's *2001: A Space Odyssey*. Bowman, having nearly been sent to a deep-space death by the malfunctioning machine, is calmly, coldly disconnecting the memory circuits that control its artificial "brain." "Dave, my mind is going," HAL says, forlornly. "I can feel it. I can feel it."

I can feel it, too. Over the past few years I've had an uncomfortable sense that someone, or something, has been tinkering with my brain, remapping the neural circuitry, reprogramming the memory. My mind isn't going—so far as I can tell—but it's changing. I'm not thinking the way I used to think. I can feel it most strongly when I'm reading. Immersing myself in a book or a lengthy article used to be easy. My mind would get caught up in the narrative or the turns of the argument, and I'd spend hours strolling through long stretches of prose. That's rarely the case anymore. Now my concentration often starts to drift after two or three pages. I get fidgety, lose the thread, begin looking for something else to do. I feel as if I'm always dragging my wayward brain back to the text. The deep reading that used to come naturally has become a struggle.

I think I know what's going on. For more than a decade now, I've been spending a lot of time online, searching and surfing and sometimes adding to the great databases of the Internet. The Web has been a godsend to me as a writer. Research that once required days in the stacks or periodical rooms of libraries can now be done in minutes. A few Google searches, some quick clicks on hyperlinks, and I've got the telltale fact or pithy quote I was after. Even when I'm not working, I'm as likely as not to be foraging in the Web's info-thickets reading and writing emails, scanning headlines and blog posts, watching videos and listening to podcasts, or just tripping from link to link to link. (Unlike footnotes, to which they're sometimes likened, hyperlinks don't merely point to related works; they propel you toward them.)

For me, as for others, the Net is becoming a universal medium, the conduit for most of the information that flows through my eyes and ears and into my mind. The advantages of having immediate access to such an incredibly rich store of information are many, and they've been widely described and duly applauded. "The perfect recall of silicon memory," *Wired*'s Clive Thompson has written, "can be an enormous boon to thinking." But that boon comes at a price. As the media theorist Marshall McLuhan pointed out in the 1960s, media are not just passive channels of information. They supply the stuff of thought, but they also shape the process of thought. And what the Net seems to be doing is chipping away my capacity for concentration and contemplation. My mind now expects to take in information the way the Net distributes it: in a swiftly moving stream of particles. Once I was a scuba diver in the sea of words. Now I zip along the surface like a guy on a Jet Ski.

I'm not the only one. When I mention my troubles with reading to friends and acquaintances—literary types, most of them—many say they're having similar experiences. The more they use the Web, the more they have to fight to stay focused on long pieces of writing. Some of the bloggers I follow have also begun mentioning the phenomenon. Scott Karp, who writes a blog about online media, recently confessed that he has stopped reading books altogether. "I was a lit major in college, and used to be [a] voracious book reader," he wrote. "What happened?" He speculates on the answer: "What if I do all my reading on the web not so much because the way I read has changed, i.e. I'm just seeking convenience, but because the way I THINK has changed?"

Bruce Friedman, who blogs regularly about the use of computers in medicine, also has described how the Internet has altered his mental habits. "I now have almost totally lost the ability to read and absorb a longish article on the web or in print," he wrote earlier this year. A pathologist who has long been on the faculty of the University of Michigan Medical School, Friedman elaborated on his comment in a telephone conversation with me. His thinking, he said, has taken on a "staccato" quality, reflecting the way he quickly scans short passages of text from many sources online. "I can't read *War and Peace* anymore," he admitted. "I've lost the ability to do that. Even a blog post of more than three or four paragraphs is too much to absorb. I skim it."

Anecdotes alone don't prove much. And we still await the long-term neurological and psychological experiments that will provide a definitive picture of how Internet use affects cognition. But a recently published study of online research habits, conducted by scholars from University College London, suggests that we may well be in the midst of a sea change in the way we read and think. As part of the five-year research program, the scholars examined computer logs documenting the behavior of visitors to two popular research sites, one operated by the British Library and one by a U.K. educational consortium, that provide access to journal articles, e-books, and other sources of written information. They found that people using the sites exhibited "a form of skimming activity," hopping from one source to another and rarely returning to any source they'd already visited. They typically read no more than one or two pages of an article or book before they would "bounce" out to another site. Sometimes they'd save a long article, but there's no evidence that they ever went back and actually read it. The authors of the study report:

> It is clear that users are not reading online in the traditional sense; indeed there are signs that new forms of "reading" are emerging as users "power browse" horizontally through titles, contents pages and abstracts going for quick wins. It almost seems that they go online to avoid reading in the traditional sense.

Thanks to the ubiquity of text on the Internet, not to mention the popularity of text-messaging on cell phones, we may well be reading more today than we did in the 1970s or 1980s, when television was our medium of choice. But it's a different kind of reading, and behind it lies a different kind of thinking—perhaps even a new sense of the self. "We are not only what we read," says Maryanne Wolf, a developmental psychologist at Tufts University and the author of *Proust and the Squid: The Story and Science of the Reading Brain.* "We are how we read." Wolf worries that the style of reading promoted by the Net, a style that puts "efficiency" and "immediacy" above all else, may be weakening our capacity for the kind of deep reading that emerged when an earlier technology, the printing press, made long and complex works of prose commonplace. When we read online, she says, we tend to become "mere decoders of information." Our ability to interpret text, to make the rich mental connections that form when we read deeply and without distraction, remains largely disengaged.

Reading, explains Wolf, is not an instinctive skill for human beings. It's not etched into our genes the way speech is. We have to teach our minds how to translate the symbolic characters we see into the language we understand. And the media or other technologies we use in learning and practicing the craft of reading play an important part in shaping the neural circuits inside our brains. Experiments demonstrate that readers of ideograms, such as the Chinese, develop a mental circuitry for reading that is very different from the circuitry found in those of us whose written language employs an alphabet. The variations extend across many regions of the brain, including those that govern such essential cognitive functions as memory and the interpretation of visual and auditory stimuli. We can expect as well that the circuits woven by our use of the Net will be different from those woven by our reading of books and other printed works.

Sometime in 1882, Friedrich Nietzsche bought a typewriter—a Malling-Hansen Writing Ball, to be precise. His vision was failing, and keeping his eyes focused on a page had become exhausting and painful, often bringing on crushing headaches. He had been forced to curtail his writing, and he feared that he would soon have to give it up. The typewriter rescued him, at least for a time. Once he had mastered touch-typing, he was able to write with his eyes closed, using only the tips of his fingers. Words could once again flow from his mind to the page.

But the machine had a subtler effect on his work. One of Nietzsche's friends, a composer, noticed a change in the style of his writing. His already terse prose had become even tighter, more telegraphic. "Perhaps you will through this instrument even take to a new idiom," the friend wrote in a letter, noting that, in his own work, his "'thoughts' in music and language often depend on the quality of pen and paper."

"You are right," Nietzsche replied, "our writing equipment takes part in the forming of our thoughts." Under the sway of the machine, writes the German media scholar Friedrich A. Kittler, Nietzsche's prose "changed from arguments to aphorisms, from thoughts to puns, from rhetoric to telegram style."

The human brain is almost infinitely malleable. People used to think that our mental meshwork, the dense connections formed among the 100 billion or so neurons inside our skulls, was largely fixed by the time we reached adulthood. But brain researchers have discovered that that's not the case. James Olds, a professor of neuroscience who directs the Krasnow Institute for Advanced Study at George Mason University, says that even the adult mind "is very plastic." Nerve cells routinely break old connections and form new ones. "The brain," according to Olds, "has the ability to reprogram itself on the fly, altering the way it functions."

As we use what the sociologist Daniel Bell has called our "intellectual technologies"— the tools that extend our mental rather than our physical capacities—we inevitably begin to take on the qualities of those technologies. The mechanical clock, which came into common use in the 14th century, provides a compelling example. In *Technics and Civilization*, the historian and cultural critic Lewis Mumford described how the clock "disassociated time from human events and helped create the belief in an independent world of mathematically measurable sequences." The "abstract framework of divided time" became "the point of reference for both action and thought."

The clock's methodical ticking helped bring into being the scientific mind and the scientific man. But it also took something away. As the late MIT computer scientist Joseph Weizenbaum observed in his 1976 book, *Computer Power and Human Reason: From Judgment to Calculation*, the conception of the world that emerged from the widespread use of timekeeping instruments "remains an impoverished version of the older one, for it rests on a rejection of those direct experiences that formed the basis for, and indeed constituted, the old reality." In deciding when to eat, to work, to sleep, to rise, we stopped listening to our senses and started obeying the clock.

The process of adapting to new intellectual technologies is reflected in the changing metaphors we use to explain ourselves to ourselves. When the mechanical clock arrived, people began thinking of their brains as operating "like clockwork." Today, in the age of software, we have come to think of them as operating "like computers." But the changes, neuroscience tells us, go much deeper than metaphor. Thanks to our brain's plasticity, the adaptation occurs also at a biological level.

The Internet promises to have particularly far-reaching effects on cognition. In a paper published in 1936, the British mathematician Alan Turing proved that a digital computer, which at the time existed only as a theoretical machine, could be programmed to perform the function of any other information-processing device. And that's what we're seeing today. The Internet, an immeasurably powerful computing system, is subsuming most of our other intellectual technologies. It's becoming our map and our clock, our printing press and our typewriter, our calculator and our telephone, and our radio and TV.

When the Net absorbs a medium, that medium is re-created in the Net's image. It injects the medium's content with hyperlinks, blinking ads, and other digital gewgaws, and it surrounds the content with the content of all the other media it has absorbed. A new e-mail message, for instance, may announce its arrival as we're glancing over the latest headlines at a newspaper's site. The result is to scatter our attention and diffuse our concentration.

The Net's influence doesn't end at the edges of a computer screen, either. As people's minds become attuned to the crazy quilt of Internet media, traditional media have to adapt to the audience's new expectations. Television programs add text crawls and pop-up ads, and magazines and newspapers shorten their articles, introduce capsule summaries, and crowd their pages with easy-to-browse info-snippets. When, in March of this year, *The New York Times* decided to devote the second and third pages of every edition to article abstracts, its design director, Tom Bodkin, explained that the "shortcuts" would give harried readers a quick "taste" of the day's news, sparing them the "less efficient" method of actually turning the pages and reading the articles. Old media have little choice but to play by the new-media rules.

Never has a communications system played so many roles in our lives—or exerted such broad influence over our thoughts—as the Internet does today. Yet, for all that's been written about the Net, there's been little consideration of how, exactly, it's reprogramming us. The Net's intellectual ethic remains obscure.

About the same time that Nietzsche started using his typewriter, an earnest young man named Frederick Winslow Taylor carried a stopwatch into the Midvale Steel plant in Philadelphia and began a historic series of experiments aimed at improving the efficiency of the plant's machinists. With the approval of Midvale's owners, he recruited a group of factory hands, set them to work on various metalworking machines, and recorded and timed their every movement as well as the operations of the machines. By breaking down every job into a sequence of small, discrete steps and then testing different ways of performing each one, Taylor created a set of precise instructions—an "algorithm," we might say today—for how each worker should work. Midvale's employees grumbled about the strict new regime, claiming that it turned them into little more than automatons, but the factory's productivity soared.

More than a hundred years after the invention of the steam engine, the Industrial Revolution had at last found its philosophy and its philosopher. Taylor's tight industrial choreography—his "system," as he liked to call it—was embraced by manufacturers throughout the country and, in time, around the world. Seeking maximum speed, maximum efficiency, and maximum output, factory owners used time-and-motion studies to organize their work and configure the jobs of their workers. The goal, as Taylor defined it in his celebrated 1911 treatise, *The Principles of Scientific Management*, was to identify and adopt, for every job, the "one best method" of work and thereby to effect "the gradual substitution of science for rule of thumb throughout the mechanic arts." Once his system was applied to all acts of manual labor, Taylor assured his followers, it would bring about a restructuring not only of industry but of society, creating a utopia of perfect efficiency. "In the past the man has been first," he declared; "in the future the system must be first."

Taylor's system is still very much with us; it remains the ethic of industrial manufacturing. And now, thanks to the growing power that computer engineers and software coders wield over our intellectual lives, Taylor's ethic is beginning to govern the realm of the mind as well. The Internet is a machine designed for the efficient and automated collection, transmission, and manipulation of information, and its legions of programmers are intent on finding the "one best method"—the perfect algorithm—to carry out every mental movement of what we've come to describe as "knowledge work."

Google's headquarters, in Mountain View, California—the Googleplex—is the Internet's high church, and the religion practiced inside its walls is Taylorism. Google, says its chief executive, Eric Schmidt, is "a company that's founded around the science of measurement," and it is striving to "systematize everything" it does. Drawing on the terabytes of behavioral data it collects through its search engine and other sites, it carries out thousands of experiments a day, according to the *Harvard Business Review*, and it uses the results to refine the algorithms that increasingly control how people find information and extract meaning from it. What Taylor did for the work of the hand, Google is doing for the work of the mind.

The company has declared that its mission is "to organize the world's information and make it universally accessible and useful." It seeks to develop "the perfect search engine," which it defines as something that "understands exactly what you mean and gives you back exactly what you want." In Google's view, information is a kind of commodity, a utilitarian resource that can be mined and processed with industrial efficiency. The more pieces of information we can "access" and the faster we can extract their gist, the more productive we become as thinkers.

Where does it end? Sergey Brin and Larry Page, the gifted young men who founded Google while pursuing doctoral degrees in computer science at Stanford, speak frequently of their desire to turn their search engine into an artificial intelligence, a HAL-like machine that might be connected directly to our brains. "The ultimate search engine is something as smart as people—or smarter," Page said in a speech a few years back. "For us, working on search is a way to work on artificial intelligence." In a 2004 interview with *Newsweek*, Brin said, "Certainly if you had all the world's information directly attached to your brain, or an artificial brain that was smarter than your brain, you'd be better off." Last year, Page told a convention of scientists that Google is "really trying to build artificial intelligence and to do it on a large scale."

Such an ambition is a natural one, even an admirable one, for a pair of math whizzes with vast quantities of cash at their disposal and a small army of computer scientists in their employ. A fundamentally scientific enterprise, Google is motivated by a desire to use technology, in Eric Schmidt's words, "to solve problems that have never been solved before," and artificial intelligence is the hardest problem out there. Why wouldn't Brin and Page want to be the ones to crack it?

Still, their easy assumption that we'd all "be better off" if our brains were supplemented, or even replaced, by an artificial intelligence is unsettling. It suggests a belief that intelligence is the output of a mechanical process, a series of discrete steps that can be isolated, measured, and optimized. In Google's world, the world we enter when we go online, there's little place for the fuzziness of contemplation. Ambiguity is not an opening for insight but a bug to be fixed. The human brain is just an outdated computer that needs a faster processor and a bigger hard drive.

The idea that our minds should operate as high-speed data-processing machines is not only built into the workings of the Internet, it is the network's reigning business model as well. The faster we surf across the Web—the more links we click and pages we view— the more opportunities Google and other companies gain to collect information about us and to feed us advertisements. Most of the proprietors of the commercial Internet have a financial stake in collecting the crumbs of data we leave behind as we flit from link to link—the more crumbs, the better. The last thing these companies want is to encourage leisurely reading or slow, concentrated thought. It's in their economic interest to drive us to distraction.

Maybe I'm just a worrywart. Just as there's a tendency to glorify technological progress, there's a countertendency to expect the worst of every new tool or machine. In Plato's *Phaedrus*, Socrates bemoaned the development of writing. He feared that, as people came to rely on the written word as a substitute for the knowledge they used to carry inside their heads, they would, in the words of one of the dialogue's characters, "cease to exercise their memory and become forgetful." And because they would be able to "receive a quantity of information without proper instruction," they would "be thought very knowledgeable when they are for the most part quite ignorant." They would be "filled with the conceit of wisdom instead of real wisdom." Socrates wasn't wrong—the new technology did often have the effects he feared—but he was shortsighted. He couldn't foresee the many ways that writing and reading would serve to spread information, spur fresh ideas, and expand human knowledge (if not wisdom).

The arrival of Gutenberg's printing press, in the 15th century, set off another round of teeth gnashing. The Italian humanist Hieronimo Squarciafico worried that the easy availability of books would lead to intellectual laziness, making men "less studious" and weakening their minds. Others argued that cheaply printed books and broadsheets would undermine religious authority, demean the work of scholars and scribes, and spread sedition and debauchery. As New York University professor Clay Shirky notes, "Most of the arguments made against the printing press were correct, even prescient." But, again, the doomsayers were unable to imagine the myriad blessings that the printed word would deliver.

So, yes, you should be skeptical of my skepticism. Perhaps those who dismiss critics of the Internet as Luddites or nostalgists will be proved correct, and from our hyperactive, data-stoked minds will spring a golden age of intellectual discovery and universal wisdom. Then again, the Net isn't the alphabet, and although it may replace the printing press, it produces something altogether different. The kind of deep reading that a sequence of printed pages promotes is valuable not just for the knowledge we acquire from the author's words but for the intellectual vibrations those words set off within our own minds. In the quiet spaces opened up by the sustained, undistracted reading of a book, or by any other act of contemplation, for that matter, we make our own associations, draw our own inferences and analogies, foster our own ideas. Deep reading, as Maryanne Wolf argues, is indistinguishable from deep thinking.

If we lose those quiet spaces, or fill them up with "content," we will sacrifice something important not only in our selves but in our culture. In a recent essay, the playwright Richard Foreman eloquently described what's at stake:

> I come from a tradition of Western culture, in which the ideal (my ideal) was the complex, dense and "cathedral-like" structure of the highly educated and articulate personality—a man or woman who carried inside themselves a personally constructed and unique version of the entire heritage of the West. [But now] I see within us all (myself included) the replacement of complex inner density with a new kind of self—evolving under the pressure of information overload and the technology of the "instantly available."

As we are drained of our "inner repertory of dense cultural inheritance," Foreman concluded, we risk turning into "'pancake people'—spread wide and thin as we connect with that vast network of information accessed by the mere touch of a button."

I'm haunted by that scene in *2001*. What makes it so poignant, and so weird, is the computer's emotional response to the disassembly of its mind: its despair as one circuit after another goes dark, its childlike pleading with the astronaut—"I can feel it. I can feel it. I'm afraid"—and its final reversion to what can only be called a state of innocence. HAL's outpouring of feeling contrasts with the emotionlessness that characterizes the human figures in the film, who go about their business with an almost robotic efficiency. Their thoughts and actions feel scripted, as if they're following the steps of an algorithm. In the world of *2001*, people have become so machinelike that the most human character turns out to be a machine. That's the essence of Kubrick's dark prophecy: as we come to rely on computers to mediate our understanding of the world, it is our own intelligence that flattens into artificial intelligence.

■ READING AND WRITING

1. What, according to Carr, is the difference between assimilating information and learning?
2. Carr writes that the "Web has been a godsend to me as a writer" but also that this "boon comes at a price." Summarize the advantages that Carr says the Internet offers as well as the drawbacks that he worries might accompany long-term use.
3. Carr uses Google's desire to develop the "perfect search engine" to discuss two kinds of intelligence. How would you describe these? Do you see any reason for concern about the influence technology might be having on intelligence?
4. Do you think Carr presents an effective argument? Why or why not? Does he address possible counterarguments? What are they?

■ DEVELOPING LONGER RESPONSES

5. Write a brief essay in which you answer the following question: Does using the Internet encourage or discourage individuality? Support your response with specific examples based on your experience and on Carr's conclusions.

> *According to his biography at TED.com, Jamais Cascio rejects the "nightmare scenarios of global catastrophe and social meltdown" we so often hear from other futurists in favor of "a different, often surprising alternative: What if human beings, and all of our technology, could actually manage to change things for the better?" In this article, first published in the July/August issue of* Atlantic Monthly, *Cascio argues that humans have the means, right now, to overcome just about anything by harnessing technology and pharmacology to boost intelligence.*

GET SMARTER Jamais Cascio

Seventy-four thousand years ago, humanity nearly went extinct. A super-volcano at what's now Lake Toba, in Sumatra, erupted with a strength more than a thousand times that of Mount St. Helens in 1980. Some 800 cubic kilometers of ash filled the skies of the Northern Hemisphere, lowering global temperatures and pushing a climate already on the verge of an ice age over the edge. Some scientists speculate that as the Earth went into a deep freeze, the population of *Homo sapiens* may have dropped to as low as a few thousand families.

The Mount Toba incident, although unprecedented in magnitude, was part of a broad pattern. For a period of 2 million years, ending with the last ice age around 10,000 B.C., the Earth experienced a series of convulsive glacial events. This rapid-fire climate change meant that humans couldn't rely on consistent patterns to know which animals to hunt, which plants to gather, or even which predators might be waiting around the corner.

How did we cope? By getting smarter. The neurophysiologist William Calvin argues persuasively that modern human cognition—including sophisticated language and the capacity to plan ahead—evolved in response to the demands of this long age of turbulence. According to Calvin, the reason we survived is that our brains changed to meet the challenge: we transformed the ability to target a moving animal with a thrown rock into a capability for foresight and long-term planning. In the process, we may have developed syntax and formal structure from our simple language.

Our present century may not be quite as perilous for the human race as an ice age in the aftermath of a super-volcano eruption, but the next few decades will pose enormous hurdles that go beyond the climate crisis. The end of the fossil-fuel era, the fragility of the global food web, growing population density, and the spread of pandemics, as well as the emergence of radically transformative bio- and nanotechnologies—each of these threatens us with broad disruption or even devastation. And as good as our brains have become at planning ahead, we're still biased toward looking for near-term, simple threats. Subtle, long-term risks, particularly those involving complex, global processes, remain devilishly hard for us to manage.

But here's an optimistic scenario for you: if the next several decades are as bad as some of us fear they could be, we can respond, and survive, the way our species has done time and again: by getting smarter. But this time, we don't have to rely solely on natural evolutionary processes to boost our intelligence. We can do it ourselves.

Most people don't realize that this process is already under way. In fact, it's happening all around us, across the full spectrum of how we understand intelligence. It's visible in the hive mind of the Internet, in the powerful tools for simulation and visualization that are jump-starting new scientific disciplines, and in the development of drugs that some people (myself included) have discovered let them study harder, focus better, and stay awake longer with full clarity. So far, these augmentations have largely been outside of our bodies, but they're very much part of who we are today: they're physically separate from us, but we and they are becoming cognitively inseparable. And advances over the next few decades, driven by breakthroughs in genetic engineering and artificial intelligence, will make today's technologies seem primitive. The nascent jargon of the field describes this as "intelligence augmentation." I prefer to think of it as "You+."

Scientists refer to the 12,000 years or so since the last ice age as the Holocene epoch. It encompasses the rise of human civilization and our co-evolution with tools and technologies that allow us to grapple with our physical environment. But if intelligence augmentation has the kind of impact I expect, we may soon have to start thinking of ourselves as living in an entirely new era. The focus of our technological evolution would be less on how we manage and adapt to our physical world, and more on how we manage and adapt to the immense amount of knowledge we've created. We can call it the Nöocene epoch, from Pierre Teilhard de Chardin's concept of the Nöosphere, a collective consciousness created by the deepening interaction of human minds. As that epoch draws closer, the world is becoming a very different place.

Of course we've been augmenting our ability to think for millennia. When we developed written language, we significantly increased our functional memory and our ability to share insights and knowledge across time and space. The same thing happened with the invention of the printing press, the telegraph, and the radio. The rise of urbanization allowed a fraction of the populace to focus on more-cerebral tasks—a fraction that grew inexorably as more complex economic and social practices demanded more knowledge work, and industrial technology reduced the demand for manual labor. And caffeine and nicotine, of course, are both classic cognitive-enhancement drugs, primitive though they may be.

With every technological step forward, though, has come anxiety about the possibility that technology harms our natural ability to think. These anxieties were given eloquent expression in these pages by Nicholas Carr, whose essay "Is Google Making Us Stupid?" (July/August 2008 *Atlantic*) argued that the information-dense, hyperlink-rich, spastically churning Internet medium is effectively rewiring our brains, making it harder for us to engage in deep, relaxed contemplation.

Carr's fears about the impact of wall-to-wall connectivity on the human intellect echo cyber-theorist Linda Stone's description of "continuous partial attention," the modern phenomenon of having multiple activities and connections under way simultaneously.

We're becoming so accustomed to interruption that we're starting to find focusing difficult, even when we've achieved a bit of quiet. It's an induced form of ADD—a "continuous partial attention-deficit disorder," if you will.

There's also just more information out there—because unlike with previous information media, with the Internet, creating material is nearly as easy as consuming it. And it's easy to mistake more voices for more noise. In reality, though, the proliferation of diverse voices may actually improve our overall ability to think. In *Everything Bad Is Good for You*, Steven Johnson argues that the increasing complexity and range of media we engage with have, over the past century, made us smarter, rather than dumber, by providing a form of cognitive calisthenics. Even pulp-television shows and video games have become extraordinarily dense with detail, filled with subtle references to broader subjects, and more open to interactive engagement. They reward the capacity to make connections and to see patterns—precisely the kinds of skills we need for managing an information glut.

Scientists describe these skills as our "fluid intelligence"—the ability to find meaning in confusion and to solve new problems, independent of acquired knowledge. Fluid intelligence doesn't look much like the capacity to memorize and recite facts, the skills that people have traditionally associated with brainpower. But building it up may improve the capacity to think deeply that Carr and others fear we're losing for good. And we shouldn't let the stresses associated with a transition to a new era blind us to that era's astonishing potential. We swim in an ocean of data, accessible from nearly anywhere, generated by billions of devices. We're only beginning to explore what we can do with this knowledge-at-a-touch.

Moreover, the technology-induced ADD that's associated with this new world may be a short-term problem. The trouble isn't that we have too much information at our fingertips, but that our tools for managing it are still in their infancy. Worries about "information overload" predate the rise of the Web (Alvin Toffler coined the phrase in 1970), and many of the technologies that Carr worries about were developed precisely to help us get some control over a flood of data and ideas. Google isn't the problem; it's the beginning of a solution.

In any case, there's no going back. The information sea isn't going to dry up, and relying on cognitive habits evolved and perfected in an era of limited information flow—and limited information access—is futile. Strengthening our fluid intelligence is the only viable approach to navigating the age of constant connectivity.

When people hear the phrase *intelligence augmentation*, they tend to envision people with computer chips plugged into their brains, or a genetically engineered race of post-human super-geniuses. Neither of these visions is likely to be realized, for reasons familiar to any Best Buy shopper. In a world of ongoing technological acceleration, today's cutting-edge brain implant would be tomorrow's obsolete junk—and good luck if the protocols change or you're on the wrong side of a "format war" (anyone want a Betamax implant?). And then there's the question of stability: Would you want a chip in your head made by the same folks that made your cell phone, or your PC?

Likewise, the safe modification of human genetics is still years away. And even after genetic modification of adult neurobiology becomes possible, the science will remain in flux; our understanding of how augmentation works, and what kinds of genetic modifications are possible, would still change rapidly. As with digital implants, the brain modification you might undergo one week could become obsolete the next. Who would want a 2025-vintage brain when you're competing against hotshots with Model 2026?

Yet in one sense, the age of the cyborg and the super-genius has already arrived. It just involves external information and communication devices instead of implants and genetic modification. The bioethicist James Hughes of Trinity College refers to all of this as "exocortical technology," but you can just think of it as "stuff you already own." Increasingly, we buttress our cognitive functions with our computing systems, no matter that the connections are mediated by simple typing and pointing. These tools enable our brains to do things that would once have been almost unimaginable:

■ powerful simulations and massive data sets allow physicists to visualize, understand, and debate models of an 11-dimension universe;

■ real-time data from satellites, global environmental databases, and high-resolution models allow geophysicists to recognize the subtle signs of long-term changes to the planet;

■ cross-connected scheduling systems allow anyone to assemble, with a few clicks, a complex, multimodal travel itinerary that would have taken a human travel agent days to create.

If that last example sounds prosaic, it simply reflects how embedded these kinds of augmentation have become. Not much more than a decade ago, such a tool was outrageously impressive—and it destroyed the travel-agent industry.

That industry won't be the last one to go. Any occupation requiring pattern-matching and the ability to find obscure connections will quickly morph from the domain of experts to that of ordinary people whose intelligence has been augmented by cheap digital tools. Humans won't be taken out of the loop—in fact, many, many *more* humans will have the capacity to do something that was once limited to a hermetic priesthood. Intelligence augmentation decreases the need for specialization and increases participatory complexity.

As the digital systems we rely upon become faster, more sophisticated, and (with the usual hiccups) more capable, we're becoming more sophisticated and capable too. It's a form of co-evolution: we learn to adapt our thinking and expectations to these digital systems, even as the system designs become more complex and powerful to meet more of our needs—and eventually come to adapt to *us*.

Consider the Twitter phenomenon, which went from nearly invisible to nearly ubiquitous (at least among the online crowd) in early 2007. During busy periods, the user can easily be overwhelmed by the volume of incoming messages, most of which are of only passing interest. But there is a tiny minority of truly valuable posts. (Sometimes they have extreme value, as they did during the October 2007 wildfires in California and the November 2008 terrorist attacks in Mumbai.) At present, however, finding the most-useful bits requires wading through messages like "My kitty sneezed!" and "I hate this taco!"

But imagine if social tools like Twitter had a way to learn what kinds of messages you pay attention to, and which ones you discard. Over time, the messages that you don't really care about might start to fade in the display, while the ones that you do want to see could get brighter. Such attention filters—or focus assistants—are likely to become important parts of how we handle our daily lives. We'll move from a world of "continuous partial attention" to one we might call "continuous augmented awareness."

As processor power increases, tools like Twitter may be able to draw on the complex simulations and massive data sets that have unleashed a revolution in science. They could become individualized systems that augment our capacity for planning and foresight, letting us play "what-if" with our life choices: where to live, what to study, maybe even where to go for dinner. Initially crude and clumsy, such a system would get better with more data and more experience; just as important, we'd get better at asking questions. These systems, perhaps linked to the cameras and microphones in our mobile devices, would eventually be able to pay attention to what we're doing, and to our habits and language quirks, and learn to interpret our sometimes ambiguous desires. With enough time and complexity, they would be able to make useful suggestions without explicit prompting.

And such systems won't be working for us alone. Intelligence has a strong social component; for example, we already provide crude cooperative information-filtering for each other. In time, our interactions through the use of such intimate technologies could dovetail with our use of collaborative knowledge systems (such as Wikipedia), to help us not just to build better data sets, but to filter them with greater precision. As our capacity to provide that filter gets faster and richer, it increasingly becomes something akin to collaborative intuition—in which everyone is effectively augmenting everyone else.

In pharmacology, too, the future is already here. One of the most prominent examples is a drug called modafinil. Developed in the 1970s, modafinil—sold in the U.S. under the brand name Provigil—appeared on the cultural radar in the late 1990s, when the American military began to test it for long-haul pilots. Extended use of modafinil can keep a person awake and alert for well over 32 hours on end, with only a full night's sleep required to get back to a normal schedule.

While it is FDA-approved only for a few sleep disorders, like narcolepsy and sleep apnea, doctors increasingly prescribe it to those suffering from depression, to "shift workers" fighting fatigue, and to frequent business travelers dealing with time-zone shifts. I'm part of the latter group: like more and more professionals, I have a prescription for modafinil in order to help me overcome jet lag when I travel internationally. When I started taking the drug, I expected it to keep me awake; I didn't expect it to make me feel smarter, but that's exactly what happened. The change was subtle but clear, once I recognized it: within an hour of taking a standard 200-mg tablet, I was much more alert, and thinking with considerably more clarity and focus than usual. This isn't just a subjective conclusion. A University of Cambridge study, published in 2003, concluded that modafinil confers a measurable cognitive-enhancement effect across a variety of mental tasks, including pattern recognition and spatial planning, and sharpens focus and alertness.

I'm not the only one who has taken advantage of this effect. The Silicon Valley insider webzine *Tech Crunch* reported in July 2008 that some entrepreneurs now see modafinil as an important competitive tool. The tone of the piece was judgmental, but the implication was clear: everybody's doing it, and if you're not, you're probably falling behind.

This is one way a world of intelligence augmentation emerges. Little by little, people who don't know about drugs like modafinil or don't want to use them will face stiffer competition from the people who do. From the perspective of a culture immersed in athletic doping wars, the use of such drugs may seem like cheating. From the perspective of those who find that they're much more productive using this form of enhancement, it's no more cheating than getting a faster computer or a better education.

Modafinil isn't the only example; on college campuses, the use of ADD drugs (such as Ritalin and Adderall) as study aids has become almost ubiquitous. But these enhancements are primitive. As the science improves, we could see other kinds of cognitive-modification drugs that boost recall, brain plasticity, even empathy and emotional intelligence. They would start as therapeutic treatments, but end up being used to make us "better than normal." Eventually, some of these may become over-the-counter products at your local pharmacy, or in the juice and snack aisles at the supermarket. Spam e-mail would be full of offers to make your brain bigger, and your idea production more powerful.

Such a future would bear little resemblance to *Brave New World* or similar narcomantic nightmares; we may fear the idea of a population kept doped and placated, but we're more likely to see a populace stuck in overdrive, searching out the last bits of competitive advantage, business insight, and radical innovation. No small amount of that innovation would be directed toward inventing the next, more powerful cognitive-enhancement technology.

This would be a different kind of nightmare, perhaps, and cause waves of moral panic and legislative restriction. Safety would be a huge issue. But as we've found with athletic doping, if there's a technique for beating out rivals (no matter how risky), shutting it down is nearly impossible. This would be yet another pharmacological arms race—and in this case, the competitors on one side would just keep getting smarter.

The most radical form of superhuman intelligence, of course, wouldn't be a mind augmented by drugs or exocortical technology; it would be a mind that isn't human at all. Here we move from the realm of extrapolation to the realm of speculation, since solid predictions about artificial intelligence are notoriously hard: our understanding of how the brain creates the mind remains far from good enough to tell us how to construct a mind in a machine.

But while the concept remains controversial, I see no good argument for why a mind running on a machine platform instead of a biological platform will forever be impossible; whether one might appear in five years or 50 or 500, however, is uncertain. I lean toward 50, myself. That's enough time to develop computing hardware able to run a high-speed neural network as sophisticated as that of a human brain, and enough time for the kids who will have grown up surrounded by virtual-world software and household robots—that is, the people who see this stuff not as "Technology," but as everyday tools—to come to dominate the field.

Many proponents of developing an artificial mind are sure that such a breakthrough will be the biggest change in human history. They believe that a machine mind would soon modify itself to get smarter—and with its new intelligence, then figure out how to make itself smarter still. They refer to this intelligence explosion as "the Singularity," a term applied by the computer scientist and science-fiction author Vernor Vinge. "Within thirty years, we will have the technological means to create superhuman intelligence," Vinge wrote in 1993. "Shortly after, the human era will be ended." The Singularity concept is a secular echo of Teilhard de Chardin's "Omega Point," the culmination of the Nöosphere at the end of history. Many believers in Singularity—which one wag has dubbed "the Rapture for nerds"—think that building the first real AI will be the last thing humans do. Some imagine this moment with terror, others with a bit of glee.

My own suspicion is that a stand-alone artificial mind will be more a tool of narrow utility than something especially apocalyptic. I don't think the theory of an explosively self-improving AI is convincing—it's based on too many assumptions about behavior and the nature of the mind. Moreover, AI researchers, after years of talking about this prospect, are already ultra-conscious of the risk of runaway systems.

More important, though, is that the same advances in processor and process that would produce a machine mind would also increase the power of our own cognitive-enhancement technologies. As intelligence augmentation allows us to make *ourselves* smarter, and then smarter still, AI may turn out to be just a sideshow: we could always be a step ahead.

So what's life like in a world of brain doping, intuition networks, and the occasional artificial mind?

Banal.

Not from our present perspective, of course. For us, now, looking a generation ahead might seem surreal and dizzying. But remember: people living in, say, 2030 will have lived every moment from now until then—we won't jump into the future. For someone going from 2009 to 2030 day by day, most of these changes wouldn't be jarring; instead, they'd be incremental, almost overdetermined, and the occasional surprises would quickly blend into the flow of inevitability.

By 2030, then, we'll likely have grown accustomed to (and perhaps even complacent about) a world where sophisticated foresight, detailed analysis and insight, and augmented awareness are commonplace. We'll have developed a better capacity to manage both partial attention and laser-like focus, and be able to slip between the two with ease—perhaps by popping the right pill, or eating the right snack. Sometimes, our augmentation assistants will handle basic interactions on our behalf; that's okay, though, because we'll increasingly see those assistants as extensions of ourselves.

The amount of data we'll have at our fingertips will be staggering, but we'll finally have gotten over the notion that accumulated information alone is a hallmark of intelligence. The power of all of this knowledge will come from its ability to inform difficult decisions, and to support complex analysis. Most professions will likely use simulation and modeling in their day-to-day work, from political decisions to hairstyle options. In a world of augmented intelligence, we will have a far greater appreciation of the consequences of our actions.

This doesn't mean we'll all come to the same conclusions. We'll still clash with each other's emotions, desires, and beliefs. If anything, our arguments will be more intense, buttressed not just by strongly held opinions but by intricate reasoning. People in 2030 will look back aghast at how ridiculously unsubtle the political and cultural disputes of our present were, just as we might today snicker at simplistic advertising from a generation ago.

Conversely, the debates of the 2030s would be remarkable for us to behold. Nuance and multiple layers will characterize even casual disputes; our digital assistants will be there to catch any references we might miss. And all of this will be everyday, banal reality. Today, it sounds mind-boggling; by then, it won't even merit comment.

What happens if such a complex system collapses? Disaster, of course. But don't forget that we already depend upon enormously complex systems that we no longer even think of as technological. Urbanization, agriculture, and trade were at one time huge innovations. Their collapse (and all of them are now at risk, in different ways, as we have seen in recent months) would be an even greater catastrophe than the collapse of our growing webs of interconnected intelligence.

A less apocalyptic but more likely danger derives from the observation made by the science-fiction author William Gibson: "The future is already here, it's just unevenly distributed." The rich, whether nations or individuals, will inevitably gain access to many augmentations before anyone else. We know from history, though, that a world of limited access wouldn't last forever, even as the technology improved: those who sought to impose limits would eventually face angry opponents with newer, better systems.

Even as competition provides access to these kinds of technologies, though, development paths won't be identical. Some societies may be especially welcoming to biotech boosts; others may prefer to use digital tools. Some may readily adopt collaborative approaches; others may focus on individual enhancement. And around the world, many societies will reject the use of intelligence-enhancement technology entirely, or adopt a cautious wait-and-see posture.

The bad news is that these divergent paths may exacerbate cultural divides created by already divergent languages and beliefs. National rivalries often emphasize cultural differences, but for now we're all still standard human beings. What happens when different groups quite literally think in very, very different ways?

The good news, though, is that this diversity of thought can also be a strength. Coping with the various world-historical dangers we face will require the greatest possible insight, creativity, and innovation. Our ability to build the future that we want—not just a future we can survive—depends on our capacity to understand the complex relationships of the world's systems, to take advantage of the diversity of knowledge and experience our civilization embodies, and to fully appreciate the implications of our choices. Such an ability is increasingly within our grasp. The Nöocene awaits.

■ READING AND WRITING

1. According to Cascio, how have we been "augmenting our ability to think for millennia"?
2. How do you feel about evolving into what Cascio calls "You+"?
3. In explaining the use of drugs to augment intelligence, Cascio writes: "From the perspective of a culture immersed in athletic doping wars, the use of such drugs may seem like cheating. From the perspective of those who find that they're much more productive using this form of enhancement, it's no more cheating than getting a faster computer or a better education." Do you agree with Cascio's point? Explain your response.
4. In "The Allegory of the Cave," Plato writes that "in the world of knowledge the idea of good appears last of all, and is seen only with an effort…" How might Cascio respond to this concept of knowledge and "the idea of good"?

■ DEVELOPING LONGER RESPONSES

5. "Get Smart" is, in part, a response to Nicholas Carr's "Is Google Making Us Stupid?" Write a brief essay in which you analyze how Cascio addresses Carr's concerns about technology's ill effects on learning and concentration. Do you find Cascio's counterarguments persuasive? Why or why not?

■ RESEARCH AND WRITING PROJECTS

1. Aristotle, Descartes, Hume, Spinoza, Hegel, and Coleridge (to name a few in the Western tradition) each developed theories of imagination as part of their philosophical projects. Create an annotated bibliography of primary texts that focus on theories of imagination. Your bibliography should consist of at least six texts from six different authors (only two of whom should come from the list above) and should include an introduction that summarizes and contextualizes your research.

2. A recurring theme throughout this chapter is the constant negotiation between what is considered to be "real" or "natural" and what is considered "artificial" or "fake." Choose two essays that explicitly engage in this negotiation. Compare the criteria each uses to arrive at definitions of the real and the artificial. In what ways does the "real" shift? How is the "artificial" characterized? Discuss the inherent weaknesses in each definition. How are these definitions helpful?

3. Using the essays by Carr and Cascio as starting points, further research the questions they raise about the effects that developing technologies are having on abilities to think and learn. Find at least four other reliable sources that explore these issues and use them to develop an argument about the consequences of the further integration of various technologies into our intellectual and imaginative lives.

2 Food for Thought

© Peter Menzel / menzelphoto.com

IMAGE 2.1 shows one of the families featured in *Hungry Planet: What the World Eats* by Peter Menzel and Faith D'Aluisio. This 2005 book presents a photographic study of families from around the world, revealing what they eat during the course of one week. The Aboubakar family, pictured here, of the Breidjing Camp in Chad spent 685 CFA Francs, or $1.23 for a week's worth of food. Think about the rhetorical effects of this photograph. How does it make you feel? What does it make you think? What arguments does it make? Compare this image with those on pages 101 and 160.

While it may be true that we are *what* we eat, the writers in this chapter present compelling evidence that we are *how* we eat, too. These academics, poets, journalists, and activists argue that the food choices we make—individually, as communities, and as a nation— can affect everything from our health to the health of the planet, from the livelihood and culture of billions of people to economic and political stability around the world. Chew on that for a while.

Michael Pollan is the Knight Professor of Journalism at the University of California, Berkeley, and the author of The Omnivore's Dilemma *and* In Defense of Food: An Eater's Manifesto. *He is also a contributing writer for the* New York Times Magazine, *where this essay was published on October 12, 2008.*

FARMER IN CHIEF Michael Pollan

Dear Mr. President-Elect,

It may surprise you to learn that among the issues that will occupy much of your time in the coming years is one you barely mentioned during the campaign: food. Food policy is not something American presidents have had to give much thought to, at least since the Nixon administration—the last time high food prices presented a serious political peril. Since then, federal policies to promote maximum production of the commodity crops (corn, soybeans, wheat and rice) from which most of our supermarket foods are derived have succeeded impressively in keeping prices low and food more or less off the national political agenda. But with a suddenness that has taken us all by surprise, the era of cheap and abundant food appears to be drawing to a close. What this means is that you, like so many other leaders through history, will find yourself confronting the fact—so easy to overlook these past few years—that the health of a nation's food system is a critical issue of national security. Food is about to demand your attention.

Complicating matters is the fact that the price and abundance of food are not the only problems we face; if they were, you could simply follow Nixon's example, appoint a latter-day Earl Butz as your secretary of agriculture and instruct him or her to do whatever it takes to boost production. But there are reasons to think that the old approach won't work this time around; for one thing, it depends on cheap energy that we can no longer count on. For another, expanding production of industrial agriculture today would require you to sacrifice important values on which you did campaign. Which brings me to the deeper reason you will need not simply address food prices but to make the reform of the entire food system one of the highest priorities of your administration: unless you do, you will not be able to make significant progress on the health care crisis, energy independence or climate change. Unlike food, these are issues you did campaign on—but as you try to address them you will quickly discover that the way we currently grow, process and eat food in America goes to the heart of all three problems and will have to change if we hope to solve them. Let me explain.

After cars, the food system uses more fossil fuel than any other sector of the economy—19 percent. And while the experts disagree about the exact amount, the way we feed ourselves contributes more greenhouse gases to the atmosphere than anything else we do—as much as 37 percent, according to one study. Whenever farmers clear land for crops and till the soil, large quantities of carbon are released into the air. But the 20th-century industrialization of agriculture has increased the amount of greenhouse gases emitted by the food system by an order of magnitude; chemical fertilizers (made from natural gas), pesticides (made from petroleum), farm machinery, modern food processing and packaging and transportation have together transformed a system that in 1940 produced 2.3 calories of food energy for every calorie of fossil-fuel energy it used into one that now takes 10 calories of fossil-fuel energy to produce a single calorie of modern supermarket food. Put another way, when we eat from the industrial-food system, we are eating oil and spewing greenhouse gases. This state of affairs appears all the more absurd when you recall that every calorie we eat is ultimately the product of photosynthesis—a process based on making food energy from sunshine. There is hope and possibility in that simple fact.

In addition to the problems of climate change and America's oil addiction, you have spoken at length on the campaign trail of the health care crisis. Spending on health care has risen from 5 percent of national income in 1960 to 16 percent today, putting a significant drag on the economy. The goal of ensuring the health of all Americans depends on getting those costs under control. There are several reasons health care has gotten so expensive, but one of the biggest, and perhaps most tractable, is the cost to the system of preventable chronic diseases. Four of the top 10 killers in America today are chronic diseases linked to diet: heart disease, stroke, Type 2 diabetes and cancer. It is no coincidence that in the years national spending on health care went from 5 percent to 16 percent of national income, spending on food has fallen by a comparable amount—from 18 percent of household income to less than 10 percent. While the surfeit of cheap calories that the U.S. food system has produced since the late 1970s may have taken food prices off the political agenda, this has come at a steep cost to public health. You cannot expect to reform the health care system, much less expand coverage, without confronting the public-health catastrophe that is the modern American diet.

The impact of the American food system on the rest of the world will have implications for your foreign and trade policies as well. In the past several months more than 30 nations have experienced food riots, and so far one government has fallen. Should high grain prices persist and shortages develop, you can expect to see the pendulum shift decisively away from free trade, at least in food. Nations that opened their markets to the global flood of cheap grain (under pressure from previous administrations as well as the World Bank and the I.M.F.) lost so many farmers that they now find their ability to feed their own populations hinges on decisions made in Washington (like your predecessor's precipitous embrace of biofuels) and on Wall Street. They will now rush to rebuild their own agricultural sectors and then seek to protect them by erecting trade barriers. Expect to hear the phrases "food sovereignty" and "food security" on the lips of every foreign leader you meet. Not only the Doha round, but the whole cause of free trade in agriculture is probably dead, the casualty of a cheap food policy that a scant two years ago seemed like a boon for everyone. It is one of the larger paradoxes of our time that the very same food policies that have contributed to overnutrition in the first world are now contributing to undernutrition in the third. But it turns out that too much food can be nearly as big a problem as too little—a lesson we should keep in mind as we set about designing a new approach to food policy.

Rich or poor, countries struggling with soaring food prices are being forcibly reminded that food is a national-security issue. When a nation loses the ability to substantially feed itself, it is not only at the mercy of global commodity markets but of other governments as well. At issue is not only the availability of food, which may be held hostage by a hostile state, but its safety: as recent scandals in China demonstrate, we have little control over the safety of imported foods. The deliberate contamination of our food presents another national-security threat. At his valedictory press conference in 2004, Tommy Thompson, the secretary of health and human services, offered a chilling warning, saying, "I, for the life of me, cannot understand why the terrorists have not attacked our food supply, because it is so easy to do."

This, in brief, is the bad news: the food and agriculture policies you've inherited—designed to maximize production at all costs and relying on cheap energy to do so—are in shambles, and the need to address the problems they have caused is acute. The good news is that the twinned crises in food and energy are creating a political environment in which real reform of the food system may actually be possible for the first time in a generation. The American people are paying more attention to food today than they have in decades, worrying not only about its price but about its safety, its provenance and its healthfulness. There is a gathering sense among the public that the industrial-food system is broken. Markets for alternative kinds of food—organic, local, pasture-based, humane—are thriving as never before. All this suggests that a political constituency for change is building and not only on the left: lately, conservative voices have also been raised in support of reform. Writing of the movement back to local food economies, traditional foods (and family meals) and more sustainable farming, *The American Conservative* magazine editorialized last summer that "this is a conservative cause if ever there was one."

There are many moving parts to the new food agenda I'm urging you to adopt, but the core idea could not be simpler: we need to wean the American food system off its heavy 20th-century diet of fossil fuel and put it back on a diet of contemporary sunshine. True, this is easier said than done—fossil fuel is deeply implicated in everything about the way we currently grow food and feed ourselves. To put the food system back on sunlight will require policies to change how things work at every link in the food chain: in the farm field, in the way food is processed and sold and even in the American kitchen and at the American dinner table. Yet the sun still shines down on our land every day, and photosynthesis can still work its wonders wherever it does. If any part of the modern economy can be freed from its dependence on oil and successfully resolarized, surely it is food.

■ How We Got Here

Before setting out an agenda for reforming the food system, it's important to understand how that system came to be—and also to appreciate what, for all its many problems, it has accomplished. What our food system does well is precisely what it was designed to do, which is to produce cheap calories in great abundance. It is no small thing for an American to be able to go into a fast-food restaurant and to buy a double cheeseburger, fries and a large Coke for a price equal to less than an hour of labor at the minimum wage—indeed, in the long sweep of history, this represents a remarkable achievement.

It must be recognized that the current food system—characterized by monocultures of corn and soy in the field and cheap calories of fat, sugar and feedlot meat on the table—is not simply the product of the free market. Rather, it is the product of a specific set of government policies that sponsored a shift from solar (and human) energy on the farm to fossil-fuel energy.

Did you notice when you flew over Iowa during the campaign how the land was completely bare—black—from October to April? What you were seeing is the agricultural landscape created by cheap oil. In years past, except in the dead of winter, you would have seen in those fields a checkerboard of different greens: pastures and hayfields for animals, cover crops, perhaps a block of fruit trees. Before the application of oil and natural gas to agriculture, farmers relied on crop diversity (and photosynthesis) both to replenish their soil and to combat pests, as well as to feed themselves and their neighbors. Cheap energy, however, enabled the creation of monocultures, and monocultures in turn vastly increased the productivity both of the American land and the American farmer; today the typical corn-belt farmer is single-handedly feeding 140 people.

This did not occur by happenstance. After World War II, the government encouraged the conversion of the munitions industry to fertilizer—ammonium nitrate being the main ingredient of both bombs and chemical fertilizer—and the conversion of nerve-gas research to pesticides. The government also began subsidizing commodity crops, paying farmers by the bushel for all the corn, soybeans, wheat and rice they could produce. One secretary of agriculture after another implored them to plant "fence row to fence row" and to "get big or get out."

The chief result, especially after the Earl Butz years, was a flood of cheap grain that could be sold for substantially less than it cost farmers to grow because a government check helped make up the difference. As this artificially cheap grain worked its way up the food chain, it drove down the price of all the calories derived from that grain: the high-fructose corn syrup in the Coke, the soy oil in which the potatoes were fried, the meat and cheese in the burger.

Subsidized monocultures of grain also led directly to monocultures of animals: since factory farms could buy grain for less than it cost farmers to grow it, they could now fatten animals more cheaply than farmers could. So America's meat and dairy animals migrated from farm to feedlot, driving down the price of animal protein to the point where an American can enjoy eating, on average, 190 pounds of meat a year—a half pound every day.

But if taking the animals off farms made a certain kind of economic sense, it made no ecological sense whatever: their waste, formerly regarded as a precious source of fertility on the farm, became a pollutant—factory farms are now one of America's biggest sources of pollution. As Wendell Berry has tartly observed, to take animals off farms and put them on feedlots is to take an elegant solution—animals replenishing the fertility that crops deplete—and neatly divide it into two problems: a fertility problem on the farm and a pollution problem on the feedlot. The former problem is remedied with fossil-fuel fertilizer; the latter is remedied not at all.

What was once a regional food economy is now national and increasingly global in scope—thanks again to fossil fuel. Cheap energy—for trucking food as well as pumping water—is the reason New York City now gets its produce from California rather than from the "Garden State" next door, as it did before the advent of Interstate highways and national trucking networks. More recently, cheap energy has underwritten a globalized food economy in which it makes (or rather, made) economic sense to catch salmon in Alaska, ship it to China to be filleted and then ship the fillets back to California to be eaten; or one in which California and Mexico can profitably swap tomatoes back and forth across the border; or Denmark and the United States can trade sugar cookies across the Atlantic. About that particular swap the economist Herman Daly once quipped, "Exchanging recipes would surely be more efficient."

Whatever we may have liked about the era of cheap, oil-based food, it is drawing to a close. Even if we were willing to continue paying the environmental or public-health price, we're not going to have the cheap energy (or the water) needed to keep the system going, much less expand production. But as is so often the case, a crisis provides opportunity for reform, and the current food crisis presents opportunities that must be seized.

In drafting these proposals, I've adhered to a few simple principles of what a 21st-century food system needs to do. First, your administration's food policy must strive to provide a healthful diet for all our people; this means focusing on the quality and diversity (and not merely the quantity) of the calories that American agriculture produces and American eaters consume. Second, your policies should aim to improve the resilience, safety and security of our food supply. Among other things, this means promoting regional food economies both in America and around the world. And lastly, your policies need to reconceive agriculture as part of the solution to environmental problems like climate change.

These goals are admittedly ambitious, yet they will not be difficult to align or advance as long as we keep in mind this One Big Idea: most of the problems our food system faces today are because of its reliance on fossil fuels, and to the extent that our policies wring the oil out of the system and replace it with the energy of the sun, those policies will simultaneously improve the state of our health, our environment and our security.

▪ I. Resolarizing the American Farm

What happens in the field influences every other link of the food chain on up to our meals—if we grow monocultures of corn and soy, we will find the products of processed corn and soy on our plates. Fortunately for your initiative, the federal government has enormous leverage in determining exactly what happens on the 830 million acres of American crop and pasture land.

Today most government farm and food programs are designed to prop up the old system of maximizing production from a handful of subsidized commodity crops grown in monocultures. Even food-assistance programs like WIC and school lunch focus on maximizing quantity rather than quality, typically specifying a minimum number of calories (rather than maximums) and seldom paying more than lip service to nutritional quality. This focus on quantity may have made sense in a time of food scarcity, but today it gives us a school-lunch program that feeds chicken nuggets and Tater Tots to overweight and diabetic children.

Your challenge is to take control of this vast federal machinery and use it to drive a transition to a new solar-food economy, starting on the farm. Right now, the government actively discourages the farmers it subsidizes from growing healthful, fresh food: farmers receiving crop subsidies are prohibited from growing "specialty crops"—farm-bill speak for fruits and vegetables. (This rule was the price exacted by California and Florida produce growers in exchange for going along with subsidies for commodity crops.) Commodity farmers should instead be encouraged to grow as many different crops—including animals—as possible. Why? Because the greater the diversity of crops on a farm, the less the need for both fertilizers and pesticides.

The power of cleverly designed polycultures to produce large amounts of food from little more than soil, water and sunlight has been proved, not only by small-scale "alternative" farmers in the United States but also by large rice-and-fish farmers in China and giant-scale operations (up to 15,000 acres) in places like Argentina. There, in a geography roughly comparable to that of the American farm belt, farmers have traditionally employed an ingenious eight-year rotation of perennial pasture and annual crops: after five years grazing cattle on pasture (and producing the world's best beef), farmers can then grow three years of grain without applying any fossil-fuel fertilizer. Or, for that matter, many pesticides: the weeds that afflict pasture can't survive the years of tillage, and the weeds of row crops don't survive the years of grazing, making herbicides all but unnecessary. There is no reason—save current policy and custom—that American farmers couldn't grow both high-quality grain and grass-fed beef under such a regime through much of the Midwest. (It should be noted that today's sky-high grain prices are causing many Argentine farmers to abandon their rotation to grow grain and soybeans exclusively, an environmental disaster in the making.)

Federal policies could do much to encourage this sort of diversified sun farming. Begin with the subsidies: payment levels should reflect the number of different crops farmers grow or the number of days of the year their fields are green—that is, taking advantage of photosynthesis, whether to grow food, replenish the soil or control erosion. If Midwestern farmers simply planted a cover crop after the fall harvest, they would significantly reduce their need for fertilizer, while cutting down on soil erosion. Why don't farmers do this routinely? Because in recent years fossil-fuel-based fertility has been so much cheaper and easier to use than sun-based fertility.

In addition to rewarding farmers for planting cover crops, we should make it easier for them to apply compost to their fields—a practice that improves not only the fertility of the soil but also its ability to hold water and therefore withstand drought. (There is mounting evidence that it also boosts the nutritional quality of the food grown in it.) The U.S.D.A. estimates that Americans throw out 14 percent of the food they buy; much more is wasted by retailers, wholesalers and institutions. A program to make municipal composting of food and yard waste mandatory and then distributing the compost free to area farmers would shrink America's garbage heap, cut the need for irrigation and fossil-fuel fertilizers in agriculture and improve the nutritional quality of the American diet.

Right now, most of the conservation programs run by the U.S.D.A. are designed on the zero-sum principle: land is either locked up in "conservation" or it is farmed intensively. This either-or approach reflects an outdated belief that modern farming and ranching are inherently destructive, so that the best thing for the environment is to leave land untouched. But we now know how to grow crops and graze animals in systems that will support biodiversity, soil health, clean water and carbon sequestration. The Conservation Stewardship Program, championed by Senator Tom Harkin and included in the 2008 Farm Bill, takes an important step toward rewarding these kinds of practices, but we need to move this approach from the periphery of our farm policy to the very center. Longer term, the government should back ambitious research now under way (at the Land Institute in Kansas and a handful of other places) to "perennialize" commodity agriculture: to breed varieties of wheat, rice and other staple grains that can be grown like prairie grasses—without having to till the soil every year. These perennial grains hold the promise of slashing the fossil fuel now needed to fertilize and till the soil, while protecting farmland from erosion and sequestering significant amounts of carbon.

But that is probably a 50-year project. For today's agriculture to wean itself from fossil fuel and make optimal use of sunlight, crop plants and animals must once again be married on the farm—as in Wendell Berry's elegant "solution." Sunlight nourishes the grasses and grains, the plants nourish the animals, the animals then nourish the soil, which in turn nourishes the next season's grasses and grains. Animals on pasture can also harvest their own feed and dispose of their own waste—all without our help or fossil fuel.

If this system is so sensible, you might ask, why did it succumb to Confined Animal Feeding Operations, or CAFOs? In fact there is nothing inherently efficient or economical about raising vast cities of animals in confinement. Three struts, each put into place by federal policy, support the modern CAFO, and the most important of these—the ability to buy grain for less than it costs to grow it—has just been kicked away. The second strut is F.D.A. approval for the routine use of antibiotics in feed, without which the animals in these places could not survive their crowded, filthy and miserable existence. And the third is that the government does not require CAFOs to treat their wastes as it would require human cities of comparable size to do. The F.D.A. should ban the routine use of antibiotics in livestock feed on public-health grounds, now that we have evidence that the practice is leading to the evolution of drug-resistant bacterial diseases and to outbreaks of E. coli and salmonella poisoning. CAFOs should also be regulated like the factories they are, required to clean up their waste like any other industry or municipality.

It will be argued that moving animals off feedlots and back onto farms will raise the price of meat. It probably will—as it should. You will need to make the case that paying the real cost of meat, and therefore eating less of it, is a good thing for our health, for the environment, for our dwindling reserves of fresh water and for the welfare of the animals. Meat and milk production represent the food industry's greatest burden on the environment; a recent U.N. study estimated that the world's livestock alone account for 18 percent of all greenhouse gases, more than all forms of transportation combined. (According to one study, a pound of feedlot beef also takes 5,000 gallons of water to produce.) And while animals living on farms will still emit their share of greenhouse gases, grazing them on grass and returning their waste to the soil will substantially offset their carbon hoof prints, as will getting ruminant animals off grain. A bushel of grain takes approximately a half gallon of oil to produce; grass can be grown with little more than sunshine.

It will be argued that sun-food agriculture will generally yield less food than fossil-fuel agriculture. This is debatable. The key question you must be prepared to answer is simply this: Can the sort of sustainable agriculture you're proposing feed the world?

There are a couple of ways to answer this question. The simplest and most honest answer is that we don't know, because we haven't tried. But in the same way we now need to learn how to run an industrial economy without cheap fossil fuel, we have no choice but to find out whether sustainable agriculture can produce enough food. The fact is, during the past century, our agricultural research has been directed toward the goal of maximizing production with the help of fossil fuel. There is no reason to think that bringing the same sort of resources to the development of more complex, sun-based agricultural systems wouldn't produce comparable yields. Today's organic farmers, operating for the most part without benefit of public investment in research, routinely achieve 80 to 100 percent of conventional yields in grain and, in drought years, frequently exceed conventional yields. (This is because organic soils better retain moisture.) Assuming no further improvement, could the world—with a population expected to peak at 10 billion—survive on these yields?

First, bear in mind that the average yield of world agriculture today is substantially lower than that of modern sustainable farming. According to a recent University of Michigan study, merely bringing international yields up to today's organic levels could increase the world's food supply by 50 percent.

The second point to bear in mind is that yield isn't everything—and growing high-yield commodities is not quite the same thing as growing food. Much of what we're growing today is not directly eaten as food but processed into low-quality calories of fat and sugar. As the world epidemic of diet-related chronic disease has demonstrated, the sheer quantity of calories that a food system produces improves health only up to a point, but after that, quality and diversity are probably more important. We can expect that a food system that produces somewhat less food but of a higher quality will produce healthier populations.

The final point to consider is that 40 percent of the world's grain output today is fed to animals; 11 percent of the world's corn and soybean crop is fed to cars and trucks, in the form of biofuels. Provided the developed world can cut its consumption of grain-based animal protein and ethanol, there should be plenty of food for everyone—however we choose to grow it.

In fact, well-designed polyculture systems, incorporating not just grains but vegetables and animals, can produce more food per acre than conventional monocultures, and food of a much higher nutritional value. But this kind of farming is complicated and needs many more hands on the land to make it work. Farming without fossil fuels—performing complex rotations of plants and animals and managing pests without petrochemicals—is labor intensive and takes more skill than merely "driving and spraying," which is how corn-belt farmers describe what they do for a living.

To grow sufficient amounts of food using sunlight will require more people growing food—millions more. This suggests that sustainable agriculture will be easier to implement in the developing world, where large rural populations remain, than in the West, where they don't. But what about here in America, where we have only about two million farmers left to feed a population of 300 million? And where farmland is being lost to development at the rate of 2,880 acres a day? Post-oil agriculture will need a lot more people engaged in food production—as farmers and probably also as gardeners.

The sun-food agenda must include programs to train a new generation of farmers and then help put them on the land. The average American farmer today is 55 years old; we shouldn't expect these farmers to embrace the sort of complex ecological approach to agriculture that is called for. Our focus should be on teaching ecological farming systems to students entering land-grant colleges today. For decades now, it has been federal policy to shrink the number of farmers in America by promoting capital-intensive monoculture and consolidation. As a society, we devalued farming as an occupation and encouraged the best students to leave the farm for "better" jobs in the city. We emptied America's rural counties in order to supply workers to urban factories. To put it bluntly, we now need to reverse course. We need more highly skilled small farmers in more places all across America— not as a matter of nostalgia for the agrarian past but as a matter of national security. For nations that lose the ability to substantially feed themselves will find themselves as gravely compromised in their international dealings as nations that depend on foreign sources of oil presently do. But while there are alternatives to oil, there are no alternatives to food.

National security also argues for preserving every acre of farmland we can and then making it available to new farmers. We simply will not be able to depend on distant sources of food, and therefore need to preserve every acre of good farmland within a day's drive of our cities. In the same way that when we came to recognize the supreme ecological value of wetlands we erected high bars to their development, we need to recognize the value of farmland to our national security and require real-estate developers to do "food-system impact statements" before development begins. We should also create tax and zoning incentives for developers to incorporate farmland (as they now do "open space") in their subdivision plans; all those subdivisions now ringing golf courses could someday have diversified farms at their center.

The revival of farming in America, which of course draws on the abiding cultural power of our agrarian heritage, will pay many political and economic dividends. It will lead to robust economic renewal in the countryside. And it will generate tens of millions of new "green jobs," which is precisely how we need to begin thinking of skilled solar farming: as a vital sector of the 21st-century post-fossil-fuel economy.

■ II. Reregionalizing the Food System

For your sun-food agenda to succeed, it will have to do a lot more than alter what happens on the farm. The government could help seed a thousand new polyculture farmers in every county in Iowa, but they would promptly fail if the grain elevator remained the only buyer in town and corn and beans were the only crops it would take. Resolarizing the food system means building the infrastructure for a regional food economy—one that can support diversified farming and, by shortening the food chain, reduce the amount of fossil fuel in the American diet.

A decentralized food system offers a great many other benefits as well. Food eaten closer to where it is grown will be fresher and require less processing, making it more nutritious. Whatever may be lost in efficiency by localizing food production is gained in resilience: regional food systems can better withstand all kinds of shocks. When a single factory is grinding 20 million hamburger patties in a week or washing 25 million servings of salad, a single terrorist armed with a canister of toxins can, at a stroke, poison millions. Such a system is equally susceptible to accidental contamination: the bigger and more global the trade in food, the more vulnerable the system is to catastrophe. The best way to protect our food system against such threats is obvious: decentralize it.

Today in America there is soaring demand for local and regional food; farmers' markets, of which the U.S.D.A. estimates there are now 4,700, have become one of the fastest-growing segments of the food market. Community-supported agriculture is booming as well: there are now nearly 1,500 community-supported farms, to which consumers pay an annual fee in exchange for a weekly box of produce through the season. The local-food movement will continue to grow with no help from the government, especially as high fuel prices make distant and out-of-season food, as well as feedlot meat, more expensive. Yet there are several steps the government can take to nurture this market and make local foods more affordable. Here are a few:

■ Four-Season Farmers' Markets. Provide grants to towns and cities to build year-round indoor farmers' markets, on the model of Pike Place in Seattle or the Reading Terminal Market in Philadelphia. To supply these markets, the U.S.D.A. should make grants to rebuild local distribution networks in order to minimize the amount of energy used to move produce within local food sheds.

■ Agricultural Enterprise Zones. Today the revival of local food economies is being hobbled by a tangle of regulations originally designed to check abuses by the very largest food producers. Farmers should be able to smoke a ham and sell it to their neighbors without making a huge investment in federally approved facilities. Food-safety regulations must be made sensitive to scale and marketplace, so that a small producer selling direct off the farm or at a farmers' market is not regulated as onerously as a multinational food manufacturer. This is not because local food won't ever have food-safety problems—it will—only that its problems will be less catastrophic and easier to manage because local food is inherently more traceable and accountable.

■ Local Meat-Inspection Corps. Perhaps the single greatest impediment to the return of livestock to the land and the revival of local, grass-based meat production is the disappearance of regional slaughter facilities. The big meat processors have been buying up local abattoirs only to close them down as they consolidate, and the U.S.D.A. does little to support the ones that remain. From the department's perspective, it is a better use of shrinking resources to dispatch its inspectors to a plant slaughtering 400 head an hour than to a regional abattoir slaughtering a dozen. The U.S.D.A. should establish a Local Meat-Inspectors Corps to serve these processors. Expanding on its successful pilot program on Lopez Island in

Puget Sound, the U.S.D.A. should also introduce a fleet of mobile abattoirs that would go from farm to farm, processing animals humanely and inexpensively. Nothing would do more to make regional, grass-fed meat fully competitive in the market with feedlot meat.

■ Establish a Strategic Grain Reserve. In the same way the shift to alternative energy depends on keeping oil prices relatively stable, the sun-food agenda—as well as the food security of billions of people around the world—will benefit from government action to prevent huge swings in commodity prices. A strategic grain reserve, modeled on the Strategic Petroleum Reserve, would help achieve this objective and at the same time provide some cushion for world food stocks, which today stand at perilously low levels. Governments should buy and store grain when it is cheap and sell when it is dear, thereby moderating price swings in both directions and discouraging speculation.

■ Regionalize Federal Food Procurement. In the same way that federal procurement is often used to advance important social goals (like promoting minority-owned businesses), we should require that some minimum percentage of government food purchases—whether for school-lunch programs, military bases or federal prisons—go to producers located within 100 miles of institutions buying the food. We should create incentives for hospitals and universities receiving federal funds to buy fresh local produce. To channel even a small portion of institutional food purchasing to local food would vastly expand regional agriculture and improve the diet of the millions of people these institutions feed.

■ Create a Federal Definition of "Food." It makes no sense for government food-assistance dollars, intended to improve the nutritional health of at-risk Americans, to support the consumption of products we know to be unhealthful. Yes, some people will object that for the government to specify what food stamps can and cannot buy smacks of paternalism. Yet we already prohibit the purchase of tobacco and alcohol with food stamps. So why not prohibit something like soda, which is arguably less nutritious than red wine? Because it is, nominally, a food, albeit a "junk food." We need to stop flattering nutritionally worthless foodlike substances by calling them "junk food"—and instead make clear that such products are not in fact food of any kind. Defining what constitutes real food worthy of federal support will no doubt be controversial (you'll recall President Reagan's ketchup imbroglio), but defining food upward may be more politically palatable than defining it down, as Reagan sought to do. One approach would be to rule that, in order to be regarded as a food by the government, an edible substance must contain a certain minimum ratio of micronutrients per calorie of energy. At a stroke, such a definition would improve the quality of school lunch and discourage sales of unhealthful products, since typically only "food" is exempt from local sales tax.

A few other ideas: Food-stamp debit cards should double in value whenever swiped at farmers' markets—all of which, by the way, need to be equipped with the Electronic Benefit Transfer card readers that supermarkets already have. We should expand the WIC program that gives farmers'-market vouchers to low-income women with children; such programs help attract farmers' markets to urban neighborhoods where access to fresh produce is often nonexistent. (We should also offer tax incentives to grocery chains willing to build supermarkets in underserved neighborhoods.) Federal food assistance for the elderly should build on a successful program pioneered by the state of Maine that buys low-income seniors a membership in a community-supported farm. All these initiatives have the virtue of advancing two objectives at once: supporting the health of at-risk Americans and the revival of local food economies.

■ III. Rebuilding America's Food Culture

In the end, shifting the American diet from a foundation of imported fossil fuel to local sunshine will require changes in our daily lives, which by now are deeply implicated in the economy and culture of fast, cheap and easy food. Making available more healthful and more sustainable food does not guarantee it will be eaten, much less appreciated or enjoyed. We need to use all the tools at our disposal—not just federal policy and public education but the president's bully pulpit and the example of the first family's own dinner table—to promote a new culture of food that can undergird your sun-food agenda.

Changing the food culture must begin with our children, and it must begin in the schools. Nearly a half-century ago, President Kennedy announced a national initiative to improve the physical fitness of American children. He did it by elevating the importance of physical education, pressing states to make it a requirement in public schools. We need to bring the same commitment to "edible education"—in Alice Waters's phrase—by making lunch, in all its dimensions, a mandatory part of the curriculum. On the premise that eating well is a critically important life skill, we need to teach all primary-school students the basics of growing and cooking food and then enjoying it at shared meals.

To change our children's food culture, we'll need to plant gardens in every primary school, build fully equipped kitchens, train a new generation of lunchroom ladies (and gentlemen) who can once again cook and teach cooking to children. We should introduce a School Lunch Corps program that forgives federal student loans to culinary-school graduates in exchange for two years of service in the public-school lunch program. And we should immediately increase school-lunch spending per pupil by $1 a day—the minimum amount food-service experts believe it will take to underwrite a shift from fast food in the cafeteria to real food freshly prepared.

But it is not only our children who stand to benefit from public education about food. Today most federal messages about food, from nutrition labeling to the food pyramid, are negotiated with the food industry. The surgeon general should take over from the Department of Agriculture the job of communicating with Americans about their diet. That way we might begin to construct a less equivocal and more effective public-health message about nutrition. Indeed, there is no reason that public-health campaigns about the dangers of obesity and Type 2 diabetes shouldn't be as tough and as effective as public-health campaigns about the dangers of smoking. The Centers for Disease Control estimates that one in three American children born in 2000 will develop Type 2 diabetes. The public needs to know and see precisely what that sentence means: blindness; amputation; early death. All of which can be avoided by a change in diet and lifestyle. A public-health crisis of this magnitude calls for a blunt public-health message, even at the expense of offending the food industry. Judging by the success of recent antismoking campaigns, the savings to the health care system could be substantial.

There are other kinds of information about food that the government can supply or demand. In general we should push for as much transparency in the food system as possible—the other sense in which "sunlight" should be the watchword of our agenda. The F.D.A. should require that every packaged-food product include a second calorie count, indicating how many calories of fossil fuel went into its production. Oil is one of the most important ingredients in our food, and people ought to know just how much of it they're eating. The government should also throw its support behind putting a second bar code on all food products that, when scanned either in the store or at home (or with a cellphone), brings up on a screen the whole story and pictures of how that product was produced: in the case of crops, images of the farm and lists of agrochemicals used in its production; in the case of meat and dairy, descriptions of the animals' diet and drug regimen, as well as live video feeds of the CAFO where they live and, yes, the slaughterhouse where they die. The very length and complexity of the modern food chain breeds a culture of ignorance and indifference among eaters. Shortening the food chain is one way to create more conscious consumers, but deploying technology to pierce the veil is another.

Finally, there is the power of the example you set in the White House. If what's needed is a change of culture in America's thinking about food, then how America's first household organizes its eating will set the national tone, focusing the light of public attention on the issue and communicating a simple set of values that can guide Americans toward sun-based foods and away from eating oil.

The choice of White House chef is always closely watched, and you would be wise to appoint a figure who is identified with the food movement and committed to cooking simply from fresh local ingredients. Besides feeding you and your family exceptionally well, such a chef would demonstrate how it is possible even in Washington to eat locally for much of the year, and that good food needn't be fussy or complicated but does depend on good farming. You should make a point of the fact that every night you're in town, you join your family for dinner in the Executive Residence—at a table. (Surely you remember the Reagans' TV trays.) And you should also let it be known that the White House observes one meatless day a week—a step that, if all Americans followed suit, would be the equivalent, in carbon saved, of taking 20 million midsize sedans off the road for a year. Let the White House chef post daily menus on the Web, listing the farmers who supplied the food, as well as recipes.

Since enhancing the prestige of farming as an occupation is critical to developing the sun-based regional agriculture we need, the White House should appoint, in addition to a White House chef, a White House farmer. This new post would be charged with implementing what could turn out to be your most symbolically resonant step in building a new American food culture. And that is this: tear out five prime south-facing acres of the White House lawn and plant in their place an organic fruit and vegetable garden.

When Eleanor Roosevelt did something similar in 1943, she helped start a Victory Garden movement that ended up making a substantial contribution to feeding the nation in wartime. (Less well known is the fact that Roosevelt planted this garden over the objections of the U.S.D.A., which feared home gardening would hurt the American food industry.) By the end of the war, more than 20 million home gardens were supplying 40 percent of the produce consumed in America. The president should throw his support behind a new Victory Garden movement, this one seeking "victory" over three critical challenges we face today: high food prices, poor diets and a sedentary population. Eating from this, the shortest food chain of all, offers anyone with a patch of land a way to reduce their fossil-fuel consumption and help fight climate change. (We should offer grants to cities to build allotment gardens for people without access to land.) Just as important, Victory Gardens offer a way to enlist Americans, in body as well as mind, in the work of feeding themselves and changing the food system—something more ennobling, surely, than merely asking them to shop a little differently.

I don't need to tell you that ripping out even a section of the White House lawn will be controversial: Americans love their lawns, and the South Lawn is one of the most beautiful in the country. But imagine all the energy, water and petrochemicals it takes to make it that way. (Even for the purposes of this memo, the White House would not disclose its lawn-care regimen.) Yet as deeply as Americans feel about their lawns, the agrarian ideal runs deeper still, and making this particular plot of American land productive, especially if the First Family gets out there and pulls weeds now and again, will provide an image even more stirring than that of a pretty lawn: the image of stewardship of the land, of self-reliance and of making the most of local sunlight to feed one's family and community. The fact that surplus produce from the South Lawn Victory Garden (and there will be literally tons of it) will be offered to regional food banks will make its own eloquent statement.

You're probably thinking that growing and eating organic food in the White House carries a certain political risk. It is true you might want to plant iceberg lettuce rather than arugula, at least to start. (Or simply call arugula by its proper American name, as generations of Midwesterners have done: "rocket.") But it should not be difficult to deflect the charge of elitism sometimes leveled at the sustainable-food movement. Reforming the food system is not inherently a right-or-left issue: for every Whole Foods shopper with roots in the counterculture you can find a family of evangelicals intent on taking control of its family dinner and diet back from the fast-food industry—the culinary equivalent of home schooling. You should support hunting as a particularly sustainable way to eat meat—meat grown without any fossil fuels whatsoever. There is also a strong libertarian component to the sun-food agenda, which seeks to free small producers from the burden of government regulation in order to stoke rural innovation. And what is a higher "family value," after all, than making time to sit down every night to a shared meal?

Our agenda puts the interests of America's farmers, families and communities ahead of the fast-food industry's. For that industry and its apologists to imply that it is somehow more "populist" or egalitarian to hand our food dollars to Burger King or General Mills than to support a struggling local farmer is absurd. Yes, sun food costs more, but the reasons why it does only undercut the charge of elitism: cheap food is only cheap because of government handouts and regulatory indulgence (both of which we will end), not to mention the exploitation of workers, animals and the environment on which its putative "economies" depend. Cheap food is food dishonestly priced—it is in fact unconscionably expensive.

Your sun-food agenda promises to win support across the aisle. It builds on America's agrarian past, but turns it toward a more sustainable, sophisticated future. It honors the work of American farmers and enlists them in three of the 21st century's most urgent errands: to move into the post-oil era, to improve the health of the American people and to mitigate climate change. Indeed, it enlists all of us in this great cause by turning food consumers into part-time producers, reconnecting the American people with the American land and demonstrating that we need not choose between the welfare of our families and the health of the environment—that eating less oil and more sunlight will redound to the benefit of both.

■ READING AND WRITING

1. Pollan's letter presents a long and multifaceted argument about food and agricultural policies. In 300 words or less, write a complete and accurate summary of Pollan's main ideas.
2. Part of Pollan's plan calls for re-establishing a "regional food economy— one that can support diversified farming and, by shortening the food chain, reduce the amount of fossil fuel in the American diet." What are the regional food options around Columbia? Where does this food come from?

■ DEVELOPING LONGER RESPONSES

3. Throughout his essay, Pollan anticipates and addresses objections to his ideas. Point to specific passages in the text where he makes concessions, rebuts opposing views, or in any other way deals with ideas and opinions that challenge his own. How does Pollan's attention to opposing viewpoints strengthen his argument?

■ **USING RESEARCH**

4. Pollan suggests several specific things that President Obama should do to begin solving America's food and farming crises. Using the library's resources and the internet, find out what the president has done to address any of the issues raised in Pollan's essay. Compile your findings into a brief informative essay.

> *Poet, novelist, and essayist Wendell Berry has spent much of his life thinking, writing, and teaching about American life in general and agricultural life in particular. As the following text makes clear, he is an eloquent and determined critic of farm and food policies that continue to move Americans further away from the land—literally and figuratively. Berry delivered "Renewing Husbandry" as a lecture at the 2004 international meeting of the American Society of Agronomy, the Crop Science Society of America, the Soil Science Society of America, and the Canadian Society of Soil Science. The speech was also adapted into an essay published in the May 6, 2005, issue of the journal* Crop Science.

RENEWING HUSBANDRY   Wendell Berry

I remember well a summer morning in about 1950 when my father sent a hired man with a McCormick High Gear No. 9 mowing machine and a team of mules to the field I was mowing with our nearly new Farmall A. That memory is a landmark in my mind and my history for reasons that are clear enough. I had been born into the way of farming represented by the mule team, and I loved it. I knew irresistibly that the mules were good ones. They were stepping along beautifully at a rate of speed in fact only a little slower than mine. But now I saw them suddenly from the vantage point of the tractor, and I remember how fiercely I resented their slowness. I saw them as "in my way." For those who have had no similar experience, I will explain that I was feeling exactly the outrage and the low-grade superiority of a hot-rodder caught behind an aged dawdler in urban traffic. It is undoubtedly significant that in the summer of 1950 I passed my sixteenth birthday and became eligible to solve all my problems by driving an automobile.

This is not an exceptional or a remarkably dramatic bit of history. I recite it here to confirm that the industrialization of agriculture is a part of my familiar experience. I don't have the privilege of looking at it as an outsider. It is not incomprehensible to me. The burden of this speech, on the contrary, is that the industrialization of agriculture is a grand oversimplification, too readily comprehensible, to me and to everybody else.

We were mowing that morning, the teamster with his mules and I with the tractor, in the field behind the barn on my father's home place, where he and before him his father had been born, and where his father had died in February of 1946. The old way of farming was intact in my grandfather's mind until the day he died at eighty-two. He had worked mules all his life, understood them thoroughly, and loved the good ones passionately. He knew tractors only from a distance, he had seen only a few of them, and he rejected them out of hand because he thought, correctly, that they compacted the soil.

Even so, four years after his death his grandson's sudden resentment of the "slow" mule team foretold what history would bear out: the tractor would stay and the mules would go. Year after year, agriculture would be adapted more and more to the technology and the processes of industry and to the rule of industrial economics. This transformation occurred with astonishing speed, and it did so because, by the measures it set for itself, it was wonderfully successful. It "saved labor," it conferred the prestige of modernity, and it was highly productive.

Though I never entirely departed from farming or at least from thoughts of farming, and my affection for my own homeland remained strong, during the fourteen years after 1950 I was much away from home and was not giving to farming the close and continuous attention I have given to it in the forty years since.

In 1964 my family and I returned to Kentucky and in a year were settled on a hillside farm in my native community, where we have continued to live. Perhaps because I was a returned traveler, intending to stay, I now saw the place more clearly than before. I saw it critically too, for it was evident at once that the human life of the place, the life of the farms and the farming community, was in decline. The old self-sufficient way of farming was passing away. The economic prosperity that had visited the farmers briefly during World War II and for a few years afterward had ended. The little towns, that once had been social and economic centers, thronged with country people on Saturdays and Saturday nights, were losing out to the bigger towns and the cities. The rural neighborhoods, once held together by common memories, common work, and the sharing of help, had begun to dissolve. There were no longer local markets for chickens or eggs or cream. The spring lamb industry, once a staple of the region, was gone. The tractors and other mechanical devices certainly were saving the labor of the farmers and farm hands who had moved away, but those who had stayed were working harder and longer than ever.

Because I remembered with affection and respect my grandparents and other country people of their generation, and because I had admirable friends and neighbors with whom I was again farming, I began to ask what was happening, and why. I began to ask what would be the effect on the land, on the community, on the natural world, and on the art of farming. And these questions have occupied me steadily ever since.

By now the effects of this process of industrialization have become so apparent, so numerous, so favorable to the agribusiness corporations, and so unfavorable to everything else, that the questions troubling me and a few others in the '60s and '70s are now being asked everywhere.

There are no doubt many ways of accounting for this change, but for convenience and brevity I am going to attribute it to the emergence of context as an issue. It has become increasingly clear that the way we farm affects the local community, and that the economy of the local community affects the way we farm; that the way we farm affects the health and integrity of the local ecosystem, and that the farm is intricately dependent, even economically, upon the health of the local ecosystem. We can no longer pretend that agriculture is a sort of economic machine with interchangeable parts, the same everywhere, determined by market forces and independent of everything else. We are not farming in a specialist capsule or a professionalist department; we are farming in the world, in a webwork of dependences and influences probably more intricate than we will ever understand. It has become clear, in short, that we have been running our fundamental economic enterprise by the wrong rules. We were wrong to assume that agriculture could be adequately defined by reductionist science and determinist economics.

If you can keep the context narrow enough (and the accounting period short enough), then the industrial criteria of labor saving and high productivity seem to work well. But the old rules of ecological coherence and of community life have remained in effect. The costs of ignoring them have accumulated, until now the boundaries of our reductive and mechanical explanations have collapsed. Now, in the midst of much unnecessary human and ecological damage, we are facing the necessity of a new start in agriculture.

And so it is not possible to look back at the tableau of team and tractor on that morning in 1950 and see it as I saw it then. That is not because I have changed, though obviously I have; it is because, in the fifty-four years since then, history and the law of consequence have widened the context of the scene as circles widen on water around a thrown stone.

My impatience at the slowness of the mules, I think, was a fairly representative emotion. I thought I was witnessing a contest of machine against organism, which the machine was bound to win. I did not see that the team arrived at the field that morning from the history of farming and from the farm itself, whereas the tractor arrived from almost an opposite history, and by means of a process reaching a long way beyond that farm or any farm. It took me a long time to understand that the team belonged to the farm and was directly supportable by it, whereas the tractor belonged to an economy that would remain alien to agriculture, and it functioned entirely by means of distant supplies and long supply lines. The tractor's arrival had signaled, among other things, agriculture's shift from an almost exclusive dependence on free solar energy to a total dependence on costly fossil fuel. But in 1950, like most people at that time, I was years away from the first inkling of the limits of the supply of cheap fuel. We had entered an era of limitlessness, or the illusion thereof, and this in itself is a sort of wonder. My grandfather lived a life of limits, both suffered and strictly observed, in a world of limits. I learned much of that world from him and others, and then I changed; I entered the world of labor-saving machines and of limitless cheap fossil fuel. After that, it took me years of reading, thought, and experience, to learn again that in this world limits are not only inescapable but indispensable.

My purpose here is not to disturb the question of the use of draft animals in agriculture—though I doubt that it will sleep indefinitely. I want instead to talk about the tractor as an influence. The means we use to do our work almost certainly affect the way we look at the world. It would be absurd to assume otherwise. If the fragment of autobiography I began with means anything, it means that my transformation from a boy who had so far grown up driving a team to a boy driving a tractor was a sight-changing experience.

Brought up as a teamster but now driving a tractor, the boy almost suddenly, almost perforce, sees the farm in a different way: as ground to be got over by a means entirely different, at an entirely different cost. The team, like the boy, would grow weary, but that weariness has all at once been subtracted, and the boy is now divided from the ground by the absence of a link enforcing sympathy as a practical value. The tractor can work at maximum speed hour after hour without tiring. There is no longer a reason to remember the shady spots where it was good to stop and rest. Tirelessness and speed enforce a second, more perilous change in the way the boy sees the farm: Now he sees it as ground to be got over as fast as possible and, ideally, without stopping. In the midst of farming he has taken on the psychology of a traveler by interstate highway or by air. In other words, the focus of attention and the point of reference have shifted from the place to the technology.

I now suspect that if we work with machines the world will seem to us to be a machine, but if we work with living creatures the world will appear to us as a living creature. Be that as it may, mechanical farming certainly makes it easy to think mechanically about the land and its creatures. It makes it easy to think mechanically even about oneself, and the tirelessness of tractors brought a new depth of weariness into human experience, at a cost to health and family life that has not been fully accounted.

Once one's farm and one's thoughts have been sufficiently mechanized, industrial agriculture's focus on production, as opposed to maintenance or stewardship, becomes merely logical. And here the trouble completes itself. The almost exclusive emphasis on production permits the productive processes to be determined, not by the nature and character of the farm in its ecosystem and in its human community, but rather by the national or the global economy and the available or affordable technology. The farm and all concerns not immediately associated with production have in effect disappeared from sight. The farmer too in effect has vanished. He is no longer working as an independent and loyal agent of his place, his family, and his community, but instead as the agent of an economy that is fundamentally adverse to him and to all that he ought to stand for.

After mechanization it is certainly possible for a farmer to maintain a proper creaturely and stewardly awareness of the lives in her keeping. If you look, you can still find farmers who are farming well on mechanized farms. After mechanization, however, to maintain this kind of awareness requires a distinct effort of will. And now we must ask what are the cultural resources that can inform and sustain such an effort of will. I believe that we will find them gathered under the heading of husbandry, and here my speech arrives finally at its subject.

The word husbandry is the name of a connection. In its original sense, it is the name of the work of a domestic man, a man who has accepted a bondage to the household. We have no cause here, I think, to raise the issue of sexual roles. We need only to say that our earthly life requires both husbandry and housewifery, and that nobody, certainly no household, is excused from a proper attendance to both.

Husbandry pertains first to the household; it connects the farm to the household. It is an art wedded to the art of housewifery. It means caretaking. To husband is to use with care, to keep, to save, to make last, to conserve. Old usage tells us that beyond the household there is a husbandry of the land, of the soil, of the domestic plants and animals—obviously because of the importance of these things to the household. And there have been times, one of which is now, when some people have tried to think of a proper human husbandry of the nondomestic creatures. One reason for this is the dependence of our households and domestic life upon the wild world. Husbandry is the name of all the practices that sustain life by connecting us conservingly to our places and our world, the art of keeping tied all the strands in the living network that sustains us.

And so it appears that most and perhaps all of industrial agriculture's manifest failures are the result of an attempt to make the land produce without husbandry. The attempt to remake agriculture as a science and an industry has excluded from it the age-old husbandry which was central and essential to it, and which denoted always the fundamental domestic connections and demanded a restorative care in the use of the land and its creatures.

This effort had its initial and probably its most radical success in separating farming from the economy of subsistence. Through World War II, farm life in my region (and, I think, nearly everywhere) rested solidly upon the garden, dairy, poultry flock, and meat animals that fed the farm's family. This was the husbandry and the housewifery by which the farm lived. It was simply unthinkable that the farm family would buy at the store any food that they could produce at home. And especially in hard times these families, and their farms too, survived by means of their subsistence economy. The industrial program, on the contrary, suggested that it was "uneconomic" for a farm family to produce its own food; the effort and the land would be better applied to commercial production. The result is utterly anomalous and strange in human experience: farm families that buy everything they eat at the store.

An intention to replace husbandry with science was made explicit in the renaming of disciplines in the colleges of agriculture. Soil husbandry became soil science, and animal husbandry became animal science. This change is worth lingering over because of what it tells us about our susceptibility to poppycock. When any discipline is made or is called a science it is thought by some to be much increased in preciseness, complexity, and prestige. When husbandry becomes science, the lowly has been exalted and the rustic has become urbane. Purporting to increase the sophistication of the study of the humble art of farming, this change in fact brutally oversimplifies it.

Soil science, as practiced by soil scientists, and even more as it has been handed down to farmers, has tended to treat the soil as a lifeless matrix in which soil chemistry takes place and nutrients are made available. And this, in turn, has made farming increasingly shallow—literally so—in its understanding of the soil. The modern farm is understood as a surface on which various mechanical operations are performed, and to which various chemicals are applied. The under-surface reality of organisms and roots is mostly ignored.

Soil husbandry is a different kind of study, involving a different kind of mind. Soil husbandry leads, in the words of Sir Albert Howard, to understanding "health in soil, plant, animal, and man as one great subject." We apply the word health only to living creatures, and to soil husbandry a healthy soil is a wilderness, mostly unstudied and unknown, but teemingly alive. The soil is at once a living community of creatures and their habitat. A good farm, like its good soil, is both a community and a dwelling place. The farm's husband, its family, its crops and animals, all are members of the soil community; all belong to the character and identity of the place. To rate the farm family merely as "labor" and its domestic plants and animals merely as "production" is thus an oversimplification, both radical and destructive.

Science is too simple a word to name the complex of relationships and connections that compose a healthy farm—a farm that is a full membership of the soil community. If we propose, not the reductive science we generally have, but a science of complexity, that too will be inadequate. A science even of complexity will not be complex enough, for any complexity that science can comprehend is going to be necessarily a human construct, and therefore too simple.

The husbandry of mere humans of course cannot be complex enough either. But husbandry always has understood that what is husbanded is ultimately a mystery. A farmer, as one of his farmer correspondents once wrote to Liberty Hyde Bailey, is "a dispenser of the 'Mysteries of God.'" The mothering instinct of animals, for example, is a mystery which husbandry must use and trust mostly without understanding. The husband, unlike the manager or the would-be objective scientist, belongs inherently to the complexity and the mystery that is to be husbanded, and so the husbanding mind is both careful and humble. Husbandry originates precautionary sayings like "Don't put all your eggs into one basket" and "Don't count your chickens before they hatch." It does not boast of technological feats that will "feed the world."

Husbandry, which is not replaceable by science, nevertheless uses science, and corrects it too. It is the more comprehensive discipline. To reduce husbandry to science, in practice, is to transform agricultural "wastes" into pollutants, and to subtract perennials and grazing animals from the rotation of crops. Without husbandry, the agriculture of science and industry has served too well the purpose of the industrial economy in reducing the number of landowners and the self-employed. It has transformed the United States from a country of many owners to a country of many employees.

Without husbandry, soil science too easily ignores the community of creatures that live in and from, that make and are made by, the soil. Similarly, animal science without husbandry forgets, almost as a requirement, the sympathy by which we recognize ourselves as fellow creatures of the animals. It forgets that animals are so called because we once believed them to be endowed with souls. Animal science has led us away from that belief or any such belief in the sanctity of animals. It has led us instead to the animal factory which, like the concentration camp, is a vision of Hell. Animal husbandry, on the contrary, comes from and again leads to the psalmist's vision of good grass, good water, and the husbandry of God.

(It is only a little off my subject to notice also that the high and essential art of housewifery, later known as home economics, has now become family and consumer science. This presumably elevates the intellectual standing of the faculty by removing family life and consumption from the context—and the economy—of a home or household.)

Agriculture must mediate between nature and the human community, with ties and obligations in both directions. To farm well requires an elaborate courtesy toward all creatures, animate and inanimate. Perhaps it is sympathy that most appropriately enlarges the context of human work. Contexts become wrong by being too small—too small, that is, to contain the scientist or the farmer or the farm family or the local ecosystem or the local community—and this is crucial. "Out of context," as Wes Jackson has said, "the best minds do the worst damage."

Needing a way to give an exact sense of this necessary sympathy, the feeling of husbandry at work, I have found it in a book entitled *Feed My Sheep* by Terry Cummins. Mr. Cummins is a man of about my age, who grew up farming with his grandfather in Pendleton County, Kentucky, in the 1940s and early '50s. In the following sentences he is remembering himself at the age of thirteen, in about 1947:

> When you see that you're making the other things feel good, it gives you a good feeling, too. The feeling inside sort of just happens, and you can't say this did it or that did it. It's the many little things. It doesn't seem that taking sweat-soaked harnesses off tired, hot horses would be something that would make you notice.

Opening a barn door for the sheep standing out in a cold rain, or throwing a few grains of corn to the chickens are small things, but these little things begin to add up in you, and you can begin to understand that you're important. You may not be real important like people who do great things that you read about in the newspaper, but you begin to feel that you're important to all the life around you. Nobody else knows or cares too much about what you do, but if you get a good feeling inside about what you do, then it doesn't matter if nobody else knows. I do think about myself a lot when I'm alone way back on the place bringing in the cows or sitting on a mowing machine all day. But when I start thinking about how our animals and crops and fields and woods and gardens sort of all fit together, then I get that good feeling inside and don't worry much about what will happen to me.[1]

This passage goes to the heart of what I am trying to say, because it goes to the heart of farming as I have known it. Mr. Cummins's sentences describe an experience regrettably and perhaps dangerously missing now from the childhood of most children. They also describe the communion between the farmer as husband and the well-husbanded farm. This communion is a cultural force that can exist only by becoming personal. To see it so described is to understand at once how necessary and how threatened it now is.

So far, I have tried to say what husbandry is, how it works, and why it is necessary. Now I want to speak of two paramount accomplishments of husbandry to which I think we will have to pay more deliberate attention, in our present circumstances, than we ever have before. These are local adaptation and local coherence of form. It is strange that a science of agriculture founded on evolutionary biology, with its practical emphasis on survival, would exempt the human species from these concerns.

True husbandry, as its first strategy of survival, has always striven to fit the farming to the farm and to the field, to the needs and abilities of the farm's family, and to the local economy. Every wild creature is the product of such an adaptive process. The same process once was a dominant influence on agriculture, for the cost of ignoring it was hunger. One striking and well-known example of local adaptation in agriculture is the number and diversity of British sheep breeds, most of which are named for the localities in which they were developed. But local adaptation must be even more refined than this example suggests, for it involves consideration of the individuality of every farm and every field.

Our recent focus upon productivity, genetic and technological uniformity, and global trade—all supported by supposedly limitless supplies of fuel, water, and soil—has obscured the necessity for local adaptation. But our circumstances are changing rapidly now, and this requirement will be forced upon us again by terrorism and other kinds of political violence, by chemical pollution, by increasing energy costs, by depleted soils, aquifers, and streams, and by the spread of exotic weeds, pests, and diseases. We are going to have to return to the old questions about local nature, local carrying capacities, and local needs. And we are going to have to resume the breeding of plants and animals to fit the region and the farm.

---

[1] Published with permission from Terry Cummins.

The same obsessions and extravagances that have caused us to ignore the issue of local adaptation have at the same time caused us to ignore the issue of form. These two issues are so closely related that it is difficult to talk about one without talking about the other. During the half century and more of our neglect of local adaptation, we have subjected our farms to a radical oversimplification of form. The diversified and reasonably self-sufficient farms of my region and of many other regions have been conglomerated into larger farms with larger fields, increasingly specialized, and subjected increasingly to the strict, unnatural linearity of the production line.

But the first requirement of a form is that it must be comprehensive; it must not leave out something that essentially belongs within it. The farm that Terry Cummins remembers is remarkably comprehensive, and it is not any one of its several enterprises alone that made him feel good, but rather "how our animals and crops and fields and woods and gardens sort of all fit together."

The form of the farm must answer to the farmer's feeling for the place, its creatures, and its work. It is a never-ending effort of fitting together many diverse things. It must incorporate the life cycle and the fertility cycles of animals. It must bring crops and livestock into balance and mutual support. It must be a pattern on the ground and in the mind. It must be at once ecological, agricultural, economic, familial, and neighborly. It must be inclusive enough, complex enough, coherent, intelligible, and durable. It must have within its limits the completeness of an organism or an ecosystem.

The making of a form begins in the recognition and acceptance of limits. The farm is limited by its topography, its climate, its ecosystem, its human neighborhood and local economy, and of course by the greater economies, and by the preferences and abilities of the farmer. The true husbandman shapes the farm within an assured sense of what it cannot be and what it should not be. And thus the problem of form returns us to that of local adaptation.

The task before us, now as always before, is to renew and husband the means, both natural and human, of agriculture. But to talk now about renewing husbandry is to talk about unsimplifying what is in reality an extremely complex subject. This will require us to accept again, and more competently than ever before, the health of the ecosystem, the farm, and the human community as the ultimate standard of agricultural performance.

Unsimplification is difficult, I imagine, in any circumstances; our present circumstances will make it especially so. Soon the majority of the world's people will be living in cities. We are now obliged to think of so many people demanding the means of life from the land, to which they will no longer have a practical connection, and of which they will have little knowledge. We are obliged also to think of the consequences of any attempt to meet this demand by large-scale, expensive, petroleum-dependent technological schemes that will ignore local conditions and local needs. The problem of renewing husbandry, and the need to promote a general awareness of everybody's agricultural responsibilities, thus becomes urgent.

How are we to do this? How can we restore a competent husbandry to the minds of the world's producers and consumers?

For a start of course we must recognize that this effort is already in progress on many farms and in many urban consumer groups scattered across our country and the world. But we must recognize too that this effort needs an authorizing focus and force that would grant it a new legitimacy, intellectual rigor, scientific respectability, and responsible teaching. There are many reasons to hope that this might be supplied by our colleges of agriculture, and there are some reasons to think that this hope is not fantastical.

With that hope in mind, I want to return to a precaution that I mentioned earlier. The effort of husbandry is partly scientific but it is entirely cultural, and a cultural initiative can exist only by becoming personal. It will become increasingly clear, I believe, that agricultural scientists, and the rest of us as well, are going to have to be less specialized, or less isolated by our specialization. Agricultural scientists will need to work as indwelling members of agricultural communities or of consumer communities. Their scientific work will need to accept the limits and the influence of that membership. It is not irrational to propose that a significant number of these scientists should be farmers, and so subject their scientific work, and that of their colleagues, to the influence of a farmer's practical circumstances. Along with the rest of us, they will need to accept all the imperatives of husbandry as the context of their work. We cannot keep things from falling apart in our society if they do not cohere in our minds and in our lives.

■ READING AND WRITING

1. Although Berry has written a policy argument—he is proposing a course of action—definition plays an integral role in his efforts to persuade. What are the key terms he defines in his speech? How does he define these terms? How does providing these definitions help Berry make a successful argument?

2. What is the effect of Berry's use of personal anecdotes and autobiographical details in his speech? Think about these effects especially as they relate to his original audience.

■ DEVELOPING LONGER RESPONSES

3. Near the end of his speech, Berry asks: "How can we restore a competent husbandry to the minds of the world's producers and consumers?" How do you think those of us who are not farmers— the consumers Berry speaks of—can help fulfill our "agricultural responsibilities" to move away from the most destructive elements of industrial farming?

■ USING RESEARCH

4. Berry's speech is framed by the tensions between what he calls "the art of farming" and the mechanization of the American farm. Using the library's databases and other internet resources, find two other perspectives on this issue—sources that explain what others have to say about it. Then, write a brief essay in which you explain and compare all three perspectives. (Note: You are *not* taking a position in this essay; your task is to inform and explain.)

© Peter Menzel / menzelphoto.com

IMAGE 2.2 shows the Revis family of North Carolina, one many families featured in *Hungry Planet: What the World Eats* by Peter Menzel and Faith D'Aluisio, a 2005 book that present a photographic study of what people around the world eat during the course of one week. The Revises spent $341.98 on their week's worth of food, compared with the $1.23 spent by the Aboubakar family of the Breidjing Camp in Chad (see page 75) and the $68.53 spent by the Ahmed family of Cairo, Egypt (see page 160). What are the rhetorical effects of viewing these images as a group? What arguments might the authors have been trying to make by collecting photographs like these from around the world?

> *Alice Waters, owner and founder of Chez Panisse Restaurant and Foundation in Berkeley, California, has championed local, organic food for more than thirty-eight years. She is introducing her ideas into public schools through Edible Education, a model garden and kitchen program. This essay was first published in the September 21, 2009 edition of* The Nation.

A HEALTHY CONSTITUTION   Alice Waters

I was moved by the way Morgan Spurlock framed a narrow long-distance shot down the corridor of a Beckley, West Virginia, middle school in his outstanding 2004 film, *Super Size Me*. The film is about the toll that fast and processed food takes on all of us. Clearly visible in the background of this particular shot were dozens of students, many of whom were overweight.

Perhaps it should come as no surprise that Beckley's cafeteria offers only processed food, which is high in fat, sodium and sugar and of very little nutritional value.

Contrast this with the Central Alternative High School in Appleton, Wisconsin. The school serves troubled youth, but teachers, parents and administrators found a way to turn things around; and when they did, discipline problems dropped sharply. Their secret? Instead of the usual processed meals, the school cafeteria offers fresh, locally grown, low-fat, low-sugar alternatives. The healthier meals are delicious. The students love them. They perform better in class and don't get sick as often.

We are learning that when schools serve healthier meals, they solve serious educational and health-related problems. But what's missing from the national conversation about school lunch reform is the opportunity to use food to teach values that are central to democracy. Better food isn't just about test scores, health and discipline. It is about preparing students for the responsibilities of citizenship.

That's why we need to talk about edible education, not just school lunch reform. Edible education is a radical yet common-sense approach to teaching that integrates classroom instruction, school lunch, cooking and gardening into the studies of math, science, history and reading.

Edible education involves not only teaching children about where food comes from and how it is produced but giving them responsibilities in the school garden and kitchen. Students literally enjoy the fruits of their labor when the food they grow is served in healthy, delicious lunches that they can help prepare.

I learned this firsthand through the Chez Panisse Foundation—the organization I helped create to inspire a network of food activists around the world with edible education programs in their own communities. Here in Berkeley, I see children in our edible education program learn about responsibility, sharing and stewardship and become more connected to themselves and their peers. In the process, they come to embody the most important values of citizenship.

Listen to what one student named Charlotte has to say: "Next we went from the blue corn to the sweet corn and each picked an ear to grill. I must say it tasted really good, even without butter." Or Mati: "I think cleaning up is as important as eating. Cleaning up is sort of fun. And we can't just leave it for the teachers, because we made the mess." Or Jose: "I remember the first time I came to the kitchen. I was afraid to do anything. But then I realized, this is my kitchen. So then I started to enjoy it."

Charlotte, Mati and Jose are learning about so much more than lunch. They're learning that farmers depend on the land; we depend on farmers; and our nation depends on all of us. That cooperation with one another is necessary to nurture the community. And that, by setting the table for one another, we also take care of ourselves. School should be the place where we build democracy, not just by teaching about the Constitution but by becoming connected to our communities and the land in more meaningful ways.

In 1785, Thomas Jefferson declared that "Cultivators of the earth are the most valuable citizens. They are the most vigorous, the most independent, the most virtuous, and they are tied to their country and wedded to its liberty and interests by the most lasting bonds."

I believe he was right. The school cafeteria, kitchen and garden, like the town square, can and should be the place where we plant and nourish the values that guide our democracy. We need to join a delicious revolution that can reconnect our children to the table and to what it means to be a steward. This is the picture of a caring society, and this is the promise of edible education.

■ READING AND WRITING

1. How, according to Waters, can food be used "to teach values that are central to democracy?"
2. Explain the link that Waters makes between healthy meals and learning. What kind of evidence does she offer to support these links? Do you think more evidence would have strengthened her argument?

■ USING RESEARCH

3. Are any schools in South Carolina serving what Waters would call "fresh, locally grown, low-fat, low-sugar" meals? Are any schools in the state involved in anything like the "edible education" program she describes?

Matthew Scully served as special assistant and deputy director of speechwriting to President George W. Bush and also wrote for vice presidents Dick Cheney and Dan Quayle. The author of Dominion: The Power of Man, the Suffering of Animals, and the Call to Mercy, *Scully wrote this essay for the May 23, 2005, issue of* The American Conservative *magazine.*

FEAR FACTORIES: THE CASE FOR COMPASSIONATE CONSERVATISM— FOR ANIMALS   Matthew Scully

A few years ago I began a book about cruelty to animals and about factory farming in particular, problems that had been in the back of my mind for a long while. At the time I viewed factory farming as one of the lesser problems facing humanity—a small wrong on the grand scale of good and evil but too casually overlooked and too glibly excused.

This view changed as I acquainted myself with the details and saw a few typical farms up close. By the time I finished the book, I had come to view the abuses of industrial farming as a serious moral problem, a truly rotten business for good reason passed over in polite conversation. Little wrongs, when left unattended, can grow and spread to become grave wrongs, and precisely this had happened on our factory farms.

The result of these ruminations was *Dominion: The Power of Man, the Suffering of Animals, and the Call to Mercy*. And though my tome never quite hit the bestseller lists, there ought to be some special literary prize for a work highly recommended in both the *Wall Street Journal* and *Vegetarian Teen*. When you enjoy the accolades of PETA and *Policy Review*, Deepak Chopra and Gordon Liddy, Peter Singer and Charles Colson, you can at least take comfort in the diversity of your readership.

The book also provided an occasion for fellow conservatives to get beyond their dislike for particular animal-rights groups and to examine cruelty issues on the merits. Conservatives have a way of dismissing the subject, as if where animals are concerned nothing very serious could ever be at stake. And though it is not exactly true that liberals care more about these issues—you are no more likely to find reflections or exposés concerning cruelty in *The Nation* or *The New Republic* than in any journal of the Right— it is assumed that animal-protection causes are a project of the Left, and that the proper conservative position is to stand warily and firmly against them.

I had a hunch that the problem was largely one of presentation and that by applying their own principles to animal-welfare issues conservatives would find plenty of reasons to be appalled. More to the point, having acknowledged the problems of cruelty, we could then support reasonable remedies. Conservatives, after all, aren't shy about discoursing on moral standards or reluctant to translate the most basic of those standards into law. Setting aside the distracting rhetoric of animal rights, that's usually what these questions come down to: what moral standards should guide us in our treatment of animals, and when must those standards be applied in law?

Industrial livestock farming is among a whole range of animal-welfare concerns that extends from canned trophy-hunting to whaling to product testing on animals to all sorts of more obscure enterprises like the exotic-animal trade and the factory farming of bears in China for bile believed to hold medicinal and aphrodisiac powers. Surveying the various uses to which animals are put, some might be defensible, others abusive and unwarranted, and it's the job of any conservative who attends to the subject to figure out which are which. We don't need novel theories of rights to do this. The usual distinctions that conservatives draw between moderation and excess, freedom and license, moral goods and material goods, rightful power and the abuse of power, will all do just fine.

As it is, the subject hardly comes up at all among conservatives, and what commentary we do hear usually takes the form of ridicule directed at animal-rights groups. Often conservatives side instinctively with any animal-related industry and those involved, as if a thing is right just because someone can make money off it or as if our sympathies belong always with the men just because they are men.

I had an exchange once with an eminent conservative columnist on this subject. Conversation turned to my book and to factory farming. Holding his hands out in the "stop" gesture, he said, "I don't want to know." Granted, life on the factory farm is no one's favorite subject, but conservative writers often have to think about things that are disturbing or sad. In this case, we have an intellectually formidable fellow known to millions for his stern judgments on every matter of private morality and public policy. Yet nowhere in all his writings do I find any treatment of any cruelty issue, never mind that if you asked him he would surely agree that cruelty to animals is a cowardly and disgraceful sin.

And when the subject is cruelty to farmed animals—the moral standards being applied in a fundamental human enterprise—suddenly we're in forbidden territory and "I don't want to know" is the best he can do. But don't we have a responsibility to know? Maybe the whole subject could use his fine mind and his good heart.

As for the rights of animals, rights in general are best viewed in tangible terms, with a view to actual events and consequences. Take the case of a hunter in Texas named John Lockwood, who has just pioneered the online safari. At his canned-hunting ranch outside San Antonio, he's got a rifle attached to a camera and the camera wired up to the Internet, so that sportsmen going to Live-shot.com will actually be able to fire at baited animals by remote control from their computers. "If the customer were to wound the animal," explains the *San Antonio Express-News*, "a staff person on site could finish it off." The "trophy mounts" taken in these heroics will then be prepared and shipped to the client's door, and if it catches on Lockwood will be a rich man.

Very much like animal farming today, the hunting "industry" has seen a collapse in ethical standards, and only in such an atmosphere could Lockwood have found inspiration for this latest innovation—denying wild animals the last shred of respect. Under the laws of Texas and other states, Lockwood and others in his business use all sorts of methods once viewed as shameful: baits, blinds, fences to trap hunted animals in ranches that advertise a "100-percent-guaranteed kill." Affluent hunters like to unwind by shooting cage-reared pheasants, ducks, and other birds, firing away as the fowl of the air are released before them like skeet, with no limit on the day's kill. Hunting supply stores are filled with lures, infrared lights, high-tech scopes, and other gadgetry to make every man a marksman.

Lockwood doesn't hear anyone protesting those methods, except for a few of those nutty activist types. Why shouldn't he be able to offer paying customers this new hunting experience as well? It is like asking a smut-peddler to please have the decency to keep children out of it. Lockwood is just one step ahead of the rest, and there is no standard of honor left to stop him.

First impressions are usually correct in questions of cruelty to animals, and here most of us would agree that Live-shot.com does not show our fellow man at his best. We would say that the whole thing is a little tawdry and even depraved, that the creatures Lockwood has "in stock" are not just commodities. We would say that these animals deserve better than the fate he has in store for them.

As is invariably the case in animal-rights issues, what we're really looking for are safeguards against cruel and presumptuous people. We are trying to hold people to their obligations, people who could spare us the trouble if only they would recognize a few limits on their own conduct.

Conservatives like the sound of "obligation" here, and those who reviewed *Dominion* were relieved to find me arguing more from this angle than from any notion of rights. "What the PETA crowd doesn't understand," Jonah Goldberg wrote, "or what it deliberately confuses, is that human compassion toward animals is an obligation of humans, not an entitlement for animals." Another commentator put the point in religious terms: "[W]e have a moral duty to respect the animal world as God's handiwork, treating animals with 'the mercy of our Maker' … But mercy and respect for animals are completely different from rights for animals—and we should never confuse the two." Both writers confessed they were troubled by factory farming and concluded with the uplifting thought that we could all profit from further reflection on our obligation of kindness to farm animals.

The only problem with this insistence on obligation is that after a while it begins to sounds like a hedge against actually being held to that obligation. It leaves us with a high-minded attitude but no accountability, free to act on our obligations or to ignore them without consequences, personally opposed to cruelty but unwilling to impose that view on others.

Treating animals decently is like most obligations we face, somewhere between the most and the least important, a modest but essential requirement to living with integrity. And it's not a good sign when arguments are constantly turned to precisely how much is mandatory and how much, therefore, we can manage to avoid.

If one is using the word "obligation" seriously, moreover, then there is no practical difference between an obligation on our end not to mistreat animals and an entitlement on their end not to be mistreated by us. Either way, we are required to do and not do the same things. And either way, somewhere down the logical line, the entitlement would have to arise from a recognition of the inherent dignity of a living creature. The moral standing of our fellow creatures may be humble, but it is absolute and not something within our power to confer or withhold. All creatures sing their Creator's praises, as this truth is variously expressed in the Bible, and are dear to Him for their own sakes.

A certain moral relativism runs through the arguments of those hostile or indifferent to animal welfare—as if animals can be of value only for our sake, as utility or preference decrees. In practice, this outlook leaves each person to decide for himself when animals rate moral concern. It even allows us to accept or reject such knowable facts about animals as their cognitive and emotional capacities, their conscious experience of pain and happiness.

Elsewhere in contemporary debates, conservatives meet the foe of moral relativism by pointing out that, like it or not, we are all dealing with the same set of physiological realities and moral truths. We don't each get to decide the facts of science on a situational basis. We do not each go about bestowing moral value upon things as it pleases us at the moment. Of course, we do not decide moral truth at all: we discern it. Human beings in their moral progress learn to appraise things correctly, using reasoned moral judgment to perceive a prior order not of our devising.

C.S. Lewis in *The Abolition of Man* calls this "the doctrine of objective value, the belief that certain attitudes are really true, and others really false, to the kind of thing the universe is and the kind of things we are." Such words as honor, piety, esteem, and empathy do not merely describe subjective states of mind, Lewis reminds us, but speak to objective qualities in the world beyond that merit those attitudes in us. "[T]o call children delightful or old men venerable," he writes, "is not simply to record a psychological fact about our own parental or filial emotions at the moment, but to recognize a quality which demands a certain response from us whether we make it or not."

This applies to questions of cruelty as well. A kindly attitude toward animals is not a subjective sentiment; it is the correct moral response to the objective value of a fellow creature. Here, too, rational and virtuous conduct consists in giving things their due and in doing so consistently. If one animal's pain—say, that of one's pet—is real and deserving of sympathy, then the pain of essentially identical animals is also meaningful, no matter what conventional distinctions we have made to narrow the scope of our sympathy. If it is wrong to whip a dog or starve a horse or bait bears for sport or grossly abuse farm animals, it is wrong for all people in every place.

The problem with moral relativism is that it leads to capriciousness and the despotic use of power. And the critical distinction here is not between human obligations and animal rights, but rather between obligations of charity and obligations of justice.

Active kindness to animals falls into the former category. If you take in strays or help injured wildlife or donate to animal charities, those are fine things to do, but no one says you should be compelled to do them. Refraining from cruelty to animals is a different matter, an obligation of justice not for us each to weigh for ourselves. It is not simply unkind behavior, it is unjust behavior, and the prohibition against it is non-negotiable. Proverbs reminds us of this—"a righteous man regardeth the life of his beast, but the tender mercies of the wicked are cruel"—and the laws of America and of every other advanced nation now recognize the wrongfulness of such conduct with our cruelty statutes. Often applying felony-level penalties to protect certain domestic animals, these state and federal statutes declare that even though your animal may elsewhere in the law be defined as your property, there are certain things you may not do to that creature, and if you are found harming or neglecting the animal, you will answer for your conduct in a court of justice.

There are various reasons the state has an interest in forbidding cruelty, one of which is that cruelty is degrading to human beings. The problem is that many thinkers on this subject have strained to find indirect reasons to explain why cruelty is wrong and thereby to force animal cruelty into the category of the victimless crime. The most common of these explanations asks us to believe that acts of cruelty matter only because the cruel person does moral injury to himself or sullies his character—as if the man is our sole concern and the cruelly treated animal is entirely incidental.

Once again, the best test of theory is a real-life example. In 2002, Judge Alan Glenn of Tennessee's Court of Criminal Appeals heard the case of a married couple named Johnson, who had been found guilty of cruelty to 350 dogs lying sick, starving, or dead in their puppy-mill kennel—a scene videotaped by police. Here is Judge Glenn's response to their supplications for mercy:

> The victims of this crime were animals that could not speak up to the unbelievable conduct of Judy Fay Johnson and Stanley Paul Johnson that they suffered. Several of the dogs have died and most had physical problems such as intestinal worms, mange, eye problems, dental problems and emotional problems and socialization problems ... . Watching this video of the conditions that these dogs were subjected to was one of the most deplorable things this Court has observed. ...
>
> [T]his Court finds that probation would not serve the ends of justice, nor be in the best interest of the public, nor would this have a deterrent effect for such gross behavior. ... The victims were particularly vulnerable. You treated the victims with exceptional cruelty. ...
>
> There are those who would argue that you should be confined in a house trailer with no ventilation or in a cell three-by-seven with eight or ten other inmates with no plumbing, no exercise and no opportunity to feel the sun or smell fresh air. However, the courts of this land have held that such treatment is cruel and inhuman, and it is. You will not be treated in the same way that you treated these helpless animals that you abused to make a dollar.

Only in abstract debates of moral or legal theory would anyone quarrel with Judge Glenn's description of the animals as "victims" or deny that they were entitled to be treated better. Whether we call this a "right" matters little, least of all to the dogs, since the only right that any animal could possibly exercise is the right to be free from human abuse, neglect, or, in a fine old term of law, other "malicious mischief." What matters most is that prohibitions against human cruelty be hard and binding. The sullied souls of the Johnsons are for the Johnsons to worry about. The business of justice is to punish their offense and to protect the creatures from human wrongdoing. And in the end, just as in other matters of morality and justice, the interests of man are served by doing the right thing for its own sake.

There is only one reason for condemning cruelty that doesn't beg the question of exactly why cruelty is a wrong, a vice, or bad for our character: that the act of cruelty is an intrinsic evil. Animals cruelly dealt with are not just things, not just an irrelevant detail in some self-centered moral drama of our own. They matter in their own right, as they matter to their Creator, and the wrongs of cruelty are wrongs done to them. As *The Catholic Encyclopedia* puts this point, there is a "direct and essential sinfulness of cruelty to the animal world, irrespective of the results of such conduct on the character of those who practice it."

Our cruelty statutes are a good and natural development in Western law, codifying the claims of animals against human wrongdoing, and, with the wisdom of men like Judge Glenn, asserting those claims on their behalf. Such statutes, however, address mostly random or wanton acts of cruelty. And the persistent animal-welfare questions of our day center on institutional cruelties—on the vast and systematic mistreatment of animals that most of us never see.

Having conceded the crucial point that some animals rate our moral concern and legal protection, informed conscience turns naturally to other animals—creatures entirely comparable in their awareness, feeling, and capacity for suffering. A dog is not the moral equal of a human being, but a dog is definitely the moral equal of a pig, and it's only human caprice and economic convenience that say otherwise. We have the problem that these essentially similar creatures are treated in dramatically different ways, unjustified even by the very different purposes we have assigned to them. Our pets are accorded certain protections from cruelty, while the nameless creatures in our factory farms are hardly treated like animals at all. The challenge is one of consistency, of treating moral equals equally, and living according to fair and rational standards of conduct.

Whatever terminology we settle on, after all the finer philosophical points have been hashed over, the aim of the exercise is to prohibit wrongdoing. All rights, in practice, are protections against human wrongdoing, and here too the point is to arrive at clear and consistent legal boundaries on the things that one may or may not do to animals, so that every man is not left to be the judge in his own case.

More than obligation, moderation, ordered liberty, or any of the other lofty ideals we hold, what should attune conservatives to all the problems of animal cruelty—and especially to the modern factory farm—is our worldly side. The great virtue of conservatism is that it begins with a realistic assessment of human motivations. We know man as he is, not only the rational creature but also, as Socrates told us, the rationalizing creature, with a knack for finding an angle, an excuse, and a euphemism. Whether it's the pornographer who thinks himself a free-speech champion or the abortionist who looks in the mirror and sees a reproductive health-care services provider, conservatives are familiar with the type.

So we should not be all that surprised when told that these very same capacities are often at work in the things that people do to animals—and all the more so in our $125 billion a year livestock industry. The human mind, especially when there is money to be had, can manufacture grand excuses for the exploitation of other human beings. How much easier it is for people to excuse the wrongs done to lowly animals.

Where animals are concerned, there is no practice or industry so low that someone, somewhere, cannot produce a high-sounding reason for it. The sorriest little miscreant who shoots an elephant, lying in wait by the water hole in some canned-hunting operation, is just "harvesting resources," doing his bit for "conservation." The swarms of government-subsidized Canadian seal hunters slaughtering tens of thousands of newborn pups—hacking to death these unoffending creatures, even in sight of their mothers—offer themselves as the brave and independent bearers of tradition. With the same sanctimony and deep dishonesty, factory-farm corporations like Smithfield Foods, ConAgra, and Tyson Foods still cling to countrified brand names for their labels—Clear Run Farms, Murphy Family Farms, Happy Valley—to convince us and no doubt themselves, too, that they are engaged in something essential, wholesome, and honorable.

Yet when corporate farmers need barbed wire around their Family Farms and Happy Valleys and laws to prohibit outsiders from taking photographs (as is the case in two states) and still other laws to exempt farm animals from the definition of "animals" as covered in federal and state cruelty statutes, something is amiss. And if conservatives do nothing else about any other animal issue, we should attend at least to the factory farms, where the suffering is immense and we are all asked to be complicit.

If we are going to have our meats and other animal products, there are natural costs to obtaining them, defined by the duties of animal husbandry and of veterinary ethics. Factory farming came about when resourceful men figured out ways of getting around those natural costs, applying new technologies to raise animals in conditions that would otherwise kill them by deprivation and disease. With no laws to stop it, moral concern surrendered entirely to economic calculation, leaving no limit to the punishments that factory farmers could inflict to keep costs down and profits up. Corporate farmers hardly speak anymore of "raising" animals, with the modicum of personal care that word implies. Animals are "grown" now, like so many crops. Barns somewhere along the way became "intensive confinement facilities" and the inhabitants mere "production units."

The result is a world in which billions of birds, cows, pigs, and other creatures are locked away, enduring miseries they do not deserve, for our convenience and pleasure. We belittle the activists with their radical agenda, scarcely noticing the radical cruelty they seek to redress.

At the Smithfield mass-confinement hog farms I toured in North Carolina, the visitor is greeted by a bedlam of squealing, chain rattling, and horrible roaring. To maximize the use of space and minimize the need for care, the creatures are encased row after row, 400 to 500 pound mammals trapped without relief inside iron crates seven feet long and 22 inches wide. They chew maniacally on bars and chains, as foraging animals will do when denied straw, or engage in stereotypical nest-building with the straw that isn't there, or else just lie there like broken beings. The spirit of the place would be familiar to police who raided that Tennessee puppy-mill run by Stanley and Judy Johnson, only instead of 350 tortured animals, millions—and the law prohibits none of it.

Efforts to outlaw the gestation crate have been dismissed by various conservative critics as "silly," "comical," "ridiculous." It doesn't seem that way up close. The smallest scraps of human charity—a bit of maternal care, room to roam outdoors, straw to lie on—have long since been taken away as costly luxuries, and so the pigs know the feel only of concrete and metal. They lie covered in their own urine and excrement, with broken legs from trying to escape or just to turn, covered with festering sores, tumors, ulcers, lesions, or what my guide shrugged off as the routine "pus pockets."

C.S. Lewis's description of animal pain—"begun by Satan's malice and perpetrated by man's desertion of his post"—has literal truth in our factory farms because they basically run themselves through the wonders of automation, and the owners are off in spacious corporate offices reviewing their spreadsheets. Rarely are the creatures' afflictions examined by a vet or even noticed by the migrant laborers charged with their care, unless of course some ailment threatens production—meaning who cares about a lousy ulcer or broken leg, as long as we're still getting the piglets?

Kept alive in these conditions only by antibiotics, hormones, laxatives, and other additives mixed into their machine-fed swill, the sows leave their crates only to be driven or dragged into other crates, just as small, to bring forth their piglets. Then it's back to the gestation crate for another four months, and so on back and forth until after seven or eight pregnancies they finally expire from the punishment of it or else are culled with a club or bolt-gun.

As you can see at www.factoryfarming.com/gallery.htm, industrial livestock farming operates on an economy of scale, presupposing a steady attrition rate. The usual comforting rejoinder we hear—that it's in the interest of farmers to take good care of their animals—is false. Each day, in every confinement farm in America, you will find cull pens littered with dead or dying creatures discarded like trash.

For the piglets, it's a regimen of teeth cutting, tail docking (performed with pliers, to heighten the pain of tail chewing and so deter this natural response to mass confinement), and other mutilations. After five or six months trapped in one of the grim warehouses that now pass for barns, they're trucked off, 355,000 pigs every day in the life of America, for processing at a furious pace of thousands per hour by migrants who use earplugs to muffle the screams. All of these creatures, and billions more across the earth, go to their deaths knowing nothing of life, and nothing of man, except the foul, tortured existence of the factory farm, having never even been outdoors.

But not to worry, as a Smithfield Foods executive assured me, "They love it." It's all "for their own good." It is a voice conservatives should instantly recognize, as we do when it tells us that the fetus feels nothing. Everything about the picture shows bad faith, moral sloth, and endless excuse-making, all readily answered by conservative arguments.

We are told "they're just pigs" or cows or chickens or whatever and that only urbanites worry about such things, estranged as they are from the realities of rural life. Actually, all of factory farming proceeds by a massive denial of reality—the reality that pigs and other animals are not just production units to be endlessly exploited but living creatures with natures and needs. The very modesty of those needs—their humble desires for straw, soil, sunshine—is the gravest indictment of the men who deny them.

Conservatives are supposed to revere tradition. Factory farming has no traditions, no rules, no codes of honor, no little decencies to spare for a fellow creature. The whole thing is an abandonment of rural values and a betrayal of honorable animal husbandry—to say nothing of veterinary medicine, with its sworn oath to "protect animal health" and to "relieve animal suffering."

Likewise, we are told to look away and think about more serious things. Human beings simply have far bigger problems to worry about than the well being of farm animals, and surely all of this zeal would be better directed at causes of human welfare.

You wouldn't think that men who are unwilling to grant even a few extra inches in cage space, so that a pig can turn around, would be in any position to fault others for pettiness. Why are small acts of kindness beneath us, but not small acts of cruelty? The larger problem with this appeal to moral priority, however, is that we are dealing with suffering that occurs through human agency. Whether it's miserliness here, carelessness there, or greed throughout, the result is rank cruelty for which particular people must answer.

Since refraining from cruelty is an obligation of justice, moreover, there is no avoiding the implications. All the goods invoked in defense of factory farming, from the efficiency and higher profits of the system to the lower costs of the products, are false goods unjustly derived. No matter what right and praiseworthy things we are doing elsewhere in life, when we live off a cruel and disgraceful thing like factory farming, we are to that extent living unjustly, and that is hardly a trivial problem.

For the religious-minded, and Catholics in particular, no less an authority than Pope Benedict XVI has explained the spiritual stakes. Asked recently to weigh in on these very questions, Cardinal Ratzinger told German journalist Peter Seewald that animals must be respected as our "companions in creation." While it is licit to use them for food, "we cannot just do whatever we want with them. ... Certainly, a sort of industrial use of creatures, so that geese are fed in such a way as to produce as large a liver as possible, or hens live so packed together that they become just caricatures of birds, this degrading of living creatures to a commodity seems to me in fact to contradict the relationship of mutuality that comes across in the Bible."

Factory farmers also assure us that all of this is an inevitable stage of industrial efficiency. Leave aside the obvious reply that we could all do a lot of things in life more efficiently if we didn't have to trouble ourselves with ethical restraints. Leave aside, too, the tens of billions of dollars in annual federal subsidies that have helped megafarms undermine small family farms and the decent communities that once surrounded them and to give us the illusion of cheap products. And never mind the collateral damage to land, water, and air that factory farms cause and the more billions of dollars it costs taxpayers to clean up after them. Factory farming is a predatory enterprise, absorbing profit and externalizing costs, unnaturally propped up by political influence and government subsidies much as factory-farmed animals are unnaturally sustained by hormones and antibiotics.

Even if all the economic arguments were correct, conservatives usually aren't impressed by breathless talk of inevitable progress. I am asked sometimes how a conservative could possibly care about animal suffering in factory farms, but the question is premised on a liberal caricature of conservatism—the assumption that, for all of our fine talk about moral values, "compassionate conservatism" and the like, everything we really care about can be counted in dollars. In the case of factory farming, and the conservative's blithe tolerance of it, the caricature is too close to the truth.

Exactly how far are we all prepared to follow these industrial and technological advances before pausing to take stock of where things stand and where it is all tending? Very soon companies like Smithfield plan to have tens of millions of cloned animals in their factory farms. Other companies are at work genetically engineering chickens without feathers so that one day all poultry farmers might be spared the toil and cost of de-feathering their birds. For years, the many shills for our livestock industry employed in the "Animal Science" and "Meat Science" departments of rural universities (we used to call them Animal Husbandry departments) have been tampering with the genes of pigs and other animals to locate and expunge that part of their genetic makeup that makes them stressed in factory farm conditions—taking away the desire to protect themselves and to live. Instead of redesigning the factory farm to suit the animals, they are redesigning the animals to suit the factory farm.

Are there no boundaries of nature and elementary ethics that the conservative should be the first to see? The hubris of such projects is beyond belief, only more because of the foolish and frivolous goods to be gained—blood-free meats and the perfect pork chop.

No one who does not profit from them can look at our modern factory farms or frenzied slaughter plants or agricultural laboratories with their featherless chickens and fear-free pigs and think, "Yes, this is humanity at our finest—exactly as things should be." Devils charged with designing a farm could hardly have made it more severe. Least of all should we look for sanction in Judeo-Christian morality, whose whole logic is one of gracious condescension, of the proud learning to be humble, the higher serving the lower, and the strong protecting the weak.

Those religious conservatives who, in every debate over animal welfare, rush to remind us that the animals themselves are secondary and man must come first are exactly right—only they don't follow their own thought to its moral conclusion. Somehow, in their pious notions of stewardship and dominion, we always seem to end up with singular moral dignity but no singular moral accountability to go with it.

Lofty talk about humanity's special status among creatures only invites such questions as: what would the Good Shepherd make of our factory farms? Where does the creature of conscience get off lording it over these poor creatures so mercilessly? "How is it possible," as Malcolm Muggeridge asked in the years when factory farming began to spread, "to look for God and sing his praises while insulting and degrading his creatures? If, as I had thought, all lambs are the Agnus Dei, then to deprive them of light and the field and their joyous frisking and the sky is the worst kind of blasphemy."

The writer B.R. Meyers remarked in *The Atlantic*, "research could prove that cows love Jesus, and the line at the McDonald's drive-through wouldn't be one sagging carload shorter the next day .... Has any generation in history ever been so ready to cause so much suffering for such a trivial advantage? We deaden our consciences to enjoy—for a few minutes a day—the taste of blood, the feel of our teeth meeting through muscle."

That is a cynical but serious indictment, and we must never let it be true of us in the choices we each make or urge upon others. If reason and morality are what set human beings apart from animals, then reason and morality must always guide us in how we treat them, or else it's all just caprice, unbridled appetite with the pretense of piety. When people say that they like their pork chops, veal, or foie gras just too much ever to give them up, reason hears in that the voice of gluttony, willfulness, or at best moral complaisance. What makes a human being human is precisely the ability to understand that the suffering of an animal is more important than the taste of a treat.

Of the many conservatives who reviewed *Dominion*, every last one conceded that factory farming is a wretched business and a betrayal of human responsibility. So it should be a short step to agreement that it also constitutes a serious issue of law and public policy. Having granted that certain practices are abusive, cruel, and wrong, we must be prepared actually to do something about them.

Among animal activists, of course, there are some who go too far—there are in the best of causes. But fairness requires that we judge a cause by its best advocates instead of making straw men of the worst. There isn't much money in championing the cause of animals, so we're dealing with some pretty altruistic people who on that account alone deserve the benefit of the doubt.

If we're looking for fitting targets for inquiry and scorn, for people with an angle and a truly pernicious influence, better to start with groups like Smithfield Foods (my candidate for the worst corporation in America in its ruthlessness to people and animals alike), the National Pork Producers Council (a reliable Republican contributor), or the various think tanks in Washington subsidized by animal-use industries for intellectual cover.

After the last election, the National Pork Producers Council rejoiced, "President Bush's victory ensures that the U.S. pork industry will be very well positioned for the next four years politically, and pork producers will benefit from the long-term results of a livestock agriculture-friendly agenda." But this is no tribute. And millions of good people who live in what's left of America's small family-farm communities would themselves rejoice if the president were to announce that he is prepared to sign a bipartisan bill making some basic reforms in livestock agriculture.

Bush's new agriculture secretary, former Nebraska Gov. Mike Johanns, has shown a sympathy for animal welfare. He and the president might both be surprised at the number and variety of supporters such reforms would find in the Congress, from Republicans like Chris Smith and Elton Gallegly in the House to John Ensign and Rick Santorum in the Senate, along with Democrats such as Robert Byrd, Barbara Boxer, or the North Carolina congressman who called me in to say that he, too, was disgusted and saddened by hog farming in his state.

If such matters were ever brought to President Bush's attention in a serious way, he would find in the details of factory farming many things abhorrent to the Christian heart and to his own kindly instincts. Even if he were to drop into relevant speeches a few of the prohibited words in modern industrial agriculture (cruel, humane, compassionate), instead of endlessly flattering corporate farmers for virtues they lack, that alone would help to set reforms in motion.

We need our conservative values voters to get behind a Humane Farming Act so that we can all quit averting our eyes. This reform, a set of explicit federal cruelty statutes with enforcement funding to back it up, would leave us with farms we could imagine without wincing, photograph without prosecution, and explain without excuses.

The law would uphold not only the elementary standards of animal husbandry but also of veterinary ethics, following no more complicated a principle than that pigs and cows should be able to walk and turn around, fowl to move about and spread their wings, and all creatures to know the feel of soil and grass and the warmth of the sun. No need for labels saying "free-range" or "humanely raised." They will all be raised that way. They all get to be treated like animals and not as unfeeling machines.

On a date certain, mass confinement, sow gestation crates, veal crates, battery cages, and all such innovations would be prohibited. This will end livestock agriculture's moral race to the bottom and turn the ingenuity of its scientists toward compassionate solutions. It will remove the federal support that unnaturally serves agribusiness at the expense of small farms. And it will shift economies of scale, turning the balance in favor of humane farmers—as those who run companies like Wal-Mart could do right now by taking their business away from factory farms.

In all cases, the law would apply to corporate farmers a few simple rules that better men would have been observing all along: we cannot just take from these creatures, we must give them something in return. We owe them a merciful death, and we owe them a merciful life. And when human beings cannot do something humanely, without degrading both the creatures and ourselves, then we should not do it at all.

■ READING AND WRITING

1. How does Scully build and support his case that cruelty to animals, especially in the factory farming system, should be a conservative cause?
2. In his essay, Scully writes: "If reason and morality are what set human beings apart from animals, then reason and morality must always guide us in how we treat them, or else it's all just caprice, unbridled appetite with the pretense of piety." What do you think Scully means by this? Do you agree with him? Explain your response.
3. Where does Scully stand on the "rights" of animals? Point to specific passages from his essay to support your response.

■ DEVELOPING LONGER RESPONSES

4. Read through the essay and identify the sources that Scully uses to support his argument. Why do you think he chose these particular people and publications? How do these sources help him reach his intended audience?

Arturo Rodriguez, president of the United Farm Workers, wrote "Cheap Food" with Alexa Delwiche, a UFW researcher, and Sheheryar Kaoosji, an analyst with Change to Win, for the book Food, Inc.: How Industrial Food Is Making Us Sicker, Fatter, and Poorer—and What You Can Do about It. *The book was designed as a companion to filmmaker Robert Kenner's 2008 documentary* Food, Inc., *described in promotional material as an "unflattering look inside America's corporate controlled food industry."*

CHEAP FOOD: WORKERS PAY THE PRICE
Arturo Rodriguez, with Alexa Delwiche and Sheheryar Kaoosji

■ Death in the Fields

Young grapevines thrive in the fierce summer sun of California's Central Valley. But the same early summer heat that helps bring life to the bountiful produce millions of Americans enjoy can also destroy. Unlike the young grapevines, assured of constant irrigation and hydration, farmworker Maria Isabel Vasquez Jimenez had to do without water as she labored in the fields in direct sunlight on a 95-degree day in May 2008.

After almost nine hours of work, Maria became dizzy and collapsed to the ground. Her boyfriend Florentino Bautista ran to her, held her in his arms, and begged for help. The foreman walked over to them and stood over the couple, reassuring Bautista and telling him that "this happens all the time." Remedies devised by the foreman and supervisor ranged from applying rubbing alcohol to placing a wet bandanna on Maria's body. Finally, Maria's boyfriend and coworkers were allowed to take her to a clinic, though the foreman told them to lie about where she was working. It took almost two hours to get the young woman to the clinic. Immediately upon her arrival, the clinic called an ambulance for the hospital. By the time she arrived at the hospital, her body temperature was 108.4 degrees.

Maria held on for two days, but her young body could not withstand the stress. Having arrived in the United States from a small village in Oaxaca only months before and having worked in the fields for only three days, seventeen-year-old Maria died, leaving her family and loving boyfriend forever. It's difficult to accept that such an injustice could occur in 2008. But tragic stories like Maria's are all too common in American agriculture.

Statistics tell part of the story. The rate of death due to heat stress for farm workers is twenty times greater than for the general population.[1] In the past five years, thirty-four

---

[1]Centers for Disease Control, "Heat-Related Deaths Among Crop Workers: United States, 1992-2006," 57, no. 24 (June 2008). Available online at http://www.cdc.gov/mmwr/preview/mmwrhtml/mm5724al.ht

farm workers have died due to heat exposure in the United States. Six of those deaths occurred in the summer of 2008 alone.[2] The actual number is likely much higher because many farmworker deaths are not recorded as heat deaths, and some are not recorded at all.

Maria's death is a poignant example of how the pressures for decreased prices in our food system inevitably lead to exploitation of the workers at the lowest end of the economic chain. Good producers and retailers have successfully abdicated responsibility for the well-being of the workforce that makes their profits possible, aided and abetted by a callous and uninvolved government.

Who is to blame for these senseless and preventable deaths? The farm labor contractors who are hired by the growers to provide them with workers? The growers who actually own the crops and employ the contractors? Or the State of California, which is tasked with enforcing labor regulations that mandate shade, drinking water, and rest breaks for farmworkers toiling in the sun-baked fields?

From a moral perspective, there is more than enough blame to go around. But the system of agricultural production our society has created is designed to shield major corporations from any legal responsibility for their actions or inactions. The layers of subcontracting built into American agriculture are designed to shift responsibility downward from the largest firms to the smallest. Charles Shaw wine, sold exclusively at Trader Joe's and nicknamed affectionately by its customers "Two Buck Chuck," is solely produced by Bronco Wine Company, the largest wine-grape grower in the United States.[3] West Coast Grape Farming, a subsidiary of Bronco Wine and owner of the vineyard in which Maria died, hired Merced Farm Labor, an independent farm labor contractor, to provide workers to harvest their grapes. While Maria and her boyfriend were not picking grapes directly for the Charles Shaw label, both Bronco Wine Company and West Coast Grape Farming are owned and operated by the same Franzia family, which singlehandedly supplies more than 360 million bottles of wine to Trader Joe's each year.

If this supply chain seems unnecessarily complicated well, that's the point. Maria Isabel's employer was neither Trader Joe's, nor Charles Shaw—producer and—winemaker Bronco Wines, but a farm labor contractor with no discernible assets and no traceable relationship to the product sold. Thus, the retailer and producer are shielded from responsibility. Maria Isabel may die, but Charles Shaw wine is still on sale for $1.99 per bottle. Trader Joe's liberal, consumer-friendly reputation is preserved. And a farm labor contractor in Merced, California, quietly goes out of business. But the system that led to Maria Isabel's death continues without change.

The precariousness of a farmworker's life extends far beyond heat deaths. Fatality and injury rates for farmwork rank second in the nation, second only to coal mining.[4] The U.S. Environmental Protection Agency (EPA) estimates that U.S. agricultural workers experience

---

[2] Garance Burke, "More Farm Deaths in Heat Despite Calif. Crackdown," Associated Press, August 21, 2008. Available online at http://www.usatoday.com/news/nation/2008-08-20-3205167992_x.htm.
[3] "California: Strawberries, Vegetables, Water" *Rural Migration News* 14, no. 3 (July 2008). Available online at http://migration.ucdavis.edu/rmn/comments.php?id=1330_0_5_0.
[4] William Kandel, "A Profile of Hired Farmworkers, a 2008 Update," Economic Research Report No. ERR-60, USDA, July 2008. Available online at http://www.ers.usda.gov/publications/err60/err60.pdf.

10,000-20,000 acute pesticide-related illnesses each year, though they also admit that this is likely a significant underestimate.[5] Drinking water and sanitary conditions—basic rights most American workers take for granted—are denied to farmworkers on a daily basis.

The plight of many farmworkers is made worse by their tenuous legal status as U.S. residents. Guest workers brought in under the government-sponsored H2-A visa program are routinely cheated out of wages, forced to pay exorbitant fees to recruiters, and virtually held captive by employers who seize their documents. Slavery—not in a metaphorical or symbolic sense, but in the literal meaning of the word—still exists on farms scattered throughout the country. In 2004, the United States Department of Justice investigated 125 cases of slave labor on American farms, involving thousands of workers.[6] Their shaky legal status helps explain farmworkers' vulnerability. Workers hesitate to report labor law violations for fear of losing their jobs or being deported. But workplace fear is just one variable in a systemic problem: the institutionalized acceptance of farmworkers as second-class citizens. The injustices farmworkers experience are by no means accidental.

Most Americans would be horrified to realize that the foods they eat are produced under conditions like these. Their lack of knowledge about these realities is attributable not to public apathy but to deliberate obfuscation by the companies that market foods and unconscionable neglect by the government agencies that should be safeguarding workers. As food production has become increasingly complex, it has become nearly impossible for consumers to gather information on their food purchases. Product labels reveal little information about a food's origin and contents and tell consumers nothing of the plight of those harvesting and processing their goods. As a result, farmworkers in America are left to suffer incredible poverty and abuse in an industry characterized by great wealth and enormous profits.

■ Retailer Power and Its Impact on Farmers

Food production in the United States is a high-technology, modern process. Produce and animal varieties are meticulously bred, designed, and genetically engineered by food scientists, supported by large academic programs at public land-grant universities across the nation and in government agencies like the USDA and FDA. Products are packaged, distributed, and sold throughout the nation and exported worldwide using the same state-of-the-art, just-in-time logistics systems that move other goods throughout the international economy.

---

[5] U.S. General Accountability Office (GAO), "Pesticides: Improvement Needed to Ensure the Safety of Farm Workers and Their Children," GAO/RCED-00-40,2000, citing a 1993 U.S. EPA study. Available online at www. gao.gov/archieve/2000/rc00040.pdf.

[6] Oxfam, "Like Machines in the Fields: Workers Without Rights in American Agriculture." Research Paper, March 2004. Available online at http://www.oxfamamerica.org/newsandpublications/research_reports/art7011. html/OA-Like_Machines_in_the_Fields.pdf.

But despite the high-tech systems that streamline and control the flow of goods to the nation's dinner tables, a farmworker's job is remarkably similar to the life of Chinese and Japanese immigrants at the turn of the twentieth century, of Mexican migrants in the 1920s, of white Dust Bowl migrants during the Depression, or black and Mexican migrant workers since the 1940s. Crops eaten raw, such as grapes, strawberries, and lettuce, require careful and steady human hands to retain the physical and visual perfection required by the modern consumer. Much of the so-called specialty crops (that is, fruits and vegetables) that the nation consumes are grown in the heat of California's Central and Coachella valleys, where day-time temperatures stay in the triple digits throughout harvesting season.

Strawberry and lettuce workers bend thousands of times a day, picking valuable produce from the rich earth of the central coast of California that John Steinbeck once wrote about. Apple workers fill bags with up to seventy pounds of produce, carrying them up and down ladders across the Yakima Valley of Washington state. The story is retold every generation, with workers toiling for minimum wages to feed the population of the United States.

Most people are surprised to learn that the conditions of farm laborers have not been dramatically improved since the days of *Grapes of Wrath*. In fact, the story has gotten worse in recent years. The growers that employ farmworkers have been experiencing a historic squeeze in prices from the retailers that purchase their produce. The retail food sector has been inexorably consolidating for decades, culminating in the dominance of Wal-Mart over the grocery industry, representing between twenty and forty percent of the sales volume of various food products in the United States. Today, the top five retailers control over sixty percent of the market.[7] Thanks to this consolidation, a relative handful of companies wield enormous power over food suppliers—power they use to demand ever-lower prices for the fruits, vegetables, and other commodities they stock. Growers have responded to these pressures, providing picture-perfect produce at deflationary prices, sourcing them from around the world in order to provide year-round supplies to the retailers.

And consumers have reaped the benefits. The average American family now spends less than ten percent of its income on food, the lowest percent in history.[8] In 1950, this figure was twenty percent. As writer and grower David Mas Masumoto described it in a poem he presented at the 2008 Slow Food Festival, "I remember $2-a-box peaches in 1961 and $2-a-box peaches in 2007."[9]

But everyday low prices for consumers (and increasing profits for the shareholders of the giant retailers) have created serious consequences for growers. Each year, farmers capture less of the consumers' food dollar. For example, in 1982, farmers received thirty-

---

[7] Ibid, citing Linda Calvin et al., *U.S. Fresh Fruit and Vegetable Marketing: Emerging Trade Practices, Trends, and Issues* (Washington, D.C.: Economic Research Service, U.S. Department of Agriculture, January 2001, Agricultural Economic Report No. 795. Available online at http://www.ers.usda.gov/publications/aer795.

[8] USDA, "Food CPI, Prices and Expenditures: Food Expenditures by Families and Individuals as a Share of Disposable Personal Income," Economic Research Service, June 17, 2008. Available online at http://www.ers.usda.gov/briefing/CPIFoodandExpenditures/Data/table7.htm.

[9] Jane Black, "Slow Food at Full Speed: They Ate It Up." *Washington Post*, September 3, 2008. Available online at http://www.washingtonpost.com/wp-dyn/content/story/2008/09/02/ST2008090202273.html.

four percent and thirty-three percent of what consumers paid for fresh vegetables and fresh fruit, respectively, at retail food stores; by 2004, these farm shares had declined to nineteen percent for fresh vegetables and twenty percent for fresh fruit.[10]

One result of this squeeze is that only gigantic agribusinesses can survive in the new farming economy. Massive state-sponsored infrastructure, especially the dam and levee system developed in California over the twentieth century, allowed large California growers to achieve unprecedented scale while successfully gobbling up smaller growers farm by farm. Such scale also benefits top retailers that depend on the considerable quantities supplied by only the largest growers. Medium-sized family growers now depend on selling prime agricultural land to the developers who are helping California cities sprawl to supplement their income. Organic growers who once hoped to provide a new model of agriculture have been pushed to the periphery by high certification costs and loose standards that allow the largest growers to dominate the mainstream organic market.

But ultimately the effects of retail consolidation have trickled down the production line to workers, causing wages and benefits for workers throughout the food system to stagnate. Today, even a modest wage increase for workers on a farm could threaten a supplier's contract with a retailer. Furthermore, growers and labor contractors often find the easiest way to minimize labor costs is by cutting corners on labor and safety standards. Some labor contractors even admit that "breaking the law is the only way you can make decent money."[11] Of course, there are exceptions, and many decent employers in the industry exist. But the system results in a constant push for lower costs, with no basic standards across the industry. There is no high road—only a low road populated by growers racing one another to reach rock bottom.

■ Agricultural "Exceptionalism" and the Subsidy Economy

This situation is not sustainable, nor is it accidental. In large measure, it can be traced back to government policies designed to produce the very system that now distorts agricultural production in this country.

The State of California, where almost half of U.S. produce is grown and forty percent of farm laborers work, provides a vivid illustration of how this process has worked. The policies pursued by California as well as by the federal government have promoted corporate agricultural interests for over a century.[12] By demanding a set of immigration

---

[10] Hayden Stewart, "How Low Has the Farm Share of Retail Food Prices Really Fallen?" *Economic Research Report* No. ERR-24, August 2006. Available online at www.ers.usda.gov/Publications/ERR24/.

[11] Daniel Rothenberg, *With These Hands: The Hidden World of Migrant Farmworkers Today* (Berkeley: University of California Press, 1998), 97.

[12] Philip Martin, "Labor Relations in California Agriculture." In *University of California Institute for Labor and Employment. The State of California Labor*, 2001. Available online at http://repositories.cdlib.org/ile/scl2001/Section7.

policies that guaranteed cheap labor and made these workers dependent on the government through assistance programs (or on the growers themselves through labor camps), a permanent underclass in the fields was cultivated.[13] This is a policy called "agricultural exceptionalism"—the exemption of agriculture from labor and other laws under the Jeffersonian theory that food production is not only a crucial U.S. industry but also a superior way of life that deserves special preservation and protection. This mindset has dominated U.S. policy in land use, labor law, and direct and indirect farm subsidies for a century.

As a result, although government exists in part to protect the powerless from the powerful, government has done little to benefit the agricultural workers who feed the nation. While most workers won historic labor protections through the Fair Labor Standards Act of 1938—which set minimum wage requirements, overtime laws, and child labor laws— powerful lobbying by agribusiness succeeded in excluding farmworkers from protection under these laws.[14] The minimum wage now applies to farmworkers in most cases, but overtime provisions still do not. Furthermore, to this day, the age limit for children working in agriculture differs from other businesses. Children under the age of 14 cannot be employed in any other industry; in agriculture the age limit is twelve. No age restrictions apply to children working on family farms.

Agribusiness also managed to exclude farmworkers from another piece of New Deal legislation, the National Labor Relations Act, which gave workers the right to form unions and bargain collectively. So when the limited rights farmworkers actually enjoy are violated, they are denied the ability to organize themselves to demand fair treatment.

One of the most egregious examples of agricultural exceptionalism has been the government's failure to reduce farmworkers' exposure to pesticides because of the profit loss growers might suffer if pesticides were more tightly regulated. Cleverly, regulation of farmworker exposure to pesticides was placed under the jurisdiction of the EPA, famous for its use of "cost-benefit analysis" when determining whether to place restrictions on the use of chemicals.[15] The phrase sounds innocuous, even reasonable, but, in practice, reliance on cost-benefit analysis means that a hazardous pesticide will not be restricted by the EPA if the economic hardship to the grower is considered to be greater than the hazards to farmworker or consumer health. If pesticide protection for farmworkers were under the jurisdiction of the Occupational Safety and Health Administration (OSHA), cost-benefit analysis would not be required—a simple finding that workers' lives were at risk would suffice to justify regulation.

More than twenty years ago, the EPA concluded that farmworkers were disproportionately affected by the use of pesticides. Indeed, a large body of scientific literature has documented this relationship. A study of 146,000 California Hispanic farmworkers concluded that, when compared to the general Hispanic population, farmworkers were more likely to develop certain types of leukemia by fifty-nine percent,

---

[13] Ibid.

[14] Keith Cunningham-Parmeter, "A Poisoned Field: Farm Workers, Pesticide Exposure, and Tort Recovery in an Era of Regulatory Failure," *New York University Review of Law & Social Change* 28:431.

[15] Ibid.

stomach cancer by seventy percent, cervical cancer by sixty-three percent, and uterine cancer by sixty-eight percent.[16] Despite this evidence, the EPA has failed to enact any mitigation procedures to address farmworkers' chronic exposure to pesticides.

Thanks to the importance of agriculture to the California economy, agribusiness has been especially powerful at the state government level. One result has been an amazingly lopsided set of water management policies: only three rivers in California remain undimmed, and eighty percent of the water collected is consumed by agriculture.[17] Both small-and large-scale growers purchase vast amounts of imported river water at just a fraction of the true price, their purchases subsidized by state and federal taxpayer dollars. Indeed, in some regions of California, the average urban water user pays seventy-five times the price of a grower. Not only have these subsidies encouraged extremely inefficient water use by agricultural producers, but they have allowed growers and retailers to profit in their ability to produce crops more cheaply than otherwise possible, all at the expense of the taxpayer. Meanwhile, more than 635 miles of rivers and streams in the Central Valley have been classified as unsafe for fishing, swimming, or drinking due to pollution from agricultural runoff.[18] And as drought risk intensifies throughout the state, the bulk of the state's water continues to be dumped, quite literally, into the Central Valley for growers either to use for crops or to resell for profit to urban water districts, desperate for the precious resource.

■ Immigration Policy As a Tool of Agribusiness

Over the last century, the most important policy perpetuating the existence of an underclass of agricultural workers has been U.S. immigration policy. Today, almost eighty percent of the 2.5 million farm workers in the United States were born outside of the United States.[19] The overwhelming majority of farmworkers are from Mexico. Estimates vary, but at least fifty percent of the workforce is not authorized to work in the United States.[20]

The roots of Mexican migration patterns lie in a series of U.S. approved guest programs created during the twentieth century specifically to address farm labor needs and in lax

[16] Margaret Reeves, Anne Katten, and Martha Guzman, "Fields of Poison," (Darby, Pa.: Diane Publishing, 2002), citing a study by P.K. Mills and S. Kwong, "Cancer Incidence in the United Farm Workers of America (UFW) 1987-1997," *American Journal of Industrial Medicine* 40 (2001): 596-603. Available online at http://www.ufw.org/white_papers/report.pdf.

[17] Liquid Gold: A California Exhibition. An Exhibit by the Water Resources Center Archives, University of California at Berkeley. Online at http://www.lib.berkeley.edu/WRCA/exhibit.html.

[18] The Environmental Justice Water Coalition, "Thirsty for Justice: A People's Blueprint for California Water," 2005. Available online at http://eee.ejcw.org/Thirsty%20for%20Justice.pdf.

[19] U.S. Department of Labor (DOL), Findings of the National Agricultural Workers Survey (NAWS) 2001-2002: A Demographic and Employment Profile of United States Farmworkers (Washington, D.C.: U.S. Department of Labor, March 2005), Research Report No. 9. Available online at http://www.dol.gove/asp/programs/agworker/report_8.pdf.

[20] Kandel.

enforcement of immigration laws by the federal government during periods in which no guest worker programs were in place.[21]

The most recent wave of labor migration to the United States was spurred by the North American Free Trade Agreement (NAFTA) and other trade liberalizing policies. The entrance of cheap, government-subsidized U.S. corn into the Mexican economy in the wake of NAFTA signaled to Mexican corn producers that there was no future left for them in agriculture. And they were right. Government investment in Mexican agriculture fell by ninety percent.[22] Almost two million subsistence farmers were displaced. Some farmers fled to urban areas in Mexico, while others decided there was nowhere else to go but north of the border.[23]

So NAFTA, after having been branded by both Republicans and Democrats as the solution to combating poverty in Mexico and reducing migrations to the United States, only deepened the problem. Rather than improving the economic situation on both sides of the border as promised, NAFTA helped produce a *decrease* in real wages in Mexico between 1995 and 2005.[24] Annual migration to the United States *increased* from 2.5 million unauthorized immigrants in 1995 to 11 million in 2005.[25] As a result of the effects of NAFTA on food production in southern Mexico, Oaxacans are now the fastest growing population of farmworkers in the United States. Today, one in five families in Mexico depends on remittances from the United States, the total averaging almost $24 billion a year.[26]

Since NAFTA's implementation, the only serious U.S. immigration policy enacted to address the influx of migrants was Operation Gatekeeper (1995), the policy of deterring migration by increasing border enforcement in the border cities of San Diego and El Paso.[27] This policy only shifted migration patterns farther east into more harsh and inhospitable desert. Mexican farmworkers leave their families and risk their lives crossing a dangerous and increasingly militarized border because there are no other options left. To risk is to hope for better.

---

[21] Martin.

[22] Public Citizen, "Down on the Farm: NAFTA's Seven-Years War on Farmers and Ranchers in the U.S., Canada and Mexico," June 2001. Available online at http://www.citizen.org/documents/ACFF2.PDF.

[23] Ibid.

[24] Giselle Henriques and Raj Patel, "Agricultural Trade Liberalization and Mexico," Food First, Policy Brief 7, 2003, available online at http://www.foodfirst.org/pubs/policy/pb7.pdf.

[25] Philip Martin, "NAFTA and Mexico—US Migration," 2005. Available online at http://giannini.ucop.edu/Mex_USMigration.pdf.

[26] Tracy Wilkinson, "Less Money Going to Mexico as US Economy Falters," *Los Angeles Times*, October 2, 2008. Available online at http://www.latimes.com/news/printedition/asection/la-fg-mexmoney2-2008oct02,0,2037607.story.

[27] Connie de la Vega and Conchita Lozano, 2005, "Advocates Should Use Applicable International Standards to Address Violations of Undocumented Workers' Rights in the United States," *Hastings Race & Poverty Law Journal* 3, 35.

Tragically, since 1995, deaths along the United States/Mexico border have doubled.[28] In 2005, 472 people died in the desert, with heat exposure and dehydration as the leading causes of death. And when migrants do survive, their best and often only shot at employment in the United States is the lowest-paid, most-dangerous, least-respected occupations of all—including agriculture. In a world of free trade for goods and closed borders for people, those who survive the passage can check their rights at the gate.

■ Farm Workers Looking Up at the Poverty Line

It's difficult for a family of four living at the official poverty level to get by, making just $21,000 per year.[29] But compare that with a farmworker family's annual wage of roughly $13,000, a sum comparable to one acre's profit for a strawberry field.[30] Farmworkers continue to be among the lowest-paid laborers in the United States, with only dishwashers earning less.[31] The majority of farmworkers live below the poverty line, with real wages hovering around minimum wage.[32] Benefits are even more meager. Less than one-tenth of workers have employer-paid health insurance for non-work related health care, and just ten percent receive paid holidays or vacation time.[33]

As we've noted, a significant factor accounting for the low wages of farmworkers is the large proportion of unauthorized immigrant workers employed in agriculture. Undocumented workers have few employment options, thus making workers more willing to accept low wages.[34] The use of farm labor contractors (FLCs), hired by growers to provide workers, also helps explain the low wages for farmworkers. FLCs are notorious for paying lower wages in order to compete with the other thousands of contractors desperate for a grower's business. Farm labor contractors provide almost fifty percent of farm labor in California, a number that grows every year both in California and in the rest of the nation.

U.S. policymakers consistently support and facilitate agricultural producers' dependence on low-wage labor. Some may believe that the poor compensation of immigrant workers will be augmented by a safety net of government assistance programs designed to help the working poor. Yet undocumented status and extreme poverty have proven to be insurmountable barriers that prevent many farmworker families from actually accessing much of this assistance.

---

[28] General Accountability Office, "Illegal Immigration: Border Crossing Deaths Have Doubled Since 1995; Border Patrol's Efforts to Prevent Deaths Have Not Been Fully Evaluated," GAO-06-770, August 2006. Available online at http://www.goa.gov/new.items/d06770.pdf.

[29] Department of Health and Human Services, "Annual Update of the HHS Poverty Guidelines," *Federal Register* 73, no. 15 (January 23, 2008): 3971-3972. Available online at http://aspe.hhs.gov/POVERTY/08fedreg.htm.

[30] Kandel.

[31] Ibid.

[32] DOL.

[33] Kandel.

[34] Ibid.

While the legal status of workers is no impediment when hiring workers for poverty-level wages, the same status excludes these workers from their only opportunities to make ends meet through government assistance. Less than one in five farmworkers use means-tested services such as Temporary Assistance to Needy Families; housing vouchers; Women, Infants, and Children; food-stamps; Medicaid; or the National School Lunch Program, citing legal status and cost as significant barriers.[35] And even though each week a percentage of farmworkers' paychecks flows into the Social Security system, most will never see a dime of it. Only two percent of farmworkers report ever receiving any social security benefits.[36] Far from being a drain to the system, those working without authorization actually provide Social Security with an average annual subsidy of nearly $7 billion.[37]

High rates of poverty contribute to shocking health problems among farmworkers. Nearly eighty percent of male farmworkers are overweight.[38] And one in five males have at least two of three risk factors for chronic disease, such as high cholesterol, high blood pressure, or obesity, putting them at heightened risk to suffer from heart disease, stroke, asthma, and diabetes. Many farmworkers have never visited a doctor's or any other type of medical facility, including an emergency room. And as migrant workers return to Mexico, the costs associated with medical treatment for their high rates of chronic disease will be borne by Mexican society, thus creating a greater strain on the already fragile Mexican economy.

Poverty rates among farmworkers extend into their housing options. Interestingly, in 2005, the three least affordable places to live in the United States, measured by the percentage of income spent on rent or mortgage payments, were areas with high farmworker populations: Salinas, CA; Watsonville, CA; and Petaluma/Santa Rosa, CA.[39] In expensive cities such as these, affordable housing options are in such short supply that workers often are forced to live wherever they can find shelter, from abandoned cars to tin-roofed shanties.

Squalid living conditions in labor camps, reminiscent of those we associate with the 1930s, still exist for farmworkers today. In May 2008, more than one hundred migrant fruit pickers from Washington were found living in tents in a Central Valley cherry orchard in California without access to clean water. They were bathing in drainage ditches.

There have been some model housing programs created in California and Florida, but generally speaking, substandard living conditions are the norm for farmworkers. While some workers live in employer-provided housing, many families instead choose to crowd into rented apartments, sharing space appropriate for a single family with as many as ten to twenty other people. Poor sanitation and proximity to pesticide-laden fields create serious

---

[35] DOL.

[36] Ibid.

[37] Eduardo Porter, "Illegal Immigrants Are Bolstering Social Security with Billions," *New York Times*, April 5, 2005. Available online at www.nytimes.om/2005/04/05/business/05immigration.html.

[38] Don Villarejo et al., "Suffering in Silence: A Report on the Health of California's Agricultural Workers," California Institute of Rural Studies, Sponsored by California Endowment, 2001. Available online at www.fachc.org/pdf/mig_suffering%20in%silence.pdf.

[39] Alina Tungend, "The Least Affordable Place to Live? Try Salinas," *New York Times*, May 7, 2006, real estate section. Available online at www.nytimes.com/2006/05/07/realestate/07california.html.

public health risks for farmworker families. But these are the conditions workers must accept when left with no other options.

■ Government's Malign Neglect

It isn't enough to demand that government should create more laws to protect farmworkers. The ones that do exist aren't enforced. Agricultural land is too vast for government to patrol; there are more than 80,000 farms in California alone, employing well over half a million workers.[40] CAL-OSHA, the state agency responsible for worker safety enforcement, conducted fewer than 300 inspections between 2007 and 2008.[41] Penalties are meager, and often violations are never even collected.

California holds the reputation for the most pro-farmworker legislation in the nation, yet the state provides many examples of the inadequacies of government enforcement. California remains the only state to enact any legislation granting farmworkers basic labor rights. The Agricultural Labor Relations Act (ALRA) of 1975 provides agricultural workers with organizing rights and protects workers from workplace retaliation from employers due to union involvement. However, even after unions gained organizing rights, the State of California ignored most of these rights once conservatives had regained the state house in 1983. The growers reasserted their ability to intimidate, and the United Farm Workers' ability to organize workers returned to the pre-law level that year, when the Republican-appointed Agricultural Labor Relations Board determined that even the cold-blooded murder of pro-union farmworker Rene Lopez by a company goon did not amount to an unfair labor practice.

Despite the existence of ALRA, union density rates among farmworkers remain low. Growers were found by the State of California to have intimidated, threatened, and offered bribes to workers at union elections in 2005 and 2006, but there have been no meaningful penalties, only an offer of another chance for workers to try to organize under such conditions.[42]

The failure to enforce heat protection laws provides another example. In 2005, California passed a law to protect workers from death due to heat stroke. The law requires that employers provide fresh water, shade, and additional breaks when the temperature goes above 95 degrees. Yet more farmworkers have died in the three years since the law's enactment than the three years prior.[43] More than one-third of the farms visited by CAL-OSHA in 2007 were out of compliance with the heat regulations.

---

[40] USDA, Census on Agriculture, 2002. Available online at http://www.nass.usda.gov/Census/Pull_Data_Census.jsp.

[41] Data were gathered from OSHA's inspection database. Query included all establishments engaged in crop or livestock production from September 1, 2007, and September 1, 2008. Available online at http://www.osha.gov/pls/imis/industry.html. 994 inspections were conducted during the same time period for all crop and livestock establishments (approximately 2.1 million farms or 938 million acres) in the United States during the same time period.

[42] *United Farm Workers v. VINCENT B. ZANINOVICH & SONS, A CALIFORNIA CORPORATION*, 34 ALRB No. 3 (2008).

[43] Burke.

Pesticide spraying provides yet another example. California leads the nation in pesticide protection for farmworkers, which includes one of only two pesticide spraying reporting systems in the nation. Even so, pesticide spraying continues at high rates, and the burden for reporting rests with the workers, keeping reporting rates low.

■ The Union Is the Solution

Farmworkers have long known that, though government may try to protect them, ultimately it will not stand with them. Workers without representation have no chance of even bringing a claim to enforcement agencies without facing threats of firing, deportation, or worse. The most effective solution for workers has been to organize and collectively demand improved wages, benefits, and working conditions. Unionized workers have the protections that allow them to speak up when something goes wrong.

Unfortunately, the policy of excluding agriculture from laws that affect the rest of the country (especially labor law) lives on. And rather than a remnant of the past, it may in fact be a harbinger of where the American economy is headed in the twenty-first century. The abused and exploited second tier of the American labor force has expanded from agricultural workers to include many food-processing workers across the nation as well as employees in other sectors dominated by people of color, such as hospitality, janitorial work, trucking, and security. Millions of these workers effectively have no rights and no chance of basic protections without organizing themselves into unions.

The history of the meatpacking industry in the twentieth century is an example of the effect unions can have on an industry. Long one of the dirtiest, lowest-paying, most-dangerous urban jobs, as depicted in Upton Sinclair's 1906 novel *The Jungle*, meatpacking was transformed in the 1930s into a well-paying, respected, and safer job because the workers organized the Meatpackers' Union. The daily tasks of these jobs were not transformed by unionization, but the union allowed its members to improve their working conditions, raise families, buy homes, and even overcome the racial discrimination that existed in postwar cities such as Chicago and Minneapolis. At the same time, food safety and quality were boosted by workers with such crucial rights as whistle-blowing and the ability to affect assembly line speeds, benefiting not just workers but consumers.

In recent years, the same price pressures from retailers such as Wal-Mart that have depressed agricultural wages have resulted in meat processing being moved to rural, nonunion facilities run by such strongly antiunion meat and poultry firms as Tyson and Smithfield. The result has been declining standards, wages, and quality in the meatpacking industry. The jobs that once supported the working class in Midwestern cities have been redesigned to exploit workers from around the world, who have no ability to complain about or question unsafe and unfair practices. Progress has turned back, to the detriment of both rural and urban economies, workers, and consumers. Once again, only big retailers and food processors win.

There is hope for better conditions. Only about five percent of U.S. farmworkers are unionized. The unionized workers don't always make much more than other farmworkers (though some do), but they do get health insurance and even a pension, which are increasingly rare even for white-collar workers. More important, union workers have the right to speak up on the job. They have the freedom to advocate for issues that matter to them without fear of dismissal. They can establish procedures with their supervisors for days it gets too hot in the fields and workers feel their health may be at risk. The value of this is remarkable both for the basic conditions of the workplace and the quality and sustainability of the food produced. And a farmworker union with higher density would be a powerful ally to the environmental justice movement that is rising across the nation, empowered to address global as well as kitchen table issues in the food processing industry.

Cesar Chavez, founder and leader of the United Farm Workers until his death in 1993, focused much of his work on environmental issues such as pesticide use, the dangers of monoculture, and the benefits of natural production methods, understanding that collective bargaining was a meaningless tool if farmworkers were still being poisoned in the fields. He recognized that pesticide use is an issue that clearly affects both workers and consumers.

The safety and well-being of farmworkers, consumers, and the environment have always been secondary to profits in the eyes of the big agricultural interests. So, when the government failed to address concerns about the harmful effects of organophosphates on workers, consumers, and the environment, Chavez and the UFW used union contracts to regulate pesticides. Union contracts in 1970 achieved what no U.S. government agency ever had: key provisions restricting the use of the five most dangerous pesticides.[44]

Unfortunately, the current system for farmworkers to choose a union is broken. The sad truth is that the federal agencies designed to oversee the food system and its workforce—the Food and Drug Administration, the U.S. Department of Agriculture, the Department of Labor, and the Environmental Protection Agency—as well as the State of California's Agricultural Labor Relations Board, have little practical ability to conduct a fair union election, let alone regulate pesticides, food safety, or worker safety in the fields.

It is even worse in other states. The agricultural exceptionalism of the 1930s remains dominant, and there is no way for farmworkers to organize in the rest of the country. Many young farmworkers don't know what a union is, having grown up in a post-NAFTA North America of economic instability, migration, and constant fear.

■ Farm Workers and Consumer Power

This litany of problems has a solution. It is to change the balance of power when it comes to our food. Workers have never had the power to balance out the strength of agribusiness. But consumers have enormous power when they are activated and informed.

---

[44] Robert Gordon, "Poisons in the Fields: The United Farm Workers, Pesticides, and Environmental Politics," *The Pacific Historical Review* 68, no. 1 (Feb. 1999): 51-77. Available online at http://links.jstor.org/sici?sici=0030-8684%28199902%2968%3A1%3C51%3APITFTU%3E2.0CO%3B2-8.

The two UFW-led grape boycotts of the 1960s and 1970s were unprecedented in their scope, duration, and effectiveness because they combined the power of the farmworker, on strike in California, and the consumer, refusing to purchase the product across the country. This boycott was able to defeat the power of the retailer and grower because the consumer, the final arbiter of the transaction, took action.

So why has the consumer abdicated this power in more recent years? Have consumers made a Faustian bargain, accepting worker exploitation in exchange for low prices? If so, the actual benefits to consumers are meager. University of California at Davis agricultural economist Philip Martin has computed that farmworker wages and benefits levy a total cost of $22 per year on each American household.[45] Furthermore, he found that to raise average farmworker wages by forty percent, bringing workers from below the poverty line to above it, would cost the average household only $8 more for produce each year.[46]

Thankfully, consumer awareness in the food system has reached unprecedented levels, and the ability to create change to the food system has made important strides because of consumer preference. The organics industry continues to grow. Wal-Mart, long criticized for its irresponsible buying practices and cheap products, now carries organics and purchases locally grown produce when possible. Concern over the treatment of animals has led to ballot propositions banning caged animals and has changed the buying practices of major fast-food outlets. The growth explosion of Whole Foods from a niche natural foods store to a $6 billion powerhouse proves that consumers are willing to pay more for quality food.

The principle of sustainability recognizes the interdependence of our food system. And worker dignity, respect, and health and safety are fundamental to a sustainable system. Purchasing organic strawberries doesn't mean much if workers are still dying in fields. This same force that exploits farmworkers also pollutes our environment, impoverishes rural communities, and sickens consumers. Unless the balance of power is shifted away from valuing profits over human life, no one is protected.

Cesar Chavez once noted, "In the old days, miners would carry birds with them to warn against poison gas. Hopefully, the birds would die before the miners. Farmworkers are society's canaries."[47] The integrity of the food system begins with just conditions for workers.

Only the consumer has the power to support farmworkers in their struggle for representation. And only with an empowered workforce will there be an organized, principled counterbalance to the food production sector, defending sustainability, safety, and other standards. When workers are empowered, consumers are protected. Working together to take the following steps, we can make our food system more just, sustainable, and healthy.

---

[45] "How We Eat: 2005," *Rural Migration News* 13, no. 3 (July 2007). Available online at http://migration.ucdavis.edu/rmn/more.php?id=1229_0_5_0.

[46] Ibid.

[47] Address by Cesar Chavez, President, United Farm Workers of America, AFL-CIO, Pacific Lutheran University, Tacoma.

■ What Can You Do?

If you share the concerns we've described in these pages, here are some practical steps you can take to support our efforts to improve the conditions of the workers who provide you with the food that you and your family eat:

■ Become educated on farmworker issues. Start by visiting the resource library at www.ufw.org.

■ Support union and other advocacy campaigns for workers in the food system.

■ Demand that retailers provide more transparent information on the working and living conditions of their suppliers' workforce.

■ When they're available, always purchase products that guarantee workers' rights and express your support and approval to retailers so they'll be encouraged to stock such products.

■ Support comprehensive immigration reform.

■ Support policies that assist the working poor, such as increasing the minimum wage, living wage ordinances, and universal health care.

■ Buy organic. Even though organic production does not provide workers with any additional wages, benefits, or respect, they are spared the detrimental effects associated with pesticides.

While it's time for consumers to mobilize and participate in reforming the food system, it is equally important for farmworker and food-system advocates from every step of the supply chain to come together and engage in a serious dialogue. It is our responsibility as advocates to create opportunities for consumers to use their power in improving the lives of food-system workers. Whether this occurs through the development of a "Socially Just" food certification label, through an extensive consumer awareness campaign, through legislation, or through an entirely new vision, now is the time to organize ourselves, to work together, to implement the type of societal transformation that we envision every morning when we get out of bed, and to renew our struggle for economic and social justice.

■ READING AND WRITING

1. While this essay is about a nationwide issue, Rodriguez and his co-authors begin with the story of one woman—Maria Isabel Vasquez Jimenez. Which rhetorical appeal is at work in this section of the essay? What do the authors accomplish by opening with Maria's story?
2. Briefly summarize the problems, as explained in the essay, that farm workers face in the United States. What role, according to the authors, can consumers play in addressing these problems?

■ DEVELOPING LONGER RESPONSES

3. What kinds of sources do Rodriguez and his co-authors use in their essay? (Don't forget to look at the footnotes throughout the essay.) Write an essay in which you analyze the authors' use of logos to support their claims and persuade their audience.

■ USING RESEARCH

4. Find the websites of the United Farm Workers and Change to Win and spend some time exploring them. What kinds of ethos do these organizations present? What does each organization do rhetorically to develop its ethos? How does knowing more about these organizations affect your reading of Rodriguez's essay?

Christine Lennon is a freelance writer in Los Angeles who regularly contributes to InStyle *and* Time *magazines. She wrote this essay for the August 2007 issue of* Food & Wine.

WHY VEGETARIANS ARE EATING MEAT
Christine Lennon

To a die-hard meat eater, there's nothing more irritating than a smug vegetarian. I feel at liberty to say this because I am one (a steak lover) and I married the other (a vegetarian with a pulpit). For me, "Do you now, or would you ever, eat meat?" has always been a question on par with "Do you ever want to get married?" and "Do you want children?" The answer to one reveals as much about a person's interior life, and our compatibility, as the response to the others. My husband Andrew's reply to all of those questions when I asked him three years ago was, "No."

Obviously, we're now married. We had twins earlier this year. And somewhere in between those two events, the answer to the third question was also re-evaluated, and the vegetarian soapbox was put to rest, too.

Yes, my husband has started eating meat again after a seven-year hiatus as an ethically motivated and health-conscious vegetarian. About a year ago, we arrived at a compromise: I would eat less meat—choosing mostly beef, pork and poultry produced by local California ranchers without the use of hormones or antibiotics—and he would indulge me by sharing a steak on occasion. But arriving at that happy medium wasn't as straightforward as it sounds. In the three years we've been together, several turns of events have made both of us rethink our choices and decide that eating meat selectively is better for the planet and our own health. And judging by the conversations we've had with friends and acquaintances, we're not the only ones who believe this to be true.

For Andrew and about a dozen people in our circle who have recently converted from vegetarianism, eating sustainable meat purchased from small farmers is a new form of activism—a way of striking a blow against the factory farming of livestock that books like Michael Pollan's *The Omnivore's Dilemma* describe so damningly. Pollan extols the virtues of independent, small-scale food producers who raise pasture-fed livestock in a sustainable and ethical manner. In contrast, he provides a compelling critique of factory farms, which cram thousands of cows, pigs or chickens into rows of cages in warehouses, feed them drugs to plump up their meat and fight off the illnesses caused by these inhumane conditions, and produce innumerable tons of environmentally destructive animal waste.

The terms "grass fed" and "pasture raised"—meaning that an animal was allowed to graze the old-fashioned way instead of being fed an unnatural and difficult-to-digest diet of mostly corn and other grain—have now entered the food-shoppers' lexicon. But Andrew and I didn't fully understand what those phrases meant until we got to know Greg Nauta of Rocky Canyon Farms. Nauta is a small-scale rancher and farmer from Atascadero, California, who grows organic vegetables and raises about 35 animals on pastureland. Since we met him at the Hollywood Farmers' Market a year ago, it has become even clearer to us that supporting guys like him—by seeking out and paying a premium for sustainably raised meat—is the right thing for us to do.

Nauta's cattle graze on 200 leased acres of pasture in central California and are fed the leftover vegetables and fruits he grows that don't sell at the farmers' market, supplemented by locally grown barley grain on occasion. "That's dessert," he says of the barley, "not a main course. That would be like us eating ice cream every day."

Three times a week, Nauta loads his truck full of coolers stocked with cattleman's steaks and handmade pork sausages and drives to the Los Angeles–area farmers' markets. Selling his vegetables and meat directly to conscientious eaters, people to whom he talks weekly about rainfall averages and organic produce, Nauta says, is "the best way small guys like me can compete." In the past several months, Nauta has noticed a handful of curious vegetarians, like Andrew, wandering over to his booth to ask questions. And they're satisfied enough with the answers to give his meat a try—and come back for more.

If preserving small-scale farming isn't a compelling enough reason to eat beef or pork, consider the nutritional advantages grass-fed meat has over the factory-fed kind. "One of the benefits of all-grass-fed beef, or 'beef with benefits,' as we say, is that it's lower in fat than conventionally raised beef," says Kate Clancy, who studies nutrition and sustainable agriculture and was until recently the senior scientist at the nonprofit Union of Concerned Scientists. "The other thing is that the meat and milk from grass-fed cattle will probably have higher amounts of omega-3 fatty acids, which may help reduce the risk of heart disease and strengthen people's immune systems. What's good for the environment, what's good for cattle, is also good for us."

Combine these findings with the questions being raised about meat replacements derived from soy and wheat gluten, and the real thing seems better by the minute. "What we know about soy is that as you process it, you lose a lot of the benefits," says Ashley Koff, a Los Angeles–based registered dietician. "Any soy-based fake meat product is incredibly processed, and you have to use chemicals to get the mock flavor. Any other whole-food diet is going to be a lot better for you." Vegetarians like Andrew—he once brought a tofu sandwich to a famous Texas barbecue restaurant—may now have a harder time justifying their "healthier" dietary choices.

Former vegetarians are some of the most outspoken proponents of eating meat. "I was vegan for 16 years, and I truly believed I was doing the right thing for my health," says the actress and model Mariel Hemingway, who is the author of *Healthy Living from the Inside Out*. "But when I was vegan, I was super-weak. I love animals, and we should not support anything but ethical ranching, but when I eat meat, I feel more grounded. I have more energy."

Even chef Mollie Katzen, author of the vegetarian bible the *Moosewood Cookbook*, is experimenting with meat again. "For about 30 years I didn't eat meat at all, just a bite of fish every once in a while, and always some dairy," she says. "Lately, I've been eating a little meat. People say, 'Ha, ha, Mollie Katzen is eating steak.' But now that cleaner, naturally fed meat is available, it's a great option for anyone who's looking to complete his diet. Somehow, it got ascribed to me that I don't want people to eat meat. I've just wanted to supply possibilities that were low on the food chain."

Recently, when responding to the invitation to her high-school reunion, Katzen had to make a choice between the vegetarian and the conventional meal. She checked the nonvegetarian box. "The people who requested the vegetarian meal got fettuccine Alfredo," she says. "It's a bowl full of flour and butterfat. I'd much rather have vegetables and grains and a few bites of chicken."

For Andrew and many of our ex-vegetarian friends, the ethical reasons for eating meat, combined with the health-related ones, have been impossible to deny. "The way I see it, you've got three opportunities every day to act on your values and have an immediate effect on something you're concerned about," Andrew says. "You're probably worried about Darfur, too, but what can you do about that every single day? Write a letter? It doesn't have the same kind of impact."

Supporting ranchers we believe in, and the stores and restaurants that sell their products, has a very tangible impact that we experience firsthand all the time. But ask most vegetarians if the battle between small, sustainable ranchers and industrial farming is at the top of their list of concerns about eating meat, and you'll probably be met with a blank stare. "For people who are against eating meat because it's wrong or offensive to eat animals, even the cleanest grass-fed beef won't be good enough," Katzen says.

Convincing those people that eating meat can improve the welfare of the entire livestock population is a tough sell. But we'll keep trying. What we've discovered is that you can hover pretty close to the bottom of the food chain and still make a difference, quietly. We've found a healthy balance somewhere between the two extremes—which, come to think of it, is also a good way to approach a marriage.

READING AND WRITING

1. Lennon is writing a causal argument, one that makes a claim about a particular trend. How does she explain the causal relationship between food activism and the eating of meat by people who had been vegetarians? Do you find her argument persuasive? Why (or why not)?

2. Lennon quotes her husband, Andrew, as saying: "The way I see it, you've got three opportunities every day to act on your values and have an immediate effect on something you're concerned about. You're probably worried about Darfur, too, but what can you do about that every single day? Write a letter? It doesn't have the same kind of impact." What is Andrew saying here about the relationship between beliefs and action? Do you agree with him? Explain.

USING RESEARCH

3. Lennon bases her argument on a small sample of people. Using the library's resources and the internet, try to find out if this trend has spread to other parts of the country.

Jessica B. Harris, a professor at the City University of New York, is the author of 10 cookbooks that document the culture and food of the African diaspora. This memoir was published in Gastropolis: Food and New York City, *a 2009 collection about New Yorkers' relationships with food.*

THE CULINARY SEASONS OF MY CHILDHOOD Jessica B. Harris

Few culinary traditions are as undocumented as those of middle-class African Americans. Scroll back to the 1950s, when segregation was still rampant in the South, and the foodways are even less well known. Although they are briefly mentioned in a few autobiographical narratives and in some fiction, the concern of most African Americans was more than throwing off the shackles of southern segregations that our forebears had come north to escape. This is reflected in our life tales more than in our recollections of meals eaten and foods purchased. The result is that most outsiders believe that ham hocks and hard times are the only remnants of our culinary past. Certainly there were plenty of ham hocks and no shortage of hard times. In fact, my New Jersey-born and-raised mother always claimed that that state could best Mississippi in the racist sweepstakes and that she had the stories to prove it! In North and South alike, middle-class African Americans ate the same cornbread and fried chicken and chitterlings and foods from the traditions of the African diaspora as did our less well-off counterparts, but we also ate differently, foods that expressed our middle classness and reflected our social and political aspirations.

Even though chitterlings might be on the menu, they could equally likely be accompanied by a mason jar of corn liquor or a crystal goblet of champagne. Southern specialties like fried porgies and collard greens show up for dinner, but they might be served along with dishes becoming common in an increasingly omnivorous United States that was just beginning its love affair with food. Nowhere is this more evident than in my own life and in the culinary season of my childhood.

A descendant of the enslaved and free Africans who made their way north in the Great Migration, I grew up in a transplanted southern culture that still remains a vibrant region of the African American culinary world. My family, like many others long separated from the South, raised me in ways that continued their eating traditions, so now I can head south and sop biscuits in gravy, suck chewy bits of fat from a pig's foot spattered with hot sauce, and yes'm and no'm with the best of 'em.

But that's not all of me. I also am a postwar baby who was the only child of striving middle-class parents who were old enough to have been young African American adults in the poverty of the Great Depression. They showered me with love and childhood coddling that makes my childhood seem like an African American version of *The Little Princess*. I also am a child at the confluence of two major African American culinary traditions. My mother's family could claim a smidge of black southern aristocracy, as they were descended from free people of color who migrated to Roanoke, Virginia. My father's family was from Tennessee and had upcountry Georgia roots that extended down the Natchez Trace. Both families showed their backgrounds at the table.

My maternal grandmother, Bertha Philpot Jones, was the quintessential African American matriarch presiding over a groaning board filled with savory goods. The role has become a visual cliché in movies like *The Nutty Professor Part II: The Klumps, Soul Food,* and *Dear Departed,* which revel in the dysfunction of African American life. No such dysfunction, however, was tolerated at Grandma Jones's table; she would not allow it. She was the matriarch and absolute sovereign of the Jones family; she ruled with a delicate but steel-boned hand, and the family marched to her tune. Watermelon-rind pickles spiced with fragrant cinnamon and whole cloves and the reassuring warmth of a full oven wafting smells of roasted joints and freshly baked bread are the aromas I most associate with her. She was a Baptist minister's wife and could put a hurtin' on some food. She had to, for as the minister's wife, she had not only her own brood of twelve children plus husband to feed, but the church folks who dropped in to take care of as well. She pickled fruits like Seckel pears, which had a curiously tart-sweet taste that comes back to me even today. The smell of Parker House rolls, the warmth of the kitchen, and the closeness of a large family all were part of the thrill of Grandma Jones's house. I didn't see her often—only on holidays and special occasions when we'd take the Holland Tunnel to head off to Plainfield, New Jersey, to visit and sit around the table.

Ida Irene Harris, my paternal grandmother, was at the other end of the culinary spectrum. I saw her much more often, at least once a week. When I travel in the South, folks are astounded to hear that as a child I had no southern roots, no grandmother to visit by segregated train or bus under the tutelage of kindly porters and with a tag pinned to my coat. Instead, my South was in the North, for Grandma Harris, in her day-to-day existence, re-created the preserved-in-amber South of her nineteenth-century rural youth in the precincts of her small apartment in the South Jamaica projects. I remember her apartment well, particularly the kitchen, with the four-burner stove on which she made lye soap, the refrigerator that always contained a pitcher of grape Kool-Aid with lemons cut up in it, and the sink in which she washed clothes, punching them with a broomstick to make sure they would get clean. Most of all, I remember the taste of the collard greens that she prepared: verdant, lush with just enough smoked pig tarts and fat for seasoning; they were the culinary embodiment of her love and, along with her silky beaten biscuits, one of the few dishes that she made well.

Grandma Harris lived in a self-created southern world. For years, she maintained a small garden plot at the back of the South Jamaica projects. This was just after the victory gardens of World War II when tenants could plant a small plot of land if they wished. Grandma Harris grew southern staples: collard and mustard greens, peanuts, snap beans, and more. I remember her weeding the peanuts and breaking off a leaf of the greens to test for ripening as the Long Island Rail Road train roared by on the tracks above. She taught me to love the slip of boiled peanuts, to sop biscuits in Alaga syrup with butter cut up in it, and to savor the tart sourness of buttermilk long before there was any romance to things southern.

I didn't understand the education she'd given me until years later, in Senegal's Theatre Daniel Sorano, I heard a griot sing. It was as though Grandma Harris had leaned down from the clouds and touched me. The timbre, the tone, the almost keening wail of the Mandinka singer captured the tuneless songs that Grandma sang as she went about her daily tasks, as much as the tastes of the Senegalese food recalled flavors from my childhood. It was then that I realized that unknown to both of us, Grandma Harris had taught me the ways of the past in her demeanor, her stalwartness, her faith, and her food. Those ways would help me survive. She also taught me to behave. I will never forget the summer day when she administered the only childhood whipping I can recall.

"Whipping" was not a word that was used in my house as I was growing up. I was a Dr. Spock baby through and through, and discipline was more about firm conversation than about Daddy's belt. At Grandma Harris's apartment, though, the rules changed and that one time, I knew I was going to get a whipping for sure.

Grandma Harris was another kind of old-line southern matriarch. It didn't matter that she lived on the third floor of the South Jamaica projects in Queens; her world was deeply rooted in the traditions of her South. She would brook no contradiction about manners. In her home, New Year's was celebrated with a mix of collard, mustard, and turnip greens that she had stewed down to a low gravy to accompany the obligatory hoppin' John and chitterlings. I always passed on the chitterlings and ate the hoppin' John, but the greens were my favorite. I had even more respect for them after they caused my downfall and earned me my only childhood whipping.

It happened on a summer's day when I was about six or seven. My mother worked, so I was sent to Grandma's apartment to spend the day in the traditional, extended-family day-care arrangement. I spent most of those urban summer days of my early childhood in her small one-bedroom apartment reading in a chair and staying out from under her feet in order to avoid going outside to play with the other kids, who invariably made fun of my private-school vowels and bookish ways. She, on the other side, spent her days insisting that I go out and play with the "nice children" who all called her Mother Harris.

On the day in question, when I had managed to avoid the dreaded piss-smelling barrels and rough boys and girls of the playground, she looked up from her sewing and said, "Jessica, come here." I was in for it. I was pleasantly surprised when, instead of ordering me downstairs, she instead went for her purse and gave me some money wrapped in a hankie with instructions to go to Miranda's, the Italian-owned corner market, and get a piece of "streak-a-lean-streak-a-fat" for the greens that she was going to cook.

Thrilled at being sent on an errand and overjoyed at escaping the barrel torture, I headed off. The walk was short, only a scant block through the maze of red-brick buildings that had not yet deteriorated into the breeding ground of hopelessness they were to become. A few small trees were in leaf, and the sounds of other children playing reminded me how grown up I was. I was on an errand. Arriving at Miranda's, I went directly to the meat counter, where, as in most African American neighborhoods, there was a vast array of pig parts both identifiable and unknown. Having not a clue about streak-a-lean-streak-a-fat but feeling exceptionally sophisticated in my seven-year-old head, I pointed to the slab bacon that my mother used to season things and asked for the requisite amount. It was brought out for my examination, and I grandly pronounced it fine. Cut off to the desired thickness and wrapped in slick brown paper, it was presented to me with solemnity. I tucked it into the net shopping bag that Grandma had provided and headed back home, proud and pleased.

I pushed open the heavy downstairs door and ran up the concrete steps, heels clanking on the metal treads that lined them. When I got to 3B, I pushed through the door that

Grandma always kept open in those kinder times and headed in to present my parcel. To my amazement, when she opened it, she began to mutter and ask me what I had gotten.

"Steak-a-lean-streak-a-fat," I replied.

"Did you ask for it?" she questioned.

"No, I pointed it out to the man," I ventured with increasing timidity.

"Well, this isn't it! I wanted what I asked for, streak-a-lean-streak-a-fat," she countered. "This is slab bacon!"

"It's the same thing, isn't it?" I queried.

"NO! Now you march right back there and get me what I asked for, streak-a-lean-streak-a-fat. Take this back!"

"But?"

"No Buts!" Just march back there, young lady! Right Now!"

I trudged back to Miranda's, each step made heavier with the thought of having to tell the butcher that I'd made an error and hoping that he'd take back the offending bacon. The joy of escape of the prior hour had soured into a longing for the nasty boys and the stinky barrels. Luckily, the man took pity on bourgie old me and took back the bacon, replacing it with a fattier piece of streaky pork that was a fraction of the price.

When I got back to the building, Grandma was sitting on the benches out front and waiting for me. She uttered the five words that I'd never heard her say: "Go cut me a switch."

Terrified, I set off and hunted for the smallest branch that I could find in this virtually treeless urban landscape, knowing what was coming next. I returned with a smallish green switch that I had unearthed lord knows where. She took a few halfhearted passes at my legs, solemnly repeating with each one, "Don't think you're smarter than your elders." Tears flowed on both sides: mine because I'd certainly learned my lesson through the humiliation of returning the bacon followed by the public whipping, Grandma's because she adored me and wanted a respectful granddaughter. Despite that childhood trauma, I still love collard greens and never eat my New Year's mess of them without remembering Grandma Harris. I always season them with what I have come to think of as streak-a-lean-streak-a-fat-cut-me-a-switch; savor their smoky, oily splendor; and think of the southern lessons she taught me with every bite.

The other days of my early summers were spent with my working parents. We left New York City for family vacations, and I can remember the ice man delivering big blocks of ice wrapped in burlap to chill the icebox of the small cabin that we rented on Three Mile Harbor Road in East Hampton long before the area attained its current vogue. The year after my whipping, when I was eight, we visited Oak Bluffs, Massachusetts, the African American summer community on Martha's Vineyard that has become much touted these days. It was love at first sight, and my parents bought a summer house there that winter.

From the time I was nine until the present, this house has been a part of every summer. Then we made long trips on the Boston Post Road and the Merritt Parkway up to the Wood's Hole ferry dock. Old habits die hard, and my parents in the 1950s would no more think of hitting the road without a shoebox full of fried chicken, deviled eggs, pound cake, oranges, and raisins and a thermos full of lemonade or some other cool drink that they would leave home without maps and a tank full of gas.

Oak Bluffs was just beginning to grow in popularity among New Yorkers; Bostonians knew about its glories long before we did. Middle-class African Americans from New York and New Jersey summered in Sag Harbor near the Hamptons, but my prescient father did not want to be so close to the city that friends could drop in unannounced on the weekends, so it was Martha's Vineyard for us. We joked that if we lost our way to the Vineyard, we could simply follow the trail of chicken bones left by fellow black New Yorkers and find the ferry pier with no problem. Like us, they were marked by segregated back doors and the lack of on-the-road facilities and also stuck to the old ways. We brought our chicken along for years until the Connecticut Turnpike was completed, and then we gradually left the chicken and deviled eggs at home and settled for the mediocre fare of the rest stops. I was thrilled several years ago when a friend, Alexander Smalls, opened a restaurant in Grand Central Terminal celebrating our traveling ways; it was called the Shoebox Café. While the menu was his own inventive interpretation of the black food of the South, I knew he was also honoring the past that many black Americans share.

My Vineyard summers were where I caught my first fish, a porgy of respectable size, and learned to strip the skin off an eel and find out just how delicious the sweet meat was, once you got over the snake look, and to pick mussels off the docks at Menemsha. The days were punctuated by sharing meals with family and friends, waiting for my father to appear on the Friday night "daddy boat" to spend the weekends, and savoring rainy days because my mother treated us with one of her fantastic blueberry cobblers prepared with berries we had picked before the storm came, from the bushes that grew wild along the roadside. July folded into August marked by county fairs, cotton candy, Illumination Night, Darling's molasses puff, swordfish at Giordano's restaurant, and movies at the Strand or Islander movie houses, accompanied by hot buttered popcorn served from a copper kettle. Soon it was time to pack the car again and head back to our house in Queens. I never really minded because autumn brought the return to school, and my world expanded one hundredfold. My school saw to that.

The United Nations International School was and is a special place. As the first non-UN-connected child to attend the school and one of very few Americans enrolled in the early years, my playmates were the world. UNIS, as the school is called by the cognoscenti, was small, then so small that it added a grade each year until it finally stretched from prekindergarten through high school. Inside Queens's Parkway Village apartments that had been transformed into classrooms, I made lifelong friends and learned how to function in a world that extended to the globe's four corners. A trip to Vasu's or Shikha's house brought smells of the Indian subcontinent, and on occasions when I was fortunate enough to be invited to birthday parties, there were tastes of rich spices and heady unknown flavors that would never have turned up on the table of my garlic-free household. The rich stews of central Europe were featured at Danuta's, and steak and kidney pie might turn up on the table at Eluned's. I can still feel the rasp of the embossed silver spoon-backs that were used on the table at Jennifer and Susan's house in Great Neck and remember their mother's wonderful way with shortbread with nostalgia that can still make my mouth water more than forty-five years later. The annual round of birthday parties was interrupted by school events like international potluck suppers. Parents brought dishes from around the globe, and students began culinary competitions like eating spaghetti with chopsticks in the days before Asian noodle bowls and the vast array of Italian pastas became common culinary currency.

As more Americans joined the school community, even they displayed amazing culinary inventiveness, and I remember being invited to a formal Coke-tail party at Anne's house, where we were served all manner of multihued nonalcoholic cocktails in delicate stemmed glassware complete with swizzle sticks, umbrella garnishes, and lots of maraschino cherries at a birthday fete that was every young girl's dream. All the class events seemed to center on international households of like-acting folk who proved to me at an early age that no matter what turned up on the table, it was to be savored and eaten with gusto.

During the twelve or so years that I attended UNIS, I grew to understand something about the world's food. My core group of friends spent many of those years together, and we became familiar with one another's households and foods and, with that growing knowledge, came to realize that the table was not only where we held our parties and our class fetes but also where we worked out our problems and got answers to questions about one another. With hindsight, I now realize that we achieved at our birthday tables and communal suppers the same détente and understanding that the parents of many of my friends worked so hard to attain at the tables at which they tried to bring peace to the world.

If my grandmothers' tables gave me a grounding in the African American past that is so much the bedrock of all that I do, and UNIS gave me an understanding of the food of the world, a palate that is open to tasting just about anything, and the knowledge that more friends are made around the table than just about anywhere else, my parents and our daily life completed the picture with the finishing touches.

I have saved my household for last, for it, more than any of the other outside influences, marked the season of my childhood eating. While I grew up at the confluence of two African American culinary traditions and lived in an international world at school, at home on Anderson Road in St. Albans, Queens, my surroundings were a wondrous combination of my parents' dueling culinary wills.

Very few African Americans are to the manor born; most of us have a past of want or need, if not for love, than for cash and the opportunities it can bring. My father, Jesse Brown Harris, was such a person. He was a black man and a striking one at that, aubergine-hued with the carriage of an emperor of Songhai. Early photos show him tall and slender, looking very proprietary about his little family of three. Daddy was not a numbers runner. Daddy was not a welfare ducker or an absentee father. Daddy was just Daddy, and the constancy of that statement and my lack of awareness that this was not the norm for all black children made me different.

As a teenager, Daddy had lived over the stables and worked as a Shabbas goy in Williamsburg, Brooklyn. Until the day he died, he was marked by a childhood of grinding poverty during which he had worn flour-bag suits to school and church, cadged coal at the railroad yard for heat, and picked dandelion leaves on the Fisk College campus for dinner. He was torn between the desire to overcome his past and provide differently for his family and the need to remember it with honor.

My father ate southern food whenever he could cajole my mother into preparing the hog maws or chitterlings that he adored. We even put a stove into the basement of our house so that the smell would not taint our living quarters. He would occasionally bring home cartons of buttermilk, which he would savor with squares of the flaky and hot cornbread that my mother baked at the drop of a hat. Sunday breakfast was his special time, and he would proudly sit at the head of the table and sop up his preferred mix of Karo dark with butter cut up in it with the hoecake that was off-limits to anyone else in the household.

He was the only one in his family of man children who did not and could not cook. My Uncle Bill, his older brother, gave me my first taste of rabbit stew, and my Uncle Jim's spaghetti sauce was the stuff of family legend. Actually, my father cared little for food, but he loved restaurants and, with his increasing affluence, dined out with the best of them. In the early years, dining out meant heading to the local silver bullet diner near our house for specials like mashed potatoes with gravy and Salisbury steak or sauerbraten (the neighborhood was German before we moved in). The bakery on Linden Boulevard, the main shopping street, sold flaky butter cookies and gingerbread at Christmas. Later, when St. Albans became blacker, we would head to Sister's Southern Diner after church on Sundays, still dressed in our Sabbath finery, for down-home feasts of smothered pork chops and greens or stewed okra and fried fish in an orgy of southern feasting that Mommy did not have to cook. In later years, restaurants like the Brasserie, La Fonda del Sol, and the Four Seasons were where we celebrated birthdays and anniversaries. There, my father's duality surfaced, and he would order wine for the bucket or "spittoon," as we had baptized it in our family jargon, and crepes suzette or Caesar salad for the flamboyant tableside service, but we three secretly knew that all the while what he really wanted was a ham hock and some butterbeans to satisfy the tastes of his youth.

My mother, though, truly loved food and had amazing taste buds that could analyze the components of a dish with startling accuracy. She would then reproduce her version of it at home, to the delight of all. Trained as a dietician, my mother reveled in entertaining and entranced her friends with her culinary inventiveness. Decades later, she revealed that at school, she had been required to sit through classes on how to keep black people out of restaurants and was discouraged from doing anything with food demonstrations that would put her in public view. After a brief stint as a dietitian at Bennett College in North Carolina and an even briefer stay in domestic service as a private dietitian, she found that she did not enjoy the field. Instead, she put her talents to use at the supper table, and I grew up eating homemade applesauce and tea sandwiches of olives and cream cheese when my friends were chowing down Gerber's finest and processed cheese spread. Weeknights featured balanced meals like breaded veal cutlets with carrots and peas and a salad, alternating with sublime fried chicken and mashed potatoes or rice and always a green vegetable and salad, or string beans, potatoes, and ham ends slow cooked into what we called a New England boiled dinner.

Parties were the occasion for pulling out all the stops. My mother would prepare ribbon and pinwheel sandwiches from whole wheat bread, cream cheese, white bread, and strips of red and green bell pepper, long before the spectrum opened up to admit such hues as orange, purple, white, and even yellow! She created cabarets in the basement—persuading her friends to come as babies or in nightclothes, hiring calypso singers, serving drinks with small umbrellas, and devising smoking centerpieces with dry ice and punch bowls—and, each Sunday, presided over table overflowing with roasts and a multiplicity of vegetables.

My mother created magic in the kitchen and made cooking exciting and fun, with a trick for every dish and a sense of adventure at the stove. As her only child, I got the benefit of this knowledge and accompanied her in the kitchen almost from my birth. In later years, she began to tire of the kitchen, but eventually, she renewed her interest in things culinary and discovered the wonder of ingredients like confit of duck, fresh garlic, pimentos, and arugula. Ever curious, her life was a constant adventure. I did not learn to cook; I simply absorbed it in her kitchen, moving from high chair to small tasks to whole dishes and entire meals.

I am very much the product of all of this, and these seasons of my personal and yet very New York childhood gave me the foods of the world on my plate. For the first years of my life, my fork ranged throughout the world from the simple country food of Grandma Harris to the more elegant Virginia repasts of Grandma Jones and the dishes of the 1950s and 1960s that were, for me, the tastes of home. I also sampled fare from the globe's four corners at the homes of my international classmates and learned that no matter where our origins or our regionalisms, when we eat together and share the commensalisms of the table, we make ourselves and our worlds better. It has been said that we are what we eat. I certainly am, and in the many seasons of my New York youth, that included an amazing amount of mighty good food.

■ READING AND WRITING

1. Though Harris has written a memoir essay, she does present an implicit argument about food. What is her claim? What kinds of support does she provide to persuade her audience?
2. How does Harris use her family history to reject and correct common stereotypes about foods that African Americans eat? How does she use food to weave together the various threads of her family background?
3. Compare Harris' essay with one of the more explicit arguments in this chapter (Pollan's, for example, or Berry's or Rodriguez's). Which do you think is more effective as an argument? Why?

■ DEVELOPING LONGER RESPONSES

4. Late in her essay, Harris writes: "My core group of friends … became familiar with one another's households and foods and, with that growing knowledge, came to realize that the table was not only where we held our parties and our class fetes but also where we worked out our problems and got answers to questions about one another." Develop a brief memoir essay in which you explore how food and the experience of preparing or sharing a meal provided more to you than simple sustenance.

Siobhan Phillips, a junior fellow at the Harvard Society of Fellows, is the author of The Poetics of the Everyday: Creative Repetition in Modern American Verse. *Her writing has also appeared in* PMLA, Prospect, Hudson Review, *and at* Salon.com, *where this essay was published on April 25, 2009.*

CAN WE AFFORD TO EAT ETHICALLY?
Siobhan Phillips

Organic food prices are daunting in a recession. But do we have to choose between our principles and our pocketbooks?

Last month, a report from England found sales of some organic food had fallen up to 31 percent. Ethical food advocates have been worrying about a similar trend in this country since the recession began: Just as the need for better food choices became more widely accepted, our economy fell apart, and consumers who once considered free-range, $5-a-dozen eggs a necessity may start eyeing the caged-hens carton for half that price. A recent *National Review* column argued that organic food was, in fact, "an expensive luxury item, something bought by those who have the resources."

I had wondered about the elitism of ethical eating ever since I started reading about the movement in books like "The Omnivore's Dilemma," "Fast Food Nation" and "Food Politics." When Alice Waters told Americans that they could dine better by forgoing "the cellphone or the third pair of Nike shoes," my monthly cellphone bill totaled zero and I owned just one pair of sneakers. When Michael Pollan urged citizens to plant a garden, I was living on the 10th floor of an urban apartment building. When Barbara Kingsolver wrote in "Animal, Vegetable, Miracle" that sustainable cooking could be thrifty, her recommendations included a plot of land and a second freezer that I didn't own. My kitchen had the dimensions of a medium-size walk-in closet. And I was better off than many in my neighborhood.

At honest moments, though, I suspected my reluctance to seek out organic rutabagas was more lazy than practical. So last year, when global food prices began to soar, I devised an experiment: My husband and I would eat conscientiously for a month, not just on our regular grocery allotment but on the government-defined, food-stamp minimum: $248 for two people in our hometown of New Haven, Conn. We would choose the SOLE-est products available—that is, the sustainable, organic, local or ethical alternative. We would start from a bare pantry, shop only at places that took food stamps and could be reached on foot, and use only basic appliances. The test would mean some painful changes; gone was my husband's customary breakfast of Honey Nut Cheerios and our favorite dinner of pepperoni pizza. But it would answer that nagging question: When shopping for food, did I have to choose between my budget and my beliefs?

Challenges began on my first grocery trip, where staples required some massive outlays of cash. It was anxiety-inducing to shell out $4 a jar for organic spices, even after I pared down my shelf to salt, pepper, oregano, basil, curry, cumin, chili and cinnamon. (I also bought some garlic, soy sauce and red wine vinegar, though these were non-local organic; I justified the carbon footprint—not to mention the price—with the thought that cheap eaters need to fill up on flavor.) It was frightening to spend $7 on a small bottle of organic olive oil in hopes it would last all month. The costliest decision was meat; I didn't want to impose a completely vegetarian diet on my carnivorous husband or on-and-off-carnivorous self, but the frozen slabs of grass-fed steak at the farmers' market seemed tough to manage. Instead, I bought a small free-range chicken for about $9 and a scant pound of local ground beef for about $6, knowing that this, along with some sustainable canned fish, was our allotment of animal flesh for four weeks. Even less expensive purchases demanded worry and adjustments; the price difference between organic fruits and vegetables, for example, prompted me to switch apples for carrots in my packed lunch.

The real work began when I lugged my haul home. The chicken had to go far: After roasting my scrawny-looking bird in the most basic way—a smear of oil across the skin, a sprinkle of salt and pepper—I sliced, hacked and pulled every piece of meat I could find off the bones and then simmered the carcass in a pot for basic stock. (I saved the fat for cooking.) Along with the meat, this broth was divided into meal-size portions and stored in my freezer for soups, sandwiches and dinners to come.

I then tackled the beef, which had to be stretched, too. The right choice, I figured, was chili, not just because my husband and I both love it but also because it's a thrifty dish— especially if you use dried beans. I hadn't before my test month, I confess, but once I did, I discarded the intimidating time charts that had stymied me and relied on a basic process of soak, then cook. Beans are forgiving. The first of my merciful batches went into a big pot along with the ground beef, some organic onion and tomatoes, and lashings of garlic and chili powder; the result smelled as good as meatier versions. It also found a place, in divided portions, among the containers of my now-crowded freezer.

The last of my initial challenges was bread. Before the experiment, I purchased our loaf bread—that "natural" kind with about 30 ingredients in 12 perfect slices and three layers of plastic packaging—but my experiment proved that it's not hard to fix something with better flavor and the same approximate shape for a lot less money. It doesn't take much energy, either; by now, all those who can type the words "no knead" into Google have probably discovered the time-saving revolution of hands-free loaves. I froze mine in slices, which kept it convenient without letting it go stale.

Bird, beans, bread: I felt better already. It took a lot of time to fix that much— most of the month's first Sunday. Yet after this bout of shopping and chopping, I spent no other concentrated stretches on food preparation in the remaining four weeks. The biggest change in my culinary efforts wasn't the amount of time but its placement; I was always working ahead. I found this rhythm less stressful, ultimately, since it ended my previous 5 p.m. habit of wondering what was for dinner. Now, I could walk in the door at the end of my workday sure of what we would eat.

So what did we eat? Breakfasts were easy: One tutorial, and my husband agreed that cooking organic quick oats in the microwave was nearly as easy as pouring out cold cereal.

Add raisins and a dash of cinnamon sugar and it tastes even better. Fair-trade, organic coffee and tea allowed us each to maintain our caffeine injection of choice. Lunch, too, was straightforward; we ate dinner leftovers, sometimes, or went with a standard sandwich of organic peanut butter on homemade organic bread. I also made several big batches of spicy black beans and rice that I kept in a pot in the fridge and spooned into single-serving Tupperware for midday meals.

Dinners demanded more variety and thought. I got help from blogs and stories about schemes similar to mine (Rebecca Blood's is the best I found) and looked especially closely at the USDA's brochure of "Recipes and Tips for Healthy, Thrifty Meals," since I assumed it would provide the most accessible advice. The government recipes proved disappointing, though, since they often presumed larger economies of scale than I could manage and relied on processed items or factory cuts. I also disliked the sense of compromise in USDA recommendations, which supposed that those on a budget should be satisfied with a bland "noodle casserole" that would never aspire to the flavor of real lasagna.

I set the government recipes aside, then, and copied out inspirational passages from two other sources. One was M.F.K. Fisher, who began "How to Cook a Wolf" during WWII rationing. The book is my favorite from her shelf because it links her sometimes self-satisfied gourmandism to a stubbornly practical spirit. A little problem like poverty is not going to prevent Fisher from enjoying her meals. Her homage to a piece of whole-wheat toast is a lesson in how to savor the basics, and her advice about preserving vegetable juices recommends pouring them into an old gin bottle: I loved the idea of a low-cost lifestyle that depends on such bottles just lying around.

I loved, too, the equal and opposite approach in my second nourishing source, the "More-With-Less" cookbook. Its author couldn't be more different than Fisher; Doris Janzen Longacre, a Mennonite church leader in 1970s Ohio, would probably have found the remains of Fisher's liquor cabinet as strange as the course of Fisher's love affairs. Like Fisher, though, Longacre presents thrifty eating as a deliberate, intelligent decision—in her case, choosing a world with more justice and less anxiety. The two authors both refuse the idea that cheap cooking bespeaks concession; to them, frugal eating can mean sophisticated tastes or developed morals.

Frugal eating can also be a course in cosmopolitanism—not the worldliness that comes from fusion cuisine at wine-paired prix fixes but the kind in which you learn more about how the rest of the world actually eats. Once I put aside make-do recipes, I had to seek out dishes that are inexpensive in their genuine forms, a search that took me around the world as it provided a plethora of options. It's more heartening to prepare a spicy biryani than it is to assemble the nondescript "bake" of economy cookbooks, even if both are built of rice and vegetables. And it's more pleasant to announce a biryani as you serve up plates, or to sit over its final forkfuls as you talk through your partner's day. You're not getting by, all of a sudden, so much as having dinner.

The dinners I have in mind all use the common, cheap staples of global cuisine: Almost every culture has one or two time-tested options based on beans, whole grains and pasta as well as several versatile methods for cheap vegetables and several adaptably thrifty types of soup or stew. The lentils of Indian dal, for example, are not those of the Middle Eastern mujadarra, but they both do wonderful, easy things with a sustainably grown legume that goes for about $1.50 a pound. I simplified a lot, and I ignored some specific ingredient directives; the same organic brown crop grown two states away made both my Chinese fried rice and Italian risotto. But that's the point: a kitchen of cosmopolitan simplicity lets a cook employ the often repetitive offerings of farmers' markets and local production without going out of her mind with monotony.

There were tribulations, naturally. I missed some baked goods, though we had a small bit of fair-trade organic cocoa for treats. Even more painful was our decrease in dairy; buying ethically meant cutting back to just a sprinkle of cheese on the top of dishes or a few shavings on a sandwich. We found, though, that good local cheddar really is more flavorful than the cheap supermarket stuff; so is organic whole milk—a small splash on hot oats provided more uplift than the soggy skim lake that once drowned our cereal pellets. Plus our discovery of better flavors was accompanied by revelations of new ones, as we tried and enjoyed things like anchovies, parsnips, polenta, sardines and scapes. Eating sustainably and frugally forces you to challenge preferences and resist ruts, since you pretty much have to buy any available item that's cheap and well-grown. Thrifty habits thus helped my husband and me to dine more adventurously, and we felt pleasantly surprised more often than deprived.

Our test methods wouldn't work for everyone, I know: I relied on the sort of reasonably flexible schedule that is a luxury in far too many households, and I started with some basic cooking knowledge. (As Salon critic Laura Miller recently suggested, food advocates may need to think more about the skills as well as the funds that are required by ethical eating.) Yet our four-week hypothetical did provide a feasible way for my husband and me to eat sustainably long-term: When the month finished—with a magisterial $1.20 left in the cache—we decided to stick with most of our experimental changes. We now eat slightly larger quantities of meat, fruit and cheese, and pepperoni pizza is back in the menu rotation. But apart from that pepperoni (and I'm still looking for an ethical source), I've yet to purchase any recurring items that aren't SOLE-justified, and our grocery bills have stayed lean.

Our meals have stayed varied, too, as sustainable grocery shopping pushes me toward regular minor novelties: making tortillas from scratch with organic flour, toasting the seeds I scooped from my local pumpkin, bringing home the variety of farmers-market kale with the super-crimped leaves. These sorts of practices no longer seem like a statement or an effort. In fact, they seem natural enough that the one question I'm left with is: Why didn't I start cooking and eating this way sooner?

READING AND WRITING

1. How does Phillips answer the question she presents in the title of her essay? What is the rhetorical effect of asking questions in an essay—and then answering them?
2. What does Phillips do in her introduction (the first three paragraphs) to put her topic into context? Though she writes from an entirely personal perspective, using only her experience as evidence, how else does Phillips make her essay relevant to a broader audience?
3. How would you characterize the ethos that Phillips presents in her essay? How does she develop this ethos? Go to the Salon website (at www. salon.com) and examine the articles, essays, and advertisements. Do you think Phillips' ethos is a good match for Salon and its audience?

USING RESEARCH

4. Phillips presents little—if any—statistical evidence of the affordability of ethical eating. Use the internet and the library's resources to look for articles or studies that include data from larger-scale research comparing the costs of organic and non-organic food. Do you think this kind of information would have strengthened Phillips' essay, given her purpose and audience?

> *Joel Salatin is a third-generation alternative farmer at Polyface Farm in Virginia's Shenandoah Valley. He and his farm have been featured in several national publications, in Michael Pollan's book* The Omnivore's Dilemma, *and in the documentary film* Food, Inc. *Salatin wrote this essay for* Food, Inc.: How Industrial Food Is Making Us Sicker, Fatter, and Poorer—and What You Can Do about It, *the companion book to that film.*

DECLARE YOUR INDEPENDENCE   Joel Salatin

Perhaps the most empowering concept in any paradigm-challenging movement is simply opting out. The opt-out strategy can humble the mightiest forces because it declares to one and all, "You do not control me."

The time has come for people who are ready to challenge the paradigm of factory-produced food and to return to a more natural, wholesome, and sustainable way of eating (and living) to make that declaration to the powers that be, in business and government, that established the existing system and continue to prop it up. It's time to opt out and simply start eating better—right here, right now.

Impractical? Idealistic? Utopian? Not really. As I'll explain, it's actually the most realistic and effective approach to transforming a system that is slowly but surely killing us.

■ What Happened to Food?

First, why am I taking a position that many well-intentioned people might consider alarmist or extreme? Let me explain.

At the risk of stating the obvious, the unprecedented variety of bar-coded packages in today's supermarket really does not mean that out generation enjoys better food options than our predecessors. These packages, by and large, having passed through the food inspection fraternity, the industrial food fraternity, and the lethargic cheap-food-purchasing consumer fraternity, represent an incredibly narrow choice. If you took away everything with an ingredient foreign to our three trillion intestinal microflora, the shelves would be bare indeed. (I'm talking here about the incredible variety of microorganisms that live in our digestive tracts and perform an array of useful functions, including training our immune systems and producing vitamins like biotin and vitamin K.) In fact, if you just eliminated every product that would have been unavailable in 1900, almost everything would be gone, including staples that had been chemically fertilized, sprayed with pesticides, or ripened with gas.

Rather than representing newfound abundance, these packages wending their way to store shelves after spending a month in the belly of Chinese merchant marines are actually the meager offerings of a tyrannical food system. Strong words? Try buying real milk—as in raw. See if you can find meat processed in the clean open air under sterilizing sunshine. Look for pot pies made with local produce and meat. How about good old unpasteurized apple cider? Fresh cheese? Unpasteurized almonds? All these staples that our great-grandparents relished and grew healthy on have been banished from today's supermarket.

They've been replaced by an array of pseudo-foods that did not exist a mere century ago. The food additives, preservatives, colorings, emulsifiers, corn syrups, and unpronounceable ingredients listed on the colorful packages bespeak a centralized control mindset that actually reduces the options available to fill Americans' dinner plates. Whether by intentional design or benign ignorance, the result has been the same—the criminalization and/or demonization of heritage foods.

The mindset behind this radical transformation of American eating habits expresses itself in at least a couple of ways.

One is the completely absurd argument that without industrial food, the world would starve. "How can you feed the world?" is the most common question people ask me when they tour Polyface Farm. Actually, when you consider the fact that millions of people, including many vast cities, were fed and sustained using traditional farming methods until just a few decades ago, the answer is obvious. America has traded seventy-five million buffalo, which required no tillage, petroleum, or chemicals, for a mere forty-two million head of cattle. Even with all the current chemical inputs, our production is a shadow of what it was 500 years ago. Clearly, if we returned to herbivorous principles five centuries old, we could double our meat supply. The potential for similar increases exists for other food items.

The second argument is about food safety. "How can we be sure that food produced on local farms without centralized inspection and processing is really safe to eat?" Here, too, the facts are opposite to what many people assume. The notion that indigenous food is unsafe simply has no scientific backing. Milk-borne pathogens, for example, became a significant health problem only during a narrow time period between 1900 and 1930, before refrigeration but after unprecedented urban expansion. Breweries needed to be located near metropolitan centers, and adjacent dairies fed herbivore-unfriendly brewery waste to cows. The combination created real problems that do not exist in grass-based dairies practicing good sanitation under refrigeration conditions.

Lest you think the pressure to maintain the industrialized food system is all really about food safety, consider that all the natural-food items I listed above can be given away, and the donors are considered pillars of community benevolence. But as soon as money changes hands, all these wonderful choices become "hazardous substances," guaranteed to send our neighbors to the hospital with food poisoning. Maybe it's not human health but corporate profits that are really being protected.

Furthermore, realize that many of the same power brokers (politicians and the like) encourage citizens to go out into the woods on a 70-degree fall day; gun-shoot a deer with possible variant Creutzfeld-Jacob's disease (like mad cow for deer); drag the carcass a mile through squirrel dung, sticks, and rocks; then drive parade-like through town in the blazing afternoon sun with the carcass prominently displayed on the hood of the Blazer. The hunter takes the carcass home, strings it up in the backyard tree under roosting birds for a week, then skins it out and feeds the meat to his children. This is all considered noble and wonderful, even patriotic. Safety? It's not an issue.

The question is, who decides what food is safe? In our society, the decisions are made by the same type of people who decided in the Dred Scott ruling that slaves were not human beings. Just because well-educated, credentialed experts say something does not make it true. History abounds with expert opinion that turned out to be dead wrong. Ultimately, food safety is a personal matter of choice, of conscience. In fact, if high-fructose corn syrup is hazardous to health—and certainly we could argue that it is—then half of the government-sanctioned food in supermarkets is unsafe. Mainline soft drinks would carry a warning label. Clearly, safety is a subjective matter.

■ RECLAIMING FOOD FREEDOM

Once we realize that safety is a matter of personal choice, individual freedom suddenly—and appropriately—takes center stage. What could be a more basic freedom than the freedom to choose what to feed my three-trillion-member internal community?

In America I have the freedom to own guns, speak, and assemble. But what good are those freedoms if I can't choose to eat what my body wants in order to have the energy to shoot, preach, and worship? The only reason the framers of the American Constitution and Bill of Rights did not guarantee freedom of food choice was that they couldn't envision a day when neighbor-to-neighbor commerce would be criminalized…when the bureaucratic-industrial food fraternity would subsidize corn syrup and create a nation of diabetes sufferers, but deny my neighbor a pound of sausage from my Thanksgiving hog killin'.

People tend to have short memories. We all assume that whatever is must be normal. Industrial food is not normal. Nothing about it is normal. In the continuum of human history, what western civilization has done to its food in the last century represents a mere blip. It is a grand experiment on an ever-widening global scale. We have not been here before. The three trillion members of our intestinal community have not been here before. If we ate like humans have eaten for as long as anyone has kept historical records, almost nothing in the supermarket would be on the table.

A reasonable person, looking at the lack of choice we now suffer, would ask for a Food Emancipation Proclamation. Food has been enslaved by so-called inspectors that deem the most local, indigenous, heritage-based, and traditional foods unsafe and make them illegal. It has been enslaved by a host-consuming agricultural parasite called "government farm subsidies." It has been enslaved by corporate-subsidized research that declared for four decades that feeding dead cows to cows was sound science—until mad cows came to dinner.

The same criminalization is occurring on the production side. The province of Quebec has virtually outlawed outdoor poultry. Ponds, which stabilize hydrologic cycles and have forever been considered natural assets, are now considered liabilities because they encourage wild birds, which could bring avian influenza. And with the specter of a

National Animal Identification System being rammed down farmers' throats, small flocks and herds are being economized right out of existence.

On our Polyface Farm nestled in Virginia's Shenandoah Valley, we have consciously opted out of the industrial production and marketing paradigms. Meat chickens move every day in floorless, portable shelters across the pasture, enjoying bugs, forage, and local grain (grown free of genetically modified organisms). Tyson-style, inhumane, fecal factory chicken houses have no place here.

The magical land-healing process we use, with cattle using mob-stocking, herbivorous, solar conversion, lignified carbon sequestration fertilization, runs opposite the grain-based feedlot system practiced by mainline industrial cattle production. We move the cows every day from paddock to paddock, allowing the forage to regenerate completely through its growth curve, metabolizing solar energy into biomass.

Our pigs aerate anaerobic, fermented bedding in the hay feeding shed, where manure, carbon, and corn create a pig delight. We actually believe that honoring and respecting the "pigness" of the pig is the first step in an ethical, moral cultural code. By contrast, today's industrial food system views pigs as merely inanimate piles of protoplasmic molecular structure to be manipulated with whatever cleverness the egocentric human mind can conceive. A society that views its plants and animals from that manipulative, egocentric, mechanistic mindset will soon come to view its citizens in the same way. How we respect and honor the least of these is how we respect and honor the greatest of these.

The industrial pig growers are even trying to find the stress gene so it can be taken out of the pig's DNA. That way the pigs can be abused but won't be stressed about it. Then they can be crammed in even tighter quarters without cannibalizing and getting sick. In the name of all that's decent, what kind of ethics encourages such notions?

In just the last couple of decades, Americans have learned a new lexicon of squiggly Latin words: camphylobacter, lysteria, E. coli, salmonella, bovine spongiform encephalopathy, avian influenza. Whence these strange words? Nature is speaking a protest, screaming to our generation: "Enough!" The assault on biological dignity has pushed nature to the limit. Begging for mercy, its pleas go largely unheeded on Wall Street, where Conquistadors subjugating weaker species think they can forever tyrannize without an eventual payback. But the rapist will pay—eventually. You and I must bring a nurturing mentality to the table to balance the industrial food mindset.

Here at Polyface, eggmobiles follow the cows through the grazing cycle. These portable laying hen trailers allow the birds to scratch through the cows' dung and harvest newly uncovered crickets and grasshoppers, acting like a biological pasture sanitizer. This biomimicry stands in stark contrast to chickens housed beak by wattle in egg factories, never allowed to see sunshine or chase a grasshopper.

We have done all of this without money or encouragement from those who hold the reins of food power, government or private. We haven't asked for grants. We haven't asked for permission. In fact, to the shock and amazement of our urban friends, our farm is considered a Typhoid Mary by our industrial farm neighbors. Why? Because we don't medicate, vaccinate, genetically adulterate, irradiate, or exudate like they do. They fear our methods because they've been conditioned by the powers that be to fear our methods.

The point of all this is that if anyone waits for credentialed industrial experts, whether government or nongovernment, to create ecologically, nutritionally, and emotionally friendly food, they might as well get ready for a long, long wait. For example, just imagine what a grass-finished herbivore paradigm would do to the financial and power structure of America. Today, roughly seventy percent of all grains go through herbivores, which aren't supposed to eat them and, in nature, never do. If the land devoted to that production were converted to perennial prairie polycultures under indigenous biomimicry management, it would topple the grain cartel and reduce petroleum usage, chemical usage, machinery manufacture, and bovine pharmaceuticals.

Think about it. That's a lot of economic inertia resisting change. Now do you see why the Farm Bill that controls government input into our agricultural system never changes by more than about two percent every few years? Even so-called conservation measures usually end up serving the power brokers when all is said and done.

■ Opting Out

If things are going to change, it is up to you and me to make the change. But what is the most efficacious way to make the change? Is it through legislation? Is it by picketing the World Trade Organization talks? Is it by dumping cow manure on the parking lot at McDonald's? Is it by demanding regulatory restraint over the aesthetically and aromatically repulsive industrial food system?

At the risk of being labeled simplistic, I suggest that the most efficacious way to change things is simply to declare our independence from the figurative kings in the industrial system. To make the point clear, here are the hallmarks of the industrial food system:

- Centralized production

- Mono-speciation

- Genetic manipulation

- Centralized processing

- Confined animal feeding operations

- Things that end in "cide" (Latin for death)

- Ready-to-Eat food

- Long-distance transportation

- Externalized costs—economy, society, ecology

- Pharmaceuticals

- Opaqueness

- Unpronounceable ingredients

- Supermarkets

- Fancy packaging

- High fructose corn syrup

- High liability insurance

- "No Trespassing" signs

Reviewing this list shows the magnitude and far-reaching power of the industrial food system. I contend that it will not move. Entrenched paradigms never move…until outside forces move them. And those forces always come from the bottom up. The people who sit on the throne tend to like things the way they are. They have no reason to change until they are forced to do so.

The most powerful force you and I can exert on the system is to opt out. Just declare that we will not participate. Resistance movements from the antislavery movement to women's suffrage to sustainable agriculture always have and always will begin with opt-out resistance to the status quo. And seldom does an issue present itself with such a daily—in fact, thrice daily—opportunity to opt out.

Perhaps the best analogy in recent history is the home-school movement. In the late 1970s, as more families began opting out of institutional educational settings, credentialed educational experts warned us about the jails and mental asylums we'd have to build to handle the educationally and socially deprived children that home-schooling would produce. Many parents went to jail for violating school truancy laws. A quarter-century later, of course, the paranoid predictions are universally recognized as wrong. Not everyone opts for home-schooling, but the option must be available for those who want it. In the same way, an opt-out food movement will eventually show the Henny Penny food police just how wrong they are.

Learn to Cook Again

I think the opt-out strategy involves at least four basic ideas.

First, we must rediscover our kitchens. Never has a culture spent more to remodel and techno-glitz its kitchens, but at the same time been more lost as to where the kitchen is and what it's for. As a culture, we don't cook any more. Americans consume nearly a quarter of all their food in their cars, for crying out loud. Americans graze through the kitchen, popping precooked, heat-and-eat, bar-coded packages into the microwave for eating-on-the-run.

That treatment doesn't work with real food. Real heritage food needs to be sliced, peeled, sautéed, marinated, pureed, and a host of other things that require true culinary skills. Back in the early 1980s when our farm began selling pastured poultry, nobody even asked for boneless, skinless breast. To be perfectly sexist, every mom knew how to cut up a chicken. That was generic cultural mom information. Today, half of the moms don't know that a chicken even has bones.

I was delivering to one of our buying club drops a couple of months ago, and one of the ladies discreetly pulled me aside and asked: "How do you make a hamburger?" I thought I'd misunderstood, and asked her to repeat the question. I bent my ear down close to hear her sheepishly repeat the same question. I looked at her incredulously and asked: "Are you kidding?"

"My husband and I have been vegetarians. But now that we realize we can save the world by eating grass-based livestock, we're eating meat, and he wants a hamburger. But I don't know how to make it." This was an upper-middle-income, college-educated, bright, intelligent woman.

The indigenous knowledge base surrounding food is largely gone. When "scratch" cooking means actually opening a can, and when church and family reunion potlucks include buckets of Kentucky Fried Chicken, you know our culture has suffered a culinary information implosion. Big time. Indeed, according to marketing surveys roughly seventy percent of Americans have no idea what they are having for supper at 4:00 pm. That's scary.

Whatever happened to planning the week's menus? We still do that at our house. In the summer, our Polyface interns and apprentices enjoy creating a potluck for all of us Salatins every Saturday evening. All week they connive to plan the meal. It develops throughout the week, morphs into what is available locally and seasonally, and always culminates in a fellowship feast.

As a culture, if all we did was rediscover our kitchens and quit buying prepared foods, it would fundamentally change the industrial food system. The reason I'm leading this discussion with the option is because too often the foodies and greenies seem to put the onus for change on the backs of farmers. But this is a team effort, and since farmers do not even merit Census Bureau recognition, non-farmers must ante up to the responsibility for the change. And both moms and dads need to reclaim the basic food preparation knowledge that was once the natural inheritance of every human being.

■ Buy Local

After rediscovering your kitchen, the next opt-out strategy is to purchase as directly as possible from your local farmer. If the money pouring into industrial food dried up tomorrow, that system would cease to exist. Sounds easy, doesn't it? Actually, it is. It doesn't take any legislation, regulation, taxes, agencies, or programs. As the money flows to local producers, more producers will join them. The only reason the local food system is still minuscule is because few people patronize it.

Even organics have been largely co-opted by industrial systems. Go to a food co-op drop, and you'll find that more than half the dollars are being spent for organic corn chips, treats, and snacks. From far away.

Just for fun, close your eyes and imagine walking down the aisle of your nearby Wal-Mart or Whole Foods. Make a note of each item as you walk by and think about what could be grown within one hundred miles of that venue. I recommend this exercise when speaking at conferences all over the world, and it's astounding the effect it has on people. As humans, we tend to get mired in the sheer monstrosity of it all. But if we break it down into little bits, suddenly the job seems doable. Can milk be produced within one hundred miles of you? Eggs? Tomatoes? Why not?

Not everything can be grown locally, but the lion's share of what you eat certainly can. I was recently in the San Joaquin Valley looking at almonds—square miles of almonds. Some eighty-five percent of all the world's almonds are grown in that area. Why not grow a variety of things for the people of Los Angeles instead? My goodness, if you're going to irrigate anyway, why not grow things that will be eaten locally rather than things that will be shipped to some far corner of the world. Why indeed? Because most people aren't asking for local. Los Angeles is buying peas from China so almonds can be shipped to China.

Plenty of venues exist for close exchange to happen. Farmers' markets are a big and growing part of this movement. They provide a social atmosphere and a wide variety of fare. Too often, however, their politics and regulations stifle vendors. And they aren't open every day for the convenience of shoppers.

Community-supported agriculture (CSA) is a shared-risk investment that answers some of the tax and liability issues surrounding food commerce. Patrons invest in a portion of the farm's products and receive a share every week during the season. The drawback is the paperwork and lack of patron choice.

Food boutiques or niche retail facades are gradually filling a necessary role because most farmers' markets are not open daily. The price markup may be more, but the convenience is real. These allow farmers to drop off products quickly and go back to farming or other errands. Probably the biggest challenge with these venues is their overhead relative to scale.

Farmgate sales, especially near cities, are wonderful retail opportunities. Obviously, traveling to the farm has its drawbacks, but actually visiting the farm creates an accountability and transparency that are hard to achieve in any other venue. To acquire food on the farmer's own turf creates a connection, relationship, and memory that heighten the intimate dining experience. The biggest hurdle is zoning laws that often do not allow neighbors to collaboratively sell. (My book *Everything I Want to Do Is Illegal* details the local food hurdles in greater detail.)

Metropolitan buying clubs (MBCs) are developing rapidly as a new local marketing and distribution venue. Using the Internet as a farmer-to-patron real-time communication avenue, this scheme offers scheduled drops in urban areas. Patrons order via the Internet from an inventory supplied by one or more farms. Drop points in their neighborhoods offer easy access. Farmers do not have farmers' market politics or regulations to deal with, or sales commissions to pay. This transaction is highly efficient because it is nonspeculative—everything that goes on the delivery vehicle is preordered, and nothing comes back to the farm. Customizing each delivery's inventory for seasonal availability offers flexibility and an info-dense menu.

Many people ask, "Where do I find local food, or a farmer?" My answer: "They are all around. If you will put as much time into sourcing your local food as many people put into picketing and political posturing, you will discover a whole world that Wall Street doesn't know exists." I am a firm believer in the Chinese proverb: "When the student is ready, the teacher will appear." This nonindustrial food system lurks below the radar in every locality. If you seek, you will find.

■ Buy What's in Season

After discovering your kitchen and finding your farmer, the third opt-out procedure is to eat seasonally. This includes "laying by" for the off season. Eating seasonally does not mean denying yourself tomatoes in January if you live in New Hampshire. It means procuring the mountains of late-season tomatoes thrown away each year and canning, freezing, or dehydrating them for winter use.

In our basement, hundreds of quarts of canned summer produce line the pantry shelves. Green beans, yellow squash, applesauce, pickled beets, pickles, relish, and a host of other delicacies await off-season menus. I realize this takes time, but it's the way for all of us to share bioregional rhythms. To refuse to join this natural food ebb and flow is to deny connectedness. And this indifference to life around us creates a jaundiced view of our ecological nest and our responsibilities within it.

For the first time in human history, a person can move into a community, build a house out of outsourced material, heat it with outsourced energy, hook up to water from an unknown source, send waste out a pipe somewhere else, and eat food from an unknown source. In other words, in modern America we can live without any regard to the ecological life raft that undergirds us. Perhaps that is why many of us have become indifferent to nature's cry.

The most unnatural characteristic of the industrial food system is the notion that the same food items should be available everywhere at once at all times. To have empty grocery shelves during inventory downtime is unthinkable in the supermarket world. When we refuse to participate in the nonseasonal game, it strikes a heavy blow to the infrastructure, pipeline, distribution system, and ecological assault that upholds industrial food.

■ Plant a Garden

My final recommendation for declaring your food independence is to grow some of your own. I am constantly amazed at the creativity shown by urban-dwellers who physically embody their opt-out decision by growing something themselves. For some, it may be a community garden where neighbors work together to grow tomatoes, beans, and squash. For others, it may be three or four laying hens in an apartment. Shocking? Why? As a culture, we think nothing of having exotic tropical birds in city apartments. Why not use that space for something productive, like egg layers? Feed them kitchen scraps and gather fresh eggs every day.

Did someone mention something about ordinances? Forget them. Do it anyway. Defy. Don't comply. People who think nothing of driving around Washington, D.C., at eighty miles an hour in a fifty-five speed limit zone often go apoplectic at the thought of defying a zoning- or building-code ordinance. The secret reality is that the government is out of money and can't hire enough bureaucrats to check up on everybody anyway. So we all need to just begin opting out and it will be like five lanes of speeders on the beltway—who do you stop?

Have you ever wanted to have a cottage business producing that wonderful soup, pot pie, or baked item your grandmother used to make? Well, go ahead and make it, sell it to your neighbors and friends at church or garden club. Food safety laws? Forget them. People getting sick from food aren't getting it from their neighbors; they are getting it from USDA-approved, industrially produced, irradiated, amalgamated, adulterated, reconstituted, extruded, pseudo-food laced with preservatives, dyes, and high fructose corn syrup.

If you live in a condominium complex, approach the landlord about taking over a patch for a garden. Plant edible landscaping. If all the campuses in Silicon Valley would plant edible varieties instead of high maintenance ornamentals, their irrigation water would actually be put to ecological use instead of just feeding hedge clippers and lawn mower engines. Urban garden projects are taking over abandoned lots, and that is a good thing. We need to see more of that. Schools can produce their own food. Instead of hiring Chemlawn, how about running pastured poultry across the yard? Students can butcher the chickens and learn about the death-life-death-life cycle.

Clearly, so much can be done right here, right now, with what you and I have. The question is not, "What can I force someone else to do?" The question is "What am I doing today to opt out of the industrial food system?" For some, it may be having one family sit-down, locally-sourced meal a week. That's fine. We haven't gotten where we've gotten overnight, and we certainly won't extract ourselves from where we are overnight.

But we must stop feeling like victims and adopt a proactive stance. The power of many individual right actions will then compound to create a different culture. Our children deserve it. And the earthworms will love us—along with the rest of the planet.

■ READING AND WRITING

1. If the industrial food system is going to change, Salatin writes, "it is up to you and me to make the change." And the best way to do this, he says, is to "declare your independence" from the status quo. How can we do this, according to Salatin? What specifically does he mean by "opting out"?

2. How would you characterize the tone of Salatin's essay? Point to passages in the text that Salatin uses to establish this tone. Do you find the tone compelling? Is it effective? Explain.

3. How does Salatin address the two major concerns he mentions about his proposal—that the world will not be able to feed itself without industrial food and that locally grown food is not always safe? Do you think his handling of these concerns is sufficient?

■ DEVELOPING LONGER RESPONSES

4. Write a formal letter to Salatin in which you raise any questions you have about his proposal—about its feasibility, for example, or its effectiveness.

RESEARCH AND WRITING PROJECTS

© Peter Menzel / menzelphoto.com

1. **IMAGE 2.3,** like the photos on pages 75 and 101, is from the book *Hungry Planet: What the World Eats* by Peter Menzel and Faith D'Aluisio. Here, the Ahmed family of Cairo, Egypt, poses with a week's supply of food, which cost them 387.85 Egyptian Pounds, or $68.53. If you look closely, you can see some packaged and apparently processed foods mixed in with the fresh produce. Several of the readings in this chapter mention the worldwide reach of America's industrial food system, but none fully explores the issue. Using library and internet resources, research the following question: How does the U.S. industrial food system—including factory farms—affect the availability, quality, and cost of food in other parts of the world? Use your research to compile an annotated bibliography of at least six informative and reliable sources that you can use in a later writing project.

2. Working with a group of classmates, investigate and catalog the sources of the food served on the University of South Carolina campus—from

dining halls to fast-food outlets. Some questions to keep in mind as you conduct your research: What companies supply the meals that are offered on campus? Where do they get the food to produce these meals? Does any of the food come from local resources (farms, ranches, or farmer's markets)? If not, why not? With your group, use your research findings to compose a report on the state of USC's food supply. Later in the semester, your instructor might ask you to develop an argument based on your research and your report.

3. Nearly every essay in this chapter speaks, in one way or another, of the need for Americans to return to the kitchen, to learn how to cook meals from scratch to avoid processed foods. Research this issue to find out if there are any organized movements—in schools, churches, or communities, for example—whose goal it is to teach Americans, especially children, to cook. Use your research and your own experience to write a policy argument that proposes an effective way to teach cooking skills.

3

Voiceovers:
Narrating Gender

IMAGE 3.1: The forces that shape us as men and women—the pieces of our gendered selves—come from a variety of sources. Think about the family, social, and professional roles you fill based on your gender. Where did the expectations for these roles originate? Who or what lets you know what is expected of you in these roles? What happens if you do not meet these expectations?

Gender is a difficult concept—one that often blends intensely personal issues with overtly political, religious, and cultural agendas. Rather than attempt to explain the many perspectives on the subject, the readings in this chapter offer stories, in a variety of genres, of people dealing with gender and its various complications. Individually, they use people and personal experience to imply powerful arguments. Taken together, they provide a vivid and often moving introduction to the subject.

Nawal El Saadawi is a psychiatrist and the celebrated author of more than 40 works of fiction and non-fiction. The novel Memoirs of a Woman Doctor, *like many of her books, reveals what she calls "the double exploitation of Egyptian women—both their general, social oppression and their private oppression, through …marriage." El Saadawi has said that* Memoirs of a Woman Doctor, *from which this piece is excerpted, portrays the circumstances and characteristics of "an Egyptian woman such as myself," but that "the work is still fiction." The novel was first published in serial format and was censored when it was published in one volume.*

from
MEMOIRS OF A WOMAN DOCTOR
Nawal el-Saadawi

The conflict between me and my femininity began very early on, before my female characteristics had became pronounced and before I knew anything about myself, my sex and my origins, indeed before I knew the nature of the cavity which had housed me before I was expelled into the wide world.

All I did know at that time was that I was a girl. I used to hear it from my mother all day long. 'Girl!' she would call, and all it meant to me was that I wasn't a boy and I wasn't like my brother.

My brother's hair was cut short but otherwise left free and uncombed, while mine was allowed to grow longer and longer and my mother combed it twice a day and twisted it into plaits and imprisoned the ends of it in ribbons and rubber bands.

My brother woke up in the morning and left his bed just as it was, while I had to make my bed and his as well.

My brother went out into the street to play without asking my parents' permission and came back whenever he liked, while I could only go out if and when they let me.

My brother took a bigger piece of meat than me, gobbled it up and drank his soup noisily and my mother never said a word. But I was different: I was a girl. I had to watch every movement I made, hide my longing for the food, eat slowly and drink my soup without a sound.

My brother played, jumped around and turned somersaults, whereas if I ever sat down and allowed my skirt to ride as much as a centimeter up my thighs, my mother would pierce me with a glance like an animal immobilizing its prey and I would cover up those shameful parts of my body.

Shameful! Everything in me was shameful and I was a child of just nine years old.

I felt sorry for myself and locked myself in my room and cried. The first real tears I shed in my life weren't because I'd done badly at school or broken something valuable but because

I was a girl. I wept over my femininity even before I knew what it was. The moment I opened my eyes on life, a state of enmity already existed between me and my nature.

I jumped down the stairs three at a time so as to be in the street before I'd counted ten. My brother and some of the boys and girls who lived nearby were waiting for me to play cops and robbers. I'd asked my mother's permission. I loved playing games and running as fast as I could. I felt an overwhelming happiness as I moved my head and arms and legs in the air or broke into a series of leaps and bounds, constrained only by the weight of my body which was dragged down earthwards time and again.

Why had God created me a girl and not a bird flying in the air like that pigeon? It seemed to me that God must prefer birds to girls. But my brother couldn't fly and this consoled me a little. I realized that despite his great freedom he was as incapable as I was of flying. I began to search constantly for weak spots in males to console me for the powerlessness imposed on me by the fact of being female.

I was bounding ecstatically along when I felt a violent shudder running through my body. My head spun and I saw something red. I didn't know what had happened to me. Fear gripped my heart and I left the game. I ran back to the house and locked myself in the bathroom to investigate the secret of this grave event in private.

I didn't understand it at all. I thought I must have been struck down by a terrible illness. I went to ask my mother about it in fear and trembling and saw laughter and happiness written all over her face. I wondered in amazement how she could greet this affliction with such a broad smile. Noticing my surprise and confusion, she took me by the hand and led me to my room. Here she told me women's bloody tale.

I took to my room for four days running. I couldn't face my brother, my father or even the house-boy. I thought they must all have been told about the shameful thing that had happened to me: my mother would doubtless have revealed my new secret. I locked myself in, trying to come to terms with this phenomenon. Was this unclean procedure the only way for girls to reach maturity? Could a human being really live for several days at the mercy of involuntary muscular activity? God must really hate girls to have tarnished them with this curse. I felt that God had favoured boys in everything.

I got up from the bed, dragged myself over to the mirror and looked at the two little mounds sprouting on my chest. If only I could die! I didn't recognize this body which sprang a new shame on me every day, adding to my weakness and my preoccupation with myself. What would grow on my body next? What other new symptom would my tyrannical femininity break out in?

I hated being female. I felt as if I was in chains—chains forged from my own blood tying me to the bed so that I couldn't run and jump, chains produced by the cells of my own body, chains of shame and humiliation. I turned in on myself to cover up my miserable existence.

I no longer went out to run and play. The two mounds on my chest were growing bigger. They bounced gently as I walked. I was unhappy with my tall slender frame, folding my arms over my chest to hide it and looking sadly at my brother and his friends as they played.

I grew. I grew taller than my brother even though he was older than me. I grew taller than the other children of my age. I withdrew from their midst and sat alone thinking. My childhood was over, a brief, breathless childhood. I'd scarcely been aware of it before it was gone, leaving me with a mature woman's body carrying deep inside it a ten-year-old child.

I saw the doorman's eyes and teeth shining in his black face as he came up to me; I was sitting alone on his wooden bench letting my eyes follow the movements of my brother and his friends in the street. I felt the rough edge of his galabiya brushing my leg and breathed in the strange smell of his clothes. I edged away in disgust. As he came closer again, I tried to hide my fear by staring fixedly at my brother and his companions as they played, but I felt his coarse rough fingers stroking my leg and moving up under my clothes. I jumped up in alarm and raced away from him. This horrible man had noticed my womanhood as well! I ran all the way up to our flat and my mother asked what the matter was. But I couldn't tell her anything, perhaps out of a feeling of fear or humiliation or a mixture of the two. Or perhaps because I thought she'd scold me and that would put an end to the special affection between us that made me tell her my secrets.

I no longer went out in the street, and I didn't sit on the wooden bench any more. I fled from those strange creatures with harsh voices and moustaches, the creatures they called men. I created an imaginary private world for myself in which I was a goddess and men were stupid, helpless creatures at my beck and call. I sat on a high throne in this world of mine, arranging the dolls on chairs, making the boys sit on the floor and telling stories to myself. Alone with my imagination and my dolls, nobody ruffled the calm of my life, except my mother with her never-ending orders for me to do tasks around the flat or in the kitchen: the hateful, constricted world of women with its permanent reek of garlic and onions. I'd scarcely retreated into my own little world when my mother would drag me into the kitchen saying, 'You're going to be married one day. You must learn how to cook. You're going to be married…' Marriage! Marriage! That loathsome word which my mother mentioned every day until I hated the sound of it. I couldn't hear it without having a mental picture of a man with a big see-through belly with a table of food inside it. In my mind the smell of the kitchen was linked with the smell of a husband and I hated the word husband just as I hated the smell of the food we cooked.

My grandmother's chatter broke off as she looked at my chest. I saw her diseased old eyes scrutinizing the two sprouting buds and evaluating them. Then she whispered something to my mother and I heard my mother saying to me, 'Put on your cream dress and go and say hello to your father's guest in the sitting-room.'
I caught a whiff of conspiracy in the air. I was used to meeting most of my father's friends and bringing them coffee. Sometimes I sat with them and heard my father telling them how well I was doing in school. This always made me feel elated and I thought that since my father had acknowledged my intelligence he would extricate me from the depressing world of women, reeking of onions and marriage.

But why the cream dress? It was new and I hated it. It had a strange gather at the front which made my breasts look larger. My mother looked at me inquiringly and asked, 'Where's your cream dress?'

'I won't wear it,' I replied angrily.

She noticed the stirrings of rebellion in my eyes and said regretfully, 'Smooth down your eyebrows then.'

I didn't look at her, and before opening the sitting-room door I ruffled up my eyebrows with my fingers.

I greeted my father's friend and sat down. I saw a strange, frightening face and eyes examining me relentlessly as my grandmother's had done shortly before.

'She's first in her group at primary school this year,' said my father.

I didn't notice any admiration in the man's eyes at these words but I saw his inquiring glances roaming all over my body before coming to rest on my chest. Scared, I stood up and ran out of the room as if a devil was after me. My mother and grandmother met me eagerly at the door and asked in unison, 'What did you do?'

I let out a single cry in their faces and ran to my room, slamming the door behind me. Then I went over to the mirror and stared at my chest. I hated them, these two protrusions, these two lumps of flesh which were determining my future! How I wished I could cut them off with a sharp knife! But I couldn't. All I could do was hide them by flattening them with a tight corset.

The heavy long hair I carried around everywhere on my head held me up in the morning, got in my way in the bath and made my neck burning hot in the summer. Why wasn't it short and free like my brother's? His didn't weigh his head down or hinder his activities. But it was my mother who controlled my life, my future and my body right down to every strand of my hair. Why? Because she'd given birth to me? But why did that give her some special merit? She went about her normal life like any other woman and conceived me involuntarily in a random moment of pleasure. I'd arrived without her knowing or choosing me, and without my choosing her. We'd been thrust arbitrarily on one another as mother and daughter. Could any human being love someone who'd been forced upon them? And if my mother loved me instinctively in spite of herself, what credit did that do her? Did it make her any better than a cat which sometimes loves its kittens and at other times devours them? I sometimes thought the harsh way she treated me hurt me more than if she'd eaten me! If she really loved me and wanted my happiness above her own, then why did her demands and desires always work against my happiness? How could she possibly love me when she put chains on my arms and legs and round my neck every day?

For the first time in my life I left the flat without asking my mother's permission. My heart was pounding as I went down the street, though my provocative act had given me a certain strength. As I walked, a sign caught my eye: 'Ladies' Hairdresser'. I had only a second's hesitation before going in.

I watched the long tresses squirm in the jaws of the sharp scissors and then fall to the ground. Were these what my mother called a woman's crowning glory? Could a woman's crown fall shattered to the ground like this because of one moment of determination? I was filled with a great contempt for womankind: I had seen with my own eyes that women believe in worthless trivia. This contempt gave me added strength. I walked back home with a firm step and stood squarely in front of my mother with my newly cropped hair.

My mother gave a shrill cry and slapped my face hard. Then she hit me again and again while I stood where I was as if rooted to the spot. My challenging of authority had turned me into an immovable force, my victory over my mother had transformed me into a solid mass, unaffected by the assault. My mother's hand struck my face and then drew back each time, as if it had hit a granite boulder.

Why didn't I cry? I usually burst into tears at the slightest snub or the gentlest of slaps. But the tears didn't come. My eyes stayed open, looking into my mother's eyes boldly and firmly. She went on slapping me for a while, then collapsed back on to the sofa, repeating in bewilderment, 'You must have gone mad!'

I felt sorry for her when I saw her features crumbling in helpless defeat. I had a strong urge to hug and kiss her and break down and cry in her arms, and say to her, 'It's not good for me always to do as you say.'

But I took my eyes away from hers so she wouldn't realize I'd witnessed her defeat, and ran off to my room. I looked in the mirror and smiled at my short hair, the light of victory in my eyes.

For the first time in my life I understood the meaning of victory; fear led only to defeat, and victory demanded courage. My fear of my mother had vanished; that great aura which had made me terrified of her had fallen away. I realized that she was just an ordinary woman. The slaps she delivered were the strongest thing about her but they no longer scared me—because they didn't hurt any more.

I hated our flat except for the room where my books were. I loved school except for the home economics period. I loved all the days of the week except Friday.

I took part in all school activities and joined the drama society, the debating society, the athletics club, and the music and art clubs. Even that wasn't enough for me so I got together with some friends and we set up a society that I called the Friendship Club. Why, I'm not sure, except that deep down inside I had an overwhelming longing for companionship, for profound, all-embracing companionship with no strings attached, for vast groups of people to be with me, talk to me, listen to me and soar up to the heavens with me.

It seemed to me that whatever heights I reached, I wouldn't be content, the flame burning within me wouldn't be extinguished. I began to hate the repetitiveness and similarity of lessons: I would read the material once and once only—to go over it again would stifle me, kill me. I wanted something new, new…all the time.

I wasn't aware of him at first when he came into my room where I sat reading and stood beside me. Then he said, 'Don't you want to relax for a bit?'

I'd been reading for ages and felt tired so I smiled and said, 'I'd like to go for a walk in the fresh air.'

'Put on your coat and let's go.'

I quickly pulled on my coat and ran to catch up with him. I was on the point of slipping my hand into his and running along together as we used to do when we were children. But then I caught his eye and suddenly remembered how many years it had been since I had last played like a child, years during which my legs had forgotten how to run and become used to moving slowly like grown-ups' legs. I put my hand in my coat pocket and walked slowly at his side.

'You've grown,' he said.

'So have you.'

'Do you remember when we used to play together?'

'You always beat me when we had races.'

'You always won at marbles.'

We laughed uproariously. The air flooded into my chest and invigorated me, making me feel as if I was recapturing something denied to me in my over-regimented childhood.

'I bet I'd win if we had a race now.'

'No, I'll beat you,' I said confidently.

'Let's see.'

We marked out a line on the ground and stood side by side. He shouted, 'One…two…three…' and we shot forward. I was about to reach the goal first when he grabbed my clothes from behind. I stumbled and fell and he fell beside me. Still panting, I looked up at him and saw him staring at me in a funny way which made the blood rush to my cheeks. I watched his arm reach out in the direction of my waist and he whispered in a rough voice, 'I'm going to kiss you.'

I was convulsed by a strange and violent trembling. For a moment which passed like lightning through my feelings, I wished he would stretch out his arm further and hold me tight, but then this odd secret desire was transformed into a wild fury.

My anger only made him more persistent and he held on to me with an iron grip. I don't know where I got the strength, but I threw off his arm and it flailed in the air while I brought my hand down hard across his face.

I turned over and over in bed in utter confusion. Strange sensations swept through me and images flashed before my eyes. One of them lodged itself in front of me and wouldn't go away: my cousin lying on the ground beside me, his arm nearly round my waist and his strange glances boring into my head. I closed my eyes and was borne along by my fantasy in which his arms moved tightly around me and his lips pressed firmly down on mine.

I buried my head under the covers, unable to believe that I'd slapped him with the hand I was now picturing quivering in his. I pulled the covers tightly over my head to shut out my strange dream but it crept back, so I put the pillow over my head and pressed it down as hard as I could to suffocate the stubborn ghost, until sleep finally overtook me.

I opened my eyes the following morning. The sunlight had chased away the darkness and all the phantoms that prowled in its shadows. I opened the window and the fresh air blew in, chasing away the last clinging traces of the night's dreams. I smiled scornfully at the cowardly part of me which trembled with fear at the stronger part when I was awake, but then crept into my bed at night and filled the darkness around me with fantasies and illusions.

In my final year at secondary school I came out top of my group…I sat wondering what to do…

I hated my femininity, resented my nature and knew nothing about my body. All that was left for me was to reject, to challenge, to resist! I would reject my femininity, challenge my nature, resist all the desires of my body; prove to my mother and grandmother that I wasn't a woman like them, that I wouldn't spend my life in the kitchen peeling onions and garlic, wasting all my days so that my husband could eat and eat.

I was going to show my mother that I was more intelligent than my brother, than the man she'd wanted me to wear the cream dress for, than any man, and that I could do everything my father did and more.

■ READING AND WRITING

1. Though it is a work of fiction, Saadawi's excerpt clearly introduces an argument about gender and femininity. What do you think that argument is? How does Saadawi use her protagonist to voice the argument?
2. Early in the excerpt, Saadawi's protagonist says, "I wept over my femininity even before I knew what it was." What kinds of expectations and obstacles does she face? What are the origins of these hurdles?
3. Saadawi's narrative is rich with imagery. List some of these images in the text and discuss their rhetorical effectiveness.

■ DEVELOPING LONGER RESPONSES

4. Read Shirin Ebadi's "From the Living Room to the Courtroom" elsewhere in this chapter and write a brief essay in which you compare Ebadi's piece with Saadawi's. Think about the genre of each text, the arguments, and the rhetorical choices the authors make in their efforts to persuade.

Mary Kay Blakely teaches magazine writing at the University of Missouri Journalism School and has been a contributing editor to Ms. *magazine since 1981. She has written essays on social and political issues for* The New York Times, The Washington Post, Mother Jones, *and many other publications. She is also the author of the critically acclaimed memoirs* Wake Me When It's Over *and* American Mom: Motherhood, Politics, and Humble Pie, *in which this essay appeared.*

A WRESTLING MOM   Mary Kay Blakely

A writer I much admire said in an essay about the trials of being the feminist mother of sons that it *pained* her to see her adolescent son suffer abuse from thuggish friends for sticking up for the rights of gay sailors and American Indians. Good God, I thought, those are the joyful moments for a feminist mother. The painful moments come when she hears her son issue a wolf whistle or talk about joining the army.

My sons have wanted to join the army, to be like Tom Cruise in *Top Gun*. They have wanted to swagger. Like Clint Eastwood, they've hankered after the respect and awe a man gets when he leaves a wake of death behind him. I have seen these macho personas come and go with my sons. So I didn't take all these theatrical characters too seriously—Indiana Jones, Luke Skywalker, Rocky Balboa. They usually didn't survive beyond the year. One did, however, and I realized after the third year that it was probably a keeper. It was not a part of my son I had grown, and it did not cheer me. Of all the role models I imagined for my sons, Hulk Hogan was not one of them.

"It's not the same as TV, Mom," Ryan said. Wrestle-Mania was just theatre, he said. "It's a joke. That isn't real wrestling." His passion for this sport would eventually engage me in a male culture for which I would never have imagined developing an affinity.

Every Friday morning during his senior year of high school, Ryan stood before the bathroom mirror carefully knotting his tie. A strictly jeans and T-shirt guy at age eighteen, he followed the high school athlete's tradition of wearing ties to notify classmates: I have a game today. Friends would wish him luck in the halls, but few would attend the afternoon meet. Unlike the football and basketball teams, wrestlers attract about the same size audience as, say, the chess club. It did not matter. His teammates and coaches—the close fraternity he aimed to please most—would observe every move. A sparse population of parents would make up in volume what we lacked in numbers.

The button at his neck felt a half-inch short of its mark, although his eyes withheld any pleasure at the measurable results of all the iron he'd pumped. Nor did his eyes concede any regret when he combed his hair around the swollen, tender tip of his "cauliflower" ear, in full bloom again this season. Admitting neither vanity nor chagrin to the mirror, a young wrestler strives to become utterly unconscious of his body—its muscle, its pain, its hunger, its sweat. It was the wrestler's mom, approaching the end of an eighteen-year intimacy with this body and this boy, who openly admired and winced through mornings such as these.

"How do I look?" he asked, more out of habit than any need for my approval. He patted his black tie familiarly. "Like a pallbearer with a tic," I replied. He laughed.

In fact, I thought he looked splendid, but saying so would have been meaningless that day. We had come to the outer edge of unconditional love, and wrestling taught both of us what some of the future conditions might be. For a boy who'd always known how to charm parents and teachers out of final ultimata, for whom friendship and fun came easily but deadlines and due dates were hard, I suspected he loved this sport precisely because it was so merciless. Give in to temptation, skip a practice, allow a distraction, underestimate an opponent—you lose. In a six-minute match, there is no room for excuses. Preparing for a test that would take him to the limits of his strength and his will, he had no use for easy praise that day.

Before he left the bathroom, he weighed himself one last time, apparently to see if combing his hair had worked off another ounce. Wrestlers are relentless dieters—if you're good at 152 pounds, they maintain, you should be dynamite at 145. Despite the saunas and workouts in layers of polyurethane, there would be high anxiety when, stripped down to mere ounces of clothing, he stepped on the scale to qualify for the meet. "Enjoy your Thanksgiving dinner," his head coach advised in November. "It will be your last full meal for three months." Not making weight was the worst kind of defeat, providing opponents the free points of a forfeit and disappointing teammates with a failure of will.

All family dinners became testy events during wrestling season. His scorn for calories interrupted my long habits of the heart, equating food with love. Rejection was inevitable. "What's *in* this?" he asked suspiciously before applying his fork to his plate. "How many grams of fat?" For someone who once thought there was no greater heaven than helping himself to a full bag of Chips Ahoy, a stick of celery held little bliss. That morning, he had a glass of water for breakfast. He would probably skip lunch.

"Are you coming today?" he asked before heading out the door, aware of my conflicts with work. Four years ago, I hadn't comprehended the urgency of his repeated invitations to the meets. As a single mom, I preferred other ways of spending our limited "quality time" together than by losing circulation in the bleachers twice a week. Initially, duty rather than enthusiasm brought me to the gym. It's hard for my family and friends to believe I became a sweaty-palmed fan of high school wrestling.

The team had already begun their stretching exercises when I took my seat in the bleachers that afternoon. Ryan sat in the center of the circle with the two other captains, Enrique and Will, surrounded by their black, white, Asian, and Hispanic teammates—all dressed in red. Like a military drill team, they moved in unison to the captains' calls: "Down...up...again...up...left...up...down..." The goofball antics that regularly erupted during practices were not indulged here. Under the scrutiny of opponents with names like the Rams, Bears, Wreckers, Vikings, or Warriors, the Greenwich Cardinals gave nothing away.

Although their movements were graceful and disciplined, adolescence lent a distinctly amateur quality to their performance: there was always a limb flailing here or there with a too-large foot. Already my throat swelled with involuntary emotion, like that buried patriotism that reveals itself when a parade marches by. An almost primal longing for a united humanity surfaced as I watched this colorfully diverse team moving in a single, unified direction.

The youngest wrestlers, smaller by half than most of the fans in the bleachers, approached the mat first. The lightweights, usually in their first varsity season, were all limbs. In any position, their eight entangled appendages resembled a dense thicket of pickup sticks. During Ryan's first season four years ago, I could never tell exactly what he was supposed to be doing down there. My cheers were feeble, limited to "Go, Ry!" But where? To what end? The rapid development in a boy between fourteen and eighteen can give a mother the bends, however prepared she may think she is for the coming man.

I had, of course, observed the results of his body-building, but until I attended a wrestling match I'd never watched him use this power on another person. At eighteen, he had the capacity to level most of the people in the gymnasium. There was a part of him that loved this power; there was a part of me that regretted it. I couldn't witness this obvious strength in my son, his joy in using it, without thinking about the ways it would change his social relationships with women. His habitual friendliness with strangers on the sidewalk, with clerks in stores and cafés, was not as readily returned anymore. Some women—not because of any thing he had done but what had been done to them—automatically feared him. The "collateral" damage of violence against women: it costs all men smiles on the street.

When the weight class below him was called to the mat, Ryan shed his warmup sweats and secured the straps of his singlet. One of the reasons he kept inviting me to his meets, I finally understood, was that he wanted to announce: "This is who I am now. See me." And see I did. Confronted by all that lycra and muscle, the various states of dress and undress, the mothers in the bleachers hardly knew where to rest their eyes. When I looked away from my own son, I soon realized that I was admiring the son of another mother, perhaps the one sitting next to me. I looked down at my feet and thought about human sexuality. I wondered if it was the same for fathers who observed their daughters in bikinis for the first time. It was hard to know the appropriate way to acknowledge the stunning physical changes in a child of the other sex, and yet not to acknowledge those changes was to ignore the most important development issues of the moment.

He put on his headgear and then began the sideline dance that wrestlers do, the loose-limbed hop from foot to foot that simultaneously pumps them up and calms them down. His eyes were focused utterly inward, concentrating on some private vision inside his head. If he knew I was watching, if he knew how much I studied and enjoyed this unselfconscious, rhythmic, juice-up dance, he would stop instantly, as if he had been caught exploring his face for morning stubble in the bathroom mirror. I thought if he kept up this freedom of expression, there was a good chance he'd be spared the urge to beat drums as a Wild Man twenty-some years from now.

For all the mockery Robert Bly's tribal rituals in suburban America have inspired, he has hit a cultural nerve in his argument for exclusively male companionship and ritual. In a lecture four years ago, Bly implied that a single mother's close relationships with sons—especially firstborns—often made it difficult for them to come to terms with the aggressive and competitive parts of themselves. He suggested there were some truths men must learn that mothers cannot teach them. Ryan learned things in the company of his coaches and teammates that I could never have taught him. This recognition brought an element of pain, as separation invariably does.

The week before, still pumped up after an invigorating victory, a phrase commonly used in the locker room slipped out in the car: it was too bad his best friend had to lose to that "fuckin' fairy" from Darien. He was sorry the minute he'd said the F-word—not the first one, which has thoroughly saturated the culture. ("The word 'fuck' is uttered 102 times during the film *The Last Boy Scouts*," according to the *Harper's* Index). No, it was the second F-word that prompted the apology. Only in the environment of the car did he remember that our extended family of friends included several fairies. The word meant nothing, he assured me. It was army.

"It's only language," I reminded him, "…only the stuff we think with." I knew crudeness was a prerequisite in the world of the locker room; he knew sexism and homophobia were enemies in mine. His defection didn't seem so innocent, so temporary, to me because this phrase was acquired during his first real experience with power. How that power was defined, for and against whom, had everything to do with how it would eventually be used. Still largely unconscious of the bigotry that began with a word, he didn't want it to matter. "Trust me," I said. "Words matter."

If my son had some discomforting moments with the language requirements of a feminist mom, I had a few unsettling months with the service obligations of a wrestling son. According to tradition, the captains' moms were responsible for raising funds for the team. Consequently, I spent most of my Saturdays that winter in the corridor outside the gymnasium serving chili-dogs with the other mothers. We were real estate managers, bank cashiers, journalists…women who had not served coffee to the men in our offices for the last ten years. Yet there we were, catering to sons who stood on the brink of "emancipated minor," fully aware that serving men leads not to gratitude but to oblivion.

I had some difficulties with the unfair assumption that a captain's dad belongs in the bleachers while a captain's mom is happiest behind the refreshment stand. Nevertheless, I felt a peculiar satisfaction fulfilling my chili-dog duties. Maybe it was a fit of nostalgia, savoring every ritual of our last season together. Or maybe it was the greater generosity one generation affords to the next. Fifteen years ago, I was a consultant for the Amax Coal Company when the first women employees entered the mines, amid great hostility and resistance. "I can get behind this liberation stuff for my daughters," one of the miners confessed privately, "but not for my wife."

My thoughts were suddenly interrupted by loud hollering below. The two coaches leaped up from their seats and were leaning over the edge of the mat as the referee crouched low, eyeball-to-eyeball with the wrestlers on the floor. Before I could join the rallying shouts, a hand slapped the mat, a whistle blew. The wrestler in blue jumped up ecstatically. A defeated Cardinal sat on the mat in limp disbelief. He threw off his headgear angrily, then quickly picked it up and left the mat before tripping into the penalty points of unsportsmanlike conduct. The head coach shrugged and raised a pair of helpless hands—sign language for "shit happens." Slipping out of his wet singlet, he put on the T-shirt bearing this month's slogan: "PAIN—It is better to give than to receive." A junior varsity player was bounced from the bench to make room for the higher ranked, defeated teammate. Membership had its privileges.

Whenever a Cardinal left the mat in despair, a grim and wordless exchange rippled through the eyes in the bleachers. It was a humbling moment to witness a son in defeat, to contemplate how much more loomed ahead, how powerless we were to prevent it. Every mother I know has battled the irrational craving to spare her children disappointment and heartache. When Ryan exploded in enraged frustration on the golf course last summer, one of my relatives advised me to teach him our family philosophy that it's just as honorable to be a good loser as it is to be a gracious winner. "I can't teach him that," I said, empathizing with his suffering. "It isn't true."

The two wrestling team alumni who came to every meet were whispering some private, last-minute advice to Ryan before he stepped onto the mat. Pete and Pat—whom the Cardinals referred to as "Pete and Repeat" and who might be eligible to found the first chapter of Adult Children of Wrestling Moms—still arranged their business and social lives around the high school team, not yet having found a fraternity as satisfying as this in the outside world. I was grateful for the straightforward affection they gave my son. Whatever the content of their private conversations, it introduced me to what complete comprehension looked like on his face. It was not an expression I'd ever seen at home.

The coaches met him at the edge of the mat. They had the credibility and authority—all but expired for most of the parents in the bleachers—to demand discipline and give orders. It was a challenge to feel entirely happy about this natural turn of events. I couldn't help wishing this authority were directing him, "Do your homework! Think about your future!" But instead I heard, "I know you can *kill* this guy! I want to see it in the first period!"

As Ryan crouched into his stance, my heartbeat accelerated, my skin dampened, my own muscles became taut. Sitting in the bleachers was an aerobic experience for me. As usual, I sat myself next to the Puebla women, Enrique's mother and two sisters, who taught the tweedier New England residents how to behave at a wrestling meet. The team loved them: "You can really *hear* them," the coach said.

I liked to sit next to the Pueblas because I never had to feel like an emotionally embarrassing relative in their company. Enrique's mother Marcia, one of my fund-raising teammates at the refreshment stand this year, spoke only Spanish while I spoke only English. We understood each other's sign language and facial expressions adequately enough to conduct our chili-dog business, but our communication in the bleachers was seamless. She screamed, I screamed, we all screamed.

An aggressive takedown in the first period resulted in a reversal. Alarm flashed into Ryan's face and stayed there. As he fought with everything he had—every muscle straining against the hold, every fiber of his being resisting defeat—the Cardinal fans tried to out-shout the deafening cheers from our opponents. The buzzer sounded, ending the period in the nick of time.

Unless someone got a bloody nose—a painless and welcome time out—it was usually necessary for one of the wrestlers to tie his shoe between periods. It was a lengthy process, tightening laces and wrapping the ankles, then taking a drink for revival. It was usually the losing wrestler who discovered he needed to relace a shoe, who needed to break the momentum of his opponent and rally his own. Perilously close to defeat, Ryan painstakingly attended his shoe. My thoughts drifted back to the first time he dressed himself, the gorgeous look of satisfaction on his three-year-old face…until he got to those damn shoes. Defeated by a shoelace, he cried in frustration. Vulnerable again, the lone figure bent in concentration on the mat raised an identical lump in my throat. If he lost his match that day, I knew he would not let himself cry.

After a second punishing round, his total exhaustion was evident: spent muscles, sweaty limbs, airless lungs, a worried face. With time running out, the third period was always the most reckless. Already, mat burns colored his cheeks, blood trickled from his mouth; his ear, I thought, must have been swelling under his headgear. He said he never felt these injuries when they were happening. I did. For the last four years, emergency rooms had been a regular feature of my existence. In these stark, tiled rooms of reverberating tensions, there were no crowds, no cheers, no coaches. Emergency rooms were where mothers wrestled alone against monstrous fears.

I thought back to the prior December when Ry's teammate, Will, grabbed my elbow before I paid my admission at the Staples High School tournament and reported that Ryan had just been taken out on a stretcher. My heart squeezed fiercely as images of broken necks, brain damage, and comas flooded my brain. "It's only his arm," Will assured me. Only an arm, only an ear…only the young can be so cavalier about their bodies. Armies are made up of youth for a reason. Ryan was a casualty of friendly fire that day: The injury happened during warm-ups with a teammate. When he lost consciousness after severely dislocating his right elbow, the trainer called an ambulance.

Fifteen minutes later, after a record number of moving violations on I-95, I reached Norwalk Hospital. Despite my wish to remain calm, I had trouble with simple interrogatory sentences at the information desk: "My son, Staples High School, about fifteen minutes ago—his arm (a spastic gesture to my right elbow)…is he here?" The nurse looked quizzically, then brightened.

"Oh, you mean *Ryan*." She smiled and pointed down a long corridor. A burly paramedic pushing an ambulance gurney noted my hesitation in the hallway. I repeated my garbled question. "Oh," he said, grinning, "you want *Ryan*." He accompanied me to his room.

Obviously no longer unconscious, my son was propped up in his bed, a very pale Cardinal in a nest of white sheets. The doctor, still smiling from some joke that preceded my arrival, picked up a pair of scissors to free the wounded arm from his pullover jacket. Their amiable chatter concluded abruptly.

"No way!" Ryan said, the color returning to his face. He sat bolt upright and insisted on pulling it over his head. When the doctor rejected that suggestion as too painful and risky, the paramedic, a former high school wrestler, came to the defense of his fellow jock.

"Doc, you can't cut his jacket—read this," he said, pointing to the word embroidered on the right shoulder: "Captain." The doctor looked at me, the only nonmember of this religion.

"Knock him out," I said. "Cut the jacket."

The patient prevailed. It took three of us to slip the jacket, undamaged, over his head and arm. It seemed a foolish kind of bravery, risking enormous pain to salvage a symbol. But in the whiplash emotions of his final wrestling season, nothing stayed the same. As the fear of permanent physical injury receded into the background, I recognized the enduring psychological benefits he'd earned from this sport. If wrestling gave him one oddball ear and six weeks in a sling, it also produced a confident, witty, capable young man, the Ryan instantly recognized by the hospital staff. He was willing to put his body between the scissors and the "Captain" because, he reminded me, "words matter."

Going into that third reckless period, he knew he needed a pin. Handicapped by the limited flexibility of this now-bandaged arm and a longer limbed opponent, he had trouble securing the leg he needed for a take-down. With thirty seconds to go, he lunged for a knee in a sudden rush of adrenaline. Now he was in a cradle, now he was out, now he had freed his arm, now he was on top pressing down…three inches to go, two inches, oh-my-God-*one*-inch! My laryngitis would inform me later that much of the thunderous noise in the bleachers came from me. He got his pin, seven seconds to spare.

Tradition required each wrestler, after the referee raised the winner's arm, to shake the hand of the opponent's coach. Although Ryan might not yet have mastered the good loser part of our family's honorable equation, his relatives would have been pleased to have seen him in the role of gracious winner. On the way back across the mat to his own bench he always stopped, win or lose, to hug his opponent. This hug was no formality but full of emotion. After four years of rising up in the same weight class together and witnessing each other's most glorious and humiliating moments, his mortal enemies from other schools had become his friends. During long breaks at all-day tournaments, they empathized with injuries and bad seasons, traded tips about summer camps and clinics, talked scholarships and women. The hug said "congratulations" or "sorry I had to pin you." In his last year, it had the bittersweet tinge of "so long."

Like the handshake of peace at the end of a church service, each team lined up after the final match and walked in a single file across the gym, shaking or slapping each hand from the opposite direction. Only once, when a racial slur tipped the defeated Cardinals beyond a strained control, did the handshake erupt in a brawl. Wrestling on a multi-racial team required coming to terms with every myth about racial superiority or inferiority. On the mat, you could hardly know a man better, be closer, understand more thoroughly that his immediate goals are exactly the same as your own.

Maybe it was this quality that wrestling had given my son—the camaraderie and experience of navigating the high tensions of an interracial world—that caused my palms to sweat so. The civil wars among our children, race against race, are so heartbreaking. Watching this handshake of peace, it became excruciatingly clear that if all of us would only do the same—if we would only mobilize our wills not to give in to temptation, skip a practice, allow a distraction, underestimate an opponent, or be careless with language—we would not have to keep losing the next generation to wars.

As the team rolled up the mats, the moms in the bleachers conferred on final plans for the annual awards banquet. Moving as far away from chili-dogs as possible we agreed on a Chinese menu, then decided to hire a caterer to serve it. We packed our gear—the video cameras, the coolers of Gatorade, the ace bandages and aspirin and ice packs we were never without. If we were entirely sane, we would not need these semi-barbaric rituals to break our hearts and thrill our souls. But we were not entirely sane. We would be back next week.

■ READING AND WRITING

1. In her memoir, Blakely refers to herself as a feminist. Based on what you have read, how do you think she defines that term? How do you define it?

2. Blakely's title works on multiple levels—yes, she becomes a "wrestling mom" to her son's team, but there's more. What is Blakely wrestling with in this excerpt? How does she work through these issues?

3. What does this text say about environment—people, places, interactions—and gender? Do you agree with Blakeley's position? Explain.

4. Who do you think is Blakeley's intended audience? What does she do in her text to connect with this audience?

According to the website of award-winning poet and essayist Nancy Mairs, the memoir Voice Lessons: On Becoming a (Woman) Writer *is "a tribute to the liberating power of literature and feminist ideas." The essay "Voice Lessons," which opens the book, eloquently shows how "finding a voice" as an essayist transformed Mairs' life.*

VOICE LESSONS
Nancy Mairs

■ 1. Pear Trees

The question I am most often asked when I speak to students and others interested in writing is, How did you find your voice? I have some trouble with this locution because "find" always suggests to me the discovery, generally fortuitous, of some lack or loss. I have found an occasional four-leaf clover I have found a mate. I have, more than once, found my way home. But is a voice susceptible of the same sort of revelation or retrieval? Hasn't mine simply always been there, from my earliest lallation to the "I love you" I called after my husband on his way to school several hours ago?

But of course, I remind myself, the question doesn't concern *my* voice at all but the voice of another woman (also named Nancy Mairs, confusingly enough) whose "utterances" are, except for the occasional public reading, literally inaudible: not, strictly speaking, a voice at all, but a fabrication, a device. And when I look again at the dictionary, I see that "find" can indeed also mean "devise." The voice in question, like the woman called into being to explain its existence, is an invention.

But of whom? For simplicity's sake, we assume that the voice in a work is that of the writer (in the case of nonfiction) or one invented by her (in the case of fiction). This assumption describes the relationship between writer (the woman in front of a luminous screen) and persona (whoever you hear speaking to you right now) adequately for most readers. And maybe for most writers, too. Until that earnest student in the second row waves a gnawed pencil over her head and asks, timidly as a rule because hers is the first question, "How did you find your voice?"

As though "you" were a coherent entity already existing at some original point, who had only to open her mouth and agitate her vocal chords—or, to be precise, pick up her fingers and diddle the keys—to call the world she had in mind into being. Not just a writer, an author. But I've examined this process over and over in myself, and the direction of this authorial plot simply doesn't ring true. In the beginning, remember, was the *Word*. Not me. And the question, properly phrased, should probably be asked of my voice: How did you find (devise, invent, contrive) your Nancy?

On the day I was married (actually, a few days beforehand, since I got rather caught up in last-minute preparations), I stopped writing. These two events (one event and one non-event, to be precise) might have been purely coincidental, but I suspect that they weren't. Although thirty years later I can see that that day marked a beginning, which, like a healthy rootstock, has burgeoned over time into beginning after beginning after beginning, I had no such sense then. On that day something came to an end, something I might call my artistic youth.

I was nineteen then, and I had been writing for at least eleven years. And I mean writing: not just dutiful school assignments, though I did plenty of those, but sheaves of poems and short stories scribbled in time stolen from school assignments—the very opposite of dutiful, downright subversive of duty. What was different about married life, I wonder, that made it resistant to subversion of this sort? Or—and I think this is the same question in different guise—what did I think writing was that my married state seemed to debar it?

The facts refute one easy explanation. My husband was not responsible for my silence. As anyone who's read Charlotte Perkins Gilman's story "The Yellow Wallpaper" will recall, some husbands wary of the way artistic endeavor resists control, will suppress it—if not outright then by ignoring, deprecating, even ridiculing it. But George always liked my writing, and he urged me to continue it. In the years since I've established myself as a writer, we've both been happier, in part, I think, because I'm doing what we've both always believed I should be doing. So, although I tend to blame George for everything from lost teaspoons to the colonies of blue mold sprouting at the back of the refrigerator and it would be both convenient and credible to blame him for the nearly fatal consequences to my writing of its collision with marriage, I'll have to look elsewhere.

I had no explicit reason, back in 1963, to believe that a married woman could not be a writer. In fact, my aunt was one—a married woman writer, that is—although the way my grandmother referred to her daughter's poetry and her psychoanalysis in the same shuddering breath was, I'll admit unnerving. Aunt Jane aside, however, I didn't have any particular reason to believe that a married woman could—or should—write more than grocery lists and thank-you notes for the christening presents. In high school I'd had a passion for historical romances, many written by women, but as an English major in college I'd been assigned virtually no works by women, married or otherwise, so women's literacy legitimacy seemed dubious. Both in classes and on my own I'd read plenty of works about women, of course. Most of these women weren't married, though they were generally trying to get that way, and the book ended when they finally made it. Those who were married seemed to have few creative options: They could knit, sometimes with powerful consequences. They could commit adultery, but then they were likely to heave themselves under the wheels of a train or gobble fistfuls of arsenic. Childbirth was all too often fatal. And if they got really out of hand, there was always the attic.

Thus, I encountered few enough figures to suggest how to function happily as a wife, much less a writing wife. But the absence of models was only one strand in an elaborate knot. Another, perhaps even more important, was spun by the need that sent me hurtling into marriage while I was still, in every way, a girl, and here both literature and psychoanalysis are again at least partially implicated. From the age of four on, I had no father. The figurative lack that some believe at once underwrites and undermines human artistic expression was accompanied, in my case, by a more literal hole, a wound even, and I desired, above everything else, to stop it up. Whatever I wrote, I wrote out of that pain, and whatever I wrote assuaged the pain a little but never enough. Everything I saw and read informed me, assured me, that what I needed to fill that void was a man. Maybe it also told me what to do with him, and with our life together, after I got him, but I neglected that part. I just wanted to get him, and plug him in, and ease the pain. Since I had written entirely out of yearning and now I yearned no more, I had neither the motivation nor the material to keep on writing.

Does this sound far-fetched? Probably it does. I'm writing about "pre-feminist" experience in an era that labels itself, more wistfully than accurately, "post-feminist." You'll just have to take my word for it: Once I was married, nothing in my life seemed worth writing about. I was, perhaps, unusually naïve. I favored the surfaces of poems by Sara Teasdale and Edna St. Vincent Millay. I'd been given the *Sonnets from the Portuguese* but never, of course, *Aurora Leigh*. Sylvia Plath was still alive on my wedding day (though not for long thereafter), but I'd never heard of her and didn't read her work for almost a decade. Anne Sexton was still alive, too, but I hadn't heard of her, either. Or of Adrienne Rich. Or of Carolyn Kizer. As a college freshman I did hear May Sarton read, my diary records, but obviously I didn't "hear" her. For some reason (not hard now to fathom, but then I didn't even wonder), the only painting by Georgia O'Keeffe in my art text was of the Brooklyn Bridge, not the secret spaces of shells or bones or flowers. Not one work in my yearlong music course had been composed by a woman.

Maybe if I'd gone to Radcliffe or Smith, my experience would have been different, but my little women's college was playing it safe. A few of the writers and artists we studied were still alive, but they were mostly men, and what they were depicting wasn't going on in my life. Later I got a job as a technical editor, and then I read Carl Sagan on the greenhouse effect on Mars and Venus and Ursula Marvin on the composition of moon rocks, but what they were depicting wasn't going on in my life, either—or anybody else's for that matter. I did read *The Feminine Mystique*, and later *The Golden Notebook*, and later still *The Second Sex*, but for a long time I couldn't (or, I now see, I wouldn't, didn't dare) discern how these might be about me.

Here's what *was* going on in my life after I was married. A final year of college. A brief, unhappy sting of grade-school teaching. The birth of a daughter. A job. An episode of depression so debilitating as to require six months of confinement in a state mental hospital. After my release, the same job for another year. The birth of a son. A different job. Also weekly sessions with a psychiatrist, summer vacations in New Hampshire, season tickets to the Charles Playhouse, occasional concerts by the Chorus Pro Musica and visits to museums and to zoos, increasing involvement in the antiwar movement. Yearnings? Yes, but not the sort I knew how to articulate and none I'd have counted as art if I had been able to speak.

After about eight years, I started committing adultery, and again at long last I had something to write about: sexual arousal masked as a troubled heart, which was more fruitful, I found, than my interminably troubled mind. The poems started coming reliably enough in a number and quality to get me into graduate school. Luckily, I refrained from throwing myself under an MBTA car (the railroads being by this time pretty well defunct) and arsenic in quantity is hard to come by nowadays. All the same, adultery proved increasingly unsatisfactory. For one thing, no matter how discreetly it's handled, it's awfully hard on a marriage. And increasingly I knew myself committed to George and the children. I couldn't have both commitment and independence: not what I meant by commitment, not what I meant by independence. For his own reasons, George never forced—never even asked—me to choose. He let me travel to the point of choice on my own.

I chose him. But did I choose only him? On my wedding day I seemed to have chosen between marriage and writing, not consciously but firmly nonetheless. I believed that choice necessary, and so I suppose it was, even though now I perceive the dilemma as a false one. The choice I made nearly twenty years later—the one to remain actively married rather than frittering away my emotional energies—circumvented the dilemma by breaking my reliance on romance for inspiration. The dilemma was beside the point. I could have both marriage and writing. The price was labor, an awful lot of it: grinding, occasionally wearisome, often scary, and absolutely without end. I had to change my intellectual and aesthetic beliefs about the world and about what I was doing in it, and I had to keep on changing them as the world changed—and I changed in it—forever. The reward: well, who knew?

The fact is that adultery had been hard on more than my marriage. It was fixing me in amber. The golden aromatic resin was thickening. I could feel its sticky pressure in my nostrils, down my throat. I was sucked in by love and loss. I had to get out. But how? What else could rouse me to write? What else did I know? *There were the babies, and the blood, the way bread yields and sighs like flesh under your fist, the death of the little dog, so sudden, unlooked for, and the way your tears choked you as you folded him into the pillowcase and heaped dirt over the linen, and then too your body, its betrayal sudden also but its diminishment protracted so that grief, you learn, will actually never end, and the babies gone, and soon the blood as well.* These were the sorts of things I knew, or was learning, and so I tried some of them out on the guys (it was just them and me that year) in a poetry workshop. "Yech," they said.

And kept on saying. That was a bad time for me, alone with the guys, who knew what writing was because they were doing it, who knew that what I was doing, to the extent that they weren't doing it, wasn't writing, not the real thing (muscular, tough-minded, penetrating, gritty), and who didn't mind telling me so. One or another has gone on telling me so ever since. "Stop squandering your time on this feminist stuff," Edward Abbey told me for years. And after he died, a reviewer for the *New York Times* caught up the tune before it faded away: "a waste of a 'talented voice,'" he wrote. I don't think any man has ever suggested I give up writing. It's just that a lot of them want me to write something *else*. (My mother does too, by the way, so I'm using the word *man* pretty loosely.)

Whether some of us like it or not, men (in the loose sense of the world) have determined and continue to dominate our culture, and that still (though who knows for how long) includes the arts. It's been men senators ranting about queer photographers and crucifixes in piss and the need to protect the taxpayers' hard-earned pennies from being squandered on obscenities (environmental degradation and the deaths of people with brown or red or yellow or black skin being something other than obscene). It was a man director of the National Endowment for the Arts who, lashed by the senators' tongues, scurried around demanding pledges of sanitation before doling out his meager funds. Women (white heterosexual middle-class educated ones, anyway) may more frequently succeed at grabbing men's goodies—the directorship of the National Endowment for the Arts among them—and call themselves post-feminist when they do, but these are still men's goodies and will be as long as men determine what they are, what you must believe and do in order to get them, and what they're worth.

As the feminist theologian Rosemary Radford Ruether points out, "It is almost impossible for an individual alone to dissent from this culture. Alternative cultures and communities must be built up to support the dissenting consciousness." If I'd been trapped forever by some evil genie in that poetry workshop with all those guys doing the polite equivalent of sticking their fingers down their throats in response to my writing, I can't imagine what would have become of me, but it might have warranted my enshrinement as the tragic heroine of some "real" work of art, along the lines of Hedda Gabler, maybe, or Blanche DuBois. As luck would have it, however, I found myself in another poetry workshop altogether, gathered under the pear trees outside a very old farmhouse in New Hampshire on summer Mondays, listening to, reflecting upon, discussing, and celebrating the poems of a small but diverse group of women.

And when (around the time I began my doctoral work) my poems began to turn to essays about a woman's life, the life of a woman's body, the life of a crippled woman's body, no one at Skimmilk Farm moved to banish me from the Monday workshop. In the ivory phallus, I had found, where poets hardly speak even to fiction writers (let alone to essayists, literary critics, and the like), the genres are like armed camps, and transgressing their boundaries can result in swift expulsion. If I'd started reading an essay in my poetry workshop there, I'd have been cut off and told to register for the nonfiction workshop meeting down the hall. At the Farm, the women simply listened to my essays very hard and laughed in all the right places. Although I have not seen many of them for years now, I still think of them as my audience. They, and all the others like them whom I've never met, are the ones I write for.

And really, what more can we—as writers, as artists, as human beings—do for one another? In the middle of a sentence I'm having trouble with, when my attention strays and I find myself cringing in anticipation of the next inevitable *yech* (and I do cringe; old habits die hard), I say: Let the masters of the written word cling to their bodiless principles. Let them pronounce what is interesting and what is not, what is a poem and what is not, what merits their grudging praise and what does not. For myself, I want another model. I want to hear *this* poem by *this* person on *this* muggy August morning under the pear trees. I want to know what it is doing in the life of her work, and in my life as well. I want to give her the courage to say the next hard thing, without fear of ridicule or expulsion if she strays across the borders of good taste, good sense, or good judgment demarcated by a tradition she has had no part in forming. I want her to do the same for me.

This is what we can *all* do to nourish and strengthen one another: listen to one another very hard, ask hard questions, too, send one another away to work again, and laugh in all the right places.

■ 2. The Groves of Academe

In fact, the autobiographical pitch and timbre distinguishing this voice that utters me developed unconsciously but not spontaneously during the years after finding community under the pear trees, when, as a doctoral student, I began at last to attend seriously to the words and intonations of women as women. I found my writing voice, and go on finding it, in precisely the same way that I came to my first utterances: by listening to the voices around me, imitating them, then piping up on my own—timidly at first, making plenty of mistakes, being corrected, correcting myself, listening some more....

Up until this point, my writing had been rooted in fertile but decidedly uneven emotional ground, and now I began to tap intellectual sources instead. No, that implicit split between ardor and intellect is the very opposite of what I mean: ideas now erupted into and became indistinguishable from my emotional and even my corporeal life. I could feel them in my flesh, quickening my breath, itching my fingers, spilling out through the nib of the black Parker fountain pen my husband gave me as an anniversary present appropriate to a writing wife. I can trace this development—as I entered, inhabited, and then slipped out of the academy—from my earliest attempts at articulating a deliberating, if sometimes falteringly, feminist vision onward: a kind of archaeology of voice.

By the time I established myself as a doctoral student in English literature with a particular interest in works by women, I was pushing forty. I'm no longer sure why I started to work on a doctorate—and probably never was. I certainly didn't burn with ambition either to "get" or to "be" a PhD. I'd come to like the classroom, however, and the Catholic high school where I'd been teaching after I finished my MFA fired me. I lacked credentials for the public schools, which I could acquire while I worked on a PhD in English education, teaching freshman composition in the bargain. The fact that I happen to like teaching freshman composition, both because I believe it to be the most important course in the university curriculum and because I feel an inarticulate passion for the mute helplessness of freshmen, signaled my unsuitability for doctoral work (no true scholar would so abase himself), but fortunately no one took it seriously.

By 1979, I'd completed the course work for a PhD in English education, all but the required course in advanced sadistics. Then, after a summer of those workshops at Skimmilk Farm, where I also devoured a shelf of books by Virginia Woolf, I returned to Tucson with permission to speak.

I came to feminism in my characteristic fashion—late. Trailing a good decade or more behind the vanguard of feminist scholars, I discovered women writers and began writing a woman's life myself. While other women had been, rumor had it, burning their bras, I was still strapping myself into mine, even though my breasts are so small that it routinely rode up and threatened to strangle me. Arriving in Tucson on an August morning when the temperature was a hundred three in the shade, I stripped it off. (My conversions, like all my acts, are experientially rather than theoretically grounded. I didn't object to my bra on principle; I just couldn't stand the grip of wet elastic around my neck.)

Similarly, although I wasn't entirely unaware of feminist issues, I could never quite see how they applied to my life and, thus, why I should act on them. And in truth, for a number of reasons, they may have impinged on me less than on some others. I had spent my formative years in a household of self-sufficient women: my grandmother, divorced long before my birth, supported herself as a bank teller, and my widowed mother worked as a school secretary until her remarriage when I was eleven. I attended a college where even in those pre-feminist days female competence was taken for granted under the stage lights, in the chemistry lab, on the hockey field, and definitely at the bridge table. My husband took part in running our household and rearing our children without the fuss and fanfare that many men make to call attention, like toddlers assisting Mommy, to their "helpfulness."

Small wonder, perhaps, that such privileged circumstances had obscured other women's pain, not to mention my own. For I had been, in spite of my good fortune, inexplicably and often bitterly unhappy for reasons that feminist readings of my experience were at last enabling me to scrutinize and then even to manage. In the spring semester of 1980, I entered my first explicitly feminist gathering; a graduate seminar entitled "Women As Sign."

The setting turned out to be extraordinary because the professor, having lost one baby and in danger of losing another, was put to bed just a week or so into the semester, and instead of canceling the course or turning it over to someone else, she moved it to her home. Every week, then, in place of the plastic and fluorescence to which we'd grown inured, we gathered in an airy space around Susan's couch: a dozen or so women, one (rather brave, as I think on it) man, and Alden, humping up higher and rounder each week, her mute presence bespeaking the knowledges our books and seminar papers refused us until, just a couple of weeks before the semester's end, she showed up in tiny but thriving person to set a kind of seal on the proceedings.

In this company, embarrassed by my stunted growth, wary, curious, and curiously afraid, I began to learn to read again and to try my hand at formal feminist criticism, straining after a tone of subtle irony. (Subtlety struck me as a great virtue in those days: I didn't want to mark myself as ingenuous by explaining some point that everyone who knew anything took for granted. But I couldn't figure out just what "everyone" knew, except that it was obviously more than I did. I still can't, and it still is, for I forgive myself for bafflement more readily now.) This voice—arch and insiderly—was not my own.

In the same semester that the "Woman As Sign" seminar awaited Alden Carroll's arrival, a departure yanked me into another opportunity for growth. I admire people who leap into larger selves with the élan of sky divers entering the ether, but I grow only if yanked, I'm afraid, and then only under protest. In this case, my reluctance was born as much of sadness as of timidity. I had known and admired Sally Perper for eight years, since first coming to the University of Arizona, and when pancreatic cancer forced her to give up teaching just days before the spring 1980 semester began, I assumed her "Composition Through Literature" without the joy I'd have felt otherwise at being permitted to teach the course.

Today I remember with pleasure every detail about that class except for a model I wrote to prepare my students for their major assignment, a documented essay about a literary work of their own choosing. The structure of my piece was clear, the ideas were accessible, and the mechanics of documentation were correct, but the tone was all wrong, designed to baffle and discomfit the ordinary reader. Bafflement and discomfiture are much the point, if not quite the whole to it, in the academy. The Haves and Have Nots of general society are paralleled there by the Knows and Know Nots. The same principle of exclusion operates, but on a linguistic rather than a material basis. To belong you need a word hoard, as the Anglo-Saxons would say: linguistic currency, in both senses of the phrase. Unfortunately, thanks to inflation, deflation, and the frequent replacement of one monetary system by another—now cowry shells, now coins, now Coleman lanterns—it can be pretty hard to figure out your worth. My use of words like "mythopoetic" obviously reflected considerable anxiety about my position. Not that "mythopoetic" isn't a perfectly good word. Not that I wouldn't still use it if I needed it. Just that the nature of that need has changed, and I would no longer risk replicating that earlier, edgy, spurious need in my students.

Not until my preliminary doctoral examination did I begin, by treating literary insight as a variety of personal experience, to hear a voice I might "own," although the emotional din of the occasion threatened to drown out those peepings. The fact that shifting to the PhD program in English literature prolonged my course of study had suited me. I was a happy student, a happy teacher, and, thanks to the chronic progressive nature of my multiple sclerosis, I was almost wholly without professional purpose. The future for which my classmates were preparing themselves diligently, yearningly—freedom from freshmen, publication in PMLA, sabbaticals at the Bodleian or in Tuscany, promotion to a full professorship, maybe even an endowed chair—was closing to me. Why hurry toward my own obscurer fate? The university had anticipated hangers-on, however, with a system of regulations designed to purge itself automatically of such indigestible bits if they failed to eliminate themselves voluntarily. My end was in view.

That it couldn't be reached except by examination isn't surprising, given that an academic degree attests to capabilities, one might even say powers, jealously guarded by those who possess them already. The difference between an academic degree and a driver's license, say, or a medical technician's certificate is that at least some academic powers may have no practical consequences, may not even manifest themselves in any quantifiable manner, and so may seem mysterious, elusive, ineffable, transcendent—an awful lot like gods. Testing godlikeness—as opposed to determining whether a person understands the meaning of an octagonal road sign or can clip a needle neatly into a vein—can be a bit tricky: the results tend to be so mixed. But preliminary doctoral examinations purport to do so.

I did not understand then, and I still do not, what of value this system was believed to reveal. Memory? If a PhD attests to the holder's capacity to retain and retrieve information without resorting to sources, then I oughtn't to have one, I can't even remember how to spell "weird" without looking it up, much less retrace Leopold Bloom's progress through Dublin—or even Clarissa Dalloway's through London, to which I feel far closer—without returning to *Ulysses* or *Mrs. Dalloway*. If not memory, perhaps writing skill? But no matter how substantial, clearly organized, and charmingly expressed a little essay I might whip up in three hours, I would always, always do better in, say, three days, and I suspect everyone else would, too. Grace under pressure? This could indeed be a valuable quality in some circumstances, but not those likely to be encountered by a professor of literature, who can always say, if asked a question he can't answer, "I don't know. Give me a day or so to think about it."

I once heard a professor challenged by a group of graduate students to defend the examination system, blurt, "Well, I had to go through it, and so should you." There's the real reason, I suspect. Examinations visit the misery of one generation on the next—the scholarly equivalent of hazing. They invited students to exhibit work that, produced under adverse circumstances involving anxiety, lack of resources, limited time, and mental and physical exhaustion, falls short of their best, and they force students to accept judgments based on that hastily conceived and frantically scribbled or uttered work. Meditation, reflection, revision—the essential elements of solid intellectual production—are deliberately debarred.

I remember walking out of my oral prelims to find my husband waiting, a bottle of Drambuie hidden in a paper bag for a toast.

"How did it go?" he asked.

"I passed!" I told him, and burst into tears. As a younger woman, I'd believed that opening oneself up to experience—all experience—offered the greatest opportunity for intellectual and spiritual growth. Now, suddenly, I saw that there are some experiences one simply ought never to have, and prelims constituted such an experience for me. Over time, my humiliation—my sense of having been required to present myself in a compromised light I would never have chosen, any more than I'd have chosen to strip my misshapen body to its skin, even less—faded, of course. But a sliver of grief remains lodged near my heart.

I was surprised, then, rereading years later the essays written for the exam, that their tone hardly sounds bleak or distressed. On the contrary, the voice is breathless with excitement, with exertion, with laughter, but not with anxiety. This woman sounds like she's having as good a time as I always do when the world drops away and I am left alone with language. Listening to her, I am carried back to a little room with one high window where I hunch intently at a grey metal desk under florescent flicker, sucking at cigarettes and red cans of Coke, pushing my fountain pen across sheet after sheet of yellow legal-size paper ... and sure enough, I'm having a wonderful time.

"Self. Life. Writing. Self-life-writing. Selflifewriting," the first essay of my prelims began.

> "Autobiography. ... a particular kind of writing, writing about a real life, one that really (maybe) happened (when?). ... At once easier and harder to write than biography—easier because the writer doesn't have to do a whole lot of research except in the archives of memory, which stay open longer hours than many of us would wish, and because she's automatically an authority, whose mistakes (if she's caught) will be forgiven as slips of memory, not excoriated as sloppy research, and because, as at once the writer and the subject, she doesn't risk the confusion of identity biographers sometimes experience; harder because ... Well, think of the pain; think of the responsibility.

Out of this half-humorous tumble of words rang my own voice. Not romantic anguish, not guy talk, not muteness or critical bombast masking intellectual cowardice, though I had learned from trying on each of those rejected styles. I would speak plainly out of my own experience, to an audience I liked and trusted, about a woman's life, making it up as I went along. I was on my way to nowhere in particular and in no hurry to get there. I would poke into the byways, much as George and I would later meander through the Cotswolds despite the tuts and stifled groans of my stepfather in the rear seat, for whom getting lost clearly did not constitute a lark. I would take my time. I would sometimes feel pained and burdened by the processes of self-creation/-discovery/-revelation, but I would also laugh out loud more than I could have anticipated, and others, weeping and laughing along with me, would provide consolation. I might *work* alone but I would never *be* alone, not as long as I could call out and muse on a response. "I" would be I.

My reward such as it might be: my voice's Nancy.

◼ Notes

[1] For we (mis)speak only out of irredeemable loss—loss of the infantile "imaginary harmony with the mother and the world," in the words of Toril Moi (*Sexual/Textual Politics: Feminist Literary Theory* [London and New York: Routledge, 1988] p. 101).

[2] Rosemary Radford Ruether, *Disputed Questions: On Being a Christian* (New York: Orbis Books, 1989), p. 128.

◼ READING AND WRITING

1. How does Mairs define "voice"? Where in her text do you see her definition come together?
2. Is this a feminist text? Point to specific elements of and passages in the text to support and explain your response.
3. How does Mairs make her very personal story speak to others? How does she make it larger than herself and her own life?

◼ USING RESEARCH

4. Use the resources available through the library and the internet to find another woman writing about being a woman writer. How does this text compare with Mairs'? Think about the central ideas in each text, the style of each, and the rhetorical choices the authors make. Which do you find to be more compelling? Why?

Charles Hirshberg is a journalist and author whose work has appeared in The Washington Post, The Los Angeles Times, *and* Life *magazine, and who has written three books about popular music. The following essay was first published in May 2002 in* Popular Science *and later collected in* The Best American Science and Nature Writing, 2003.

MY MOTHER, THE SCIENTIST Charles Hirshberg

In 1966, Mrs. Weddle's first grade class at Las Lomitas Elementary School got its first homework assignment: We were to find out what our fathers did for a living, then come back and tell the class. The next day, as my well-scrubbed classmates boasted about their fathers, I was nervous. For one thing, I was afraid of Mrs. Weddle: I realize now that she was probably harmless, but to a shy, elf-size, nervous little guy she looked like a monstrous, talking baked potato. On top of that, I had a surprise in store, and I wasn't sure how it would be received.

"My daddy is a scientist," I said, and Mrs. Weddle turned to write this information on the blackboard. Then I dropped the bomb: "And my mommy is a scientist!"

Twenty-five pairs of first-grade eyes drew a bead on me, wondering what the hell I was talking about. It was then that I began to understand how unusual my mother was.

Today, after more than four decades of geophysical research, my mother, Joan Feynman, is getting ready to retire as a senior scientist at NASA's Jet Propulsion Laboratory. She is probably best known for developing a statistical model to calculate the number of high-energy particles likely to hit a spacecraft over its lifetime, and for her method of predicting sun spot cycles. Both are used by scientists worldwide. Beyond this, however, my mother's career illustrates the enormous change in how America regards what was, only a few decades ago, extremely rare: a scientist who's a woman and also a mother.

To become a scientist is hard enough. But to become one while running a gauntlet of lies, insults, mockeries, and disapproval—this was what my mother had to do. If such treatment is unthinkable (or, at least, unusual) today, it is largely because my mother and other female scientists of her generation proved equal to every obstacle thrown in their way.

My introduction to chemistry came in 1970, on a day when my mom was baking challah bread for the Jewish New Year. I was about 10, and though I felt cooking was unmanly for a guy who played shortstop for Village Host Pizza in the Menlo Park, California, Little League, she had persuaded me to help. When the bread was in the oven, she gave me a plastic pill bottle and a cork. She told me to sprinkle a little baking soda into the bottle, then a little vinegar, and cork the bottle as fast as I could. There followed a violent and completely unexpected pop as the cork flew off and walloped me in the forehead. Exploding food: I was ecstatic! "That's called a chemical reaction," she said, rubbing my shirt clean. "The vinegar is an acid and the soda is a base, and that's what happens when you mix the two."

After that, I never understood what other kids meant when they said that science was boring.

One of my mother's earliest memories is of standing in her crib at the age of about 2, yanking on her 11-year-old brother's hair. This brother, her only sibling, was none other than Richard Feynman, destined to become one of the greatest theoretical physicists of his generation: enfant terrible of the Manhattan Project, pioneer of quantum electrodynamics, father of nanotechnology, winner of the Nobel Prize, and so on. At the time, he was training his sister to solve simple math problems and rewarding each correct answer by letting her tug on his hair while he made faces. When he wasn't doing that, he was often seen wandering around Far Rockaway, New York, with a screwdriver in his pocket, repairing radios—at age 11, mind you.

My mother worshipped her brother, and there was never any doubt about what he would become. By the time she was 5, Richard had hired her for 2 cents a week to assist him in the electronics lab he'd built in his room. "My job was to throw certain switches on command," she recalls. "I had to climb up on a box to reach them. Also, sometimes I'd stick my finger in a spark gap for the edification of his friends." At night, when she called out for a glass of water, Riddy, as he was called, would demonstrate centrifugal force by whirling it around in the air so that the glass was upside down during part of the arc. "Until, one night," my mother recalls, "the glass slipped out of his hand and flew across the room."

Richard explained the miraculous fact that the family dog, the waffle iron, and Joan herself were all made out of atoms. He would run her hand over the corner of a picture frame, describe a right triangle and make her repeat that the sum of the square of the sides was equal to the square of the hypotenuse. "I had no idea what it meant," she says, "but he recited it like a poem, so I loved to recite it too." One night, he roused her from her bed and led her outside, down the street, and onto a nearby golf course. He pointed out washes of magnificent light that were streaking across the sky. It was the aurora borealis. My mother had discovered her destiny.

That is when the trouble started. Her mother, Lucille Feynman, was a sophisticated and compassionate woman who had marched for women's suffrage in her youth. Nonetheless, when 8-year-old Joanie announced that she intended to be a scientist, Grandma explained that it was impossible. "Women can't do science," she said, "because their brains can't understand enough of it." My mother climbed into a living room chair and sobbed into the cushion. "I know she thought she was telling me the inescapable truth. But it was devastating for a little girl to be told that all of her dreams were impossible. And I've doubted my abilities ever since."

The fact that the greatest chemist of the age, Marie Curie, was a woman gave no comfort. "To me, Madame Curie was a mythological character," my mother says, "not a real person whom you could strive to emulate." It wasn't until her 14th birthday—March 31, 1942—that her notion of becoming a scientist was revived. Richard presented her with a book called *Astronomy*. "It was a college textbook. I'd start reading it, get stuck, and then start over again. This went on for months, but I kept at it. When I reached page 407,

I came across a graph that changed my life." My mother shuts her eyes and recites from memory: "'Relative strengths of the Mg+ absorption line at 4,481 angstroms ... from *Stellar Atmospheres* by Cecilia Payne.' Cecilia Payne! It was scientific proof that a woman was capable of writing a book that, in turn, was quoted in a text. The secret was out, you see."

My mother taught me about resonances when I was about 12. We were on a camping trip and needed wood for a fire. My brother and sister and I looked everywhere, without luck. Mom spotted a dead branch up in a tree. She walked up to the trunk and gave it a shake. "Look closely," she told us, pointing up at the branches. "Each branch waves at a different frequency." We could see that she was right. So what? "Watch the dead branch," she went on. "If we shake the tree trunk in just the right rhythm, we can match its frequency and it'll drop off." Soon we were roasting marshmallows.

The catalog of abuse to which my mother was subjected, beginning in 1944 when she entered Oberlin College, is too long and relentless to fully record. At Oberlin, her lab partner was ill-prepared for the advanced-level physics course in which they were enrolled, so my mother did all the experiments herself. The partner took copious notes and received an A. My mother got a D. "He understands what he's doing," the lab instructor explained, "and you don't." In graduate school, a professor of solid state physics advised her to do her Ph.D. dissertation on cobwebs, because she would encounter them while cleaning. She did not take the advice; her thesis was titled "Absorption of infrared radiation in crystals of diamond-type lattice structure." After graduation, she found that the "Situations Wanted" section of The New York Times was divided between Men and Women, and she could not place an ad among the men, the only place anyone needing a research scientist would bother to look.

At that time, even the dean of women at Columbia University argued that "sensible motherhood" was "the most useful and satisfying of the jobs that women can do." My mother tried to be a sensible mother and it damn near killed her. For three years, she cooked, cleaned, and looked after my brother and me, two stubborn and voluble babies.

One day in 1964 she found herself preparing to hurl the dish drain through the kitchen window and decided to get professional help. "I was incredibly lucky," she remembers, "to find a shrink who was enlightened enough to urge me to try to get a job. I didn't think anyone would hire me, but I did what he told me to do." She applied to Lamont-Doherty Observatory and, to her astonishment, received three offers. She chose to work part-time, studying the relationship between the solar wind and the magnetosphere. Soon she would be among the first to announce that the magnetosphere—the part of space in which Earth's magnetic field dominates and the solar wind doesn't enter—was open-ended, with a tail on one side, rather than having a closed-teardrop shape, as had been widely believed. She was off and running.

My mother introduced me to physics when I was about 14. I was crazy about bluegrass music, and learned that Ralph Stanley was coming to town with his Clinch Mountain Boys. Although Mom did not share my taste for hillbilly music, she agreed to take me. The highlight turned out to be fiddler Curly Ray Cline's version of "Orange Blossom Special," a barn burner in which the fiddle imitates the sound of an approaching and departing train. My mother stood and danced a buck-and-wing and when, to my great relief, she sat down, she said, "Great tune, huh? It's based on the Doppler effect." This is not the sort of thing one expects to hear in reference to Curly Ray Cline's repertoire. Later, over onion rings at the Rockybilt Cafe, she explained: "When the train is coming, its sound is shifting to higher frequencies. And when the train is leaving, its sound is shifting to lower frequencies. That's called the Doppler shift. You can see the same thing when you look at a star: if the light source is moving toward you, it shifts toward blue; if it's moving away, it shifts toward red. Most stars shift toward red because the universe is expanding."

I cannot pretend that, as a boy, I liked everything about having a scientist for a mother. When I saw the likes of Mrs. Brady on TV, I sometimes wished I had what I thought of as a mom with an apron. And then, abruptly, I got one.

It was 1971 and my mother was working for NASA at Ames Research Center in California. She had just made an important discovery concerning the solar wind, which has two states, steady and transient. The latter consists of puffs of material, also known as coronal mass ejections, which, though long known about, were notoriously hard to find. My mother showed they could be recognized by the large amount of helium in the solar wind. Her career was flourishing. But the economy was in recession and NASA's budget was slashed. My mother was a housewife again. For months, as she looked for work, the severe depression that had haunted her years before began to return.

Mom had been taught to turn to the synagogue in times of trouble, and it seemed to make especially good sense in this case, because our synagogue had more scientists in it than most Ivy League universities. Our rabbi, a celebrated civil rights activist, was arranging networking parties for unemployed eggheads. But when my mother asked for an invitation to one of these affairs, he accused her of being selfish. "After all-there are men out of work just now."

"But Rabbi," she said, "it's my life."

I remember her coming home that night, stuffing food into the refrigerator, then pulling out the vacuum cleaner. She switched it on, pushed it back and forth across the floor a few times, then switched it off and burst into tears. In a moment, I was crying too and my mother was comforting me. We sat there a long time.

"I know you want me here," she told me. "But I can either be a part-time mama, or a full-time madwoman."

A few months later, Mom was hired as a research scientist at the National Center for Atmospheric Research, and we moved to Boulder, Colorado. From then on, she decided to "follow research funding around the country, like Laplanders follow the reindeer herds." She followed it to Washington, D.C., to work for the National Science Foundation, then to the Boston College Department of Physics, and finally, in 1985, to JPL, where she's been ever since. Along the way, she unlocked some of the mysteries of the aurora. Using data from Explorer 33, she showed that auroras occur when the magnetic field of the solar wind interacts with the magnetic field of the Earth.

In 1974, she became an officer of her professional association, the American Geophysical Union, and spearheaded a committee to ensure that women in her field would be treated fairly. She was named one of JPL's elite senior scientists in 1999 and the following year was awarded NASA's Exceptional Scientific Achievement Medal.

Soon she'll retire, except that retirement as my mother the scientist envisions it means embarking on a new project: comparing recent changes in Earth's climate with historic ones. "It's a pretty important subject when you consider that even a small change in the solar output could conceivably turn Long Island into a skating rink—just like it was some 10,000 years ago."

The first thing I did when I came home from Mrs. Weddle's class that day in 1966 was to ask my mother what my father did. She told me that he was a scientist, and that she was a scientist too. I asked what a scientist was, and she handed me a spoon. "Drop it on the table," she said. I let it fall to the floor. "Why did it fall?" she asked. "Why didn't it float up to the ceiling?" It had never occurred to me that there was a "why" involved. "Because of gravity," she said. "A spoon will always fall, a hot-air balloon will always rise." I dropped the spoon again and again until she made me stop. I had no idea what gravity was, but the idea of "Why?" kept rattling around in my head. That's when I made the decision: the next day, in school, I wouldn't just tell them what my father did. I'd tell them about my mother too.

■ READING AND WRITING

1. "To become a scientist is hard enough," Hirshberg writes. "But to become one while running a gauntlet of lies, insults, mockeries, and disapproval—this was what my mother had to do." How does Hirshberg use his mother's story to compose an argument about gender? What is his claim?
2. Reread the italicized sections of the essay. What does Hirshberg achieve by setting these sections apart from the rest of the narrative? How do these sections support his argument?
3. How would you characterize Hirshberg's ethos? How does he convey this ethos to his audience?

■ DEVELOPING LONGER RESPONSES

4. Hirshberg, Shirin Ebadi, and Nancy Mairs all write about women and their work. All three pieces are memoirs, though Mairs and Ebadi tell their own stories while Hirshberg tells his mother's. After reading each of these texts, write a brief essay in which you explain the rhetorical advantages and disadvantages of using memoir to present an argument.

Shirin Ebadi, a lawyer and activist, won the Nobel Peace Price in 2003 for her efforts to promote democracy and human rights in Iran, especially for her focus on the rights of women and children. The Washington Post *called her 2006 book* Iran Awakening: A Memoir of Revolution and Hope *"a riveting account of a brave, lonely struggle to take Islamist jurists to task for betraying the promises of their own revolution" in Iran. "From the Living Room to the Courtroom," a chapter from that memoir, vividly recounts her struggle and the victims of injustice Ebadi risked her career and her safety to help.*

FROM THE LIVING ROOM TO THE COURTROOM   Shirin Ebadi, with Azadeh Moaveni

Leila Fathi disappeared one sunny day in the summer of 1996 while picking wildflowers in the hills behind her village, near the northwestern Kurdish city of Sanandaj. Her parents, like many in the region, struggled to get by, and eleven-year-old Leila was collecting the wild plants and flowers the family would then dry and sell in the local bazaar. She and her cousin had set out with their woven baskets in the late morning and had interrupted their picking to play among the tall grasses. Growing up near Sanandaj, where people picnicked outdoors, held weddings under the open sky, and danced alongside the riverbanks, they ran about as though the hills were an extension of their tiny living room, with nothing like the intuitive watchfulness of urban children. Bent over filling her skirt with petals, Leila didn't notice the three men approaching. They emerged from the back side of the hill, moving quietly until they were almost atop her, and then closed in swiftly. One twisted her thin arms behind her back, while another tried to clasp her thrashing legs together. Her cousin managed to escape, and he hid behind a tree, watching the men drag a fighting, kicking Leila over to a slope. He watched them tear off her peasant skirt and rape her, strike a fatal blow to her head, and then hurl her battered body over a cliff in the craggy hillside.

The local police arrested the three men, but after the prime suspect confessed to the crime, he mysteriously hung himself in prison. Odd that in a prison where inmates are not even allowed to wear watches, he had conveniently found a meter of braided rope, just the length for hanging. The other two suspects denied complicity, but the court found them guilty of rape and sentenced them to death.

I mentioned earlier that under the Islamic penal code instituted after the revolution, a man's life is worth twice that of a woman. In most Islamic countries, laws determining compensation apply only in financial cases, such as inheritance. The Islamic Republic, however, applies compensation, or "blood money" provisions, in criminal cases. Under Islamic law, the family of a victim of homicide or manslaughter has the right to choose between legal punishment and financial compensation, referred to as blood money. Many Islamic scholars hold that blood money should be blind to gender, but Iran practices a discriminatory interpretation. Under the Iranian code, the worth of a woman's life equals half of a man's, a point that often leads to grotesque legal judgments that effectively punish the victim. In this instance, the judge ruled that the "blood money" for the two men was worth more than the life of the murdered nine-year-old girl, and he demanded that her family come up with thousands of dollars to finance their executions.

Leila's father sold all of his few worldly possessions, including the little clay hut where his family slept. Homeless but convinced that they would at least reclaim their honor, they offered the money to the court. It was not enough. The family took to sleeping at the shrine of Ayatollah Khomeini, a vast mausoleum on the road to Qom, while trying to raise the remaining cash. First Leila's father volunteered to sell a kidney, but his organ was rejected because of his past drug abuse. Next Leila's brother offered his up, but the doctor refused because he was handicapped by polio. "Why," asked the doctor, "are you two so insistent on selling your kidneys?" Out poured the tale. They could not return to their village, they explained, stained by the shame of Leila's rape. Family honor rests on the virtue of women, and nothing less than the perpetrators' execution could erase their shame.

Horrified by this bizarre tale, the doctor wrote to the head of the judiciary and threatened to report the case to an international organization, Doctors Without Borders, unless the state treasury made up the difference needed for the execution. The judiciary chief agreed, but in a further unbelievable twist, just days before the scheduled execution one of the convicts escaped from prison, and, in the meantime, Leila's disconsolate family had erected a ramshackle cloth tent on the sidewalk outside the courthouse. The family was shocked to learn that the court had reopened the case. Perhaps it was because the ambiguities inherent in the Iranian legal system mean that even a closed case always remains subject to further review. Perhaps, as Leila's family claimed, it was because one of the accused used a relative, a conservative member of parliament to influence the outcome. The case was unraveling.

It was at this point that I heard about the case and decided to take a look at the file. At first I was skeptical. Criminal justice in the post-revolutionary legal system was flawed; it denied female victims of violence equal restitution. But the case of Leila's family suggested that it was effectively pathological, capable of destroying the livelihoods of those who petitioned for justice on behalf of their victimized loved ones. I paid a visit to the family at their tent outside the courthouse, and after listening to their account of the long, sordid tale, I agreed to represent them.

The outlines of the case were stark, and I constructed a simple, elegant defense: it was unjust for a girl to be raped and killed, and for her family to have lost every possession and become homeless through the legal proceedings that followed; it was unjust that the victims were now being victimized further by the law. "Do not criticize Islamic law," the judge sternly warned me in court. "I'm only asking if justice has been served," I retorted.

As the session neared its close, someone whispered in my ear that Leila's brothers had concealed kitchen knives in their coats and were planning to attack the remaining defendant as he left the court. I asked for a recess and called the boys out into the hall.

"Please," I said, "please give me a chance to see what I can do in court first."

Both of them sat on a bench and wept. "If we had paid a professional assassin *half* of what we paid the court," one of them cried, "Justice would have been carried out. Now we're homeless, while one of them is free and the other is about to walk."

"I know," I whispered. "I know. But let's try."

Over the course of the proceedings, the court acquitted both defendants, overturned the acquittals, and then relaunched the investigation. The family's grief slowly descended into madness. Leila's mother took to sitting outside the courthouse in a white funeral shroud, holding a placard that described her daughter's violation. During one trial, she threatened to set herself on fire, and began screaming profanities at the court. As though the whole proceeding was not dramatic enough, the judge held her in contempt of court and filed legal charges against her that took us weeks of mediation to settle.

It would tire your patience if I detailed the legal proceedings any further, but suffice it to say that the case was not resolved, and remains open to this day. I did not succeed in getting the legal system to mete out anything approximating justice, but I do think we accomplished something else: we made a national showcase of the flaws in Iranian law concerning the rights of women and children. The case swiftly turned into a public issue, so much so that candidates in Leila's province ran on platforms that included stances on her case. The Iranian press took on Leila's story as an egregious illustration of the social problems of the Islamic Republic.

The trial reverberated long after the final court session. It played itself out in the newspapers as well as the courtroom, and the publicity established my reputation as a lawyer whose work focused on the rights of women and children. I learned very quickly that one of the most powerful tools at the disposal of the legally powerless was the media. My prominence in turn made me more effective at defending my clients, because the judge knew that both he and the judiciary would be forced to justify their decision in the court of public opinion. Oftentimes they simply did not care, but at those times I reminded myself that raising people's awareness of their rights was in itself a contribution.

In the course of the dark months when I watched Leila's family fall apart in despair, as the case garnered more attention, I was struck by how few women even knew that the legal system discriminated against them so severely. Most women had some sense of the laws governing child custody and divorce, because at some point exiting a marriage occurs to many. But by and large, murder or accidental death did not touch the lives of the majority of women; they had no occasion to hear or learn about what sort of fate might lay in store for them, what sort of legal morass awaited them, should they be so unlucky as to have an incident like Leila's befall their family.

I decided to write an article for the magazine *Iran-t Farda*, in approachable language, rather than in an overly intellectual or legalistic style, that would set out in stark terms women's inferior status in the penal code. The section of the code devoted to blood money, *diyeh*, holds that if a man suffers an injury that damages his testicles, he is entitled to compensation equal to a woman's life. I put it this way in my article: if a professional woman with a PhD is run over in the street and killed and an illiterate thug gets one of his testicles injured in a fight, the value of her life and his damaged testicle are equal. There is a vulgar expression in Persian that conveys deep contempt for someone "You're not even worth one of my testicles." I politely invoked this in my article, to explain in terms no Iranian could mistake just how outrageous these laws were, how they treated women as non-people. In the end I posed a question: Is this really how the Islamic Republic regards its women?

The article both titillated and electrified literate Tehran. The editor had published it eagerly, aware that it would, like much of the magazine's content, provoke the hard-line judiciary. The issue sold out immediately, and people showed up at the magazine's offices, begging for even a photocopy of the article. I was stunned. I had expected that it might circulate widely, but I'd never thought it would resound this way throughout the city. A hard-line member of parliament threatened me publicly, telling reporters, "Someone stop this woman, or we'll shut her up ourselves." When I heard this, I realized for the first time that the system might actually fear me and the growing public resonance with my work.

In 1996, the year Leila's case went to court, the Islamic regime tolerated little criticism of its repressive ways. The suppression of political dissent had mellowed some from the early, brutal days of the revolution, when the papers were full of the photos and names of the summarily executed, but the system still punished any perceived challenge to its authority severely. We lived with daily examples of even prominent grand ayatollahs who had been defrocked (unheard of in Shia Islam) or placed under house arrest for speaking out against executions and harsh forms of criminal punishment, such as the chopping off of hands. If the system was willing to disgrace and effectively imprison distinguished senior theologians who had participated actively in the revolution, why should it hesitate for a moment in punishing me, a nonrevolutionary, a non-cleric, and, as a woman, a nonperson?

I was nervous. While I was arguing Leila's case, the judge repeatedly accused me of speaking against Islam and its sacred laws. In the politico-religious worldview of such traditionalists, a person who challenges Islam is easily considered an apostate. And the power of interpretation—the power to differentiate between a respectful criticism of a worldly law and an attack on a holy tenet—was in their hands. I was fighting on their battlefield. And I could not simply pull out a copy of the Universal Declaration of Human Rights and wave it in the faces of clerics who found seventh-century penal practice instructive. To argue that Leila's family should not have to finance the execution of her killer or to argue that a woman's life should equal a man's before the law, I too had to draw on Islamic principles and precedents in Islamic law.

My two daughters were growing old enough that they came home from school each day with a barrage of questions. *Thud.* They would toss their backpacks in the hallway. *Thud thud.* They would run down the hall, fingers sticky from a snack on the way home. Navigating the Islamic Republic as a woman was getting more tricky, and so was navigating Islamic Republic motherhood. Maman, is it really wrong for me to go in front of my male cousins without a veil? Maman, is America truly the source of all that is toxic in the world? Maman, was Mossadegh really a bad man? It was a delicate balance, trying to teach my daughters progressive values and the emptiness behind the revolutionary dogma they were fed in school, while ensuring that they learned and superficially obeyed all that dogma anyway, so the could pass through the education system. "A lot of this is simply wrong," I would usually say, "but you need to study it anyway, so you can pass your exams and go to college."

My husband, Javad, as usual, left these delicate lessons to me. Just as he left the cooking, the shopping, the cleaning, the balancing of the checkbook, and the shuttling of the girls to and from their classes to me. With the caseload I was taking on, balancing the attention the girls needed at home and my work was getting harder. And now the girls didn't need just bedtime stories anymore. They needed our guidance in dealing with adolescence in Tehran, with all its lures and chaos. "Just tell me if you need any help," Javad would say. And that struck me as most unfair of all, because I certainly never waited for him to ask, "Shirin *jan*, can you please cook dinner tonight?" I cooked dinner every single night because it was obvious to me that it was my responsibility. This was the running theme of our arguments. He wanted me to tell him what to do, and I thought he should figure it out without being told.

Between my practice in the morning and working on articles in the evening, I had started my next book, a treatise on the rights of refugees. Before I started my legal practice, the book writing kept my mind engaged, but now, combined with representing clients, it resulted in an often overwhelming workload. I managed to keep the household running smoothly only by planning well in advance. There was really no such institution as takeout, and the expectations of an Iranian wife include that she will cook. Leaving a sink full of dirty dishes or a hamper full of laundry is simply not an option. If I needed to travel or take a short trip for work, I arranged all the family's meals in advance. They would know to look on the top shelf of the refrigerator for that evening's cutlet, and then in the freezer for the meals labeled for the following days of the week. I even made just the right amount of fresh salad dressing and put that in the refrigerator too. I don't mean to suggest that I was a brilliant housewife or a superb cook; by Iranian standards I'm sure I could have been faulted on an array of small details and neglects. But from the beginning I had run a household that was cozier than clinically spotless, and the family was accustomed to this informality. Perhaps it was a shade fatalistic, the sometimes casual approach I took to the present. But ever since my brother-in-law Fuad's execution, when the gravity of death first touched me, I'd found preoccupation with the minutiae of daily life meaningless. If we all ultimately die, and turn to dust in the ground, should it ever truly upset us if the floor hasn't been swept quite recently enough. This didn't mean that I wasn't concerned with the details of my children's lives; it just meant that I distinguished carefully which details mattered.

To bridge my worry about spending so much time away from the house, I made a point of bringing my work home in the evening and involving the girls in what I was thinking or writing about each day. Better that they be drawn into my orbit of preoccupations, I figured, than wonder why I was so absorbed in things beyond them. I suppose deep down I hoped they would inherit my beliefs, my sensitivity to injustice, and my compulsion to push the boundaries.

The night the voting results came in for the 1996 parliamentary elections, I gathered my daughters around me on the sofa and narrated to them. Sometimes I tried to tell them about my work, to make abstract concepts such as women's rights come alive through the characters who passed through their lives. They knew, for example, that my friend Shahla Sherkat had four years ago started a women's publication called *Zanan*. It was Shahla who'd first called to tell me about Leila's case and asked whether I could offer their family legal advice. In a way, my daughters could trace the evolution in women's role through my life and the lives of those they knew as close family friends. Before 1992, I couldn't even get a permit to work as an attorney. Shahla directed a government-owned weekly aimed at conservative, religious women. The same year I secured a license and began taking on cases, Shahla started up *Zanan*, which at first tentatively and then more forcefully took up the issues that a broader spectrum of women in Iran faced each day. Sometimes she referred cases to me; sometimes I wrote articles for her magazine.

Our budding activism was premised on a few basic facts: we lived under an Islamic Republic that was neither going anywhere nor inclined to recast its governing ethos as secular; the legal system was underpinned by Islamic law; and every facet of a woman's place in society—from access to birth control to divorce rights to compulsory veiling— was determined by interpretations of the Koran.

If we wanted to make a tangible difference in the lives of the women around us and in the lives of people like Leila and her family, we had no choice but to advocate for female equality in an Islamic framework. In this, our personal sensibilities and political worldview were wholly irrelevant. It so happened that I believed in the secular separation of religion and government because, fundamentally, Islam, like any religion, is subject to interpretation. It can be interpreted to oppress women or interpreted to liberate them. In an ideal world, I would choose not to be vulnerable to the caprice of interpretation, because the ambiguity of theological debates spirals back to the seventh century; there will never be a definitive resolution, as that is the nature and spirit of Islamic interpretation, a debate that will grow and evolve with the ages but never be resolved. I am a lawyer by training, and know only too well the permanent limitations of trying to enshrine inalienable rights in sources that lack fixed terms and definitions. But I am also a citizen of the Islamic Republic, and I know the futility of approaching the question any other way. My objective is not to vent my own political sensibilities but to push for a law that would save a family like Leila's from becoming homeless in their quest to finance the executions of their daughter's convicted murderers. If I'm forced to ferret through musty books of Islamic jurisprudence and rely on sources that stress the egalitarian ethics of Islam, then so be it. Is it harder this way? Of course it is. But is there an alternative battlefield? Desperate wishing aside, I cannot see one.

One summer morning in 1997, as I leafed through a newspaper in my office, I came across a story about a battered child who had died in a local hospital after suffering repeated blows to the head. The photo that ran with the story showed a bent little girl with thin limbs covered in cigarette burns. The photo was so painful to look at that I quickly folded it over and read on. The little girl was named Arian Golshani. After her parents' divorce, the court granted custody of Arian to her father, a brutal man with a police record for fraud and drug addiction. According to the neighbors, the father kept Arian in dungeon-like conditions. The nine-year-old weighed only thirty-three pounds, her arms had been broken several times and plastered with makeshift casts at home, and after the schoolteacher called her father to inquire about the cigarette burn marks all over her body, she was kept home from school for months. Arian's mother went to the court and pleaded for custody; she explained her daughter's condition, explained that her ex-husband was guilty of horrific abuse. The court impassively declined to grant her custody.

All morning, the image of that scarred child remained etched in my mind. Something must be done, I felt, but what? A couple of hours later, the phone rang. A photographer friend had also seen Arian's photo in the newspaper. "Shirin, we must do something," she said. "I know, let me think," I replied. That afternoon, we convened a meeting with a few friends from a children's rights society and conferred over little cups of Turkish coffee. In the end, we devised a stealthy plan: we would arrange a ceremony ostensibly to mourn her death, but we would also use it as an occasion to protest the civil code that was its cause. We reserved space at a large mosque in central Tehran, Al-Ghadir, and took out ads in the newspaper announcing the death of Arian Golshani and the funeral ceremony in her honor. I asked Javad's uncle, a cleric, to speak about child abuse and to tell the story of her short, brutal life.

The Islamic Revolution had anointed the Muslim family the centerpiece of its ideology of nation. The revolutionaries envisioned the domesticated Muslim mother, confined to the house and caring for her multiplying brood, as key to the restoration of traditional and authentic values. Yet it seemed in no way contradictory to them to then institute a family law that automatically tore children away from mothers in the event of divorce, or made polygamy as convenient as a second mortgage. The question of child custody had weighed heavy on my own mind for years, for my older sister had long felt bound to her failing marriage partly out of fear of losing her children. It numbered among the most destructive of the system's legal codes, and articles and public outcry against the custody law had grown louder with each passing year.

On the day of the ceremony, in the fall of 1997, we lined the funeral hall with flowers and set a small table with plump dates at the entrance. Shortly before the ceremony started, several women walked through the mosque with dazed expressions, their tears flowing. They were Arian's mother and aunts. "I didn't know my daughter had so many friends," her mother said in a strangled voice, searching my face in confusion. "If so, why did she die alone?" I swallowed hard and gently led her to a seat in the front.

Javad's uncle was a gifted orator, and his speech moved the audience from the beginning. Toward the middle, a man named Alavi walked up to him holding the hand of a small child. "Here is another Arian," he said, and he recounted the child's story, his custody granted to his father but the boy desperately wishing to live with his mother. Mr. Alavi lifted the child high into the air and declared to the audience, "People, do something for these children!"

Suddenly the atmosphere grew very charged, and everyone began crying. I strode up to the microphone in the women's section and said, "Today we are here to defend the rights of other Arians. We must reform the law that led to this death." People began shouting slogans, and we asked them to disperse the flowers on the streets on their way out. The whole hall moved toward the doors at once, chanting, "The law must be reformed!" and plucking the petals from their stems.

Within half an hour, the busy streets surrounding the mosque were strewn with white petals, and the taxi drivers and commuters crawling through traffic paused to look at the mosque. Newspapers covered the story, and universities began holding seminars on child abuse. Suddenly, women's custody rights were at the center of a self-generated campaign of public awareness. My office phone, which had begun ringing more frequently ever since Leila's case, now pretty much rang incessantly. And not simply with potential clients but with journalists and international human rights monitors who needed an Iranian interlocutor on the ground to explain how the system worked and how women—not yet organized in those days—were working to change its ways.

When the trial began, I represented Arian's mother and charged the girl's father and stepbrother with torture and murder, respectively. Reporters, including broadcast journalists, crowded the courtroom, and as soon as the trial started the second row whipped out a banner reading, THE PRICE OF ARIAN'S DEATH IS A CHANGE IN THE LAWS IN FAVOR OF IRANIAN CHILDREN. Because the case had become so sensitive, the head of the branch court, a cleric, presided.

My opening statement didn't require much embellishment; the tragedy of Arian's case spoke for itself. I told the court of how she grew weak, malnourished, and disoriented after weeks of torture, how she had started to touch herself, and when her stepbrother found her with her hands between her legs, he kicked her violently, sending her tiny body flying across the floor. I described how her head cracked against the wall, sustaining the concussion that within hours killed her. I made sure to linger on the laws themselves, not simply Arian's case. I paced back and forth, my low heels clicking against the floor of the courtroom, essentially putting the law—rather than these particular defendants—on trial.

When I finished, the head of the branch court took the microphone from me. "Islam," he began ponderously, "is a religion of equality, but the Koran stipulates that a woman's inheritance is half that of a man."

How irrelevant! We were not even discussing inheritance. It was a pretext to accuse me of defaming religion.

I asked the judge permission to speak. "I am not criticizing Islam," I declared flatly. "May the tongue of anyone who does be cut. I am criticizing a law that has been passed by the Iranian parliament. Is it fair," I asked, turning toward the court, "for a child to be abused by her father so cruelly, and for the court to deny her mother custody? Is it fair to expect a mother whose child has just been killed to pay for the execution of justice?"

"Don't worry," said the judge, assuring me that the blood money would be taken from the public treasury.

"But we don't want our taxes to go to murderers!" I said, exasperated.

The judge sentenced Arian's stepbrother to death, and her father and stepmother to one year in prison. Arian's mother eventually consented to stay the stepbrother's execution. I admired her for her compassion, as the stepbrother had been a child of the father's second marriage, and he himself had been taken from his mother after their divorce. His abuse was monstrous, but he was also a victim of the same system.

The trial's end attracted worldwide attention. CNN correspondent Christiane Amanpour interviewed me with Arian's mother, and as I watched her distraught face at home on the television, I felt heartened for a moment: though Arian's death had been senseless, at least her legacy served enormous purpose. Perhaps the Islamic Republic resisted accountability to its citizens, but it wished with each passing year to shed its pariah status in the global community. Slowly, it grew more aware that a nation on uneven footing with the West could not afford to trample its citizens' rights.

When I watched that broadcast, aware that it was being beamed around the world, I also realized for the first time that I had become what you might call famous. Prominence is something that accrues gradually. You work and speak, write articles and lecture, meet with clients and defend them, day after day, night after night, and then you wake up one day and notice that there is a long trial behind you that constitutes a reputation. That's how it happened for me, anyway. How unimportant it was to me as a person, but how useful it became to my work. It meant journalists would listen if I approached them with a case and would help publicize it both inside the country and abroad. It meant that human rights observers around the world knew and trusted me, and launched swift appeals for urgent cases I brought to their attention. It meant there was now a face and a name attached to the abstract term "human rights" in Iran, and that finally millions of women who could not articulate their frustrations and desires had someone to speak on their behalf. I would never assume such a role for myself, but in the Islamic Republic, we have a problem with representation. Our diplomats around the world are, naturally, loyal to the regime, and the regime's credibility is not such that it reflects the true opinions of the people. The responsibility falls, then, on unofficial ambassadors to relate Iranians' perceptions and hopes to the world.

Between my ever-growing reputation and the world's curiosity about how women fared in a society like Iran's, it seemed more possible each year to make the system pay an international price for its refusal to reform its laws at home.

■ READING AND WRITING

1. How does the story of Leila Fathi and her family function in this piece, rhetorically and thematically?
2. What gender issues does Ebadi raise in her piece? What is her central argument? How does she support her claims?
3. What does Edabi reveal about herself in her text? How does this information affect your view of her argument?

■ USING RESEARCH

4. Find Ebadi's Nobel Peace Prize lecture online, read the text, and write a 150- to 200-word summary of Ebadi's main points. How are these themes reflected in "From the Living Room to the Courtroom"? Which text do you think presents the more effective argument? Why?

Poet, political activist, and author Ewuare X. Osayande is co-founder and director of POWER (People Organized Working to Eradicate Racism) and creator of Project ONUS: Redefining Black Manhood. The following essay was included in the 2008 collection Men Speak Out: Views on Gender, Sex, and Power.

REDEFINING MANHOOD:
RESISTING SEXISM Ewuare X. Osayande

"Don't you grow up to be a black man!" The words would echo in my young and impressionable mind for years. They belonged to my mother. The source of her message was the combination of internalized oppression as a black woman living in a white supremacist society, and her pain and frustration with the men in her life who abused and misused her. I came to understand my mother's outcry as a desperate plea for her son not to grow up and be like the men she knew.

I saw the worst of patriarchal abuse in the tragic murder of my father, caught in the path of a jealous man who thought that women were his property. Despite these traumatic experiences, I am today a proud, self-loving, heterosexual black man. I have decided to respond to my mother's lament by working to redefine what manhood means to me and to the men I come in contact with. This means confronting racism, sexism, and masculine violence when and where I see it.

I did not have many men to look up to during my childhood. Soon after I was born, my father joined the Army and eventually ended up stationed in Germany. My mother's first marriage was to a man who was hardly ever around. When he was, he never showed any real interest in my life. As I became a teenager, I promised myself that I would never be like either of my fathers. Although I did not know what to do, I certainly knew what not to do. But it wasn't until I got married that I came face to face with my own issues of manhood.

The marriage lasted less than three years. I quickly realized that I was not able to fulfill the socially ascribed role of being the "man of the house," even though I tried to the best of my ability. The pressure of providing for a growing family and finding affirming work became overwhelming. The marriage quickly dissolved even as my self-criticism and awareness was beginning to evolve. There is nothing about masculinity in that period of my life that makes me happy or proud. I am ashamed of the man I was, and I remain ever-vigilant to prevent the man I was from becoming the man I am. But my early confusion led me to a process of political self-awareness that has rooted me ever since.

I don't remember how I first came across the work of feminist writer bell hooks, but I do know that I read her book, *Sisters of the Yam*, in one sitting. Although written for black women, this book helped me make sense of the problems I experienced in my marriage and it helped me make sense of myself. I had heard about feminism before, but never paid it much mind. I dismissed it as "that white women's stuff."

I had long been involved in black liberation struggle. I went from being a staunch black student activist in college to being a respected community activist in Philadelphia. Like many black men, I believed that racism was the only oppression that required our community's attention. Reading bell hooks helped correct my vision and revise my understanding. I now see that sexism is as important as racism in liberation struggle. Black women and men have to address white dominant society as well as male domination from both within and outside the black community. Black feminist thought has broadened my understanding of how various forms of oppression criss-cross and often collide.

I now also see that my experience of trying to live up to a "man-of-the-house" sex role is shared by many of the men in my family. I watch my male relatives mask their depression with jokes that project their sense of worthlessness onto the women in their lives. I worry for them and more so for the women they claim to love. I see how the men's penchant for domination in the home has wreaked havoc on their partners. There is a cloud of anxiety that covers these women. That cloud is the threat of violence that lingers in the air after the man has publicly ridiculed, demeaned, or yelled at her. I am torn up inside even as I try to figure out how to intervene.

I once feared that any act of intervention would be met with resistance by the men and would result in increased violence in the home. I now better understand the root causes of this pain and anger. Rather than being a model for healthy relationships, patriarchy is actually the very force responsible for their demise.

I try to speak affirmatively to these men in my family, offering them alternative ways of viewing themselves as men, keeping myself accountable to the pain and anguish that I know very well. I know that I must not wait for a tragedy to occur. I must remain in constant communication with the hope that conversation can offer a process for change. I share with my family and with myself the belief that love is justice in its most intimate embrace. As such, we men must make every effort to see the women in our lives as equal partners and we must respect them as individuals with ambitions and desires that transcend our own.

It has been ten years since I embraced feminist thought as a guide for my personal life and political activism. In that time, I have given talks and workshops on resisting negative socialization and internalized oppression. One of the issues I am constantly confronted with is how to talk about the matrix of oppressions in a way that is both direct and accessible. I find that all too often some folk want to hide behind their personal oppression. For example, when I give talks on racism and how race impacts our understanding of sexist oppression in the United States, it's not unusual to meet resistance from white women in the audience. More than one white woman has tried to deflect any consideration of how she may experience white privilege even as she must contend with sexism. At the same time, I often meet white men who claim a pro-feminist outlook but who approach me with questions that suggest male domination only exists within the black community. There is a continuing challenge to appreciate the ways that race and class impact how sexism is experienced in this country.

There is a different gendered experience for a black woman or a woman of color and a white woman. Women of color scholars and activists have written about this for years. I have witnessed an increased interest in feminist thought in the black community thanks to the works of bell hooks, Angela Davis, Alice Walker, Joy James, Barbara Smith, Audre Lorde, and many others. My black female peers are pioneering a body of scholarship and engaging in feminist activism that speaks directly to the hip-hop-inspired generation. Yet progress is still slow. While the legacy of racism has made it difficult for feminist thought to have the radicalizing effect it could have within the black community, sexist black men have used that racism to trump any real discussion of sexism within the black community.

In the United States, black masculinity is a manhood that, in the main, has braced itself against the onslaught of a biased and bigoted society. Racism constantly threatens our well being and our very existence. This defensive posturing often leaves us detached from our feelings. In a society that views us as predator and prey, we are inclined to be on guard at all times. Yet our self-protective posturing often manifests in a hypermasculinity that is predicated upon domination and that sees violence as a primary option to resolve problems.

This perversion of manhood took its ultimate and most personal form in the murder of my father in January 2000. My father had recently begun dating a woman who had left an abusive relationship. My father's murderer was this woman's former lover who resorted to the most violent expression of male domination. In his sexist mind, the woman was his property. He did not recognize her agency or her right to create a life outside of his desires. When she began dating my father, this man struck out. He ambushed and attacked my father and his woman friend. My father was stabbed so severely that he died before the rescue workers arrived. The woman spent a few days in the hospital recovering from her wounds.

The murderer was a respected man of the community who was considered upstanding by most people who knew him. He was not crazy. He was socialized to view women as mere property and to exercise power even to the point of violence, especially when he believed his so-called manhood was being challenged.

As long as domination and violence are considered central parts of masculinity, I worry for the future for my two boys. At ages eleven and eight, they are still becoming aware of themselves in the world. I am learning how quickly sexist socialization can take place. The system is relentless; it bombards my sons with sexist and racist messages on a daily basis. Their mother and I go to great lengths to provide our sons with alternative ways of understanding themselves as boys so that they can resist sexist indoctrination. Yet, despite all our intervention, it seems that every aspect of their young lives is filled with sexist instruction. The same old sexism has been revamped for the computer age.

Female cartoon characters are portrayed as damsels in distress who are in constant need of a male hero to save them. In video games, the same is true but with added violence and grossly sexualized images of the female body. My response is to aid my sons in making better choices about the kinds of cartoons they watch and video games they play. I read books with them about women athletes who excel in sports. Their mother has taken them to see the WNBA play live.

It is my fervent hope that anti-sexist, anti-racist interventions will serve my sons well as they grow from boys into men. I will certainly be there to provide an example of manhood that is not an expression of force, superiority, and violence but rather an expression of love, respect, justice, accountability, integrity, and peace.

■ READING AND WRITING

1. How does Osayande define manhood? How do feminist principles figure in this definition?
2. Explain the link Osayande makes between the "man-of-the-house" role that many men in his family try to fill and the violence that these men inflict against the women in their lives.
3. What does Osayande mean when he talks about the "matrix of oppressions" he tries to address as part of his activism? Where does violence against women fit into this matrix?
4. What is the rhetorical function of Osayande's story about the murder of his father?

■ USING RESEARCH

5. Osayande mentions the profound influence that feminist thinker and writer bell hooks had on him as he redefined his masculinity. Use the library or the internet to find an essay by hooks in which she discusses race and gender issues. Write a 150- to 200-word summary of this essay and then explain how reading it affected your understanding of Osayande's text.

IMAGE 3.2: The readings in this chapter explore personal, social, and professional roles that are influenced by traditional gender expectations and stereotypes. They also show how our thinking about these stereotypes can be slow to change. What characteristics do you associate with men and masculinity? And with women and femininity? How different would your parents' and grandparents' responses be from your own?

Joshua E. Borgmann received his MFA in Creative Writing from the University of South Carolina in 2005 and teaches composition, creative writing, and literature at Southwestern Community College in Creston, Iowa. His prose poem "Unattractive Male Seeks Human Female" was published in the 2002 collection The Emergence of Man Into the 21st Century.

UNATTRACTIVE MALE SEEKS
HUMAN FEMALE   Joshua E. Borgmann

Straight up, here I am: SWM 25 seeking SF 18-35. Looks, race, other shit unimportant, but must be willing to tolerate fat bald man interested in music, primarily the British band Cradle of Filth; books: *American Psycho*, *White Noise*, and maybe *Wise Blood;* movies: *Pulp Fiction*, *Texas Chainsaw Massacre*, *Dogma*, *Pornogothic*, *Blair Witch*—digs *Star Trek* and *South Park* for sociopolitical discourse—overall a very underground black death doom grind kinda groove looking for someone who can just sit back with some Type-O-Negative playing 'cause I do that a lot when I write 'cause I'm a poet and yes I've written love poems even though I haven't had many dates. Back some years I wrote one I called "Black is the Only Color in the World" and later, after I gave up this dancer I was seeing, I traded the poppies for telephones that never ring and even though I wasn't Alan Jackson or even Garth Brooks I felt like I needed a cowboy hat 'cause I was sure stuck writing that damn "she done gone left me and I'm so sad" song, so I moved on and wrote one on the girl I stalked in sixth grade and that one went over well but hey I'm rambling so back to business. Morally I'm for this carpe diem do as thou will shit but politics is kinda tricky 'cause really that's economics and some days I feel socialist and others libertarian so I just vote Democrat but I'm anti-censorship and don't mind pornography. It's better work than McDonalds and besides how else is a guy like me going to see naked women anyway but hey don't take that wrong 'cause like I've said somewhere else sex doesn't equal success.

Note: Children tolerated, pets welcomed; however, if you're an overzealous Christian or a sorority type and you're still reading please stop (all other responses will be considered for replies).

■ READING AND WRITING

1. What gender issues does Borgmann allude to in his poem? What does the poem say about these issues?
2. How would you characterize the speaker of the poem? What does Borgmann do to develop the speaker's character?
3. Can a poem present an effective argument? Explain your response.

> *Using sarcasm and wit to deliver cutting social critiques, David Sedaris has become one of America's most popular humor writers. "Chicken in the Henhouse," from the 2004 collection* Dress Your Family in Corduroy and Denim, *showcases Sedaris' ability to use seemingly ordinary details from daily life to slice through the "cultural euphemisms and political correctness," as his online biography puts it, that so many of us tend to accept or ignore.*

CHICKEN IN THE HENHOUSE   David Sedaris

It was one of those hotels without room service, the type you wouldn't mind if you were paying your own bill but would complain about if someone else was paying. I was not paying my own bill, and so the deficiencies stuck out and were taken as evidence of my host's indifference. There was no tub, just a plastic shower stall, and the soap was brittle and smelled like dishwashing detergent. The bedside lamp was missing a bulb, but that could have been remedied easily enough. I could have asked for one at the front desk, but I didn't want a light bulb. I just wanted to feel put-upon.

It started when the airline lost my luggage. Time was lost filling out forms, and I'd had to go directly from the airport to a college an hour north of Manchester, where I gave a talk to a group of students. Then there was a reception and a forty-five-minute drive to the hotel, which was out in the middle of nowhere. I arrived at one A.M. and found they had booked me into a basement room. Late at night it didn't much matter, but in the morning it did. To open the curtains was to invite scrutiny, and the people of New Hampshire stared in without a hint of shame. There wasn't much to look at, just me, sitting on the edge of the bed with a phone to my ear. The airline had sworn my suitcase would arrive overnight, and when it didn't, I called the 800 number printed on the inside of my ticket jacket. My choices were either to speak to a machine or to wait for an available human. I chose the human, and after eight minutes on hold I hung up and started looking for someone to blame.

"I don't care if it's my son, my congressman, what have you. I just don't approve of that lifestyle." The speaker was a woman named Audrey who'd called the local talk-radio station to offer her opinion. The Catholic Church scandal had been front-page news for over a week, and when the priest angle had been exhausted, the discussion filtered down to pedophilia in general and then, homosexual pedophilia, which was commonly agreed to be the worst kind. It was for talk radio, one of those easy topics, like tax hikes or mass murder. "What do you think of full-grown men practicing sodomy on children?"

"Well, I'm *against* it!" This was always said as if it was somehow startling, a minority position no one had yet dared lay claim to.

I'd been traveling around the country for the past ten days, and everywhere I went I heard the same thing. The host would congratulate the caller on his or her moral fortitude, and wanting to feel that approval again, the person would rephrase the original statement, freshening it up with an adverb or qualifier. "Call me old-fashioned, but I just hugely think it's wrong." Then, little by little, they'd begin interchanging the words *homosexual* and *pedophile*, speaking as if they were one and the same. "Now they've even got them on TV," Audrey said. "And in the schools! Talk about the proverbial chicken in the henhouse."

"Fox," the host said.

"Oh, they're the worst," Audrey said. "*The Simpsons* and such—I never watch that station."

I meant in the henhouse," the host said. "I believe the saying is 'the fox in the henhouse,' not 'the chicken in the henhouse.'"

Audrey regrouped. "Did I say chicken? Well, you get my point. These homosexuals can't reproduce themselves, and so they go into the schools and try to recruit our young people."

It was nothing I hadn't heard before, but I was crankier than usual and found myself in the middle of the room, one sock on and one sock off, shouting at the clock radio. "Nobody recruited *me*, Audrey. And I *begged* for it."

It was *her* fault I was stuck in a basement room with no luggage, her and all the people just like her: the satisfied families trotting from the parking lot to the first-floor restaurant, the hotel guests with whirlpool baths and rooms overlooking the surrounding forest. *Why waste the view on a homosexual? He only looks at schoolboys' rectums. And a suitcase? Please! We all know what they do with those.* They might not have come out and said it, but they are sure thinking it. I could tell.

It stood to reason that if the world was conspiring against me, my Mr. Coffee machine was broken. It sat on the bathroom counter, dribbling cold water, and after a brief, completely unsatisfying cry, I finished getting dressed and left the room. There was a staircase at the end of the hall, and beside it a little cleared area where a dozen or so elderly women knelt upon the carpet, piecing together a patchwork quilt. They looked up as I passed, one of them turning to ask me a question. "Yoin' shurch?" Her mouth was full of pins and it took me a moment to realize what she was saying—You going to church? It was an odd question, but then I remembered that it was a Sunday, and I was wearing a tie. Someone at the college had loaned it to me the night before, and I'd put it on in hopes it might distract from my shirt, which was wrinkled and discolored beneath the arms. "No," I told her, "I'm *not* going to church." Oh, I was in a horrible mood. Midway up the stairs I stopped and turned back around. "I *never* go to church," I said. "Never. And I'm not about to start now."

"Shute shelf," she said.

Past the restaurant and gift shop, in the center of the lobby, was a complimentary beverage stand. I thought I'd get a coffee and take it outdoors, but just as I approached, a boy swooped in and began mixing himself a cup of hot chocolate. He looked like all of the kids I'd been seeing lately, in airports, in parking lots: the oversize sweatshirts stamped with team emblems, the baggy jeans and jazzy sneakers. His watch was fat and plastic, like a yo-yo strapped to his wrist, and his hair looked as if it had been cut with the lid of a can, the irregular hanks stiffened with gel and coaxed to stand at peculiar angles.

It was a complicated business, mixing a cup of hot chocolate. You had to spread the powdered cocoa from one end of the table to the other and use as many stirrers as possible, making sure to thoroughly chew the wetted ends before tossing them upon the stack of unused napkins. This is what I like about children: complete attention to one detail and complete disregard of another. When finally finished, he scooted over to the coffee urn, filling two cups, black, and fitting them with lids. The drinks were stacked into a tower, then tentatively lifted off the table. "Whoa," he whispered. Hot chocolate seeped from beneath the lid of the bottom cup and ran down his hand.

"Do you need some help with those?" I asked.

The boy looked at me for a moment. "Yeah," he said. "Carry these upstairs." There was no *please* or *thank you*, just "I'll take the hot chocolate myself."

He set the coffees back on the table, and as I reached for them it occurred to me that maybe this was not such a good idea. I was a stranger, an admitted homosexual traveling through a small town, and he was, like, ten. And alone. The voice of reason whispered in my ear. *Don't do it, buster. You're playing with fire.*

I withdrew my hands, then stopped, thinking, *Wait a minute. That's not reason. It's Audrey, that crackpot from the radio.* The real voice of reason sounds like Bea Arthur, and when it failed to pipe up, I lifted the coffees off the table and carried them toward the elevator, where the boy stood mashing the call button with his chocolate-coated fingers.

A maid passed and rolled her eyes at the desk clerk. "Cute kid."

Before the church scandal I might have said the same thing, only without the sarcasm. Now, though, any such observation seemed suspect. Though Audrey would never believe it, I am not physically attracted to children. They're like animals to me, fun to watch but beyond the bounds of my sexual imagination. That said, I am a person who feels guilty for crimes I have not committed, or have not committed in years. The police search the train station for a serial rapist and I cover my face with a newspaper, wondering if maybe I did it in my sleep. The last thing I stole was an eight-track tape, but to this day I'm unable to enter a store without feeling like a shoplifter. It's all the anxiety with none of the free stuff. To make things just that much worse, I seem to have developed a remarkable perspiration problem. My conscience is cross-wired with my sweat glands, but there's a short in the system and I break out over things I didn't do, which only makes me look more suspect. Innocently helping to lighten a child's burden was a *good* thing—I knew this—yet moments after lifting the coffees off the table I was soaking wet. As usual, the sweat was fiercest on my forehead, under my arms, and, cruelly, on my ass, which is a great mystery to me. If the stress is prolonged, I'll feel the droplets inching down the back of my legs, trapped, finally, by my socks, which are cotton and bought expressly for their absorbent powers.

If there was a security camera in the lobby, this is what it would have shown: A four-and-a-half-foot-tall boy stands mashing and then pounding the elevator call button. Beside him is a man, maybe a foot taller, dressed in a shirt and tie and holding a lidded cup in each hand. Is it raining outside? If not, perhaps he just stepped from the shower and threw on his clothes without drying himself. His eyes shift this way and that, giving the impression that he is searching for somebody. Could it be this silver-haired gentleman? He's just walked up, looking very dapper in his tweed jacket and matching cap. He talks to the boy and lays a hand on the back of his head, scolding him probably, which is good, as somebody needed to. The other man, the wet one, is just standing there, holding the cups and trying to wipe his forehead with his sleeve at the same time. A lid pops off and something—it looks like coffee—spills down the front of his shirt. He leaps about, prancing almost, and pulls the fabric away from his skin. The boy seems angry now and says something. The older gentleman offers a handkerchief, and the man sets down one of his cups and runs—literally runs, panting—off camera, returning thirty seconds later with another lidded cup, a replacement. By this time the elevator has arrived. The gentleman holds open the door, and he and the boy wait as the man picks the other cup off the floor and joins them. Then the door closes, and they are gone.

"So, who have we got here?" the gentleman asked. His voice was jovial and enthusiastic. "What do you call yourself, big fella?"

"Michael," the boy said.

"Well, that's a grown-up name, isn't it."

Michael guessed that it was, and the man caught my eye and winked, the way people do when they're establishing a partnership. *We'll just put on the small fry, what do you say?* "I bet a big guy like you must have a lot of girlfriends," he said. "Is that true?"

"No."

"You *don't*? Well, what's the problem?"

"I don't know. I just don't have one. That's all," Michael said.

I had always hated it when men asked the girlfriend question. Not only was it corny, but it set you in their imaginations in a way that seemed private to me. Answer yes and they'd picture your wee courtship: the candlelit dinner of hot dogs and potato chips, the rumpled Snoopy sheets. Answer no and you were blue-balled, the frustrated bachelor of the second grade. It was an idea of children as miniature adults, which was about as funny to me as the dog in sunglasses.

"Well, there must be *someone* you have your eye on."

The boy did not answer, but the man persisted in trying to draw him out. "Is Mommy sleeping in this morning?"

Again, nothing.

The man gave up and turned to me. Your wife," he said. "I take it she's still in bed?"

He thought I was Michael's father, and I did not correct him. "Yes," I said. "She's upstairs … passed out." I don't know why I said this, or then again, maybe I do. The man had constructed a little family portrait, and there was a pleasure in defacing it. Here was Michael, here was Michael's dad, and now, here was Mom, lying face down on the bathroom floor.

The elevator stopped on three, and the man tipped his hat. "All right, then," he said. "You two enjoy the rest of the morning." Michael had pressed the button for the fifth floor no less than twenty times, and now he gave it an extra few jabs just for good measure. We were alone now, and something unpleasant entered my mind.

Sometimes when I'm in a tight situation, I'll feel a need to touch somebody's head. It happens a lot on airplanes. I'll look at the person seated in front of me, and within a moment the idea will have grown from a possibility to a compulsion. There is no option—I simply have to do it. The easiest method is to make like I'm getting up, to grab the forward seat for support and just sort of pat the person's hair with my fingers. "Oh, I'm sorry," I say.

"No problem."

Most often I'll continue getting out of my seat, then walk to the back of the plane or go to the bathroom and stand there for a few minutes, trying to fight off what I know is inevitable: I need to touch the person's head again. Experience has taught me that you can do this three times before the head's owner either yells at you or rings for the flight attendant. "Is something wrong?" she'll ask.

"I don't think so, no."

"What do you mean 'no,'" the passenger will say. "This freak keeps touching my head."

"Is that true, sir?"

It's not always a head. Sometimes I need to touch a particular purse or briefcase. When I was a child this sort of compulsive behavior was my life, but now I practice it only if I'm in a situation where I can't smoke: planes—as I mentioned—and elevators.

Just touch the boy's head, I thought. *The old man did it, so why can't you?*

To remind myself that this is inappropriate only makes the voice more insistent. The thing must be done *because* it is inappropriate. If it weren't, there'd be no point in bothering with it.

He won't even notice it. Touch him now, quick.

Were we traveling a long distance, I would have lost the battle, but fortunately we weren't going far. The elevator arrived on the fifth floor and I scrambled out the door, set the coffees on the carpet, and lit a cigarette. "You're going to have to give me a minute here," I said.

"But my room's just down the hall. And this is non-smoking."

"I know, I know."

"It's not good for you," he said.

"That's true for a lot of people," I told him. "But it *really is* good for me. Take my word for it."

He leaned against a door and removed the DO NOT DISTURB sign, studying it for a moment before sticking it in his back pocket.

I only needed to smoke for a minute, but realized when I was finished that there was no ashtray. Beside the elevator was a window, but of course it was sealed shut. Hotels. They do everything in their power to make you want to jump to your death, and then they make certain that you can't do it. "Are you finished with your cocoa?" I asked.

"No."

"Well, are you finished with the lid?"

"I guess so."

He handed it to me and I spit into the center—no easy task, as my mouth was completely dry. Fifty percent of my body water was seeping out my ass, and the other half was in transit.

"That's gross," he said. "Yeah, well, you're just going to have to forgive me." I stubbed the cigarette into the spit, set the lid on the carpet, and picked up the coffees. "Okay. Where to?"

He pointed out a long corridor and I followed him, gnawing on a question that's been troubling me for years. What if you had a baby and you just … you just needed to touch it where you knew you shouldn't. I don't mean that you'd want to. You wouldn't *desire* the baby any more than you desire a person whose head you've just touched. The act would be compulsive rather than sexual, and while to you there'd be a big difference, you couldn't expect a prosecutor, much less an infant, to recognize it. You'd be a bad parent, and once the child could talk and you told it not to tell anyone, you would become a manipulator—a monster, basically—and the reason behind your actions would no longer matter.

The closer we got to the end of the hall, the more anxious I became. I had not laid a finger on the boy's head. I have never poked or prodded either a baby or a child, so why did I feel so dirty? Part of it was just my makeup, the deep-seated belief that I deserve a basement room, but a larger, uglier part had to do with the voices I hear on talk radio, and my tendency, in spite of myself, to pay them heed. The man in the elevator had not thought twice about asking Michael personal questions or about laying a hand on the back of his head. Because he was neither a priest nor a homosexual, he hadn't felt the need to watch himself, worrying that every word or gesture might be misinterpreted. He could unthinkingly wander the halls with a strange boy, while for me it amounted to a political act—an insistence that I was as good as the next guy. Yes, I am a homosexual; yes, I am soaking wet; yes, I sometimes feel an urge to touch people's heads, but still I can safely see a ten-year-old back to his room. It bothered me that I needed to prove something this elementary. And prove it to people whom I could never hope to convince.

"This is it," Michael said. From the other side of the door I heard the sound of a television. It was one of those Sunday-morning magazine programs, a weekly hour where all news is good news. Blind Jimmy Henderson coaches a volley ball team. An ailing groundhog is fitted for a back brace. That type of thing. The boy inserted his card key into the slot, and the door opened onto a bright, well-furnished room. It was twice the size of mine, with higher ceilings and a sitting area. One window framed a view of the lake, and the other a stand of scarlet maples.

"Oh, you're back," a woman said. She was clearly the boy's mother, as their profiles were identical, the foreheads easing almost imperceptibly into blunt freckled noses. Both too had spiky blond hair, though for her I imagined the style was accidental, the result of the pillows piled behind her head. She was lying beneath the covers of a canopy bed, examining one of the many brochures scattered across the comforter. A man slept beside her, and when she spoke, he shifted slightly and covered his face with the crook of his arm. "What took you so long?" She looked toward the open door, and her eyes widened as they met mine. "What the …"

There was a yellow robe at the foot of the bed, and the woman turned her back to me as she got up and stepped into it. Her son reached for the coffees, and I tightened my grip, unwilling to surrender what I'd come to think of as my props. They turned me from a stranger to a kindly stranger, and I'd seen myself holding them as his parents rounded on me, demanding to know what was going on.

"Give them to me," he said, and rather than making a scene, I relaxed my grip. The coffees were taken, and I felt my resolve starting to crumble. Empty-handed, I was just a creep, the spooky wet guy who'd crawled up from the basement. The woman crossed to the dresser, and as the door started to close she called out to me. "Hey," she said. "Wait a minute," I turned, ready to begin the fight of my life, and she stepped forward and pressed a dollar into my hand. "You people run a very nice hotel," she told me. "I just wish we could stay longer."

The door closed and I stood alone in the empty corridor, examining my tip and thinking, *Is that all?*

■ READING AND WRITING

1. What arguments does Sedaris make about sexuality, stereotypes, and intolerance? How does he use himself as his primary "evidence"?
2. How does Sedaris use humor to convey his feelings about Audrey and her homophobic comments? Why is humor a more effective rhetorical tool in this case than anger or indignation?
3. How would you describe the ethos that Sedaris presents in his text? What does he do to convey this ethos to his audience?

■ RESEARCH AND WRITING PROJECTS

1. Based on the reading you have done in this chapter, craft a formal definition of "feminism." Then, research the library's databases to find other definitions of the term as it is used in academia, politics, and public discourse. What do these definitions have in common? How are they different? What does this tell you about the complexity of the term?
2. Most of the texts in this chapter present implicit arguments. Choose one of these texts and write an essay in which you make the implicit argument explicit. Because you are not writing a memoir essay, you will have to identify the argument in the original text and then develop an explicit claim of your own. You will also have to conduct research to find sources to support your position.
3. Use the library's resources and the internet to explore how gender roles and expectations differ in four countries or regions outside the United States.

4 Our Monsters, Ourselves

IMAGE 4.1: If this photo seems at all ominous, it might be because we "have apocalypse on the brain … from terrorism, the war, [and] natural disasters like Katrina," according to Kyle Bishop's essay "Dead Man Still Walking." Or maybe, as Annalee Newtiz argues in "Capitalist Monsters," it's because we see ourselves in the dark images. How would you explain the remarkable popularity over the past few years of vampires, zombies, and other monsters in pop culture?

What keeps you awake at night? Swine flu? Terrorism? War? The economy? Your next exam? Whatever your fear, there seems to be a monster lurking somewhere to embody it. We need these creatures for a variety of reasons, according to the readings in this chapter. And that's why vampires, zombies, and other monsters will always be with us—and will continue to leave their gory imprint on pop culture through books, films, television, music, and fashion.

217

Bram Stoker's Dracula *was first published in 1897 in London. In the years since, the novel's popularity and influence have grown: The book has spawned scores of adaptations and imitations in several genres and media, from stage and film productions to television series, graphic novels, and, of course, other works of fiction. Stoker himself was a theater critic and a manager for the celebrated actor Henry Irving before turning to fiction writing in his 40s. In addition to* Dracula, *he wrote several other novels and short stories, though none achieved the critical acclaim or eventual popularity of his masterpiece. The excerpt that follows includes Chapters 2 and 3 of the novel, which is told in the epistolary form—that is, it is made up primarily of diary and journal entries of individual characters and of letters between characters. The two principals in the excerpt are Jonathan Harker, a young solicitor from England, and Dracula, a mysterious count who lives in a crumbling castle in the Carpathian Mountains. Harker has traveled to Dracula's home to help him conduct a real estate transaction.*

from
DRACULA   Bram Stoker

■ Chapter II

5 MAY—I must have been asleep, for certainly if I had been fully awake I must have noticed the approach of such a remarkable place. In the gloom the courtyard looked of considerable size, and as several dark ways led from it under great round arches, it perhaps seemed bigger than it really is. I have not yet been able to see it by daylight.

When the calèche stopped, the driver jumped down and held out his hand to assist me to alight. Again I could not but notice his prodigious strength. His hand actually seemed like a steel vice that could have crushed mine if he had chosen. Then he took out my traps, and placed them on the ground beside me as I stood close to a great door, old and studded with large iron nails, and set in a projecting doorway of massive stone. I could see even in the dim light that the stone was massively carved, but that the carving had been much worn by time and weather. As I stood, the driver jumped again into his seat and shook the reins; the horses started forward, and trap and all disappeared down one of the dark openings.

I stood in silence where I was, for I did not know what to do. Of bell or knocker there was no sign; through these frowning walls and dark window openings it was not likely that my voice could penetrate. The time I waited seemed endless, and I felt doubts and fears crowding upon me. What sort of place had I come to, and among what kind of people? What sort of grim adventure was it on which I had embarked? Was this a customary incident in the life of a solicitor's clerk sent out to explain the purchase of a

London estate to a foreigner? Solicitor's clerk! Mina would not like that. Solicitor—for just before leaving London I got word that my examination was successful; and I am now a full-blown solicitor! I began to rub my eyes and pinch myself to see if I were awake. It all seemed like a horrible nightmare to me, and I expected that I should suddenly awake, and find myself at home, with the dawn struggling in through the windows, as I had now and again felt in the morning after a day of overwork. But my flesh answered the pinching test, and my eyes were not to be deceived. I was indeed awake and among the Carpathians. All I could do now was to be patient, and to wait the coming of the morning.

Just as I had come to this conclusion I heard a heavy step approaching behind the great door, and saw through the chinks the gleam of a coming light. Then there was the sound of rattling chains and the clanking of massive bolts drawn back. A key was turned with the loud grating noise of long disuse, and the great door swung back.

Within, stood a tall old man, clean shaven save for a long white moustache, and clad in black from head to foot, without a single speck of color about him anywhere. He held in his hand an antique silver lamp, in which the flame burned without chimney or globe of any kind, throwing long quivering shadows as it flickered in the draught of the open door. The old man motioned me in with his right hand with a courtly gesture, saying in excellent English, but with a strange intonation:

"Welcome to my house! Enter freely and of your own will!" He made no motion of stepping to meet me, but stood like a statue, as though his gesture of welcome had fixed him into stone. The instant, however, that I had stepped over the threshold, he moved impulsively forward, and holding out his hand grasped mine with a strength which made me wince, an effect which was not lessened by the fact that it seemed as cold as ice—more like the hand of a dead than a living man. Again he said:—

"Welcome to my house. Come freely. Go safely; and leave something of the happiness you bring!" The strength of the handshake was so much akin to that which I had noticed in the driver, whose face I had not seen, that for a moment I doubted if it were not the same person to whom I was speaking; so to make sure, I said interrogatively:—

"Count Dracula?" He bowed in a courtly way as he replied:—

"I am Dracula; and I bid you welcome, Mr. Harker, to my house. Come in; the night air is chill, and you must need to eat and rest." As he was speaking, he put the lamp on a bracket on the wall, and stepping out, took my luggage; he had carried it in before I could forestall him. I protested but he insisted:—

"Nay, sir, you are my guest. It is late, and my people are not available. Let me see to your comfort myself." He insisted on carrying my traps along the passage, and then up a great winding stair, and along another great passage, on whose stone floor our steps rang heavily. At the end of this he threw open a heavy door, and I rejoiced to see within a well-lit room in which a table was spread for supper, and on whose mighty hearth a great fire of logs, freshly replenished flamed and flared.

The Count halted, putting down my bags, closed the door, and crossing the room, opened another door, which led into a small octagonal room lit by a single lamp, and seemingly without a window of any sort. Passing through this, he opened another door, and motioned me to enter. It was a welcome sight; for here was a great bedroom well lighted and warmed with another log fire,—also added to but lately, for the top logs were fresh—

which sent a hollow roar up the wide chimney. The Count himself left my luggage inside and withdrew, saying, before he closed the door:—

"You will need, after your journey, to refresh yourself by making your toilet. I trust you will find all you wish. When you are ready, come into the other room, where you will find your supper prepared."

The light and warmth and the Count's courteous welcome seemed to have dissipated all my doubts and fears. Having then reached my normal state, I discovered that I was half famished with hunger; so making a hasty toilet, I went into the other room.

I found supper already laid out. My host, who stood on one side of the great fireplace, leaning against the stonework, made a graceful wave of his hand to the table, and said:—

"I pray you, be seated and sup how you please. You will, I trust, excuse me that I do not join you; but I have dined already, and I do not sup."

I handed to him the sealed letter which Mr. Hawkins had entrusted to me. He opened it and read it gravely; then, with a charming smile, he handed it to me to read. One passage of it, at least, gave me a thrill of pleasure.

"I must regret that an attack of gout, from which malady I am a constant sufferer, forbids absolutely any travelling on my part for some time to come; but I am happy to say I can send a sufficient substitute, one in whom I have every possible confidence. He is a young man, full of energy and talent in his own way, and of a very faithful disposition. He is discreet and silent, and has grown into manhood in my service. He shall be ready to attend on you when you will during his stay, and shall take your instructions in all matters."

The Count himself came forward and took off the cover of a dish, and I fell to at once on an excellent roast chicken. This, with some cheese and a salad and a bottle of old Tokay, of which I had two glasses, was my supper. During the time I was eating it the Count asked me many questions as to my journey, and I told him by degrees all I had experienced.

By this time I had finished my supper, and by my host's desire had drawn up a chair by the fire and begun to smoke a cigar which he offered me, at the same time excusing himself that he did not smoke. I had now an opportunity of observing him, and found him of a very marked physiognomy.

His face was a strong—very strong—aquiline, with high bridge of the thin nose and peculiarly arched nostrils; with lofty domed forehead, and hair growing scantily around the temples but profusely elsewhere. His eyebrows were very massive, almost meeting over the nose, and with bushy hair that seemed to curl in its own profusion. The mouth, so far as I could see it under the heavy moustache, was fixed and rather cruel-looking, with peculiarly sharp white teeth; these protruded over the lips, whose remarkable ruddiness showed astonishing vitality in a man of his years. For the rest, his ears were pale, and at the tops extremely pointed; the chin was broad and strong, and the cheeks firm though thin. The general effect was one of extraordinary pallor.

Hitherto I had noticed the backs of his hands as they lay on his knees in the firelight, and they had seemed rather white and fine; but seeing them now close to me, I could not but notice that they were rather coarse—broad, with squat fingers. Strange to say, there were hairs in the center of the palm. The nails were long and fine, and cut to a sharp point.

As the Count leaned over me and his hands touched me, I could not repress a shudder. It may have been that his breath was rank, but a horrible feeling of nausea came over me, which do what I would, I could not conceal. The Count, evidently noticing it, drew back; and with a grim sort of smile, which showed more than he had yet done his protuberant teeth, sat himself down again on his own side of the fireplace. We were both silent for a while; and as I looked towards the window I saw the first dim streak of the coming dawn. There seemed a strange stillness over everything; but as I listened I heard as if from down below in the valley the howling of many wolves. The Count's eyes gleamed, and he said:—

"Listen to them—the children of the night. What music they make!" Seeing, I suppose, some expression in my face strange to him, he added:—

"Ah, sir, you dwellers in the city cannot enter into the feelings of the hunter." Then he rose and said:—

"But you must be tired. Your bedroom is all ready, and tomorrow you shall sleep as late as you will. I have to be away till the afternoon; so sleep well and dream well!" With a courteous bow, he opened for me himself the door to the octagonal room, and I entered my bedroom. …

I am all in a sea of wonders. I doubt; I fear; I think strange things, which I dare not confess to my own soul. God keep me, if only for the sake of those dear to me!

7 MAY—It is again early morning, but I have rested and enjoyed the last twenty-four hours. I slept till late in the day, and awoke of my own accord. When I had dressed myself I went into the room where we had supped, and found a cold breakfast laid out, with coffee kept hot by the pot being placed on the hearth. There was a card on the table, on which was written:—

"I have to be absent for a while. Do not wait for me.—D." I set to and enjoyed a hearty meal. When I had done, I looked for a bell, so that I might let the servants know I had finished but I could not find one. There are certainly odd deficiencies in the house, considering the extraordinary evidences of wealth which are around me. The table service is of gold, and so beautifully wrought that it must be of immense value. The curtains and upholstery of the chairs and sofas and the hangings of my bed are of the costliest and most beautiful fabrics, and must have been of fabulous value when they were made, for they are centuries old, though in excellent order. I saw something like them in Hampton Court, but there they were worn and frayed and moth-eaten. But still in none of the rooms is there a mirror. There is not even a toilet glass on my table, and I had to get the little shaving glass from my bag before I could either shave or brush my hair. I have not yet seen a servant anywhere, or heard a sound near the castle except the howling of wolves. Sometime after I had finished my meal—I do not know whether to call it breakfast or dinner, for it was between five and six o'clock when I had it—I looked about for something to read, for I did not like to go about the castle until I had asked the Count's permission. There was absolutely nothing in the room, book, newspaper, or even writing materials; so I opened another door in the room and found a sort of library. The door opposite mine I tried, but found it locked.

In the library I found, to my great delight, a vast number of English books, whole shelves full of them, and bound volumes of magazines and newspapers. A table in the center was littered with English magazines and newspapers, though none of them were of very recent date. The books were of the most varied kind—history, geography, politics, political economy, botany, geology, law—all relating to England and English life and customs and manners. There were even such books of references as the London Directory, the "Red" and "Blue" books, Whitaker's Almanac, the Army and Navy Lists, and —it somehow gladdened by heart to see it—the Law List.

Whilst I was looking at the books, the door opened, and the Count entered. He saluted me in a hearty way, and hoped that I had had a good night's rest. Then he went on:—

"I am glad you found your way in here, for I am sure there is much that will interest you. These companions"—and he laid his hand on some of the books—"have been good friends to me, and for some years past, ever since I had the idea of going to London, have given me many, many hours of pleasure. Through them I have come to know your great England; and to know her is to love her. I long to go through the crowded streets of your mighty London, to be in the midst of the whirl and rush of humanity, to share its life, its change, its death, and all that makes it what it is. But alas! As yet I only know your tongue through books. To you, my friend, I look that I know it to speak."

"But, Count," I said, "you know and speak English thoroughly!" He bowed gravely.

"I thank you, my friend, for your all too-flattering estimate, but yet I fear that I am but a little way on the road I would travel. True, I know the grammar and the words, but yet I know not how to speak them."

"Indeed," I said, "you speak excellently."

"Not so," he answered. "Well, I know that, did I move and speak in your London, none there are who would not know me for a stranger. That is not enough for me. Here I am noble; I am *boyar*; the common people know me, and I am master. But a stranger in a strange land, he is no one; men know him not—and to know him not is to care not for. I am content if I am like the rest, so that no man stops if he sees me, or pause in his speaking if he hear my words, 'Ha, ha! A stranger!' I have been so long master that I would be master still—or at least that none other should be master of me. You come to me not alone as agent of my friend Peter Hawkins, of Exeter, to tell me all about my new estate in London. You shall, I trust, rest here with me awhile, so that by our talking I may learn the English intonation; and I would that you tell me when I make error, even of the smallest, in my speaking. I am sorry that I had to be away so long today; but you will, I know, forgive one who has so many important affairs in hand."

Of course I said all I could about being willing, and asked if I might come into the room when I chose. He answered: "Yes, certainly" and added:—

"You may go anywhere you wish in the castle, except where the doors are locked, where of course you will not wish to go. There is reason that all things are as they are, and did you see with my eyes and know with my knowledge, you would perhaps better understand." I said I was sure of this, and then he went on:—

"We are in Transylvania; and Transylvania is not England. Our ways are not your ways, and there shall be to you many strange things. Nay, from what you have told me of your experiences already, you know something of what strange things there may be."

This led to much conversation; and as it was evident that he wanted to talk, if only for a talking's sake, I asked him many questions regarding things that have already happened to me or come within my notice. Sometimes he sheered off the subject, or turned the conversation by pretending not to understand; but generally he answered all I asked most frankly. Then as time went on, and I had got somewhat bolder, I asked him of some of the strange things of the preceding night, as, for instance, why the coachman went to the places where he had seen the blue flames. He then explained to me that it was commonly believed that on a certain night of the year—last night, in fact, when all evil spirits are supposed to have unchecked sway—a blue flame is seen over any place where treasure has been concealed. "That treasure has been hidden," he went on, "in the region through which you came last night, there can be but little doubt; for it was the ground fought over for centuries by the Wallachian, the Saxon, and the Turk. Why, there is hardly a foot of soil in all this region that has not been enriched by the blood of men, patriots or invaders. In old days there were stirring times, when the Austrian and the Hungarian came up in hordes, and the patriots went out to meet them—men and women, the aged and the children too—and waited their coming on the rocks above the passes, that they might sweep destruction on them with their artificial avalanches. When the invader was triumphant he found but little, for whatever there was had been sheltered in the friendly soil."

"But how," said I, "can it have remained so long undiscovered, when there is a sure index to it if men will but take the trouble to look?" The Count smiled, and as his lips ran back over his gums, the long, sharp, canine teeth showed out strangely; he answered:—

"Because your peasant is at heart a coward and a fool! Those flames only appear on one night; and on that night no man of this land will, if he can help it, stir without his doors. And, dear sir, even if he did he would not know what to do. Why, even the peasant that you tell me of who marked the place of the flame would not know where to look in daylight even for his own work. Even you would not, I dare be sworn, be able to find these places again?"

"There you are right," I said. "I know no more than the dead where even to look for them." Then we drifted into other matters.

"Come," he said at last, "tell me of London and of the house which you have procured for me." With an apology for my remissness, I went into my own room to get the papers from my bag. Whilst I was placing them in order I head a rattling of china and silver in the next room, and as I passed through, noticed that the table had been cleared and the lamp lit, for it was by this time deep into the dark. The lamps were also lit in the study or library, and I found the Count lying on the sofa, reading, of all things in the world, an English Bradshaw's Guide. When I came in he cleared the books and papers from the table; and with him I went into plans and deeds and figures of all sorts. He was interested in everything, and asked me a myriad questions about the place and its surroundings. He clearly had studied beforehand all he could get on the subject of the neighborhood, for he evidently at the end knew very much more than I did. When I remarked this, he answered:—

"Well, but, my friend, is it not needful that I should? When I go there I shall be all alone, and my friend Harker Jonathan—nay, pardon me, I fall into my country's habit of putting your patronymic first—my friend Jonathan Harker will not be by my side to correct and aid me. He will be in Exeter, miles away, probably working at papers of the law with my other friend, Peter Hawkins. So!"

We went thoroughly into the business of the purchase of the estate at Purfleet. When I had told him the facts and got his signature to the necessary papers, and had written a letter with them ready to post to Mr. Hawkins, he began to ask me how I had come across so suitable a place. I read to him the notes which I had made at the time, and which I inscribe here:—

"At Purfleet, on a by-road, I came across just such a place as seemed to be required, and where was displayed a dilapidated notice that the place was for sale. It is surrounded by a high wall, of ancient structure, built of heavy stones, and has not been repaired for a large number of years. The closed gates are of heavy old oak and iron, all eaten with rust.

"The estate is called Carfax, no doubt a corruption of the old *Quatre Face*, as the house is four-sided, agreeing with the cardinal points of the compass. It contains in all some twenty acres, quite surrounded by the solid stone wall above mentioned. There are many trees on it, which make it in places gloomy, and there is a deep, dark-looking pond or small lake, evidently fed by some springs, as the water is clear and flows away in a fair-sized stream. The house is very large and of all periods back, I should say to mediæval times, for one part is of stone immensely thick, with only a few windows high up and heavily barred with iron. It looks like part of a keep, and is close to an old chapel or church. I could not enter it, as I had not the key of the door leading to it from the house, but I have taken with my kodak views of it from various points. The house has been added to but in a very straggling way, and I can only guess at the amount of ground it covers, which must be very great. There are but few houses close at hand, one being a very large house only recently added to and formed into a private lunatic asylum. It is not, however, visible from the grounds."

When I finished, he said:—

"I am glad that it is old and big. I myself am of an old family, and to live in a new house would kill me. A house cannot be made habitable in a day; and, after all, how few days go to make up a century. I rejoice also that there is a chapel of old times. We Transylvanian nobles love not to think that our bones may lie amongst the common dead. I seek not gaiety nor mirth, not the bright voluptuousness of much sunshine and sparkling waters which please the young and gay. I am no longer young; and my heart, through weary years of mourning over the dead, is not attuned to mirth. Moreover, the walls of my castle are broken; the shadows are many, and the wind breathes cold through the broken battlements and casements. I love the shade and the shadow, and would be alone with my thoughts when I may." Somehow his words and his look did not seem to accord, or else it was that his cast of face made his smile look malignant and saturnine.

Presently, with an excuse, he left me, asking me to put all my papers together. He was some little time away, and I began to look at some of the books around me. One was an atlas, which I found opened naturally at England, as if that map had been much used. On looking at it I found in certain places little rings marked, and on examining these I noticed that one was near London on the east side, manifestly where his new estate was situated; the other two were Exeter, and Whitby on the Yorkshire coast.

It was the better part of an hour when the Count returned. "Aha!" he said; "still at your books? Good! But you must not work always. Come; I am informed that your supper is ready." He took my arm, and we went into the next room, where I found an excellent supper ready on the table. The Count again excused himself, as he had dined out on his being away from home. But he sat as on the previous night, and chatted whilst I ate. After supper I smoked, as on the last evening, and the count stayed with me, chatting and asking questions on every conceivable subject, hour after hour. I felt that it was getting very late indeed, but I did not say anything, for I felt under obligation to meet my host's wishes in every way. I was not sleepy, as the long sleep yesterday had fortified me; but I could not help experiencing that chill which comes over one at the coming of the dawn, which is like, in its way, the turn of the tide. They say that people who are near death die generally at the change to the dawn or at the turn of the tide; anyone who has when tired, and tied as it were to his post, experienced this change in the atmosphere can well believe it. All at once we heard the crow of a cock coming up with preternatural shrillness through the clear morning air; Count Dracula, jumping to his feet, said:—

"Why, there is the morning again! How remiss I am to let you stay up so long. You must make your conversation regarding my dear new country of England less interesting, so that I may not forget how time flies by us," and, with a courtly bow, he quickly left me.

I went into my own room and drew the curtains, but there was little to notice; my window opened into the courtyard, all I could see was the warm grey of quickening sky. So I pulled the curtains again, and have written of this day.

8 May—I began to fear as I wrote in this book that I was getting too diffuse; but now I am glad that I went into detail from the first, for there is something so strange about this place and all in it that I cannot but feel uneasy. I wish I were safe out of it, or that I had never come. It may be that this strange night-existence is telling on me; but would that that were all! If there were any one to talk to I could bear it, but there is no one. I have only the Count to speak with, and he!—I fear I am myself the only living soul within the place. Let me be prosaic so far as facts can be; it will help me to bear up, and imagination must not run riot with me. If it does I am lost. Let me say at once how I stand—so seem to.

I only slept a few hours when I went to bed, and feeling that I could not sleep any more, got up. I had hung my shaving glass by the window, and was just beginning to shave. Suddenly I felt a hand on my shoulder, and heard the Count's voice saying to me, "Good-morning." I started, for it amazed me that I had not seen him, since the reflection of the glass covered the whole room behind me. In starting I had cut myself slightly, but did not notice it at the moment. Having answered the Count's salutation, I turned to the glass again to see how I had been mistaken. This time there could be no error, for the man was close to me, and I could see him over my shoulder. But there was no reflection of him in the mirror! The whole room behind me was displayed; but there was no sign of a man in it, except myself. This was startling, and, coming on the top of so many strange things, was beginning to increase that vague feeling of uneasiness which I always had when the Count is near; but at the instant I saw that the cut had bled a little, and the blood was trickling over my chin. I laid down the razor, turning as I did so half round to look for some sticking plaster. When the Count saw my face, his eyes blazed with a sort of demoniac fury, and he suddenly made a grab at my throat. I drew away, and his hand touched the string of beads which held the crucifix. It made an instant change in him, for the fury passed so quickly that I could hardly believe that it was ever there.

"Take care," he said, "take care how you cut yourself. It is more dangerous than you think in this country." Then seizing the shaving glass, he went on: "And this is the wretched thing that has done the mischief. It is a foul bauble of man's vanity. Away with it!" and opening the heavy window with one wrench of his terrible hand, he flung out the glass, which was shattered into a thousand pieces on the stones of the courtyard far below. Then he withdrew without a word. It is very annoying, for I do not see how I am to shave, unless in my watch-case or the bottom of the shaving-pot, which is fortunately of metal.

When I went into the dining-room, breakfast was prepared; but I could not find the Count anywhere. So I breakfasted alone. It is strange that as yet I have not seen the Count eat or drink. He must be a very peculiar man! After breakfast I did a little exploring in the castle. I went out on the stairs, and found a room looking towards the South. The view was magnificent, and from where I stood there was every opportunity of seeing it. The castle is on the very edge of a terrible precipice. A stone falling from the window would fall a thousand feet without touching anything! As far as the eye can reach is a sea of green tree tops, with occasionally a deep rift where there is a chasm. Here and there are silver threads where the rivers wind in deep gorges through the forests.

But I am not in heart to describe beauty, for when I had seen the view I explored further; doors, doors, doors everywhere, and all locked and bolted. In no place save from the windows in the castle walls is there an available exit.

The castle is a veritable prison, and I am a prisoner!

■ Chapter III

When I found that I was a prisoner a sort of wild feeling came over me. I rushed up and down the stairs, trying every door and peering out of every window I could find; but after a little the conviction of my helplessness overpowered all other feelings. When I look back after a few hours I think I must have been mad for the time, for I behaved much as a rat does in a trap. When, however, the conviction had come to me that I was helpless I sat down quietly—as quietly as I have ever done anything in my life—and began to think over what was best to be done. I am thinking still, and as yet have come to no definite conclusion. Of one thing only am I certain; that it is no use making my ideas known to the Count. He knows well that I am imprisoned; and as he has done it himself, and has doubtless his own motives for it, he would only deceive me if I trusted him fully with the facts. So far as I can see, my only plan will be to keep my knowledge and my fears to myself, and my eyes open. I am, I know, either being deceived, like a baby, by my own fears, or else I am in desperate straits; and if the latter be so, I need, and shall need, all my brains to get through.

I had hardly come to this conclusion when I heard the great door below shut, and knew that the Count had returned. He did not come at once to the library, so I went cautiously to my own room and found him making the bed. This was odd, but only confirmed what I had all along thought—that there were no servants in the house. When later I saw him through the chink of the hinges of the door laying the table in the dining-room, I was assured of it; for if he does himself all these menial offices, surely it is proof that there is no one else to do them. This gave me a fright, for if there is no one else in the castle, it must have been the Count himself who was the driver of the coach that brought me here. This is a terrible thought; for if so, what does it mean that he could control the wolves, as he did, by only holding up his hand in silence. How was it that all the people at Bistriz and on the coach had some terrible fear for me? What meant the giving of the crucifix, of the garlic, of the wild rose, of the mountain ash? Bless that good, good woman who hung the crucifix round my neck! for it is a comfort and a strength to me whenever I touch it. It is odd that a thing which I have been taught to regard with disfavor and as idolatrous should in a time of loneliness and trouble be of help. Is it that there is something in the essence of the thing itself, or that it is a medium, a tangible help, in conveying memories of sympathy and comfort? Some time, if it may be, I must examine this matter and try to make up my mind about it. In the meantime I must find out all I can about Count Dracula, as it may help me to understand. Tonight he may talk of himself, if I turn the conversation that way. I must be very careful, however, not to awake his suspicion.

MIDNIGHT—I have had a long talk with the Count. I asked him a few questions on Transylvania history, and he warmed up to the subject wonderfully. In his speaking of things and people, and especially of battles, he spoke as if he had been present at them all. This he afterwards explained by saying that to a *boyar* the pride of his house and name is his own pride, and their glory is his glory, that their fate is his fate. Whenever he spoke of his house he always said, "we," and spoke almost in the plural, like a king speaking. I wish I could put down all he said exactly as he said it, for to me it was most fascinating. It seemed to have in it a whole history of the country. He grew excited as he spoke, and walked about the room pulling his great white moustache and grasping anything on which he laid his hands as though he would crush it by main strength. One thing he said which I shall put down as nearly as I can; for it tells in its way the story of his race:—
"We Szekelys have a right to be proud, for in our veins flows the blood of many brave races who fought as the lion fights, for lordship. Here, in the whirlpool of European races, the Ugric tribe bore down from Iceland the fighting spirit which Thor and Wodin gave them, which their Berserkers displayed to such fell intent on the seaboards of Europe, ay, and of Asia and Africa too, till the peoples thought that the wolves themselves had come. Here, too, when they came, they found the Huns, whose warlike fury had swept the earth like a living flame, till the dying peoples held that in their veins ran the blood of those old witches, who, expelled from Scythia had mated with the devils in the desert. Fools, fools! What devil or what witch was ever so great as Atila, whose blood is in these veins?" He held up his arms. "Is it a wonder that we were a conquering race; that we were proud; that when the Magyar, the Lombard, the Avar, the Bulgar, or the Turk poured his thousands on our frontiers, we drove them back? Is it strange that when Arpad and his legions swept through the Hungarian fatherland he found us here when he reached the frontier; that the Honfoglalas was completed there? And when the Hungarian flood swept eastward, the Szekelys were claimed as kindred by the victorious Magyars, and to us for centuries was trusted the guarding of the frontier of Turkey-land; ay, and more than that, endless duty of the frontier guard, for, as the Turks say, 'water sleeps, and enemy is sleepless.' Who more gladly than we throughout the Four Nations received the 'bloody sword,' or at its warlike

call flocked quicker to the standard of the King? When was redeemed that great shame of my nation, the shame of Cassova, when the flags of the Wallach and the Magyar went down beneath the Crescent? Who was it but one of my own race who is Voivode crossed the Danube and beat the Turk on his own ground? This was a Dracula indeed! Woe was it that his own unworthy brother, when he had fallen, sold his people to the Turk and brought the shame of slavery on them! Was it not this Dracula, indeed, who inspired that other of his race who in a later age again and again brought his forces over the great river into Turkey-land; who, when he was beaten back, came again, and again, and again, though he had to come alone from the bloody field where his troops were being slaughtered, since he knew that he alone could ultimately triumph! They said that he thought only of himself. Bah! What good are peasants without a leader? Where ends the war without a brain and heart to conduct it? Again, when, after the battle of Mohács, we threw off the Hungarian yoke, we of the Dracula blood were amongst their leaders, for our spirit would not brook that we were not freed. Ah, young sir, the Szekelys—and the Dracula as their heart's blood, their brains, and their swords—can boast a record that mushroom growths like the Hapsburgs and the Romanoffs can never reach. The warlike days are over. Blood is too precious a thing in these days of dishonorable peace; and the glories of the great races are as a tale that is told."

It was by this time on morning, and we went to bed. (*Mem.*, this diary seems horribly like the beginning of the "Arabian Nights," for everything has to break off at cockcrow—or like the ghost of Hamlet's father.)

12 MAY—Let me begin with facts—bare, meager facts, verified by books and figures, and of which there can be no doubt. I must not confuse them with experiences which will have to rest on my own observation, or my memory of them. Last evening when the Count came from his room he began by asking me questions on legal matters and on the doing of certain kinds of business. I had spent the day wearily over books, and simply to keep my mind occupied, went over some of the matters I had been examined in at Lincoln's Inn. There was a certain method in the Count's inquiries, so I shall try to put them down in sequence; the knowledge may somehow or sometime be useful to me.

First, he asked if a man in England might have two solicitors or more. I told him he might have a dozen if he wished, but that it would not be wise to have more than one solicitor engaged in one transaction, as only one could act at a time, and that to change would be certain to militate against his interest. He seemed thoroughly to understand, and went on to ask if there would be any practical difficulty in having one man to attend, say, to banking, and another to look after shipping, in case local help were needed in a place far from the home of the banking solicitor. I asked him to explain more fully, so that I might not by any chance mislead him, so he said:—

"I shall illustrate. Your friend and mine, Mr. Peter Hawkins, from under the shadow of your beautiful cathedral at Exeter, which is far from London, buys for me through your good self my place at London. Good! Now here let me say frankly, lest you should think it strange that I have sought the services of one so far off from London instead of someone resident there, that my motive was that no local interest might be served save my wish only; and as one of London residence might, perhaps, have some purpose of himself or friend to serve, I went thus afield to seek my agent, whose labors should be only to my interest. Now, suppose I, who have much of affairs, wish to ship goods, say, to Newcastle, or Durham, or Harwich, or Dover, might it not be that it could with more ease be done by consigning to one in these ports?" I answered that certainly it would be most easy, but that we solicitors had a system of agency one for the other, so that local work could be done locally on instruction from any solicitor, so that the client, simply placing himself in the hands of one man, could have his wishes carried out by him without further trouble.

"But," said he, "I could be at liberty to direct myself. Is it not so?"

"Of course," I replied; and "such is often done by men of business, who do not like the whole of their affairs to be known by any one person."

"Good!" he said, and then went on to ask about the means of making consignments and the forms to be gone through, and of all sorts of difficulties which might arise, but by forethought could be guarded against. I explained all these things to him to the best of my ability, and he certainly left me under the impression that he would have made a wonderful solicitor, for there was nothing that he did not think of or foresee. For a man who was never in the country, and who did not evidently do much in the way of business, his knowledge and acumen were wonderful. When he had satisfied himself on these points of which he had spoken, and I had verified all as well as I could by the books available, he suddenly stood up and said:—

"Have you written since your first letter to our friend Mr. Peter Hawkins, or to any other?" It was with some bitterness in my heart that I answered that I had not, that as yet I had not seen any opportunity of sending letters to anybody.

"Then write now, my young friend," he said, laying a heavy hand on my shoulder: "write to our friend and to any other; and say, if it will please you, that you shall stay with me until a month from now."

"Do you wish me to stay so long?" I asked, for my heart grew cold at the thought.

"I desire it much; nay, I will take no refusal. When your master, employer what you will, engaged that someone should come on his behalf, it was understood that my needs only were to be consulted. I have not stinted. Is it not so?"

What could I do but bow acceptance? It was Mr. Hawkins' interest, not mine, and I had to think of him, not myself; and besides, while Count Dracula was speaking, there was that in his eyes and in his bearing which made me remember that I was a prisoner, and that if I wished it I could have no choice. The Count saw his victory in my bow, and his mastery in the trouble of my face, for he began at once to use them, but in his own smooth, resistless way:—

"I pray you, my good young friend, that you will not discourse of things other than business in your letters. It will doubtless please your friends to know that you are well, and that you look forward to getting home to them. Is it not so?" As he spoke he handed me three sheets of note-paper and three envelopes. They were all of the thinner foreign post, and looking at them, then at him and noticing his quiet smile, with the sharp, canine teeth lying over the red underlip, I understood as well as if he had spoken that I should be careful what I wrote, for he would be able to read it. So I determined to write only formal notes now, but to write fully to Mr. Hawkins in secret, and also to Mina, for to her I could write in shorthand, which would puzzle the Count, if he did see it. When I had written my two letters I sat quiet, reading a book whilst the Count wrote several notes, referring as he wrote them to some books on his table. Then he took up my two and placed them with his own, and put by his writing materials, after which, the instant the door had closed behind him, I learned over and looked at the letters, which were face down on the table. I felt no compunction in doing so, for under the circumstances I felt that I should protect myself in every way I could.

One of the letters was directed to Samuel F. Billington, No. 7, The Crescent, Whitby, another to Herr Leutner, Varna; the third to Coutts & Co., London, and the fourth to Herren Klopstock & Billreuth, bankers, Buda-Pesth. The second and fourth were unsealed. I was just about to look at them when I saw the door-handle move. I sank back in my seat, having just had time to replace the letters as they had been and to resume my book before the Count, holding still another letter in his hand, entered the room. He took up the letters on the table and stamped them carefully, and then turning to me, said:—

"I trust you will forgive me, but I have much work to do in private this evening. You will, I hope, find all things as you wish." At the door he turned, and after a moment's pause said:

"Let me advise you, my dear young friend—nay, let me warn you with all seriousness, that should you leave these rooms you will not by any chance go to sleep in any other part of the castle. It is old, and has many memories, and there are bad dreams for those who sleep unwisely. Be warned! Should sleep now or ever overcome you, or be like to do, then haste to your own chambers or to these rooms, for your rest will then be safe. But if you be not careful in this respect, then"—He finished his speech in a gruesome way, for he motioned with his hands as if he were washing them. I quite understood; my only doubt was as to whether any dream could be more terrible than the unnatural, horrible net of gloom and mystery which seemed closing around me.

LATER—I endorse the last words written, but this time there is no doubt in question. I shall not fear to sleep in any place where he is not. I have placed the crucifix over the head of my bed—I imagine that my rest is thus freer from dreams; and there it shall remain.

When he left me I went to my room. After a little while, not hearing any sound, I came out and went up the stone stair to where I could look out towards the South. There was some sense of freedom in the vast expanse, inaccessible though it was to me, as compared with the narrow darkness of the courtyard. Looking out of this, I felt that I was indeed in prison, and I seemed to want a breath of fresh air, though it were of the night. I am beginning to feel this nocturnal existence tell on me. It is destroying my nerve. I start at my own shadow, and am full of all sorts of horrible imaginings. God knows that there is ground for my terrible fear in this accursed place! I looked out over the beautiful expanse, bathed in soft yellow moonlight till it was almost as light as day. In the soft light the distant hills became melted, and the shadows in the valleys and gorges of velvety blackness. The mere beauty seemed to cheer me; there was peace and comfort in every breath I drew. As I leaned from the window my eye was caught by something moving a storey below me, and somewhat to my left, where I imagined, from the order of the rooms, that the windows of the Count's own room would look out. The window at which I stood was tall and deep, stone-mullioned, and though weatherworn, was still complete;

but it was evidently many a day since the case had been there. I drew back behind the stonework, and looked carefully out.

What I saw was the Count's head coming out from the window. I did not see the face, but I knew the man by the neck and the movement of his back and arms. In any case I could not mistake the hands which I had had so many opportunities of studying. I was at first interested and somewhat amused, for it is wonderful how small a matter will interest and amuse a man when he is a prisoner. But my very feelings changed to repulsion and terror when I saw the whole man slowly emerge from the window and begin to crawl down the castle wall over that dreadful abyss, *face down* with his cloak spreading out around him like great wings. At first I could not believe my eyes. I thought it was some trick of the moonlight, some weird effect of shadow; but I kept looking, and it could be no delusion. I saw the fingers and toes grasp the corners of the stones, worn clear of the mortar by the stress of years, and by thus using every projection and inequality move downwards with considerable speed, just as a lizard moves along a wall.

What manner of man is this, or what manner of creature is it in the semblance of man? I feel the dread of this horrible place overpowering me; I am in fear—in awful fear—and there is no escape for me; I am encompassed about with terrors that I dare not think of. ...

15 MAY—Once more have I seen the Count go out in his lizard fashion. He moved downwards in a sidelong way, some hundred feet down, and a good deal to the left. He vanished into some hole or window. When his head had disappeared, I leaned out to try and see more, but without avail—the distance was too great to allow a proper angle of sight. I knew he had left the castle now, and thought to use the opportunity to explore more than I had dared to do as yet. I went back to the room, and taking a lamp, tried all the doors. They were all locked, as I had expected, and the locks were comparatively new; but I went down the stone stairs to the hall where I had entered originally. I found I could pull back the bolts easily enough and unhook the great chains; but the door was locked, and the key was gone! That key must be in the Count's room; I must watch should his door be unlocked, so that I may get it and escape. I went on to make a thorough examination of the various stairs and passages, and to try the doors that opened from them. One or two small rooms near the hall were open, but there was nothing to see in them except old furniture, dusty with age and moth-eaten. At last, however, I found one door at the top of the stairway which, though it seemed to be locked, gave a little under pressure. I tried it harder, and found that it was not really locked, but that the resistance came from the fact that the hinges had fallen somewhat, and the heavy door rested on the floor. Here was an opportunity which I might not have again, so I exerted myself, and with many efforts forced it back so that I could enter. I was now in a wing of the castle further to the right than the rooms I knew and a storey lower down. From the windows I could see that the suite of rooms lay along on the south of the castle, the windows of the end room looking out both west and south. On the latter side, as well as to the former, there was a great precipice. The castle was built on the corner of a great rock, so that on three sides it was quite impregnable, and great windows were placed here where sling, or bow, or culverin could not reach, and consequently light and comfort, impossible to a position which had to be guarded, were secured. To the west was a great valley, and then, rising far away, great jagged mountain fastnesses, rising peak

on peak, the sheer rock studded with mountain ash and thorn, whose roots clung in cracks and crevices and crannies of the stone. This was evidently the portion of the castle occupied by the ladies in bygone days, for the furniture had more air of comfort than any I had seen. The windows were curtainless, and the yellow moonlight, flooding in through the diamond panes, enabled one to see even colors, whilst it softened the wealth of dust which lay over all and disguised in some measure the ravages of time and the moth. My lamp seemed to be of little effect in the brilliant moonlight, but I was glad to have it with me, for there was a dread loneliness in the place which chilled my heart and made my nerves tremble. Still, it was better than living alone in the rooms which I had come to hate from the presence of the Count, and after trying a little to school my nerves, I found a soft quietude come over me. Here I am, sitting at a little oak table where in old times possibly some fair lady sat to pen, with much thought and many blushes, her ill-spent love-letter, and writing in my diary in shorthand all that has happened since I closed it last. It is nineteenth century up-to-date with a vengeance. And yet, unless my senses deceive me, the old centuries had, and have, powers of their own which mere "modernity" cannot kill.

LATER: THE MORNING OF 16 MAY—God preserve my sanity, for to this I am reduced. Safety and the assurance of safety are things of the past. Whilst I live on here there is but one thing to hope for, that I may not go mad, if, indeed, I be not mad already. If I be sane, then surely it is maddening to think that of all the foul things that lurk in this hateful place the Count is the least dreadful to me; that to him alone I can look for safety, even though this be only whilst I can serve his purpose, Great God! Merciful God! Let me be calm, for out of that way lies madness indeed. I began to get new lights on certain things which have puzzled me. Up to now I never quite knew what Shakespeare meant when he made Hamlet say:—

"My tablets! quick, my tablets!
'Tis meet that I put it down," etc.,

For now, feeling as though my own brain was unhinged or as if the shock had come which must end in its undoing, I turn to my diary for repose. The habit of entering accurately must help to soothe me.

The Count's mysterious warning frightened me at the time; it frightens me more now when I think of it, for in future he has a fearful hold upon me. I shall fear to doubt what he may say!

When I had written in my diary and had fortunately replaced the book and pen in my pocket I felt sleepy. The Count's warning came into my mind, but I took a pleasure in disobeying it. The sense of sleep was upon me, and with it the obstinacy which sleep brings as outrider. The soft moonlight soothed, and the wide expanse without gave a sense of freedom which refreshed me. I determined not to return tonight to the gloom-haunted rooms, but to sleep here, where, of old, ladies had sat and sung and lived sweet lives whilst their gentle breasts were sad for their menfolk away in the midst of remorseless wars. I drew a great couch out of its place near the corner, so that as I lay, I could look at the lovely view to east and south, and unthinking of and uncaring for the dust, composed myself for sleep. I suppose I must have fallen asleep; I hope so, but I fear, for all that followed was startlingly real—so real that now sitting here in the broad, full sunlight of the morning, I cannot in the least believe that it was all sleep.

I was not alone. The room was the same, unchanged in any way since I came into it; I could see along the floor, in the brilliant moonlight, my own footsteps marked where I had disturbed the long accumulation of dust. In the moonlight opposite me were three young women, ladies by their dress and manner. I thought at the time that I must be dreaming when I saw them, for, though the moonlight was behind them, they threw no shadow on the floor. They came close to me, and looked at me for some time, and then whispered together. Two were dark, and had high aquiline noses, like the Count, and great dark, piercing eyes, that seemed to be almost red when contrasted with the pale yellow moon. The other was fair, as fair as can be, with great wavy masses of golden hair and eyes like pale sapphires. I seemed somehow to know her face, and to know it in connection with some dreamy fear, but I could not recollect at the moment how or where. All three had brilliant white teeth that shone like pearls against the ruby of their voluptuous lips. There was something about them that made me uneasy, some longing and at the same time some deadly fear. I felt in my heart a wicked, burning desire that they would kiss me with those red lips. It is not good to note this down; lest someday it should meet Mina's eyes and cause her pain; but it is the truth. They whispered together, and then they all three laughed—such a silvery, musical laugh, but as hard as though the sound never could have come through the softness of human lips. It was like the intolerable, tingling sweetness of water-glasses when played on by a cunning hand. The fair girl shook her head coquettishly, and the other two urged her on. One side:—

"Go on! You are first, and we shall follow; yours is the right to begin." The other added:—

"He is young and strong; there are kisses for us all." I lay quiet, looking out under my eyelashes in an agony of delightful anticipation. The fair girl advanced and bent over me till I could feel the movement of her breath upon me. Sweet it was in one sense, honey-sweet, and sent the same tingling through the nerves as her voice, but with a bitter underlying the sweet, a bitter offensiveness, as one smells in blood.

I was afraid to raise my eyelids, but looked out and saw perfectly under the lashes. The girl went on her knees, and bent over me, simply gloating. There was a deliberate voluptuousness which was both thrilling and repulsive, and as she arched her neck she actually licked her lips like an animal, till I could see in the moonlight the moisture shining on the scarlet lips and on the red tongue as it lapped the white sharp teeth. Lower and lower went her head as the lips went below the range of my mouth and chin and seemed about to fasten on my throat. Then she paused, and I could hear the churning sound of her tongue as it licked her teeth and lips, and could feel the hot breath on my neck. Then the skin of my throat began to tingle as one's flesh does when the hand that is to tickle it approaches nearer—nearer. I could feel the soft, shivering touch of the lips on the super-sensitive skin of my throat, and the hard dents of two sharp teeth, just touching and pausing there. I closed my eyes in a languorous ecstasy and waited—waited with beating heart.

But at that instant, another sensation swept through me as quick as lightning. I was conscious of the presence of the Count, and of his being as if lapped in a storm of fury.

As my eyes opened involuntarily I saw his strong hand grasp the slender neck of the fair woman and with giant's power draw it back, the blue eyes transformed with fury, the white teeth champing with rage, and the fair cheeks blazing with passion. But the Count! Never did I imagine such wrath and fury, even to the demons of the pit. His eyes were positively blazing. The red light in them was lurid, as if the flames of hell-fire blazed behind them. His face was deathly pale, and the lines of it were hard like drawn wires; the thick eyebrows that met over the nose now seemed like a heaving bar of white-hot metal. With a fierce sweep of his arm, he hurled the woman from him, and then motioned to the others, as though he were beating them back; it was the same imperious gesture that I had seen used to the wolves. In a voice which, though low and almost in a whisper seemed to cut through the air and then ring round the room he said:—

"How dare you touch him, any of you? How dare you cast eyes on him when I had forbidden it? Back, I tell you all! This man belongs to me! Beware how you meddle with him, or you'll have to deal with me." The fair girl, with a laugh of ribald coquetry, turned to answer him:—

"You yourself never loved; you never love!" On this the other women joined, and such a mirthless, hard, soulless laughter rang through the room that it almost made me faint to hear; it seemed like the pleasure of fiends. Then the Count turned, after looking at my face attentively and said in a soft whisper:—

"Yes, I too can love; you yourself can tell it from the past. Is it not so? Well, now I promise you that when I am done with him you shall kiss him at your will. Now go! go! I must awaken him, for there is work to be done."

"Are we to have nothing tonight?" said one of them, with a low laugh, as she pointed to the bag which he had thrown upon the floor, and which moved as though there were some living thing within it. For answer he nodded his head. One of the women jumped forward and opened it. If my ears did not deceive me there was a gasp and a low wail, as of a half-smothered child. The women closed round, whilst I was aghast with horror; but as I looked they disappeared, and with them the dreadful bag. There was no door near them, and they could not have passed me without my noticing. They simply seemed to fade into the rays of moonlight and pass out through the window, for I could see outside the dim, shadowy forms for a moment before they entirely faded away.

Then the horror overcame me, and I sank down unconscious.

■ READING AND WRITING

1. Though this excerpt is a fraction of the novel, it does vividly introduce the reader to Count Dracula. What is monstrous about the count? Why might Stoker's original audience have found him particularly frightening?
2. What is a *boyar* and what is the significance of the term for understanding the character of Count Dracula?
3. The Count reveals in conversation with Harker that he is eager to perfect his English. Why is the mastery of the English language so important to the Count? What does this detail tell us about the Count and about the era?
4. What are the rhetorical effects of presenting fiction in the epistolary form? What are the rhetorical and literary advantages of this form? What are its limitations?

■ USING RESEARCH

5. *Dracula* was published in 1897 by a native of Ireland who was also writing for the book-buying public of the English mainland. Research the relationship, particularly during the 19th century, between the nations of Ireland, where Stoker was born, and England, where the book was published. How does this knowledge change the way you read the text?

CAPITALIST MONSTERS   Annalee Newitz

They've got us in the palm of their big hand
When we pretend that we're dead
They can't hear a word we said
When we pretend that we're dead

—17, from *Bricks Are heavy* (1992)

At the turn of the century, critics hailed two movies as exciting reinventions of the horror genre: *the Sixth Sense* and *Blair Witch Project*. Both are about dead people who refuse to stay that way. The signature line from Sixth Sense, Haley Joel Osment's whispered, creepy "I see dead people," was an instant pop cultural meme. T-shirts with this phrase and morphed versions of it ("I see stupid people") were everywhere at the dawn of the new millennium, as were parodies and rip-offs of M. Night Shyamalan's terse, quiet movie about a little boy plagued by needy ghosts.

Osment's character Cole sees spirits who cannot rest until they get some kind of closure on their lives. He's begun to go insane when Malcolm, a child psychologist, helps him understand that the dead are not there to hurt or frighten him—they just need to be heard by one of the only human beings who can. Every dead person has story that Cole must interpret. Only by talking with these terrifying creatures, who often appear to him soaked in blood or with their brains dripping out, can he bring peace to himself and his preternatural counterparts.

Of course, some ghosts could give a crap about closure. Certainly this is the case with the bloodthirsty spirits who haunt the remote Maryland woods in *Blair Witch*. When a bunch of art students decide to slum it around the countryside to get footage for a sarcasm-laced film they're making about the legend of these spirits, they discover what documentary filmmakers have known for almost a century: the natives don't appreciate their condescending attitude. Murdered in mysterious, supernatural fashion, the students in *Blair Witch* are reduced to little knots of hair and teeth because they've refused to heed stories the locals tell about the Blair Witch's power to kill from beyond the grave.

Nothing is more dangerous than a monster whose story is ignored.

Like all ghosts, the dead people in *Sixth Sense* and *Blair Witch* come to the human world bearing messages. They remind us of past injustices, of anguish too great to survive, of jobs left undone, and of truths we try to forget. Gloopy zombies and entrail-covered serial killers are allegorical figures of the modern age, acting out with their broken bodies and minds the conflicts that rip our social fabric apart. Audiences taking in a monster story aren't horrified by the creature's otherness, but by its uncanny resemblance to ourselves.

One type of story that has haunted America since the late nineteenth century focuses on humans turned into monsters by capitalism. Mutated by backbreaking labor, driven insane by corporate conformity, or gorged on too many products of a money-hungry media industry, capitalism's monsters cannot tell the difference between commodities and people. They confuse living beings with inanimate objects. And because they spend so much time working, they often feel dead themselves.

The capitalist monster is not always horrifying. Something it is, to borrow a phrase from radical geneticist Richard Goldschmidt, a "hopeful monster."[1] Instead of telling a story about the destructiveness of a society whose members live at the mercy of the marketplace, this creature offers an allegory about surmounting class barriers or workplace drudgery to build a better world.

Regardless of whether its story is terrifying or sweet, capitalist monsters embody the contradictions of a culture where making a living often feels like dying.

■ Economic Disturbances

Stories about monstrosity are generally studied from psychoanalytic and feminist perspectives, but I argue that an analysis of economic life must be synthesized with both in order to understand how we define "monsters" in US popular culture. Capitalist monsters are found in literature and art films as well as commercial fiction and movies. Certainly we can find dramatic differences between its literary and B-movie incarnations. But, even as they cross the line between one form of media and another, the stories' fundamental messaging remains the same: capitalism creates monsters who want to kill you.

It's crucial to acknowledge that the people creating the books and movies I analyze in *Pretend We're Dead* may not have self-consciously intended to draw connections between what is monstrous and what people do for money. The "capitalist" part of capitalist monsters is usually a subtext and may not even be the most important part of a narrative. It lurks in the background, shaping events and infecting the plot line.

And it must be contained, figured, talked around, repressed. Stories where economic concerns rise to the surface and become overt are generally marginal affairs, embraced only by audiences of the highly educated or hardcore fans.

As an example, consider the strange case, of Brian Yuzna's brilliant 1989 monster movie *Society*. Set in Beverly Hills, this low-budget gore fest follows the paranoid adventures of teenager William Whitney, who discovers that his adoptive parents and sister are polymorphous, incestuous, human-eating aliens who have raised him for food. As the story unfolds, Yuzna draws an overt connection between the ruling class and evil beasts who eat the poor for fun. While *Society* is intentionally ironic and playful at times, the message is unmistakable: the rich are repulsive alien monsters. Further, these elite aliens are literally incestuous, so we are unable to avoid the implication that wealth is being hoarded by a few inbred elites who have no intention of sharing it with anyone who isn't part of their "family." *Society* culminates in a grotesque, skin-dripping orgy at the mayor's house where all the rich white folks of Beverly Hills melt into one, throbbing body which sucks the flesh off a human "meal."

While *Society* boasts all the standard fare of a horror film, complete with gloppy makeup effects and gratuitous nubile teenagers, it was never released theatrically in the United States. Theatergoers in England got a chance to see it on the wide screen, and gave it rave reviews, but in the United States it went straight to video. Yuzna speculates that this discrepancy has everything to do with how Americans view class. Interviewed about *Society*, he said:

> I realized that the British don't have a hard time realizing that there are classes. Americans, it's like messing with their mythology; you're threatening their whole world. The American world view is predicated on this idea that those who have more really deserve it. ... One of the points of *Society* is that not only do a very small number of people control the world, but ... whatever class you are born in is the class you will grow up in.[2]

Clearly, Yuzna's open depiction of class warfare made his film too disturbing, too economically horrifying, for a mainstream American audience. Even *The Psychotronic Video Guide,* known for its promotion of weird, underground films, describes *Society* as "very anti-establishment."[3] Thus, while we might say *Society* is a success artistically and certainly within its own terms as a capitalist monster movie, it hardly qualifies as "popular." It rests on the extreme edge of the pop culture spectrum, a film too overt for its own good. Like one of the nineteenth-century literary novels I will talk about in chapter 2, Frank Norris' *McTeague, Society* reaches only a small audience which is already willing to accept the basic idea that wealth generates monstrosity.

A more "standard" entry in the capitalist monster genre might be *Silence of the Lambs* (1991), a popular and Academy award-winning horror film about serial killers, released just two years after *Society*. Certainly one would not want to argue that *Silence* is an unself-conscious production; Jonathan Demme, its director/*auteur*, is well known for his thoughtful, critical films about US culture. Yet *Silence* is hardly the blanket condemnation of class warfare that *Society* is.

We are reminded repeatedly in *Silence*, through flashbacks and scenes between hero Agent Starling and seductive psycho Hannibal Lecter, that Starling's traumas are related to her class background (Lecter calls her a "rube"), yet her preoccupation with her poor, rural background is sutured neatly into a splashier narrative about gender and the art of violence. Judith Halberstam notes that *Silence* "dramatizes precisely ... [how] monstrosity in postmodern horror films finds its place in what Baudrillard has called the obscenity of 'immediate visibility' and what Linda Williams has dubbed 'the frenzy of the visible.'"[4] It participates in a hypervisual and distracting gone aesthetic of oozing wounds and skinned flesh. The spectacles of murdered and mutilated bodies are so heavily foregrounded that the questions about social class and economic mobility which fuel the narrative are safely contained as a subtext.

■ Dead Labor

A number of theorists and literary critics such as Halberstam have dealt with monster stories as something more than sheer entertaining spectacle. Perhaps most famously, Carol Clover's groundbreaking study, *Men, Women and Chainsaws: Gender in the Modern Horror Film*, paved the way for an analysis of monsters as rooted in anxieties around masculinity, urbanization and sexual desire. Other critics, such as David J. Skal and William Paul, have investigated the political and social meanings of horror in film. Some studies of the horror genre, such as James Twitchell's *Dreadful Pleasures,* Drake Douglas' *Horrors!*, and even David Kerekes' and David Slater's *Killing for Culture: An Illustrated History of the Death Film from Mondo to Snuff*, offer a way of blending aesthetic appreciation with cultural criticism.[5] I think the "appreciation" approach is still by far the most common in work on monsters, which indicates the degree to which many people remain uncertain as to whether one can call something "aesthetic" if it is also disgusting or outright goofy the way many monster movies are.

I take it for granted that pop culture stories are worth analyzing in my work. What matters to me is not aesthetics, but why monster stories are one of the dominant allegorical narratives used to explore economic life in the United States. As Clover explains, something about the flagrant violence of generic horror lends itself well to allegorical reading. Addressing the problem of gender in slasher films, she writes:

> The qualities that locate the slasher film outside the usual aesthetic system … are the very qualities that make it such a transparent source for (sub)cultural attitudes toward sex and gender in particular … the slasher film, not despite but exactly because of its crudity and compulsive repetitiveness, gives us a clearer picture of current sexual attitudes, at least among the segment of the population that forms its erstwhile audience.[6]

Like slashers, narratives in the capitalist monster genre are often too violent to fit within "the usual aesthetic system." And yet, as I will argue, such violence offers an intensely raw expression of what it means to live through financial boom and bust, class warfare, postcolonial economic turmoil, and even everyday work routines. Like gender, capitalism is a social construction which gets passed off as natural only by means of psychological repression and various forms of public coercion. Understandably, then, it is in extreme images of violence and misery that we find uncensored fears of capitalism.

Perhaps above all else, capitalist monsters represent the subjective experience of alienation. As Karl Marx and other philosophers have explained, there is a particular kind of social alienation attached to labor in free market capitalism. Marx describes alienation as the sensation of being brutalized and deadened by having to sell oneself for money. Alienation is what it feels like to be someone else's commodity, to be subject to a boss who "owns" you for a certain amount of time. Capitalist forms of work, Marx writes:

> Mutilate the laborer into a fragment of a man, degrade him to the level of an appendage of a machine, destroy every remnant of charm in his work and turn it into a hated toil … they transform his life-time into working-time … Accumulation of wealth at one pole is, therefore, at the same time accumulation of misery, agony of toil, slavery, ignorance, brutality, mental degradation, at the opposite pole.[7]

Elsewhere, Marx has stated simply that "capital is dead labor." Of course, the accumulation of wealth does not literally mean the death of laborers, although often it does; more importantly, capitalist work implies a symbolic death. It is the death of individual freedom, of pleasurable, rewarding activity, and of a rich social life. In short, it is the transformation of "lifetime into working-time" Capitalism, as its monsters tell us more or less explicitly, makes us pretend that we're dead in order to live. This pretense of death, this willing sacrifice of our own lies simply for money, is the dark side of our economic system.

◼ Great Monsters in American History

In this book, I deal with five types of monsters: serial killers, made doctors, the undead, robots; and people involved in the media industry. I use each chapter to trace the evolution of stories about these monsters from their late-nineteenth- and early-twentieth-century incarnations up through early twenty-first century ones. As we tell and retell these monster stories over time, their meanings gradually shift to reflect changing social conditions and economic anxieties. Moreover, these monsters tend to jump from one form of media to another. They can be found in movies, pulp fiction, and classic American novels. My choice of texts from all these media reflects this diversity of venues.

Every monster story I discuss in this book is North American, and all except for a tiny subset were created in the United States.[8] I chose to narrow my focus in this way so that I could focus explicitly on the kinds of fantasies produced by a nation devoted to capitalism as both an economic and a moral system. Many of the financial concerns shared by people in the United States are quite different from those experienced by people in Japan, Brazil, Italy, and other countries whose pop culture is full of stories about ghosts and otherworldly beasts. Analyzing stories about monsters produced in the United States gives us a window into what Fredrick Jameson would call the "political unconscious"[9] of a powerful but troubled nation.

I've also chosen to examine monster stories beginning with tomes published in the 1880s and continuing through to the present day. I start with the 1880s because it was an important turning point in U.S. economic history. Aside from being a time of tremendous financial crisis, it was also the era immediately following the Civil War Reconstruction.

The United States no longer depended on slave labor to fuel a large portion of its economy, and labor unions were beginning to make their presence felt. Moreover, civil rights for people of color and several waves of immigrants meant that new workers were pouring into the free market and changing its character forever. At the same time, technological innovations allowed the United States to develop industries devoted to the manufacture and maintenance of communications devices, among them the machines that later became radios, cameras, film projectors, and televisions. Analysts later termed the economic relations spawned by these devices "the culture industry." The culture industry changed the way we tell stories in such a profound way that its hegemony could be compared to the rise of print culture after Gutenberg built the first press.

The monsters in this book reflect the character of the American economy in the years since the 1880s. They rampage through narratives preoccupied with post-slavery economics, the culture industry, and new definitions of labor.

I locate the literary roots of capitalist monster stories in late nineteenth century naturalism rather than in gothic romanticism of the same era. Halberstam and many other theorists such as Marie-Helene Huet[10] have made a strong case for tracing monstrosity in literature back to the gothic and romantic traditions. But I argue that the naturalist novel, featuring what Donald Pizer has called "melodramatic sensationalism and moral confusion," provides perhaps the first glimpse of certain thematic and spectacular obsessions that come to dominate the capitalist monster genre."[11] Stephen Crane's attention to gore in his naturalist classic *the Red Badge of Courage* certainly influenced later disturbing images in film and fiction related to economic horror, and the overt connections between class, brutality, and murder in Frank Norris' *McTeague* might be said to make his novel a slightly more staid and realistic version of Yuzna's *Society*. A concern with yoking the surreal extremes of human behavior with socioeconomic status make naturalist aesthetics an obvious precursor of capitalist monster tales.[12]

The twentieth-century modernist and postmodernist fixations on what Theodor Adorno and Max Horkheimer call "the culture industry" are also deeply important to capitalist monster narratives, especially after the 1950s.[13] As the market in images, culture, and information came to replace industrial mass production, the issues foregrounded in these stories shifted. Simultaneously, the mid-century movement toward decolonization in the United States and abroad changed the stakes for global capital and for race relations. Put simply, forms of ownership and production that were immediately relevant in the early twentieth century became what Raymond Williams calls "residual formations" within dominant culture."[14]

The media industry may be an "emergent formation" that is still in the process of achieving market hegemony, but it nevertheless underwrites the ways we have experienced and expressed alienation over the past fifty years. Frank Norris represented a monster created by capitalism in the 1880s by putting a gigantic mining drill into the hands of his demented protagonist McTeague; in the 1980s, David Cronenberg offered us a similar kind of monster in *Videodrome* (1983) by surrealistically inserting a mind-controlling videocassette into the body of his media mogul antihero. Both stories disturb us by showing what it means to become the "appendage of a machine," but the forms of capitalist production associated with these machines are very different.

◼ The Nightmare of Social Construction

Capitalist monsters may be the bearers of stories, but they are also protagonists in them, individuals propelled by (and often attempting to propel) social circumstances they cannot control. For this reason, a cluster of issues which came to be called "identity politics" in the late twentieth century are central to how economic horror maps its social terrain. Gender, race, sexuality, and national identity are crucial to how we are asked to imagine (or not imagine) our economic identities in these stories. I don't mean to imply that any of these categories come to stand in for class. Rather, they provide a context for economic crisis; they complicate the idea of class by providing alternate models of oppression and liberation; and most importantly, they operate alongside capitalism as overwhelming social forces which help to create monsters as often as they create "normal" individuals. A capitalist monster story is, like a naturalist one, quite profoundly interested in social structures. But it is also focused on how specific individuals—often marginalized ones—cope with them.

What the monsters I deal with in this book share in common are position(s) which place them at the mercy of social, rather than "natural," forces. Theirs is a monstrosity that grows out of what Judith Butler has called "subjection,"[15] the process by which an individual is granted psychological interiority—subjectivity—only by assimilating (often unspoken) social norms and taboos. That subjection results in monsters points up the degree to which economic horror narratives are trying to articulate a connective between "civilization" and human disturbance. By contrast, many other horror genres locate "terror" in the realm of nature: humans in such tales are menaced by wild animals, creepy nonhuman beings, aliens, natural disasters, etc. Capitalist monsters are, to put it succinctly, freaks of culture, not freaks of nature.

It is therefore no surprise that the monsters I examine here are all *made* monstrous, rather than *born* monstrous. Serial killers are created by "bad environments;" mad doctors build or concoct monsters in their labs; the undead are reanimated as monsters; robots are always built by someone else; and of course people in the media industry are only made monstrous by virtue of the narratives they produce and consume. Indeed, the constructedness of these monsters is often at the crux of their stories. It underscores their connection to human-made institutions like the economy, demonstrating the degree to which ideology is "made material" in individuals as well as their social apparatus.[16]

One might say that in the stories I look at in this book, monsters are always constructed. This forces us to question the human agency behind their creation, socialization, and education.

Westworld (1973), Michael Crichton's proto-*Jurassic Park* film about a cyborg revolt at a theme park, foregrounds the horrifying implications of what it means to construct identities for the sole purpose of maintaining a service labor force. Protagonists Peter and John visit the "Delos" park, which promises "vacations of the future." Peopled by cyborgs who are "there to serve you and paid for by the exorbitant 1,000-dollar-a-day guest fees, the park is divided into Medieval World, Roman World, and Westworld, each populated by robot "natives." Peter and John stay in Westworld, a simulation of the Old West complete with gunfights, prostitutes, and wild saloons. As it turns out, all the most exciting forms of entertainment in Westworld require using the robots: John has a gleeful adventure shooting a sheriff robot, both men get in a barroom brawl with more robots, and later they enjoy a night of sex with robot whores. Yet Peter is made uneasy by the robots' obvious resemblance to slaves and kept women. Late at night, we see workers hauling away all the robots who have been "killed" by their human masters. Clearly, the robots' constructed social position at the park is more than a little disturbing. Seeing their dead bodies left behind like so much litter underscores just how problematic the human/robot relationships in Westworld actually are.

Created by and for the entertainment economy, the robots of *Westword* are effectively slaves of the culture industry. Yet due to their programming, the robots' options for revolt are fairly limited: they manage to kill several humans but can't escape the park's boundaries. This, finally, is the dark side of social construction, the moment when subjection becomes teratogenesis in *Westworld*, as in other narratives, we see how the market (inflected by a history of racial slavery and sexism) helps to create antisocial monsters who are destructive of human life precisely *because* of how and why they were constructed. *Westworld's* cyborgs were *made* dangerous to fill a market niche for specialty vacations and to fulfill a human desire for interactive entertainment. Allegorically speaking, individuals in this fabricated race of cyborgs are so thoroughly alienated during the subjection process that they can only imagine an end to suffering in violence and murder. But ultimately, humans are the biggest problem in this movie. They are so thoroughly alienated themselves that they get amusement out of producing servants they can kill without guilt. The monster's construction is simply a more literal version of his human counterpart's.

Capitalist monsters are the fantasy outcome of social constructivism in a class-stratified world. Their tales demonstrate why identity constructed under capitalism is a nightmare.

■ Pretend We're Dead

I have divided my analysis of economic horror into three clusters: mental monstrosity, bodily monstrosity, and narrative monstrosity. What's at stake here are three basic ways that economic forces "mark" us. The economy structures not just the way we think, but also (as many people have noted) the shape and health of our bodies. It also affects how we tell stories about transformations in both our psychological and physical states under capitalism.

In chapters which focus on serial killers and mad doctors, I explore mental monstrosity in tales about people who go insane because they lead lives which they perceive as forced on them by profit-driven institutions. I argue that the serial killer is a figure whose brutality condemns methods of capitalist production by taking them to their extreme, ultimately mass producing dead bodies. This grisly mass production is what drives the "publicity machine" in Norman Mailer's *the Executioner's Song*. As Mailer details how serial killer Gary Gilmore turned himself into a commodity image for the culture industry with his public pleas for execution, it becomes clear that the professional media are an integral part of Gilmore's homicidal mania. I consider *The Executioner's Song* in the historical context of naturalist fiction, especially Stephen Crane's *The Real Badge of Courage*, and in light of movies about serial killers made during and after the 1970s. Tracing their aesthetic origin to Mathew Brady's Civil War photographs of dead bodies, I ascribe the relevance of films like *Henry: Portrait of a Serial Killer* and *Private Parts* to a continuing cultural association between image consumption and the act of serial killing.

I turn next to the madness of doctors in narratives that are about the importance of professional middle-class work. Doctors in the Jekyll/Hyde tradition (in which I include Frank Norris' crazed dentist from *McTeague*) are driven mad partly because they feel they must be at work all the time, performing intellectual labor which involves selling off one's ideas to professional institutions. To express their nonprofessional sides, they made monsters of themselves.

Bodily monstrosity comes to the fore in my chapters on the undead and robots, beings who are, in many cases, physically disfigured by the very economic practices which grant them immortality and superhuman powers. The undead, in my analysis of short stories by H.P. Lovecraft and a variety of zombie movies, represent the horrifying returns of beings whose identities were forged in a colonial-era, slave-based economy. Comparing fantastical horror stories with D.W. Griffith's racist epic *Birth of a Nation*, I explore why both whites and people of color live in fear that their colonial ancestors will rise again to bring the world back to an earlier, more overtly brutal phase in capitalist history.

Robots are also marked as physically "other," but not in a racial sense. They are a "lower class," usually cast as the new manual laborers in a global capitalist future. Having assimilated technology into its body, or vice versa, the robot is a monster who is programmed and manufactured to serve a specific purpose: Usually, its job is to perform intensive labor and to fight for a human society which does not view cyborgs as human equals. Beginning my analysis with Charles Chaplin's *Modern Times* and Isaac Asimov's classic *I, Robot* and continuing with contemporary movies like *RoboCop* and cyberpunk novels by William Gibson, Rudy Rucker, and Marge Piercy, I connect representations of the robot's mechanical body to its degraded social status. I conclude my chapters on the undead and cyborgs with an analysis of how both monsters are portrayed as engaging in revolutionary acts aimed at overthrowing the people who created them.

I concluded with a chapter on narrative monstrosity, which deals with the hideous and sometimes pathetic creatures who participate in the culture industry as producers and consumers. From hack writers and bloodthirsty actresses trapped in Hollywood hell to prisoners of television and video games, these are media monsters whose lives are ruled by commodity images and corporate propaganda. Trapped inside a storytelling machine which exists solely to make money, characters in these tales struggle to tell the difference between narrative truth and the slick, commercial lies that do well at the box office. Often, their conflicts turn them into rampaging monsters—or worse, pieces of media themselves come to life and eat the audiences who watch them.

Pretend We're Dead is ultimately an extended meditation on how works about monsters represent economic crisis. The extreme horror we see in these stories—involving graphic depictions of death, mutilation, and mental anguish—is one way popular and literary fictions allegorize extremes of economic boom and bust in the United States during the past century. What becomes clear when we analyze monster stories is that the capitalist culture industry hasn't simply generated happy fantasies of self-made men with good, clean work ethics. It is just as likely to spawn gore-soaked narratives of social destruction. The history of capitalism can be told as a monster story from beginning to end.

■ Notes

[1]Goldschmidt, in his 1940 work *The Material Basis of Evolution,* argues that evolution is not gradual but proceeds in leaps and bounds. As a result, sudden, drastic mutations produce useless, maladapted animals but also, sometimes, hopeful monsters whose mutations make them ideally suited to their environment. Goldschmidt's work was a critique of Darwinian evolutionary theory, which held that all species change took place over long periods of time.

[2]Wiater, *Dark Visions*, 216.

[3]Weldon, *The Psychotronic Video Guide*, 518.

[4]Halberstam, *Skin Shows*, 1.

[5]For further reference, see Skal, *The Monster Show*; Paul, *Laughing Screaming*; Twitchell, *Dreadful Pleasures*; Douglas, *Horrors!*; and Kerekes and Slater, *Killing for Culture*.

[6]Clover, *Men, Women, and Chainsaws,* 22-23.

[7]From Marx, *Capital*, vol. 1, excerpted in Tucker, *The Marx-Engels Reader*, 430-31.

[8]I include a few Canadian films in the mix, not without realizing that Canadian monster stories merit their own volume of essays.

[9]Jameson, *The Political Unconscious.*

[10]Huet, *Monstrous Imagination.* Huet traces the idea of monstrosity to the early modern period in this fascinating study of teratology and ways that we imagine procreation.

[11]Pizer, *The Theory and Practice of Literary Naturalism*, 87.

[12]I do grapple with the gothic tradition in a chapter on robots, but by and large the gothic elements in this genre are related to their status as romances rather than horror fictions. Thus, the gothic comes in as part of a genre hybrid of economic horror/romance.

[13]I'm thinking of their treatment of this in *Dialectic of Enlightenment.*

[14]Williams, *Problems in Materialism and Culture*, 41.

[15]See Butler, *The Psychic Life of Power*.

[16]I'm referring to Louis Althusser's famous claim that ideology is "material." See his "Ideology and Ideological State Apparatuses," in *Lenin and Philosophy and Other Essays*.

■ READING AND WRITING

1. Newitz argues that monsters serve as "allegorical figures" that dramatize prevalent anxieties about America's capitalist economic system. What anxieties in particular does she cite? Can you think of any examples from movies or television programs you've seen recently that seem either to confirm or contradict her thesis?
2. What does Newitz mean when she says that American monsters are "freaks of culture, not freaks of nature"? How does Newitz use Judith Butler's idea of "subjection" in her argument?

■ DEVELOPING LONGER RESPONSES

3. Newitz's analysis of monster movies and books includes texts that many people might not think of as part of the genre. What, specifically, is her definition of a monster story? Do you find this definition convincing? Using Newitz's piece as a starting point, write a brief essay in which you present your own definition of a monster story.

■ USING RESEARCH

4. Newitz limits her study to texts produced in America after 1880. Use the internet and the library's resources to explore whether textual representations of monsters in other nations or from earlier than 1880 complicate her argument or support it.

IMAGE 4.2

IMAGE 4.3

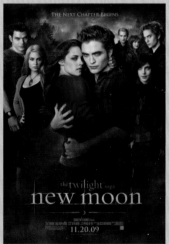

IMAGE 4.4

IMAGE 4.2: Max Schreck as Count Orlok in the 1922 vampire film *Nosferatu*. The movie was an unauthorized adaptation of Bram Stoker's *Dracula*. **IMAGE 4.3:** Bela Lugosi and Carrol Borlund in 1935's *Mark of the Vampire*, in which Lugosi played Count Dracula. **IMAGE 4.4:** The cast of the fall 2009 release *Twilight: New Moon*. What might the evolution of vampires on film—from the hideous to the dashing to the young, pale, and beautiful—say about the fears and desires of the audiences that paid to watch these monsters?

> Fabio Parasecoli studies and teaches food history and culture in Rome and New York and is president of the Association for the Study of Food and Society, an international organization dedicated to exploring the complex relationships among food, culture, and society. The following piece is a chapter from his 2008 book Bite Me: Food in Popular Culture.

VAMPIRES AND OTHER VORACIOUS MONSTERS Fabio Parasecoli

Imagine to find yourself traveling at the end of the universe, and to realize suddenly that you are starving. Where would you go? It is definitely not an easy situation.

The History of every major Galactic Civilization tends to pass through three distinct and recognizable phases, those of Survival, Inquiry and Sophistication, otherwise known as the How, Why and Where phases. For instance, the first phase is characterized by the question How can we eat? The second by the question Why do we eat? And the third by the question Where shall we eat? (Adams 1995: 215)

This predicament is the premise of *The Restaurant at the End of the Universe* (1980), the second book in the series *The Hitchhiker's Guide to the Galaxy* by Douglas Adams, whose first installment has been turned into a movie in 2005 by Garth Jennings with a screenplay by Adams himself. Zaphod Beeblebrox, the two-headed, three-armed president of the Galaxy, decides to take Arthur Dent, the only survivor from Earth, and the rest of his crew for a quick bite at the Restaurant at the End of the Universe. What ensues deserves to be quoted extensively.

> A large dairy animal approached Zaphod Beeblebrox's table, a large fat meaty quadruped of the bovine type with large watery eyes, small horns and what might almost have been an ingratiating smile on its lips.
>
> "Good evening," it lowed and sat back heavily on its haunches, "I am the main Dish of the Day. May I interest you in parts of my body?" It harrumphed and gurgled a bit, wriggled its hind quarters into a more comfortable position and gazed peacefully at them. ...
>
> "Something off the shoulder perhaps?" suggested the animal. "Braised in a white wine sauce?"
>
> "Er, *your* shoulder?" said Arthur in a horrified whisper.
>
> "But naturally my shoulder, sir," mooed the animal contentedly, "nobody else's is mine to offer." ...
>
> "What's the problem, Earthman?" said Zaphod ....
>
> "I just don't want to eat an animal that's standing there inviting me to," said Arthur. "It's heartless."

"Better than eating an animal that doesn't want to be eaten," said Zaphod …

"Look," said Zaphod, "we want to eat, we don't want to make a meal of the issues. Four rare steaks, please, and hurry. …"

"A very wise choice, sir, if I may say so. Very good," it said. "I'll just nip off and shoot myself."

He turned and gave a friendly wink to Arthur.

"Don't worry, sir," he said, "I'll be very humane."

It waddled unhurriedly off to the kitchen (Adams 1995: 115-117)

The goal of this scene is, of course, to poke fun at all those carnivores who require that animals are treated more humanely, especially when slaughtered. We will not get into this debate, which is actually quite sensitive and deeply fraught with ethical issues. Instead, we will try to understand why the dialog makes us subtly, but undoubtedly, uncomfortable. Since the environment in which the scene unfolds is all in all quite familiar, despite the location at the end of the universe, it is easy for us to recognize it and to relate to its dynamics. At the same time, presumably none of us have ever witnessed a meal presenting itself and inviting us to consume it. By addressing the guests, the animal reveals feelings like patience and pride. Suddenly, the divide between what devours and what is devoured turns out to be quite blurred. The bovine acts like a human being, while some of the human-like characters, ready to eat a sentient and speaking creature, appear to be at least partially devoid of what we would consider human traits. The strange intensity of this apparently funny scene and its troubling effect on the reader requires some explication. Why is it so powerful in its simplicity? We know that humor is often able to reach deep into us, allowing us to deal with issues that otherwise would bother or even frighten us. Why does the bovine make us laugh and shudder at the same time? I believe that the speaking animal embodies one of deepest, primal fears of all humans: the dread of being eaten and the correspondent anxiety that we might end up eating somebody.

One of the contemporary masters of horror, Stephen King, allows us to face these fears in the short story "Lunch at the Gotham Café," from the novella collection *Everything's Eventual* (2003). In a restaurant, a maître d' suddenly goes bonkers, and starts stabbing the patrons.

The maître d' brought his left hand out from behind his back. In it was the largest butcher's knife I have ever seen. It had to have been two feet long, with the top part of its cutting edge slightly belled, like a cutlass in an old pirate movie …

"Eeeeee! EEEEEEE!" the maître d' screamed, and swung the butcher-knife flat through the air. It made a kind of whickering sound, like a whispered sentence. The period was the sound of the blade burying itself in William Humboldt's right cheek. Blood exploded out of the wound in a furious spray of tiny droplets. They decorated the tablecloth in a fan-shaped stipplework, and I clearly saw (I will never forget it) one bright red drop fall into my waterglass and then dive for the bottom into a pinkish filament like a tail stretching out behind it. It looked like a bloody tadpole. …

If there had been a paralysis in the room—I can't actually say if there was or not, although I seem to have seen a great deal, and remember it all—that broke it. There were more screams and other people got up. Several tables were overturned. Glasses and china shattered on the floor. (King 2003: 414-416)

The tale strikes and unsettles us because it overturns the usual situation of a restaurant. The patrons get butchered and bleed over white tablecloths. The roles are inverted, and the illusion of a safe, stable reality is shattered, as the broken glasses and china aptly symbolize. The patrons, usually the eaters, end up dead and in pieces, metaphorically ready to be ingested and consumed.

Restaurants appear also in horror movies and TV shows. In Robert Rodriguez's 1996 *From Dusk Till Dawn*, written together with Quentin Tarantino, a family is taken hostage by criminals but they end up in a road-side café that at night turns into a vampire den, where occasional and unknowing clients end up on the menu. In the Season 6 episode "Doublemeat Palace" in the hugely successful series *Buffy the Vampire Slayer*, the blonde monster-killer gets a job in a fast-food joint where employees keep disappearing. In the end, nobody is actually being turned into hamburgers, but the unpleasant doubts linger.

These stories bother us because they show the fragility of what we consider as normality. In a heartbeat, ordinary people turn into men-eating monsters. Where do these unsettling fears come from? Why are we afraid of being killed and ingested? Why are we fascinated by characters that express their limitless hunger at all costs, to the point of dismembering and consuming human beings? Horror stories are mainstays in fiction: flesh-eating monsters and evil witches ready to cook us crowd our imagination from childhood. They cannot just be an instrument used by adults to impose discipline on their offspring; if this were the case, we could not fully explain why icons such as vampires, cannibals, and other monstrous characters have always been popular, and not only in Western cultures.

Using examples taken from contemporary pop culture, I will argue that these scary creatures express drives and desires that we would find otherwise unacceptable, like the unbridled hunger and the single-minded longing for ingestion that seem to define us as infants and later on—in sublimated and controlled ways—as adults. As newborns, all we want and need is to be fed, but our source of nourishment happens to be a human being. However, in the opinion of many psychologists, even at that young age, we cannot fully accept those drives, so intense that they would not stop until full satisfaction: the consequence is guilt, which has to be addressed and relieved. For this reason, every culture seems to find ways to deal with what we can define as cannibalistic desires, despite the ethical and social refusal to acknowledge their very existence and to accept them as a constitutive part of normal dynamics in the development of autonomous individuals and the functional dynamics of social communities. Certain civilizations apparently codified and limited the expression of these drives to very specific situations and conditions of ritual cannibalism. Otherwise these instincts are perceived as a threat and as the ultimate negation of all proper social interactions and negotiations.

Yet they exist, occasionally emerging both at the personal and at the social level, despite all attempts at denying them. Refused and stigmatized, cannibalistic desires resist again the social and cultural rules that condemn them by assuming different qualities under various historical conditions. For instance, since the emergency of absolute kings and nation states in Europe, they have surfaced as political metaphors to describe political power in terms of a devouring entity. Political science, philosophy, but also popular culture have often employed these food-related images to critique invasive governments and controlling authorities of all kinds. Thomas Hobbes, one of the first thinkers to analyze the absolute power of the state, considered human beings in their natural condition as willing to destroy each other as famished beasts; in his opinion, centralized governments set up by social contract to control these destructive tendencies had to be as powerful as a Leviathan, the voracious and vicious sea monster that the Judaic-Christian tradition often identified with absolute Evil (Hobbes 1982).

Where does the strength of these images come from? What kind of chords do they strike at the individual level? And what social and political mechanisms do they uncover, making them visible and understandable in very immediate and direct way?

■ Embodied Appetites

In the previous chapter, we analyzed the development and the functions of the brain to achieve a better understanding of why pop culture has such a compelling grip on us: recent developments in neuroscience seem to indicate that emotions, passions, and pleasure constitute essential elements in all mental processes, including the ones we would like to believe to be totally rational—a fact of which marketers have long been aware. We have also illustrated how pop culture perceives the mind, describing it at times as a computer completely independent from the body, at times as a mix of memories, feelings, and sensations heavily dependent on physical experiences. We can now proceed to analyze the main engine of market-oriented pop culture: consumption—and, in the case of Western affluent cultures, uninterrupted and all encompassing consumption. Food, as the primary and primal form of consumption, cannot but play a fundamental role in this discussion.

Once again, it can be useful to begin from the basic mechanisms that seem to regulate our bodies and our inner lives. We need to go back to our times as newborns to start this journey into our fears and dreams, and to understand how they relate to food and ingestion. Infants' need to be nourished constitutes the motivation for one of the first connections to the reality outside their own bodies: eating. These contacts with the world aim at absorbing all the elements that provide the energy necessary to survival and growth. When the source of nourishment disappears, or it is not able totally to satisfy the hunger, infants experience their first frustrations and disappointments, often expressed as crying and wailing, as all parents, infancy professionals, and anybody who has been around a newborn know very well.

Being one of our first interactions with the external world, it is likely that the feeding experience somehow determines the modality of our relation with reality at large, not only limited to the physiological mechanisms of nutrition, but also regarding emotional and rational aspects. Our dependence on food is after all "one of the most common and pervasive sources of value in human experience" (Curtin and Heldke 1992: xiii).

Hunger and the desire for incorporation—although inherently destructive—are a constitutive dimension of human life, stubborn, and for this reason scary. The irrepressible instinct for ingestion and the guilt that comes with it needs to be managed to ensure the emotional stability of the individual; the result is often unconscious denial.

Psychoanalysts such as Sigmund Freud, Melanie Klein, and Jacques Lacan located the source of this process—known as repression—in the early phases of our development as autonomous individuals. As a matter of fact, it could be considered as an inevitable byproduct of our growth process and of the simultaneous acquisition of language, which also marks the introduction into the world of culture and sociality outside the protective and caring boundaries of the immediate family. The painful process of learning rules and practices whose sense often escapes us and that aim to regulate body functions like eating, defecating, and even moving cannot but be perceived as a deprivation and as a fall from the full satisfaction of our emotional and biological needs that the relationship with our parents seemed to ensure.

These experiences, according to most psychoanalytic theories, remain emotionally effective and active at a subconscious level, even when most of us are totally unaware of them. To cope with them, we create defense mechanisms protecting our conscious processes and, above all, our self-esteem. One of the most effective among these mechanisms is to project the feelings connected with distressful experiences outside of ourselves, so that we can deal with them more easily. These dynamics create a pattern that we can apply, later on, to any disturbing event in our adult lives.

Sigmund Freud was the first therapist to work on the hypothesis that unconscious fears, uncontrollable drives, and unacceptable desires, otherwise unmanageable by the conscious self, are often expressed—at the individual level—in the forms of dreams, involuntary verbal expression and actions, psychosomatic symptoms, and, in the worst cases, paranoia and full-blown neurosis. Nevertheless, the forms that individuals choose to externalize these inner demons are not random or whimsical. On the contrary, the modality of these expression is deeply embedded in culture and society; after all, even our subconscious needs languages and codes to express itself. These behaviors also apply when it comes to eating. We are all fully aware of the key role that food, ingestion, and body images play as an outlet for these kinds of disturbances. Conditions such as anorexia and bulimia have been acknowledged as dangerous social plagues, and new neuroses such as the excessive fixation on physical exercise and orthorexia, the compulsive need to eat correctly, i.e. healthy, nutritionally balanced food, are on the rise. These neurotic expressions are not arbitrary and unsystematic, but rather they seem to articulate themselves in predictable and classifiable forms. Individuals seem to choose from a predetermined set of possible expressions in a bodily and performative language that can be communicated and understood. In other words, they have recourse to culturally determined codes and expressions to convey their most intimate fears and desires. The same fears and desires, repressed at the personal and communal level, become part of shared narratives that cultures create to neutralize any disruptive element that could become detrimental to its smooth functioning. Legends and tales, mythical figures and historical characters, traditions and customs all seem to fulfill this purpose as acceptable modalities of expression and representation of memories, feelings, and experiences that determine our development as infants and that we tend to suppress or even foreclose in adult life.

In vampires, cannibals, and various monsters—cruel but fascinating characters—we can externalize the elements of our inner life that most haunt and scare us, by giving them life and flesh (blood included, of course) (Dundes 1998: 159-175). We make them into autonomous agents with a life of their own, for whose actions we carry no responsibilities. As a matter of fact, in the fictional worlds we create we ourselves are at risk of becoming the victims of their ungodly instincts. Our innocence is safe.

This would explain why Anne Rice, arguably the most popular vampire-story writer of today, often connects—more or less patently and consciously—children's attitudes, food, and the vampires' craving for blood. Here is a passage from the first book of her most famous series, *Interview with the Vampire* (1977), where the vampire Louis tells the story of his first feeding: "I drank, sucking the blood out of the holes, experiencing for the first time since infancy the special pleasure of sucking nourishment, the body focused with the mind upon one vital source. ... How pathetic it is to describe these things, which can't truly be described" (Rice 1977: 19). The parallel between the vampire's blood sucking and the infant's suckling is so obvious that it is not even necessary to linger on it. Describing his body as absolutely concentrated on the feeding act, the vampire re-enacts the instinctive, stubborn, single-minded hunger of infants, who from birth are able to identify their source of nourishment. Furthermore, it is an experience that cannot be expressed in words. This is another important clue to the constitutive similarity between the monster and infants: they are both placed in a world beyond language, a world that does not know culture and symbols, laws and rules. It is a fantasy world where pleasure can be accessed directly, without the mediation of words, enjoyed total bliss.

The parallel between infants and vampires becomes even more manifest in one of the most disturbing characters ever created by Anne Rice, the young vampire girl Claudia, stuck in an eternal present as a child by her transformation into a destructive monster. She is described as extremely obstinate in all her manifestations: "For little child she was, but also fierce killer now capable of the ruthless pursuit of blood with all a child's demanding" (Rice (1997: 98). The obnoxious, stubborn, and almost mindless repetitiveness of the vampire's killing and sucking activities is striking, as Anne Rice herself points out: "What truly lies before you is vampire nature, which is killing. ... You will be filled, Louis, as you were meant to be, with all the life that you can hold; and you will have hunger when that's gone for the same, and the same, and the same" (Rice 1997: 83).

For vampires, killing is not only the inevitable outcome of a need for nourishment and survival. It appears to constitute their whole reality, the nature of their inner selves. Sucking blood reflects unbridled drives beyond simple hunger, pointing to some fundamental experience that all of us share in some measure. Otherwise, how could we explain the never-ending success of books and movies dedicated to these creatures of darkness? Their analysis can reveal interesting elements not only about the structure and dynamics of society (at least the Western, consumerist one), but also about the psychological mechanisms of individuals (Žižek 1992).

Condemned to feed on blood, vampires cannot share their repasts with humans. Just as the experience of feeding on blood cannot be expressed in any structured language, it cannot be organized in any structured meal. Yet the sensuality of food as experienced by mortals often reveals connections with the vampire's hunger. Both share the same sensual nature, even when they are placed on the opposite sides of culture.

> I moved silently over the narrow street and met the thick aromas of the kitchen rising on the air past the gate. The slightly nauseating smell of cooking meat. ... She stirred the mixtures in the kettle. I caught the sweet smell of the spices and the fresh green of marjoram and bay; and then in a wave came the horrid smell of the cooking meat, the blood and fresh decaying in the boiling fluids. ... The juices of the pot foamed on the lip and pit in the glowing coals below. Her dark odor came to me, her dusky spiced perfume, stronger than the curious mixture from the pot. (Rice 1977: 155)

Being an aspect of culture, prepared meals seem revolting to vampires, who position themselves beyond the distinction between the raw and the cooked that anthropologist Claude Lévi-Strauss presupposed at the base of every culinary culture (Lévi-Strauss 1968).

Furthermore, vampires can only move at night, when the rest of humankind (or at least its respectable parts) is asleep; they exist outside the human collectivity in a dimension where neither culture nor nurture has any meaning. Vampires are the undead, surviving beyond the limited life of humans. These elements reinforce the non-cultural character of the vampire experience, revealed by the impossibility for words to express it. The vampire's urge to feed on humans cannot be an object of knowledge; it cannot be symbolized, and become part of culture.

Nevertheless, humans and vampires share the same enjoyment in satisfying their hunger, as the following passage hints.

> "Your slave," Armand whispered with a deep intake of breath that was passionate. And he watched, as the boy drank deeply. I could see him savoring the wet lips, the mobile flesh of the throat as the wine went down. And now the boy took a morsel of white meat, making that same salute, and consumed it slowly, his eyes fixed on Armand. It was as though Armand feasted upon the feast, drinking in that part of life which he could not share any longer except with his eyes. (Rice 1977: 252-253)

Here the human shows utter bliss in eating his food, mimicking the vampire's sensuality and transport. Vampires' victims seem to experience a deep and uncontrolled pleasure in becoming food themselves, revealing a profound ambivalence towards devouring and being devoured.

> I saw the mortal boy watching me, and I smelled the hot aroma of his flesh.... Never had I felt like this, never had I experienced it, this yielding of a conscious mortal. ... He was pressing the length of his body against me now, and I felt the hard strength of his sex beneath his clothes pressing against my leg. A wretched gasp escaped my lips, but he bent close, his lips on what must have been so cold, so lifeless for him; and I sank my teeth into his skin, my body rigid, that hard sex

driving against me, and I lifted him in passion off the floor. Wave after wave of his beating heart passed into me as, weightless, I rocked with him, devouring him, his ecstasy, his conscious pleasure. (Rice 1977: 231-232)

This element is also evident in the forefather of all vampire tales, Bram Stoker's *Dracula* (1867). Here is the description of the encounter between the young Jonathan Harker and the three vampire women living in Dracula's castle.

There was something about them that made me uneasy, some longing and at the same time some deadly fear. … I could feel the soft, shivering touch of the lips on the supersensitive skin of my throat, and the hard dents of two sharp teeth, just touching and pausing there. I closed my eyes in a languorous ecstasy and waited—waited with beating heart. (Stocker 2003: 43-44)

Several literary critics have noticed these sexual undertones. "Dracula is the symptom of a wish, largely sexual, that we wish we did not have. The effect of repression is to turn a hunger into horror; the image of a repressed longing as it appears in a dream or a fiction is a sinister shape that threatens with what it promises, that insinuates the desire beneath the fear" (Stade 1982: vi).

In the moment of the embrace, followed by the fatal bite, victim and monster temporarily lose their individuality; as a matter of fact, they seem to experience sensual pleasure precisely because they get lost in a sort of blurring of their boundaries, a feeling that provokes both bliss and panic.

This move is excluded from Western culture, at least from its components based on the Greco-Christian oppositions of desires and emotions vs. reason, of body vs. soul, of matter vs. spirit, where humans are considered as absolutely autonomous and individual selves with clearly distinct—though arbitrary—borders (Bordo 1993: 1-42; Foucault 1988: 133-144). Vampires, feeding on others, blur these boundaries: they are inherently relational, unable to separate themselves from their prey. Their survival depends on the existence of others, even if the others become their victims, in a conundrum that opposes limitless hunger and destruction of the source of nourishment.

Because of their insatiability, vampires could also be interpreted as representations of certain aspects of our bodily experience, associated in many traditional Western cultures to the image of women as "hungering, voracious, all-needing and all-wanting" (Bordo 1993: 160). Since the Middle Ages, women's association with the preparation and serving of meals seems to have given rise to men's fear about feminine control over ingestion and consumption. Building in part of this connection between food and the feminine, medieval theologians tended to relate women to matter and the body, while men were equated to the spiritual and the rational (Bynum 1984 and 1987). Since the spiritual had pre-eminence over the physical, this dualism also led to the attribution to women of traits such as unruliness, lack of self-control, and unbridled appetite, in terms of both food and sex. Besides other philosophical implications, these elements could also be interpreted as the rationalization of the infant's fear regarding the end of the limitless access to the mother's body, and "the terrifying erotic independence of every baby's mother" (Dinnerstein 1976: 62). In other words, we can detect a strong ambivalence when it comes to the endless, unspeakable, and symbiotic source of nourishment that the mother constitutes for the infant: it can be the origin of infinite pleasure, but also of fear and potential starvation when denied.

The consummate science fiction writer Octavia E. Butler reflected on these troublesome issues in her last full-length novel, *Fledgling*, published in 2005, one year before her death. Approaching vampire stories from the same feminist point of view that made her voice unique in science fiction writing, she imagined a world where vampires actually live in symbiosis with humans, who are given the choice to voluntarily become a part of families where humans, both men and women, provide blood and the vampire, does not matter whether male or female, ensures pleasure, love, longer spans of life, and protection. The novel's protagonist, the young female vampire Shori, has lost her memories and only slowly she realizes her true nature when she bites a male human.

> He tasted wonderful, and he had fed me without trying to escape or to hurt me. I licked the bite until it stopped bleeding. I wished I could make it heal, wished I could repay him by healing him.
>
> He sighed and held me, leaning back in his seat and letting me lean against him. "So what was that?" he asked after a while. "How did you do that? And why the hell did it feel so fantastic?"
>
> He had enjoyed it—maybe as much as I had. I felt pleased, felt myself smile. That was right somehow. (Butler 2005: 18)

All boundaries of sex, gender, class, and even victim and victimizer, are completely blurred. Humans do not become vampires when bitten; and vampires, who live much longer than humans, suffer deeply every time one of their symbiotic partners dies of old age: "Once I had tasted them, they enjoyed the way I made them feel. Instead of being afraid or angry, they were first confused, then trusting and welcoming, eager for more of the pleasure that I could give them. It happened that way each time" (Butler 2005: 32). In Butler's novel, the enjoyment that humans sense in the vampire's embrace uncovers the subtle identification of viewers and readers with the monsters at which previous narratives had only timidly hinted. The recurrent theme of the bliss found in the vampire's bite seems to point to the uncomfortable revelation that somehow, deep down, we want to lose our individuality and that we all could find the monster in ourselves.

What makes vampires really scary is that they confront us with what we could become if we let go, if we gave way to instincts and drives that we are afraid might be buried inside us. It would not take much for us to turn into monsters; this fear is metaphorically expressed in the fact that once bitten, the victims become themselves vampires. It is something that spreads easily and fast, like an infectious disease. This theme acquires greater relevance and political undertones in modern stories such as *I Am Legend* by Richard Matheson. In this 1954 novel, becoming in 2007 a movie starring Will Smith, the protagonist Robert Neville is the last human being in a world where everybody else has turned into vampires. Every night he has to endure the unrelenting siege of his home, while during the day he wanders around killing monsters and trying to figure out how to stop the contagion. Neville lives in what seems to be middle America, yet one where reality seems to have gone mad. Or has it really? During one of the long nights, Neville gets to think about the reason why the vampire is so hated:

> Are his needs more shocking than the needs of other animals and men? Are his needs more outrageous than the deeds of the parent who drained the spirit of his child? The vampire may foster quickened heartbeats and levitated hair. But is he worse than the parent who gave to society a neurotic child who became a politician? Is he worse than the manufacturer who set up belated foundations with the money he made by handing bombs and guns to suicidal nationalists? Is he worse than the distiller who gave bastardized grain juice to stultify further the brains of those who, sober, were incapable of a progressive thought? (Nay, I apologize for this calumny; I nip the brew that feeds me). Is he worse than the publisher who filled ubiquitous racks with lust and death wishes? Really, now, search your soul, lovie—is the vampire so bad?
>
> All he does is drink blood. (Matheson 1995: 32)

After all, Matheson seems to warn us, we are all vampires. Or at least it would not take us much to turn into monsters. A generation later, in 1975, Stephen King again gave voice to these dreads. In his novel *Salem's Lot*, two vampires under the aspect of businessmen move into an old abandoned mansion in a small American town, which in a short time turns into a sort of ghost town where more and more citizens are turned into vampires. The novel is frightening because it shows a bunch of peaceful middle-Americans becoming monsters through slight changes in their daily routines, especially in eating and drinking. As one of the vampires explains:

> The folk here are still rich and full-blooded, folk who are stuffed with the aggression and the darkness so necessary to ... There is no English word for it. *Pokol: vurderlak; eyalik*... The people have not cut off the vitality which flows from their mother, the earth, with a shell of concrete and cement. Their hands are plunged into the very waters of life. They have ripped the life from the earth, whole and beating. (King 2000: 256)

It is enough to dig a little deeper to find energies and drives that only need to be set free to express themselves in ways that terrorize us. This unbridled vitality, the voraciousness and the wild craving for ingestion that vampires awake in Salem's Lot's citizens is the same that we often recognize in infants, especially in hungry ones.

■ Hunger and Development

The connection between vampires and infants can be approached from different points of view. As we mentioned, the representations of vampires' victims in pop culture hint at both their fear of being destroyed, and their wish to lose themselves in the monsters. When the creatures of the night bite, their targets seem to lose their individuality and pleasurably abandon themselves. At the same time, vampires' prey are terrified by the bites from the monsters, which are dangerous and deadly. This ambivalence can be explained if we assume that we readers somehow can identify not only with the prey, but also with the hunters. In other words, the constant success of vampires in Western pop culture makes sense if we can find some trait of the undead bloodsuckers in ourselves, particularly in our fantasies and in our drives.

At this point, it might be useful to explore what psychology and psychoanalysis have to say about these issues, to achieve a better understanding not only of vampires, but also of ingestion and, more broadly, of the consumption drives that constitute the back-bone of market-driven pop culture.

As a matter of fact traditional psychoanalysis tended to limit the impact of eating and ingestion, and hence consumption, only to the development of the early phases of life, with little or no consequence once the individual reaches adulthood. An inherent contradiction seems to haunt Freud's approach to hunger. He definitely acknowledges its importance, to the point that, in his three seminal essays on the theory of sexuality, originally published in 1905, and specifically in "the Sexual Aberrations," he resorts twice to hunger as a metaphor for the libido.

> The fact of existence of sexual needs in human beings and animals is expressed in biology by the assumption of a "sexual instinct," on the analogy of the instinct of nutrition, that is of hunger. Everyday language possesses no counterpart to the word "hunger," but science makes use of the word "libido" for that purpose. (Freud 2000:1)
> The normal sexual aim is regarded as being the union of the genitals in the act known as copulation, which leads to a release of sexual tension and a temporary extinction of the sexual instinct—a satisfaction analogous to the sating of hunger. (Freud 2000:15)

The psychoanalyst describes hunger as a drive, and an extremely powerful one, that needs satisfaction just like the sexual instinct and that anybody can understand, since it is familiar to any human being. As a matter of fact, in "Infantile Sexuality" Freud argues that the first stage of the sexual development of infants is closely connected to eating and food.

> The first of these [phases] is the oral or, as it might be called, cannibalistic pregenital sexual organization. Here sexual activity has not yet been separated from the ingestion of food. ... The sexual aim consists in the incorporation of the object—the prototype of a process which, in the form of identification, is later to play such an important psychological part. (Freud 2000: 64)
> The child's lips, in our view, behave like an erotogenic zone, and no doubt stimulation by the warm flow of milk is the cause of the pleasurable sensation. The satisfaction of the erotogenic zone is associated, in the first instance, with the satisfaction of the need for nourishment. To begin with, sexual activity attaches itself to functions serving the purpose of self-preservation and does not become independent of them until later. No one who

has ever seen a baby sinking back satiated from the breast and falling asleep with flushed cheeks and a blissful smile can escape the reflection that this picture persists as a prototype of the expression of sexual satisfaction in later life. (Freud 2000: 47-48)

It is significant that the passage is part of a section on autoerotism. Freud seems to emphasize that in his opinion there are no external objects of pleasure, and he stresses this concept several times in the essay. On the other hand, Freud also makes the assertion that the breast is the first sexual object, previous to autoerotism. In "Transformation of Puberty," he affirms: "A child suckling at his mother's breast has become the prototype of every relation of love. The finding of an object is in fact a refinding of it" (Freud 2000: 88). Later on, in "on Narcissism" (1914), he appears quite unresolved, stating that the child has originally two objects, himself and the mother who feeds him. As it has been noted, this is no secondary matter, since it engendered the competing psychoanalytic theories based on the mutually exclusive assumptions that the libido is originally pleasure-seeking (inward) or object-seeking (outward) (Chodorow 2000: xv-xvi).

Freud argues that fantasies of devouring are particularly disturbing, because they are based on the earliest pleasure drive: oral gratification. Developing children desire to consume their parents, and these unacceptable longings inspire fear of retaliation. It is not by chance that bedtime stories and children's tales, such as the brothers Grimm's Hansel and Gretel or Little Red Riding Hood, are full of cannibalistic acts.

Whatever importance Freud gives to hunger and nourishment in infancy, he seems to underestimate their role in later stages of the sexual development of the human being, unless in the form of "hysterical vomiting" following repression and disgust about food (Freud 2000: 48). How can the influence of an activity that remains crucial during the whole span of life become so negligible in classic psychoanalytical theory? Do human beings stop eating, or experiencing pleasure or disgust through food?

Freud left many issues open to further examination, some of which were addressed by child psychologist Melanie Klein in the 1920s.

Her point of departure was the narcissistic attitude of newborns, that is to say, their exclusive focus on themselves and their needs, whose satisfaction brings pleasure. "Children form relations with the outside world by directing to objects from which pleasure is obtained the libido that was originally attached exclusively to the child's own ego " (Klein 1987a: 58). From the earlier stages of her career, she understood that the psychoanalytic methods developed by Freud were based on language, a skill still not fully mastered by young children. This realization led her to develop a new approach that she called "play technique:" this consisted in observing children play with toys and objects to analyze their behavior, which she assumed was a reflection of their inner world. Following this intuition, she moved towards the study of objects relations, considered as the ego's earlier mechanisms of defense.

Now the first object to which infants relate is their mothers' breast (or any substitute for it), on which they depend for the pleasurable satisfaction of their vital needs. When babies are content and well fed, they feel one with it. But if they sense that their needs are not met, then the breast is experienced as a separate entity, becoming their first psychological object and a cause of anxiety. The withdrawal of the breast probably constitutes the infant's first experience of object loss, which can be exorcized by games such as peek-a-boo and hide-and-seek, re-enacting the loss but reassuring the child about its positive ending with the finding of the lost object (Frankiel 1993).

At this point, infants end up perceiving the breast as split into a good part, which they identify with themselves and which provides hallucinatory pleasure, and a bad part, which becomes the object of the oral-sadistic, or cannibalistic, desires of the infant. In these phantasies (in Klenian language, phantasies are the representations that allow babies to relate psychically to the conjunction of their inner and outer world), children bite, devour, and ingest the breast, but as a consequence of the guilt provoked by this desire they dread a punishment corresponding to the offense. The object of their attack becomes a source of danger because infants fear similar retaliatory attacks from it. This early oral-sadistic phase will be overcome only when, with the beginning of the genital phase, the children's ego becomes able to take in the mother as a whole person, with her good and bad parts.

In Klein's analysis, the role played by feeling in the development of the subject cannot be easily dismissed. Worried that their sadistic impulses might destroy the objects of their drive, and afraid of retaliation from the objects that have been attacked in phantasy, infants move to different, more external objects that related symbolically to the ones left behind. In Klein's theory, the transfer of desires and anxieties from object to object, training infants to substitution and representation, also introduces them into the symbolic and semiotic dimension, which constitutes the basis for language and learning. If we interpret aggressive impulses as incorporation of knowledge, it becomes clear that our hunger, and our desire for ingestion, push us along the path of symbol formation, socialization, and culture.

Nevertheless, to be part of culture and of society, growing infants must learn to repress their destructive, ingestion-based drives, which nevertheless, in adult life, will constitute the core for all desires for control and power, perceived as potentially dangerous for collective life. For these reasons they must be transformed and expressed—sublimated, in psychoanalytical language—in acceptable and constructive forms. But they keep on exerting a deep influence on the way we deal with reality as adults.

The permanence of the anxieties, drives, and fear connected with the ambivalent relationship to the mother's breast (or any source of nourishment) would explain why we identify not only with the victims of vampires, but also with the monsters themselves: although we have repressed our infant memories, we might still subconsciously maintain some cannibalistic instincts (Copjec 1991: 34). The recurrence of these monster-like figures in pop culture can only be explained as an embodiment of the drives connected to our daily and necessary feeding experiences, which ostensibly remain relevant throughout our adult life, even though psychoanalysis seems to focus on them only during the first phases of life. We should speak not of transitory phases that once finished are gone forever, but rather of long-lasting attitudes and approaches towards the external word.

■ Hunger as Void

The relative lack of interest of psychoanalysis in the role of eating and food in adult life continued also with the French analyst and theorist Jacques Lacan, who, however, as will see in Chapter 4, dedicated much attention to body images. In the later portions of his career, Lacan interpreted children's desire for the absolute fulfillment of their own necessities as an impossible symbiotic fantasy centered on total fusion with the mother, a bodily *jouissance* (absolute enjoyment) that constitutes the ultimate experience of the Real, in Lucan's theory a dimension that cannot be talked about and categorized, beyond symbolic culture and even imagination. However, this bliss can never be achieved because it actually never existed, creating the constitutive lack and longing that lie at the core of human beings and their desires. From the moment when children learn to verbalize their needs by acceding to the symbolic realm of culture and language, the demands addressed to mothers are more a plea for recognition and unconditional love than an actual request for them to meet a given necessity. Whatever the response, children can never be absolutely certain of their mother's love. As a consequence, what is left of the demand after the specific needs have been satisfied emerges as desire, which actually expresses the wish for the fantasized total unity with the mother. For Lacan, human subjects are centered on this fundamental gap, a void that he called *béance* and that explains their deepest motivations and wants. It is as if a bottomless hunger was placed at the core of what we are: whatever we acquire, ingest, and consume could never fulfill it. We face again the insatiable voraciousness of vampires, their unspeakable desire, and their existence beyond social or cultural boundaries.

Jacques Lacan also examined infants' destructive, cannibalistic drives. Investigating young children's behavior, he pointed to their "motor impotence and nursling dependence," determined by a "veritable specific prematurity of birth (Lacan 2002: 4, 6). The organic inadequacy and lack of bodily integrity frustrate children, who as we will see in Chapter 4, try to find the completeness and wholeness they need in their own images reflected in mirrors According to Lacan, the infants' fragmentary body experience is manifested in later life in sadomasochistic fantasies and dreams centered on body fragmentation (*corps morcelé*). This fantasy is also connected with the may be produced by the anxiety caused by the infants' own aggressive impulses toward the mother's breast, from which they fear retaliation in the form of devouring. Lucan finds the origin of aggressive tendencies in the frustration deriving from the disturbing realization of the gap between the children's lived experience of the fragmented body and their narcissistic identifications. These tendencies build on an already present fantasy aggression toward the bad breast and the ensuing fears of retaliation. In "Aggressiveness in Psychoanalysis" (1948), Lacan contended that this tendency might find its roots precisely in "the images of castration, emasculation, mutilation, dismemberment, dislocation, evisceration, devouring, and bursting open of the body, in short, the images that I have grouped together under the heading 'images of the fragmented body'" (Lacan 2002: 13). Nevertheless, the interest in the ambivalence towards eating and being eaten that Lacan tackled in his early writings almost disappears in his later works, where he shifted his increasingly abstract analysis to fantasies and drives. He concentrated on sexuality, fetishes, the gaze, even on the voice, leaving aside good, plain hunger.

Despite the fact that in the work of some of the most influential psychologists and psychiatrists the interest in these themes is often limited to the earliest phases of human development, we are led to admit that hunger and more generally desire for consumption do play an important role in our adult life. Sometimes they can become so intense that they make us uncomfortable. From childhood, we are taught various forms of self-control, aimed at easing our life in families, communities, and society. Unbridled desire is frowned upon, if not condemned. Only children, at times, are able to get away with it; after all, they are considered adults in training. For this reason, pop culture has often used young characters to poke fun at the defects and vices of adults. The movie *Willy Wonka and the Chocolate Factory* (1971) and its recent remake by the visionary filmmaker Tim Burton, *Charlie and the Chocolate Factory* (2005), both based on the book *Charlie and the Chocolate Factory* written in 1964 by British author Roald Dahl, are in different ways a gentle critique of excessive consumption. All the characters embody one form or another of limitless, stupid greed that inevitably leads to self-destruction, even if imaginary. At the same time, though, they offer an interesting insight into the voraciousness and the drives that lurk in all of us; that is probably the reason for the success of the movie with both young viewers and adults. Through the various characters, we indulge vicariously in our vices, knowing that even the worst punishment is not for real. All of the winners of the famous Golden Ticket granting entrance to the mysterious chocolate factory, together with their chaperones, are clearly blown away when they access the core of Wonka's reign: the room with the chocolate river, where everything is edible. At one moment or another, all of them give in to their curiosities and cravings, even good little Charlie. For our discussion, Augustus Gloop is the most interesting among the children who are invited to visit the fabled factory. In the 1971 movie he is represented as a hefty German boy; we see him for the first time when he is interviewed in a traditional *Stube*-style restaurant together with his parents, all of them overweight and stuffing their face with sausages and other meats. In both movies he ends up falling into the chocolate river and disappearing into the pipes of the factory. The substance he was trying to ingest so greedily metaphorically devours him, while the Oompa Loompas, mysterious little creatures working for Wonka, offer a moral commentary on the events, in a spirit not too distant from Dante's while he travels through the different levels of Hell in the *Divine Comedy*. After all, the Florentine poet also dedicated a special position to the gluttonous, in Cantica VI: a smelly place where they are hit by an endless rain of dirty water, snow, and hail. The whole *Divine Comedy* works according to the logic of the *contrappasso*, or retaliation: each category of sinners is punished by a torture that is closely connected with their sin, often its contrary. The same rules work in Wonka's Chocolate Factory.

Sometimes pop culture characters are not punished for their greed: this is the case for the satirical cartoon series *South Park* created by Matt Stone and Trey Parker, with its cohort of excessive, vulgar, and politically incorrect characters. Eric Cartman, a child overfed by his single mother, who tries to overcompensate for the absence of a father and her quite unruly sexual drive (in one episode she appears on the cover of *Crack Whore* magazine), perfectly represents the bottomless voraciousness of the infant. Although capable of articulating his desire in words, Cartman is led by a bottomless hunger, and more generally a drive towards all sorts of consumption, that cannot be controlled and does not abide by laws of propriety or even simple humanity. In episode 2 of the first season, "Weight Gain 4000," Cartman has to appear on TV because he has cheated his way into winning a national "Save our Fragile Planet" writing contest. Aware of his poor shape he decides to bulk up, lured into using a product, Weight Gain 4000, that assures "over 4000 grams of saturated fat per serving." With the battle cry of "Beefcake," Cartman sets to consume ridiculous amounts of the substance, proud of becoming so big he cannot even get on the school bus. Finally he ends up on a TV talk show about obese people; still all he can see and appreciate is that he can consume and grow without limits.

In episode 8 of the first season, "Starvin' Marvin," at Thanksgiving Cartman and his friends see a TV commercial for distance adoptions: $5 a month to sponsor a child in Ethiopia, and a sports watch for those who call to start the adoption paying by credit card. By mistake, instead of the watch, they receive a child, quickly named Starvin' Marvin. The little Ethiopian gets a crash course in consumerism. He is taken to an all-you-can-eat buffet, where Cartman manages to eat all his food. In the meanwhile, a mad scientist creates a genetically modified breed of Thanksgiving Turkey that reproduces very fast and attacks the citizens of South Park. Could there be a more direct expression of the fear of being ingested by the objects of our hunger? Also Cartman is punished by retaliation: Starvin' Marvin succeeds in sending him to Ethiopia in his place. The little fat white boy finds himself among starving people, until Marvin gets back to Ethiopia, bringing all the killer turkeys, which in the meanwhile have been killed.

The dread of being devoured often surfaces in the show. In episode 2 of the second season, "Cartman's Mom is Still a Dirty Slut," the citizens of South Park become anthropophagic when they get stuck in a snowstorm. The absurd but significant twist is that they begin drawing straws to decide who will be sacrificed for the others' survival just four hours into the storm, after a very abundant breakfast and with plenty of food still around. By the end of the storm, they have eaten three people, and they decide to bring the leftovers home in doggie bags. *South Park* makes us laugh, but also makes us squirm in our seats. In its absurd irony it confronts us with questions about and insights into ourselves that we would rather not face. In some way, comedy accomplishes the same function as scary stories. Both operate as imaginary representations and collective discharges of subconscious elements that are culturally perceived as unclean, if not dangerous.

■ The Famished Undead

Vampires, zombies, and other devouring creatures, including cannibals, have been around for a long time in Western culture. There are different theories about the origin of the word "vampire" itself. It could come from the Turkish *uber*, witch, and its Slavic derivatives *upior* and *upir*, or from the Greek verbal root *pi*, meaning "to drink." It seems that the expression "vampire" itself appeared for the first time at the end of the seventeenth century in France, and became more common in the eighteenth century, with *Dissertations sur les Apparitions et sur les Revenants et les Vampires*, published by Dom Calmet in 1746 (Dundes 1998: 4-5). It became a common word in the rest of Europe more or less in the same period, although it was not used in Eastern Europe, where the superstitions regarding vampires were actually common and where these monsters were rather called *strigoi, moroii,* or *varcolaci* (Klaniczay 1990). Vampires already showed traits that would later appear also in Western pop culture: they were considered as a sort of reanimated corpses, which could only be defeated by totally destroying, cutting, and burning their bodies. They can take "power" away from people, and in particular milk from nursing mothers (an interesting reference to the breast). In other legends they suck human blood. Perhaps surprisingly, there is no actual reference to the fact that a fifteenth-century prince from Romania, the Voivode Dracul, a sworn enemy of the Turkish invaders, whom he massacred by the hundreds, was a vampire.

At this point, we cannot avoid a historical question with heavy social and political undertones: why does a stable kernel, which we have demonstrated reveals close connections with the psychological development of human infants, appear under different forms at different times and places? The answer, which we will try to clarify in the following paragraphs, is that this constant core element of the human experience, which as adults we tend to forget about or to deny, surfaces in forms that mutate and vary in order to fit in the network of ideas, values, practices, discourses, and material realities of different cultures and societies at different moments of their historical transformation. This would explain why the uneasiness about our "cannibalistic" drives expresses itself as a humorous critique of unbridled consumerism and shameless gluttony in pieces of pop culture like *Willy Wonka* or *South Park* in America at the turn of the twenty-first century.

In the case of vampire legends, historian Gàbor Klaniczay argues that they emerged in the Austro-Hungarian empire during the seventeenth century when witchcraft became less culturally relevant, under the new mentality influenced by rationalism and scientific advances that were investigating blood (Klaniczay 1990: 168-188). The same factors might have determined the success of vampire stories in Western Europe, later amplified by the Romantic taste for the mysterious and the horrific, often interpreted as a cultural reaction to the rationalism promoted by the Enlightenment.

Some elements that we find in vampirism within Western traditions, i.e., the undead or the returning dead and the thirst for blood, can be traced also in other traditions, like Voudoun in all its incarnations, both in the original cradle in Benin and in the Americas (Voodoo in Haiti, Condomblé in Brazile, Obia in Jamaica, Santeria in Cuba).

Voodoo sacrifices follow the classical pattern of immolation rites. The following paragraph will rely on the research of the anthropologist Alfred Métraux, which to this day is still one of the best works on the subject.

> The act of killing is always preceded by a rite which is akin both to Communion and divination. The victim can only be put to death if he has first eaten some food and drunk some liquid of a sacred nature. ... As soon as the animal has eaten or drunk, it becomes the property of the *loa* (voodoo divine entity, note) and partakes of his divine nature. ... This participation in the sacred nature of the victim can be taken as a total identification of the people performing the sacrifice with the creature sacrificed. (Métraux 1972: 170)

Here we find again the element of ambivalence that we have recognized in many phenomena connected with ingestion and consumption: a form of identification between the eater and the eaten.

In Haiti the thirst for blood is the main trait of the so called *loups-garous* (werewolves), female vampires who make small children die by sucking their blood.

> To suck the little victim's blood, a werewolf gets into the house in the form of a cockroach or some other insect, or slides a straw through the wattling so that it rests against the child's cheek. Opinions differ as to how vampires operate. Some say they "drain" a child gradually, others that they have only to take three drops of blood for the child to die of an illness, caused magically. (Métraux 1972: 304)

The insatiable desire for incorporation puts *loups-garous* outside the realm of humanity, to the point where they can change their shape at will.

In the case of Voodoo and similar religions, it is quite difficult to trace the development of beliefs and practices before their arrival in the New World. And after that, for centuries the only written documents we can access originated, of course, in the environment of colonial culture and practices (Bodin 1990; Burton 1997; Fernàndez Olmos and Paravisini-Gebert 2003). However, it is not unreasonable to make a case for the influence of the slave-master relationships in the development of the core concepts of Afro-Caribbean religions and in the creation of myths, ceremonies, and traditions. Food played an important role in the Voodoo cult: to each divine entity corresponded certain produce and substances, including blood (Rigaud 1985: 91-100). We must not forget that food was precisely a sensitive point in the power relations between the white masters, who depend on the slave for the production, transformation, and even service of food, and the slave, who often struggled to secure enough food to survive. Somehow, the white masters were not only using the food produced by the slaves, but also consuming the slaves themselves, sucking their vital energy. It is likely that this grim reality gave depth to mythical figures such as zombies and *loups-garous*, whose traits also reflected the fundamental ambivalence about devouring that we have already discussed.

This hypothesis is sustained also by historian Luis White in her work on rumors and stories about vampires in colonial East Africa.

> Vampire stories offer a better, clearer, more analytical picture of the colonial experience than other sources do. . . Vampires themselves are revealing beings: a separate race of bloodsucking creatures, living among humans on fluids that they extract from human bodies; vampires mark a way in which relations of race, of bodies, and of tools of extraction can be debated, theorized, and explained. (White 2000: 307)

In East Africa stories, firemen, game rangers, and mine managers become blood-takers, using modern instruments like injections and working on behalf of the white colonizers, who crave the vital fluids of the Africans. The core element for these legends might be of Indian origin. The first word used for vampire is East Africa is in fact *mumiani*, which appeared in Swahili dictionaries in the nineteenth century. It would refer to a mummy, about also to a medicine. At about the same time, the word *momiai* was used on the west coast of India to indicate a sort of medicine based on blood. In Indian lore, this blood was often thought of as extracted through torture in hospitals, probably because these institutions were identified with the colonizers, and most people did not understand too well what was going on inside them. Indian soldiers working for the British could have brought these stories to Africa (Pels 1992). Whatever their origin might have been, the legends were absorbed in the web of the culture, the mentality, and the material realities of the specific colonial power structures, assuming new meanings that helped make sense of a different situation.

■ Cultured Cannibals

Many Africans believed that white colonizers were eager not only to drink their blood but also to eat their very flesh. These kinds of stories probably began circulating when the arrival of the European explorers first, and the slave merchants after, radically changed the customs and the economic flows traditionally connected with slavery in Africa. In colonial Katanga, today's Congo, people believed that Africans were hired to capture other Africans, make then "dumb" with injections, fatten them, and them give them for white men to eat on special occasions like Christmas (White 2000: 207). Similar legends and contemporary urban myths can be found also in other countries that have a colonial past, such as Brazil and Bolivia (Scheper-Hughes 1992; Watchel 1994).

In Western cultures, however, when we think of cannibals we tend to refer to the anthropophagic customs of barbaric or anyway savage populations. Anthropophagy has actually been present in Western collective imagination since its origin. In Homer's *Iliad*, the hero Achilles wishes he were able to unleash his fury to the point of desiring to eat his enemies, marking this act as the ultimate taboo that would set him apart from humankind, while in the *Odyssey* Ulysses faces the man-devouring Cyclops (Buchan 2001). Also Ovid, in the *Metamorphoses*, refers to this practice (Kilgour 1990: 28-45). Later on, Romans accused the Christians, and the Christians in turn accused the Jews, of consuming human flesh. Literary critics and theorists have been very sensitive to the theme of incorporation, often analyzed in terms of a scrambling of the fundamental dichotomy between inside and outside that constitutes one of the bases for the development of autonomous individuals. As philosopher Judith Butler maintained, "a movement of boundary itself appeared to be quite central to what bodies are" (J. Butler 1993: ix). All that finds itself outside the boundaries defining one's identity can be perceived as threatening. This need for a stable and contoured integrity leads individuals and social groups to push whatever they perceive as unfamiliar toward the outside, creating an external space of absolute difference, which can never be part of the subject and which at the same time defines the subject. "Abject and abjection are my safeguards. The primers of my cultures," affirmed the French cultural theorist Julia Kristeva, who also noted: "Food loathing is perhaps the most elementary and most archaic form of abjection … it is not lack of cleanliness or health that cause abjection but what disturbs identity, system, order. What does not respect borders, positions, rules. The in-between, the ambiguous, the composite" (Kristeva 1982: 2-4). Individuals identify with the norms regulating their eating habits, which, together with sex, play a key role in defining taboos and pollution fears, as the British anthropologist Mary Douglas demonstrated in the studies about purity (Douglas 1969). The lack of boundaries and distinctions constitutes a pending danger for any social structure. When individuals or groups share the same desire, or, better, when they happen to desire the same thing, they erase the distinction between each other, the differences that define them as individuals and that constitute the basis of any social interaction. This negation of boundaries can lead to an explosion of violence, precipitating society into chaos, argued the French philosopher René Girard, who defined this phenomenon as a "mimetic crisis" (Girard 1979).

What I am interested in pointing out is that starting from the fifteenth century, when Columbus first met the natives in the Caribbean, anthropophagy became in the mind of many "cannibalism," a word that itself derives from the name of those populations, the Caribs. I will not get into the highly debated question of whether cannibalism actually ever existed, and if so, what its function was in the societies that adopted it. What is significant in our context is that a concept already existing in Western culture in connection with eating and ingestion, and with all the ambivalences and the psychological relevance that we have examined, was used to reinforce the boundary between civilization and savagery, as a screen for colonial violence at a historical moment when European powers were spreading their influence all over the globe.

Some political theorists see in the apparition of cannibals an expression of the European proto-capitalist appetite. After all, in *Capital*, Karl Marx compared capitalists to werewolves, vampires, and parasites living off labor (Marx 1990: 353, 367, 645). To this day, the term "cannibalization" is used in business language to incorporate a competitor's market share (Bartolovich 1998: 208). This element actually reminds us of the inner contradictions and ambivalence that we find every time we deal with ingestion:

> [Capitalism] continuously comes up against the "physical obstacle" to its own consumption, which it then must meet with ingenious methods to consume more labor power without killing off its agent. … To the extent that proto-capitalists did feel drive toward exhaustive consumption, they were working against their own long-term interest which it took them some time to learn. The training of appetite, unsurprisingly, becomes a preoccupation of period commentators on trade, discovery and production. (Bartolovich 1998: 213, 216)

In other words, devouring always comes with the fear of destruction.

Cannibals have become a common feature in many contemporary pieces of pop culture. In 1993 a U.S. movie, *The Miracle of the Andes*, told the story of the Uruguayan Air Force Flight 571 disaster in the Andes, where the survivors ended up eating each other. In the 1970s a few Italian moviemakers originated a whole genre of low-budget cannibal B-movies that enjoyed a certain success for some years and were characterized by a tendency to pure splatter and heavy sexual undertones. Usually the main characters find themselves in a horrific situation during anthropological expeditions or quests for lost loved ones, which always take place in beautiful, lush, and uncontaminated nature. The first of these films was *Ultimo Mondo Cannibale* (Last Cannibal World, 1977) by Ruggero Deodato, followed in the same year by *Emmanuelle e gli Ultimi Cannibali* (Emmanuelle and the Last Cannibals, 1977) by Joe D' Amato and *La Montagna del Dio Cannibale* (The Cannibal God's Mountain, 1978) by Sergio Martino, starring Ursula Andress, and what is considered the masterpiece of the genre, *Cannibal Holocaust* (1980), again the work of Mr. Deodato. The genre flourished until the mid-1980s, and enjoyed a certain commercial success abroad. It is interesting that those were precisely the years when Italy was profoundly shaken by internal terrorism, both from the extreme right and from the extreme left. Assassinations, urban guerrillas, and even major massacres made evident to all citizens a different side of politics. Just a few years earlier Marco Ferreri had filmed *La Grande Bouffe* (1973), in which four successful bourgeois characters decide to get together to kill themselves by binging, and Federico Fellini had created a movie version of the Latin writer Petronius' *Satyricon* (1969), with a memorable and excessive dinner scene where power and overeating are clearly connected.

Cannibalism appears also in comedies: the first example is probably *Sweeney Todd: The Demon Barber of Fleet Street* (1936), which then became a musical with lyrics by Stephen Sondheim and in 2007 was made into the film by Tim Burton starring Johnny Depp. In the play, Sweeney's thirst for revenge ends up in a flourishing business in pies filled with human meat. In the same spirit, we can mention the film *Delicatessen*, a 1991 black comedy written and directed by Jean-Pierre Jeunet and Marc Caro, centered on a butcher who serves to his clients the flesh of his apprentices, and *Eating Raoul*, a 1982 black comedy by Paul Bartel where a mild-mannered married couple gather the money they need to open their restaurant by advertising themselves as an S&M escort duo and killing whoever shows up for their services. In a more serious key, in 1989 Peter Greenaway directed the visually amazing *The Cook, the Thief, His Wife and Her Lover*, where in the end the thief of the title is forced to eat his wife's lover, whom he has killed. In *301/302* (2004) the Korean filmmaker Chul-sook Park depicted the love/hate relation between two women, one fixated on cooking and the other anorexic, which ends up in tragedy with the former eating the latter. The most famous pop culture cannibal both in books and on film is arguably Hannibal Lecter, played by a fantastic Anthony Hopkins in Jonathan Demme's 1991 *The Silence of the Lambs* (a role he reprised in *Hannibal*, 2001, and *Red Dragon*, 2003). The tense and charged relationship between the detective Clarice Starling (Jodie Foster) and the psychiatrist-turned-anthropophagist who helps her to capture other criminals delves deep into all the complexity related to ingestion of symbolic—and at times physical—otherness.

■ Hungry Powers

The recurring fear of being transformed into food and the dread about one's own devouring instincts and the taboo placed on anthropophagy have been considered as the origin of table manners.

> Table manners are social agreements; they are devised precisely because violence could so easily erupt at dinner. Eating is aggressive by nature, and the implements

required for it could quickly become weapons; table manners are, most basically, a system of taboos designed to ensure that violence remains out of the question. (Visser 1992: xii)

In *Totem and Taboo*, Freud imagines that the beginning of society was the murder of the original father by his sons and their shared consumption of his flesh.

> One day the expelled brothers joined forces, slew and ate the father, and thus put an end to the father's horde.... Now they accomplish their identification with him by devouring him and each acquired a part of his strength. The totem feast, which is perhaps mankind's first celebration, would be the repetition and commemoration of this memorable, criminal act with which so many things began, social organization, moral restrictions, and religion. (Freud 1998: 122)

Meals connect those who share them, confirming their identities as individuals and as social groups, all while excluding those who do not participate in them. As the German political writer Hannah Arendt wrote, "to live together in the world means essentially that a world of things is between those who have it in common, as a table is located between those who sit around it; the world, like every in-between, relates and separates at the same time" (Arendt 1958: 48). The political relevance of communal eating emerges in the work of many political scientists. The ambivalent fears and desires connected to it, as we have already seen, are not culturally acceptable, since they constitute a negation of culture itself as social interaction and negotiation. Yet they play a fundamental role in the constitution of power, as the Nobel Prize recipient Elias Canetti poignantly exposed it. In a section aptly called "The Entrails of Power" from his masterpiece *Crowds and Power*, Canetti argues that teeth are "the very first manifestation of order," "The most striking natural instrument of power" (Canetti 1984: 207). More precisely, smoothness and order, which allow teeth to fulfill their task, and their shape reminiscent of a prison, have become attributes of power. Indeed for Canetti, power is a form of digestion, often sucking all substances from the subjects it supposedly represents. As in the case with the body, if this process of ingestion and digestion is interrupted, the result is death, the dissolution of power. It is not by chance that in the past the king or anybody holding any kind of power had to show their authority by an unusual capacity of consumption, which was often visible in full bodies and huge bellies.

> It may be useful to have a look at eating in general, independent of the eater's position in the social scale. A certain esteem for each other is clearly evident in all who eat together. This is already expressed by the fact of their sharing.... But the touch of solemnity in their attitude cannot be explained by this alone; their mutual esteem also means that they will not eat each other.... People eat together, bare their teeth and eat and, even at this critical moment, feel no desire to eat each other. (Canetti 1984: 220-221)

Now things have changed, and power tries to disguise itself in slim and toned bodies that are submitted to all kinds of stress to display eternal youth and vigor. Obesity and lack of physical fitness are considered traits of the lower classes, unable to control their impulses and to adopt a good diet. However, the implicit danger lurking in this kind of digestive power is still cannibalism, the fear of being destroyed and consumed by those who are stronger: a fear that is the direct reflection of our own drives aimed at ingesting the world to bring it under control within ourselves.

■ Works Cited

Adams, Douglas. 1995 (1980). *The Restaurant at the End of the Universe.* New York: Ballantine Books.

Arendt, Hannah. 1958. *The Human Condition.* Garden City, NY: Doubleday Anchor Books.

Bartolovich, Crystal. 1998. "Consumerism, or the Cultural Logic of Late Cannibalism." In *Cannibalism and the Colonial World*, ed. Francis Barker, Peter Hulme, and Margaret Iversen. Cambridge: Cambridge University Press.

Bodin, Ron. 1990. *Voodoo: Past and Present.* Lafayette, LA: University of Southwestern Louisiana.

Bordo, Susan. 1993. *Unbearable Weight.* Berkeley and Los Angeles: University of California Press.

Buchan, Mark. 2001. "Food for Thought: Achilles and the Cyclops." In *Eating Their Words: Cannibalism and the Boundaries of Cultural Identity,* ed. Kristen Guest. Albany: State University of New York Press.

Burton, Richard D.E. 1997. *In/different Spaces.* Berkeley and Los Angeles: University of California Press.

Butler, Judith. 1993. *Bodies That Matter.* New York: Routledge.

Butler, Octavia E. 2005. *Fledging.* New York: Seven Stories Press.

Bynum, Caroline Walker. 1984. "Fast, Feast, and Flesh: The Religious Significance of Food to Medieval Women." In *Representations* 11:1-25.

Bynum, Caroline Walker. 1987. *Holy Feast and Holy Fast: The Religious Significance of Food to Medieval Women.* Berkeley and Los Angeles: University of California Press.

Canetti, Elias. 1984 (1960). *Crowds and Power.* New York: The Noonday Press.

Copjec, Joan. 1991. "Vampires, Breast-Feeding, and Anxiety." In *October* 58: 25-43.

Curtin, Deane W. and Lisa M Heldke. 1992. "Introduction." In *Cooking, Eating, Thinking*, ed. Deane W. Curtin and Lisa M Heldke. Bloomington and Indianapolis: Indiana University Press.

Dinnerstein, Dorothy. 1976. *The Mermaid and the Minotaur: Sexual Arrangements and the Human Malaise.* New York: Harper and Row.

Douglas, Mary. 1969. *Purity and Danger.* London: Routledge and Kegan Paul.

Dundes, Alan. 1998. *The Vampire: A Casebook.* Madison: University of Wisconsin Press.

Fernandez Olmos, Margarite and Lizabeth Paravisini-Gebert. 2003. *Creole Religions of the Caribbean.* New York: New York University Press.

Foucault, Michel. *The History of Sexuality, Vol. III: The Care of the Self.* New York: Vintage Books.

Frankiel, R.V. 1993. "Hide-and-Seek in the Playroom: On Object Loss and Transference in Child Treatment." In *Psychoanalytic Review* 80: 351-9.

Freud, Sigmund. 1998 (1913). *Totem and Taboo.* Mineola, NY: Dover Publications.

Freud, Sigmund. 2000 (1905). *Three Essays on the Theory of Sexuality.* New York: Basic Books.

Girard, René. 1979. *Violence and the Sacred.* Baltimore: Johns Hopkins University Press.

Hobbes, Thomas. 1982 (1651). *Leviathan.* New York and London: Penguin Classics.

Kilgour, Maggie. 1990. *From Communion to Cannibalism: An Anatomy of Metaphors of Incorporations.* Princeton: Princeton University Press.

King, Stephen. 2000 (1975). *Salem's Lot.* New York: Pocket Books.

King, Stephen. 2003. *Everything's Eventual.* New York: Pocket Books.

Klaniczay, Gabor. 1990. "The Decline of Witches and the Rise of Vampires under the Eighteenth-Century Hapsburg Monarchies." In *The Uses of Supernatural Power: The Transformation of Popular Religion in Medieval and Early Modern Europe.* Princeton: Princeton University Press.

Klein, Melanie. 1987a (1926). "The Psychological Principles of Infant Analysis." In *The Selected Melanie Klein,* ed. Juliet Mitchell. New York: The Free Press.

Kristeva, Julia. 1982. *Powers of Horror.* New York: Columbia University Press.

Lacan, Jacques. 2002 (1966). *Écrits: A Selection.* New York and London: W.W. Norton & Company.

Lévi-Strauss, Claude. 1968. *L'Origine des manières de table.* Paris: Plon.

Marx, Karl. 1990 (1867). *Capital, Vol. 1.* Harmondsworth: Penguin.

Matheson, Richard. 1995 (1954). *I Am Legend.* New York: Orb Edition.

Métraux, Alfred. 1972. *Voodoo in Haiti.* New York: Schocken Books.

Pels, Peter. 1992. "Mumiani: The White Vampire. A Neo-diffusionist Analysis of Rumor." In *Ethnofoor* 5(1-2): 315-30.

Rice, Anne: 1977. *Interview with the Vampire.* New York: Ballantine Books.

Rigaud, Milo. 1985 (1953). *Secrets of Voodoo.* San Francisco: City Lights Books.

Scheper-Hughes, Nancy. 1992. *Death without Weeping: The Violence of Everyday Life in Brazil.* Berkeley and Los Angeles: University of California Press.

Stoker, Bram. 2003 (1867). *Dracula,* introduction by Brooke Allen. New York: Barnes & Noble Classics.

Visser, Margaret. 1992. *The Rituals of Dinner* New York: Penguin Books.

Watchel, Nathan. 1994. *God and Vampires: Return to Chipaya.* Chicago: University of Chicago Press.

White, Luise. 2000. *Speaking with Vampires: Rumor and History in Colonial Africa.* Berkeley and Los Angeles: University of California Press.

Žižek, Slavoj. 1992. *Looking Awry.* Cambridge, MA: MIT Press.

READING AND WRITING

1. What is Parasecoli's central argument is this essay? How does he explain our enduring fascination with vampires, zombies, and other monsters?
2. Parasecoli proposes the unconventional idea that the victims of vampire attacks enjoy, to a certain extent, their status as prey. What textual evidence does he offer to support this idea? What implications does he draw from this apparent ambivalence about being consumed?
3. Parasecoli cites a number of texts, both popular and obscure, from different historical periods and across a variety of media—everything from an 18th century French predecessor of *Dracula* to recent *South Park* episodes. What are the rhetorical effects of his use of these sources? How do they contribute to his ethos? How do they help him develop his argument? Which of his sources do you think are the most effective?

DEVELOPING LONGER RESPONSES

4. What parallels exist between the popular interest in the vampire/zombie fiction of consumption and the contemporary issues of food that Chapter 2 asks us to consider? Why is eating, as Parasecoli suggests, such an essential feature of our culture's monster tales?

USING RESEARCH

5. Parasecoli's essay draws heavily on psychoanalytic theory, especially the work of Sigmund Freud and Jacques Lacan. Use the library's resources to learn more about psychoanalytic theory and how it is applied to literary texts. Report your findings in a brief essay that explains how theories of the mind can help us understand literature.

Caitlin Flanagan writes book reviews and cultural criticism for The Atlantic *magazine, where this essay was published in December 2008. She is also the author of* To Hell with All That, *a 2006 book about the lives of modern women.*

WHAT GIRLS WANT   Caitlin Flanagan

Children's books about divorce—which are unanimously dedicated to bucking up those unfortunate little nippers whose families have gone belly-up—ask a lot of their authors. Their very premise, however laudable, so defies the nature of modern children's literature (which, since the Victorian age, has centered on a sentimental portrayal of the happy, intact family) that the enterprise seems doomed from the title. Since the 1950s, children have delighted in the Little Bear books (Mother Bear: "I never did forget your birthday, and I never will")—but who wants to find a copy of Cornelia Maude Spelman's *Mama and Daddy Bear's Divorce* wedged onto the shelf? Still, the volumes fill a need: helping children understand that life on the other side of the custody hearing can still be happy and hopeful, that a broken family is not a ruined one.

But pick up a novel written for adolescents in which the main character is a child of divorce, and you're in very different waters. Divorce in a young-adult novel means what being orphaned meant in a fairy tale: vulnerability, danger, unwanted independence. It also means that the protagonists must confront the sexuality of their parents at the moment they least want to think about such realities. It introduces into a household the adult passions and jealousies that have long gone to ground in most middle-aged parents, a state of affairs that is particularly difficult for girls, who have a more complicated attitude toward their own emerging sexuality than do boys, and who are far more rooted in the domestic routines and traditions of their families, which constitute the vital link between the sweet cocooning of childhood and their impending departure from it.

The only thing as difficult for a girl as a divorce—if we are to judge from stories aimed at the teen market—is a move. Relocating is what led to the drug addiction, prostitution, and death that freaked out a generation of readers in *Go Ask Alice*, and to the teenybopper dipsomania of *Sarah T.: Portrait of a Teenage Alcoholic*. In the most perfectly constructed young-adult novel of the past few decades, *Are You There God? It's Me, Margaret*, Judy Blume heightened the anxiety in her tale of a girl awaiting her first period by beginning the story with Margaret's move to the suburbs. The drama and anguish with which girls confront such disruptions to their domestic lives are typical both of the narcissism that can make living with a teenage girl one of the most unpleasant experiences God metes out to the unsuspecting, and of the ways that, for women, puberty is the most psychologically complex and emotionally alive experience of their lives. Why wouldn't a girl buck against leaving her hometown? Never again will she have such intense friendships, such a burning need to be in constant contact with the circle of girls (the best friend, the second-best friend, the whole court as carefully considered and clearly delineated as a bridal party) who sustain her through their shared experience of the epic event of female adolescence.

TWILIGHT IS THE FIRST in a series of four books that are contenders for the most popular teen-girl novels of all time. (The movie based on the first book was released in November.) From the opening passage of the first volume, the harbingers of trouble loom: 17-year-old Bella Swan is en route to the Phoenix airport, where she will be whisked away from her beloved, sunny hometown and relocated to the much-hated Forks, Washington, a nearly aquatic hamlet of deep fogs and constant rains. The reason for the move is that Mom (a self-absorbed, childlike character) has taken up with a minor-league baseball player, and traveling with him has become more appealing than staying home with her only child. Bella will now be raised by her father, an agreeable-enough cipher, who seems mildly pleased to have his daughter come to live with him, but who evinces no especial interest in getting to know her; they begin a cohabitation as politely distant and mutually beneficial as a particularly successful roommate matchup off *Craigslist.* Bella's first day at her new school is a misery: the weather is worse than she could ever have imagined, and the one silvery lining to the disaster is the mystery and intrigue presented by a small group of students—adopted and foster children of the same household—who eat lunch together, speak to no one else, are mesmerizingly attractive, and (as we come rather quickly to discover) are vampires. Bella falls in love with one of them, and the novel—as well as the three that follow it—concerns the dangers and dramatic consequences of that forbidden love.

I hate Y.A. novels; they bore me. That's a disappointing fact of my reading life, because never have I had such an intense relationship with books as when I was a young girl. I raged inside them and lived a double emotional life (half real girl, half inhabitant of a distant world). *To Sir, With Love* and *A Tree Grows in Brooklyn, Forever* and *Rebecca, Mr. and Mrs. Bo Jo Jones* and *Mrs. Mike, Gone With the Wind* and *Rich Man, Poor Man,* and even *Valley of the Dolls* (an astonishing number of whose 8 million readers turned out to be teenagers) and *Peyton Place,* as well as any movie-star biography I could get my hands on (Judy Garland, Greta Garbo—in those days, you had to have been long dead or seriously faded to be worthy of such a biography) and a slew of far less famous books written exclusively for the teen-girl market and published in paperback, never to be heard of again—all of these books consumed me in a way that no other works of art or mass culture ever have. I chose books neither because of, nor in spite of, their artistic merit, only for their ability to pull me through the looking glass.

When I read in "The Dead" that Lily was "literally run off her feet," I did not care about, or even notice, the misuse of the word *literally,* nor did it occur to me to observe that this subtle deployment of a Dublin colloquialism hinted at the story's point of view. What I cared about, intensely, was what it would feel like to be sent running up and down the stairs of a house as a teenage maid, with holiday gaieties in full force, and everyone being mean to me, instead of pampering and babying me the way my parents did on Christmas Eve. I can remember lying on my bed in a Dublin row house at 15, so immersed in Margaret Mitchell that I faked three days of illness to keep reading, and I remember lying in my own bed in Berkeley—the cat dozing at my feet, the bay wind brushing the tree branches against my dormer windows—and roaring through *A Tree Grows in Brooklyn* completely at home in turn-of-the-century Williamsburg, a place I had never even heard of before picking up the book but which I could navigate, in the landscape of my imagination, as easily as I could the shady streets and secret hillside staircases that connected my house to the record shop and ice-cream parlor down on Euclid Avenue.

The salient fact of an adolescent girl's existence is her need for a secret emotional life—one that she slips into during her sulks and silences, during her endless hours alone in her room, or even just when she's gazing out the classroom window while all of Modern European History, or the niceties of the *passé composé*, sluice past her. This means that she is a creature designed for reading in a way no boy or man, or even grown woman, could ever be so exactly designed, because she is a creature whose most elemental psychological needs—to be undisturbed while she works out the big questions of her life, to be hidden from view while still in plain sight, to enter profoundly into the emotional lives of others— are met precisely by the act of reading.

TWILIGHT IS FANTASTIC. It's a page-turner that pops out a lurching, frightening ending I never saw coming. It's also the first book that seemed at long last to rekindle something of the girl-reader in me. In fact, there were times when the novel—no work of literature, to be sure, no school for style; hugged mainly to the slender chests of very young teenage girls, whose regard for it is on a par with the regard with which just yesterday they held *Hannah Montana*—stirred something in me so long forgotten that I felt embarrassed by it. Reading the book, I sometimes experienced what I imagine long-married men must feel when they get an unexpected glimpse at pornography: slingshot back to a world of sensation that, through sheer force of will and dutiful acceptance of life's fortunes, I thought I had subdued. The *Twilight* series is not based on a true story, of course, but within it is *the* true story, the original one. *Twilight* centers on a boy who loves a girl so much that he refuses to defile her, and on a girl who loves him so dearly that she is desperate for him to do just that, even if the wages of the act are expulsion from her family and from everything she has ever known. We haven't seen that tale in a girls' book in a very long time. And it's selling through the roof.

Bella and Edward meet on that unpleasant first day of school, in biology class. The only free spot in the room is next to Edward, a vacancy she initially falls into with a glimmer of excitement—like Dracula's Lucy and Mina, and like every other young woman who has ever come to the attention of a vampire, Bella is enthralled. But Edward demonstrates none of the pickup-artist smoothness of his kind. As she glances shyly at him before sitting down, he meets her eyes "with the strangest expression on his face—it was hostile, furious." As she takes the seat beside him, he leans away from her, "sitting on the extreme edge of his chair and averting his face like he smelled something bad."

In short, Edward treats Bella not as Count Dracula treated the objects of his desire, but as Mr. Rochester treated Jane Eyre. He evinces the most profound disdain and distaste for this girl. Even after they have confessed their love for each other, he will still occasionally glare at and speak sharply to her. At the end of that long first day at Forks High, Bella goes to the school office to drop off some paperwork, and who is there but Edward—trying to get himself transferred out of the class they share.

And yet they are such kindred spirits! They are both crackerjack biology students (Bella because she took an AP course back in Phoenix, and Edward because he has taken the class God knows how many times, given that he is actually 104 years old); they both love the arts; they share a dim view of the many young men who would be Bella's suitors if only she would take an interest in them. All of these facts, combined with Edward's languid, androgynous beauty—slim and feline, possessed of tousled hair and golden eyes—predictably anger and confuse Bella, although they do nothing to cool her awakening physical passion for her smoldering, obdurate antagonist. (This poignant aspect of the female heart proves once again a theory advanced by a high-school chum of mine, an improbable lothario who replied when I demanded that he explain his freakish success with the ladies: "Chicks thrive on rejection.") Edward puts the young girl into a state of emotional confusion and vulnerability that has been at the heart of female romantic awakening since the beginning of time.

Bella is an old-fashioned heroine: bookish, smart, brave, considerate of others' emotions, and naturally competent in the domestic arts (she immediately takes over the grocery shopping and cooking in her father's household, and there are countless, weirdly compelling accounts of her putting dinner together—wrapping two potatoes in foil and popping them into a hot oven, marinating a steak, making a green salad—that are reminiscent of the equally alluring domestic scenes in Rosemary's Baby). Indeed, the book, which is set in contemporary America and centers on teenage life and culture, carries a strange—and I imagine deeply comforting to its teenage-girl readers—aura of an earlier time in American life and girlhood. The effect is subtle, and probably unintentional on the part of its author, a first-time novelist, who was home with three small boys when she blasted out this marvelous book. Like the Harry Potter series, the *Twilight* books are ostensibly set in the present, but—in terms of the mores, attitudes, and even the central elements of daily life portrayed within them—clearly evoke the culture of the author's adolescence. The Harry Potter series, feats of wizardry aside, is grounded in a desperate curiosity about the life of the English public school, which was a constant in the imaginative lives of middle- and working-class children in the Britain of J. K. Rowling's youth, and was also a central subject of the comics and novels produced for British children. Stephenie Meyer has re-created the sort of middle-class American youth in which it was unheard-of for a nice girl to be a sexual aggressor, and when the only coin of the realm for a boy who wanted to get lucky was romance and a carefully waged campaign intended to convince the girl that he was consumed by love for her.

Twilight is a 498-page novel about teenagers in which a cell phone appears only toward the very end, and as a minor plot contrivance. The kids don't have iPods; they don't text-message each other; they don't have MySpace pages or Facebook accounts. Bella does have a computer on which she dutifully e-mails her mother now and then, but the thing is so slow and dial-up that she almost never uses it, other than on the morning that she decides to punch the word *vampire* into her wood-burning search engine to learn a thing or two about her squeeze. But the world of the past is alive in other, more significant ways: Bella's friends, all in search of "boyfriends," spend weeks thinking about whom they will invite to a Sadie Hawkins dance. After a friend (toward whom Bella has gently been directing one of her own admirers) finally goes on a big "date" (a lost world right there, in a simple word), she phones Bella, breathless: "Mike kissed me! Can you believe it?" It was a scene that could have existed in any of the books I read when I was an adolescent; but in today's world of Y.A. fiction, it constitutes an almost bizarre moment. (Few things are as bewildering to contemporary parents as the sexual mores and practices of today's adolescents. We were prepared to give our children a "sex is a beautiful thing" lecture; they were prepared to have oral sex in the eighth grade.)

Think, for a moment, of the huge teen-girl books of the past decade. *The Sisterhood of the Traveling Pants* is about female empowerment as it's currently defined by the kind of jaded, 40-something divorcées who wash ashore at day spas with their grizzled girlfriends and pollute the Quiet Room with their ceaseless cackling about the uselessness of men. They are women who have learned certain of life's lessons the hard way and think it kind to let young girls understand that the sooner they grasp the key to a happy life (which essentially boils down to a distaff version of "Bros before hos"), the better. In *Sisterhood*, four close friends might scatter for the summer—encountering everything from ill-advised sex with a soccer coach to the unpleasant discovery that Dad's getting remarried—but the most important thing, the only really important thing, is that the four reunite and that the friendships endure the vicissitudes of boys and romance. Someday, after all, they will be in their 50s, and who will be there for them—really there for them—then? The boy who long ago kissed their bare shoulders, or the raspy-voiced best friend, bleating out hilarious comments about her puckered fanny from the next dressing room over at Eileen Fisher? *Gossip Girl*, another marketing sensation, replaces girls' old-fashioned need for male love and tenderness—these chippies could make a crack whore look like Clara Barton—with that for shopping and brand names. Notoriously set in an Upper East Side girls school that seems to combine elements of Nightingale-Bamford with those of a women's correctional facility after lights-out, the book gives us a cast of young girls whose desire for luxury goods (from Kate Spade purses to Ivy League–college admissions) is so nakedly hollow that the displacement of their true needs is pathetic. *Prep*—a real novel, not the result of a sales-team brainstorm—derives much of its pathos from the fact that the main character is never sure whether the boy she loves so much, and has had so many sexual encounters with, might actually constitute that magical, bygone character: her "boyfriend." The effect of *Prep* on teenagers is reminiscent of that of *The Catcher in the Rye*: both books describe that most rarefied of social worlds, the East Coast boarding school, and yet young readers of every socioeconomic level have hailed them for revealing the true nature of their inner life. In *Prep*, the heroine wants something so fundamental to the emotional needs of girls that I find it almost heartbreaking: she wants to know that the boy she loves, and with whom she has shared her body, loves her and will put no other girl in her place.

Bella, despite all of her courage and competence, manages to end up in scrape after scrape: finding herself in the path of a runaway car, fainting at school, going shopping in a nearby city and getting cornered by a group of malevolent, taunting men. And over and over, out of nowhere, shoving the speeding car out of her way, or lifting her up in his arms, or scaring the bejesus out of the men who would harm her, is Edward. And at last, while she is recuperating from the near-rape, with a plate of ravioli in a café near the alley, he reveals all. Not since Maxim de Winter's shocking revelation—"You thought I loved Rebecca? … I hated her"—has a sweet young heroine received such startling and enrapturing news.

As he gradually explains, Edward has been avoiding and scorning Bella not because he loathes her but because he is so carnally attracted to her that he cannot trust himself to be around her for even a moment. The mere scent of her hair is powerful enough that he is in a constant struggle to avoid taking—and thereby destroying—her. This is a vampire novel, so it is a novel about sex, but no writer, from Bram Stoker on, has captured so precisely what sex and longing really mean to a young girl.

THE EROTIC RELATIONSHIP between Bella and Edward is what makes this book—and the series—so riveting to its female readers. There is no question about the exact nature of the physical act that looms over them. Either they will do it or they won't, and afterward everything will change for Bella, although not for Edward. Nor is the act one that might result in an equal giving and receiving of pleasure. If Edward fails—even once—in his great exercise in restraint, he will do what the boys in the old pregnancy-scare books did to their girlfriends: he will ruin her. More exactly, he will destroy her, ripping her away from the world of the living and bringing her into the realm of the undead. If a novel of today were to sound these chords so explicitly but in a nonsupernatural context, it would be seen (rightly) as a book about "abstinence," and it would be handed out with the tracts and bumper stickers at the kind of evangelical churches that advocate the practice as a reasonable solution to the age-old problem of horny young people. (Because it takes three and a half very long books before Edward and Bella get it on—during a vampiric frenzy in which she gets beaten to a pulp, and discovers her Total Woman—and because Edward has had so many decades to work on his moves, the books constitute a thousand-page treatise on the art of foreplay.) That the author is a practicing Mormon is a fact every reviewer has mentioned, although none knows what to do with it, and certainly none can relate it to the novel; even the supercreepy "compound" where the boring half of *Big Love* takes place doesn't have any vampires. But the attitude toward female sexuality—and toward the role of marriage and childbearing—expressed in these novels is entirely consistent with the teachings of that church. In the course of the four books, Bella will be repeatedly tempted—to have sex outside of marriage, to have an abortion as a young married woman, to abandon the responsibilities of a good and faithful mother—and each time, she makes the "right" decision. The series does not deploy these themes didactically or even moralistically. Clearly Meyer was more concerned with questions of romance and supernatural beings than with instructing young readers how to lead their lives. What is interesting is how deeply fascinated young girls, some of them extremely bright and ambitious, are by the questions the book poses, and by the solutions their heroine chooses.

Bella's fervent hope—one that will not be realized until the final novel—is that Edward will ravage her, and that they will be joined forever; the harrowing pain that is said to be the victim's lot at the time of consummation means nothing to her. She loves him and wants to make a gift to him of her physical body—an act fraught with ambiguous dangers (the *Twilight* series so resonates with girls because it perfectly encapsulates the giddiness and the rapture—and the menace—that inherently accompany romance and sex for them). The ways in which his refusal and her insistence are accommodated are at the heart not only of this novel but of the entire series, and that inspires the rapture young girls feel for the books. This is not your seventh-grade human-development teacher passing around a dental dam and thereby making you want to send a plume of fifth-period taco salad and Gatorade into her outstretched palm. This is sex and romance fully—ecstatically, dangerously—engaged with each other. At last, at last.

AS I WRITE this, I am sitting on the guest-room bed of a close friend, and down the hall from me is the bedroom of the daughter of the house, a 12-year-old reader extraordinaire, a deep-sea diver of books. She was the fourth person through the doors of the Westwood Barnes & Noble the midnight that the series' final volume, *Breaking Dawn*, went on sale, and she read it—a doorstop, a behemoth—in six hours, and then turned back to page one as though it were the natural successor to the last page.

Posted on this girl's door—above the fading sticker of a cheery panda hopping over a pink jump rope, and one of a strawberry and a lollipop (their low placement suggesting the highest reach of a very small child), and to the right of an oval-shaped decal bearing the single, angry imperative STOP GLOBAL WARMING—is a small, black, square-shaped sticker that reads MY HEART BELONGS TO EDWARD. In the middle is a photograph of a pair of shapely female hands proffering a red Valentine heart. Also taped to this girl's closed door is a single piece of lined paper, on which she has written, in a carefully considered amalgam of block letters and swirly penmanship and eight different colors of crayon:

EDWARD'S FAN CLUB
YOU MAY ONLY ENTER IF YOU KNOW THE PASSWORD

That she had made her declaration for Edward on such a pretty, handmade sign was all-girl—as was her decision to leave up the old stickers from her childhood. One of the signal differences between adolescent girls and boys is that while a boy quickly puts away childish things in his race to initiate a sexual life for himself, a girl will continue to cherish, almost to fetishize, the tokens of her little-girlhood. She wants to be both places at once—in the safety of girl land, with the pandas and jump ropes, and in the arms of a lover, whose sole desire is to take her completely. And most of all, as girls work all of this out with considerable anguish, they want to be in their rooms, with the doors closed and the declarations posted. The biggest problem for parents of teenage girls is that they never know who is going to come barreling out of that sacred space: the adorable little girl who wants to cuddle, or the hard-eyed young woman who has left it all behind.

Years and years ago, when I was a young girl pressing myself into novels and baking my mother pretty birthday cakes, and writing down the 10 reasons I should be allowed to purchase and wear to the eighth-grade dance a pair of L'eggs panty hose, I knew that password. But one night a few years after that dance, I walked into a bedroom at a party and saw something I shouldn't have, and a couple of months after that I unwisely accepted a ride to the beach from a boy I hardly knew, and then I was a college girl carrying a copy of Hart's *History of Renaissance Art* across campus and wondering whether I should take out a loan and go to graduate school, and somewhere along the way—not precisely on the day I got my first prescription for birth control, and not exactly on the afternoon I realized I had fallen out of love with one boy and had every right to take up with another—somewhere along the way, I lost the code. One day I was an intelligent girl who could pick up almost any bit of mass-market fiction that shed light on the mysteries of love and sex, and the practicalities by which one could merge the two, and read it with a matchless absorption. *Valley of the Dolls* had been so crucial in my life not because of its word to the wise about the inadvisability of mixing Seconal and Scotch, but for the three sentences that explained how to go about getting undressed before the first time you have sex: go into the bathroom, take your clothes off, and reemerge with a towel wrapped around yourself. One day I was that girl, and one day I was not, and from then on, if you wanted to tempt me to read a bit of trash fiction, I was going to need more compelling information than that.

Midway through *Twilight*, after Edward and Bella have declared their feelings for one another, she emerges from a classroom with a pal, uncertain whether she will eat lunch with Edward, or whether he will once again have vanished into the air, as he has a tendency to do. "But outside the door to our Spanish class, leaning against the wall—looking more like a Greek god than anyone had a right to—Edward was waiting for me."

It's a small moment in the book, but it lit aglow some tiny room of memory, if only for a maddening moment. I thought about how romantically charged high schools are for their young inmates. In 12th grade, I had a class next to the student parking lot. As I sat there one grayish day, I saw my boyfriend emerge from a side door of the massive school, along with half a dozen of his friends. They were clearly in the grip of some new plan, and they stood around their parked cars for a few minutes, talking. Where were they going, and why couldn't I go along?

The boy I was dating leaned against his car and listened to them, and he laughed, but then something happened—I could see he had changed his mind, and as the others drove away, he stood there for a while, looking after them, and then he pushed away from the car and disappeared back into school. Maybe, at long last, he was taking seriously his father's warnings that he might not graduate if he kept ditching school.

The bell rang, the room emptied—and there he was, in the hallway outside my class. "Let's ditch," he said.

I was in worse academic shape than he was; my graduation and college admission depended on passing—as a senior!—my eighth-period geometry class (many trusted souls had assured me that I'd have a bright future, provided that I passed that damn course). And standing in front of me was a boy who had just abandoned his friends to spend the afternoon with me.

I can't remember a thing about geometry except the useless phrase *side-angle-side*, but for the rest of my life I'll remember the bottle of red wine we bought at a package store a mile from school, and the certainty (since proved) that in the scheme of things, I had made exactly the right decision.

■ READING AND WRITING

1. How does Flanagan's title create a sense of expectation on the part of her audience? What, according to the essay, do girls want?

2. Reviews, even feature reviews like Flanagan's that deal with a range of issues, are evaluative arguments. As such, they must be based on criteria to be successful. What criteria does Flanagan use to evaluate *Twilight*? How does she present and explain these criteria to her audience?

3. Flanagan's ethos is a significant rhetorical element in her essay. How does she wish to be perceived by her audience? What does she do to persuade her audience to think of her in this way? Do you think she is successful?

4. Flanagan discusses a range of topics in her essay, from divorce and young adult fiction to the emotional needs of adolescent girls and Edward Cullen. How does she link these various topics and use these links to advance her argument?

Grady Hendrix, a New York writer, runs the New York Asian Film Festival. He wrote this essay for the July 28, 2009, "Fine Whine" section of the online magazine Slate.

VAMPIRES SUCK. ACTUALLY, THEY DON'T. AND THAT'S THE PROBLEM. Grady Hendrix

Last week at Comic-Con, the big story wasn't comic books—it was vampires. Some 2,000 young women set up a tent city outside the San Diego Convention Center on Tuesday, sleeping rough so that they could attend the Thursday panel on *New Moon,* the upcoming sequel to vampire blockbuster *Twilight.*

It's just another sign of the massive popularity of vampires. Yet, like many people who acquire mega-celebrity, the vampire has developed an eating disorder. Read the books. Watch the movies. You'll see vampires who manage nightclubs, build computer databases, work as private investigators, go to prep school, lobby Congress, chat with humans, live near humans, have sex with humans, and pine over humans, but the one thing you won't see them do is suck the blood of humans.

No, bloodsucking is so yesterday. It's so 1994. It's so Anne Rice. Today's vampire is a good listener. He cares about our love lives and our problems, which is strange because we're supposed to be his food. Humans just assume that we are the center of the universe and so, faced with a literary creation that should, by all rights, just conk us over the head and suck us down like Slurpees, we've decided that we're too fascinating to be eaten. And so the modern vampire stalks, seduces, sleeps with, and cries over us. They don't eat us.

The original Dracula in *Dracula* loved to drink blood. He has "white sharp teeth, behind the full lips of the blood-dripping mouth." He forces Mina Harker to his bosom, where "[h]er white nightdress was smeared with blood, and a thin stream trickled down [his] bare chest," and he compels her to drink his blood, like a "child forcing a kitten's nose into a saucer of milk. ..." This bodily fluid fetishism was par for the course for the next 79 years, until Anne Rice's *Interview With the Vampire,* when Ms. Rice started to tweak up the Gothness. In her books, vampires were better known for being immortal than for sucking blood, which makes their fascination with humans even more mysterious: After living among us for hundreds of years, haven't they heard all of our jokes by now?

At least Anne Rice's vampires were still primarily bloodsuckers. The first sign that something was awry came with the introduction of Angel in "Buffy the Vampire Slayer." A prime example of the brooding, crying-on-the-inside, leather-jacketed emo boy of the '90s (see also: Dylan McKay, "Beverly Hills, 90210"; James Hurley, "Twin Peaks"), Angel was a vampire who had a soul. He fell in love with Buffy, teared up a lot, and believed in random acts of kindness. Angel, in short, sucked. Or, rather, he didn't suck, which was the problem. When he did suck, he took limited amounts of blood from consenting human women, or sucked blood against his will, or sucked rat blood.

Rat blood.

Think about it. Faced with the impact of his diet on humans, Angel accepts a yucky, cruelty-free substitute, then endlessly lectures other vampires about their moral failings because they don't do the same. He's not a vampire—he's a vegan.

But the ladies loved him, and he launched a sensitive-vampire industry. These days, you have Laurel K. Hamilton's Anita Blake: *Vampire Hunter* series, Charlaine Harris' *Sookie Stackhouse* novels (from which we derive "True Blood"), Richelle Mead's *Vampire Academy* books, and Leslie Esdaile Banks' *Vampire Huntress Legends* series featuring Damali Richards, a spoken-word artist who fights vampires, a detail which guarantees that I'm rooting for the vampires. But most damaging of all are Stephenie Meyer's *Twilight* books.

At least Angel, Anita Blake's vampires, Sookie Stackhouse, and most of the rest of them have a lot of sex. But Edward Cullen, immortal star of the *Twilight* books, does not have sex. Edward tells Bella, his human paramour, that they *need* to wait until they're married before doing the deed. In the meantime, he's fascinated by her, beguiled by her, he can't stay away from her—but he can't touch her. Instead, he lies next to her in bed and moons over her as she sleeps. Leaving aside the fact that he's a 90-year-old man, this is what stalkers do, not boyfriends.

Just as America's young men are being given deeply erroneous ideas about sex by what they watch on the Web, so, too, are America's young women receiving troubling misinformation about the male of the species from *Twilight*. These women are going to be shocked when the sensitive, emotionally available, poetry-writing boys of their dreams expect a bit more from a sleepover than dew-eyed gazes and chaste hugs. The young man, having been schooled in love online, will be expecting extreme bondage and a lesbian three-way.

The bigger problem here is that we're breeding sexually incompatible human beings, and vampires are to blame. I can see a time coming when the birth rate is going to precipitously decline. And what that means is that vampires are going to run out of food. But if Charlaine Harris, Laurel K. Hamilton, Stephenie Meyer, and all the others are right about the souls of their emo, Goth, velvet-wearing, crybaby vampire spawn, then maybe some kind of mass, Kurt Cobain-inspired, "You'll miss me when I'm gone," species-wide suicide is what vampires have been after all along.

READING AND WRITING

1. In setting up his argument, Hendrix gives us a brief history vampires, from Bram Stoker's Count Dracula to the "sensitive-vampire industry" of today. How has the vampire changed, according to Hendrix? What is behind these changes?
2. Hendrix makes it clear that non-threatening, attractive vampires are a problem. Explain his reasoning. Do you find his argument convincing?
3. How does Hendrix use humor to connect with his audience and to advance his argument?

DEVELOPING LONGER RESPONSES

4. Both Hendrix and Cailtin Flanagan, in the essay that precedes this one, discuss vampires, desire, and sex. How do the authors differ in their approach to these issues? Which discussion do you find more effective rhetorically? Why?

Kyle Bishop is an assistant professor in the Department of English at Southern Utah University. He has presented and published a variety of papers on popular culture and cinematic adaptations, including Metropolis, Night of the Living Dead, Fight Club, White Zombie, Buffy the Vampire Slayer, *and* Dawn of the Dead. *This essay was published in the Spring 2009 issue of the* Journal of Popular Film and Television.

DEAD MAN STILL WALKING: EXPLAINING THE ZOMBIE RENAISSANCE Kyle Bishop

Wars and other tragedies affect cultural consciousness like the blast from a high-yield explosive or a massive earthquake. The ensuing shockwaves reach far and wide, and one of the best ways to recognize and understand these undulations is by analyzing the literature and film of the times. For instance, the use of atomic weapons at the end of World War II ushered in nuclear paranoia narratives like the films *Godzilla* (1954) and *Them!* (1954), and fear of the encroaching Communist threat inspired alien invasion stories like Jack Finney's novel *Invasion of the Body Snatchers* (1955) and the movie *Invaders from Mars* (1953). The terrorist attacks of September 11, 2001, caused perhaps the largest wave of paranoia for Americans since the McCarthy era. Since the beginning of the war on terror, American popular culture has been colored by the fear of possible terrorist attacks and the grim realization that people are not as safe and secure as they might have once thought. This shift in cultural consciousness can be most readily seen in narrative fiction, particularly through zombie cinema.

Since 2002, the number of both studio and independent zombie movies has been on a steady rise. Hollywood has re-embraced the genre with revisionist films like *28 Days Later* (2002), video game-inspired action movies like *Resident Evil* (2002), big-budget remakes like *Dawn of the Dead* (2004), and comedies like *Shaun of the Dead* (2004). The zombie craze continued with 2007 seeing the theatrical releases of *Planet Terror, 28 Weeks Later,* and *Resident Evil: Extinction*—the Sundance Film Festival even featured two zombie films that season[1]—and with a remake of *Day of the Dead*, Romero's own *Diary of the Dead,* and *Zombie Strippers* all coming out in 2008. David Oakes's *Zombie Movie Data Base* Website confirms this increased interest in zombie cinema with data showing a marked rise in all kinds of zombie narratives over the past ten years: more than 575 titles are listed for 2006 alone.[2] Peter Dendle, Pennsylvania State University professor and zombie scholar, observes that the number of amateur zombie movies has "mushroomed considerably" since 2000 (interview). Although the quality of many of these backyard, straight-to-video, and Internet-based productions remains a matter of debate, the striking surge in the genre's popularity and frequency cannot be denied.

The fundamental genre conventions of zombie cinema fit post-9/11 cultural consciousness well. During the latter half of the twentieth century, zombie movies graphically represented the inescapable realities of unnatural death (via infection, infestation, or violence) and presented a grim view of a modern apocalypse in which society's infrastructure breaks down. The twenty-first-century zombie movies are no different from their historical antecedents but society has changed markedly since the World Trade Center towers were destroyed. Scenes depicting deserted metropolitan streets, abandoned human corpses, and gangs of lawless vigilantes have become more common than ever, appearing on the nightly news as often as on the movie screen. Because the after-effects of war, terrorism, and natural disasters so closely resemble the scenarios of zombie cinema, such images of death and destruction have all the more power to shock and terrify a population that has become otherwise jaded by more traditional horror films.

■ The Developmental Cycle of Zombie Cinema: Establishing the Renaissance

The modern zombie movie has been around for almost forty years and, like other genres, it has gone through periods of feast and famine.[3] According to film scholar Darryl Jones, the genre was born in 1968 with the release of George A. Romero's *Night of the Living Dead* (161), in which a motley group of people, led by an African American anti-hero named Ben (Duane Jones), must spend the night in a besieged country house, waiting for the authorities to arrive. When the county militia finally does show up, its first response is to shoot and kill Ben, the only survivor of the supernatural abattoir. The violence and graphic images in this low-budget film were unprecedented at the time, and the movie functions largely as a metaphor of the atrocities of Vietnam and racism.[4] Called "hippie Gothic" by film theorist Joseph Maddrey (51), *Night* protests the war by graphically confronting audiences with the horrors of death and dismemberment and by openly criticizing those who use violence to solve their problems. The politically subversive film gained a cult following and eventually made more than $30 million worldwide ("Business Data for *Night*").

Recognizing the potential market and profitability of such movies, other filmmakers began to experiment with the story line in little-known films like *Garden of the Dead* (1972), *Return of the Evil Dead* (1973), and *Horror of the Zombies* (1974). In 1978, Romero released *Dawn of the Dead*, a lampoon of capitalism and rampant consumerism. It depicts a group of reporters and SWAT team members forced to barricade themselves for weeks into an abandoned shopping mall surrounded by zombies.[5] *Dawn* was almost immediately followed by Lucio Fulci's unofficial sequel *Zombie* (1979), about a global zombie infestation originating on a voodoo-laden Caribbean island. The two films firmly defined the genre, with *Dawn* becoming a huge hit that grossed $55 million worldwide ("Business Data for *Dawn*"), and they spawned a veritable surge of classical zombie movies, such as *Night of the Zombies* (1981), *Revenge of the Zombies* (1981), *Mansion of the Living Dead*(1982), and *Kung Fu Zombie* (1982).

In spite of the proliferation of these movies and their success on B-reel screens, they seem to have played themselves out by the mid-1980s, especially after the arrival of Michael Jackson's "Thriller" video in 1983. This campy short film tried to be uncanny and frightening, but once the walking dead started to dance and jive with the King of Pop, zombies became nothing more than a joke. Although Romero tried to revitalize zombie films in 1985 with *Day of the Dead* (the metaphor this time addressing Cold War fears and paranoia[6]), the genre was in its death throes. *Day* failed at the box office, and Maddrey supposes that "audiences in the carefree, consumer-friendly 1980s apparently did not feel the need for such a serious examination of personal and societal values" (129). Instead consumers wanted comedic movies like Dan O'Bannon's *Return of the Living Dead* (1985), which flagrantly abuses Romero's genre rules by featuring zombies that can talk and by introducing the now-quintessential eating of brains. With such unmemorable titles as *Zombie Brigade* (1986) and *I Was a Teenage Zombie* (1987), things only got worse as budgets plummeted and camp took the place of scripts.

Historically, zombie cinema had always represented a stylized reaction to cultural consciousness and particularly to social and political injustices, and America in the 1990s saw perhaps too much complacency and stability for zombie movies to fit the national mood. The Cold War was over, the Berlin Wall had fallen, Ronald Reagan's Star Wars defense system was proven unnecessary, and George H.W. Bush's Gulf War had apparently been resolved. In fact, aside from some skirmishes in third-world countries, Americans were largely insulated from global warfare. Furthermore, in the Clinton decade, sexual impropriety took headlines away from global genocide and tyrannical massacres. With nothing specific to react to or protest against, cinematic versions of the zombie genre declined steadily throughout the 1990s, although Peter Jackson's *Dead Alive* (1992) provided some fresh ideas by inventing a subgenre commonly called "splatstick" comedy, where blood and guts are the primary comedic medium. Nevertheless, virtually no new or original stories were produced in the decade at all, although Dendle observes that no-budget, direct-to-video productions continued to flourish (*Zombie Movie* 10).

Even though zombies were no longer a source of terror on the silver screen, young people found renewed interest in zombies through violent video games. In 1993, id Software released a revolutionary first-person shooter game called *Doom*, which features zombified marines; however, these basically two-dimensional foes use guns instead of teeth, and the game's plot is more science fiction than horror. While zombies continued to play bit parts in other games, the first true zombie video game—Capcom's *Biohazard* (since renamed *Resident Evil*)—did not appear until 1996. This game takes its central story line directly from Romero's movies, for players must explore an isolated country manor while shooting reanimated corpses and trying to avoid being eaten—although unlike Romero's movies, there is a lot more "fight" than "flight." Nevertheless, the terror and action of zombie movies translated quite logically from the big screen to the video screen, and a nontraditional form of narrative incubated the genre until it was ready to re-emerge in theaters in 2002 with the release of two mainstream movies.

By returning to the classical form of Romero's films, British director Danny Boyle began the zombie renaissance with the first truly frightening zombie movie in years. Riding high from his *Trainspotting* (1996) success, Boyle created a new version of the zombie story with *28 Days Later*, in which a man wakes from a coma to find London abandoned and full of decaying corpses. Boyle also introduced faster, more feral zombie creatures, keeping the monsters alive rather than dead, and audiences responded as if the genre were new, instead of just newly re-visioned. The film's $8 million budget eventually resulted in a $45 million gross in the United States alone ("Business Data for *28 Days Later*"). At about the same time, mainstream Hollywood was also trying to kick-start the genre by capitalizing on the popularity of the video game circuit with Paul W.S. Anderson's *Resident Evil*, an action-packed science fiction movie that is more video game than narrative. More big-budget films have followed, like the two *Resident Evil* sequels (2004 and 2007), remakes of *Dawn of the Dead* (2006), the revisionist comedy *Shaun of the Dean*, and Romero's return with 2005's *Land of the Dead*.

The popularity of the zombie continues to inundate other media as well. The shooting-gallery nature of zombie survival—the more you kill, the more keep popping up—still spawns new video games every year in which players become part of the action. The *Biohazard* series now has over a dozen titles, and Romero's latest zombie movie inspired the game *Land of the Dead: Road to Fiddler's Green* (2005). The zombie also found a logical home in graphic novels, most notably Steve Nile's *George A. Romero's Dawn of the Dead* (2004) and Robert Kirkman's ongoing epic series *The Walking Dead* (2004-present). Zombies can be found outside of narrative fiction in the humorous yet strangely eerie *Zombie Survival Guide* (2003). This parody of popular survival guides is a straight-faced, seemingly nonfiction effort by Max Brooks to prepare the public for an actual zombie infestation. Even a number of hard-rock bands have jumped aboard the zombie bandwagon (e.g., Zombie Ritual and their 2004 album *Night of the Zombie Party*).

However, in spite of this evidence of a resurgence in the popularity of the zombie monster, no one identified the movement as having an official "renaissance" until Romero—the "Shakespeare of zombie cinema" (Dendle, *Zombie Movie* 121)—re-entered the game with *Land of the Dead*. In early 2006, Steven Wells wrote an article reacting to Showtime's made-for-TV movie *Homecoming* (2004), in which "Americans killed in Iraq rise from their flag-draped coffins and slaughter their way to the polling booths so they can vote out a warmongering president" (2). Wells shows an even broader impact, claiming that "there were zombies everywhere in 2005," from an all-zombie production of *Romero and Juliet* to online zombie blogs and a zombie appearance on *American Idol* (2). Zombies even showed up in the sixth Harry Potter novel, if only for a brief cameo.

The appearance of zombies in print media other than graphic novels is perhaps the most notable evidence of a renaissance for the more mainstream public. According to Don D'Auria, an editor of horror novels, "Until three years ago [zombies] were really unseen. Then they just seemed to pop up everywhere" (qtd. in St. John 2). In a 2006 *New York Times* article, Warren St. John provides a number of examples of the zombie literary invasion: Brian Keene's *The Rising*, a novel about "smart zombies;" David Willington's *Monster Island*, about a zombie infestation in Manhattan; and *World War Z: An Oral History of the Zombie War*, another faux nonfiction creation from Brooks (1, 13). In addition, Stephen King, the unequivocal master of modern literary horror, finally released a full-blown version of the zombie story with his 2006 novel *Cell*, a chilling morality tale in which unnamed terrorists turn the majority of Americans into enraged cannibals by brainwashing them with a mind-scrambling cell phone signal.

While the zombie renaissance is basically a given to zombie scholars and fans, such coverage from mainstream publications like the *New York Times* gives Wells' observations greater credibility as well as publicity. The return of the zombie, most obviously and prolifically in film, has fully come to the public's attention. St. John summarizes the renaissance: "In films, books and video games, the undead are once again on the march, elbowing past werewolves, vampires, swamp things and mummies to become the post-millennial ghoul of the moment" (1). All this evidence points to one unavoidable fact: "zombies are back" (2).

■ The Primary Characteristics of Zombie Cinema: Understanding the Genre

The twenty-first century zombie movie renaissance seems fueled in part by the popularity of zombies in other media and by the relatively low cost and ease of making splatterfest films.[7] But to explain this phenomenon and to understand the post-9/11 social relevance of zombie cinema, the essential characteristics of such films must be examined and the genre must be differentiated from other horror genres. Unlike many other tales of terror and the supernatural, the classical zombie story has very specific criteria that govern its plot and development. These genre protocols include not only the zombies and the imminent threat of violent deaths, but also a post-apocalyptic backdrop, the collapse of societal infrastructures, the indulgence of survivalist fantasies, and the fear of other surviving humans. All of these plot elements and motifs are present in pre-9/11 zombie films, but they have become more relevant to a modern, contemporary audience.

The most conspicuous feature of zombie movies is naturally the zombies themselves—both what the creatures *are* and, perhaps more important, what they are *not*. Audiences fear these ghouls for a number of obvious reasons: they are corpses raised from the dead, and, more significantly, they are the corpses of the known dead, what horror scholar R.H.W. Dillard calls "dead kindred" (15). In addition, the zombies pursue living humans with relentless dedication and kill people merciless by eating them alive. Because zombies are technically "dead" rather than the more romantic "undead" (i.e., ghosts and vampires), they possess merely a rotting brain and have no real emotional capacity. Toward that end, zombies cannot be reasoned with, appealed to, or dissuaded by logical discourse. Other supernatural foes devised by authors and Hollywood filmmakers are generally conscious, thinking individuals. In fact, in recent years, traditional supernatural monsters have become sympathetic protagonists and misunderstood heroes, like the ghosts in *The Sixth Sense* (1999) or *The Others* (2001), the vampires in Anne Rice's tales, or characters like Angel and Spike in the television series *Buffy the Vampire Slayer* (1997-2003) and *Angel* (1999-2004). Such qualities for zombies are logical impossibilities.[8]

What's more, in contrast to other supernatural or undead creatures, the zombie directly manifests the visual horrors of death; unlike most ghosts and vampires, zombies are in an active state of decay. Simon Pegg, co-writer and star of *Shaun of the Dead*, observes, "Metaphorically the classic creature embodies a number of our greatest fears. Most obviously, it is our own death, personified. The physical manifestation of that thing we fear the most" (133). It is no coincidence that the modern cinematic zombie cycle began "on the eve of the Tet offense in Vietnam" (Maddrey 122), when the general populace was being exposed to graphic images of death and violence on the nightly news. In addition, the inescapable realities of mortality ensure that every viewer could both fear and relate to the zombie: although no one expects to rise from the grave as a cannibalistic ghoul, everyone will die and rot.

As audiences have become more familiar with special effects and more accustomed to images of violence, cinematic depictions of zombies have had to become progressively more naturalistic and horrific. In *Night of the Living Dead*, the ghouls are basically just pasty-faced actors; even the scenes of cannibalistic acts are less shocking because the film is in black and white rather than color. By *Dawn of the Dead*, the zombies have become more realistic (yet strangely blue), and scenes of death and dismemberment are shockingly graphic and naturalistic—thanks for the most part to special effects wizard Tom Savini, who claimed that "much of my work for *Dawn of the Dead* was like a series of portraits of what I have seen for real in Vietnam" (qtd in Skal 311). Now, after thirty more years of global warfare and bloodshed, the twenty-first-century audience, largely desensitized by graphically violent video games and other media, almost demands an upping of the ante. In response, *28 Days Later* and *Land of the Dead* feature zombies with missing limbs, decaying flesh, and only partially constituted heads and faces; even the rather light *Shawn of the Dead* (a self-proclaimed "romantic comedy" zombie film) has some particularly gruesome ghouls and nauseating dismemberment scenes.[9]

Yet even though zombies are certainly uncanny and frightening by themselves, such monsters would not prove much of a threat if they appeared in the modern-day world; certainly the police or military would be around to exterminate the monsters. But zombie movies are almost always set during (or shortly after) the apocalypse, when those reassuring infrastructures cease to exist. In *Night of the Living Dead*, the zombie infestation seems limited to just one backwoods county, but by *Dawn of the Dead*, the impression is rather clear that the whole world is overrun. Romero's feckless survivors hide out in a shopping mall for an indeterminate amount of time, waiting in vain for the resumption of media broadcasts and for help that never arrives. *28 Days Later* is based on the premise that all of the United Kingdom has been decimated in just under a month, and *Land of the Dead* is even bleaker: the film is set in a zombie-dominated world, where Pittsburgh has been set up as a city-state unto itself. In all of these scenarios, the virus, plague, or infestation has been so rapid and complete that cities are quickly overrun, buildings abandoned, posts deserted, and airwaves silenced.

One of the greatest—or at least the most detailed—literary imaginings of the apocalypse is King's *The Stand,* a novel with no zombies but with most of the other zombie motifs: the story explores both the utter fall and eventual resurrection of the United States following a devastating and global viral pandemic.[10] King's novel blames the end of modern society on the governmental military complex, tailoring the deterioration of America's infrastructure on William Butler Yeats's description of the end of the world: "Things fall apart; the center cannot hold." This poignant image is central to zombie cinema; Brooks describes the new world order in his *Zombie Survival Guide*:

> When the living dead triumph, the world degenerates into utter chaos. All social order evaporates. Those in power, along with their families and associates, hold up in bunkers and secure areas around the country. Secure in these shelters, originally built for the Cold War, they survive. Perhaps they continue the façade of a government command structure. Perhaps the technology is available to communicate with other agencies or even other protected world leaders. For all practical purposes, however, they are nothing more than a government-in-exile. (155)

Once people start to die at an uncontrollable rate, panic rages through all levels of the government and the military, and most would be more interested in saving themselves and their families than in doing their jobs.[11]

The breakdown of social order leads to one of the more curious allures of zombie films: their ability to play out survivalist fantasies. Extreme followers of the survivalist credo hoard food-stuffs and ammunition in their isolated mountain cabins and basement bunkers, just hoping for the day when society will collapse and their paranoia will finally be justified. Like Brooks' book parodies, numerous survival manuals and Websites—such as Jack A. Spigarelli's *Crisis Preparedness Handbook* (2002) and Joshua Piven and David Borgenicht's *The Complete Worst-Case Scenario Survival Handbook* (2007)—encourage and direct such behavior, and apocalypse narratives allow their followers some cathartic enjoyment. Furthermore, as realized in movies like *The Omega Man* (1971) and *Night of the Comet* (1984), the end of the world means the end of capitalism, and everything becomes free for the taking. As a matter of survival, looting becomes basically legal—or at the very least, there is no law enforcement presence to prevent wanton theft. Anyone can own a Porsche, wear the latest Paris fashions, or go on an unbridled shopping spree.

The best depictions of this contradictory "fun amidst the terror" are found in the 1978 *Dawn of the Dead* and the 2004 remake by Zach Snyder. Both films take place primarily in shopping malls, locations that afford both security and sustenance. In the '78 version, Romero presents a light-hearted montage showing the four remaining survivors at play among the many shops available to them—playing basketball, eating exotic foods, and putting on makeup and expensive clothes—living out what horror scholar David J. Skal calls "consumerism gone mad" (309). Snyder's film includes a similar montage: finding themselves relatively safe from everything but boredom, the survivors play games, try on expensive clothes and shoes, watch movies on big-screen televisions, and even play golf. In a sick way, the mall is the ultimate vacation resort—they just can't ever go outside. An abbreviated version of the same idea is present in *28 Days Later*: in a parody of game shows like *Supermarket Sweep* (1990-2003), the four survivors race around a grocery store, filling their carts with all the goods they can carry.

Such sequences show that once the survivors take both the law and their protection into their own hands, establishing some kind of defensible stronghold—like a shopping mall, a bunker, an ordinary house, or the neighborhood pub—the zombies cease to be much of a direct threat and become more animals to be avoided. Instead, the real fear comes from the other human survivors—those who can still think plot and act.[12] As Dillard points out, "The living people are dangerous to each other, both because they are potentially living dead should they die and because they are human with all of the ordinary human failings" (22). In most zombie films, the human protagonists eventually argue, fight, and even turn against one another; cabin fever can make those inside the strongholds more dangerous than the zombies on the outside (Jones 161-162). In addition, the journey from survivor to vigilante is a short one; with the total collapse of all governmental law-enforcement systems, survival of the fittest becomes a very literal and grim reality. Those with power, weapons, and numbers simply take whatever they want. However, in the new zombie economy, everything is free—except other humans, of course. For lawless renegades, the only real sports left are slavery, torture, rape, and murder, which appease base appetites that cannot be satisfied by simply going to the mall.

In the 1978 *Dawn of the Dead*, the peaceful haven of the shopping mall is destroyed by the violent arrival of a vigilante biker gang. These bandits, whose primary aim is to loot the stores, disrupt the careful balance established between the zombies and the remaining survivors; as a result of the bikers' intrusion, more people die and all security is lost. In *28 Days Later*, this vigilante scenario is all the more frightening because the primary thread comes from the military, soldiers who are supposed to protect citizens, not abuse them. In a misguided attempt to repopulate the world, the soldiers threaten the female protagonists with rape, and Jim (Cillian Murphy) narrowly escapes execution for defending them. The threat of the zombies remains a fundamentally frightening part of the movie, but because the threat of bodily harm and rape are real-world potentialities, they are all the more terrifying.

◼ The Twenty-First-Century Zombie: Explaining the Renaissance

The post-9/11 zombie film remains remarkably true to the genre's original protocols. Although the zombies are not always literally dead, as in Romero's films, the apparent apocalypse and collapse of social infrastructure remain central features. In addition, the genre tends to emphasize certain causes for the end of the world, including infectious disease, biological warfare, euthanasia, terrorism, and even immigration. Although the genre is forty years old, these concepts resonate more strongly with present-day Americans than ever before, where events like the September 11 attacks, the war in Iraq, and Hurricane Katrina provide comparable forms of shocking ideas and imagery.

The end of the world is the ultimate societal fear, made all the more real by current weapons of mass destruction, and Snyder's remake of *Dawn of the Dead* depicts this apocalypse through a sequence of shocking events most zombie films simply imply. Ana (Sarah Polley), the film's protagonist, wakes one morning to find the world she knew collapsing around her. Her husband is trying to kill her, neighbors are shooting one another with handguns, and explosions of unknown origins rock the skyline. The chaos, disorientation, fear, and destruction she witnesses are disturbingly similar to the initial news footage broadcast on September 11, 2001. Although Jim in *28 Days Later* wakes after the apocalypse is essentially over, the film nevertheless presents a disturbing sequence of images of a metropolitan London void of all human presence. At the time of its conception, this moment in the screenplay was probably intended to simply shock audiences with its foreignness, but after September 11, the eerie street scenes take on new meaning.

Screenwriter Alex Garland joins Boyle on the *28 Days Later* DVD commentary track, where they discuss the historical antecedents of the film's imagery. The screenplay was written and filming had begun before September 11, so Garland and Boyle drew from other international crises and disasters for apocalyptic images. The scene in which Jim picks up stray pound notes off London's empty streets was directly inspired by footage from the "killing fields" of Cambodia during and after the reign of Pol Pot. The street billboard displaying hundreds of photos and notes seeking missing loved ones, which has a direct tie to 9/11 now, was based on an actual street scene following a devastating earthquake in China. The abandoned city, overturned buses, and churches full of corpses were all inspired by existing moments of actual civil unrest and social collapse.

Such images of metropolitan desolation and desertion certainly resonate strongly with contemporary audiences. According to Brooks, "People have apocalypse on the brain right now. … It's from terrorism, the war, [and] natural disasters like Katrina" (qtd. in St. John 13). During and after the collapse of the World Trade Center towers in New York, numerous journalists and bystanders commented on how the events seemed unreal— like something out of a movie. After Hurricane Katrina, Kevin Lair, who lived with his family near where the 17th Street levee burst, told reporters, "The whole thing looks like something out of a science fiction movie" (qtd in "It's Like"). Additionally, John Graydon, who rode out the aftermath of the storm in the Superdome, called his father in England and said, "It's like a scene from *Mad Max* in there" (qtd. in Beard). Nightly news clips showed the deserted streets of New Orleans as if the city were a film set, with abandoned cars, drifting newspapers, and stray dogs. Of course, these events may not directly affect the production of zombie movies, but they certainly affect an audience's reception of those films.

Romero's movies, like all great fantasy texts, have always offered critical metaphors, and the great twenty-first-century zombie films continue in this vein. According to Andy Coghlan of *New Scientist* magazine. "Infectious diseases are indeed the new paranoia that's striking Western society" (qtd. in James); fittingly, *28 Days Later* is about the risks of an unstoppable pandemic, in which a blood-borne virus can wipe out the entire United Kingdom in just under a month's time. Furthermore, the film makes the somewhat abstract potential of zombification a much more visceral reality. Boyle's characters refer to the ravenous monsters as "infected," not "zombies"—the creatures are not technically dead at all, but hapless people infected with a psychological virus that makes them ultra-aggressive and violent. This kind of zombie is more frightening than the traditional fantasy monster, and instead of just being a horror movie, *28 Days Later* crosses into science fiction: It *could* happen. In fact, Boyle calls the movie "a warning for us as well as an entertainment" (qtd. In James).

The psychotic plague of *28 Days Later* is mostly likely a reference to AIDS, but it could just as easily reference cholera, smallpox, or anthrax. In fact, in an unsettling irony, England experienced a devastating outbreak of foot-and-mouth disease during the filming of *28 Days Later*, resulting in the slaughter of millions of livestock (Boyle and Garland). Similarly, the *Dawn of the Dead* remake was shot during another scare: the SARS epidemic of 2003. Snyder noticed the alarming parallels between his film and the nightly news; both were fraught with panic and misinformation (Snyder and Newman). The threat of infestation and other biohazards is hardly less significant today: It is hard to view either film—or any zombie movie, for that matter—without thinking of the recent threat of bird flu or avian influenza.

The idea of a terminal, debilitating illness or infection leads to the less obvious issue present in all zombie movies: euthanasia. These films raise the quest: is it better to murder loved ones or to allow them to become something monstrous? In Romero's *Land of the Dead*, those bitten by zombies are given the choice of being killed immediately, since the virus takes time to work. Like a terminally ill patient, those infected by the zombie virus have time to say goodbye, put some affairs in order, and determine the method of their own death, enacting a kind of morbidly poignant "living will."[13] In *28 Days Later*, however, anyone infected must be killed at once—and often brutally; the virus takes only twenty seconds to fully manifest its insanity. When Selena's (Naomie Harris) traveling companion is bitten in a zombie attack, Selena immediately hacks off his injured limb and butchers him with a machete. In an even more pathetic scene, young Hannah (Megan Burns) barely gets the chance to say goodbye to her father (Brendan Gleeson) before the British military shoot him. The slaughter of the infected living becomes an essential form of mercy killing: the choices of the zombie landscape are hard ones, but survival is the top priority.

All of these narrative motifs and cinematic images can resonate strongly with modern viewers of the zombie movie, but the primary metaphor in the post-9/11 zombie world is terrorism. According to St. John,

> It does not take much of a stretch to see the parallel between zombies and anonymous terrorists who seek to convert others within society to their deadly cause. The fear that anyone could be a suicide bomber or a hijacker parallels a common trope of zombie films, in which healthy people are zombified by contact with other zombies and become killers. (13)

The transmission of the zombie infection is a symbolic form of radical brainwashing. Because anyone can become infected (i.e., conditioned) at any time, everyone is a potential threat; thus, paranoia becomes almost as important as survival. Those bitten often hide the injury, so even friends and family members cannot be fully trusted. In fact, the first zombie encountered in the *Dawn of the Dead* remake is a young girl, her apparent innocence making her violence all the more shocking.

Romero's *Land of the Dead* depicts a post-zombied society, a world where the enemy is literally at the gates. Pittsburgh has been converted into an island stronghold, with rivers and electric fencing keeping the zombies out (and the residents safely in). Class division is more critical than in other zombie films: the upper class lives an opulent lifestyle in Fiddler's

Green, a luxurious high-rise, while ignoring the problem; the commoners, however, must face reality while living in the slums below. In a documentary by Marian Mansi about the making of *Land of the Dead*, Romero comments, "Thematically, what the film is about is a bunch of people trying to live as though nothing has changed. Or at least that's what the administration believes. The protagonists understand that the world has completely changed." To keep the wealthy properly fed and supplied, the poor and industrious must risk their lives by venturing outside the city's fortifications, scavenging the countryside in an ever-increasing radius. They see the grim horrors of death and infection every day, much like soldiers on the front line of combat.

The wealthy elite in Fiddler's Green are literally isolated from the grim facts that make their lifestyle possible. To ensure the status quo, Dennis Hopper's Kaufman, the self-appointed leader of Pittsburgh, constructs the world's most extreme border security—blown up and barricaded bridges make the rivers impassable, and electric fences and armed guards protect the area from any intrusion; in an extreme example of xenophobia, soldiers shoot any intruders on sight. These forms of immigration control have become even more jarringly familiar with recent debates about erecting a fence between the United States and Mexico and the redeployment of National Guard troops to guard the United States' southern border during George W. Bush's presidency. *Land of the Dead* is certainly not subtle in its critique of modern American foreign policy; in fact, in Mansi's documentary, Romero goes so far as to identify the fascist Kaufman as Donald Rumsfeld and the Fiddler's Green tenants board as the Bush administration. Like Americans in the years immediately after the 9/11 terrorist attacks, the residents in *Land of the Dead* are asked both to continue their lives as if no real threat existed and to behave in certain ways because of the threat that *does* exist.

■ Conclusion

Although the conventions of the zombie genre remain largely unchanged, the movies' relevance has become all the more clear—a post-9/11 audience cannot help but perceive the characteristics of zombie cinema through the filter of terrorist threats and apocalyptic reality. Dendle emphasizes that the problem is "sorting out whether the movies really are doing something different in the post-9/11 world, or whether it's simply that audiences can't help but see them differently now" (interview). Most twenty-first-century zombies are faster, more deadly, and symbolically more transparent, but otherwise the films follow the mold Romero invented back in the 1960s. Yet they *are* different now, at least from the perspective of reception. As Dendle says, "we'll all view the world differently now, and … filmmakers and audiences alike are inherently attuned to read themes and motifs through different lenses than they would have before" (interview).

Initially, zombie movies shocked audiences with their unfamiliar images; today, they are all the more shocking because of their familiarity. In fact, fans of horror films, particularly apocalypse narratives like zombie movies, may find that the movies even help prepare them for reality. Dendle was approached in the summer of 2005 by a law student who had survived the horrors of September 11 firsthand. Although the experience was understandably shocking, this student claimed he had been emotionally prepared for the tragedy not by his family, community, or government, but by his long appreciation for zombie movies (interview). Perhaps zombie cinema is not merely a reflection of modern society, but a type of pre-emptive panacea, and that potential gives the genre both cultural significance and value.

■ Notes

1 These were Andrew Currie's *Fido* and *The Signal*, written and directed by David Bruckner, Dan Bush, and Jacob Gentry.

2 Oakes uses a rather liberal definition of zombie movies on his *Zombie Movie Data-Base,* including in his numbers any film that features undead or otherwise reanimated creatures, such as golems, mummies, and creatures possessed by demons.

3 This article is limited in scope to those films that openly embrace the genre conventions established by George A. Romero in his series of zombie movies (i.e. stories that feature hordes of cannibalistic human corpses that relentlessly pursue an isolated group of survivors and can only be killed by a gunshot or blow to the head). While zombies can be found in a variety of films prior to 1968, the majority of zombie movies made since September 11 follow Romero's genre lead, not those films addressing voodoo enslavement or alien invasion.

4 For more detailed readings of *Night of the Living Dead*, see Maddrey 49-51, 122-124; Jones 160-163; Dillard; and Paul Wells 8082. For an in-depth psychoanalytical reading of the film and an investigation of terror in general, see Connolly 422-424.

5 For a discussion of the symbolism and capitalist critique in *Dawn of the Dead*, see Jones 163; Maddrey 126; Paul Wells 82; and Wood 125-127.

6 For more detailed discussions of *Day of the Dead*, see Jones 163-164 and Maddrey 128.

7 For instance, the direct-to-video films *Rise of the Undead* (2005) and *Swamp Zombies* (2005) boast total production budgets of $10,000 and $12,000 respectively, according to the "Business Data" sites for both films.

8 Two notable exceptions must be addressed. First, in the non-canonical "zombedies" of the 1980s and '90s, like *Return of the Living Dead* and *I Was a Teenage Zombie*, the protagonists do become zombies, and the plots of such films often revolve around turning the hapless heroes back to normal. As mentioned earlier, however, such films are not true zombie horror films. Second, Romero has been experimenting with the idea of zombie evolution, a concept progressing toward sentient ghouls. For example, in *Day of the Dead*, a quasi-domesticated zombie named "Bub" is taught to use a razor, pick up the phone, and hold and fire a gun; in *Land of the Dead*, a former gas station attendant named "Big Daddy" leads a zombie attack, figuring out how to circumvent the humans' fortifications. Such an evolution seems illogical, but it is hard to argue against Romero, should he choose to adjust his own genre. Nevertheless, in spite of these experiments, the true zombie protagonist has not yet arrived.

9 *Shaun of the Dead* is certainly the most thought provoking and relevant of the zombedies, although the comedy is one of satire rather than just jokes and slapstick. Director Edgar Wright is suggesting that a zombie infestation would probably go unnoticed by the average middle-class worker; as depicted by Simon Pegg's Shaun, modern society has already turned everyone into zombies.

10 In fact, Romero considered filming a screen adaptation of *The Stand*, which Maddrey points out "would have been the one [of King's works] most suited to Romero's vision of America" (127).

11   This unpleasant possibility, that those hired to protect would actually cut and run was manifested in New Orleans during Hurricane Katrina, when a number of local law-enforcement officers fled with their families ("N.O. Police").

12   This is one of the more interesting aspects of the zombie scenario, but it is one that cannot be fully explored in a two-hour film. Romero's *Land of the Dead* shows the breakdown of social structure most fully, but it would be best demonstrated by serialized narratives, such as Kirkman's graphic novels or a television series.

13   Once again, a zombie movie eerily echoes contemporary headlines: *Land of the Dead* was released the same summer that Americans debated the tragic case of Terri Schiavo, who ultimately was taken off life support at the behest of her husband.

■ Works Cited

Beard, Matthew. "Hurricane Katrina: 'Like a Scene from Mad Max:' British Couple." *Independent.* BNet Business Network, 3 Sept., 2005. Web 27 Feb. 2009.

Boyle, Danny, dir. *28 Days Later.* 2002. Twentieth Century Fox, 2003. DVD.

Boyle, Danny, and Alex Garland. Commentary. *28 Days Later*. Dir. Danny Boyle.

Brooks, Max. *The Zombie Survival Guide.* New York: Three Rivers. 2003. Print.

"Business Data for *Dawn of the Dead* (1978)." *Internet Movie Database*. IMDb.com, n.d. Web. 3 May 2006.

"Business Data for *Night of the Living Dead*." *Internet Movie Database*. IMDb.com, n.d. Web. 3 May 2006.

"Business Data for *Rise of the Undead*." *Internet Movie Database*. IMDb.com, n.d. Web. 3 May 2006.

"Business Data for *Swamp Zombies*." *Internet Movie Database*. IMDb.com, n.d. Web. 3 May 2006.

"Business Data for *28 Days Later*." *Internet Movie Database*. IMDb.com, n.d. Web. 3 May 2006.

Connolly, Angela. "Psychoanalytic Theory in Times of Terror." *Journal of Analytical Psychology* 48 (2003): 407-431. Print.

Dendle, Peter. E-mail interview. 20 Oct. 2005.

———. *The Zombie Movie Encyclopedia.* Jefferson: McFarland, 2001. Print.

Dillard, R.H.W. "*Night of the Living Dead:* It's Not Like Just a Wind That's Passing Through." *American Horrors*. Ed. Gregory A. Waller. Chicago: U of Illinois P, 1987. 14-29. Print.

"It's Like a Sci-Fi Movie." *News24.com*. 24.com, 10 Jan. 2005. Web. 27 Feb. 2009.

James, Toby, dir. *Pure Rage: The Making of* 28 Days Later. *28 Days Later*. Dir. Danny Boyle. 2002. Twentieth Century Fox, 2003. DVD.

Jones, Darryl. *Horror: A Thematic History in Fiction and Film.* London: Arnold, 2002. Print.

King, Stephen. *The Stand.* New York: Doubleday. 1990. Print.

Maddrey, Joseph *Nightmares in Red, White and Blue: The Evolution of the American Horror Film*. Jefferson: McFarland, 2004. Print.

Mansi, Marian, dir. *Undead Again: The Making of* Land of the Dead. Land of the Dead. Dir. George A. Romero. 2005. Unrated Director's Cut. Universal, 2005, DVD.

"N.O. Police Fire 51 for Desertion." *Fox News.* Fox News Corporation, 30 Oct. 2005. Web. 27 Feb. 2009.

Oakes, David, ed. *Zombie Movie Data-Base.* Trash Video, n.d. Web. 27 Oct. 2007.

Pegg, Simon. Afterword. *Miles Behind Us.* By Robert Kirkman. Berkeley: Image Comics, 2004. Print Vol. 2 of *The Walking Dead.*

Romero, George A., dir. *Dawn of the Dead.* 1978. Ultimate Ed. Anchor Bay, 2004. DVD.

———, dir. *Day of the Dead.* 1985. Anchor Bay, 2003. DVD.

———, dir. *Land of the Dead.* 2005. Unrated Director's Cut. Universal, 2005. DVD.

———, dir. *Night of the Living Dead.* 1968. Millennium Ed. Elite, 1994. DVD.

Skal, David J. *The Monster Show.* New York: Faber, 1993. Print.

Snyder, Zach, dir. *Dawn of the Dead.* 2004. Unrated Director's Cut. Universal, 2004. DVD.

Snyder, Zach, and Eric Newman. Commentary. *Dawn of the Dead.* Dir. Zach Snyder.

St. John, Warren. "Market for Zombies? It's Undead (Aaahhh!)." *New York Times* 26 Mar. 2006, sec. 9: 1+. Print.

Wells, Paul. *The Horror Genre: From Beelzebub to Blair Witch.* New York: Wildflower, 2002. Print.

Wells, Steven. "G2: Shortcuts: Zombies Come Back from the Dead." *Guardian* [London] 2 Jan. 2006, Features: 2. Print.

Wood, Robin. "Neglected Nightmares" *Horror Film Reader.* Ed. Alain Silver and James Ursini. New York: Limelight Editions, 2000. 111-27. Print.

Wright, Edgar, dir. *Shaun of the Dead.* 2004. Universal, 2004. DVD.

Yeats, William Butler. "The Second Coming." 1919. *The Norton Introduction to Literature.* Ed Jerome Beaty et al. 8th ed. New York: Norton, 2002. 1325. Print.

■ READING AND WRITING

1. Bishop presents a causal argument in his essay. What is his claim? What evidence does he provide to explain the causal relationships that he identifies? Do you find his argument convincing? Explain your response.
2. How does Bishop define the zombie genre? What role does this definition play in his larger argument?
3. What social benefit(s) does Bishop suggest viewers might gain from watching zombie movies? Do you agree with his analysis?

■ USING RESEARCH

4. Use one of the library's news media databases, such as LexisNexis Academic, to find several reviews of zombie films made after September 11, 2001. Do these reviewers make the connections between the terrorist attacks and the renaissance of zombie films that Bishop suggests? Or do they propose other connections between zombie movies and broader social trends? Write a brief essay that summarizes your findings, and include a works cited page or bibliography.

Originally from San Francisco, Cintra Wilson has written books, short stories, essays, and screenplays. She wrote this piece for the September 18, 2008, Fashion & Style section of The New York Times.

YOU JUST CAN'T KILL IT Cintra Wilson

Don't know how it happened. It felt more like a gradual, irresistible drift, but in retrospect, it might have been a sudden, overnight conversion. Maybe our local video store rented "The Hunger" one too many times.

Perhaps one teenager too many lay awake after midnight, unable to get Edward Gorey's disturbing Black Doll image out of his head. Maybe a girl with 14 piercings in each ear sang Siouxsie and the Banshees's "Cities in Dust" to her cat enough times to warp the entire light spectrum.

But there was a distinct point in San Francisco, in the late 1980s, when all the post-punk wardrobes of my extended tribe—a lower Haight-Ashbury aggregate of motorcyclists, college dropouts, would-be artists and nightclub workers—turned as abruptly and completely black as if a wall of ink had crept up from the Pacific and saturated everything, save for occasional outcroppings of little silver skulls.

Secretly I nursed grandiose ideas that my funereal vintage attire aligned me with beatniks, existentialists, Zen Buddhists, French Situationists, 1930s movie stars and samurai. (In reality, my style could probably have been more aptly described as "Biker Madonna with mood disorder.")

We were all young and poor: If your clothes were all black, everything matched and was vaguely elegant (especially if you squinted). Entropy was a thrifty, built-in style; if your tights ripped into cobwebs, that, too, was a look.

We lived in squalid tenements and worked until 4 a.m. Goth was a fashion response to doing infrequent laundry and never seeing the sun. A Northern California anti-tan could be an advantage if you made yourself even paler. On the bright side, our new monochromism was helpful to community building: We were able to recognize our neighbors as well as if we had all adopted regional folk costume. You knew you could rely on your blackly attired ilk to answer questions like, "Hey, where should I go to get my 1978 Triumph Bonneville repaired/get green dreadlocks/get the word Golgotha tattooed in five-inch letters across my back/buy jimson weed/cast a reverse love spell for under $14/(insert your vaguely but harmlessly sinister demimonde activity here)?"

"'Gothic' is an epithet with a strange history, evoking images of death, destruction, and decay," the fashion historian Valerie Steele writes in "Gothic: Dark Glamour" (Yale University Press), a new coffee-table book, written with Jennifer Park. An exhibition of the same name, curated by Ms. Steele at the Museum at the Fashion Institute of Technology, unpacks the evolution of goth in fashion from its early beginnings in Victorian mourning to its most current expressions.

"It is not just a term that describes something (such as a Gothic cathedral), it is also almost inevitably a term of abuse, implying that something is dark, barbarous, gloomy and macabre," she wrote. "Ironically, its negative connotations have made it, in some respects, ideal as a symbol of rebellion. Hence its significance for youth subcultures."

But goth fashion is not just for maladjusted latchkey kids. A recent proliferation of Haute Goth on the runways of designers like Alexander McQueen, Rick Owens, Gareth Pugh and the spidery crochet webs of Rodarte (not to mention various darkly inclined Belgian designers) suggests, once again, that black still is, and probably always will be the new black.

The goth subculture, however, for those who live it, is more than the sum of its chicken bones, vampire clichés and existential pants. It remains a visual shortcut through which young persons of a certain damp emotional climate can broadcast to the other members of their tribe who they are. Goth is a look that simultaneously expresses and cures its own sense of alienation.

This sentiment was echoed by Wendy Jenkins of Powell, Ohio, whom I contacted via a goth group on Facebook. "To me, Goth is like an escape," wrote Ms. Jenkins, who is 18 and attends Olentangy Liberty High School.

"No one really judges each other," she continued. "It doesn't matter if you are tall, short, black, white, heavy, thin. Goth can fit everyone! I think it is a great way to bond with others who are different and who are just like you at the same time! Because we are wearing black most the time we are EZ to find!"

Missy Graf, 20, of Edmonton, Alberta, became fascinated by the goths at her Catholic high school. "One of the goth girls was in the choir with me," she wrote in an e-mail message, "and we talked about depression and God's apparent absence from her life. It was one of my first encounters with the world outside of the 'Christian bubble.'"

"I guess I slowly became (eh-em) 'goth' starting a year and a half ago," she added. "I was afraid of what my mom would think (she is still convinced that goth is associated with Satan-worshipping and that dying my hair black is one more step into the oblivion ... oh mom! You dye your hair red. Don't you know that Satan panties are red, not black?). Whatever. Eventually I got to the point where I stopped trying to make people accept me."

The Bay Area was home to a number of influential goths. Courtney Love successfully introduced the kinderwhore look: filmy Victorian nightgowns with fright-wig doll hair and heavy makeup. The band Specimen kept an apartment in the Mission District strewn with artificial cobwebs. Diamanda Galas frequently gabbled in demonic tongues on concert stages with her grand piano. I was privileged to direct the poet/performance artist/goth icon Danielle Willis in "Breakfast in the Flesh District," her candidly hilarious, autobiographical one-woman show about working in the Tenderloin's strip clubs as a self-styled vampire.

Ms. Willis, who embraced goth the second she saw Tim Curry's "sweet transvestite from Transylvania" in "The Rocky Horror Picture Show," used to write great articles on the ironies of goth fashion, like "Lord Damien Stark's Makeup Tips for the Bleak" (originally printed in Ghastly Magazine):

"Whiteface should create the illusion that you really are that pale, and not that you have a bunch of makeup from Walgreens caked all over your face. Done badly, Gothic makeup can look painfully stupid. After spending money on a decent base, take the trouble to apply it evenly. It's appalling how many Goths overlook something so basic and vital to their entire aesthetic. Equally bad and unfortunately just as frequent is the tendency to overpowder and the tendency to end one's pallor at the jawbone. I can understand someone having difficulty with liquid eyeliner, but some mistakes are just inexcusably stupid. Don't make them."

I just wore black, but Danielle Willis was a Satanic blood fetishist who had her own 19th-century phlebotomy kit, permanent fangs dentally bonded to her eyeteeth and serious drug problems. I once teased her about her decorative penchant for red velvet chaises, heavy curtains, ball-and-claw side tables, stigmata and other forms of morbid opulence, saying that they didn't necessarily mean she was goth, just Italian. She clocked me pretty hard.

THE ORIGINS of contemporary goth style are found in the Victorian cult of mourning.

"Victorians had a joke when women got into fashionable mourning dress—they called it 'the trap rebaited.'" Ms. Steele said, showing me one of the highlights of the F.I.T. exhibition: a 1905 Victorian cult-of-mourning gown by Desbuisson & Hudelist that was off-the-shoulder, had a plunging neckline and was covered with matte-black sequins.

The show also makes a healthy foray into what Ms. Steele calls the "diabolism, dandyism and decadence" of Dracula. "Just as the devil is the prince of darkness, the dandy is the black prince of elegance," she explained. "And the paradigm of the gothic man is a dandy vampire aristocrat."

The vampire introduces the idea of the "erotic macabre" into gothic fashion. There are stunning examples in the show of vampiric sex appeal—e.g., a voluminous blood-red gown by John Galliano for Dior, printed with a Marquis de Sade quotation: "Is it not by murder that France is free today?" (Which, accessorized with its huge chain and cross made of railway spikes, would inspire even the Easter Bunny to absinthe and Emocore.)

One display acknowledges the fetish culture's influence on goth ("kinky nihilism," as Ms. Steele describes it): buckled PVC corsets and other snazzy bondage accoutrements in addition to the usual Morticia Addams styles.

But to Wendy Jenkins, vampires represent more than just a hot batch of spooky formalwear. They provide a romantic narrative for sympathizing with her own perceived abnormalities. She wrote to me: "I think vampires are freaking sweet because they have such true emotions that no mere mortals can express! I too at times think I am a vampire being with my hate of garlic and how my eyes r sensitive to light."

This sense of pathos-dripping, emotional fragility draws no small ridicule to the idea of "goth." The word still brings to mind Anne Rice à la Renaissance Faire, moody bodice-ripper connotations, as well as ruffled shirts, tarot cards and sad girls who wistfully change their names to Pandora and Esmeralda (a tendency finally ridiculed to death in the "Saturday Night Live" sketch Goth Talk, with its teenage hosts, Azrael Abyss, "Prince of Sorrows," and his friend, Circe Nightshade).

Nocturne Midnight, aka Josh Klooster from Millet, Alberta, a 17-year-old student at Leduc Composite High School in Edmonton (and another goth in the Facebook group), prefers "a suave gentleman style," he wrote. "Dress shirt, dress pants, top hat, spiked collar, light make-up. It makes me feel like an aristocrat."

Tia Senat, 15, a sophomore at Ellsworth High School in Ellsworth, Kan., identifies her goth-influenced style as "emo."

"Some Goth people seem different, but really they're just normal people hidden behind a sort of personality 'curtain,'" she said. "Emo is being extremely sensitive and showing your emotions.

"What drew me to it was because it basically explained how I acted. You can't just decide to be. It really just happens. Many people believe that all teens such as me participate in self-mutilation, or cutting, and that they whine about their life and how bad it is compared to other people. Not all Emo kids do this unless something very, very traumatic happens, believe me."

Mr. Midnight takes exception. "Emos tend to take themselves far too seriously," he said. "Every emotion they have is one extreme or another. Extremely happy, crushingly sad, screaming rage. Just too much emotion. All the time."

Looking back at my own experience, it seems that black clothes were a response to certain catastrophic influences that came up with terrible regularity. We had all lost, or were in the process of losing, friends to AIDS, addictions and accidents. There were always disappointments in romance, and no surplus of mental health or functional families. Boots, black and leather provided a certain group with a certain emotional exoskeleton, a blustering attempt to express an edgy, careless willingness to hurl ourselves into oblivion. But the writing on the collective black flag, for all our reckless posturing, may have been best articulated as: "Ow, I'm hypersensitive. Please don't hurt me again."

Nocturne Midnight explains the importance of being goth: "It's a part of who I am," he said. "Nothing else worked. Goth just seemed to fit. I suppose Goth invokes in me a feeling of happiness, of belonging."

Later Wendy Jenkins wrote to tell me: "Case you didn't know, I am in a wheelchair."

There are certainly worse ways to misspend a youth than living it in a vampire costume. After all, sometimes the most sympathetic character in a story is the villain.

But being goth doesn't mean you have no sense of humor.

"Gothic style should be as opulent, decadent and individual as possible," Danielle Willis wrote. "If you're not up to making the effort necessary to carry off this most high maintenance of affectations, try wearing plaid shirts and listening to Nirvana instead."

READING AND WRITING

1. Based on Wilson's article, what does it mean to "be goth"? How does fashion play in to this identity?
2. How does Wilson organize and develop her exploration of this topic? What kinds of evidence does she use to support her claims? Do you find her claims persuasive?
3. How does Wilson position herself as the author in this piece? How does she want to be perceived by her audience? How does she develop this ethos?

DEVELOPING LONGER RESPONSES

4. Wilson quotes fashion historian Valerie Steele as saying that "gothic" is "almost inevitably a term of abuse, implying that something is dark, barbarous, gloomy and macabre. Ironically, its negative connotations have made it, in some respects, ideal as a symbol of rebellion. Hence its significance for youth subcultures." What, based on your reading of Wilson's piece, do you think members of the goth subculture are rebelling against? Why is this kind of rebellion so appealing to young people?

■ RESEARCH AND WRITING PROJECTS

1. Annalee Newitz and Kyle Bishop suggest in their essays that monsters are allegorical figures who reflect the widespread and often unconscious fears experienced by particular cultures in particular eras. Read all of Stoker's *Dracula* and use the library and the internet to explore what life was like in late 19th century Great Britain. Then, compose an argument in which you answer the following question: What cultural anxieties might Count Dracula represent for the British people at the time of the book's publication? You will need to support your claim with evidence from the primary text (*Dracula*) and from your research.

2. The pantheon of iconic monsters in literature and film is dominated by male characters. Why do you think this is the case? Use resources available through the library and the internet to explore this question and to find examples of female monsters. After completing your research, compose a causal argument in which you present and support a claim about the reasons behind this tradition of male-dominated monster stories. Or you may argue that this tradition is changing and examine the causes behind this change.

3. While the vampires discussed in this chapter are drawn from the folklore and literature of Europe, similar monsters—such as the Chupacabra—appear in a number of other cultures. Research the representations of a blood-sucking monster in another part of the world and explain what this monster means to the culture that produced it. Then, compare your findings with the conclusions drawn in this chapter about the meaning of monsters in European and American cultures. Finally, compose an essay in which you analyze the social and cultural functions and implications of monsters in the West and in the region you researched.

4. The film industry is certainly a driving force behind the resurgent popularity of vampire stories. And movie marketing has always been a vital part of the industry. Using the library's resources and the internet, find examples of vampire movie posters from the following time periods: 1920-1950, 1951-1980, 1981-2010. Select at least one poster from each time period and analyze the rhetoric at work in each of them. To do this, you'll have to also get a sense of each poster's original rhetorical

context—it's time, it's target audience, and it's purpose. And, according to the readings in this chapter, you'll also have to understand the widespread cultural anxieties of each time period. Use your research to compose a comparative analysis of the rhetorical choices each poster makes.

5 Responsibility and Response

IMAGE 5.1: "I cannot see an outstretched hand and not put something there," Elie Wiesel says in "Am I My Brother's Keeper?" How do you respond when you see others in need?

What do we owe our fellow human beings? Compassion? Understanding? Action? What are our obligations when we learn of injustice or tragedy, whether it's across the hall or a world away? Is joining a *Facebook* group enough? Or wearing a bracelet? Clearly, these are difficult questions. And as the essays and articles in this chapter show, answering them in meaningful ways is a complicated process.

Holocaust survivor and Nobel laureate Elie Wiesel is a teacher, a writer, and one of the world's most persistent and eloquent voices for peace and moral responsibility. His best-known book is Night, a memoir about his time in a Nazi death camp as a child, though he has written scores of other books, speeches, and essays. Richard D. Heffner is a professor of communications and public policy at Rutgers University and the producer and longtime host of the radio program The Open Mind. The text that follows is from the 2001 book Conversations with Elie Wiesel.

AM I MY BROTHER'S KEEPER?
Elie Wiesel and Richard D. Heffner

Elie, this is a question that perhaps is not understood too well by a good many people in our time. What does it mean to you?

It is a question that Cain asked of God, having killed Abel: "Am I my brother's keeper?" And the answer, of course, is, we are all our brothers' keepers. Why? Either we see in each other brothers, or we live in a world of strangers. I believe that there are no strangers in God's creation. There are no strangers in a world that becomes smaller and smaller. Today I know right away when something happens, whatever happens, anywhere in the world. So there is no excuse for us not to be involved in these problems. A century ago, by the time the news of a war reached another place, the war was over. Now people die and the pictures of their dying are offered to you and to me while we are having dinner. Since I know, how can I not transform that knowledge into responsibility? So the key word is "responsibility." That means I must keep my brother.

Yet it seems that despite the fact that we live in an age of rapid, immediate communications, we know so little about what is happening to our brothers.

We are careless. Somehow life has been cheapened in our own eyes. The sanctity of life, the sacred dimension of every minute of human existence, is gone. The main problem is that there are so many situations that demand our attention. There are so many tragedies that need our involvement. Where do you begin? We know *too* much. No, let me correct myself. We are *informed* about too many things. Whether information is transformed into knowledge is a different story, a different question.

But we are in the world of communication. Nothing has caught the fantasy, the imagination, of the world these last years as communication has. So many radio stations, so many television stations, so many publications, so many talk shows. It's always more and more information that is being fed. And I'm glad that these things are happening, because I think people should be informed.

However, let us say that on a given day a tragedy has taken place. For a day we are all glued to the television. Three days later, we are still glued. A week later, another tragedy occurs and then the first tragedy is overshadowed by the next one. I remember when I saw the hungry children of Biafra for the first time. I didn't sleep. I tried everything I could to address the problem—to write articles and call up people and organize activities to send food to those children. But if you had shown those pictures for a whole month, by the second month people would not have been moved by them. What happened to the information there? It is still stored, but yet we don't act upon it, because we are summoned by the current event.

There seems to be almost an inevitability about what you are describing, because extending and perfecting the means of communication is certainly a major thrust of our times.

I would like to be able to say to my students that there are so many things in the world that solicit your attention and your involvement that you can choose any one. I really don't mind where that particular event is taking place. But I would like my students to be fully involved in *some* event. Today, for instance, they will say, "I go to zone A, and then I go to zone B." But as long as zone A has not been covered fully, as long as it is a human problem, I don't think we can abandon it. All the areas must be covered. I would not want to live in a world today in which a person or a community, because of color, because of religion, because of ethnic origin, or because of social conditions, would feel totally neglected or abandoned. There must be someone who speaks to and for that group, every group.

Is there any question but that we have seen the faces of those who suffer and yet we are not moved sufficiently?

I plead your case: In 1945, all the newspapers and magazines in the United States showed the pictures of the concentration camps. And yet for another five years, displaced persons remained in those camps. How many were allowed to come to America? They were told, "Those who want to go to Palestine, good. All the others, come and we shall give you what you really need most—human warmth?" Furthermore, look at what happened in South Africa. Apartheid was a blasphemy. We saw these white racists killing. I remember images that moved me to anger— images of funeral processions. Whites had killed blacks because they were black. And then the whites disrupted the funerals, killing more black people. That is the limit of endurance, the limit of any tolerance. We should have protested louder. And yet we didn't.

We talk about a world that is, perhaps, too much with us, so much so that there is no time to focus. How do you help your students deal with that?

I mentioned Cain and Abel. Why did Cain kill Abel? It is not because he was jealous. According to the text that we read and comment upon, it was because Cain spoke to Abel, his younger brother, and he told him of his pain, of his abandonment, of his solitude—that God didn't want to accept his offering. In the Bible it's said, "And Cain spoke to Abel." And we don't even know whether Abel listened. There was no dialogue. So the first act, really, among brothers, was a lack of communication.

So what I would teach my students is communication. I believe in dialogue. I believe if people talk, and they talk sincerely, with the same respect that one owes to a close friend or to God, something will come out of that, something good. I would call it presence. I would like my students to be present whenever people need a human presence. I urge very little upon my students, but that is one thing I do. To people I love, I wish I could say, "I will suffer in your place." But I cannot. Nobody can. Nobody should. I can be present, though. And when you suffer, you need a presence.

When you say "communicate," you mean to accept communication, don't you?

To be able to give and to receive at the same time.

Does it seem to you that we're not listening to the world around us, that we're so much involved in our individual pursuits?

Absolutely. I think the noise around us has become deafening. People talk but nobody listens. People aren't afraid of that silence. Have you seen those youngsters and not-so-young people go around in the street with a Walkman on their ears? They don't want to hear anything. They want to hear only their own music. Which is the same music, by the way, that they heard yesterday. It's a kind of repetition which is deafening. People don't want to hear the world. The world is, I think, in need of being heard.

Elie, I find that as I get older and older still, I so often find that I want to shut things out, because I can't focus on what needs to be focused on if I'm listening to everything. That seems to me to be where we began, in a sense.

To me too, of course. So often I want to turn off everything and say, "Look, it's easier to talk about *Romeo and Juliet* than to talk about what's happening today anywhere in the world." Naturally. Because in that play, there is a text and there is a story. It's a story I can turn in any direction I want, really. You think that *Romeo and Juliet* is a story of love. It's a story of hate. So whatever subject I discuss, I can always turn it one way or another. It's familiar, graspable. I prefer to discuss Plato, naturally. But we must open our eyes, and—

I don't want to be a devil's advocate here. I understand the subjective need not to feel that I am my brother's keeper, the subjective need to shut out the pain—

Sure. You couldn't take it. There is a need to remember, and it may last only a day or a week at a time. We cannot remember all the time. That would be impossible; we would be numb. If I were to remember all the time, I wouldn't be able to function. A person who is sensitive, always responding, always listening, always ready to receive someone else's pain … how can one live? One must forget that we die; if not, we wouldn't live.

So what do we do? Can we both attend to our own needs and to the various needs of our family and friends and still extend the notion of "Am I my brother's keeper?" way beyond Abel to the far points of the world?

Perhaps we cannot, but we must try. Because we cannot, we must, even though Kant used to say, "We can, therefore we must." There is so much forgetfulness, so much indifference today, that we must **fight** it. We must fight for the sake of our own future. Is this the nature of human beings? Yes, it's part of our nature.

I know it all seems like too much—even in our own city, New York. There is so much hate and so much mistrust and distrust that you wonder what can reach these people who live together, who can live together, who after all must live together. Where do you begin? Now, I always feel very strongly about the person who needs me. I don't know who that person is, but if the person needs me, I somehow must think of that person more than about myself. Why? Because I see my own life in him or her. I remember there were times when I needed people, and they were not there. If there is a governing precept in my life, it is that: If somebody needs me, I must be there.

When I ask the question that we began with—"Am I my brother's keeper?"—I most often receive a blank stare. Obviously that stare comes from people for whom the concept is, if not anathema, at least terribly foreign. More so now, don't you think?

More so, because it involves us more deeply, because it goes further. If I say yes, then I have to do something about it. Then it really goes further than that: What does it mean? Who is my brother? It's a definition. Who is my brother? Is any person in the street my brother? Is a person in Somalia my brother? Is a person in Armenia my brother? Come on. If I say, "My brother," what do I mean? Have I seen them? Have I met them? So of course it could be a poetic expression, which means very little. But if you say that there are people in the world who need a brother, I will say, "Then I would like to be that brother." I don't always succeed, of course. I cannot. I am only an individual. I am alone, as you are alone. What can we do? We can be the brother to one person and then another person, to ten people, a hundred people in our whole life. Does it mean that we are brothers to everybody in the world? No, we cannot be. So even if we say that at least we can tell a story about a brother who is looking for a brother and finds one, I think that's quite enough.

Yes, but aren't we experiencing a new kind of isolationism today? "Please, I can't solve these problems. Don't burden me with them. I'm not my brother's keeper!"

> Today brothers become strangers. How do you expect strangers to become brothers? People who live in the same country today are strangers to one another. Take what's happened in Eastern Europe when the reactionary, exclusionary forces rule. They are neighbors, close to one another, but they see in each other a threat, a source of suspicion, a conqueror, not a brother. I think it's an historical phenomenon, which is worrisome.

Elie, what's the scriptural response to the question "Am I my brother's keeper?"

> It is actually written as a dialogue, a scenario. Cain kills Abel. And God says to him, "Hi, good morning, how are you?" "All right," says Cain. Then God says, "By the way, where is your brother?" "I don't know," is the answer. "What do you mean, you don't know?" asks God. The answer: "I don't know. Am I my brother's keeper?" And then God says, "Come on, you know. I hear the voice of your brother's blood coming from the bowels of the earth. And you want to cheat me." The whole thing is a little bit silly. Does it mean that God didn't know where Abel was? God is playing a game. It's simply a story which I like to interpret as meaning that it is possible, unfortunately, throughout history, for two brothers to be brothers and yet to become the victim and/or the assassin of the other. However, I go one step further and I try to teach my students that we learn another lesson: Whoever kills, kills his brother.

Kills his brother or kills some part of himself?

> It's possible, as I interpret it, that Cain and Abel were only one person. Cain killed Abel in Cain.

The Darwinian response to "Am I my brother's keeper?" is: "Of course not. If you pretend to be, you are interfering with natural selection." How do we build again upon the more ancient notion that indeed we are our brothers' keepers in many, many, ways?

> But remember again, Cain was *not* his brother's keeper. He killed him.

But the question asked by God—

> The question is good.

I know that's your specialty—questions.

> I love questions, true. Because there is "quest" in "question." I love that. But today, I would like to put a face on words. When I see words, I see a face. When

you speak about, let's say, "my brother's keeper," I see faces of people I knew or know, or people I've just seen this morning. Crossing the street, there is an old man with his hand outstretched. Now, am I his keeper?

Are you?

I must tell you that when I see that, I always feel strange. Because on the one hand, reason tells me that if I give him a dollar, he will go and buy alcohol. But then I say to myself, So what? Who am I to decide what he will do with the money that I give him? I cannot see an outstretched hand and not put something there. It's impossible. I know sometimes it's a weakness. I want to feel better, not to feel bad about it. But in fact I cannot.

You talked about communications before. If we don't "listen" by providing, presumably our brother will rise up and strike us down.

Or we would strike him down. Who are we? Children of Cain or children of Abel?

What's your answer?

You know, in my tradition, there is a marvelous way out. We are neither the children of Cain nor the children of Abel. There was a third son that Adam and Eve had afterward called Seth. And we are children of Seth. Which means you can be both.

Is that a cop-out?

No, not really. I think we are always oscillating between the temptation for evil and an attraction to goodness. It's enough for me to close my eyes and remember what men are capable of doing, to become terribly, profoundly, totally pessimistic, because they haven't changed. But then again, I open my eyes and close them again and say, "It would be absurd not to absorb some images and turn them into good consciousness." And it's up to us to choose. We are free to choose.

Don't you think that in our country at this time we're less concerned with, have less compassion for, those who suffer?

Absolutely. But it's really about what you are doing all your life. Can we really help more than the people around us? I go around the world, I travel, and whenever I hear about someone suffering, I try to go there and bear witness. That's my role, at least to bear witness. To say, "I've seen, I was there." Sometimes it inspires others to do what I am doing. More often than not, it doesn't.

If the moral imperative that you pose is one that seemingly is rejected in our time, why do you maintain this posture: "We must be caring, rather than careless?"

> Because I don't have a position of power. Maybe that's the reason. You and I can afford to speak on moral issues. We don't have to make a decision on them. I am sure that if you had someone facing you here who had power, a senator or a member of the Cabinet, he or she would say, "We cannot do this or that." Why? "Because so much money would be needed. We don't have the money. Housing would be required. We don't have the housing." So I can afford, really, only to pose questions, and I know that.

Yes, but I'm convinced that you raise questions because you know what the right moral answers are.

> That's true.

And you believe that by raising those questions, we will come to those answers.

> I would like to think that. But even if I knew that I would not succeed, I would still raise those questions.

Why?

> Otherwise, why am I here? I have the feeling, honestly, that my life is an offering. I could have died every minute between '44 and '45. So once I have received this gift, I must justify it. And the only way to justify life is by affirming the right to life of anyone who needs such affirmation.

Aren't you affirming, too, a conviction that something will be done in response to your question?

> Here and there one person might listen and do something. Another person might listen and not do something. But I prefer to think, that here and there, there are small miracles. And there are: a good student, a good reader, a friend. I think we spoke about it years ago: Once upon a time, I was convinced I could change the whole world. Now I'm satisfied with small measures of grace. If we could open the door of one jail and free one innocent person … if I could save one child from starvation, believe me, to me it would be worth as much as, if not more than, all the work that I am doing and all the recognition that I may get for it.

You've spoken about those who put people in the death camps and brought about their deaths directly. You also speak about others who stood around indifferently. Do you feel that that is increasingly a theme in our own times?

Oh, more and more. I have the feeling that everything I do is a variation on the same theme. I'm simply trying to pull the alarm and say, "Don't be indifferent." Simply because I feel that indifference now is equal to evil. Evil, we know more or less what it is. But indifference to disease, indifference to famine, indifference to dictators, somehow it's here and we accept it. And I have always felt that the opposite of culture is not ignorance; it is indifference. And the opposite of morality is not immorality; it's again indifference. And we don't realize how indifferent we are simply because we cannot *not* be a little indifferent. We cannot think all the time of all the people who die. If, while I sit with you, I could see the children who are dying now while we talk, we wouldn't be able to talk, you and I. We would have to take a plane, go there and do something. We wouldn't be able to continue to try to be logical and rational.

You've said that if we ignore suffering, we become accomplices, as so many did during the Holocaust. Where is it written that we are not moral accomplices?

But we are.

But what can you expect of us?

Learning. After all, I don't compare situations. I don't compare any period to the period of the Second World War. But we have learned something. I have the feeling that sometimes it takes a generation for an event to awaken our awareness. But if now, so many years after that event, we are still behaving as though it did not occur, then what is the purpose of our work as teachers, as writers, as men and women who are concerned with one another's lives?

We have a tradition in this country of extending ourselves through our wealth, our material well-being. That tradition was set aside somewhat for some time. Do you think we will recapture it more fully?

I hope so. I hope that there will be enough students and teachers and writers and poets and communicators to bring back certain values. If a father cannot feed his children, then his human rights are violated. We are such a wealthy society. I think of the United States and am overtaken by gratitude. This nation has gone to war twice in its history to fight for other people's freedoms. Then, after the wars, consider the economic help, the billions of dollars that we have given to those poor countries ravaged, destroyed by the enemy. And even now, what would the free world do without us? We have always been ready to help.

So why not? It would show that we still have compassion. Now, those are nice words, I know. But what else do we have? We have words, and sometimes we try to act upon them.

■ READING AND WRITING

1. Definitions play an important role in Wiesel's comments. What does he mean when he distinguishes between information and knowledge? How does he define responsibility? How does he link knowledge and responsibility? How does he define presence?
2. What role does listening play in Wiesel's world view?
3. How does Wiesel use references to God, religion, and religious texts in his argument? Think especially about his audience and his ethos.
4. Weisel's comments about our responsibilities, and our desensitization to those responsibilities, implicate technology and the media. Technology allows us to know more than ever before about the sufferings of our "brothers and sisters" throughout the world, he argues, but it also can overwhelm us to the point that a kind of numbness sets in. How, according to Wiesel, can we deal with this conundrum?

■ DEVELOPING LONGER RESPONSES

5. Wiesel argues that we should show hands-on, practical compassion to victims of misfortune and oppression—the more concrete, the better. Yet the language in which he makes this argument is unremittingly abstract. Find five places in the text where Wiesel uses abstract language or concepts to make his points. Does this detract from his overall meaning? Why or why not?

> *Martin Luther King, Jr. (1929-1968), the most prominent leader of the U.S. civil rights movement and recipient of the Nobel Peace Prize in 1964, wrote this letter in April 1963 while jailed in Birmingham, Alabama, for "parading without a permit." According to Stanford University's Martin Luther King, Jr. Research and Education Institute, the letter was initially circulated as a mimeographed copy and later published as a pamphlet and as an article in* Christian Century, Christianity and Crisis, *the* New York Post, *and* Ebony *magazine. King revised the letter and presented it as a chapter in his 1964 memoir of the Birmingham Campaign,* Why We Can't Wait.

LETTER FROM BIRMINGHAM JAIL
Martin Luther King, Jr.

Author's note: This response to a published statement by eight fellow clergymen from Alabama (Bishop C.C.J. Carpenter, Bishop Joseph A. Durick, Rabbi Hilton L. Grafman, Bishop Paul Hardin, Bishop Holan B. Harmon, the Reverend George M. Murray. the Reverend Edward V. Ramage and the Reverend Earl Stallings) was composed under somewhat constricting circumstance. Begun on the margins of the newspaper in which the statement appeared while I was in jail, the letter was continued on scraps of writing paper supplied by a friendly Negro trusty, and concluded on a pad my attorneys were eventually permitted to leave me. Although the text remains in substance unaltered, I have indulged in the author's prerogative of polishing it for publication.

April 16, 1963

My Dear Fellow Clergymen:

While confined here in the Birmingham city jail, I came across your recent statement calling my present activities "unwise and untimely."

Seldom do I pause to answer criticism of my work and ideas. If I sought to answer all the criticisms that cross my desk, my secretaries would have little time for anything other than such correspondence in the course of the day, and I would have no time for constructive work. But since I feel that you are men of genuine good will and that your criticisms are sincerely set forth, I want to try to answer your statement in what I hope will be patient and reasonable terms.

I think I should indicate why I am here in Birmingham, since you have been influenced by the view which argues against "outsiders coming in." I have the honor of serving as president of the Southern Christian Leadership Conference, an organization operating in every southern state, with headquarters in Atlanta, Georgia. We have some eighty-five affiliated organizations across the South, and one of them is the Alabama Christian Movement for Human Rights. Frequently we share staff, educational, and financial resources with our affiliates. Several months ago the affiliate here in Birmingham asked us to be on call to engage in a nonviolent direct-action program if such were deemed necessary. We readily consented, and when the hour came we lived up to our promise. So I, along with several members of my staff, am here because I was invited here. I am here because I have organizational ties here.

But more basically, I am in Birmingham because injustice is here. Just as the prophets of the eighth century B.C. left their villages and carried their "thus saith the Lord" far beyond the boundaries of their home towns, and just as the Apostle Paul left his village of Tarsus and carried the gospel of Jesus Christ to the far corners of the Greco-Roman world, so am I compelled to carry the gospel of freedom beyond my own home town. Like Paul, I must constantly respond to the Macedonian call for aid.

Moreover, I am cognizant of the interrelatedness of all communities and states. I cannot sit idly by in Atlanta and not be concerned about what happens in Birmingham. Injustice anywhere is a threat to justice everywhere. We are caught in an inescapable network of mutuality, tied in a single garment of destiny. Whatever affects one directly, affects all indirectly. Never again can we afford to live with the narrow, provincial "outside agitator" idea. Anyone who lives inside the United States can never be considered an outsider anywhere within its bounds.

You deplore the demonstrations taking place in Birmingham. But your statement, I am sorry to say, fails to express a similar concern for the conditions that brought about the demonstrations. I am sure that none of you would want to rest content with the superficial kind of social analysis that deals merely with effects and does not grapple with underlying causes. It is unfortunate that demonstrations are taking place in Birmingham, but it is even more unfortunate that the city's white power structure left the Negro community with no alternative.

In any nonviolent campaign there are four basic steps: collection of the facts to determine whether injustices exist; negotiation; self-purification; and direct action. We have gone through all these steps in Birmingham. There can be no gain saying the fact that racial injustice engulfs this community. Birmingham is probably the most thoroughly segregated city in the United States. Its ugly record of brutality is widely known. Negroes have experienced grossly unjust treatment in the courts. There have been more unsolved bombings of Negro homes and churches in Birmingham than in any other city in the nation. These are the hard, brutal facts of the case. On the basis of these conditions, Negro leaders sought to negotiate with the city fathers. But the latter consistently refused to engage in good-faith negotiation.

Then, last September, came the opportunity to talk with leaders of Birmingham's economic community. In the course of the negotiations, certain promises were made by the merchants—for example, to remove the stores' humiliating racial signs. On the basis of these promises, the Reverend Fred Shuttlesworth and the leaders of the Alabama Christian Movement for Human Rights agreed to a moratorium on all demonstrations. As the weeks and months went by, we realized that we were the victims of a broken promise. A few signs, briefly removed, returned; the others remained.

As in so many past experiences, our hopes had been blasted, and the shadow of deep disappointment settled upon us. We had no alternative except to prepare for direct action, whereby we would present our very bodies as a means of laying our case before the conscience of the local and the national community. Mindful of the difficulties involved, we decided to undertake a process of self-purification. We began a series of workshops on nonviolence, and we repeatedly asked ourselves: "Are you able to accept blows without retaliating?" "Are you able to endure the ordeal of jail?" We decided to schedule our direct-action program for the Easter season, realizing that except for Christmas, this is the main shopping period of the year. Knowing that a strong economic withdrawal program would be the by-product of direct action, we felt that this would be the best time to bring pressure to bear on the merchants for the needed change.

Then it occurred to us that Birmingham's mayoral election was coming up in March, and we speedily decided to postpone action until after election day. When we discovered that the Commissioner of Public Safety, Eugene "Bull" Connor, had piled up enough votes to be in the run-off, we decided again to postpone action until the day after the runoff so that the demonstrations could not be used to cloud the issues. Like many others, we wanted to see Mr. Connor defeated, and to this end we endured postponement after postponement. Having aided in this community need, we felt that our direct-action program could be delayed no longer.

You may well ask, "Why direct action? Why sit-ins, marches, and so forth? Isn't negotiation a better path?" You are quite right in calling for negotiation. Indeed, this is the very purpose of direct action. Nonviolent direct action seeks to create such a crisis and foster such a tension that a community which has constantly refused to negotiate is forced to confront the issue. It seeks so to dramatize the issue that it can no longer be ignored. My citing the creation of tension as part of the work of the nonviolent resister may sound rather shocking. But I must confess that I am not afraid of the word "tension." I have earnestly opposed violent tension, but there is a type of constructive, nonviolent tension which is necessary for growth. Just as Socrates felt that it was necessary to create a tension in the mind so that individuals could rise from the bondage of myths and half-truths to the unfettered realm of creative analysis and objective appraisal, so must we see the need for nonviolent gadflies to create the kind of tension in society that will help men rise from the dark depths of prejudice and racism to the majestic heights of understanding and brotherhood.

The purpose of our direct-action program is to create a situation so crisis-packed that it will inevitably open the door to negotiation. I therefore concur with you in your call for negotiation. Too long has our beloved Southland been bogged down in a tragic effort to live in monologue rather than dialogue.

One of the basic points in your statement is that the action that I and my associates have taken in Birmingham is untimely. Some have asked: "Why didn't you give the new city administration time to act?" The only answer that I can give to this query is that the new Birmingham administration must be prodded about as much as the outgoing one, before it will act. We are sadly mistaken if we feel that the election of Albert Boutwell as mayor will bring the millennium to Birmingham. While Mr. Boutwell is a much more gentle person than Mr. Connor, they are both segregationists, dedicated to maintenance of the status quo.

I have hoped that Mr. Boutwell will be reasonable enough to see the futility of massive resistance to desegregation. But he will not see this without pressure from devotees of civil rights. My friends, I must say to you that we have not made a single gain in civil rights without determined legal and nonviolent pressure. Lamentably, it is an historical fact that privileged groups seldom give up their privileges voluntarily. Individuals may see the moral light and voluntarily give up their unjust posture, but, as Reinhold Niebuhr has reminded us, groups tend to be more immoral than individuals.

We know through painful experience that freedom is never voluntarily given by the oppressor; it must be demanded by the oppressed. Frankly, I have yet to engage in a direct-action campaign that was "well timed" in the view of those who have not suffered unduly from the disease of segregation. For years now I have heard the word "Wait!" It rings in the ear of every Negro with piercing familiarity. This "Wait" has almost always meant "Never." We must come to see, with one of our distinguished jurists, that "justice too long delayed is justice denied."

We have waited for more than 340 years for our constitutional and God-given rights. The nations of Asia and Africa are moving with jet-like speed toward gaining political independence, but we still creep at horse-and-buggy pace toward gaining a cup of coffee at a lunch counter. Perhaps it is easy for those who have never felt the stinging darts of segregation to say, "Wait." But when you have seen vicious mobs lynch your mothers and fathers at will and drown your sisters and brothers at whim; when you have seen hate-filled policemen curse, kick, and even kill your black brothers and sisters; when you see the vast majority of your twenty million Negro brothers smothering in an airtight cage of poverty in the midst of an affluent society; when you suddenly find your tongue twisted and your speech stammering as you seek to explain to your six-year-old daughter why she can't go to the public amusement park that has just been advertised on television, and see tears welling up in her eyes when she is told that Funtown is closed to colored children, and see ominous clouds of inferiority beginning to form in her little mental sky, and see her beginning to distort her personality by developing an unconscious bitterness toward white people; when you have to concoct an answer for a five-year-old son who is asking, "Daddy, why do white people treat colored people so mean?"; when you take a cross-country drive and find it necessary to sleep night after night in the uncomfortable corners of your automobile because no motel will accept you; when you are humiliated day in and day out by nagging signs reading "white" and "colored"; when your first name becomes "nigger," your middle name becomes "boy" (however old you are) and your last name becomes "John," and your wife and mother are never given the respected title "Mrs."; when you are harried by day and haunted by night by the fact that you are a Negro, living constantly at tiptoe stance, never quite knowing what to expect next, and are plagued with inner fears and outer resentments; when you are forever fighting a degenerating sense of "nobodiness"—then you will understand why we find it difficult to wait. There comes a time when the cup of endurance runs over, and men are no longer willing to be plunged into the abyss of despair. I hope, sirs, you can understand our legitimate and unavoidable impatience.

You express a great deal of anxiety over our willingness to break laws. This is certainly a legitimate concern. Since we so diligently urge people to obey the Supreme Court's decision of 1954 outlawing segregation in the public schools, at first glance it may seem rather paradoxical for us consciously to break laws. One may well ask: "How can you advocate breaking some laws and obeying others?" The answer lies in the fact that there are two types of laws: just and unjust. I would be the first to advocate obeying just laws. One has not only a legal but a moral responsibility to obey just laws. Conversely, one has a moral responsibility to disobey unjust laws. I would agree with St. Augustine that "an unjust law is no law at all."

Now, what is the difference between the two? How does one determine whether a law is just or unjust? A just law is a man-made code that squares with the moral law or the law of God. An unjust law is a code that is out of harmony with the moral law. To put it in the terms of St. Thomas Aquinas: An unjust law is a human law that is not rooted in eternal law and natural law. Any law that uplifts human personality is just. Any law that degrades human personality is unjust. All segregation statutes are unjust because segregation distorts the soul and damages the personality. It gives the segregator a false sense of superiority and the segregated a false sense of inferiority. Segregation, to use the terminology of the Jewish philosopher Martin Buber, substitutes an "I-it" relationship for an "I-thou" relationship and ends up relegating persons to the status of things. Hence segregation is not only politically, economically, and sociologically unsound, it is morally wrong and sinful. Paul Tillich has said that sin is separation. Is not segregation an existential expression of man's tragic separation, his awful estrangement, his terrible sinfulness? Thus it is that I can urge men to obey the 1954 decision of the Supreme Court, for it is morally right; and I can urge them to disobey segregation ordinances, for they are morally wrong.

Let us consider a more concrete example of just and unjust laws. An unjust law is a code that a numerical or power majority group compels a minority group to obey but does not make binding on itself. This is difference made legal. By the same token, a just law is a code that a majority compels a minority to follow and that it is willing to follow itself. This is sameness made legal.

Let me give another explanation. A law is unjust if it is inflicted on a minority that, as a result of being denied the right to vote, had no part in enacting or devising the law. Who can say that the legislature of Alabama which set up that state's segregation laws was democratically elected? Throughout Alabama all sorts of devious methods are used to prevent Negroes from becoming registered voters, and there are some counties in which, even though Negroes constitute a majority of the population, not a single Negro is registered. Can any law enacted under such circumstances be considered democratically structured?

Sometimes a law is just on its face and unjust in its application. For instance, I have been arrested on a charge of parading without a permit. Now, there is nothing wrong in having an ordinance which requires a permit for a parade. But such an ordinance becomes unjust when it is used to maintain segregation and to deny citizens the First-Amendment privilege of peaceful assembly and protest.

I hope you are able to see the distinction I am trying to point out. In no sense do I advocate evading or defying the law, as would the rabid segregationist. That would lead to anarchy. One who breaks an unjust law must do so openly, lovingly, and with a willingness to accept the penalty. I submit that an individual who breaks a law that conscience tells him is unjust, and who willingly accepts the penalty of imprisonment in order to arouse the conscience of the community over its injustice, is in reality expressing the highest respect for law.

Of course, there is nothing new about this kind of civil disobedience. It was evidenced sublimely in the refusal of Shadrach, Meshach, and Abednego to obey the laws of Nebuchadnezzar, on the ground that a higher moral law was at stake. It was practiced superbly by the early Christians, who were willing to face hungry lions and the excruciating pain of chopping blocks rather than submit to certain unjust laws of the Roman Empire. To a degree, academic freedom is a reality today because Socrates practiced civil disobedience. In our own nation, the Boston Tea Party represented a massive act of civil disobedience.

We should never forget that everything Adolf Hitler did in Germany was "legal" and everything the Hungarian freedom fighters did in Hungary was "illegal." It was "illegal" to aid and comfort a Jew in Hitler's Germany. Even so, I am sure that, had I lived in Germany at the time, I would have aided and comforted my Jewish brothers. If today I lived in a Communist country where certain principles dear to the Christian faith are suppressed, I would openly advocate disobeying that country's anti-religious laws.

I must make two honest confessions to you, my Christian and Jewish brothers. First, I must confess that over the past few years I have been gravely disappointed with the white moderate. I have almost reached the regrettable conclusion that the Negro's great stumbling block in his stride toward freedom is not the White Citizen's Counciler or the Ku Klux Klanner, but the white moderate, who is more devoted to "order" than to justice; who prefers a negative peace which is the absence of tension to a positive peace which is the presence of justice; who constantly says, "I agree with you in the goal you seek, but I cannot agree with your methods of direct action"; who paternalistically believes he can set the timetable for another man's freedom; who lives by a mythical concept of time and who constantly advises the Negro to wait for a "more convenient season." Shallow understanding from people of good will is more frustrating than absolute misunderstanding from people of ill will. Lukewarm acceptance is much more bewildering than outright rejection.

I had hoped that the white moderate would understand that law and order exist for the purpose of establishing justice and that when they fail in this purpose they become the dangerously structured dams that block the flow of social progress. I had hoped that the white moderate would understand that the present tension in the South is a necessary phase of the transition from an obnoxious negative peace, in which the Negro passively accepted his unjust plight, to a substantive and positive peace, in which all men will respect the dignity and worth of human personality. Actually, we who engage in nonviolent direct action are not the creators of tension. We merely bring to the surface the hidden tension that is already alive. We bring it out in the open, where it can be seen and dealt with. Like a boil that can never be cured so long as it is covered up but must be opened with all its ugliness to the natural medicines of air and light, injustice must be exposed, with all the tension its exposure creates, to the light of human conscience and the air of national opinion, before it can be cured.

In your statement you assert that our actions, even though peaceful, must be condemned because they precipitate violence. But is this a logical assertion? Isn't this like condemning a robbed man because his possession of money precipitated the evil act of robbery? Isn't this like condemning Socrates because his unswerving commitment to truth and his philosophical inquiries precipitated the act by the misguided populace in which they made him drink hemlock? Isn't this like condemning Jesus because his unique God-consciousness and never-ceasing devotion to God's will precipitated the evil act of crucifixion? We must come to see that, as the federal courts have consistently affirmed, it is wrong to urge an individual to cease his efforts to gain his basic constitutional rights because the quest may precipitate violence. Society must protect the robbed and punish the robber.

I had also hoped that the white moderate would reject the myth concerning time in relation to the struggle for freedom. I have just received a letter from a white brother in Texas. He writes: "All Christians know that the colored people will receive equal rights eventually, but it is possible that you are in too great a religious hurry. It has taken Christianity almost two thousand years to accomplish what it has. The teachings of Christ take time to come to earth." Such an attitude stems from a tragic misconception of time, from the strangely irrational notion that there is something in the very flow of time that will inevitably cure all ills. Actually, time itself is neutral; it can be used either destructively or constructively. More and more I feel that the people of ill will have used time much more effectively than have the people of good will. We will have to repent in this generation not merely for the hateful words and actions of the bad people, but for the appalling silence of the good people. Human progress never rolls in on wheels of inevitability; it comes through the tireless efforts of men willing to be co-workers with God, and without this hard work, time itself becomes an ally of the forces of social stagnation. We must use time creatively, in the knowledge that the time is always ripe to do right. Now is the time to make real the promise of democracy and transform our pending national elegy into a creative psalm of brotherhood. Now is the time to lift our national policy from the quicksand of racial injustice to the solid rock of human dignity.

You speak of our activity in Birmingham as extreme. At first I was rather disappointed that fellow clergymen would see my nonviolent efforts as those of an extremist. I began thinking about the fact that I stand in the middle of two opposing forces in the Negro community. One is a force of complacency, made up in part of Negroes who, as a result of long years of oppression, are so drained of self-respect and a sense of "somebodiness" that they have adjusted to segregation; and in part of a few middle-class Negroes who, because of a degree of academic and economic security and because in some ways they profit by segregation, have become insensitive to the problems of the masses. The other force is one of bitterness and hatred, and it comes perilously close to advocating violence. It is expressed in the various black nationalist groups that are springing up across the nation, the largest and best-known being Elijah Muhammad's Muslim movement. Nourished by the Negro's frustration over the continued existence of racial discrimination, this movement is made up of people who have lost faith in America, who have absolutely repudiated Christianity, and who have concluded that the white man is an incorrigible "devil."

I have tried to stand between these two forces, saying that we need emulate neither the "do-nothingism" of the complacent nor the hatred and despair of the black nationalist. For there is the more excellent way of love and nonviolent protest. I am grateful to God that, through the influence of the Negro church, the way of nonviolence became an integral part of our struggle.

If this philosophy had not emerged, by now many streets of the South would, I am convinced, be flowing with blood. And I am further convinced that if our white brothers dismiss as "rabblerousers" and "outside agitators" those of us who employ nonviolent direct action, and if they refuse to support our nonviolent efforts, millions of Negroes will, out of frustration and despair, seek solace and security in black-nationalist ideologies—a development that would inevitably lead to a frightening racial nightmare.

Oppressed people cannot remain oppressed forever. The yearning for freedom eventually manifests itself, and that is what has happened to the American Negro. Something within has reminded him of his birthright of freedom, and something without has reminded him that it can be gained. Consciously or unconsciously, he has been caught up by the Zeitgeist, and with his black brothers of Africa and his brown and yellow brothers of Asia, South America, and the Caribbean, the United States Negro is moving with a sense of great urgency toward the promised land of racial justice. If one recognizes this vital urge that has engulfed the Negro community, one should readily understand why public demonstrations are taking place. The Negro has many pent-up resentments and latent frustrations, and he must release them. So let him march; let him make prayer pilgrimages to the city hall; let him go on freedom rides—and try to understand why he must do so. If his repressed emotions are not released in nonviolent ways, they will seek expression through violence; this is not a threat but a fact of history. So I have not said to my people, "Get rid of your discontent." Rather, I have tried to say that this normal and healthy discontent can be channeled into the creative outlet of nonviolent direct action. And now this approach is being termed extremist.

But though I was initially disappointed at being categorized as an extremist, as I continued to think about the matter I gradually gained a measure of satisfaction from the label. Was not Jesus an extremist for love: "Love your enemies, bless them that curse you, do good to them that hate you, and pray for them which despitefully use you, and persecute you." Was not Amos an extremist for justice: "Let justice roll down like waters and righteousness like an ever-flowing stream." Was not Paul an extremist for the Christian gospel: "I bear in my body the marks of the Lord Jesus." Was not Martin Luther an extremist: "Here I stand; I cannot do otherwise, so help me God." And John Bunyan: "I will stay in jail to the end of my days before I make a butchery of my conscience." And Abraham Lincoln: "This nation cannot survive half slave and half free." And Thomas Jefferson: "We hold these truths to be self-evident, that all men are created equal. ..." So the question is not whether we will be extremists, but what kind of extremists we will be. Will we be extremists for hate or for love? Will we be extremists for the preservation of injustice or for the extension of justice? In that dramatic scene on Calvary's hill three men were crucified. We must never forget that all three were crucified for the same crime—the crime of extremism. Two were extremists for immorality, and thus fell below their environment. The other, Jesus Christ, was an extremist for love, truth, and goodness, and thereby rose above his environment. Perhaps the South, the nation, and the world are in dire need of creative extremists.

I had hoped that the white moderate would see this need. Perhaps I was too optimistic; perhaps I expected too much. I suppose I should have realized that few members of the oppressor race can understand the deep groans and passionate yearnings of the oppressed race, and still fewer have the vision to see that injustice must be rooted out by strong, persistent, and determined action. I am thankful, however, that some of our white brothers in the South have grasped the meaning of this social revolution and committed themselves to it. They are still all too few in quantity, but they are big in quality. Some—such as Ralph McGill, Lillian Smith, Harry Golden, James McBridge Dabbs, Ann Braden, and Sarah Patton Boyle—have written about our struggle in eloquent and prophetic terms. Others have marched with us down nameless streets of the South. They have languished in filthy, roach-infested jails, suffering the abuse and brutality of policemen who view them as "dirty nigger-lovers." Unlike so many of their moderate brothers and sisters, they have recognized the urgency of the moment and sensed the need for powerful "action" antidotes to combat the disease of segregation.

Let me take note of my other major disappointment. I have been so greatly disappointed with the white church and its leadership. Of course, there are some notable exceptions. I am not unmindful of the fact that each of you has taken some significant stands on this issue. I commend you, Reverend Stallings, for your Christian stand on this past Sunday, in welcoming Negroes to your worship service on a nonsegregated basis. I commend the Catholic leaders of this state for integrating Spring Hill College several years ago.

But despite these notable exceptions, I must honestly reiterate that I have been disappointed with the church. I do not say this as one of those negative critics who can always find something wrong with the church. I say this as a minister of the gospel, who loves the church; who was nurtured in its bosom; who has been sustained by its spiritual blessings and who will remain true to it as long as the cord of life shall lengthen.

When I was suddenly catapulted into the leadership of the bus protest in Montgomery, Alabama, a few years ago, I felt we would be supported by the white church. I felt that the white ministers, priests, and rabbis of the South would be among our strongest allies. Instead, some have been outright opponents, refusing to understand the freedom movement and misrepresenting its leaders; all too many others have been more cautious than courageous and have remained silent behind the anesthetizing security of stained-glass windows.

In spite of my shattered dreams, I came to Birmingham with the hope that the white religious leadership of this community would see the justice of our cause and, with deep moral concern, would serve as the channel through which our just grievances could reach the power structure. I had hoped that each of you would understand. But again I have been disappointed.

I have heard numerous southern religious leaders admonish their worshipers to comply with a desegregation decision because it is the law, but I have longed to hear white ministers declare: "Follow this decree because integration is morally right and because the Negro is your brother." In the midst of blatant injustices inflicted upon the Negro, I have watched white churchmen stand on the sideline and mouth pious irrelevancies and sanctimonious trivialities. In the midst of a mighty struggle to rid our nation of racial and economic injustice, I have heard many ministers say: "Those are social issues, with which the gospel has no real concern." And I have watched many churches commit themselves to a completely otherworldly religion which makes a strange, un-Biblical distinction between body and soul, between the sacred and the secular.

I have traveled the length and breadth of Alabama, Mississippi, and all the other southern states. On sweltering summer days and crisp autumn mornings I have looked at the South's beautiful churches with their lofty spires pointing heavenward. I have beheld the impressive outlines of her massive religious-education buildings. Over and over I have found myself asking: "What kind of people worship here? Who is their God? Where were their voices when the lips of Governor Barnett dripped with words of interposition and nullification? Where were they when Governor Wallace gave a clarion call for defiance and hatred? Where were their voices of support when bruised and weary Negro men and women decided to rise from the dark dungeons of complacency to the bright hills of creative protest?"

Yes, these questions are still in my mind. In deep disappointment I have wept over the laxity of the church. But be assured that my tears have been tears of love. There can be no deep disappointment where there is not deep love. Yes, I love the church. How could I do otherwise? I am in the rather unique position of being the son, the grandson, and the great-grandson of preachers. Yes, I see the church as the body of Christ. But, oh! How we have blemished and scarred that body through social neglect and through fear of being nonconformists.

There was a time when the church was very powerful—in the time when the early Christians rejoiced at being deemed worthy to suffer for what they believed. In those days the church was not merely a thermometer that recorded the ideas and principles of popular opinion; it was a thermostat that transformed the mores of society. Whenever the early Christians entered a town, the people in power became disturbed and immediately sought to convict the Christians for being "disturbers of the peace" and "outside agitators." But the Christians pressed on, in the conviction that they were "a colony of heaven," called to obey God rather than man. Small in number, they were big in commitment. They were too God-intoxicated to be "astronomically intimidated." By their effort and example they brought an end to such ancient evils as infanticide and gladiatorial contests.

Things are different now. So often the contemporary church is a weak, ineffectual voice with an uncertain sound. So often it is an archdefender of the status quo. Far from being disturbed by the presence of the church, the power structure of the average community is consoled by the church's silent—and often even vocal—sanction of things as they are.

But the judgment of God is upon the church as never before. If today's church does not recapture the sacrificial spirit of the early church, it will lose its authenticity, forfeit the loyalty of millions, and be dismissed as an irrelevant social club with no meaning for the twentieth century. Every day I meet young people whose disappointment with the church has turned into outright disgust.

Perhaps I have once again been too optimistic. Is organized religion too inextricably bound to the status quo to save our nation and the world? Perhaps I must turn my faith to the inner spiritual church, the church within the church, as the true *ekklesia* and the hope of the world. But again I am thankful to God that some noble souls from the ranks of organized religion have broken loose from the paralyzing chains of conformity and joined us as active partners in the struggle for freedom. They have left their secure congregations and walked the streets of Albany, Georgia, with us. They have gone down the highways of the South on tortuous rides for freedom. Yes, they have gone to jail with us. Some have been dismissed from their churches, have lost the support of their bishops and fellow ministers. But they have acted in the faith that right defeated is stronger than evil triumphant. Their witness has been the spiritual salt that has preserved the true meaning of the gospel in these troubled times. They have carved a tunnel of hope through the dark mountain of disappointment.

I hope the church as a whole will meet the challenge of this decisive hour. But even if the church does not come to the aid of justice, I have no despair about the future. I have no fear about the outcome of our struggle in Birmingham, even if our motives are at present misunderstood. We will reach the goal of freedom in Birmingham and all over the nation, because the goal of America is freedom. Abused and scorned though we may be, our destiny is tied up with America's destiny. Before the pilgrims landed at Plymouth, we were here. Before the pen of Jefferson etched the majestic words of the Declaration of Independence across the pages of history, we were here. For more than two centuries our forebears labored in this country without wages: they made cotton king; they built the homes of their masters while suffering gross injustice and shameful humiliation—and yet out of a bottomless vitality they continued to thrive and develop. If the inexpressible cruelties of slavery could not stop us, the opposition we now face will surely fail. We will win our freedom because the sacred heritage of our nation and the eternal will of God are embodied in our echoing demands.

Before closing I feel impelled to mention one other point in your statement that has troubled me profoundly. You warmly commended the Birmingham police force for keeping "order" and "preventing violence." I doubt that you would have so warmly commended the police force if you had seen its dogs sinking their teeth into unarmed, nonviolent Negroes. I doubt that you would so quickly commend the policemen if you were to observe their ugly and inhumane treatment of Negroes here in the city jail; if you were to watch them push and curse old Negro women and young Negro girls; if you were to see them slap and kick old Negro men and young boys; if you were to observe them, as they did on two occasions, refuse to give us food because we wanted to sing our grace together. I cannot join you in your praise of the Birmingham police department.

It is true that the police have exercised a degree of discipline in handling the demonstrators. In this sense they have conducted themselves rather "nonviolently" in public. But for what purpose? To preserve the evil system of segregation. Over the past few years I have consistently preached that nonviolence demands that the means we use must be as pure as the ends we seek. I have tried to make clear that it is wrong to use immoral means to attain moral ends. But now I must affirm that it is just as wrong, or perhaps even more so, to use moral means to preserve immoral ends. Perhaps Mr. Connor and his policemen have been rather nonviolent in public, as was Chief Pritchett in Albany, Georgia, but they have used the moral means of nonviolence to maintain the immoral end of racial injustice. As T.S. Eliot has said: "The last temptation is the greatest treason: To do the right deed for the wrong reason."

I wish you had commended the Negro sit-inners and demonstrators of Birmingham for their sublime courage, their willingness to suffer, and their amazing discipline in the midst of great provocation. One day the South will recognize its real heroes. They will be the James Merediths, with the noble sense of purpose that enables them to face jeering and hostile mobs, and with the agonizing loneliness that characterizes the life of the pioneer. They will be old, oppressed, battered Negro women, symbolized in a seventy-two-year-old woman in Montgomery, Alabama, who rose up with a sense of dignity and with her people decided not to ride segregated buses, and who responded with ungrammatical profundity to one who inquired about her weariness: "My feets is tired, but my soul is at rest." They will be the young high school and college students, the young ministers of the gospel and a host of their elders, courageously and nonviolently sitting in at lunch counters and willingly going to jail for conscience' sake. One day the South will know that when these disinherited children of God sat down at lunch counters, they were in reality standing up for what is best in the American dream and for the most sacred values in our Judaeo-Christian heritage, thereby bringing our nation back to those great wells of democracy which were dug deep by the founding fathers in their formulation of the Constitution and the Declaration of Independence.

Never before have I written so long a letter. I'm afraid it is much too long to take your precious time. I can assure you that it would have been much shorter if I had been writing from a comfortable desk, but what else can one do when he is alone in a narrow jail cell, other than write long letters, think long thoughts, and pray long prayers?

If I have said anything in this letter that overstates the truth and indicates an unreasonable impatience, I beg you to forgive me. If I have said anything that understates the truth and indicates my having a patience that allows me to settle for anything less than brotherhood, I beg God to forgive me.

I hope this letter finds you strong in the faith. I also hope that circumstances will soon make it possible for me to meet each of you, not as an integrationist or a civil-rights leader but as a fellow clergyman and a Christian brother. Let us all hope that the dark clouds of racial prejudice will soon pass away and the deep fog of misunderstanding will be lifted from our fear-drenched communities, and in some not too distant tomorrow the radiant stars of love and brotherhood will shine over our great nation with all their scintillating beauty.

Yours for the cause of Peace and Brotherhood,
Martin Luther King, Jr.

READING AND WRITING

1. Write a 100- to 200-word summary of King's central argument in the "Letter."

2. As King explains in his introduction, his "Letter" is a response to a public statement by eight Alabama clergymen who had advocated patience within the black community. (You can find the statement online at <http://www.stanford.edu/group/King//frequentdocs/clergy.pdf>.) Find five places in King's text where he clearly responds to points raised by the clergymen. What tips you off that these passages are written as responses? How does this rhetorical strategy—addressing opposing positions—strengthen King's argument?

3. "I must confess that I am not afraid of the word 'tension,'" King writes. How does he explain the usefulness to his cause of creating social tensions? How does he propose that social tensions be resolved?

4. Nonviolence, as advocated by King and by others (Gandhi, Cesar Chavez, Dietrich Bonhoeffer), is often dismissed as a naïve tactic. How does King get around this accusation? Is his argument successful on this all-important point?

5. In his text, King writes that "over the past few years I have been gravely disappointed with the white moderate." How does he define "the white moderate"? What is the source of King's disappointment?

DEVELOPING LONGER RESPONSES

6. In his "Letter," King makes references to the Bible and to religious figures, even comparing himself to some of these figures: "Just as the prophets of the eighth century B.C. left their villages and carried their 'thus saith the Lord' far beyond the boundaries of their home towns, and just as the Apostle Paul left his village of Tarsus and carried the gospel of Jesus Christ to the far corners of the Greco-Roman world, so am I compelled to carry the gospel of freedom beyond my own home town." Write a brief essay in which you analyze the role faith plays in the development of King's ethos. As you work, keep in mind King's original purpose and audience.

David Grann is a staff writer at The New Yorker *magazine, where this article was published in September 2009. He has written about everything from New York City's antiquated water tunnels to the hunt for the giant squid to the presidential campaign. In this piece, Grann uses the storytelling techniques of a crime procedural to develop his claim that Texas may have executed an innocent man in 2004.*

TRIAL BY FIRE   David Grann

The fire moved quickly through the house, a one-story wood-frame structure in a working-class neighborhood of Corsicana, in northeast Texas. Flames spread along the walls, bursting through doorways, blistering paint and tiles and furniture. Smoke pressed against the ceiling, then banked downward, seeping into each room and through crevices in the windows, staining the morning sky.

Buffie Barbee, who was eleven years old and lived two houses down, was playing in her back yard when she smelled the smoke. She ran inside and told her mother, Diane, and they hurried up the street; that's when they saw the smoldering house and Cameron Todd Willingham standing on the front porch, wearing only a pair of jeans, his chest blackened with soot, his hair and eyelids singed. He was screaming, "My babies are burning up!" His children—Karmon and Kameron, who were one-year-old twin girls, and two-year-old Amber—were trapped inside.

Willingham told the Barbees to call the Fire Department, and while Diane raced down the street to get help he found a stick and broke the children's bedroom window. Fire lashed through the hole. He broke another window; flames burst through it, too, and he retreated into the yard, kneeling in front of the house. A neighbor later told police that Willingham intermittently cried, "My babies!" then fell silent, as if he had "blocked the fire out of his mind."

Diane Barbee, returning to the scene, could feel intense heat radiating off the house. Moments later, the five windows of the children's room exploded and flames "blew out," as Barbee put it. Within minutes, the first firemen had arrived, and Willingham approached them, shouting that his children were in their bedroom, where the flames were thickest. A fireman sent word over his radio for rescue teams to "step on it."

More men showed up, uncoiling hoses and aiming water at the blaze. One fireman, who had an air tank strapped to his back and a mask covering his face, slipped through a window but was hit by water from a hose and had to retreat. He then charged through the front door, into a swirl of smoke and fire. Heading down the main corridor, he reached the kitchen, where he saw a refrigerator blocking the back door.

Todd Willingham, looking on, appeared to grow more hysterical, and a police chaplain named George Monaghan led him to the back of a fire truck and tried to calm him down. Willingham explained that his wife, Stacy, had gone out earlier that morning, and that he had been jolted from sleep by Amber screaming, "Daddy! Daddy!"

"My little girl was trying to wake me up and tell me about the fire," he said, adding, "I couldn't get my babies out."

While he was talking, a fireman emerged from the house, cradling Amber. As she was given C.P.R., Willingham, who was twenty-three years old and powerfully built, ran to see her, then suddenly headed toward the babies' room. Monaghan and another man restrained him. "We had to wrestle with him and then handcuff him, for his and our protection," Monaghan later told police. "I received a black eye." One of the first firemen at the scene told investigators that, at an earlier point, he had also held Willingham back. "Based on what I saw on how the fire was burning, it would have been crazy for anyone to try and go into the house," he said.

Willingham was taken to a hospital, where he was told that Amber—who had actually been found in the master bedroom—had died of smoke inhalation. Kameron and Karmon had been lying on the floor of the children's bedroom, their bodies severely burned. According to the medical examiner, they, too, died from smoke inhalation.

News of the tragedy, which took place on December 23, 1991, spread through Corsicana. A small city fifty-five miles northeast of Waco, it had once been the center of Texas's first oil boom, but many of the wells had since dried up, and more than a quarter of the city's twenty thousand inhabitants had fallen into poverty. Several stores along the main street were shuttered, giving the place the feel of an abandoned outpost.

Willingham and his wife, who was twenty-two years old, had virtually no money. Stacy worked in her brother's bar, called Some Other Place, and Willingham, an unemployed auto mechanic, had been caring for the kids. The community took up a collection to help the Willinghams pay for funeral arrangements.

Fire investigators, meanwhile, tried to determine the cause of the blaze. (Willingham gave authorities permission to search the house: "I know we might not ever know all the answers, but I'd just like to know why my babies were taken from me.") Douglas Fogg, who was then the assistant fire chief in Corsicana, conducted the initial inspection. He was tall, with a crew cut, and his voice was raspy from years of inhaling smoke from fires and cigarettes. He had grown up in Corsicana and, after graduating from high school, in 1963, he had joined the Navy, serving as a medic in Vietnam, where he was wounded on four occasions. He was awarded a Purple Heart each time. After he returned from Vietnam, he became a firefighter, and by the time of the Willingham blaze he had been battling fire—or what he calls "the beast"—for more than twenty years, and had become a certified arson investigator. "You learn that fire talks to you," he told me.

He was soon joined on the case by one of the state's leading arson sleuths, a deputy fire marshal named Manuel Vasquez, who has since died. Short, with a paunch, Vasquez had investigated more than twelve hundred fires. Arson investigators have always been considered a special breed of detective. In the 1991 movie "Backdraft," a heroic arson investigator says of fire, "It breathes, it eats, and it hates. The only way to beat it is to think like it. To know that this flame will spread this way across the door and up across the ceiling." Vasquez, who had previously worked in Army intelligence, had several maxims of his own. One was "Fire does not destroy evidence—it creates it." Another was "The fire tells the story. I am just the interpreter." He cultivated a Sherlock Holmes-like aura of invincibility. Once, he was asked under oath whether he had ever been mistaken in a case. "If I have, sir, I don't know," he responded. "It's never been pointed out."

Vasquez and Fogg visited the Willinghams' house four days after the blaze. Following protocol, they moved from the least burned areas toward the most damaged ones. "It is a systematic method," Vasquez later testified, adding, "I'm just collecting information. ... I have not made any determination. I don't have any preconceived idea."

The men slowly toured the perimeter of the house, taking notes and photographs, like archeologists mapping out a ruin. Upon opening the back door, Vasquez observed that there was just enough space to squeeze past the refrigerator blocking the exit. The air smelled of burned rubber and melted wires; a damp ash covered the ground, sticking to their boots. In the kitchen, Vasquez and Fogg discerned only smoke and heat damage—a sign that the fire had not originated there—and so they pushed deeper into the nine-hundred-and-seventy-five-square-foot building. A central corridor led past a utility room and the master bedroom, then past a small living room, on the left, and the children's bedroom, on the right, ending at the front door, which opened onto the porch. Vasquez tried to take in everything, a process that he compared to entering one's mother-in-law's house for the first time: "I have the same curiosity."

In the utility room, he noticed on the wall pictures of skulls and what he later described as an image of "the Grim Reaper." Then he turned into the master bedroom, where Amber's body had been found. Most of the damage there was also from smoke and heat, suggesting that the fire had started farther down the hallway, and he headed that way, stepping over debris and ducking under insulation and wiring that hung down from the exposed ceiling.

As he and Fogg removed some of the clutter, they noticed deep charring along the base of the walls. Because gases become buoyant when heated, flames ordinarily burn upward. But Vasquez and Fogg observed that the fire had burned extremely low down, and that there were peculiar char patterns on the floor, shaped like puddles.

Vasquez's mood darkened. He followed the "burn trailer"—the path etched by the fire—which led from the hallway into the children's bedroom. Sunlight filtering through the broken windows illuminated more of the irregularly shaped char patterns. A flammable or combustible liquid doused on a floor will cause a fire to concentrate in these kinds of pockets, which is why investigators refer to them as "pour patterns" or "puddle configurations."

The fire had burned through layers of carpeting and tile and plywood flooring. Moreover, the metal springs under the children's beds had turned white—a sign that intense heat had radiated beneath them. Seeing that the floor had some of the deepest burns, Vasquez deduced that it had been hotter than the ceiling, which, given that heat rises, was, in his words, "not normal."

Fogg examined a piece of glass from one of the broken windows. It contained a spiderweb-like pattern—what fire investigators call "crazed glass." Forensic textbooks had long described the effect as a key indicator that a fire had burned "fast and hot," meaning that it had been fuelled by a liquid accelerant, causing the glass to fracture.

The men looked again at what appeared to be a distinct burn trailer through the house: it went from the children's bedroom into the corridor, then turned sharply to the right and proceeded out the front door. To the investigators' surprise, even the wood under the door's aluminum threshold was charred. On the concrete floor of the porch, just outside the front door, Vasquez and Fogg noticed another unusual thing: brown stains, which, they reported, were consistent with the presence of an accelerant.

The men scanned the walls for soot marks that resembled a "V." When an object catches on fire, it creates such a pattern, as heat and smoke radiate outward; the bottom of the "V" can therefore point to where a fire began. In the Willingham house, there was a distinct "V" in the main corridor. Examining it and other burn patterns, Vasquez identified three places where fire had originated: in the hallway, in the children's bedroom, and at the front door. Vasquez later testified that multiple origins pointed to one conclusion: the fire was "intentionally set by human hands."

By now, both investigators had a clear vision of what had happened. Someone had poured liquid accelerant throughout the children's room, even under their beds, then poured some more along the adjoining hallway and out the front door, creating a "fire barrier" that prevented anyone from escaping; similarly, a prosecutor later suggested, the refrigerator in the kitchen had been moved to block the back-door exit. The house, in short, had been deliberately transformed into a death trap.

The investigators collected samples of burned materials from the house and sent them to a laboratory that could detect the presence of a liquid accelerant. The lab's chemist reported that one of the samples contained evidence of "mineral spirits," a substance that is often found in charcoal-lighter fluid. The sample had been taken by the threshold of the front door.

The fire was now considered a triple homicide, and Todd Willingham—the only person, besides the victims, known to have been in the house at the time of the blaze—became the prime suspect.

Police and fire investigators canvassed the neighborhood, interviewing witnesses. Several, like Father Monaghan, initially portrayed Willingham as devastated by the fire. Yet, over time, an increasing number of witnesses offered damning statements. Diane Barbee said that she had not seen Willingham try to enter the house until after the authorities arrived, as if he were putting on a show. And when the children's room exploded with flames, she added, he seemed more preoccupied with his car, which he moved down the driveway. Another neighbor reported that when Willingham cried out for his babies he "did not appear to be excited or concerned." Even Father Monaghan wrote in a statement that, upon further reflection, "things were not as they seemed. I had the feeling that [Willingham] was in complete control."

The police began to piece together a disturbing profile of Willingham. Born in Ardmore, Oklahoma, in 1968, he had been abandoned by his mother when he was a baby. His father, Gene, who had divorced his mother, eventually raised him with his stepmother, Eugenia. Gene, a former U.S. marine, worked in a salvage yard, and the family lived in a cramped house; at night, they could hear freight trains rattling past on a nearby track. Willingham, who had what the family called the "classic Willingham look"—a handsome face, thick black hair, and dark eyes—struggled in school, and as a teen-ager began to sniff paint. When he was seventeen, Oklahoma's Department of Human Services evaluated him, and reported, "He likes 'girls,' music, fast cars, sharp trucks, swimming, and hunting, in that order." Willingham dropped out of high school, and over time was arrested for, among other things, driving under the influence, stealing a bicycle, and shoplifting.

In 1988, he met Stacy, a senior in high school, who also came from a troubled background: when she was four years old, her stepfather had strangled her mother to death during a fight. Stacy and Willingham had a turbulent relationship. Willingham, who was unfaithful, drank too much Jack Daniel's, and sometimes hit Stacy—even when she was pregnant. A neighbor said that he once heard Willingham yell at her, "Get up, bitch, and I'll hit you again."

On December 31st, the authorities brought Willingham in for questioning. Fogg and Vasquez were present for the interrogation, along with Jimmie Hensley, a police officer who was working his first arson case. Willingham said that Stacy had left the house around 9 A.M. to pick up a Christmas present for the kids, at the Salvation Army. "After she got out of the driveway, I heard the twins cry, so I got up and gave them a bottle," he said. The children's room had a safety gate across the doorway, which Amber could climb over but not the twins, and he and Stacy often let the twins nap on the floor after they drank their bottles. Amber was still in bed, Willingham said, so he went back into his room to sleep. "The next thing I remember is hearing 'Daddy, Daddy,'" he recalled. "The house was already full of smoke." He said that he got up, felt around the floor for a pair of pants, and put them on. He could no longer hear his daughter's voice ("I heard that last 'Daddy, Daddy' and never heard her again"), and he hollered, "Oh God— Amber, get out of the house! Get out of the house!'"

He never sensed that Amber was in his room, he said. Perhaps she had already passed out by the time he stood up, or perhaps she came in after he left, through a second doorway, from the living room. He said that he went down the corridor and tried to reach the children's bedroom. In the hallway, he said, "you couldn't see nothing but black." The air smelled the way it had when their microwave had blown up, three weeks earlier—like "wire and stuff like that." He could hear sockets and light switches popping, and he crouched down, almost crawling. When he made it to the children's bedroom, he said, he stood and his hair caught on fire. "Oh God, I never felt anything that hot before," he said of the heat radiating out of the room.

After he patted out the fire on his hair, he said, he got down on the ground and groped in the dark. "I thought I found one of them once," he said, "but it was a doll." He couldn't bear the heat any longer. "I felt myself passing out," he said. Finally, he stumbled down the corridor and out the front door, trying to catch his breath. He saw Diane Barbee and yelled for her to call the Fire Department. After she left, he insisted, he tried without success to get back inside.

The investigators asked him if he had any idea how the fire had started. He said that he wasn't sure, though it must have originated in the children's room, since that was where he first saw flames; they were glowing like "bright lights." He and Stacy used three space heaters to keep the house warm, and one of them was in the children's room. "I taught Amber not to play with it," he said, adding that she got "whuppings every once in a while for messing with it." He said that he didn't know if the heater, which had an internal flame, was turned on. (Vasquez later testified that when he had checked the heater, four days after the fire, it was in the "Off" position.) Willingham speculated that the fire might have been started by something electrical: he had heard all that popping and crackling.

When pressed whether someone might have a motive to hurt his family, he said that he couldn't think of anyone that "cold-blooded." He said of his children, "I just don't understand why anybody would take them, you know? We had three of the most pretty babies anybody could have ever asked for." He went on, "Me and Stacy's been together for four years, but off and on we get into a fight and split up for a while and I think those babies is what brought us so close together ... neither one of us ... could live without them kids." Thinking of Amber, he said, "To tell you the honest-to-God's truth, I wish she hadn't woke me up."

During the interrogation, Vasquez let Fogg take the lead. Finally, Vasquez turned to Willingham and asked a seemingly random question: had he put on shoes before he fled the house?

"No, sir," Willingham replied.

A map of the house was on a table between the men, and Vasquez pointed to it. "You walked out this way?" he said.

Willingham said yes.

Vasquez was now convinced that Willingham had killed his children. If the floor had been soaked with a liquid accelerant and the fire had burned low, as the evidence suggested, Willingham could not have run out of the house the way he had described without badly burning his feet. A medical report indicated that his feet had been unscathed.

Willingham insisted that, when he left the house, the fire was still around the top of the walls and not on the floor. "I didn't have to jump through any flames," he said. Vasquez believed that this was impossible, and that Willingham had lit the fire as he was retreating—first, torching the children's room, then the hallway, and then, from the porch, the front door. Vasquez later said of Willingham, "He told me a story of pure fabrication. … He just talked and he talked and all he did was lie."

Still, there was no clear motive. The children had life-insurance policies, but they amounted to only fifteen thousand dollars, and Stacy's grandfather, who had paid for them, was listed as the primary beneficiary. Stacy told investigators that even though Willingham hit her he had never abused the children—"Our kids were spoiled rotten," she said—and she did not believe that Willingham could have killed them.

Ultimately, the authorities concluded that Willingham was a man without a conscience whose serial crimes had climaxed, almost inexorably, in murder. John Jackson, who was then the assistant district attorney in Corsicana, was assigned to prosecute Willingham's case. He later told the Dallas *Morning News* that he considered Willingham to be "an utterly sociopathic individual" who deemed his children "an impediment to his lifestyle." Or, as the local district attorney, Pat Batchelor, put it, "The children were interfering with his beer drinking and dart throwing."

On the night of January 8, 1992, two weeks after the fire, Willingham was riding in a car with Stacy when SWAT teams surrounded them, forcing them to the side of the road. "They pulled guns out like we had just robbed ten banks," Stacy later recalled. "All we heard was 'click, click.' ... Then they arrested him."

Willingham was charged with murder. Because there were multiple victims, he was eligible for the death penalty, under Texas law. Unlike many other prosecutors in the state, Jackson, who had ambitions of becoming a judge, was personally opposed to capital punishment. "I don't think it's effective in deterring criminals," he told me. "I just don't think it works." He also considered it wasteful: because of the expense of litigation and the appeals process, it costs, on average, $2.3 million to execute a prisoner in Texas—about three times the cost of incarcerating someone for forty years. Plus, Jackson said, "What's the recourse if you make a mistake?" Yet his boss, Batchelor, believed that, as he once put it, "certain people who commit bad enough crimes give up the right to live," and Jackson came to agree that the heinous nature of the crime in the Willingham case—"one of the worst in terms of body count" that he had ever tried—mandated death.

Willingham couldn't afford to hire lawyers, and was assigned two by the state: David Martin, a former state trooper, and Robert Dunn, a local defense attorney who represented everyone from alleged murderers to spouses in divorce cases—a "Jack-of-all-trades," as he calls himself. ("In a small town, you can't say 'I'm a so-and-so lawyer,' because you'll starve to death," he told me.)

Not long after Willingham's arrest, authorities received a message from a prison inmate named Johnny Webb, who was in the same jail as Willingham. Webb alleged that Willingham had confessed to him that he took "some kind of lighter fluid, squirting [it] around the walls and the floor, and set a fire." The case against Willingham was considered airtight.

Even so, several of Stacy's relatives—who, unlike her, believed that Willingham was guilty—told Jackson that they preferred to avoid the anguish of a trial. And so, shortly before jury selection, Jackson approached Willingham's attorneys with an extraordinary offer: if their client pleaded guilty, the state would give him a life sentence. "I was really happy when I thought we might have a deal to avoid the death penalty," Jackson recalls.

Willingham's lawyers were equally pleased. They had little doubt that he had committed the murders and that, if the case went before a jury, he would be found guilty, and, subsequently, executed. "Everyone thinks defense lawyers must believe their clients are innocent, but that's seldom true," Martin told me. "Most of the time, they're guilty as sin." He added of Willingham, "All the evidence showed that he was one hundred percent guilty. He poured accelerant all over the house and put lighter fluid under the kids' beds." It was, he said, "a classic arson case": there were "puddle patterns all over the place—no disputing those."

Martin and Dunn advised Willingham that he should accept the offer, but he refused. The lawyers asked his father and stepmother to speak to him. According to Eugenia, Martin showed them photographs of the burned children and said, "Look what your son did. You got to talk him into pleading, or he's going to be executed."

His parents went to see their son in jail. Though his father did not believe that he should plead guilty if he were innocent, his stepmother beseeched him to take the deal. "I just wanted to keep my boy alive," she told me.

Willingham was implacable. "I ain't gonna plead to something I didn't do, especially killing my own kids," he said. It was his final decision. Martin says, "I thought it was nuts at the time—and I think it's nuts now."

Willingham's refusal to accept the deal confirmed the view of the prosecution, and even that of his defense lawyers, that he was an unrepentant killer.

In August, 1992, the trial commenced in the old stone courthouse in downtown Corsicana. Jackson and a team of prosecutors summoned a procession of witnesses, including Johnny Webb and the Barbees. The crux of the state's case, though, remained the scientific evidence gathered by Vasquez and Fogg. On the stand, Vasquez detailed what he called more than "twenty indicators" of arson.

"Do you have an opinion as to who started the fire?" one of the prosecutors asked.

"Yes, sir," Vasquez said. "Mr. Willingham."

The prosecutor asked Vasquez what he thought Willingham's intent was in lighting the fire. "To kill the little girls," he said.

The defense had tried to find a fire expert to counter Vasquez and Fogg's testimony, but the one they contacted concurred with the prosecution. Ultimately, the defense presented only one witness to the jury: the Willinghams' babysitter, who said she could not believe that Willingham could have killed his children. (Dunn told me that Willingham had wanted to testify, but Martin and Dunn thought that he would make a bad witness.) The trial ended after two days.

During his closing arguments, Jackson said that the puddle configurations and pour patterns were Willingham's inadvertent "confession," burned into the floor. Showing a Bible that had been salvaged from the fire, Jackson paraphrased the words of Jesus from the Gospel of Matthew: "Whomsoever shall harm one of my children, it's better for a millstone to be hung around his neck and for him to be cast in the sea."

The jury was out for barely an hour before returning with a unanimous guilty verdict. As Vasquez put it, "The fire does not lie."

II

When Elizabeth Gilbert approached the prison guard, on a spring day in 1999, and said Cameron Todd Willingham's name, she was uncertain about what she was doing. A forty-seven-year-old French teacher and playwright from Houston, Gilbert was divorced with two children. She had never visited a prison before. Several weeks earlier, a friend, who worked at an organization that opposed the death penalty, had encouraged her to volunteer as a pen pal for an inmate on death row, and Gilbert had offered her name and address. Not long after, a short letter, written with unsteady penmanship, arrived from Willingham. "If you wish to write back, I would be honored to correspond with you," he said. He also asked if she might visit him. Perhaps out of a writer's curiosity, or perhaps because she didn't feel quite herself (she had just been upset by news that her ex-husband was dying of cancer), she agreed. Now she was standing in front of the decrepit penitentiary in Huntsville, Texas—a place that inmates referred to as "the death pit."

She filed past a razor-wire fence, a series of floodlights, and a checkpoint, where she was patted down, until she entered a small chamber. Only a few feet in front of her was a man convicted of multiple infanticide. He was wearing a white jumpsuit with "DR"—for death row—printed on the back, in large black letters. He had a tattoo of a serpent and a skull on his left biceps. He stood nearly six feet tall and was muscular, though his legs had atrophied after years of confinement.

A Plexiglas window separated Willingham from her; still, Gilbert, who had short brown hair and a bookish manner, stared at him uneasily. Willingham had once fought another prisoner who called him a "baby killer," and since he had been incarcerated, seven years earlier, he had committed a series of disciplinary infractions that had periodically landed him in the segregation unit, which was known as "the dungeon."

Willingham greeted her politely. He seemed grateful that she had come. After his conviction, Stacy had campaigned for his release. She wrote to Ann Richards, then the governor of Texas, saying, "I know him in ways that no one else does when it comes to our children. Therefore, I believe that there is no way he could have possibly committed this crime." But within a year Stacy had filed for divorce, and Willingham had few visitors except for his parents, who drove from Oklahoma to see him once a month. "I really have no one outside my parents to remind me that I am a human being, not the animal the state professes I am," he told Gilbert at one point.

He didn't want to talk about death row. "Hell, I live here," he later wrote her. "When I have a visit, I want to escape from here." He asked her questions about her teaching and art. He expressed fear that, as a playwright, she might find him a "one-dimensional character," and apologized for lacking social graces; he now had trouble separating the mores in prison from those of the outside world.

When Gilbert asked him if he wanted something to eat or drink from the vending machines, he declined. "I hope I did not offend you by not accepting any snacks," he later wrote her. "I didn't want you to feel I was there just for something like that."

She had been warned that prisoners often tried to con visitors. He appeared to realize this, subsequently telling her, "I am just a simple man. Nothing else. And to most other people a convicted killer looking for someone to manipulate."

Their visit lasted for two hours, and afterward they continued to correspond. She was struck by his letters, which seemed introspective, and were not at all what she had expected. "I am a very honest person with my feelings," he wrote her. "I will not bullshit you on how I feel or what I think." He said that he used to be stoic, like his father. But, he added, "losing my three daughters ... my home, wife and my life, you tend to wake up a little. I have learned to open myself."

She agreed to visit him again, and when she returned, several weeks later, he was visibly moved. "Here I am this person who nobody on the outside is ever going to know as a human, who has lost so much, but still trying to hold on," he wrote her afterward. "But you came back! I don't think you will ever know of what importance that visit was in my existence."

They kept exchanging letters, and she began asking him about the fire. He insisted that he was innocent and that, if someone had poured accelerant through the house and lit it, then the killer remained free. Gilbert wasn't naïve—she assumed that he was guilty. She did not mind giving him solace, but she was not there to absolve him.

Still, she had become curious about the case, and one day that fall she drove down to the courthouse in Corsicana to review the trial records. Many people in the community remembered the tragedy, and a clerk expressed bewilderment that anyone would be interested in a man who had burned his children alive.

Gilbert took the files and sat down at a small table. As she examined the eyewitness accounts, she noticed several contradictions. Diane Barbee had reported that, before the authorities arrived at the fire, Willingham never tried to get back into the house—yet she had been absent for some time while calling the Fire Department. Meanwhile, her daughter Buffie had reported witnessing Willingham on the porch breaking a window, in an apparent effort to reach his children. And the firemen and police on the scene had described Willingham frantically trying to get into the house.

The witnesses' testimony also grew more damning after authorities had concluded, in the beginning of January, 1992, that Willingham was likely guilty of murder. In Diane Barbee's initial statement to authorities, she had portrayed Willingham as "hysterical," and described the front of the house exploding. But on January 4th, after arson investigators began suspecting Willingham of murder, Barbee suggested that he could have gone back inside to rescue his children, for at the outset she had seen only "smoke coming from out of the front of the house"—smoke that was not "real thick."

An even starker shift occurred with Father Monaghan's testimony. In his first statement, he had depicted Willingham as a devastated father who had to be repeatedly restrained from risking his life. Yet, as investigators were preparing to arrest Willingham, he concluded that Willingham had been *too* emotional ("He seemed to have the type of distress that a woman who had given birth would have upon seeing her children die"); and he expressed a "gut feeling" that Willingham had "something to do with the setting of the fire."

Dozens of studies have shown that witnesses' memories of events often change when they are supplied with new contextual information. Itiel Dror, a cognitive psychologist who has done extensive research on eyewitness and expert testimony in criminal investigations, told me, "The mind is not a passive machine. Once you believe in something—once you expect something—it changes the way you perceive information and the way your memory recalls it."

After Gilbert's visit to the courthouse, she kept wondering about Willingham's motive, and she pressed him on the matter. In response, he wrote, of the death of his children, "I do not talk about it much anymore and it is still a very powerfully emotional pain inside my being." He admitted that he had been a "sorry-ass husband" who had hit Stacy—something he deeply regretted. But he said that he had loved his children and would never have hurt them. Fatherhood, he said, had changed him; he stopped being a hoodlum and "settled down" and "became a man." Nearly three months before the fire, he and Stacy, who had never married, wed at a small ceremony in his home town of Ardmore. He said that the prosecution had seized upon incidents from his past and from the day of the fire to create a portrait of a "demon," as Jackson, the prosecutor, referred to him. For instance, Willingham said, he had moved the car during the fire simply because he didn't want it to explode by the house, further threatening the children.

Gilbert was unsure what to make of his story, and she began to approach people who were involved in the case, asking them questions. "My friends thought I was crazy," Gilbert recalls. "I'd never done anything like this in my life."

One morning, when Willingham's parents came to visit him, Gilbert arranged to see them first, at a coffee shop near the prison. Gene, who was in his seventies, had the Willingham look, though his black hair had gray streaks and his dark eyes were magnified by glasses. Eugenia, who was in her fifties, with silvery hair, was as sweet and talkative as her husband was stern and reserved. The drive from Oklahoma to Texas took six hours, and they had woken at three in the morning; because they could not afford a motel, they would have to return home later that day. "I feel like a real burden to them," Willingham had written Gilbert.

As Gene and Eugenia sipped coffee, they told Gilbert how grateful they were that someone had finally taken an interest in Todd's case. Gene said that his son, though he had flaws, was no killer.

The evening before the fire, Eugenia said, she had spoken on the phone with Todd. She and Gene were planning on visiting two days later, on Christmas Eve, and Todd told her that he and Stacy and the kids had just picked up family photographs. "He said, 'We got your pictures for Christmas,'" she recalled. "He put Amber on the phone, and she was tattling on one of the twins. Todd didn't seem upset. If something was bothering him, I would have known."

Gene and Eugenia got up to go: they didn't want to miss any of the four hours that were allotted for the visit with their son. Before they left, Gene said, "You'll let us know if you find anything, won't you?"

Over the next few weeks, Gilbert continued to track down sources. Many of them, including the Barbees, remained convinced that Willingham was guilty, but several of his friends and relatives had doubts. So did some people in law enforcement. Willingham's former probation officer in Oklahoma, Polly Goodin, recently told me that Willingham had never demonstrated bizarre or sociopathic behavior. "He was probably one of my favorite kids," she said. Even a former judge named Bebe Bridges—who had often stood, as she put it, on the "opposite side" of Willingham in the legal system, and who had sent him to jail for stealing—told me that she could not imagine him killing his children. "He was polite, and he seemed to care," she said. "His convictions had been for dumb-kid stuff. Even the things stolen weren't significant." Several months before the fire, Willingham tracked Goodin down at her office, and proudly showed her photographs of Stacy and the kids. "He wanted Bebe and me to know he'd been doing good," Goodin recalled.

Eventually, Gilbert returned to Corsicana to interview Stacy, who had agreed to meet at the bed-and-breakfast where Gilbert was staying. Stacy was slightly plump, with pale, round cheeks and feathered dark-blond hair; her bangs were held in place by gel, and her face was heavily made up. According to a tape recording of the conversation, Stacy said that nothing unusual had happened in the days before the fire. She and Willingham had not fought, and were preparing for the holiday. Though Vasquez, the arson expert, had recalled finding the space heater off, Stacy was sure that, at least on the day of the incident—a cool winter morning—it had been on. "I remember turning it down," she recalled. "I always thought, Gosh, could Amber have put something in there?" Stacy added that, more than once, she had caught Amber "putting things too close to it."

Willingham had often not treated her well, she recalled, and after his incarceration she had left him for a man who did. But she didn't think that her former husband should be on death row. "I don't think he did it," she said, crying.

Though only the babysitter had appeared as a witness for the defense during the main trial, several family members, including Stacy, testified during the penalty phase, asking the jury to spare Willingham's life. When Stacy was on the stand, Jackson grilled her about the "significance" of Willingham's "very large tattoo of a skull, encircled by some kind of a serpent."

"It's just a tattoo," Stacy responded.

"He just likes skulls and snakes. Is that what you're saying?"

"No. He just had—he got a tattoo on him."

The prosecution cited such evidence in asserting that Willingham fit the profile of a sociopath, and brought forth two medical experts to confirm the theory. Neither had met Willingham. One of them was Tim Gregory, a psychologist with a master's degree in marriage and family issues, who had previously gone goose hunting with Jackson, and had not published any research in the field of sociopathic behavior. His practice was devoted to family counseling.

At one point, Jackson showed Gregory Exhibit No. 60—a photograph of an Iron Maiden poster that had hung in Willingham's house—and asked the psychologist to interpret it. "This one is a picture of a skull, with a fist being punched through the skull," Gregory said; the image displayed "violence" and "death." Gregory looked at photographs of other music posters owned by Willingham. "There's a hooded skull, with wings and a hatchet," Gregory continued. "And all of these are in fire, depicting—it reminds me of something like Hell. And there's a picture—a Led Zeppelin picture of a falling angel. ... I see there's an association many times with cultive-type of activities. A focus on death, dying. Many times individuals that have a lot of this type of art have interest in satanic-type activities."

The other medical expert was James P. Grigson, a forensic psychiatrist. He testified so often for the prosecution in capital-punishment cases that he had become known as Dr. Death. (A Texas appellate judge once wrote that when Grigson appeared on the stand the defendant might as well "commence writing out his last will and testament.") Grigson suggested that Willingham was an "extremely severe sociopath," and that "no pill" or treatment could help him. Grigson had previously used nearly the same words in helping to secure a death sentence against Randall Dale Adams, who had been convicted of murdering a police officer, in 1977. After Adams, who had no prior criminal record, spent a dozen years on death row—and once came within seventy-two hours of being executed—new evidence emerged that absolved him, and he was released. In 1995, three years after Willingham's trial, Grigson was expelled from the American Psychiatric Association for violating ethics. The association stated that Grigson had repeatedly arrived at a "psychiatric diagnosis without first having examined the individuals in question, and for indicating, while testifying in court as an expert witness, that he could predict with 100-percent certainty that the individuals would engage in future violent acts."

After speaking to Stacy, Gilbert had one more person she wanted to interview: the jailhouse informant Johnny Webb, who was incarcerated in Iowa Park, Texas. She wrote to Webb, who said that she could see him, and they met in the prison visiting room. A man in his late twenties, he had pallid skin and a closely shaved head; his eyes were jumpy, and his entire body seemed to tremble. A reporter who once met him described him to me as "nervous as a cat around rocking chairs." Webb had begun taking drugs when he was nine years old, and had been convicted of, among other things, car theft, selling marijuana, forgery, and robbery.

As Gilbert chatted with him, she thought that he seemed paranoid. During Willingham's trial, Webb disclosed that he had been given a diagnosis of "post-traumatic stress disorder" after he was sexually assaulted in prison, in 1988, and that he often suffered from "mental impairment." Under cross-examination, Webb testified that he had no recollection of a robbery that he had pleaded guilty to only months earlier.

Webb repeated for her what he had said in court: he had passed by Willingham's cell, and as they spoke through a food slot Willingham broke down and told him that he intentionally set the house on fire. Gilbert was dubious. It was hard to believe that Willingham, who had otherwise insisted on his innocence, had suddenly confessed to an inmate he barely knew. The conversation had purportedly taken place by a speaker system that allowed any of the guards to listen—an unlikely spot for an inmate to reveal a secret. What's more, Webb alleged that Willingham had told him that Stacy had hurt one of the kids, and that the fire was set to cover up the crime. The autopsies, however, had revealed no bruises or signs of trauma on the children's bodies.

Jailhouse informants, many of whom are seeking reduced time or special privileges, are notoriously unreliable. According to a 2004 study by the Center on Wrongful Convictions, at Northwestern University Law School, lying police and jailhouse informants are the leading cause of wrongful convictions in capital cases in the United States. At the time that Webb came forward against Willingham, he was facing charges of robbery and forgery. During Willingham's trial, another inmate planned to testify that he had overheard Webb saying to another prisoner that he was hoping to "get time cut," but the testimony was ruled inadmissible, because it was hearsay. Webb, who pleaded guilty to the robbery and forgery charges, received a sentence of fifteen years. Jackson, the prosecutor, told me that he generally considered Webb "an unreliable kind of guy," but added, "I saw no real motive for him to make a statement like this if it wasn't true. We didn't cut him any slack." In 1997, five years after Willingham's trial, Jackson urged the Texas Board of Pardons and Paroles to grant Webb parole. "I asked them to cut him loose early," Jackson told me. The reason, Jackson said, was that Webb had been targeted by the Aryan Brotherhood. The board granted Webb parole, but within months of his release he was caught with cocaine and returned to prison.

In March, 2000, several months after Gilbert's visit, Webb unexpectedly sent Jackson a Motion to Recant Testimony, declaring, "Mr. Willingham is innocent of all charges." But Willingham's lawyer was not informed of this development, and soon afterward Webb, without explanation, recanted his recantation. When I recently asked Webb, who was released from prison two years ago, about the turnabout and why Willingham would have confessed to a virtual stranger, he said that he knew only what "the dude told me." After I pressed him, he said, "It's very possible I misunderstood what he said." Since the trial, Webb has been given an additional diagnosis, bipolar disorder. "Being locked up in that little cell makes you kind of crazy," he said. "My memory is in bits and pieces. I was on a lot of medication at the time. Everyone knew that." He paused, then said, "The statute of limitations has run out on perjury, hasn't it?"

Aside from the scientific evidence of arson, the case against Willingham did not stand up to scrutiny. Jackson, the prosecutor, said of Webb's testimony, "You can take it or leave it." Even the refrigerator's placement by the back door of the house turned out to be innocuous; there were two refrigerators in the cramped kitchen, and one of them was by the back door. Jimmie Hensley, the police detective, and Douglas Fogg, the assistant fire chief, both of whom investigated the fire, told me recently that they had never believed that the fridge was part of the arson plot. "It didn't have nothing to do with the fire," Fogg said.

After months of investigating the case, Gilbert found that her faith in the prosecution was shaken. As she told me, "What if Todd really was innocent?"

III

In the summer of 1660, an Englishman named William Harrison vanished on a walk, near the village of Charingworth, in Gloucestershire. His bloodstained hat was soon discovered on the side of a local road. Police interrogated Harrison's servant, John Perry, and eventually Perry gave a statement that his mother and his brother had killed Harrison for money. Perry, his mother, and his brother were hanged.

Two years later, Harrison reappeared. He insisted, fancifully, that he had been abducted by a band of criminals and sold into slavery. Whatever happened, one thing was indisputable: he had not been murdered by the Perrys.

The fear that an innocent person might be executed has long haunted jurors and lawyers and judges. During America's Colonial period, dozens of crimes were punishable by death, including horse thievery, blasphemy, "man-stealing," and highway robbery. After independence, the number of crimes eligible for the death penalty was gradually reduced, but doubts persisted over whether legal procedures were sufficient to prevent an innocent person from being executed. In 1868, John Stuart Mill made one of the most eloquent defenses of capital punishment, arguing that executing a murderer did not display a wanton disregard for life but, rather, proof of its value. "We show, on the contrary, most emphatically our regard for it by the adoption of a rule that he who violates that right in another forfeits it for himself," he said. For Mill, there was one counterargument that carried weight—"that if by an error of justice an innocent person is put to death, the mistake can never be corrected."

The modern legal system, with its lengthy appeals process and clemency boards, was widely assumed to protect the kind of "error of justice" that Mill feared. In 2000, while George W. Bush was governor of Texas, he said, "I know there are some in the country who don't care for the death penalty, but ... we've adequately answered innocence or guilt." His top policy adviser on issues of criminal justice emphasized that there is "super due process to make sure that no innocent defendants are executed."

In recent years, though, questions have mounted over whether the system is fail-safe. Since 1976, more than a hundred and thirty people on death row have been exonerated. DNA testing, which was developed in the eighties, saved seventeen of them, but the technique can be used only in rare instances. Barry Scheck, a co-founder of the Innocence Project, which has used DNA testing to exonerate prisoners, estimates that about eighty per cent of felonies do not involve biological evidence.

In 2000, after thirteen people on death row in Illinois were exonerated, George Ryan, who was then governor of the state, suspended the death penalty. Though he had been a longtime advocate of capital punishment, he declared that he could no longer support a system that has "come so close to the ultimate nightmare—the state's taking of innocent life." Former Supreme Court Justice Sandra Day O'Connor has said that the "execution of a legally and factually innocent person would be a constitutionally intolerable event."

Such a case has become a kind of grisly Holy Grail among opponents of capital punishment. In his 2002 book "The Death Penalty," Stuart Banner observes, "The prospect of killing an innocent person seemed to be the one thing that could cause people to rethink their support for capital punishment. Some who were not troubled by statistical arguments against the death penalty—claims about deterrence or racial disparities—were deeply troubled that such an extreme injustice might occur in an individual case." Opponents of the death penalty have pointed to several questionable cases. In 1993, Ruben Cantu was executed in Texas for fatally shooting a man during a robbery. Years later, a second victim, who survived the shooting, told the Houston *Chronicle* that he had been pressured by police to identify Cantu as the gunman, even though he believed Cantu to be innocent. Sam Millsap, the district attorney in the case, who had once supported capital punishment ("I'm no wild-eyed, pointy-headed liberal"), said that he was disturbed by the thought that he had made a mistake.

In 1995, Larry Griffin was put to death in Missouri, for a drive-by shooting of a drug dealer. The case rested largely on the eyewitness testimony of a career criminal named Robert Fitzgerald, who had been an informant for prosecutors before and was in the witness-protection program. Fitzgerald maintained that he happened to be at the scene because his car had broken down. After Griffin's execution, a probe sponsored by the N.A.A.C.P.'s Legal Defense and Educational Fund revealed that a man who had been wounded during the incident insisted that Griffin was not the shooter. Moreover, the first police officer at the scene disputed that Fitzgerald had witnessed the crime.

These cases, however, stopped short of offering irrefutable proof that a "legally and factually innocent person" was executed. In 2005, a St. Louis prosecutor, Jennifer Joyce, launched an investigation of the Griffin case, upon being presented with what she called "compelling" evidence of Griffin's potential innocence. After two years of reviewing the evidence, and interviewing a new eyewitness, Joyce said that she and her team were convinced that the "right person was convicted."

Supreme Court Justice Antonin Scalia, in 2006, voted with a majority to uphold the death penalty in a Kansas case. In his opinion, Scalia declared that, in the modern judicial system, there has not been "a single case—not one—in which it is clear that a person was executed for a crime he did not commit. If such an event had occurred in recent years, we would not have to hunt for it; the innocent's name would be shouted from the rooftops."

"My problems are simple," Willingham wrote Gilbert in September, 1999. "Try to keep them from killing me at all costs. End of story."

During his first years on death row, Willingham had pleaded with his lawyer, David Martin, to rescue him. "You can't imagine what it's like to be here, with people I have no business even being around," he wrote.

For a while, Willingham shared a cell with Ricky Lee Green, a serial killer, who castrated and fatally stabbed his victims, including a sixteen-year-old boy. (Green was executed in 1997.) Another of Willingham's cellmates, who had an I.Q. below seventy and the emotional development of an eight-year-old, was raped by an inmate. "You remember me telling you I had a new celly?" Willingham wrote in a letter to his parents. "The little retarded boy. ... There was this guy here on the wing who is a shit sorry coward (who is the same one I got into it with a little over a month ago). Well, he raped [my cellmate] in the 3 row shower week before last." Willingham said that he couldn't believe that someone would "rape a boy who cannot even defend himself. Pretty damn low."

Because Willingham was known as a "baby killer," he was a target of attacks. "Prison is a rough place, and with a case like mine they never give you the benefit of a doubt," he wrote his parents. After he tried to fight one prisoner who threatened him, Willingham told a friend that if he hadn't stood up for himself several inmates would have "beaten me up or raped or"—his thought trailed off.

Over the years, Willingham's letters home became increasingly despairing. "This is a hard place, and it makes a person hard inside," he wrote. "I told myself that was one thing I did not want and that was for this place to make me bitter, but it is hard." He went on, "They have [executed] at least one person every month I have been here. It is senseless and brutal. ... You see, we are not living in here, we are only existing." In 1996, he wrote, "I just been trying to figure out why after having a wife and 3 beautiful children that I loved my life has to end like this. And sometimes it just seems like it is not worth it all. . . In the 3½ years I been here I have never felt that my life was as worthless and desolate as it is now." Since the fire, he wrote, he had the sense that his life was slowly being erased. He obsessively looked at photographs of his children and Stacy, which he stored in his cell. "So long ago, so far away," he wrote in a poem. "Was everything truly there?"

Inmates on death row are housed in a prison within a prison, where there are no attempts at rehabilitation, and no educational or training programs. In 1999, after seven prisoners tried to escape from Huntsville, Willingham and four hundred and fifty-nine other inmates on death row were moved to a more secure facility, in Livingston, Texas. Willingham was held in isolation in a sixty-square-foot cell, twenty-three hours a day. He tried to distract himself by drawing—"amateur stuff," as he put it—and writing poems. In a poem about his children, he wrote, "There is nothing more beautiful than you on this earth." When Gilbert once suggested some possible revisions to his poems, he explained that he wrote them simply as expressions, however crude, of his feelings. "So to me to cut them up and try to improve on them just for creative-writing purposes would be to destroy what I was doing to start with," he said.

Despite his efforts to occupy his thoughts, he wrote in his diary that his mind "deteriorates each passing day." He stopped working out and gained weight. He questioned his faith: "No God who cared about his creation would abandon the innocent." He seemed not to care if another inmate attacked him. "A person who is already dead inside does not fear" death, he wrote.

One by one, the people he knew in prison were escorted into the execution chamber. There was Clifton Russell, Jr., who, at the age of eighteen, stabbed and beat a man to death, and who said, in his last statement, "I thank my Father, God in Heaven, for the grace he has granted me—I am ready." There was Jeffery Dean Motley, who kidnapped and fatally shot a woman, and who declared, in his final words, "I love you, Mom. Goodbye." And there was John Fearance, who murdered his neighbor, and who turned to God in his last moments and said, "I hope He will forgive me for what I done."

Willingham had grown close to some of his prison mates, even though he knew that they were guilty of brutal crimes. In March, 2000, Willingham's friend Ponchai Wilkerson—a twenty-eight-year-old who had shot and killed a clerk during a jewelry heist—was executed. Afterward, Willingham wrote in his diary that he felt "an emptiness that has not been touched since my children were taken from me." A year later, another friend who was about to be executed—"one of the few real people I have met here not caught up in the bravado of prison"—asked Willingham to make him a final drawing. "Man, I never thought drawing a simple Rose could be so emotionally hard," Willingham wrote. "The hard part is knowing that this will be the last thing I can do for him."

Another inmate, Ernest Ray Willis, had a case that was freakishly similar to Willingham's. In 1987, Willis had been convicted of setting a fire, in West Texas, that killed two women. Willis told investigators that he had been sleeping on a friend's living-room couch and woke up to a house full of smoke. He said that he tried to rouse one of the women, who was sleeping in another room, but the flames and smoke drove him back, and he ran out the front door before the house exploded with flames. Witnesses maintained that Willis had acted suspiciously; he moved his car out of the yard, and didn't show "any emotion," as one volunteer firefighter put it. Authorities also wondered how Willis could have escaped the house without burning his bare feet. Fire investigators found pour patterns, puddle configurations, and other signs of arson. The authorities could discern no motive for the crime, but concluded that Willis, who had no previous record of violence, was a sociopath—a "demon," as the prosecutor put it. Willis was charged with capital murder and sentenced to death.

Willis had eventually obtained what Willingham called, enviously, a "bad-ass lawyer." James Blank, a noted patent attorney in New York, was assigned Willis's case as part of his firm's pro-bono work. Convinced that Willis was innocent, Blank devoted more than a dozen years to the case, and his firm spent millions, on fire consultants, private investigators, forensic experts, and the like. Willingham, meanwhile, relied on David Martin, his court-appointed lawyer, and one of Martin's colleagues to handle his appeals. Willingham often told his parents, "You don't know what it's like to have lawyers who won't even believe you're innocent." Like many inmates on death row, Willingham eventually filed a claim of inadequate legal representation. (When I recently asked Martin about his representation of Willingham, he said, "There were no grounds for reversal, and the verdict was absolutely the right one." He said of the case, "Shit, it's incredible that anyone's even thinking about it.")

Willingham tried to study the law himself, reading books such as "Tact in Court, or How Lawyers Win: Containing Sketches of Cases Won by Skill, Wit, Art, Tact, Courage and Eloquence." Still, he confessed to a friend, "The law is so complicated it is hard for me to understand." In 1996, he obtained a new court-appointed lawyer, Walter Reaves, who told me that he was appalled by the quality of Willingham's defense at trial and on appeal. Reaves prepared for him a state writ of habeas corpus, known as a Great Writ. In the byzantine appeals process of death-penalty cases, which frequently takes more than ten years, the writ is the most critical stage: a prisoner can introduce new evidence detailing such things as perjured testimony, unreliable medical experts, and bogus scientific findings. Yet most indigent inmates, like Willingham, who constitute the bulk of those on death row, lack the resources to track down new witnesses or dig up fresh evidence. They must depend on court-appointed lawyers, many of whom are "unqualified, irresponsible, or overburdened," as a study by the Texas Defender Service, a nonprofit organization, put it. In 2000, a Dallas *Morning News* investigation revealed that roughly a quarter of the inmates condemned to death in Texas were represented by court-appointed attorneys who had, at some point in their careers, been "reprimanded, placed on probation, suspended or banned from practicing law by the State Bar." Although Reaves was more competent, he had few resources to reinvestigate the case, and his writ introduced no new exculpatory evidence: nothing further about Webb, or the reliability of the eyewitness testimony, or the credibility of the medical experts. It focused primarily on procedural questions, such as whether the trial court erred in its instructions to the jury.

The Texas Court of Criminal Appeals was known for upholding convictions even when overwhelming exculpatory evidence came to light. In 1997, DNA testing proved that sperm collected from a rape victim did not match Roy Criner, who had been sentenced to ninety-nine years for the crime. Two lower courts recommended that the verdict be overturned, but the Court of Criminal Appeals upheld it, arguing that Criner might have worn a condom or might not have ejaculated. Sharon Keller, who is now the presiding judge on the court, stated in a majority opinion, "The new evidence does not establish innocence." In 2000, George W. Bush pardoned Criner. (Keller was recently charged with judicial misconduct, for refusing to keep open past five o'clock a clerk's office in order to allow a last-minute petition from a man who was executed later that night.)

On October 31, 1997, the Court of Criminal Appeals denied Willingham's writ. After Willingham filed another writ of habeas corpus, this time in federal court, he was granted a temporary stay. In a poem, Willingham wrote, "One more chance, one more strike / Another bullet dodged, another date escaped."

Willingham was entering his final stage of appeals. As his anxieties mounted, he increasingly relied upon Gilbert to investigate his case and for emotional support. "She may never know what a change she brought into my life," he wrote in his diary. "For the first time in many years she gave me a purpose, something to look forward to."

As their friendship deepened, he asked her to promise him that she would never disappear without explanation. "I already have that in my life," he told her.

Together, they pored over clues and testimony. Gilbert says that she would send Reaves leads to follow up, but although he was sympathetic, nothing seemed to come of them. In 2002, a federal district court of appeals denied Willingham's writ without even a hearing. "Now I start the last leg of my journey," Willingham wrote to Gilbert. "Got to get things in order."

He appealed to the U.S. Supreme Court, but in December, 2003, he was notified that it had declined to hear his case. He soon received a court order announcing that "the Director of the Department of Criminal Justice at Huntsville, Texas, acting by and through the executioner designated by said Director ... is hereby DIRECTED and COMMANDED, at some hour after 6:00 p.m. on the 17th day of February, 2004, at the Department of Criminal Justice in Huntsville, Texas, to carry out this sentence of death by intravenous injection of a substance or substances in a lethal quantity sufficient to cause the death of said Cameron Todd Willingham."

Willingham wrote a letter to his parents. "Are you sitting down?" he asked, before breaking the news. "I love you both so much," he said.

His only remaining recourse was to appeal to the governor of Texas, Rick Perry, a Republican, for clemency. The process, considered the last gatekeeper to the executioner, has been called by the U.S. Supreme Court "the 'fail safe' in our criminal justice system."

IV

One day in January, 2004, Dr. Gerald Hurst, an acclaimed scientist and fire investigator, received a file describing all the evidence of arson gathered in Willingham's case. Gilbert had come across Hurst's name and, along with one of Willingham's relatives, had contacted him, seeking his help. After their pleas, Hurst had agreed to look at the case pro bono, and Reaves, Willingham's lawyer, had sent him the relevant documents, in the hope that there were grounds for clemency.

Hurst opened the file in the basement of his house in Austin, which served as a laboratory and an office, and was cluttered with microscopes and diagrams of half-finished experiments. Hurst was nearly six and half feet tall, though his stooped shoulders made him seem considerably shorter, and he had a gaunt face that was partly shrouded by long gray hair. He was wearing his customary outfit: black shoes, black socks, a black T-shirt, and loose-fitting black pants supported by black suspenders. In his mouth was a wad of chewing tobacco.

A child prodigy who was raised by a sharecropper during the Great Depression, Hurst used to prowl junk yards, collecting magnets and copper wires in order to build radios and other contraptions. In the early sixties, he received a Ph.D. in chemistry from Cambridge University, where he started to experiment with fluorine and other explosive chemicals, and once detonated his lab. Later, he worked as the chief scientist on secret weapons programs for several American companies, designing rockets and deadly fire bombs—or what he calls "god-awful things." He helped patent what has been described, with only slight exaggeration, as "the world's most powerful nonnuclear explosive": an Astrolite bomb. He experimented with toxins so lethal that a fraction of a drop would rot human flesh, and in his laboratory he often had to wear a pressurized moon suit; despite such precautions, exposure to chemicals likely caused his liver to fail, and in 1994 he required a transplant. Working on what he calls "the dark side of arson," he retrofitted napalm bombs with Astrolite, and developed ways for covert operatives in Vietnam to create bombs from local materials, such as chicken manure and sugar. He also perfected a method for making an exploding T-shirt by nitrating its fibres.

His conscience eventually began pricking him. "One day, you wonder, What the hell am I doing?" he recalls. He left the defense industry, and went on to invent the Mylar balloon, an improved version of Liquid Paper, and Kinepak, a kind of explosive that reduces the risk of accidental detonation. Because of his extraordinary knowledge of fire and explosives, companies in civil litigation frequently sought his help in determining the cause of a blaze. By the nineties, Hurst had begun devoting significant time to criminal-arson cases, and, as he was exposed to the methods of local and state fire investigators, he was shocked by what he saw.

Many arson investigators, it turned out, had only a high-school education. In most states, in order to be certified, investigators had to take a forty-hour course on fire investigation, and pass a written exam. Often, the bulk of an investigator's training came on the job, learning from "old-timers" in the field, who passed down a body of wisdom about the telltale signs of arson, even though a study in 1977 warned that there was nothing in "the scientific literature to substantiate their validity."

In 1992, the National Fire Protection Association, which promotes fire prevention and safety, published its first scientifically based guidelines to arson investigation. Still, many arson investigators believed that what they did was more an art than a science—a blend of experience and intuition. In 1997, the International Association of Arson Investigators filed a legal brief arguing that arson sleuths should not be bound by a 1993 Supreme Court decision requiring experts who testified at trials to adhere to the scientific method. What arson sleuths did, the brief claimed, was "less scientific." By 2000, after the courts had rejected such claims, arson investigators increasingly recognized the scientific method, but there remained great variance in the field, with many practitioners still relying on the unverified techniques that had been used for generations. "People investigated fire largely with a flat-earth approach," Hurst told me. "It looks like arson—therefore, it's arson." He went on, "My view is you have to have a scientific basis. Otherwise, it's no different than witch-hunting."

In 1998, Hurst investigated the case of a woman from North Carolina named Terri Hinson, who was charged with setting a fire that killed her seventeen-month-old son, and faced the death penalty. Hurst ran a series of experiments re-creating the conditions of the fire, which suggested that it had not been arson, as the investigators had claimed; rather, it had started accidentally, from a faulty electrical wire in the attic. Because of this research, Hinson was freed. John Lentini, a fire expert and the author of a leading scientific textbook on arson, describes Hurst as "brilliant." A Texas prosecutor once told the Chicago *Tribune,* of Hurst, "If he says it was an arson fire, then it was. If he says it wasn't, then it wasn't."

Hurst's patents yielded considerable royalties, and he could afford to work pro bono on an arson case for months, even years. But he received the files on Willingham's case only a few weeks before Willingham was scheduled to be executed. As Hurst looked through the case records, a statement by Manuel Vasquez, the state deputy fire marshal, jumped out at him. Vasquez had testified that, of the roughly twelve hundred to fifteen hundred fires he had investigated, "most all of them" were arson. This was an oddly high estimate; the Texas State Fire Marshals Office typically found arson in only fifty per cent of its cases.

Hurst was also struck by Vasquez's claim that the Willingham blaze had "burned fast and hot" because of a liquid accelerant. The notion that a flammable or combustible liquid caused flames to reach higher temperatures had been repeated in court by arson sleuths for decades. Yet the theory was nonsense: experiments have proved that wood and gasoline-fuelled fires burn at essentially the same temperature.

Vasquez and Fogg had cited as proof of arson the fact that the front door's aluminum threshold had melted. "The only thing that can cause that to react is an accelerant," Vasquez said. Hurst was incredulous. A natural-wood fire can reach temperatures as high as two thousand degrees Fahrenheit—far hotter than the melting point for aluminum alloys, which ranges from a thousand to twelve hundred degrees. And, like many other investigators,

Vasquez and Fogg mistakenly assumed that wood charring beneath the aluminum threshold was evidence that, as Vasquez put it, "a liquid accelerant flowed underneath and burned." Hurst had conducted myriad experiments showing that such charring was caused simply by the aluminum conducting so much heat. In fact, when liquid accelerant is poured under a threshold a fire will extinguish, because of a lack of oxygen. (Other scientists had reached the same conclusion.) "Liquid accelerants can no more burn under an aluminum threshold than can grease burn in a skillet even with a loose-fitting lid," Hurst declared in his report on the Willingham case.

Hurst then examined Fogg and Vasquez's claim that the "brown stains" on Willingham's front porch were evidence of "liquid accelerant," which had not had time to soak into the concrete. Hurst had previously performed a test in his garage, in which he poured charcoal-lighter fluid on the concrete floor, and lit it. When the fire went out, there were no brown stains, only smudges of soot. Hurst had run the same experiment many times, with different kinds of liquid accelerants, and the result was always the same. Brown stains were common in fires; they were usually composed of rust or gunk from charred debris that had mixed with water from fire hoses.

Another crucial piece of evidence implicating Willingham was the "crazed glass" that Vasquez had attributed to the rapid heating from a fire fuelled with liquid accelerant. Yet, in November of 1991, a team of fire investigators had inspected fifty houses in the hills of Oakland, California, which had been ravaged by brush fires. In a dozen houses, the investigators discovered crazed glass, even though a liquid accelerant had not been used. Most of these houses were on the outskirts of the blaze, where firefighters had shot streams of water; as the investigators later wrote in a published study, they theorized that the fracturing had been induced by rapid cooling, rather than by sudden heating—thermal shock had caused the glass to contract so quickly that it settled disjointedly. The investigators then tested this hypothesis in a laboratory. When they heated glass, nothing happened. But each time they applied water to the heated glass the intricate patterns appeared. Hurst had seen the same phenomenon when he had blowtorched and cooled glass during his research at Cambridge. In his report, Hurst wrote that Vasquez and Fogg's notion of crazed glass was no more than an "old wives' tale."

Hurst then confronted some of the most devastating arson evidence against Willingham: the burn trailer, the pour patterns and puddle configurations, the V-shape and other burn marks indicating that the fire had multiple points of origin, the burning underneath the children's beds. There was also the positive test for mineral spirits by the front door, and Willingham's seemingly implausible story that he had run out of the house without burning his bare feet.

As Hurst read through more of the files, he noticed that Willingham and his neighbors had described the windows in the front of the house suddenly exploding and flames roaring forth. It was then that Hurst thought of the legendary Lime Street Fire, one of the most pivotal in the history of arson investigation.

On the evening of October 15, 1990, a thirty-five-year-old man named Gerald Wayne Lewis was found standing in front of his house on Lime Street, in Jacksonville, Florida, holding his three-year-old son. His two-story wood-frame home was engulfed in flames. By the time the fire had been extinguished, six people were dead, including Lewis's wife. Lewis said that he had rescued his son but was unable to get to the others, who were upstairs.

When fire investigators examined the scene, they found the classic signs of arson: low burns along the walls and floors, pour patterns and puddle configurations, and a burn trailer running from the living room into the hallway. Lewis claimed that the fire had started accidentally, on a couch in the living room—his son had been playing with matches. But a V-shaped pattern by one of the doors suggested that the fire had originated elsewhere. Some witnesses told authorities that Lewis seemed too calm during the fire and had never tried to get help. According to the Los Angeles *Times*, Lewis had previously been arrested for abusing his wife, who had taken out a restraining order against him. After a chemist said that he had detected the presence of gasoline on Lewis's clothing and shoes, a report by the sheriff's office concluded, "The fire was started as a result of a petroleum product being poured on the front porch, foyer, living room, stairwell and second floor bedroom." Lewis was arrested and charged with six counts of murder. He faced the death penalty.

Subsequent tests, however, revealed that the laboratory identification of gasoline was wrong. Moreover, a local news television camera had captured Lewis in a clearly agitated state at the scene of the fire, and investigators discovered that at one point he had jumped in front of a moving car, asking the driver to call the Fire Department.

Seeking to bolster their theory of the crime, prosecutors turned to John Lentini, the fire expert, and John DeHaan, another leading investigator and textbook author. Despite some of the weaknesses of the case, Lentini told me that, given the classic burn patterns and puddle configurations in the house, he was sure that Lewis had set the fire: "I was prepared to testify and send this guy to Old Sparky"—the electric chair.

To discover the truth, the investigators, with the backing of the prosecution, decided to conduct an elaborate experiment and re-create the fire scene. Local officials gave the investigators permission to use a condemned house next to Lewis's home, which was about to be torn down. The two houses were virtually identical, and the investigators refurbished the condemned one with the same kind of carpeting, curtains, and furniture that had been in Lewis's home. The scientists also wired the building with heat and gas sensors that could withstand fire. The cost of the experiment came to twenty thousand dollars. Without using liquid accelerant, Lentini and DeHaan set the couch in the living room on fire, expecting that the experiment would demonstrate that Lewis's version of events was implausible.

The investigators watched as the fire quickly consumed the couch, sending upward a plume of smoke that hit the ceiling and spread outward, creating a thick layer of hot gases overhead—an efficient radiator of heat. Within three minutes, this cloud, absorbing more gases from the fire below, was banking down the walls and filling the living room. As the cloud approached the floor, its temperature rose, in some areas, to more than eleven hundred degrees Fahrenheit. Suddenly, the entire room exploded in flames, as the radiant heat ignited every piece of furniture, every curtain, every possible fuel source, even the carpeting. The windows shattered.

The fire had reached what is called "flashover"—the point at which radiant heat causes a fire in a room to become a room on fire. Arson investigators knew about the concept of flashover, but it was widely believed to take much longer to occur, especially without a liquid accelerant. From a single fuel source—a couch—the room had reached flashover in four and a half minutes.

Because all the furniture in the living room had ignited, the blaze went from a fuel-controlled fire to a ventilation-controlled fire—or what scientists call "post-flashover." During post-flashover, the path of the fire depends on new sources of oxygen, from an open door or window. One of the fire investigators, who had been standing by an open door in the living room, escaped moments before the oxygen-starved fire roared out of the room into the hallway—a fireball that caused the corridor to go quickly into flashover as well, propelling the fire out the front door and onto the porch.

After the fire was extinguished, the investigators inspected the hallway and living room. On the floor were irregularly shaped burn patterns that perfectly resembled pour patterns and puddle configurations. It turned out that these classic signs of arson can also appear on their own, after flashover. With the naked eye, it is impossible to distinguish between the pour patterns and puddle configurations caused by an accelerant and those caused naturally by post-flashover. The only reliable way to tell the difference is to take samples from the burn patterns and test them in a laboratory for the presence of flammable or combustible liquids.

During the Lime Street experiment, other things happened that were supposed to occur only in a fire fuelled by liquid accelerant: charring along the base of the walls and doorways, and burning under furniture. There was also a V-shaped pattern by the living-room doorway, far from where the fire had started on the couch. In a small fire, a V-shaped burn mark may pinpoint where a fire began, but during post-flashover these patterns can occur repeatedly, when various objects ignite.

One of the investigators muttered that they had just helped prove the defense's case. Given the reasonable doubt raised by the experiment, the charges against Lewis were soon dropped. The Lime Street experiment had demolished prevailing notions about fire behavior. Subsequent tests by scientists showed that, during post-flashover, burning under beds and furniture was common, entire doors were consumed, and aluminum thresholds melted.

John Lentini says of the Lime Street Fire, "This was my epiphany. I almost sent a man to die based on theories that were a load of crap."

Hurst next examined a floor plan of Willingham's house that Vasquez had drawn, which delineated all the purported pour patterns and puddle configurations. Because the windows had blown out of the children's room, Hurst knew that the fire had reached flashover. With his finger, Hurst traced along Vasquez's diagram the burn trailer that had gone from the children's room, turned right in the hallway, and headed out the front door. John Jackson, the prosecutor, had told me that the path was so "bizarre" that it had to have been caused by a liquid accelerant. But Hurst concluded that it was a natural product of the dynamics of fire during post-flashover. Willingham had fled out the front door, and the fire simply followed the ventilation path, toward the opening. Similarly, when Willingham had broken the windows in the children's room, flames had shot outward.

Hurst recalled that Vasquez and Fogg had considered it impossible for Willingham to have run down the burning hallway without scorching his bare feet. But if the pour patterns and puddle configurations were a result of a flashover, Hurst reasoned, then they were consonant with Willingham's explanation of events. When Willingham exited his bedroom, the hallway was not yet on fire; the flames were contained within the children's bedroom, where, along the ceiling, he saw the "bright lights." Just as the investigator safely stood by the door in the Lime Street experiment seconds before flashover, Willingham could have stood close to the children's room without being harmed. (Prior to the Lime Street case, fire investigators had generally assumed that carbon monoxide diffuses quickly through a house during a fire. In fact, up until flashover, levels of carbon monoxide can be remarkably low beneath and outside the thermal cloud.) By the time the Corsicana fire achieved flashover, Willingham had already fled outside and was in the front yard.

Vasquez had made a videotape of the fire scene, and Hurst looked at the footage of the burn trailer. Even after repeated viewings, he could not detect three points of origin, as Vasquez had. (Fogg recently told me that he also saw a continuous trailer and disagreed with Vasquez, but added that nobody from the prosecution or the defense ever asked him on the stand about his opinion on the subject.)

After Hurst had reviewed Fogg and Vasquez's list of more than twenty arson indicators, he believed that only one had any potential validity: the positive test for mineral spirits by the threshold of the front door. But why had the fire investigators obtained a positive reading only in that location? According to Fogg and Vasquez's theory of the crime, Willingham had poured accelerant throughout the children's bedroom and down the hallway. Officials had tested extensively in these areas—including where all the pour patterns and puddle configurations were—and turned up nothing. Jackson told me that he "never did understand why they weren't able to recover" positive tests in these parts.

Hurst found it hard to imagine Willingham pouring accelerant on the front porch, where neighbors could have seen him. Scanning the files for clues, Hurst noticed a photograph of the porch taken before the fire, which had been entered into evidence. Sitting on the tiny porch was a charcoal grill. The porch was where the family barbecued. Court testimony from witnesses confirmed that there had been a grill, along with a container of lighter fluid, and that both had burned when the fire roared onto the porch during post-flashover. By the time Vasquez inspected the house, the grill had been removed from the porch, during cleanup. Though he cited the container of lighter fluid in his report, he made no mention of the grill. At the trial, he insisted that he had never been told of the grill's earlier placement. Other authorities were aware of the grill but did not see its relevance. Hurst, however, was convinced that he had solved the mystery: when firefighters had blasted the porch with water, they had likely spread charcoal-lighter fluid from the melted container.

Without having visited the fire scene, Hurst says, it was impossible to pinpoint the cause of the blaze. But, based on the evidence, he had little doubt that it was an accidental fire—one caused most likely by the space heater or faulty electrical wiring. It explained why there had never been a motive for the crime. Hurst concluded that there was no evidence of arson, and that a man who had already lost his three children and spent twelve years in jail was about to be executed based on "junk science." Hurst wrote his report in such a rush that he didn't pause to fix the typos.

V

"I am a realist and I will not live a fantasy," Willingham once told Gilbert about the prospect of proving his innocence. But in February, 2004, he began to have hope. Hurst's findings had helped to exonerate more than ten people. Hurst even reviewed the scientific evidence against Willingham's friend Ernest Willis, who had been on death row for the strikingly similar arson charge. Hurst says, "It was like I was looking at the same case. Just change the names." In his report on the Willis case, Hurst concluded that not "a single item of physical evidence ... supports a finding of arson." A second fire expert hired by Ori White, the new district attorney in Willis's district, concurred. After seventeen years on death row, Willis was set free. "I don't turn killers loose," White said at the time. "If Willis was guilty, I'd be retrying him right now. And I'd use Hurst as my witness. He's a brilliant scientist." White noted how close the system had come to murdering an innocent man. "He did not get executed, and I thank God for that," he said.

On February 13th, four days before Willingham was scheduled to be executed, he got a call from Reaves, his attorney. Reaves told him that the fifteen members of the Board of Pardons and Paroles, which reviews an application for clemency and had been sent Hurst's report, had made their decision.

"What is it?" Willingham asked.

"I'm sorry," Reaves said. "They denied your petition."

The vote was unanimous. Reaves could not offer an explanation: the board deliberates in secret, and its members are not bound by any specific criteria. The board members did not even have to review Willingham's materials, and usually don't debate a case in person; rather, they cast their votes by fax—a process that has become known as "death by fax." Between 1976 and 2004, when Willingham filed his petition, the State of Texas had approved only one application for clemency from a prisoner on death row. A Texas appellate judge has called the clemency system "a legal fiction." Reaves said of the board members, "They never asked me to attend a hearing or answer any questions."

The Innocence Project obtained, through the Freedom of Information Act, all the records from the governor's office and the board pertaining to Hurst's report. "The documents show that they received the report, but neither office has any record of anyone acknowledging it, taking note of its significance, responding to it, or calling any attention to it within the government," Barry Scheck said. "The only reasonable conclusion is that the governor's office and the Board of Pardons and Paroles ignored scientific evidence."

LaFayette Collins, who was a member of the board at the time, told me of the process, "You don't vote guilt or innocence. You don't retry the trial. You just make sure everything is in order and there are no glaring errors." He noted that although the rules allowed for a hearing to consider important new evidence, "in my time there had never been one called." When I asked him why Hurst's report didn't constitute evidence of "glaring errors," he said, "We get all kinds of reports, but we don't have the mechanisms to vet them." Alvin Shaw, another board member at the time, said that the case didn't "ring a bell," adding, angrily, "Why would I want to talk about it?" Hurst calls the board's actions "unconscionable."

Though Reaves told Willingham that there was still a chance that Governor Perry might grant a thirty-day stay, Willingham began to prepare his last will and testament. He had earlier written Stacy a letter apologizing for not being a better husband and thanking her for everything she had given him, especially their three daughters. "I still know Amber's voice, her smile, her cool Dude saying and how she said: I wanna hold you! Still feel the touch of Karmon and Kameron's hands on my face." He said that he hoped that "some day, somehow the truth will be known and my name cleared."

He asked Stacy if his tombstone could be erected next to their children's graves. Stacy, who had for so long expressed belief in Willingham's innocence, had recently taken her first look at the original court records and arson findings. Unaware of Hurst's report, she had determined that Willingham was guilty. She denied him his wish, later telling a reporter, "He took my kids away from me."

Gilbert felt as if she had failed Willingham. Even before his pleas for clemency were denied, she told him that all she could give him was her friendship. He told her that it was enough "to be a part of your life in some small way so that in my passing I can know I was at last able to have felt the heart of another who might remember me when I'm gone." He added, "There is nothing to forgive you for." He told her that he would need her to be present at his execution, to help him cope with "my fears, thoughts, and feelings."

On February 17th, the day he was set to die, Willingham's parents and several relatives gathered in the prison visiting room. Plexiglas still separated Willingham from them. "I wish I could touch and hold both of you," Willingham had written to them earlier. "I always hugged Mom but I never hugged Pop much."

As Willingham looked at the group, he kept asking where Gilbert was. Gilbert had recently been driving home from a store when another car ran a red light and smashed into her. Willingham used to tell her to stay in her kitchen for a day, without leaving, to comprehend what it was like to be confined in prison, but she had always found an excuse not to do it. Now she was paralyzed from the neck down.

While she was in an intensive-care unit, she had tried to get a message to Willingham, but apparently failed. Gilbert's daughter later read her a letter that Willingham had sent her, telling her how much he had grown to love her. He had written a poem: "Do you want to see beauty—like you have never seen? / Then close your eyes, and open your mind, and come along with me."

Gilbert, who spent years in physical rehabilitation, gradually regaining motion in her arms and upper body, says, "All that time, I thought I was saving Willingham, and I realized then that he was saving me, giving me the strength to get through this. I know I will one day walk again, and I know it is because Willingham showed me the kind of courage it takes to survive."

Willingham had requested a final meal, and at 4 P.M. on the seventeenth he was served it: three barbecued pork ribs, two orders of onion rings, fried okra, three beef enchiladas with cheese, and two slices of lemon cream pie. He received word that Governor Perry had refused to grant him a stay. (A spokesperson for Perry says, "The Governor made his decision based on the facts of the case.") Willingham's mother and father began to cry. "Don't be sad, Momma," Willingham said. "In fifty-five minutes, I'm a free man. I'm going home to see my kids." Earlier, he had confessed to his parents that there was one thing about the day of the fire he had lied about. He said that he had never actually crawled into the children's room. "I just didn't want people to think I was a coward," he said. Hurst told me, "People who have never been in a fire don't understand why those who survive often can't rescue the victims. They have no concept of what a fire is like."

The warden told Willingham that it was time. Willingham, refusing to assist the process, lay down; he was carried into a chamber eight feet wide and ten feet long. The walls were painted green, and in the center of the room, where an electric chair used to be, was a sheeted gurney. Several guards strapped Willingham down with leather belts, snapping buckles across his arms and legs and chest. A medical team then inserted intravenous tubes into his arms. Each official had a separate role in the process, so that no one person felt responsible for taking a life.

Willingham had asked that his parents and family not be present in the gallery during this process, but as he looked out he could see Stacy watching. The warden pushed a remote control, and sodium thiopental, a barbiturate, was pumped into Willingham's body. Then came a second drug, pancuronium bromide, which paralyzes the diaphragm, making it impossible to breathe. Finally, a third drug, potassium chloride, filled his veins, until his heart stopped, at 6:20 P.M. On his death certificate, the cause was listed as "Homicide."

After his death, his parents were allowed to touch his face for the first time in more than a decade. Later, at Willingham's request, they cremated his body and secretly spread some of his ashes over his children's graves. He had told his parents, "Please don't ever stop fighting to vindicate me."

In December, 2004, questions about the scientific evidence in the Willingham case began to surface. Maurice Possley and Steve Mills, of the Chicago *Tribune*, had published an investigative series on flaws in forensic science; upon learning of Hurst's report, Possley and Mills asked three fire experts, including John Lentini, to examine the original investigation. The experts concurred with Hurst's report. Nearly two years later, the Innocence Project commissioned Lentini and three other top fire investigators to conduct an independent review of the arson evidence in the Willingham case. The panel concluded that "each and every one" of the indicators of arson had been "scientifically proven to be invalid."

In 2005, Texas established a government commission to investigate allegations of error and misconduct by forensic scientists. The first cases that are being reviewed by the commission are those of Willingham and Willis. In mid-August, the noted fire scientist Craig Beyler, who was hired by the commission, completed his investigation. In a scathing report, he concluded that investigators in the Willingham case had no scientific basis for claiming that the fire was arson, ignored evidence that contradicted their theory, had no comprehension of flashover and fire dynamics, relied on discredited folklore, and failed to eliminate potential accidental or alternative causes of the fire. He said that Vasquez's approach seemed to deny "rational reasoning" and was more "characteristic of mystics or psychics." What's more, Beyler determined that the investigation violated, as he put it to me, "not only the standards of today but even of the time period." The commission is reviewing his findings, and plans to release its own report next year. Some legal scholars believe that the commission may narrowly assess the reliability of the scientific evidence. There is a chance, however, that Texas could become the first state to acknowledge officially that, since the advent of the modern judicial system, it had carried out the "execution of a legally and factually innocent person."

Just before Willingham received the lethal injection, he was asked if he had any last words. He said, "The only statement I want to make is that I am an innocent man convicted of a crime I did not commit. I have been persecuted for twelve years for something I did not do. From God's dust I came and to dust I will return, so the Earth shall become my throne."

■ READING AND WRITING

1. Summarize the key elements in the case that Grann builds for Willingham's innocence.
2. Much like a fiction writer, Grann uses characterization, plot development, and suspense to tell Willingham's story—and to build his own argument. What are the rhetorical effects of these literary devices? Explain how they help—or hinder—Grann's argument.
3. Do you think there is any way to guarantee that innocent people are never executed for crimes in the United States? Explain your answer.
4. If Texas ever acknowledges that Willingham was innocent, what do you think the state's leaders should do? How do you think the federal government should respond? Do you think ordinary citizens would be obligated to respond, as well?

■ DEVELOPING LONGER RESPONSES

5. Some readers are shocked upon learning Willingham's story; others are hardly surprised at all. These reactions have a lot to do with individual assumptions about the U.S. justice system. Think about the assumptions and expectations you brought to this article. How would you characterize our system of justice? Where do your opinions about the system come from? Did reading this piece change your thinking in any way?

■ USING RESEARCH

6. At the time this textbook went to press, Texas Governor Rick Perry continued to face criticism for his handling of Willingham's case. Grann's essay thus reminds us that conversations about justice are ongoing. Using the internet or the library's databases, find out where the investigation into Willingham's possible innocence stands now.

Ashraf Rushdy is chair of the African American Studies Program and a professor of English at Wesleyan University in Connecticut. He is the author of The Empty Garden, *a study of Milton, and* Neo-Slave Narratives, *on the African American novel since the 1960s. In this essay, published in 2000 in the journal* Transition, *Rushdy explores how graphic photos of lynching victim Emmett Till were used in the effort to expose and fight injustice. And he suggests that "images of terror—used responsibly—can foster a climate in which terror is no longer tolerated."*

EXQUISITE CORPSE   Ashraf H. A. Rushdy

In an earlier time, a lynch mob would display the body of its victim with impunity, often gathering around it for a group photograph. These images, and the bodies they represented, were the icons of white supremacy. Circulated in newspapers, the pictures displayed the power of the white mob and the powerlessness of the black community. After the highly publicized lynching of Claude Neal in 1934, photographers took hundreds of shots of his mutilated body and sold them for fifty cents each. The photograph of Neal's hanging body eventually became a postcard. One group of white people, gathered around a burned black body, was communicating to another group in another county: they had done their part, asserted their place in the world. The image was certain to incite other communities to follow their example: this was the golden age of lynching.

The body of the victim assumed a magical quality for the lynch mob: the corpse was an object to be tortured, mutilated, collected, displayed. To snuff out life was rarely enough: more ritual was required. In 1937, when a Georgia mob was unable to lynch Willie Reid because the police had already killed him, they broke into the funeral home where he lay, carried his body to a baseball diamond, and burned it. Even a mob that had already hanged, maimed, and burned a man might still feel compelled to exhume his body in order to inflict further indignities; so it was with the corpse of George Armwood, in 1933.

As the historian Jacquelyn Dowd Hall has noted, the spectacle of lynching dramatized a social hierarchy where whites and blacks, women and men, knew their place. Blacks were terrorized, white women were vulnerable, and white men were on top, invulnerable and free. Still, whites projected immense sexual power onto blacks; the terror of lynching reflected their own anxieties. Indeed lynching also seems to be the expression of a peculiar necrophilia, manifest in the desire to possess the bodies of victims, in the passion with which dead bodies were handled and displayed—as if they were talismans of life itself. The East Texas lynch mob that killed David Gregory in 1933 pulled out his heart and cut off his penis before tossing his body onto a pyre: those were the most potent emblems of vitality. Such actions bespeak nothing so much as a perverse fondness for the dead body.

While lynch mobs subjected the corpses of their victims to the most spectacular abuse, victims' families were more concerned with matters of the spirit. Most often they buried their loved ones in silence: for these families, the corpse was less important than the soul.

The same can be said of those families who refused to bury lynch victims. In 1889, after a mob broke into a Barnwell, South Carolina, jail and lynched eight African American men, the local black community displayed its solidarity at the funeral. More than five hundred people lined the street, and several women implored the Lord to "burn Barnwell to the ground." The community refused to bury six of the men, claiming that the whites who killed them should bear that responsibility. In Virginia, Joseph McCoy's aunt refused to bury the body of her nephew, who was lynched in 1897. "As the people killed him, they will have to bury him," she explained. The body, whether buried or left to the elements, had become a symbol of the injustice and barbarism of the white community, the failure of the nation's founding principles: Let the dead bury their dead.

* * *

When Emmett Till was lynched in 1955, Mamie Till Bradley refused to hide her son's corpse. His mutilated and decomposed body was found in the Tallahatchie River three days after he died. Despite the sheriff's opposition, she insisted that her son be returned to Chicago. Bradley opened the casket as soon as it arrived at Illinois Central terminal, and promptly announced that she wanted an open-casket funeral so everyone could "see what they did to my boy." On the first day the casket was open for viewing, ten thousand people saw it; on the day of the funeral, at least two thousand mourners stood outside the packed church where the services were held. The body of Emmett Till—"his head ... swollen and bashed in, his mouth twisted and broken"—became a new kind of icon. Emmett Till showed the world exactly what white supremacy looked like.

According to one report, Till's funeral created an "emotional explosion": "thousands of cursing, shrieking, fainting Negroes" responded to the "corpse ... displayed 'as is.'" The Southern media denounced Bradley's decision as "macabre exhibitionism" and cheap political "exploitation." But African Americans who attended the funeral or saw pictures of Till's body were transformed. One reader congratulated the *Amsterdam News* for "putting the picture of the murdered Till boy on the front page"; a writer for the *Pittsburgh Courier* predicted that Mrs. Bradley's decision might "easily become the opening gun in a war on Dixie which can reverberate around the world." A photo-essay in *Jet* magazine proved electrifying: Representative Charles Diggs remarked that the "picture in *Jet* magazine showing Emmett Till's mutilation ... stimulated ... anger on the part of blacks all over the country." A black sociologist later wrote that "the *Jet* magazine photograph of Emmett Till's grotesque body left an indelible impression on young Southern blacks"; they went on to become "the vanguard of the Southern student movement."

The influence of the *Jet* magazine photographs has been well documented. As a girl, civil rights activist Joyce Ladner kept clippings in a scrapbook. She responded to the picture of Till's bloated body in *Jet* magazine "with horror that transformed itself into a promise to alter the political and racial terrain where such a crime could happen." Cleveland Sellers, an activist and field director in the Student Nonviolent Coordinating Committee, remembers how pictures of the corpse in black newspapers and magazines—showing "terrible gashes and tears in the flesh ... the appearance of a ragged, rotting sponge"—created a stir about civil rights when he was a youth in South Carolina. A thirteen-year-old boy named Cassius Clay stood on a street corner in Louisville, transfixed by pictures of Emmett Till in black newspapers and magazines: in one picture, smiling and happy; in the other, a gruesome mockery of a face. Muhammad Ali says he admired Mrs. Bradley, who had "done a bold thing" in forcing the world to look at her son. Fifteen years later, Ali met Brother Judge Aaron, a man who had survived a Klan lynching attempt in the 1960s. (They had carved the letters "KKK" into his chest and castrated him to send a "message" to "smart-alecky ... niggers like Martin Luther King and Reverend Shuttleworth.") Ali responded by dedicating all his future fights to "the unprotected people, to the victims."

* * *

By the time of Emmett Till's murder, lynching had begun to decline, and pictures of lynching victims were becoming scarce. What had once been viewed with pride now seemed like barbarity: the victim's body became less an icon of white supremacy than a denunciation of it. As popular opinion turned against lynching, the sight of lynched bodies became an embarrassment for white communities squirming under the glare of national and international scrutiny. In fact, these corpses became potent weapons in the political struggle to enact a law against lynching—a struggle that continues today.

The 1959 murder of Mack Charles Parker was representative of this new climate. The lynch mob wore masks to hide the identity of its members; they gave up on their original plan to castrate their victim and hang the body from a bridge: instead, they weighted the body and dumped it into the river. When Parker's body was recovered ten days later, town officials worked furiously to keep it from being entered as evidence before the Senate during deliberations on anti-lynching legislation. Police officers and state troopers guarded the body in a funeral home, and after *Chicago Defender* reporter Tony Rhoden managed to sneak in and take a picture of the badly mutilated body, there was a frantic search for him and his camera. Two hours after the coroner's inquest, before Parker's mother had even heard that his body had been recovered, he was buried in a hasty ceremony.

It is not clear what happened to Rhoden's photograph of Parker's body. If it was not published, it might have been because of the censorship that has restrained mainstream photojournalism in times of extremity. *Life* magazine had to wait eight months while government censors debated whether it could publish a picture of a dead American soldier on Buna Beach, New Guinea, in 1943. While pictures of dead bodies were widely published during the Vietnam War, a *Detroit Free Press* photographer had to beg military censors to approve a photograph of an American soldier crying over a body bag during the Persian Gulf War. And even in the absence of official censorship, Americans' delicate sensibilities have prevented the widespread dissemination of gruesome pictures. A *New York Times* reader wrote an angry letter to complain about a photograph of a Kosovo massacre victim in October 1998. His brief comment—"This is not something I wish to see alongside my breakfast"—aptly characterizes a reading public that does not expect graphic violence in the responsible media.

* * *

In June 1998 an African American man named James Byrd was murdered in Jasper, Texas, by a white ex-con named John William King and two accomplices. It was determined that Byrd's body had been dragged from a pickup truck and that the body had been dismembered along the route: the head, neck, and right arm were severed from the torso. During King's trial in February 1999, the prosecution presented photographs that documented Byrd's suffering: his knees, heels, buttocks, and elbows were ground to the bone; eight of his left ribs and nine of his right were broken; his ankles were cut to the bone by the chains that attached him to the truck. A pathologist testified that Byrd's "penis and testicles [were] shredded from his body," and we learned, with horror, that "Mr. Byrd was alive up to the point where he hit the culvert and his head separated from his body." For months, the story of James Byrd's brutal slaying transfixed the nation.

No picture of James Byrd's corpse has ever been published. Indeed, when the *New York Times* interviewed several editors for a story on newspaper photography, none had seen the prosecution's photographs. In a strange twist of fate, however, King's own body served as evidence in the state's case against him: it seems he had a passion for racist tattoos. Prosecutors showed thirty-three slides and photographs of the images inscribed on King's body: a cross with a black man hanging from it, a swastika, the insignia of Hitler's SS, a woodpecker peeking out from a Ku Klux Klan hood, the Virgin Mary holding a horned baby Jesus, images of Church, of Satan founder Anton La Vey, goat heads, Valentine hearts turned upside down, playing cards showing eights and aces (the dead man's poker hand), a dragon emblazoned with the words "Beto I" (the Texas prison where King was incarcerated from 1995 to 1997), the slogan "Aryan Pride," and several allusions to "peckerwoods"—rednecks—in prison. (It had been reported earlier that King had a tattoo of Tinkerbell on his penis; the D.A. declined to mention this.) It was King's body, not Byrd's, that became an advertisement for white supremacy, and judging by the John William King tribute pages that have sprung up on the Internet, the advertisement has been successful.

It is not likely that anyone other than the lawyers, the jury, and the courtroom spectators will ever see the photographs that the court accepted as evidence. In the only well-known image of Byrd, he is wearing a Colorado Rockies baseball cap, looking directly into the camera. The most graphic picture appeared on the cover of the Boston Globe on June 12, 1998: it showed the dried blood that stained the Jasper street where Byrd's torso had been dragged.

The Byrd family was singularly gracious in promoting reconciliation and defusing racial hatred in the aftermath of the murder, and it may have been out of respect for their feelings that photographs of James Byrd's body were not published. Indeed, for about six weeks after the murder, the major story in Jasper was the tension between the Byrd family's desire for privacy and activists' eagerness for publicity. Even as reporters set up a media circus around the funeral, they wrote compassionately of the pain that politicians and political advocacy groups created for the Byrds. When the Klan gathered for a rally to distance themselves from John William King and his cohorts, and the Dallas-based New Black Panthers gathered to respond to the Klan, the Byrd family tried to remain above the fray. As the *Houston Chronicle* reported, "Byrd's family was uncomfortable with the idea of turning him into a national symbol, and would have preferred to have had a quieter service without the political rallying cries."

Despite these pleas, this case demanded national attention. In newspaper stories that pit a grieving family wishing for peace and quiet against a flock of politically motivated vultures intent on creating a self-serving spectacle, the true complexity of the Jasper saga is lost. It is despicable, of course, to use Byrd's funeral to promote racism, as the Klan did; and it is wrongheaded to use the event to promote armed self-defense, as the New Black Panthers did. But there are other considerations—considerations that are at least as compelling as a family's grief. Those who attempted to situate the murder in its historical context, while respecting the family's wishes for a degree of privacy, should be praised.

At James Byrd's funeral, Jesse Jackson said that "Brother Byrd's innocent blood alone could very well be the blood that changes the course of our country, because no one has captured the nation's attention like this tragedy." Jackson asked the town of Jasper to erect a monument in Byrd's memory, "as a tangible protest against hate crimes." I applaud Jackson's sense of urgency, but his proposal is in the wrong tenor. Indeed, I would suggest that Jackson went wrong precisely when he departed from his insight: spilled blood is a valuable representation of the search for justice. In his resolve to create a monument, he shifted his focus from blood to image, from body to stone.

* * *

The connections between the Till and Byrd lynchings are striking. Part of the evidence against King was an *Esquire* magazine article on the Till lynching that he had kept in his apartment: this suggested that his actions were premeditated. Mamie Till Bradley spoke about the Jasper murder on a New York radio talk show; two weeks later, she held the hand of James Byrd's father at a Harlem memorial service. There were some coincidences, too: after the trial of Till's lynchers, newspapers reported that Till's father had been hanged in 1944, after he was convicted of rape and murder while stationed in Italy with the Army; after the trial in the Jasper case, it was revealed that John William King's uncle had been acquitted of killing a gay man in 1939. More than half a century of hate crimes has ensnared these families—the Tills, the Byrds, the Kings—in America's quiet history of guilt and grief.

But there are disparities. In 1955, the American public learned about Emmett Till's life and they saw his death: the contrast between a vibrant youth and a violent end helped ignite the outcry that followed. In 1998, even as contemporary readers learned about James Byrd's life, they were denied the pictures that might have inspired a greater and more productive outrage. On February 24, 1999, the same day the *New York Times* reported the jury's verdict in the Jasper trial, it ran two other stories about hate crimes: in Virginia, a jury convicted a white teenager of burning a cross on the lawn of an interracial couple; and in Louisiana, a white man was sentenced to twenty years in prison for trying to set fire to two cars and their African American occupants. Hatred is far more pervasive than we would like to admit, and representations of it are critical to the education of the majority of white Americans who believe that racism was a phenomenon that ended sometime in the sixties.

Of course, publishing pictures of James Byrd's corpse might fan the flames of white supremacy. There were reports of copycat crimes within a week of Byrd's murder: in Louisiana, where three white men taunted a black man with racial epithets while trying to drag him alongside their car; and in Illinois, where three white boys assaulted a black teenager in almost exactly the same way. Three months later, New York City police officers and firefighters parodied Byrd's murder by imitating it in a Labor Day parade float. And while the trial was underway, a Washington, D.C., radio announcer—the "Greaseman"—responded to a clip from a song by soul singer Lauryn Hill by commenting, "No wonder people drag them behind trucks." (He was fired the next day.) In a climate where people still respond to lynching with jokes and mimicry, pictures of James Byrd's body might have fed this evil appetite.

So why do we need to see the corpse? It is possible that pictures of graphic violence still have the power to make an impression. At least one member of the jury found the pictures of Byrd's body almost unbearable; she had to force herself to turn each page. Indeed, one Jasper resident suggested that the lynchers should be sentenced to life in a cell "with pictures of James Byrd's body parts pasted all over the walls"—expressing the hope that even the murderers would find such images sickening. This kind of shock therapy might work for the public at large. It would have been difficult for policemen and firemen in New York, or a DJ in Washington, to joke about the murder of James Byrd if their jokes summoned images of the horrific crimes they were taking so lightly.

These photographs could also turn the tides of history once again. African American men have long been portrayed as comic buffoons or dangerous criminals, and a large segment of this nation remains incapable of imagining black suffering. A study concerning the effects of race on the death penalty found that there is "neither strong nor consistent" evidence of discrimination against black defendants in death penalty trials. But the study also concluded that the race of the victim matters greatly in juries' decisions to sentence a murderer to death. Convicted murderers who kill a white victim are more than four times as likely to be condemned to death as those who kill a black victim. Only eight whites have been executed for murdering black Americans since the death penalty was reinstated in 1977, but 123 blacks have been put to death for murdering whites. Predominantly white juries seem unable to sympathize with black crime victims. It is possible that this crime, fixed in memory, could transform the nation's moral imagination.

To have wounded the Byrd family any more would have been intolerable; and pictures of their relative's body would have wounded them. To have created conditions that satisfied the blood lust of white supremacists would have been criminal; and photographs of the remains of James Byrd would have given them glee. To lower the already low level of public discourse would be shameful; and publishing more photographs of violence is not likely to elevate it. But our primary concern must be to prevent another family from feeling as the Byrd family now feels; we cannot determine how best to combat hatred by focusing on the response of the most incorrigible purveyors of hatred. The past teaches us that images of terror—used responsibly—can foster a climate in which terror is no longer tolerated. I suggest that we aspire to the courageous example of Mamie Till Bradley, not the cautious compromises of newspaper editors who fear to offend their readerships. A citizenry alert to the horror of hate crimes would be compensation enough.

■ READING AND WRITING

1. What is Rushdy's claim? What kind of evidence does he present to support his claim? Do you think his argument is effective? Explain why or why not.

2. After murdering David Gregory in 1933, a white mob mutilated the corpse in ways that Rushdy argues "bespeak nothing so much as a perverse fondness for the dead body." In what sense do you think Rushdy means "fondness," since he obviously doesn't mean the word in its usual sense? Are there other ways that we might interpret the mob's highly symbolic (but also horribly real) mutilation of Gregory?

3. Many cultural commentators—including Elie Wiesel, in "Am I My Brother's Keeper?"— argue that our easy access to images of horror and devastation can lead to weariness and desensitization. Rushdy makes no acknowledgment of this possibility, suggesting that a display of James Byrd's tortured corpse might have lead to a "[g]reater and more productive outrage" against racism. One way to synthesize these two positions—Wiesel's and Rushdy's—would be by looking again at Rushdy's suggestion that the images be used "responsibly" and clarifying what this means. How could a newspaper editor use these images in a responsible way? What would qualify as responsible use of these images by an organization devoted to fighting racism, such as the NAACP or the Southern Poverty Law Center? What would constitute an irresponsible use of such images?

■ USING RESEARCH

4. In the spring of 2009, the Pentagon lifted a ban on video and photos of the caskets of fallen troops returning to domestic soil, a prohibition that had been in place since 1991. Research news databases or websites to find out what the new policy is, why the ban was put in place in 1991, and the reasoning behind the change. How might Rushdy's argument about the responsible use of disturbing images apply in this situation?

IMAGE 5.2: A graffiti artist's commentary on the state of the world: "Sad Bear looked at the world and did not like what he saw." Most of the readings in this chapter either state or imply that we are obligated to make the world a better place. Do you agree with this position? Do you think it is feasible?

> *Jeremy Kahn is an independent journalist who writes about international affairs, politics, business, the environment and the arts. His work has appeared in many media outlets, including* Newsweek International, The New York Times, The New Republic, Slate, *and* The Atlantic, *where this article was published in April 2007.*

THE STORY OF A SNITCH   Jeremy Kahn

John Dowery Jr. was happy to be working again. He had recently spent 11 months cooped up, a prisoner in his own home. In November 2003, two officers investigating the sound of gunfire in East Baltimore had arrested him after a car and foot chase. They said that Dowery, who had been riding in the back of a blue Mitsubishi, had jumped out of the car, placed a loaded .38-caliber handgun on the ground, and tried to flee. A 36-year-old heroin addict with a felony drug conviction, Dowery was facing federal prosecution and the prospect of up to eight years without parole. While he awaited trial, he had been "put on the box"—confined to his house, his whereabouts monitored by a transmitter locked around his ankle.

Staring down almost a decade behind bars can change a man, make him long for a second chance. And now it seemed Dowery had been given one. In October 2004, he had cut a deal, agreeing to become a witness in a murder trial. In exchange for his testimony, and as a result of good behavior, the feds had eased the terms of his pretrial detention. He had entered a drug-treatment program and landed a job working the graveyard shift at a condiment factory in the suburbs. For the first time in years, he was clean and sober, and life was looking up.

Each night, Dowery rode the commuter rail from the city to the plant; each morning, he rode it home again. He didn't mind the odd hours; having worked as a baker, he was accustomed to being nocturnal. Shortly after dawn on October 19, 2005, he got off the train as usual. It was a brisk morning, with clouds dappling the sky but no hint of rain. He decided to skip the bus and walk the mile to his house on Bartlett Avenue.

He ambled past the massive Board of Education building, with its columns, and headed down North Avenue to Greenmount Cemetery. There he turned left, passing the abandoned row houses where the "corner boys" were already opening for business, hoping to find a junkie in need of a morning fix. Farther on, past still-shuttered hair salons and check-cashing outfits, he turned down East 24th toward Bartlett. Just after seven o'clock, he reached his front porch and called out for his girlfriend, Yolanda, to let him in. Then he sensed something behind him.

He spun around to find two men dressed in black standing in his small front yard. One held a gun. As Dowery scrambled for his neighbor's porch, the man pulled the trigger. Dowery leaped from the porch and raced around the side of his house, the two men close behind him, the gunman firing the whole way. He managed to stagger through his back door before his legs gave out. The attackers, believing their work accomplished, took off. A neighbor would later tell police that she heard one of them say, "We busted his motherfucking ass."

Dowery had been shot in the back and in both arms and legs—six times in all. Only the skilled hands of the surgeons at Johns Hopkins spared his life. And yet, in the eyes of many people in the blocks around Bartlett, John Dowery had gotten what was coming to him.

*****

In many Baltimore neighborhoods, talking to the law has become a mortal sin, a dishonorable act punishable by social banishment—or worse. Prosecutors in the city can rattle off a litany of brutal retaliations: houses firebombed, witnesses and their relatives shot, contract hits on 10-year-olds. Witness intimidation, they say, badly hampers their ability to fight crime, and it affects nearly every murder case they try.

Prosecutors in most major U.S. cities tell similar stories. Two years ago in Philadelphia, a drug kingpin was convicted of witness intimidation after he was taped threatening to kill those who testified against him. Five relatives of one witness in the case had already died, in a house fire that prosecutors believe was the drug lord's doing. Last year in San Francisco, two gang members beat a murder rap after the state's star witness turned up dead. Several years ago in Denver, a key homicide witness was sexually assaulted in what prosecutors believe was a "contract" attack designed to frighten him out of testifying.

Police and prosecutors have been contending with reluctant witnesses for decades. But according to law-enforcement experts, the problem is getting dramatically worse, and is reflected in falling arrest and conviction rates for violent crimes. In cities with populations between half a million (for example, Tucson) and a million (Detroit), the proportion of violent crimes cleared by an arrest dropped from about 45 percent in the late 1990s to less than 35 percent in 2005, according to the FBI. Conviction rates have similarly dropped. At the same time, crime has spiked. Murder rates have risen more or less steadily since 2000. Last December, the FBI voiced concern over a jump in violent crime, which in 2005 showed its biggest increase in more than a decade.

The reasons for witnesses' reluctance appear to be changing and becoming more complex, with the police confronting a new cultural phenomenon: the spread of the gangland code of silence, or omertá, from organized crime to the population at large. Those who cooperate with the police are labeled "snitches" or "rats"—terms once applied only to jailhouse informants or criminals who turned state's evidence, but now used for "civilian" witnesses as well. This is particularly true in the inner cities, where gangsta culture has been romanticized through rap music and other forms of entertainment, and where the motto "Stop snitching," expounded in hip-hop lyrics and emblazoned on caps and T-shirts, has become a creed.

The metastasis of this culture of silence in minority communities has been facilitated by a gradual breakdown of trust in the police and the government. The erosion began during the civil-rights era, when informants were a favorite law-enforcement tool against groups like the Black Panthers. But it accelerated because of the war on drugs. David Kennedy, the director of the Center for Crime Prevention and Control at the John Jay

College of Criminal Justice, in New York, told me: "This is the reward we have reaped for 20 years of profligate drug enforcement in these communities." When half the young black men in a neighborhood are locked up, on bail, or on parole, the police become the enemy. Add to this the spread of racialized myths—that crack was created by the CIA to keep blacks in their place, for example—and you get a toxic mix. Kennedy thinks the silence of many witnesses doesn't come from fear, but from anger.

The growing culture of silence helps to legitimize witness intimidation. At the same time, criminals have become more adept at enforcing the code, using increasingly sophisticated methods to bribe, intimidate, and harm witnesses. Defendants and their surrogates have obtained witnesses' supposedly confidential grand-jury testimony and tacked it to their doors, along with threatening notes. They have adopted new technology like cell-phone cameras and text-messaging to spread the word about who is snitching; threats have even been text-messaged to the phones of sequestered witnesses. And every incident in which a witness is assaulted or murdered heightens the climate of fear and mistrust—the sense that the law either can't or won't protect ordinary people.

*****

On October 13, 2004, a year before he was shot while returning home from work, John Dowery was still electronically shackled to his house. Sometime after 3 p.m. that day, he looked out his front window and saw his friend James Wise coming up the street. Dowery and Wise, whom everyone called Jay, shared a love of basketball—and of heroin. Today Jay was with a younger man Dowery didn't recognize. They stopped outside the chain-link fence around Dowery's front yard. Jay called to Dowery, then came up to the door. He seemed nervous. He wanted Dowery's advice.

Jay said the other man had a gun. They were planning to rob an old drug dealer named Reds, who operated from a vacant lot a few doors down. Dowery told him it was a bad idea. At 40, Jay was no innocent, but neither was he an experienced stickup artist. Even if the two men could pull off the robbery, stickup boys in East Baltimore don't usually live long: On the street, robbing a dealer is a capital offense. "I told him basically not to do it," Dowery would later say. "But he ain't listen."

Dowery looked on from his front door as the two men walked down the street and entered the "cut" where Reds worked. He watched a flock of dope fiends suddenly flee the alley, like ducks flushed from the reeds. Seconds later, Reds darted out too. Then Jay and his partner emerged and raced down the street.

The two had timed their escape poorly. Sauntering up the street just then was Tracy Love, an athletic 20-year-old with cornrows and a meticulously trimmed beard and mustache, whom everyone knew as "Boo-Boo." Prosecutors later alleged that Boo-Boo oversaw the Bartlett Avenue drug operation. Jay and his accomplice brushed right past him. As Dowery watched, Boo-Boo pivoted and began to follow them down the hill.

Fifteen minutes later, Dowery heard the wail of police sirens and the thump-thump of a helicopter overhead. Boo-Boo strode back up Bartlett with his younger half-brother, Tamall Parker, who went by "Moo-Moo." "I got that motherfucker, six times in the chest," Dowery later recalled Boo-Boo shouting—ostensibly to his crew down the street, but loudly enough that anyone out on the block could hear. "Next time, one of y'all gonna do it. I'm tired of doing this shit."

According to police and prosecutors, this is what happened after Jay and his partner, a man police would identify as Joseph Bassett, robbed Reds and left Bartlett Avenue: Boo-Boo went to find Moo-Moo. They got into a white Lexus with sparkling chrome hubcaps and began cruising the neighborhood, hunting for Jay and Bassett. Unaware they were being pursued, Jay and Bassett met up with a couple of prostitutes a few blocks away. Jay knew one of them, Doris Dickerson. He told her about the robbery and offered her drugs. She said she would catch up with him in a minute, and walked into an alley. Bassett also left for a few minutes. Just as Doris and Jay were about to meet back up, at the corner of Bonaparte and Robb, Boo-Boo and Moo-Moo spotted Jay. Boo-Boo let Moo-Moo out of the car, then drove around the corner and waited. Moo-Moo tugged the hood of his sweatshirt up around his face, approached Jay, and pulled out a 9-mm handgun. He opened up, firing at least 13 times. The bullets punched holes in Jay's chest and abdomen; at least one smashed into his skull.

James Sylvester Wise Jr. was dead—the 229th murder of the year in a city that would rack up 278 by the end of December. Although 10 people called 911 to report the shooting, many refused to give their names. Six told the emergency operators that they did not want to talk to the police when they arrived. One caller, John Craddock, said he had seen a man running down the street and jumping into a white Lexus. He could not see the man's face, but he thought he could make out part of the license plate—a blue-and-white temporary tag with the numbers 3, 4, and 9. Police dispatchers put out a description of the car, but to no avail. Officers canvassed the block but turned up no additional witnesses or information. None of the three who knew the most about the killing—Dowery, Bassett, or Dickerson—came forward.

*****

A man gunned down on a busy street. No identifying witnesses; no suspects. In this, James Wise's murder was typical. Colonel Frederick Bealefeld III, Baltimore's chief of detectives, says the police used to be able to rely on people's consciences and sense of civic duty to generate leads in murder investigations. But today, few witnesses are willing to offer information, even anonymously. "How hard is it for someone to get on the phone and say … 'The guy who shot up this block—it is wrong, here's who that person is'?" Bealefeld asks. "Yet we don't get a ton of those kinds of calls. And if we graphed it out, if we tracked it over the years, you would see a very clear decline."

A 26-year veteran of the force and the grandson of a cop, Bealefeld has seen these changes firsthand. His grandfather walked a beat on Greenmount Avenue, not far from Bartlett. In 30 years with the department, he fired his gun exactly once in the line of duty. "No way he could walk that beat and do that now," Bealefeld says. "He took it for granted that the community respected him. Today's police can't take that for granted." By the time Bealefeld joined the force, in 1980, things had become much more dangerous for both the police and the citizens of Baltimore. But during the '80s, working narcotics, he could still find confidential informants with relative ease. Over time, that too started to change.

Bealefeld says he does not want to underestimate the fear people feel on the streets, or their lack of trust in the law. But he thinks witness intimidation has also become a cover for indifference. "How do I separate your intransigence to take part in a civic responsibility, and a moral responsibility, from your alleged fear?" he asks, the anger rising in his voice. "'I am not doing it, because I am afraid'—that is easy to say. You may not be doing it because you are a jerk and don't care about anybody but yourself and have no love for your fellow man."

Bealefeld is right that disentangling fear from other factors is not easy. But when I spoke with people in the blocks near where James Wise was murdered, it was the fear that was most palpable. "Round here it's not a good idea to talk to the police," Jacob Smith, a thoughtful 13-year-old walking home from school in East Baltimore, told me. "People, they like, if they know you talk to the police, they don't be around you. And if people talk on them and they get locked up, their friends come up on you and hurt you or something." (The ostracism and retaliation he spoke of got wide airing as a plotline last season in HBO's *The Wire*, set in Baltimore and created by David Simon, a former crime reporter, and Ed Burns, a former police officer: A teenager thought by his peers to have snitched was beaten, and eventually his house was firebombed.)

All over Baltimore, whenever I asked people about cooperating with the law, I got the same response. "Why would you talk to the police? All you are doing is putting a label on yourself," said Barry Nelson, a 42-year-old part-time handyman who was waiting for a meal from a charity the day I met him. "They ain't going to be back to protect you after you done told on some cats." Randolph Jones, a retiree who was sweeping leaves from the sidewalk in front of his house in Northwest Baltimore, said he would call the police if something happened on his block. But the drug dealing and shootings on the next block over? He won't pick up the phone. Jones said the police try, but as soon as they arrest one corner boy, another moves in. "You got to live here, and the police can't do much," he said. "You don't want to end up like that family in East Baltimore, the Dawsons."

The Dawsons come up in almost every conversation about reluctant witnesses in Baltimore. Angela Dawson had tried to shoo drug dealers away from the sidewalk outside the East Baltimore row house where she lived with her husband, Carnell, and their five children. She had frequently called the police. The dealers decided to strike back. In October 2002, the Dawsons' house was firebombed. Angela Dawson and all her children were killed in the blaze; Carnell Dawson died in the hospital a week later. A drug dealer named Darrell Brooks was convicted of the crime and is serving life without parole. But the sentence has done little to reassure potential witnesses. More than four years later, the Dawsons still haunt the city.

*****

John Dowery knew Boo-Boo and Moo-Moo had shot someone; he prayed that it wasn't Jay, that it was the other guy. But the next day's newspaper confirmed his fear about his friend. Jay's death shook Dowery. But it also made him more determined to get his life back on track. And in the tragedy of his friend's murder, Dowery sensed opportunity. If he told the police what he knew about the killing, perhaps he could get a lighter sentence on his gun charge. On the other hand, talking was dangerous: If Boo-Boo and Moo-Moo found out, they might come after him or his family. So Dowery struggled with the decision. A day went by, then a week. Then he picked up the phone and called his public defender.

On October 27, Dowery, along with his lawyer and the prosecutor handling his gun charge, met with Michael Baier, the Baltimore homicide detective assigned to Jay's murder. Dowery told Baier what he knew about the killing. He also said that Boo-Boo and Moo-Moo, who were still hanging around Bartlett, had ditched their distinctive white Lexus. His statement provided a crucial break in the case.

Another break came the following week, when Joseph Bassett, Jay's accomplice, was busted selling heroin to undercover cops. With his long rap sheet, Bassett knew he was in trouble. He tried offering up an illegal .32 he kept at home, in the hope that the officers would let him go in exchange for getting the gun off the street. When that failed, he said he might know something about a murder on Bonaparte. The officers brought Bassett downtown to homicide, where he told Baier about robbing Reds. He also said he had seen two men in a white Lexus circling the block, and that he saw the car stop and a man get out and shoot Jay. Baier showed him a photo lineup. Bassett identified Tracy Love as the driver of the car and Tamall Parker as the shooter.

Parker and Love were picked up two days later. Baier had several other pieces of evidence: The two suspects' mother had recently returned to the dealership a white Lexus with the temporary license tag 38491L. Video from a warehouse surveillance camera near the murder scene had captured what appeared to be a white Lexus circling the block in the minutes before Jay was killed. An analysis of Love's cell phone records determined that the phone had not left East Baltimore that day, a finding that directly contradicted Love and Parker's alibi: They said they had spent the day in their mother's hair salon, in West Baltimore.

Baier did not have a confession or a murder weapon, however. So at trial, a lot would depend on the testimony of Dowery and Bassett—convicted felons who had come forward at least in part because they were facing charges themselves. Eventually they would be joined by a third witness, also in trouble with the law: Doris Dickerson, picked up for prostitution, told police that she was heading toward Jay when she heard shots. She saw Jay fall to the ground and Moo-Moo run away. She too identified Parker as the killer from a photo lineup.

Witnesses of this sort would once have made a prosecutor blanch. Now, they are usually all prosecutors have. One problem with such witnesses is that defense attorneys can use their records to attack their credibility. The fewer witnesses the state has and the more a defense attorney expects to be able to discredit them, the more likely she is to advise her client against a plea bargain. This means more cases go to trial, at significant expense to the state. And at trial, there is a decent chance—in Baltimore, about 50 percent in a nonfatal shooting, and 38 percent in a murder—that the defendant will walk.

Witnesses in the drug trade are also highly susceptible to being coerced into changing their stories or not showing up in court. If a witness goes missing, his prior statements generally aren't admissible. And a witness who "backs up"—legal slang for recanting—can create doubt, including reasonable doubt, in the minds of jurors.

Not surprisingly, defense attorneys have a different take. Elizabeth Julian, Baltimore's chief public defender, believes the problems of witness intimidation are overstated. She told me that the real issue is police tactics that encourage suspects to lie about their knowledge of other crimes, and she pointed out that it is perfectly legal for police to mislead potential witnesses into thinking they won't have to testify in court. "If you are being asked, and you are getting a 'Get Out of Jail Free' card tonight, people take it. That's human nature," she says. In her view, many witnesses who back up are telling the truth on the stand. It's their initial statements that were false—either outright fabrications or some mixture of fact and rumor. Julian jokes that the word on the street, rather than "Stop snitching," ought to be "Stop lying."

*****

As it happened, Dowery decided to become a witness—just as witness intimidation in the city was about to explode into a national story. The spark was an underground DVD titled *Stop Fucking Snitching* that began circulating in Baltimore in November 2004. In it Rodney Thomas, a rapper known locally as Skinny Suge, talks about what he thinks should happen to informants: "To all you snitches and rats … I hope you catch AIDS in your mouth, and your lips the first thing to die, yo bitch." The DVD also includes numerous segments in which young men on the street rail against snitches.

In its subject matter, the DVD was more evolution than revolution. The slogan "Stop snitching" had been around since at least 1999, when it was popularized by the Boston rapper Tangg da Juice. The video would have remained a local curiosity except for one thing: It includes a cameo by Carmelo Anthony, a Baltimore native who became an NBA star with the Denver Nuggets. Anthony appears in only six of the film's 108 minutes, and spends most of that time poking fun at a former coach and a rival player. As he later told *The Baltimore Sun*, "I was back on my block, chillin'. I was going back to show love to everybody, thinking it was just going to be on the little local DVD, that it was just one of my homeboys recording." But his celebrity, combined with the DVD's charged subject matter, created a sensation.

For Baltimore's police, prosecutors, and judges, eager to raise awareness about witness intimidation, *Stop Fucking Snitching* was a gift. "Think how bold criminals must be to make a DVD," Baltimore Circuit Judge John M. Glynn told the local press. "It shows that threatening snitches has become mainstream." Patricia Jessamy, the state's attorney for Baltimore, had hundreds of copies made and distributed them to politicians and the national media. The publicity helped her win passage of a tougher witness-intimidation law, one the Maryland legislature had voted down the year before. The police department made a show of arresting the DVD's stars, including a man accused of carrying out contract killings, and created its own video, *Keep Talking*, to encourage future witnesses to come forward.

Stop Fucking Snitching was produced by Rodney Bethea, a 33-year-old barber and entrepreneur. I met him in his small West Baltimore store, One Love Underground, which pulls double duty as a barbershop and a boutique from which he sells his own line of urban fashions. Bethea told me the authorities and media had misinterpreted the DVD. It was not intended to encourage violence against witnesses, he said; he had simply set out to make a freestyle documentary, and snitching happened to emerge as a major theme. He also said that the term snitch has a very specific meaning on the streets and in the video. "They are referring to people that are engaged in illegal activities, making a profit from it, and then when it comes time for the curtains to close—you do the crime, you do the time—now no one wants to go to jail," he told me, pulling on his goatee. "That is considered a snitch. The old lady that lives on the block that call the police because guys are selling drugs in front of her house, she's not a snitch, because she is what would be considered a civilian."

Bethea believes there is a double standard—and perhaps a tinge of racism—in law enforcement's criticism of the "Stop snitching" culture. "When you think about it, I mean, who likes a snitch?" he said. "The government don't like a snitch. Their word for it is treason. What is the penalty for treason?" He pointed out that the police have their own code of silence, and that officers who break it by reporting police misconduct are stigmatized in much the same way as those who break the code of silence on the street.

Bethea's argument has a certain elegance. But the distinction he draws between the drug dealer who flips and the civilian who is just trying to get dealers off her stoop has ceased to mean much. Just ask the Dawsons. Or Edna McAbier, a community activist who tried to clean up drugs in her North Baltimore neighborhood. The local chapter of the Bloods considered blowing her head off with a shotgun but settled for firebombing her house, in January 2005—not long after *Stop Fucking Snitching* made news. McAbier escaped with her life, and her house was not badly damaged; those responsible received long prison sentences. But though the gang members didn't succeed in killing her, they did silence her: She left Baltimore out of fear for her safety. And the city got the message: If you break the code, you are in danger—even if you are a "civilian."

*****

By the time of the McAbier firebombing, John Dowery was starting to reap the rewards of his decision to testify in the state's prosecution of Tracy Love and Tamall Parker. His own trial had been postponed indefinitely. He had been released from home confinement, his drug-treatment program was going well, and he had started working.

So far, Baier had kept Dowery's name out of the investigative records, referring to him simply as "a Federal Suspect" and "the Source" so the state would not have to disclose him as a witness until closer to the trial date. He had also deferred taking a taped statement from Dowery, out of concern for his safety. These were sound precautions: On several occasions, prosecutors have intercepted "kites"—letters from a defendant, smuggled out of jail—detailing the prosecution's witness list and instructing friends or relatives to "talk" to those on it. But Baier could not keep Dowery's name a secret forever. Sooner or later, the government would have to tell defense lawyers that he was going to testify. In the meantime, suspicions about Dowery had already begun to circulate in the neighborhood. "Somebody approached me saying 'Yeah, you snitching on us,'" he told Baier.

The case against Love and Parker languished. A trial was set for early April 2005 and then postponed until May, and then postponed again, and then again—seven times in all. In Baltimore, as in most major U.S. cities, the large number of cases and the shortage of judges, courtrooms, and lawyers make such delays common. Some cases have been postponed more than 30 times and have dragged on for more than five years. And each postponement increases the risk that witnesses who were cooperative will cease to be so— that they will move and leave no forwarding address, change their stories, genuinely forget facts, or turn up dead. "The defense attorneys play this game," says Brian Matulonis, the lieutenant in charge of Baltimore's Homicide Operations Squad. "If the witness is not there, they are ready to go. If the witness is there, they ask for a postponement."

On May 20, 2005, Baier finally took a taped statement from Dowery. It was delivered to defense lawyers in June. Soon afterward, Dowery got a phone call from Love.

"That's fucked, man. Why you gonna do me like that?" the defendant seethed.

"I said I didn't know what he was talking about," Dowery would tell the jurors during the trial. "I was testifying the whole time. But I just act like I didn't know what he was talking about."

A few weeks later, Love called Dowery again. "He like, 'Man, other guy, he say he ain't gonna testify. What about you?'"

Dowery again played dumb. "I say, 'Man, he lied. I don't know whatcha talking about. You cool.'" Love seemed satisfied. "It was, like, a friendlier conversation the second time," Dowery would testify.

Dowery was nervous about the calls and about becoming known in the neighborhood as a snitch. But he didn't believe he was in immediate danger. The trial kept getting pushed back. Summer gave way to fall. Then came the morning when two men met him at his front door with a gun.

*****

One of Jessamy's primary weapons against witness intimidation is her office's witness-assistance program. Unlike the federal witness-protection program—the one most people know about from the movies—Baltimore's program can't provide marshals to guard witnesses around the clock for years. It can't offer witnesses a new identity in some distant city. Instead, the Baltimore program—run by a staff of two, with an annual budget of $500,000—tries to get witnesses out of harm's way by putting them in low-budget hotels that serve as temporary safe houses. The average stay is 90 days. The program also helps witnesses relocate permanently, generally within Maryland, providing a security deposit or first month's rent, moving costs, and vouchers for food and transportation. If necessary, it helps with job placement and drug treatment.

In most cases, this is enough to keep witnesses safe. Few Baltimore drug gangs have much reach beyond a couple of blocks, let alone outside the city. Still, many witnesses refuse the help. Almost a third of the 255 witnesses whom prosecutors referred to the program last year did not even come to an initial meeting. Of the 176 who did, only 36 entered safe housing. "Many of these people have never left their neighborhood," says Heather Courtney, a witness-assistance coordinator. "A lot of people can't handle it. They just can't be out of that neighborhood. That is all they know."

Even after the shooting, Dowery did not want to leave East Baltimore. He had spent his whole life there. His entire family—aunts, uncles, cousins—lived nearby, most on or near Bartlett. This included many of his nine children. In a neighborhood of absentee fathers, Dowery doted on his kids. Two of them lived with him and Yolanda. And he tried to stay involved in the lives of the others.

Eventually the witness coordinators prevailed upon Yolanda, who in turn convinced Dowery that they should leave. After less than two weeks in a hotel, Dowery, Yolanda, and their five-year-old daughter moved to a house outside the city. Most of his relatives remained in the old neighborhood.

*****

The trial of Tracy Love and Tamall Parker for the murder of James Wise began on January 26, 2006, in the cramped courtroom of Baltimore Circuit Judge Sylvester Cox. During opening arguments, Christopher Nosher, the boyish assistant state's attorney prosecuting the case, appeared confident. Although Judge Cox had barred any reference to the shooting attack on Dowery, ruling that the defendants had not been definitively linked to the incident, Dowery would be allowed to testify about the phone calls from Love. For Nosher, this was a coup: jurors can be instructed to interpret a threat against a witness as "consciousness of guilt." Evidence of intimidation can also help juries understand why witnesses may back up on the stand.

Nosher had another reason to be confident: He knew that all of his witnesses would show. John Craddock, the man who had caught three numbers of the Lexus's license plate, had never wavered during the long pretrial process. Bassett, Jay's accomplice, had been convicted of his drug charges and was serving a seven-year sentence, so he wasn't going anywhere. And both Dowery and Doris Dickerson had remained cooperative.

In this respect, the trial was unusual. Witnesses so commonly miss court dates in Baltimore, whether from fear or irresponsibility, that Jessamy's office has resorted to arresting them just to compel their appearance. Jessamy acknowledges that arresting witnesses is hardly ideal—it tends to make them hostile to the prosecution and more likely to back up, and it further sours police-community relations. "But if you've done everything you can to get them to come voluntarily, then you do what you have to do," she says.

That afternoon, Dowery took the stand. He had always been skinny, but in the witness box he looked gaunt. His long, loose-fitting black shirt covered a colostomy bag, a result of the October 2005 shooting. Dowery spoke in a deep, soft voice as Nosher walked him through the events he witnessed on the day James Wise was murdered.

As he began his testimony, a commotion electrified the hallway outside. Several friends of Boo-Boo and Moo-Moo tried to rush into the courtroom carrying cell phones, which they held near their thighs, fingers resting on the camera buttons. Detective Baier was also in the hall, awaiting his turn to testify. He spotted the cell phones and stepped in front of the men, barring their path to the door. "Whoa, you can't come in here," he told them. "It's a closed courtroom." This was not true, but it kept the men from entering. Then, for laughs, Baier took out his own cell phone and took pictures of them.

Incidents of intimidation at the courthouse are no longer aberrations. Gang members sometimes line the courthouse steps, forming a gantlet that witnesses and jurors must walk through. Family members of defendants have come to court wearing Stop Snitching

T-shirts and hats. In a Pittsburgh case last year, a key (though hostile) prosecution witness came to court in Stop Snitching gear. He was ejected because his garb was considered intimidating to other witnesses, and without his testimony, the district attorney dropped the charges. At the close of a Baltimore trial two years ago, jurors were so frightened of the defendants and of gang members in the gallery that the forewoman refused to read the guilty verdict aloud; so did another juror asked to do so by the judge. The judge eventually read the verdict herself and, as a precaution, had sheriff's deputies accompany the jurors out of the building.

*****

Dowery endured a withering cross-examination, but he escaped the stand largely undamaged. Nosher's two other eyewitnesses did not. Dickerson developed sudden memory loss, claiming not to recall key details of what she had seen. Then Love's lawyer got her to admit she was probably high on heroin when the shooting took place. As for Bassett, he backed up right away. "First, I would like to say I don't appreciate being here against my will," he said in a high, squeaky voice that seemed incongruous coming from a man of his bulk. He went on to say that he never saw Jay after the robbery, never saw anyone shoot Jay, never saw a white Lexus at the end of Bonaparte, and never told Baier that he had seen any of these things. When Nosher showed him the photo lineup he had signed, in which he had identified Parker as the shooter, Bassett said that Baier "basically picked the dude out for me." What about his taped statement? He had been forced to make it, he said. "I gave them the plot of the story; they put their own characters with it."

The jury heard from other prosecution witnesses: Craddock talked about seeing the Lexus and part of the license tag. Baier testified about the investigation, stating that he had not coerced Bassett or helped him pick photos from the lineup. A telecommunications expert testified about the location of Love's cell phone. Video from the warehouse surveillance camera was shown to the jury. The defense put on no witnesses of its own. But after two days of deliberation, the jury announced that it could not reach a unanimous verdict. Judge Cox was forced to declare a mistrial.

*****

At first, the prosecutors planned to retry the case. But over the summer, the federal government decided to take over. (With Dowery's cooperation, it had already been working on a case against Love, Parker, and James Dinkins, a man police believe was involved in Dowery's shooting.) In late August, Parker, Love, and Dinkins were indicted on federal charges of conspiracy to distribute heroin. As of this writing, the trial is scheduled to begin in late March.

Federal prosecutions are one method cities are using to combat witness intimidation. A law passed by Congress last December explicitly makes witness intimidation in a state case grounds for federal prosecution. Rod Rosenstein, the U.S. attorney for Maryland, says the federal government has a big advantage over the states in breaking through the code of silence: leverage. Federal sentencing guidelines provide for long prison terms and, unlike the state system, do not allow for probation or parole. "We don't appeal to their sense of civility and morality," Rosenstein says. "We get a hammer over their heads. They realize that cooperating is the only way they can get out from under these hefty federal sentences."

Some states are looking to bring their laws into line with federal practices. The Maryland law Jessamy helped pass elevates witness intimidation from a misdemeanor to a felony punishable by a minimum of five years. It also allows prosecutors to introduce a witness's prior statements even if the witness isn't at the trial, if they can provide "clear and convincing evidence" that the defendant was responsible for the witness's absence. Still, Jessamy isn't satisfied. The new law excludes child-abuse and domestic-violence cases. And rarely can prosecutors obtain the kind of evidence of intimidation it requires. Even when they can, Jessamy says, trying to persuade judges to apply the law "is like pouring water on a stone."

Cities are also pushing to increase funding for witness assistance. The federal law passed in December allows the U.S. attorney general to dispense grants to states for witness protection. But Congress appropriated only $20 million annually for these grants through 2010. By contrast, a bill that Representative Elijah Cummings of Maryland introduced two years ago would have provided $90 million annually to support state witness-assistance programs; that bill died in committee. Since the start of the new congressional session, in January, several bills to strengthen the protection of witnesses in state cases have been introduced; as of this writing, they are all still in committee.

Federal prosecutions, new laws, more money—these are the blunt instruments of policy-makers. They might chip away at the edges of the problem. But to really reduce witnesses' reluctance to participate in the judicial process will require something beyond the abilities of cops and courts: a cultural transformation in America's inner cities. In Philadelphia, Boston, and Washington, D.C., authorities have tried to prohibit the sale of Stop Snitching clothing (they succeeded in Washington). But there is no indication that criminalizing a fashion and political statement will alter the underlying sentiment. Leonard Hamm, a long-serving Baltimore police officer who returned to head the city's department in 2004 after an eight-year absence, sees the problem this way: "I think that the community is going to have to get sick and tired of the shootings and the killings and the memorial services. And all we can do as police is be there when they say they are ready." But what if the community is never ready? Many inner-city neighborhoods have no community. The institutions that once held them together—the churches, the associations, the businesses— are shells of what they were, if they exist at all.

*****

For Dowery, the mistrial was unnerving. Yet in some ways it was better than a guilty verdict. He was still planning to testify for the federal government against Love, Parker, and Dinkins. This would further postpone his gun case. In addition, as a federal witness, he began receiving some token financial assistance from the FBI.

Dowery's family would visit him in the suburbs. Still, he missed them, and he missed his friends. So he occasionally sneaked back to the old neighborhood for a day or two, usually staying with his mother and trying to keep a low profile. In the spring, he proudly watched his two eldest sons graduate from high school. And he didn't want to skip Thanksgiving at his aunt's house, on Bartlett Avenue. "He was tired of hiding out," his aunt, Joyce Garner, told me.

On Thanksgiving night, more than 20 members of Dowery's family gathered for a feast. Dowery was in a good mood, reminiscing about old times. Garner remembers that he came to talk to her as she was cooking. She asked if he was worried about being back in the neighborhood. "He just talked about the Lord to us and gave us a big hug and said, 'God's got it,'" she recalled. Toward the end of dinner, Dowery excused himself. He wanted to run across the street to buy a pack of cigarettes and have a beer.

The sign over its beige stucco facade calls the Kozy Korner a "Cut-Rate & Lounge." Two doors separate the bar from the street. The first opens onto a grungy vestibule where a cashier sells beer and liquor from behind a bulletproof window. The second is locked; customers must be buzzed through. Once inside, they are greeted by a dark, narrow room. A Baltimore Ravens poster is affixed to one wall. A rendering of the Last Supper, with a black Jesus and black disciples, decorates the other. Three video gambling machines flash and hum.

When Dowery arrived, a dozen other patrons were packed into the space. He recognized one of them: a former girlfriend called Toot. They chatted inside the doorway while he smoked and sipped a beer. Just after 10 o'clock, the door opened, and two men entered. This time Dowery's sixth sense—the feeling that had told him to turn around on his porch that morning a year earlier—failed him. One of the men drew a gun, pointed it at Dowery's head, and fired. Then the other did the same. This time, the doctors couldn't save him.

And although the bar was crowded, no one has come forward to say they saw a thing. It's just another homicide in inner-city America, with no suspects, and no witnesses.

■ READING AND WRITING

1. Kahn's article offers different perspectives on what "snitching" means. How do the various groups represented in Kahn's piece—police and prosecutors, the public, suspects and witnesses—view the term differently? How do you define "snitching"?
2. Kahn explores the "Stop Snitching" subculture among poor, mostly black residents of Baltimore. What, according to the article, led to the development of this subculture? What other kinds of communities or groups impose codes of silence on their members? How do these groups justify their codes?
3. The dilemma of whether to report a crime and cooperate with police relates directly to the question of what we, as citizens and neighbors, owe our communities. But it is complicated by other issues—including personal safety and family obligations—as the stories of John Dowery, Jr., Edna McAbier, and the Dawson family clearly show. At what point do our obligations to the health of society cancel out what we owe to those closest to us? Does Kahn suggest an answer to this question?

■ DEVELOPING LONGER RESPONSES

4. Although he doesn't present a clear claim, Kahn does imply an argument. Write a brief essay in which you summarize Kahn's position and explain how he develops and presents his argument implicitly.

Nicholas D. Kristof is a New York Times Op-Ed columnist and Sheryl WuDunn is a former Times correspondent who works in finance and philanthropy. This essay, published August 23, 2009, in the Times, is adapted from their new book Half the Sky: Turning Oppression Into Opportunity for Women Worldwide. You can learn more about Half the Sky at www.nytimes.com/ontheground

THE WOMEN'S CRUSADE
Nicholas D. Kristof and Sheryl WuDunn

IN THE 19TH CENTURY, the paramount moral challenge was slavery. In the 20th century, it was totalitarianism. In this century, it is the brutality inflicted on so many women and girls around the globe: sex trafficking, acid attacks, bride burnings and mass rape.

Yet if the injustices that women in poor countries suffer are of paramount importance, in an economic and geopolitical sense the opportunity they represent is even greater. "Women hold up half the sky," in the words of a Chinese saying, yet that's mostly an aspiration: In a large slice of the world, girls are uneducated and women marginalized, and it's not an accident that those same countries are disproportionately mired in poverty and riven by fundamentalism and chaos. There's a growing recognition among everyone from the World Bank to the U.S. military's Joint Chiefs of Staff to aid organizations like CARE that focusing on women and girls is the most effective way to fight global poverty and extremism. That's why foreign aid is increasingly directed to women. The world is awakening to a powerful truth: Women and girls aren't the problem; they're the solution.

One place to observe this alchemy of gender is in the muddy back alleys of Pakistan. In a slum outside the grand old city of Lahore, a woman named Saima Muhammad used to dissolve into tears every evening. A round-faced woman with thick black hair tucked into a head scarf, Saima had barely a rupee, and her deadbeat husband was unemployed and not particularly employable. He was frustrated and angry, and he coped by beating Saima each afternoon. Their house was falling apart, and Saima had to send her young daughter to live with an aunt, because there wasn't enough food to go around.

"My sister-in-law made fun of me, saying, 'You can't even feed your children,'" recalled Saima when Nick met her two years ago on a trip to Pakistan. "My husband beat me up. My brother-in-law beat me up. I had an awful life." Saima's husband accumulated a debt of more than $3,000, and it seemed that these loans would hang over the family for generations. Then when Saima's second child was born and turned out to be a girl as well, her mother-in-law, a harsh, blunt woman named Sharifa Bibi, raised the stakes.

"She's not going to have a son," Sharifa told Saima's husband, in front of her. "So you should marry again. Take a second wife." Saima was shattered and ran off sobbing. Another wife would leave even less money to feed and educate the children. And Saima herself would be marginalized in the household, cast off like an old sock. For days Saima walked around in a daze, her eyes red; the slightest incident would send her collapsing into hysterical tears.

It was at that point that Saima signed up with the Kashf Foundation, a Pakistani microfinance organization that lends tiny amounts of money to poor women to start businesses. Kashf is typical of microfinance institutions, in that it lends almost exclusively to women, in groups of 25. The women guarantee one another's debts and meet every two weeks to make payments and discuss a social issue, like family planning or schooling for girls. A Pakistani woman is often forbidden to leave the house without her husband's permission, but husbands tolerate these meetings because the women return with cash and investment ideas.

Saima took out a $65 loan and used the money to buy beads and cloth, which she transformed into beautiful embroidery that she then sold to merchants in the markets of Lahore. She used the profit to buy more beads and cloth, and soon she had an embroidery business and was earning a solid income—the only one in her household to do so. Saima took her elder daughter back from the aunt and began paying off her husband's debt.

When merchants requested more embroidery than Saima could produce, she paid neighbors to assist her. Eventually 30 families were working for her, and she put her husband to work as well—"under my direction," she explained with a twinkle in her eye. Saima became the tycoon of the neighborhood, and she was able to pay off her husband's entire debt, keep her daughters in school, renovate the house, connect running water and buy a television.

"Now everyone comes to me to borrow money, the same ones who used to criticize me," Saima said, beaming in satisfaction. "And the children of those who used to criticize me now come to my house to watch TV."

Today, Saima is a bit plump and displays a gold nose ring as well as several other rings and bracelets on each wrist. She exudes self-confidence as she offers a grand tour of her home and work area, ostentatiously showing off the television and the new plumbing. She doesn't even pretend to be subordinate to her husband. He spends his days mostly loafing around, occasionally helping with the work but always having to accept orders from his wife. He has become more impressed with females in general: Saima had a third child, also a girl, but now that's not a problem. "Girls are just as good as boys," he explained.

Saima's new prosperity has transformed the family's educational prospects. She is planning to send all three of her daughters through high school and maybe to college as well. She brings in tutors to improve their schoolwork, and her oldest child, Javaria, is ranked first in her class. We asked Javaria what she wanted to be when she grew up, thinking she might aspire to be a doctor or lawyer. Javaria cocked her head. "I'd like to do embroidery," she said.

As for her husband, Saima said, "We have a good relationship now." She explained, "We don't fight, and he treats me well." And what about finding another wife who might bear him a son? Saima chuckled at the question: "Now nobody says anything about that." Sharifa Bibi, the mother-in-law, looked shocked when we asked whether she wanted her son to take a second wife to bear a son. "No, no," she said. "Saima is bringing so much to this house. ... She puts a roof over our heads and food on the table."

Sharifa even allows that Saima is now largely exempt from beatings by her husband. "A woman should know her limits, and if not, then it's her husband's right to beat her," Sharifa said. "But if a woman earns more than her husband, it's difficult for him to discipline her."

WHAT SHOULD we make of stories like Saima's? Traditionally, the status of women was seen as a "soft" issue—worthy but marginal. We initially reflected that view ourselves in our work as journalists. We preferred to focus instead on the "serious" international issues, like trade disputes or arms proliferation. Our awakening came in China.

After we married in 1988, we moved to Beijing to be correspondents for The New York Times. Seven months later we found ourselves standing on the edge of Tiananmen Square watching troops fire their automatic weapons at prodemocracy protesters. The massacre claimed between 400 and 800 lives and transfixed the world; wrenching images of the killings appeared constantly on the front page and on television screens.

Yet the following year we came across an obscure but meticulous demographic study that outlined a human rights violation that had claimed tens of thousands more lives. This study found that 39,000 baby girls died annually in China because parents didn't give them the same medical care and attention that boys received—and that was just in the first year of life. A result is that as many infant girls died unnecessarily every week in China as protesters died at Tiananmen Square. Those Chinese girls never received a column inch of news coverage, and we began to wonder if our journalistic priorities were skewed.

A similar pattern emerged in other countries. In India, a "bride burning" takes place approximately once every two hours, to punish a woman for an inadequate dowry or to eliminate her so a man can remarry—but these rarely constitute news. When a prominent dissident was arrested in China, we would write a front-page article; when 100,000 girls were kidnapped and trafficked into brothels, we didn't even consider it news.

Amartya Sen, the ebullient Nobel Prize-winning economist, developed a gauge of gender inequality that is a striking reminder of the stakes involved. "More than 100 million women are missing," Sen wrote in a classic essay in 1990 in The New York Review of Books, spurring a new field of research. Sen noted that in normal circumstances, women live longer than men, and so there are more females than males in much of the world. Yet in places where girls have a deeply unequal status, they vanish. China has 107 males for every 100 females in its overall population (and an even greater disproportion among newborns), and India has 108. The implication of the sex ratios, Sen later found, is that about 107 million females are missing from the globe today. Follow-up studies have calculated the number slightly differently, deriving alternative figures for "missing women" of between 60 million and 107 million.

Girls vanish partly because they don't get the same health care and food as boys. In India, for example, girls are less likely to be vaccinated than boys and are taken to the hospital only when they are sicker. A result is that girls in India from 1 to 5 years of age are 50 percent more likely to die than boys their age. In addition, ultrasound machines have allowed a pregnant woman to find out the sex of her fetus—and then get an abortion if it is female.

The global statistics on the abuse of girls are numbing. It appears that more girls and women are now missing from the planet, precisely because they are female, than men were killed on the battlefield in all the wars of the 20th century. The number of victims of this routine "gendercide" far exceeds the number of people who were slaughtered in all the genocides of the 20th century.

For those women who live, mistreatment is sometimes shockingly brutal. If you're reading this article, the phrase "gender discrimination" might conjure thoughts of unequal pay, underfinanced sports teams or unwanted touching from a boss. In the developing world, meanwhile, millions of women and girls are actually enslaved. While a precise number is hard to pin down, the International Labor Organization, a U.N. agency, estimates that at any one time there are 12.3 million people engaged in forced labor of all kinds, including sexual servitude. In Asia alone about one million children working in the sex trade are held in conditions indistinguishable from slavery, according to a U.N. report. Girls and women are locked in brothels and beaten if they resist, fed just enough to be kept alive and often sedated with drugs—to pacify them and often to cultivate addiction. India probably has more modern slaves than any other country.

Another huge burden for women in poor countries is maternal mortality, with one woman dying in childbirth around the world every minute. In the West African country Niger, a woman stands a one-in-seven chance of dying in childbirth at some point in her life. (These statistics are all somewhat dubious, because maternal mortality isn't considered significant enough to require good data collection.) For all of India's shiny new high-rises, a woman there still has a 1-in-70 lifetime chance of dying in childbirth. In contrast, the lifetime risk in the United States is 1 in 4,800; in Ireland, it is 1 in 47,600. The reason for the gap is not that we don't know how to save lives of women in poor countries. It's simply that poor, uneducated women in Africa and Asia have never been a priority either in their own countries or to donor nations.

ABBAS BE, A BEAUTIFUL teenage girl in the Indian city of Hyderabad, has chocolate skin, black hair and gleaming white teeth—and a lovely smile, which made her all the more marketable.

Money was tight in her family, so when she was about 14 she arranged to take a job as a maid in the capital, New Delhi. Instead, she was locked up in a brothel, beaten with a cricket bat, gang-raped and told that she would have to cater to customers. Three days after she arrived, Abbas and all 70 girls in the brothel were made to gather round and watch as the pimps made an example of one teenage girl who had fought customers. The troublesome girl was stripped naked, hogtied, humiliated and mocked, beaten savagely and then stabbed in the stomach until she bled to death in front of Abbas and the others.

Abbas was never paid for her work. Any sign of dissatisfaction led to a beating or worse; two more times, she watched girls murdered by the brothel managers for resisting. Eventually Abbas was freed by police and taken back to Hyderabad. She found a home in a shelter run by Prajwala, an organization that takes in girls rescued from brothels and teaches them new skills. Abbas is acquiring an education and has learned to be a bookbinder; she also counsels other girls about how to avoid being trafficked. As a skilled bookbinder, Abbas is able to earn a decent living, and she is now helping to put her younger sisters through school as well. With an education, they will be far less vulnerable to being trafficked. Abbas has moved from being a slave to being a producer, contributing to India's economic development and helping raise her family.

Perhaps the lesson presented by both Abbas and Saima is the same: In many poor countries, the greatest unexploited resource isn't oil fields or veins of gold; it is the women and girls who aren't educated and never become a major presence in the formal economy. With education and with help starting businesses, impoverished women can earn money and support their countries as well as their families. They represent perhaps the best hope for fighting global poverty.

In East Asia, as we saw in our years of reporting there, women have already benefited from deep social changes. In countries like South Korea and Malaysia, China and Thailand, rural girls who previously contributed negligibly to the economy have gone to school and received educations, giving them the autonomy to move to the city to hold factory jobs. This hugely increased the formal labor force; when the women then delayed childbearing, there was a demographic dividend to the country as well. In the 1990s, by our estimations, some 80 percent of the employees on the assembly lines in coastal China were female, and the proportion across the manufacturing belt of East Asia was at least 70 percent.

The hours were long and the conditions wretched, just as in the sweatshops of the Industrial Revolution in the West. But peasant women were making money, sending it back home and sometimes becoming the breadwinners in their families. They gained new skills that elevated their status. Westerners encounter sweatshops and see exploitation, and indeed, many of these plants are just as bad as critics say. But it's sometimes said in poor countries that the only thing worse than being exploited in a sweatshop is not being exploited in a sweatshop. Low-wage manufacturing jobs disproportionately benefited women in countries like China because these were jobs for which brute physical force was not necessary and women's nimbleness gave them an advantage over men—which was not the case with agricultural labor or construction or other jobs typically available in poor countries. Strange as it may seem, sweatshops in Asia had the effect of empowering women. One hundred years ago, many women in China were still having their feet bound. Today, while discrimination and inequality and harassment persist, the culture has been transformed. In the major cities, we've found that Chinese men often do more domestic chores than American men typically do. And urban parents are often not only happy with an only daughter; they may even prefer one, under the belief that daughters are better than sons at looking after aging parents.

WHY DO MICROFINANCE organizations usually focus their assistance on women? And why does everyone benefit when women enter the work force and bring home regular pay checks? One reason involves the dirty little secret of global poverty: some of the most wretched suffering is caused not just by low incomes but also by unwise spending by the poor—especially by men. Surprisingly frequently, we've come across a mother mourning a child who has just died of malaria for want of a $5 mosquito bed net; the mother says that the family couldn't afford a bed net and she means it, but then we find the father at a nearby bar. He goes three evenings a week to the bar, spending $5 each week.

Our interviews and perusal of the data available suggest that the poorest families in the world spend approximately 10 times as much (20 percent of their incomes on average) on a combination of alcohol, prostitution, candy, sugary drinks and lavish feasts as they do on educating their children (2 percent). If poor families spent only as much on educating their children as they do on beer and prostitutes, there would be a breakthrough in the prospects of poor countries. Girls, since they are the ones kept home from school now, would be the biggest beneficiaries. Moreover, one way to reallocate family expenditures in this way is to put more money in the hands of women. A series of studies has found that when women hold assets or gain incomes, family money is more likely to be spent on nutrition, medicine and housing, and consequently children are healthier.

In Ivory Coast, one research project examined the different crops that men and women grow for their private kitties: men grow coffee, cocoa and pineapple, and women grow plantains, bananas, coconuts and vegetables. Some years the "men's crops" have good harvests and the men are flush with cash, and other years it is the women who prosper. Money is to some extent shared. But even so, the economist Esther Duflo of M.I.T. found that when the men's crops flourish, the household spends more money on alcohol and tobacco. When the women have a good crop, the households spend more money on food. "When women command greater power, child health and nutrition improves," Duflo says.

Such research has concrete implications: for example, donor countries should nudge poor countries to adjust their laws so that when a man dies, his property is passed on to his widow rather than to his brothers. Governments should make it easy for women to hold property and bank accounts—1 percent of the world's landowners are women—and they should make it much easier for microfinance institutions to start banks so that women can save money.

OF COURSE, IT'S FAIR to ask: empowering women is well and good, but can one do this effectively? Does foreign aid really work? William Easterly, an economist at New York University, has argued powerfully that shoveling money at poor countries accomplishes little. Some Africans, including Dambisa Moyo, author of "Dead Aid," have said the same thing. The critics note that there has been no correlation between amounts of aid going to countries and their economic growth rates.

Our take is that, frankly, there is something to these criticisms. Helping people is far harder than it looks. Aid experiments often go awry, or small successes turn out to be difficult to replicate or scale up. Yet we've also seen, anecdotally and in the statistics, evidence that some kinds of aid have been enormously effective. The delivery of vaccinations and other kinds of health care has reduced the number of children who die every year before they reach the age of 5 to less than 10 million today from 20 million in 1960.

In general, aid appears to work best when it is focused on health, education and microfinance (although microfinance has been somewhat less successful in Africa than in Asia). And in each case, crucially, aid has often been most effective when aimed at women and girls; when policy wonks do the math, they often find that these investments have a net economic return. Only a small proportion of aid specifically targets women or girls, but increasingly donors are recognizing that that is where they often get the most bang for the buck.

In the early 1990s, the United Nations and the World Bank began to proclaim the potential resource that women and girls represent. "Investment in girls' education may well be the highest-return investment available in the developing world," Larry Summers wrote when he was chief economist of the World Bank. Private aid groups and foundations shifted gears as well. "Women are the key to ending hunger in Africa," declared the Hunger Project. The Center for Global Development issued a major report explaining "why and how to put girls at the center of development." CARE took women and girls as the centerpiece of its anti-poverty efforts. "Gender inequality hurts economic growth," Goldman Sachs concluded in a 2008 research report that emphasized how much developing countries could improve their economic performance by educating girls.

Bill Gates recalls once being invited to speak in Saudi Arabia and finding himself facing a segregated audience. Four-fifths of the listeners were men, on the left. The remaining one-fifth were women, all covered in black cloaks and veils, on the right. A partition separated the two groups. Toward the end, in the question-and-answer session, a member of the audience noted that Saudi Arabia aimed to be one of the Top 10 countries in the world in technology by 2010 and asked if that was realistic. "Well, if you're not fully utilizing half the talent in the country," Gates said, "you're not going to get too close to the Top 10." The small group on the right erupted in wild cheering.

Policy makers have gotten the message as well. President Obama has appointed a new White House Council on Women and Girls. Perhaps he was indoctrinated by his mother, who was one of the early adopters of microloans to women when she worked to fight poverty in Indonesia. Secretary of State Hillary Rodham Clinton is a member of the White House Council, and she has also selected a talented activist, Melanne Verveer, to direct a new State Department Office of Global Women's Issues. On Capitol Hill, the Senate Foreign Relations Committee has put Senator Barbara Boxer in charge of a new subcommittee that deals with women's issues.

Yet another reason to educate and empower women is that greater female involvement in society and the economy appears to undermine extremism and terrorism. It has long been known that a risk factor for turbulence and violence is the share of a country's population made up of young people. Now it is emerging that male domination of society is also a risk factor; the reasons aren't fully understood, but it may be that when women are marginalized the nation takes on the testosterone-laden culture of a military camp or a high-school boys' locker room. That's in part why the Joint Chiefs of Staff and international security specialists are puzzling over how to increase girls' education in countries like Afghanistan—and why generals have gotten briefings from Greg Mortenson, who wrote about building girls' schools in his best seller, "Three Cups of Tea." Indeed, some scholars say they believe the reason Muslim countries have been disproportionately afflicted by terrorism is not Islamic teachings about infidels or violence but rather the low levels of female education and participation in the labor force.

SO WHAT WOULD an agenda for fighting poverty through helping women look like? You might begin with the education of girls—which doesn't just mean building schools. There are other innovative means at our disposal. A study in Kenya by Michael Kremer, a Harvard economist, examined six different approaches to improving educational performance, from providing free textbooks to child-sponsorship programs. The approach that raised student test scores the most was to offer girls who had scored in the top 15 percent of their class on sixth-grade tests a $19 scholarship for seventh and eighth grade (and the glory of recognition at an assembly). Boys also performed better, apparently because they were pushed by the girls or didn't want to endure the embarrassment of being left behind.

Another Kenyan study found that giving girls a new $6 school uniform every 18 months significantly reduced dropout rates and pregnancy rates. Likewise, there's growing evidence that a cheap way to help keep high-school girls in school is to help them manage menstruation. For fear of embarrassing leaks and stains, girls sometimes stay home during their periods, and the absenteeism puts them behind and eventually leads them to drop out. Aid workers are experimenting with giving African teenage girls sanitary pads, along with access to a toilet where they can change them. The Campaign for Female Education, an organization devoted to getting more girls into school in Africa, helps girls with their periods, and a new group, Sustainable Health Enterprises, is trying to do the same.

And so, if President Obama wanted to adopt a foreign-aid policy that built on insights into the role of women in development, he would do well to start with education. We would suggest a $10 billion effort over five years to educate girls around the world. This initiative would focus on Africa but would also support—and prod—Asian countries like Afghanistan and Pakistan to do better. This plan would also double as population policy, for it would significantly reduce birthrates—and thus help poor countries overcome the demographic obstacles to economic growth.

But President Obama might consider two different proposals as well. We would recommend that the United States sponsor a global drive to eliminate iodine deficiency around the globe, by helping countries iodize salt. About a third of households in the developing world do not get enough iodine, and a result is often an impairment in brain formation in the fetal stages. For reasons that are unclear, this particularly affects female fetuses and typically costs children 10 to 15 I.Q. points. Research by Erica Field of Harvard found that daughters of women given iodine performed markedly better in school. Other research suggests that salt iodization would yield benefits worth nine times the cost.

We would also recommend that the United States announce a 12-year, $1.6 billion program to eradicate obstetric fistula, a childbirth injury that is one of the worst scourges of women in the developing world. An obstetric fistula, which is a hole created inside the body by a difficult childbirth, leaves a woman incontinent, smelly, often crippled and shunned by her village—yet it can be repaired for a few hundred dollars. Dr. Lewis Wall, president of the Worldwide Fistula Fund, and Michael Horowitz, a conservative agitator on humanitarian issues, have drafted the 12-year plan—and it's eminently practical and built on proven methods. Evidence that fistulas can be prevented or repaired comes from impoverished Somaliland, a northern enclave of Somalia, where an extraordinary nurse-midwife named Edna Adan has built her own maternity hospital to save the lives of the women around her. A former first lady of Somalia and World Health Organization official, Adan used her savings to build the hospital, which is supported by a group of admirers in the U.S. who call themselves Friends of Edna Maternity Hospital.

For all the legitimate concerns about how well humanitarian aid is spent, investments in education, iodizing salt and maternal health all have a proven record of success. And the sums are modest: all three components of our plan together amount to about what the U.S.

has provided Pakistan since 9/11—a sum that accomplished virtually nothing worthwhile either for Pakistanis or for Americans.

ONE OF THE MANY aid groups that for pragmatic reasons has increasingly focused on women is Heifer International, a charitable organization based in Arkansas that has been around for decades. The organization gives cows, goats and chickens to farmers in poor countries. On assuming the presidency of Heifer in 1992, the activist Jo Luck traveled to Africa, where one day she found herself sitting on the ground with a group of young women in a Zimbabwean village. One of them was Tererai Trent.

Tererai is a long-faced woman with high cheekbones and a medium brown complexion; she has a high forehead and tight cornrows. Like many women around the world, she doesn't know when she was born and has no documentation of her birth. As a child, Tererai didn't get much formal education, partly because she was a girl and was expected to do household chores. She herded cattle and looked after her younger siblings. Her father would say, "Let's send our sons to school, because they will be the breadwinners." Tererai's brother, Tinashe, was forced to go to school, where he was an indifferent student. Tererai pleaded to be allowed to attend but wasn't permitted to do so. Tinashe brought his books home each afternoon, and Tererai pored over them and taught herself to read and write. Soon she was doing her brother's homework every evening.

The teacher grew puzzled, for Tinashe was a poor student in class but always handed in exemplary homework. Finally, the teacher noticed that the handwriting was different for homework and for class assignments and whipped Tinashe until he confessed the truth. Then the teacher went to the father, told him that Tererai was a prodigy and begged that she be allowed to attend school. After much argument, the father allowed Tererai to attend school for a couple of terms, but then married her off at about age 11.

Tererai's husband barred her from attending school, resented her literacy and beat her whenever she tried to practice her reading by looking at a scrap of old newspaper. Indeed, he beat her for plenty more as well. She hated her marriage but had no way out. "If you're a woman and you are not educated, what else?" she asks.

Yet when Jo Luck came and talked to Tererai and other young women in her village, Luck kept insisting that things did not have to be this way. She kept saying that they could achieve their goals, repeatedly using the word "achievable." The women caught the repetition and asked the interpreter to explain in detail what "achievable" meant. That gave Luck a chance to push forward. "What are your hopes?" she asked the women, through the interpreter. Tererai and the others were puzzled by the question, because they didn't really have any hopes. But Luck pushed them to think about their dreams, and reluctantly, they began to think about what they wanted.

Tererai timidly voiced hope of getting an education. Luck pounced and told her that she could do it, that she should write down her goals and methodically pursue them. After Luck and her entourage disappeared, Tererai began to study on her own, in hiding from her husband, while raising her five children. Painstakingly, with the help of friends, she wrote down her goals on a piece of paper: "One day I will go to the United States of America," she began, for Goal 1. She added that she would earn a college degree, a master's degree and a Ph.D.—all exquisitely absurd dreams for a married cattle herder in Zimbabwe who had less than one year's formal education. But Tererai took the piece of paper and folded it inside three layers of plastic to protect it, and then placed it in an old can. She buried the can under a rock where she herded cattle.

Then Tererai took correspondence classes and began saving money. Her self-confidence grew as she did brilliantly in her studies, and she became a community organizer for Heifer. She stunned everyone with superb schoolwork, and the Heifer aid workers encouraged her to think that she could study in America. One day in 1998, she received notice that she had been admitted to Oklahoma State University.

Some of the neighbors thought that a woman should focus on educating her children, not herself. "I can't talk about my children's education when I'm not educated myself," Tererai responded. "If I educate myself, then I can educate my children." So she climbed into an airplane and flew to America.

At Oklahoma State, Tererai took every credit she could and worked nights to make money. She earned her undergraduate degree, brought her five children to America and started her master's, then returned to her village. She dug up the tin can under the rock and took out the paper on which she had scribbled her goals. She put check marks beside the goals she had fulfilled and buried the tin can again.

In Arkansas, she took a job working for Heifer—while simultaneously earning a master's degree part time. When she had her M.A., Tererai again returned to her village. After embracing her mother and sister, she dug up her tin can and checked off her next goal. Now she is working on her Ph.D. at Western Michigan University.

Tererai has completed her course work and is completing a dissertation about AIDS programs among the poor in Africa. She will become a productive economic asset for Africa and a significant figure in the battle against AIDS. And when she has her doctorate, Tererai will go back to her village and, after hugging her loved ones, go out to the field and dig up her can again.

There are many metaphors for the role of foreign assistance. For our part, we like to think of aid as a kind of lubricant, a few drops of oil in the crankcase of the developing world, so that gears move freely again on their own. That is what the assistance to Tererai amounted to: a bit of help where and when it counts most, which often means focusing on women like her. And now Tererai is gliding along freely on her own—truly able to hold up half the sky.

READING AND WRITING

1. Summarize the central elements of Kristof and WuDunn's argument, including the problems they present, the solutions they suggest, and the evidence they use to persuade their audience.
2. How do Kristof and WuDunn intertwine appeals rooted in pathos and logos to advance their argument?
3. Why, according to Kristof and WuDunn, are microfinance loans such an effective way to help improve the lives of poor families in some parts of the world? Why do microfinance organizations lend almost exclusively to women?
4. What is the portrait of men that emerges from this article? Consider (as Ashraf Rushdy would hasten to remind us) that images of non-white or poor men as criminal, lazy, or foolish have frequently had the effect of inflaming racism and violence. In portraying the abuse of third-world women, does this article risk representing men in ways that align with dangerous stereotypes? How could Kristof and WuDunn have made their argument in a different way?

DEVELOPING LONGER RESPONSES

5. Keeping Ashraf Rushdy's essay "Exquisite Corpse" in mind, examine WuDunn and Kristof's descriptions of bodily abuse and how these images function in the article. (Think, for example, of the descriptions of women tortured and murdered by sex traffickers to maintain control over others.) Compose an analysis of these images and their effects on readers. Do these textual displays of violence and abuse support Rushdy's contention that "images of terror—used responsibly—can foster a climate in which terror is no longer tolerated"?

■ RESEARCH AND WRITING PROJECTS

1. Find at least six sources from the national media dealing with the controversy surrounding Willingham's execution. After reading and analyzing these, develop a thesis about the way this issue has been framed by the media. Some questions you might consider: How do the media present the principals in the case—Willingham, Vasquez, Perry, and the prosecutors? Whose problem do your sources consider Willingham's case to be—the state of Texas's, Rick Perry's, ours, the world's? Your instructor may also ask you to develop an essay based on your thesis.

2. Consider how "snitching"—breaking some cultural code of silence to inform on those who commit criminal acts—relates to the larger idea of witnessing discussed in Chapter 1, particularly in the essay by John Durham Peters. Using the library, find at least three sources (*not* dictionaries or encyclopedias) that define the act of witnessing. Based on your research and on the Peters and Kahn essays, think about the ways that snitching relates to or contradicts witnessing and compose a definitional argument in which you address the following question: Is snitching—even with its negative connotations of betrayal—a form of witnessing? Your paper should make use of at least three sources in addition to the essays by Peters and Kahn.

3. Jeremy Kahn's "The Story of a Snitch" inspired lively discussion in the mainstream press and the blogosphere. This response was part of an even larger debate about the relationship between law enforcement and African Americans that goes back to this country's founding. Kahn makes small references to this history to explain why some black communities are reluctant to work with police. What is the source of this suspicion, mistrust, and fear of law enforcement? Do these feelings seem justified? How can law enforcement agencies overcome this problem? Use the library's resources to explore these questions. One course of inquiry you may wish to consider is the government's use of questionable practices and false eyewitness testimony to infiltrate and break up activist groups during the civil rights movement.

4. In "Letter from Birmingham Jail," Martin Luther King, Jr. explains the differences between just and unjust laws and concludes that, "One has

not only a legal but a moral responsibility to obey just laws. Conversely, one has a moral responsibility to disobey unjust laws." King was not the first person to make these distinctions or to act on them—he quotes St. Augustine in his letter, for example, as saying that "'an unjust law is no law at all.'" Use the library and the internet to find at least four other thinkers and activists who have justified "breaking some laws and obeying others," as King puts it, in the name of a greater good. Based on your research into this issue, compose an argument that clearly states and supports your position on our "moral responsibility to disobey unjust laws."

5. Each of the essays in this chapter outlines a significant social issue or problem. Some also propose means to address these problems and to achieve significant social change—you've read King's call for civil disobedience, Rushdy's argument for using images of bodily violence, and Kristof and WuDunn's call for microloans for women in developing countries. Grann and Kahn, on the other hand, focus more on bringing the problems they're writing about to life—on making their audiences care—and less on explaining how to correct these problems. Using Wiesel's claim that we are morally obligated to turn knowledge of injustice into responsibility and, sometimes, into action, develop an argument that proposes an appropriate response to the problems raised in either Grann's or Kahn's article. You should use the readings in this chapter to help you compose and support your claims, and your instructor may require that you conduct further research.

Index of Authors and Titles

Credits

Chapter One

The Allegory of the Cave by Plato from *The Dialogues of Plato*, translation by Benjamin Jowett. Copyright ©
2001 Random House.

Witnessing by John Durham Peters. Reprinted in *Media Witnessing: Testimony in the Age of Mass Communication.*
Edited by Paul Frosh and Amit Pinchevski. Copyright © 2008. Reproduced with permission of Palgrave
Macmillan.

The Wreck of Time: Taking Our Century's Measure by Annie Dillard. Harper's Magazine, Jan. 1998, Vol. 296
Issue 1772, pp. 51–56.

Phenomenology of Reading by Georges Poulet from *New Literary History.* Copyright © 1969.

Imagination and Reality by Jeanette Winterson from *Art Objects: Essays on Ecstasy and Effrontery.* Copyright
© 1997.

The Blue Machinery of Summer by Yusef Komunyakaa.

Is Google Making Us Stupid by Nicholas Carr. Copyright © 2008 by Nicholas Carr. The Atlantic Monthly, July/
August 2008. Reprinted with permission of the author.

Get Smarter by Jamais Cascio. Atlantic Monthly, Jul/Aug 2009, Vol. 304 No. 1, pp. 94–100.

Chapter Two

Farmer in Chief by Michael Pollan. New York Times, Oct. 12, 2008, pg. MM62.

Renewing Husbandry by Wendell Berry. Copyright © 2005 Crop Science Society of America. Used with
permission.

A Healthy Constitution by Alice Waters. The Nation, Sept. 21, 2009, Vol. 289 Issue 8, pp. 11–15.

Fear Factories: The Case for Compassionate Conservatism-for Animals by Matthew Scully. Copyright © 2005
The American Conservative. Reprinted with permission.

Cheap Food: Workers Pay the Price by Arturo Rodriguez with Alexa Delwiche and Sheheryar Kaoosji. *Food,
Inc.* Edited by Karl Weber. Copyright © 2009 Perseus Books Group.

Why Vegetarians Are Eating Meat by Christine Lennon. Food and Wine, Aug. 2007.

The Culinary Seasons of my Childhood by Jessica B. Harris from *Gastropolis: Food and New York City.* Copyright
© 2009 Columbia University Press. Reprinted with permission.

Can We Afford to Eat Ethically by Siobhan Phillips first appeared in Salon.com at *http://www.Salon.com.* An
online version remains in the Salon archives. Reprinted with permission.

Declare Your Independence by Joel Salatin. *Food, Inc.* Edited by Karl Weber. Copyright © 2009 Perseus Books
Group.

Chapter Three

Memoirs of a Woman Doctor by Nawal el-Saadawi. An excerpt from *Memoirs of a Woman Doctor.* Copyright © 1988 Saqi Books.

A Wrestling Mom by Mary Kay Blakely from *American Mom: Motherhood, Politics, and Humble Pie.* Copyright © 1994 Algonquin Books.

Voice Lessons by Nancy Mairs. Copyright © 1997 Beacon Press. Used by permission.

My Mother, the Scientist by Charles Hirshberg. Popular Science, May 2002, Vol. 260 Issue 5, pg. 66.

From the Living Room to the Courtroom by Shirin Ebadi, with Azadeh Moaveni from *Iran Awakening: One Woman's Journey to Reclaim Her Life and Country.* Copyright © 2006 Random House.

Redefining Manhood: Resisting Sexism by Ewuare X. Osayande from *Men Speak Out: Views on Gender, Sex, and Power. Edited by Shira Tarrant. Copyright © 2008 Routledge. Reprinted with permission.*

Unattractive Male Seeks Human Female by Joshua E. Borgmann from *The Emergence of Man Into the 21st Century.* Editors Patricia Munhall, Ed Madden, and Virginia Fitzimons. Copyright © 2002 Jones and Bartlett Publishers. Reprinted with permission.

Chicken in the Henhouse from *Dress Your Family in Corduroy and Denim* by David Sedaris. Copyright © 2004 by David Sedaris. By Permission of Little Brown and Company.

Chapter Four

Dracula by Bram Stocker. New York: Random House.

Capitalist Monsters by Annalee Newitz from *Pretend We're Dead,* pp. 1–12. Copyright © 2006 Duke University Press. All rights reserved. Used by permission of the publisher.

Vampires and Other Voracious Monsters by Fabio Parasecoli from *Bite Me: Food in Popular Culture.* Copyright © 2008 Palgrave Macmillan.

What Girls Want by Caitlin Flanagan. Atlantic Monthly, Jul/Aug. 2009, Vol. 304 No. 1, pp. 94–100.

Vampires Suck. Actually, They Don't and That's the Problem by Grady Hendrix. Slate.com. Posted Tuesday, July 28, 2009.

Dean Man Still Walking: Explaining the Zombie by Kyle Bishop from *Journal of Popular Film and Television,* Vol. 37.1, Spring 2009, pp.16–25. Reprinted with permission.

You Just Can't Kill It by Cintra Wilson from The New York Times, Style Section, 9/18/2008 Issue, Page 1. Reprinted with permission.

Chapter Five

Am I My Brother's Keeper by Elie Wiesel and Richard D. Heffner from *Conservations with Elie Wiesel.* Copyright © 2001 by Random House.

Letter from Birmingham Jail by Martin Luther King, Jr. Copyright © the Estate of Martin Luther King, Jr. Reprinted with permission.

the attendees that "the enemy of our enemy is not our friend" and warned WAP to think carefully about advocating any position that hinted at attempted censorship. Bella Abzug spoke to the issue with her usual confidence: "My position on pornography is not contrary to my lifetime position as a civil libertarian. I do not believe it is necessary for us to interfere with anyone's constitutional right to produce pornography. But that doesn't require us to encourage and assist in the proliferation of pornographic materials on the streets and in the stores."

What about pornography that portrayed *violence* against women? Did it not thereby encourage rape and battering? Dorchen Leidholdt, a former rape crisis counselor and one of WAP's founders, presented the conference attendees with specific data linking porn and violence: some one hundred psychiatrists, she noted, had reported to the 1967 Commission on Pornography that in their practices they had male patients who felt strongly that pornography *had* incited them to heightened aggression against women. She quoted as well the work of two academic psychologists, Ed Donnerstein and Neil Malamuth, whose research suggested a connection between the viewing of violent pornography and the triggering of "real-life" physical attacks against women. But others in the audience challenged that connection and criticized WAP for failing to offer a concrete definition of "pornography"—and jumping off from that, a coherent policy statement on the issue.[11]

In one of the many NYU workshops, the respected political essayist Ellen Willis vigorously insisted that pornography and violence were *not* interrelated: "You cannot define pornography," she said, "as any eroticism you don't like." In an influential article she wrote for the *Village Voice* immediately after the conference, Willis spelled out her views: "There are many varieties of porn, some pernicious, some more or less benign . . . nearly all porn is sexist in that it is the product of a male imagination and aimed at a male market. . . . If feminists define pornography, per se, as the enemy, the result will be to make a lot of women ashamed of their sexual feelings and afraid to be honest about them. And the last thing women need is more sexual shame, guilt, and hypocrisy—this time served up as feminism."[12]

WAP organizers, Willis went on, maintained that pornography is not really about sex but about violence against women, and made much of the fact "that Charles Manson and David Berkowitz [Son of Sam] had porn collections. . . . But if *Hustler* were to vanish from the shelves tomorrow, I doubt that rape or wife-beating statistics would decline." Willis recounted the distinction Robin Morgan and Gloria Steinem had made at the conference between pornography and erotica. Porn, they'd argued (in Willis' words), "reflects a dehumanized sexuality based on male domination and exploitation of women," whereas erotica expresses "an integrated sexuality based on mutual affection and desire between equals."

In Willis' opinion, the distinction failed to hold up: the erotica-versus-porn approach, in her view, "endorsed the portrayal of sex as we might like it to be and condemned the portrayal of sex as it too often is, whether in action or only in fantasy. But if pornography is to arouse, it must appeal to the feelings we have, not those that by some utopian standard we ought to have . . . the view of sex that most often emerges from talk about 'erotica' is as sentimental and euphemistic as the word itself: lovemaking should be beautiful, romantic, soft, nice, and devoid of messiness. . . . This goody-goody concept of eroticism is not feminist but feminine."

Furthermore, according to Willis, "in the movement's rhetoric pornography is a code word for vicious male lust. To the objection that some women get off on porn, the standard reply is that this only shows how thoroughly women have been brainwashed by male values." The crusade against pornography, Willis predicted, will bolster "the good girl–bad girl split." She accused Susan Brownmiller and other WAP organizers as endorsing the Supreme Court's contention "that obscenity is not protected speech," a position that Willis and others regarded "as a clear infringement of First Amendment rights." Brownmiller [according to Willis] insisted "that the First Amendment was designed to protect political dissent, not expressions of woman-hating violence. But to make such a distinction is to defeat the amendment's purpose, since it implicitly cedes to the government the right to define 'political' . . . it makes no sense to oppose pornography on the grounds that it's sexist propaganda, then turn around and argue that it's not political."

Andrea indirectly replied to Willis' critique in a response she wrote to two *New York Times* editorials that had denounced WAP's "strident and overwrought" attempt to undermine the First Amendment, and which had quoted from Andrea's earlier article, "Pornography: The New Terrorism." The *Times* refused to publish her response, as did a number of other publications, including the *Washington Post*, *The Nation*, the *Village Voice*, and her own touted *Mother Jones* (it was finally published in the 1980 anthology, *Take Back the Night*). In her letter to the *Times*, Andrea contrasted the paper's defense of "freedom of speech" in regard to pictures that showed "women sexually violated and humiliated, bound, gagged, sliced up, tortured in a multiplicity of ways" with its failure to speak out against "the enforced silence of women through the centuries."[13]

She further pointed out that the Constitution had been written "exclusively by white men who owned land and black slaves" and who denied the vote—the right to be heard on political issues—to all women. Both the law and pornography, she insisted, "express male contempt for women: they have in the past and they do now." Rape and battery were widespread, but "there is not a feminist alive who could possibly look to the male legal system for real protection from the systematized sadism of men." Women who protest pornography as both an expression of male sadism and a further incitement to it were once again being counseled to remain silent—in the name, bizarrely, of freedom of speech.

Andrea joined WAP's October 20, 1979, "March on Times Square" and gave one of the speeches at the subsequent rally in Bryant Park. She spoke out forcefully—and got a tumultuous response when she insisted that women "will never again accept any depiction of us that has as its first principle, its first premise, that we want to be abused, that we enjoy being hurt, that we like being forced." Those are *male* assumptions about *women's* lives. "Some people say that pornography is only fantasy. What part of it is fantasy? Women are beaten and raped and forced and whipped and held captive. The violence depicted is real. The acts of violence depicted in pornography are actual acts committed against real women and real female children. The fantasy is that women want to be abused."[14]

———

Subsequent to the Bryant Park rally, Andrea decided that she needed, above all else, to return to sustained work on her book, to be
free for a time from the maelstrom of "the war against pornography" and to devote herself to isolating and analyzing the underlying
issues and assumptions at stake. Her sense that *that* would be her
major contribution to the politics of pornography had been earlier
reinforced when she'd met a young law professor named Catharine
("Kitty" to her close friends and family) MacKinnon, who'd contacted her after reading *Woman Hating* and invited her to speak to
one of her classes at Yale on pornography. "It was wonderful for
me to have you here," Kitty wrote after the Yale event. "I feel good
about the slow-moving, careful way we are with each other, the gentleness, the regard, the exploration, the caution." It was the beginning of what would be a lasting friendship, and a collaboration of
profound consequence. For Andrea, the cordiality—though she and
Kitty would have their disagreements—was a great relief after what
she called "the exhausting fighting among feminists . . . strange,
divisive, huge melodramas. They get to me."[15]

Kitty was the gifted, attractive daughter of a Republican congressman from Minnesota. Tall, decisive, and stylish, Kitty cut an
imposing, dramatic figure in her severely elegant suits, reinforced
by the energetic clarity of her mind and manner. In the early stages
of her career, when she and Andrea first met, Kitty was already
immersed in fighting for the recognition of sexual harassment as a
form of sex discrimination. By the end of the decade, in a celebrated
1979 book, *Sexual Harassment of Working Women*, she originated the
legal claim for sexual harassment as sex discrimination, which in
1986 the Supreme Court would affirm under Title VII of the 1964
Civil Rights Act.

Though MacKinnon would eventually have a long and distinguished academic career, the controversial causes she espoused
and the intensity with which she uncompromisingly pursued them
proved a predictable liability in the struggle to gain a tenured law
school appointment. She spent a dozen years "living on the road,"
with occasional appointments as a visiting professor, pegged to a
low salary. Her political collaboration with Andrea proceeded at a
gradual pace, as they both during the seventies became increasing-

ly immersed in the issues spawned by the pornography debate. By the summer of 1978, they were sharing and critiquing each other's manuscripts, and as they did so their mutual admiration grew: "The intellectual acuity and rigor of yr arguments are illuminating and challenging," Andrea wrote her at one point.[16]

Andrea and Kitty felt secure enough in their relationship to read each other's work with an eye toward *improving*, not simply admiring, it (though they usually did). When Kitty, for example, read Andrea's book *Pornography* in manuscript, she pulled no punches: "You take certain things on the level of their own self-presentation, which is myth, and hold them to that standard, rather than criticizing deeper realities, which in each case are even more open to attack. Example . . . where you say 'the objective scientists' find such and such, it is not clear whether you are faulting their objectivity or questioning objectivity itself. It seems more like the former, and I think the latter is more devastating and telling." Conversely, though Andrea praised Kitty's speech "Violence Against Women—A Perspective" as "wonderful," she felt free to tell her that "I think it is just patently wrong to say that 'lesbian eroticism' per se is not from the male standpoint, and also that therefore from the male standpoint it is the most obscene. . . . *The Well of Loneliness* is I think saturated with the 'male viewpoint.'"[17]

That mixture of admiration and admonishment is every writer's definition of an ideal editor, and both women knew they'd been lucky to have found it in each other. Still, a loving friendship no less than a loving marriage is inescapably subject to periodic misunderstandings. Not all of them, in the case of Andrea and Kitty, came under the rubric of intellectual disagreements. A dozen years later, Andrea (in a letter to a third party) referred to the "many differences" on "many things" that had developed between them. She put them down to their dissimilar backgrounds: "I am Jewish from an East European family decimated by the Holocaust and she is . . . Anglo-Saxon and privileged . . . I find her ignorance about the history of Jews and the Holocaust upsetting and difficult." (Kitty's family background was in fact Celtic and on her father's side working class).

Most people, unlike MacKinnon, seemed unable to understand

why writing a book about pornography would drain whatever energy Andrea had, but as she explained to a friend, "women tied to
cars, in spiked heels, asses exposed for fucking, and the like"—these
"are photographs I can't recover from. . . . I get physically sick, and
have to work in a state of nausea. . . . When I can't communicate
how terrible it is—for instance, to all the liberal-leftists who can't
understand what's so terrible—I get so angry I could explode, and
it wastes me, so I stay isolated." On top of the anguish of constantly
staring at and writing about women being degraded and abused, she
was feeling desperate again about money: "*how* to finish the pornography book is the question."

Just then—after some twenty or so publishers had rejected the
manuscript at various stages—Doubleday, to everyone's considerable surprise, decided to option it; yet when Andrea again ran out
of money in the spring of 1979, she was turned down for a further advance. A book of her previously published essays that she'd
somehow managed to put together had also been turned down
everywhere, and the paying magazines, with the exception of *Ms.*,
remained closed to her. *Mother Jones* did accept the chapter on the
Marquis de Sade from the pornography manuscript, but when they
edited it in such a way as to make (in Andrea's phrase) "pop-bad-
hamburger of it," she—characteristically—threatened to withdraw
it. Elaborate negotiations followed and *a* version was finally put
together that met Andrea's formidable standards.

She'd learned early on in her career as a writer that editors "made
changes in my work without my knowledge," sometimes changing
the content ("knowingly or without realizing it"), and she became
a stickler for reading final proofs. None of which meant that she
would automatically refuse critical input (indeed, she accepted them
"many times and very gratefully"), but she would always remain
determined to protect the integrity of her work; even when her need
for money was acute, she'd withdraw a piece if she felt it had been
editorially mangled. "I live in a fairly hostile world," she once wrote
the features editor of *Gay Community News*, and "don't like being
vilified for things I don't believe or things I didn't actually write,
which is what happens more often than not."[18]

It came as a surprise to Andrea when Adrienne Rich "insisted" on seeing the three chapters of her pornography book that she'd already completed. Surprised because a certain amount of ill will, its origin somewhat obscure, had recently developed between the two. Toward the end of 1976, Andrea had enigmatically written Kathy Norris, her friend from Bennington days, "Adrienne just managed to injure me too, again. She has the power to review *Our Blood* in the Times Book Review, but won't, cause she hates it, or objects to it, or something. Her manner is very hard to take, she radiates a disapproval, self-righteousness, that injures."[19]

Nor did matters improve. Six months later, in another letter to Kathy, Andrea wrote, "I can't deal with her [Adrienne] at all. She has a small, strange, totalitarian mind . . ." Six months after that, Andrea complained to Robin Morgan that Adrienne continued to treat her with a "condescension" she found "entirely inappropriate," since she had "honored and defended" Adrienne's work "so different from my own, often and long." She didn't mean to imply, Andrea explained, that this "in any sense obligates her to reciprocate," but she remained "mystified" at "the reasons for this entrenched antagonism."

Despite the accumulated antipathy, Adrienne read the three chapters rapidly and called Andrea to say "how powerful" she found them. They made an appointment to talk further about it, though Andrea, perhaps gratefully, doubted "that we will ever discuss the past. I need every bit of strong feminist support I can get, because this [the pornography book] is the hardest thing I have ever done." She was soon happily reporting to Robin Morgan that Adrienne "has been warmly supportive of late."

The early months of 1980 proved a difficult time for Andrea, perhaps because they followed hard on a period of intense public activity and nearly daily engagement with other people, all of which got in the way of completing *Pornography*; besides, her preferred state was isolation. This time, even with John's support and encouragement, she felt "extremely discouraged," even going so far at one point as to write Kitty MacKinnon that "my spirit is broken." Yet she'd finally found a publisher for a slender forty-eight-page collection of short stories (full of the warmth and humor Andrea was widely thought to lack) entitled *the new woman's broken heart* that Elaine Markson had previously been unable to sell. The buyer was a tiny feminist house in California called Frog in the Well. Up to that point it had published only pamphlets, including those by Andrea, John, and Barbara Deming. Andrea's short stories would be the group's first "book-length" work, and her hope was that "at this time of extreme economic hardship for feminist writers we can establish a viable, interesting, and important new feminist publishing house."[20]

The hope, as would soon become apparent, wouldn't be realized—neither for the press in the long run nor for Andrea's stories in the short. There was no money for ads, and Andrea turned to directly soliciting reviews for the book from writers and friends who'd earlier expressed admiration for her work. But they, too, shied away. Leah Fritz, who'd long been a staunch supporter, typified the reaction: the manuscript "disturbs me too much. Perhaps it is because I am so close to you that I feel its despair so keenly. . . . Please forgive me for failing you in this instance."[21]

Mother Jones did nothing to improve Andrea's spirits when it published a piece about what it called the "New Victorian prudes"—i.e., anti-porn feminists. In protest, Andrea sent the magazine a long response and a short private one to its editor, Deirdre English, who she knew and respected. Her letter to English was in essence a lament, her anger and misery pouring out over the longstanding misinterpretation of her own position: "I am so tired, especially of being called a prude for working on the issue, not to mention a fascist, not to mention a censor, and last but not least, I have been screamed at by so many lawyers in public places for being a threat to free speech when I just want it for myself and for other women." Every feminist involved in discussions of pornography, Andrea went on, "who can't leave it alone, even if they don't quite know why . . . has to keep conquering the effects of these epithets and attributions, the chilling effect, as the lawyers would say." Deirdre English responded with openness and grace: "I welcomed your letter and your reactions, critical as they were, and understood them to come from a spirit of honest and open communication." She did not, however, respond to the substance of Andrea's complaints.[22]

In her long letter to *Mother Jones*, Andrea reined in her sense of personal exhaustion and wrote a tightly controlled, lucid response. "Every attempt to discuss the meaning of pornography to women," she wrote, "has been treated as an assault on free speech rather than an exercise of it." Every insult is hurled at feminists attempting to point out that the central themes of male pornography are "forced sex and insatiable sluts": the woman is forced to discover "that she loves abuse"; that pretense ended, she then enthusiastically delights in male domination. Contrary to *Mother Jones*, Andrea went on, feminists are not "retreating into an old-fashioned moralism" but rather insisting on leading "sexually self-determined lives." Besides, Andrea insisted—and this would subsequently prove the most contentious point—pornography *does* influence sexual behavior; it is not, as is often declared, mere entertainment or fantasy. She wasn't claiming that the relationship between pornography and sexual abuse was simple, but only "that pornography effectively promotes abusive sex as viable, exciting, and properly within the scope of normal male sexual behavior."[23]

Yet another source of demoralization during the opening months of 1980 centered on lecture fees, on which Andrea relied for economic survival. She wasn't getting as many invitations to speak as earlier, and when she did, the financial terms offered were low, haggled over in a humiliating way, and not always honored after the event was successfully concluded. One case in point was an invitation to speak at the rally preceding a large "Take Back the Night" march down Hollywood Boulevard in Los Angeles. Given the disastrous state of her finances at the time, Andrea could only accept a speaking engagement if all her expenses were paid along with the lecture fee. Andrea asked the L.A. sponsors for $500, but the organizers bargained her down to $300; she was so poor at this point in her life that she had to accept. On top of that humiliation, she was told after the event that her airfare and other expenses would be paid once the necessary funds were raised, though her understanding had been that the money was in hand from the start. After months of charges and counter-charges, and heartsick at the

debasement, Andrea decided to end the hurtful squabble and settled for a check that failed by a considerable margin to meet her
expenses. "Situations like this," Andrea wrote one of the organizers,
"make it impossible for any but the rich to participate as I did in
your march—don't you understand that?"

Then came the worst blow of all: Anchor/Doubleday rejected the
nearly completed manuscript, *Pornography*, in which she'd invested three years of work—and at the same time, weirdly, refused to
release her from the contract. This gave sadism a whole new dimension; the traditionally genteel world of publishing chose one of its
prime critics for an undisguised display of the power imbalance
between author and editor. The "horrible blow" deepened Andrea's
depression and led her, in desperation, to do what she most hated:
ask friends to loan her money.[24]

Hearing the rumor that Doubleday was busy assigning blame for
the rejection of *Pornography* on the deficiencies of the manuscript
itself, Andrea, determined to at least salvage her reputation, wrote
a long letter to her Doubleday editor carefully outlining the history of the project: "I am told that the book I submitted to you,
from yr point of view, is not the book I promised you. . . . I showed
you chapter by chapter what I was doing. I don't think I exaggerate
when I say that you encouraged me at every turn, seemed to love
the work, encouraged the direction I was going in. . . . I changed
the nature of the project and its projected length several times with
yr complete approval and encouragement. You told me—and these
are words I treasure—that you thought it the greatest book you had
been involved in publishing." The letter may have been necessary
balm for Andrea's state of mind, but, predictably, it had no effect on
Doubleday's decision. It did, however, finally agree to release her
from the contract.[25]

It had been a dreary six months, suddenly broken by the news
early in August that Wendy Goldwyn, an editor at St. Martin's,
wanted to pick up the contract. Andrea learned that the president
of the firm, Tom McCormick, "hates the book and has done everything possible to discourage Wendy from acquiring it, and me from
accepting the offer." McCormick reluctantly agreed to a contract
that Andrea described as "foul—one that no self-respecting writer

would sign" (the loss of British rights, for example); but she did, desperate for the small advance and comforted by the fact that Wendy "has put her job on the line for the book" and that St. Martin's "is small and ambitious with an interesting list and good relations with small, independent booksellers."

Knowing *Pornography* would definitely see the light of day gave her spirits a needed boost. She vowed, as she wrote Gloria Steinem, "to outwit and get past the male critical establishment, to get the book out and read, not to let it die . . . I feel very aggressive about the book—scared, very scared, but very aggressive." She called on Gloria for help, and other friends too, in advising her where to send the manuscript or galleys, how to "place parts of it in mass market women's magazines that reach different readers than *Ms.*," and how to reach a male audience "who are or who pretend to be feminists." Andrea wrote as well to thank Adrienne Rich for what she learned had been her "incredible support" in persuading St. Martin's to do the book, and asking for her comments on the manuscript. "I cannot tell you how much happier I am now," she wrote Adrienne. "I actually smile. My dreams are only moderately terrible. Feeling is beginning to enter my body. Sometimes hours pass and I am not in knots. It's wonderful."

A mere two weeks later, it all came crashing down. Again. Andrea had agreed as part of the deal to reorganize the material in the book—to put the chapter on the Marquis de Sade, for example, up front—and to write both a new afterword and an introduction; on her own she'd also intended another go-round on the entire manuscript to sharpen and clarify some of her arguments. She had never agreed, as her editor, Wendy Goldwyn, suddenly claimed, to write another *ten* chapters. That demand, coming out of the blue, floored her. Wendy also claimed that St. Martin's had only recently discovered that *Woman Hating* had sold badly (it had, in fact, sold nine thousand copies—quite good for a serious, "mid-list" book).[26]

The truth of the matter was that St. Martin's had gotten cold feet (with Tom McCormick, no doubt, pouring on ice cubes in a steady stream). Andrea knew she was powerless to change his mind, but bitter and disheartened, she was determined on sending Wendy an *accurate* account of what had transpired: "My integrity forbids

me accepting yr bullshit version of the story. . . . I did everything
I agreed to do. Elaine and I were completely upfront with you on
every level about everything. . . . I have absolutely no respect on any
level for what you have done to me; but don't blame me for it—and
don't think for a minute that I buy it." For good measure, Andrea
sent copies of her letter to Gloria, Adrienne, Shere Hite, and Robin
Morgan. Wendy did not respond, though St. Martin's let Elaine
know that they were canceling the contract. As Andrea wrote Adrienne, "On the one hand, I am completely confident and militant
inside; and on the other, I keep crumbling. . . . I'm sorry to sound
so melodramatic but I am getting tired and impatient and with that
goes both arrogance and self-pity. . . . If I could take all the editors
in the world and put them in a bottle and throw them into the sea,
I would I swear."[27]

In the meantime, she continued to make the publishing rounds;
Elaine managed to set up a number of meetings with editors at
other houses, and Andrea, feeling vaguely punch-drunk, continued
to attend them. "And so it goes," she told Adrienne, "long intense
conversations with editors who love the book but essentially want
everything different, and even if someone were right I am afraid
that I have endured so much pure stupidity that I have become stupid and would not know it. Now I'm dealing with a lot of male editors and am seeing incredible gender-polarized readings of the book
that astonish: they keep looking for the woman's voice in the book
that pleads, begs, apologizes—."

Meanwhile, at home in their fifth-floor walkup at 231 Second
Avenue, a hamburger joint had recently opened on the ground
floor and was continuing to send up the dumbwaiter shaft a steady
stream of noxious fumes that permeated the apartment and made
them feel headachy and nauseated much of the time. As Andrea
later described it, "the gas could pass through anything, and did:
a clenched fist; layers of human fat; the porous walls of this particular slum dwelling; the human heart and brain and especially
the abdomen, where it turned spike-like and tore into the lower
intestine with sharp bitter thrusts." John had recently gone to work
at *Essence* (from 1981 to 1985 he'd become its managing editor) and
was out of the apartment during the day, when the fumes were at

their worst. Andrea had to keep the windows open "no matter how cold or wet or ugly or dusty or hot or wretched," and for relief she'd take long, long walks through the city, then crawl back home "like a slug, dragging the day's fatigue behind me." They stopped paying rent and would ultimately bring a lawsuit against the landlord.[28]

Then out of nowhere an editor at Perigee named Sam Mitnick expressed interest, and after what Andrea described as "excruciating negotiations re content, which I won," decided to offer her a contract for *Pornography*. Andrea described Mitnick to Gloria as "tense, neurotic, Jewish, 36, two heart attacks, open heart surgery, very smart, very driven—thrives on the opposition to the book in house." He was, she decided, "a gay Jewish prince," and she liked him: not only was he "very bright" but he "actually likes to read—a superior virtue, and an unusual one, in an editor." Working with Mitnick, Andrea felt she finally understood why the manuscript had "contaminated" its earlier female editors: "they were perceived as one with it, as if it was their opinion. With a male editor, no one even thinks to make that assumption of association."[29]

True or not, meeting Mitnick marked a genuine turning point. Not only did he publish Andrea's book on pornography in 1981, but that same year he got Perigee to put out the paperback edition of *Our Blood*—a goal that had eluded Andrea and Elaine for five years. Still further, Mitnick was able to get Andrea a contract for the next book she wanted to write—a study of rightwing women. "So things are looking up for the first time in a long time," Andrea wrote Robin Morgan. She added, humorously, that henceforth she might even have to give up referring to her writing career as "in the Greek tragic mode," which John had naturalized into the phrase "the House of Camden."[30]

On completing *Pornography*, Andrea, in relief, set down her thoughts: "I had never expected the process . . . to be, in a sense, so ruthless and awful . . . if this is what it does to me, and I know all the material that isn't here, all that is left out, what will it do to others? . . . I don't know, except that I wrote it as truthfully as I knew how—except the last sentence, where I told what might be truth, what might be a lie, knowingly: 'The boys are betting. The boys are wrong' ['The boys are betting on our compliance, our ignorance, our fear. We have always refused to face the worst that men have done to us. The boys count on it.'] Are they [wrong]? Maybe. But about three weeks ago I came across this excerpt from a Kafka letter . . .

"'If the book we are reading does not wake us, as with a foot hammering on our skull, why then do we read it? . . . what we must have are those books which come upon us like ill fortune and distress us deeply, like the death of one we love better than ourselves, like suicide. A book must be an ice-axe to break the sea frozen inside us.' I will probably keep wondering if I have managed something like what Kafka meant, because I think that if it is less, it isn't justified."[31]

Having spent some four years researching the subject—and the text of *Pornography* attests to the depth of that research—Andrea now knew a great deal more than she had as a younger woman, and the new knowledge had transformed her views. She no longer saw pornography as benign—let alone as providing liberating inspiration for the artist, which she *had* thought as a teenager. She'd long since faced "what the content of pornography actually is and how the acts of forced sex in it correspond to the reality of women's lives." In her opinion, even the pornography that could be described "as not being violent, objectifies women in a way which" she now believed "is the precondition for violence . . . dehumanizing someone makes it a lot easier to hurt them." The most pervasive scenario in both written and visual heterosexual pornography, she'd come to believe, centrally involved scenes of (male) dominance and (female) submission. Nor, she now belatedly realized, should that have come as a surprise. How could it be otherwise?

In *Pornography*, Andrea argued that the destructive "meta-message" of most porn, reflecting the society in which it was created, "is that the female in her pure sexuality is sadistic, a conviction articulated not only by the pornographers but also by the enlightened philosophers on all levels. The Christians called women carnal and evil and killed nine million as witches. The enlightened thinkers secularize the conviction, turn faith to idea." Thus Havelock Ellis, in his classic 1933 work *Studies in the Psychology of Sex*, justified "the male force used against women in sex by positing a more fundamental female sadism." Half a century later, Georges Bataille's

1928 *Story of the Eye*, proclaimed profound by a host of contemporary pundits, including Sartre, Foucault, Roland Barthes, and Susan Sontag—particularly Sontag, who Andrea decided "is an honorary man and doesn't intend to give it up"—argued "that pornography of high quality—gracefully conceived and written—is art." "High quality" because, according to Bataille's intellectual admirers, he has revealed "the authentic nexus between sex and death." What his admirers have failed to notice, Andrea believed, is that Bataille has "obscured the meaning of force in sex . . . as the essential dynamic."[32]

"This is 'big news,'" Andrea mockingly writes, "to women whose lives are circumscribed by the sexual sadism of males; but it is good news to those males who justify their abuse of women by believing that women are sexually sadistic at heart and that the sadism of women is formidable despite the fact that it is not socially or historically self-evident. The cage is justified because the animal inside it is wild and thus dangerous. . . . As long as this alleged female sadism is controlled by men, it can be manipulated to give men pleasure: dominance in the male system is pleasure."

Andrea's treatment in *Pornography* of the Marquis de Sade's intellectual admirers is no less pungent. She mocks the claims of his then most recent biographer, Donald Thomas, that "the cruelties of his fiction are quite at variance with almost all of Sade's conduct" and that his sexual desires were "indulged largely in his fiction." Such characterizations are not merely false history, Andrea charges, but they also serve "to trivialize Sade's brutalities against women." What such a defense amounts to, she tellingly charges, is that "the victims of Sade's sexual terrorism are less important than 'philosophical disquisitions.'" To demonstrate that Thomas' apologia typifies the approach of Sade's biographers, Andrea quotes from another: "He [Sade] had given a few girls and women a little pain, but not so much really. . . . Most of the women he had used in his orgies had come to him willingly enough, for payment, or, oddly enough, because they liked him." Tellingly, Andrea makes one of Sade's victims, Rose Keller, the co-dedicatee (along with John Stoltenberg) of her book.[33]

In *Pornography* Andrea also takes on—and eviscerates—almost along the way, such present-day admirers of Sade's as the literary critic Richard Gilman and the cultural historian Christopher Lasch. She dismisses Gilman's "banal prose" rather quickly, with a quote from his 1980 book *Decadence*: Sade "is the first compelling enunciator in modern times of the desire . . . to act otherwise than existing moral structures coerced one into doing." Substitute the name of any villain—Hitler, Stalin—for Sade, and the absurdity of Gilman's admiration becomes apparent. Andrea was only slightly more respectful of Lasch. She cites his statement that Sade anticipated a "defense of woman's sexual rights—their rights to dispose of their own bodies, as feminists would put it today"—though he did so, according to Lasch, "more clearly than the feminists." Andrea's response is scorching: "The notion that Sade presages feminist demands for women's sexual rights is rivaled in self-serving absurdity only by the opinion of Gerald and Caroline Greene, in *S-M: The Last Taboo*, that 'if there was one thing de Sade was not, it was a sexist.'"

To the assertion of some of her critics that "women do have more freedom than they had, say, a hundred, 150 years ago," thus demonstrating that change is possible, Andrea's response was that "the kind of change I'm interested in is when women are no longer defined in relation to and by contrast with men. And the kind of change I'm interested in has to do with an end to a gender system that I think is specious, that I think is not . . . [an accurate] categorization of human beings . . . a woman is born into this system and her destiny is predetermined from birth. The coercive nature of that predetermination is what we're struggling against . . . one of the reasons that we don't have answers is that we have refused to describe the sexual system in which we live accurately." She felt that to the extent she'd made a contribution, it was in "describing this system the way that it is. . . . We're going to have to find a way to organize an economy from the ground up that is not based on the sex-class labour of women, including reproductive labour. Socialist or Marxist societies have not done that. . . . What I believe we have to do is everything. I know that ends up sounding like no answer, but it is what we have to do." It wasn't a job, in her view, that the intellectual left was prepared to take on. It had, as Andrea saw it, "*advocated* pornography as crucial to liberation," and an endless line of prominent left supporters, from Ramsay Clark to Dick Gregory to Paul Krassner and an "unbelievable array of leftist newspapers and writers," had actually claimed Larry Flynt, publisher of *Hustler*, as a working-class hero.

With the publication of *Pornography: Men Possessing Women*, Andrea got back as good as she'd given out. Her legion of critics were quick to tell her that she had not managed much more than a screech in the night. Fortunately, Kitty had read the book while it was still in manuscript, had recognized it as Andrea's most important work to date, and had told her so before the critical deluge descended. "This is just an incredible book," she'd written Andrea, "and fundamental to all of our work on every level." Kitty singled out as "overwhelmingly excellent" Andrea's discussion of fetishism and objectification and her arresting treatment of racism—namely, that "poverty forces . . . [the black woman into pornography], but it is the sexual valuation of her skin that *predetermines* her *poverty*."[34]

A few other assessments appeared that grasped the significance of *Pornography*, including Leah Fritz's three cheers for Andrea's deft skewering of the reigning male cultural gods, including Norman Mailer and his "essentially racist" work, *The White Negro*. And when Dorothy Allison wrote what was at least a mixed review, Andrea wrote her to say that "after the vicious stuff I've been getting on my book, I was pretty grateful to you because you granted me something, quite a lot actually." But those few friendly voices aside, Andrea took a severe critical drubbing; it was almost as if the deeper her perceptions went, the louder the shrieks that rent the air.[35]

Many of the reviews of the book were woundingly personal: as a lesbian she hated all men; her rage distorted her judgment; overweight and "unsightly," she invited male rejection. She was accused as well of a host of intellectual crimes: that she'd created a dualistic system—abusive men, submissive women—that was not only ahistorical, but philosophically sterile; and, some of her critics charged—quite misreading Andrea's utopian side—that she believed that male supremacy would, necessarily, *always* be in the saddle, with only momentary glimpses of freedom possible for women. As Andrea's friend Leah Fritz put it, "The rage spewed forth by these critics, both male and female, can only be compared to the riots that occurred when Picasso's paintings were exhibited at the famous Armory show in 1913."[36]

One of the most negative reviews came in the most important press outlet: the *New York Times*. Ellen Willis, the reviewer, acknowledged that pornography, like "all cultural images influence behavior . . . they articulate and legitimize feelings that already exist." Pornography, in other words, was a symptom not a cause of the violence endemic in the culture. What Ellis omitted and implicitly denied was in fact at the heart of Andrea's argument—that along with *representing* the amount of violence in the culture, pornography also *amplified* that violence. In place of acknowledging the breadth and sophistication of Andrea's analysis, Willis settled for calling it "a book-length sermon, preached with a rhetorical flourish and a single-minded intensity that meet somewhere between poetry and rant."[37]

Andrea had a long history behind her of being ignored or belittled or misunderstood, and she tried to be philosophical about Willis' put-down even though she was aware that a pan in the *Times* all but guaranteed truncated sales. As she wrote her friend Ellen Frankfort, "If the book were in cloth that would be the end of it. Since it's in paper it has a chance . . . [though] the reviews around the country, with about two exceptions, have been absolutely devastating: 'the book is sexual bigotry, hatred of men', etc. Nothing about what I actually did. Nothing about what pornography actually is . . . it's a crazy kind of hostility, completely out of control on every level." When Andrea sent the book out to "lots of feminists of many different kinds," the response was different—was "overwhelmingly enthusiastic."

Being human, Andrea suffered from the reception. "I am having a hard time with it," she wrote a friend. "I had no idea it could affect me this way." Yet she stood her ground. She insisted that she had *not* chosen "out-of-the-ordinary" examples of pornography but rather representative ones: "I did not weight the argument," she told a reporter from the feminist publication *Sojourner*, "by picking anything that was particularly bizarre"; to begin her chapter on "Force," for example, she purposely chose a picture "that most people would not view as violent"—and then persuasively dissected its essentially ugly misogyny. The overall message of *Pornography* was clear-cut: the industry directly and accurately reflected social psychology— the existing *power* differential between men and women.

7

Lovelace; Trans; and Right-Wing Women

A ndrea's dismay over the reception of *Pornography* was a match for the negative mood of the country as a whole in regard to the issues relating to gender and sexuality about which she most cared. One key development in the late seventies and early eighties involved the transformation of both national political parties: in accelerating numbers, the Southern Democrats shifted allegiance to the Republican Party, which simultaneously began to purge itself of its own pro-choice minority. In the 1980 election, reversing a long-standing historical trend, more white women (by a margin of nearly 10 percent) voted Democratic than voted Republican. The parties were becoming more polarized, and the Republicans decidedly more conservative. In his inaugural address, Ronald Reagan spoke of the need to "protect the unborn" and, in a transparent attack on racial busing, pledged to "end the manipulation of schoolchildren by utopian planners."

The backlash against the women's movement was palpable. Attacks on abortion rights steadily mounted, spurred on by pressure groups like the Eagle Forum and the Moral Majority. Poor women suffered most: when the Supreme Court, in *Harris v. McRae*, confirmed the constitutionality of the 1976 Hyde Amendment (which banned the use of federal funding to pay for abortions through Medicaid), it greatly increased the odds that some 45 million low-income women would lose access to *safe* abortions. The Reagan administration heightened their plight when it shifted responsibility for a host of other social service programs—rape crisis centers, food pantries, battered women's shelters, etc.—from the federal government to the states or to the private sector, neither of which had the resources to meet the demand.

Meanwhile, the demise of the Equal Rights Amendment looked assured as the right poured money and troops into the struggle to kill it on the state level. In another, quite different sign of the times, the books of George Gilder began to grace the *New York Times* bestseller lists. Especially popular was his *Sexual Suicide*, which stressed the biologically determined differences between men and women and denounced feminists as a profound threat to the "natural" unit of the nuclear family (which Gilder further glorified in *Wealth and Poverty*, a book that sold over a million copies).

The radical feminist movement itself was in considerable disarray, with the issues of pornography and sadomasochism increasingly dividing it—abetted, on a more elevated plane, by the division between feminists committed to the view that men and women were biologically different (and complementary) and those like Andrea, who saw gender as socially constructed. Deflated expectations took hold across the board; as Andrea herself predicted soon after Reagan's triumph, "We lost an awful lot in this [1980] election and most of us are in a state of anguish. We face a loss of abortion rights [and] the defeat of the ERA is assured." Legal protection for rape within marriage was still on the books in all states but three, and "we have 28 million battered wives."[1]

In an interview with *Feminist Studies* in 1981, Andrea told the interviewer that the feminist movement had been helping women, "saving their lives," but "we're not changing the institutions that keep the women getting hurt. . . . We're sitting here talking about some improvement in some laws . . . [but] we have to use pornography as a tool to understand the system in which we live, and to change it. We would be fools," she said, "to think that we would have inner lives that are entirely dissociated from the actual system in which we live. . . . I think that men commit acts of forced sex against women systematically" and that was precisely what the women's movement had begun to realize.

Not Betty Friedan's movement. Not the leadership, as opposed to the grassroots membership, of NOW. Not the brilliant *Village Voice* columnist Ellen Willis, who derisively insisted that "in Andrea Dworkin's moral universe the battle of the sexes is a Manichaean clash between absolute power and absolute powerlessness, absolute villains and absolute victims." Barbara Deming pointed out to Willis that Andrea "considers male sexual aggression not innate, but learned." As she'd written in *Pornography*, such aggression is "institutionalized in sports, the military, acculturated sexuality, the history and mythology of heroism, it is taught to boys until they become its advocates . . . advocates of that which they most fear." Barbara herself differed from Andrea in thinking "that men are more divided in themselves than [she] allows"; when boys "abandon their mothers, learn contempt for them," Barbara wrote, "a *part* of them regrets the choice, sees it as a lying act, and always will. This regret [is] rarely conscious of course."[2]

In regard to Friedan, Andrea was scornful. Friedan "has been insisting for several years now," Andrea wrote late in 1979, "about how to maintain our wondrous equality which we have already achieved according to her. *We* are concerned about wife battery, marital rape, incest, and the many forms of child abuse. We are concerned about the poverty of women as a class. . . . We are concerned about the sexual harassment suffered by working women and students. We are concerned about the rights of lesbian mothers and homosexual children. We are concerned about the proliferation of woman-hating propaganda. . . . We are concerned about the reproductive rights of women and girls. . . . We are concerned about the most basic issues of material survival. Friedan is concerned about issues of privilege and comfort. Most women do not have that luxury."[3]

The closest thing to a publicity campaign for *Pornography* resulted not from favorable reviews or Perigee's ads for the book, but from the accidents of friendship. Andrea's close friend, the photographer Elsa Dorfman, was married to the liberal lawyer Harvey Silverglate, and he in turn was friendly with the lawyer and academic Alan Dershowitz. From that string of connections emerged a Dworkin/Dershowitz debate at Radcliffe's Longfellow Hall on May 13, 1981. The place was packed, with people sitting in the aisles and standing along the walls. The pending event, according to one reporter, "was the hottest topic in town, and most local newspapers and radio stations carried stories on it." In an interview she gave the evening before the debate, Andrea explained her own reasons for accepting the invitation: "He offered me access to his institutional power, and I had to accept. It hurts me terribly to be so powerless in this society that I have to accept his chivalry." Doubtless, too, she viewed the debate as a chance to counteract the landslide of negative reviews, and to spread word of the book's *actual* contents.

Andrea opened the debate in a tone that a reporter described as "soft-spoken and very eloquent." (People meeting Andrea for the first time and having only read her vehement prose were often shocked at how gentle and "nice" she was on a personal level, and what a generous "good listener"; her private voice was kind and empathetic.) Julie Bindel, for one, loved her "dry humour, unwavering integrity, and shy vulnerability . . . [she was] warm, open-minded . . . with feminists from all sides of the debate, Andrea would patiently and respectfully listen."[4]

On the platform, she did often sound fierce, and her soft-spoken speech that night at Radcliffe wasn't typical. She did, though, successfully convey the essence of her defense against the standard charge that curtailing pornography was an affront to the First Amendment's guarantee of free speech: "women as a class are excluded from being able to exercise speech—rape, battery, and incest all being ways of keeping a class of people from being able to speak at all." The overflow crowd remained hushed throughout her talk—and gave her a standing ovation at its close.

Dershowitz, for his part, was apparently not having one of his "chivalrous" evenings. Instead of using the podium and microphone, as Andrea had, he remained seated (translation: "this was not an occasion one was required to 'rise' to"). According to a reporter from *Sojourner*, he "almost immediately alienated the audience by calling Dworkin and her ideas 'dangerous.'" He then minimized the "fuss" over pornography by declaring that the women involved had "obviously" volunteered to be photographed. Was Dworkin suggesting that they be denied the right to do so? In answer to his own question, he opened a magazine that he said was written by a group of "S & M lesbians" and read a passage from it denouncing any and all efforts to censor pornographic material. If censorship came to pass, Dershowitz warned the audience—apparently assuming it was composed solely of gay people—"your own interests could be the first ones ruled out." He managed to antagonize the crowd to the point where several spectators angrily shouted out that he was a "sexist" and a "pornographer." Andrea declined to respond, other than to say that Dershowitz had misrepresented her views and turned the event into "a mind fuck."[5]

Simultaneous with the Radcliffe debate, Andrea and Kitty were gradually being drawn into a controversy that centered precisely on Dershowitz's claim that women voluntarily participated in pornographic productions. The dispute focused on Linda Boreman, the birth name of the woman who'd come to be known as Linda Lovelace, star of the hugely successful 1972 hardcore film *Deep Throat* (even the *New York Times* reviewed it). In 1980, Linda had published her autobiography, *Ordeal*, which described in convincing detail how her abusive manager, pimp, and husband, Chuck Traynor, had coerced her into prostitution and into performing in porn films ("My initiation was a gang rape by five men, arranged by Mr. Traynor. . . . I felt like garbage, I engaged in sex acts in pornography against my will to avoid being killed").

It was Gloria Steinem who told Andrea that she had to read *Ordeal*. She did, though no one had to convince her that such horror stories, which paralleled her own, *did* happen, and with some frequency. That Linda herself had been living a nightmare was supported by polygraph tests and by a professional psychiatric diagnosis of complex PTSD. Once having read *Ordeal*, Andrea was unable to stop thinking about it, and she began to wonder if Linda's grievances against the pornographers couldn't be brought as a civil suit for damages. At that point she didn't know MacKinnon well, but she invited her to a book party for her short story collection, *a new woman's broken heart*.[6]

They talked together in a corner about *Ordeal* and MacKinnon particularly remembers Andrea saying "We got the Klan, why can't we get the pornographers?" Intrigued, MacKinnon mulled the matter over and then phoned Andrea to say that she thought a civil suit against the makers of the porn film *Deep Throat* (in which Linda had been forced to perform prodigious feats of fellatio) might be a possible way to go. At a subsequent WAP event, to which Andrea had invited MacKinnon, they met Linda, then eight months pregnant with her second child. Gloria Steinem had already briefed Linda about a possible suit, and she told MacKinnon, "I hear you have some legal ideas about *Deep Throat*." When MacKinnon said she did, Linda suggested a meeting at her house on Long Island, where she lived with her second husband, Larry Marciano.[7]

The group that soon after drove out to Long Island consisted of Andrea, Kitty, Gloria, Stan Pottinger, a former Department of Justice Civil Division lawyer close to Gloria, and Kent Harvey, a colleague of Kitty's. As Andrea later put it, they spent "about six hours drilling Linda like banshies from hell. . . . I was very, very rough on her—much more than Kitty was. And I came out of it believing not only every word that she said but that she was tough enough to be able to do this. So we sort of set the parameters of basically making a civil rights claim that covered marital rape, abduction, rape, prostitution, and the making of pornography."

Through the auspices of WAP, a press conference was arranged that included Linda, Andrea, Kitty, and Gloria (and in supportive attendance, the ERA activist Valerie Harper, who during much of the 1970s had played Rhoda Morgenstern on *The Mary Tyler Moore Show*). From that point on, the case would absorb a fair amount of Andrea and Kitty's available time. A few additional people were gradually brought into the discussion, including Linda's husband and a lawyer who represented a number of Vietnam vets. What became clear early on was that the statute of limitations had already run out—a serious impediment to bringing the lawsuit (not to mention that as recently as 1975, marital rape had been legal in all fifty states). Eventually, they all put their opinions on the table, with the final decision left up to Linda. Andrea and Kitty wanted to go forward, but none of the men did, and Gloria (who Linda trusted entirely) sided with the men. Kitty came up with the unique theory that a viable way around the statute of limitations might be possible under a court ruling that declared sex discrimination a conspiracy to violate civil rights.

The risks for Linda were formidable, and (according to Kitty) for quite some time she held up "strongly under all of this." Kitty herself was prepared to proceed, though at the time she was an underpaid, untenured university professor who would personally—Andrea being too poor—bear the brunt of the considerable legal expenses entailed. As Linda mulled over the decision of whether to proceed, Kitty, through long letters, kept her thoroughly informed, never minimizing the risky consequences of a judge's ruling against them. Linda seemed to grow more determined by the day, and at one point Kitty triumphantly wrote Andrea that "every time Linda asserts herself . . . I am an audience of thousands of women's voices cheering . . ." Yet in the end, Linda—who now had two young children to take care of—decided not to go ahead with the lawsuit; it was simply too risky, both psychically and financially. Kitty remained her lawyer.[8]

In the fall of 1981, Kitty and Andrea planned to teach a graduate seminar on feminist theory together at Stanford, where Kitty was currently on a "hand-to-mouth" appointment. But as it turned out, the feminist studies department wasn't keen on inviting Andrea to the campus, and Kitty, though "livid and rageful," made the strategic decision to postpone submitting the course proposal. Andrea interpreted the temporary retreat as a permanent defeat and, deeply insulted at Stanford's cold shoulder, refused to pursue the project further. Kitty wittily noted that "we must have crossed some line from being friends into being a long-term relationship, in that you are having prideful explosions at me" (Andrea had hung up on her at one point). No, Kitty added, "I am not just like you—why does that mean I cannot be trusted?"[9]

Andrea apologized for hanging up, but otherwise (temporarily) stood her ground: when you told "me you had given up our course because of the threats in order to get a [university] contract, you also said this was something (a kind of thing, a category of act) you had never done before in yr life. You recognized the character of it, what it was and what it meant. I recognize what it was too. That's all. It shocked and hurt me terribly . . . giving up that proposal for a joint course was giving in to McCarthyism, political blackmail, and the ostracization of a radical, in this case me. . . . I don't like this kind of shit, Kitty. . . . I want to keep working together on Linda, pornography, the issues . . . but I do not want to come out there." And they did continue to work together, closely, on the issues—which in turn led to enough meetings and personal contact to rapidly reintroduce warmth and trust into the relationship.

During the early months of 1982, Andrea was absorbed in finishing *Right-Wing Women*. That consuming effort would alone have necessitated a considerable retreat from activism, but the divisions and denunciations that had increasingly marked feminist politics made the retreat something of a welcome respite. It was a time of disgruntlement in the nation as a whole, as well as in the feminist movement; despite a large tax cut and a steep rise in military spending, 10 percent of the labor force was unemployed. As for feminism, polarization on the West Coast was particularly pronounced; much of it focused on the public actions of Samois, a lesbian S/M group, and its publications (*Coming to Power* and Pat Califia's *Sapphistry*). Middle-of-the-road heterosexual feminists were appalled, and— somewhat to Andrea's surprise—Betty Friedan's NOW passed a resolution condemning S/M. The issue of race further divided the movement. African American and Hispanic women, feeling their special perspectives and needs largely ignored, formed their own publishing collective, Kitchen Table Press; its anthology *This Bridge Called My Back*, edited by Gloria Anzaldua and Cherrie Moraga, became an instant classic.

Andrea was feeling both the economic pinch and the escalating feminist warfare. Her East Village apartment building, already beset by noxious fumes, had also become overrun with rats. She and John were desperate to move but couldn't afford to, and Andrea settled into what she herself described as a "sullen, morbid, deathlike" mood, finding reliable comfort only in John and in the absorption of work. "It is impossible to be part of a movement," she wrote a friend, "that embraces the swastika as sex toy" (a reference to the symbol that now and then appeared on the leather outfits of S/M dykes). "The courage required to face and change the real condition of women under men is not here."

John shared Andrea's negative view of sadomasochism. In his own 1980 article in *Gay Community News*, "What Is the Meaning of S&M?," deploring its spreading appeal, he argued that its roots were to be found "in the social structure of male-over-female domination"—in eroticized violence and powerlessness: "In order to believe that relationships between sadists and masochists are 'liberated,'" he wrote, "one would have to believe that contempt is caring, that humiliation is respect, that brutality is affection, and that bondage is freedom."[10]

Andrea recognized that her current pessimistic mood might be exaggerated: "I think my limits are real—I think there is plenty I don't see—I am sure of it." Still, it was hard not to be in what she called "a misogynistic snit" when pro-S/M and pro-pornography forces seemed to have taken over the movement and some of her own basic beliefs had come under fire. In her view, feminists were currently "underestimating the magnitude of male power" and, perhaps even more important, seemed increasingly wedded to what she viewed as the mistaken notion that "gender" had a biological basis, was an intrinsic given. "I don't believe in gender," Andrea wrote a friend, "and for what it's worth, I hope I will die not believing in it, whatever else I start or stop believing. I don't believe that gender exists outside a social system of oppression . . . and female friendship within this system has a revolutionary consequence that is intrinsic to it . . . it can be as close to freedom as we can get—but it is also as tattered and ragged and ruined as our various bodies and souls."

As the strength of the radical wing of feminism weakened, Andrea not only held her ground, but extended it. In her very first book, *Woman Hating*, published in 1974, she'd taken a firm and positive view not only of the gender model of androgyny but also of those who insisted on the integrity of a "transsexual" identity (today more commonly referred to as transgender). Empathy in the face of human suffering was a hallmark of Andrea's character, and as early as 1974 she insisted that "every transsexual is entitled to a sex-change operation, and it should be provided by the community as one of its functions." (Nor did she ever change her mind on the subject.) Back then she'd also been way ahead of the cultural curve in insisting that there were not two genders but rather many, predicting that "we will discover cross-sexed phenomena in proportion to our ability to see them." The "multi-sexual nature of people," she argued, must be "accepted into the forms of human community."[11]

Half a dozen years later, as the emphasis on male/female biological differences continued to gain cultural ground, Andrea stood firm on her earlier conviction that gender was fluid and multi-faceted. For a time in the seventies, she'd been somewhat friendly with Janice Raymond, whose transphobic 1979 book *The Transsexual Empire: The Making of a She-Male*, deplored the "medicalization" of gender that encouraged surgical intervention to create "a woman according to man's image." It was a view that Andrea deplored, and she let Raymond know it at some length: "I knew of transsexuals in Europe as a small, vigorously persecuted minority, without any recourse to civil or political protection. They lived in absolute exile, as far as I could see, conjuring up for me the deepest reaches of Jewish experience. They were driven by their ostracization to prostitution, drugs, and suicide, conjuring up for me the deepest reaches of female experience. Their sense of gender dislocateness [sic] was congruent with mine, in that my rage at the cultural and so-called biological definitions of womanhood and femininity was absolute. I perceived their suffering as authentic. . . . Looking back, I can see other, unknown at the time, sources of my own particular empathy. Male-to-female transsexuals were in rebellion against the phallus and so was I. Female-to-male transsexuals were seeking a freedom only possible to males in patriarchy, and so was I. The means were different, but the impulses were related. I haven't changed my mind." Kitty entirely agreed with Andrea: "Jan Raymond is wrong. . . . She is thinking that our problem is gender. I think that our problem is sexuality."[12]

Andrea felt, too—and deeply regretted—that so many political women now seemed to believe "that talking to all kinds of women means abandoning their own style and their own principles. What are they afraid of? Guilt by association? Is this what the feminist movement has come to?—that women can be discredited, or fear they'll be accused of sharing their politics if they *talk* to conservative women, or middle-class women, or women in high heels or women in dresses or women who wear make-up." Any woman who feels that "having a politically correct line" and associates only with those who share it were, in Andrea's view, "hallucinating an autonomy that women by definition in a male supremacist society cannot have."[13]

In regard to men, Andrea felt that the women's movement as a whole hadn't concentrated nearly enough on talking to and educating men—an opinion, had it been widely known, that would have shocked those multitudes, then and since, who have cavalierly dismissed her as a man-hater, and probably a pathological one. The feminist sociologist Michael Kimmel, himself heterosexual, has been one of the few men to question the dogmatic view that Andrea thought "all men are rapists"; Kimmel insisted that in fact "all manner of furious male-bashing, man-hating, and anti-sex ideas have been projected onto her."

What Andrea actually felt was that among younger men especially (as she told an interviewer in 1982), "in the last four or five years I've begun to see a substantial and vocal and active minority of men that is profoundly anti-sexist. And I think we have to understand that we've really made an impact there, it's one that we haven't even recognized, we don't even know we've done it. . . . And 'educate' is an euphemism for put pressure on, coerce, do activism around everything, the whole spectrum of action from the most militant to the most communicative."

Andrea completed *Right-Wing Women* in late March of 1982. Only a few weeks later, in mid-April, more than eight hundred women gathered at Barnard College for what would become a historic conference on female sexuality. Andrea wasn't there by choice, though the invitation to attend had been an "open call." The conference had a number of plenary sessions and some seventeen workshops devoted to a wide variety of issues (including abortion rights, psychotherapy, popular sex advice literature, and disability rights). WAP distorted the actual breadth of the conference in claiming that it was essentially about three issues only: S/M, lesbian butch/femme roles, and pornography (in fact, there was only one workshop on butch/femme, and none specifically focused on S/M, though that topic was often referenced in other workshops). WAP was closer to the mark when it insisted that no special effort had been made to enlist any of its members in the eight months of planning sessions that led up to the conference "to tell the truth about our politics," is how the WAP protest leaflet that they handed out at the conference put it.[14]

WAP and two other anti-porn groups staged a protest at the conference garbed in T-shirts that on one side read "For Feminist Sexuality" and on the other "Against S/M," and also circulated a two-page leaflet accusing the organizers of shutting out "a major part of the feminist movement" in favor of "the very sexual institutions and values that oppress all women." In response to a barrage of phone calls from women identifying themselves as members of anti-porn groups and critical of the conference for advancing "patriarchal values," the Barnard administrators buckled under the pressure and on the eve of the event confiscated 1,500 copies of the seventy-two-page handbook *Diary of a Conference*, which its organizers had put together as a guide to the event. Carole Vance, coordinator of the conference, subsequently ascribed the protest to the anti-pornographers' "loss of control over the discourse."

The arguments within feminism remained at fever pitch through most of the 1980s. When the journal *Feminist Studies* subsequently printed documents relating to the conference in its Spring 1983 issue (followed in its Fall 1983 issue by fourteen pages of letters denouncing WAP), that organization's steering committee sent *Feminist Studies* an eleven-page letter of protest correcting what it insisted had been the many distortions in the journal's coverage. *Feminist Studies* refused to print it.

The letter contained a concise summary of what WAP insisted were its *actual* positions, as opposed to the distorted versions (so WAP asserted) ascribed to it at the conference and repeated in *Feminist Studies*—and by a number of historians since. Though Andrea hadn't participated in the conference, and hadn't formally joined WAP, her own views adhered closely to those in the WAP steering committee letter. She wasn't "anti-sex"—she was against what she viewed as stereotypic role-playing (butch-femme) and rituals of dominance and submission (S/M). Nor had she "sought out" an alliance with the right ("Feminists who did anything against pornography were accused of being in bed with the right," Andrea insisted. "We have never worked with the right. . . . We have never wanted to and so we never have . . . part of the media coverage has been to create an alliance that has never existed"). The related accusation of "playing into the Right's traditional values," moreover, was the equivalent of saying that one should refrain from criticizing Israel for confiscating Palestinian land because it would feed anti-Semitism.[15]

Of prime importance—both to Andrea and to WAP—was what they insisted had been the conference's misrepresentation of their position regarding biological determinism. Throughout the conference, WAP members had been referred to as "cultural feminists"—that is, advocates of the view that women and men were fundamentally, innately, different from each other. So-called cultural feminists focused on their own subculture, art, and spirituality. And they insisted that male *values*—not *men*—were the enemy, and in particular, *machismo* and normative heterosexuality.[16]

The opposing forces within feminism weren't always clearly demarked, and many feminists went back and forth between the opposing camps. But at the unwavering heart of cultural feminism was the conviction that biology determined that women are fundamentally alike—and fundamentally different from men. Andrea's view, to the contrary, was that although sex roles *were* currently dichotomous, both the structure and content of those roles were culturally constructed; neither men nor women were naturally this way or that. Her vehemence in denouncing men as selfish, violent, and woman-hating could sometimes seem the echo of a determinist position, but her core belief was that a gender-just world *could* come into existence; nothing in our hormones or genes prevented it (though the oppressive weight and imprinting of historical *experience* might).

When John Stoltenberg took part in a panel on pornography at a different conference, he put the matter succinctly: "I want a world in which gender is not a battle for power differences. In fact, I could really do without gender"—that is, as currently defined. To achieve a social order free of female subordination and abuse, the epiphenomena—pornography, sadomasochism, and dichotomous sex roles (like butch-femme)—that reflected and deepened a split-gender view of humanity had to be uncompromisingly resisted. In Andrea's view, the defenders of porn, S/M, and butch-femme were deluded: they saw themselves as radical heroes, unconventional pioneers of sexual pleasure bent on rethinking feminist orthodoxy that viewed women as victims devoid of agency, whereas in fact, Andrea believed, they were profoundly conformist, offering strict allegiance to the *pre-existing* division of sex roles between those who dominate and those who submit.[17]

Right-Wing Women, released early in 1983, was by a considerable margin Andrea's most impressive achievement to date, though arguable in some of its particulars and necessarily dated in others (women today are not *as* segregated in "female job ghettos"; nor is politics any longer "an all-male clique of power"). The book's sustained tone is one of solemn authority—the sort of mature even-temperedness foretold but not sustained in her earlier books, which periodically succumbed to eruptions of thunderous moralizing. *Right-Wing Women* reflects more fully than any of Andrea's previous work the many-faceted strands of her temperament, ranging (without contradiction) from brooding desolation and gloom-ridden sooth-saying, to a sensitive receptivity, even tenderness, toward those she opposed politically—in this case, right-wing women, who most radical feminists of her generation contemptuously dismissed as ignorant puppets of their masters. Fittingly, Andrea dedicated the book to two other multi-faceted and generous women: Gloria Steinem and Muriel Rukeyser.

At the heart of *Right-Wing Women* is Andrea's obstinate insistence not only of their humanity, but also of their *agency*: they know what they're doing; their choices are deliberate, even shrewd. They're not stupid, they're not dupes, they're not unfeeling robots. They may have made their pact with the Devil, but as a survival tactic, and not as sacrificial lambs. The right-wing woman, in Andrea's view, conforms to a pre-assigned role, but does so as a necessary safety measure. "No one," Andrea writes, "can bear to live a meaningless life"; by attaching themselves to men and to "the values honored by men," these women "seek to acquire value." Which is what we all do, or try to.

The Right offers women (or claims to) valuable protection—from disorder, from homelessness, from shame. It abides by the rules of the game: domesticity and child-bearing; if adhered to, it guarantees protection from a dangerous outside world. Andrea illustrates the difficult trade-off with some surprising examples, pre-eminently the anti-homosexual crusader Anita Bryant, who in 1983, with AIDS now a full-blown catastrophe, would hardly seem a likely subject for sympathy. Andrea uses Bryant's autobiography, *Mine Eyes Have Seen the Glory*, to document the brutal poverty, material and emotional, of her childhood. When her father deserted the family, Anita blamed herself, in particular her "driving ambition." As an adult, guilty over her "abnormal" wish to win fame as a singer, she proved easy prey for Bob Green, a Miami disc jockey, who manipulated her into marriage and then took over her life. "One sees a woman," Andrea writes, "hemmed in, desperately trying to please a husband . . . whose control of her life on every level is virtually absolute" and sometimes violent. Torn between her desire for a career and her assigned role as a "good wife and mother," religion became Anita's only real solace, Jesus her "true husband." Her notoriously bigoted testimony against the Dade County homosexual rights ordinance was given, in Andrea's view, reluctantly—anything less, Bob Green had insisted, would be to condone sin, to fall short in her Christian duty. Eventually Anita succeeded in freeing herself from Green, and Andrea, in a final benediction, writes "*Pace*, sister."

Not all of *Right-Wing Women* is quite so benign. As part of her research, Andrea attended the National Women's Conference in Houston and tried to talk with some of the conservative women in attendance; she found their conversation "ludicrous, terrifying, bizarre, instructive"—and only intermittently moving. Many of the women refused to talk with her at all. Those who did told her that lesbians are "rapists, certified committers of sexual assault against women and girls." Nor were the women more kindly disposed toward Jews; she was told they were "Christ-killers, communists and usurers." Dialogue proved impossible: the women were impervious to counter-views. Yet Andrea—here *denying* them agency—placed the blame not on the women themselves but on the men who "almost totally" controlled the right-wing movement, and built it "on the fear and ignorance of women."

The women knew, as Andrea saw it, that "men hate intelligence in women," and in *Right-Wing Women* she indicts the men for bringing "home half-truths, ego-laden lies," which they then use "to demand solace or sex or housekeeping." The intelligence of the women had scant chance of being expressed, let alone nurtured: "without the light of public life, discourse, and action," intelligence dies. Yet women's innate *capacity*, Andrea stresses, is hardly in doubt: the three greatest writers in the English language were surely, she believed, George Eliot, Jane Austen, and Virginia Woolf.

Andrea makes it clear in *Right-Wing Women* that she isn't suggesting men employ overt force in reducing the women in their lives to submission, nor that most women are consciously discontented with their lot. Her focus is on how woman-hating has been institutionalized and how those institutions—like the law—serve to keep women in their place. Certainly in the 1980s, and even today, marital rape and battering are difficult to prove in court, even when women do find the considerable courage necessary to bring suit. Nor does Andrea put all the blame for women's unequal position on right-wing men; she's profoundly angry at men on the *left* for their opposition to abortion and their generally patronizing attitude toward their female compatriots. She even takes her lesbian sisters to task for their self-satisfaction in being cultural rebels when in fact all that they've done is to "break a few rules." And she has no patience for cultural feminists who portray themselves as *inherently* nurturant and closer to nature than men are. Nor, in fact, does Andrea see men as irredeemable; their smug sense of superiority is the product of a given set of social values, and society *can* be renovated, its values changed.

The only instance in *Right-Wing Women* where Andrea consistently loses her footing is when she leaves the contemporary scene and turns to historical examples to make her points—assuming, in the process, an unchanging continuity from past to present. She equates, for example, the obstacles and mockery that greeted the remarkable Victoria Woodhull in the late nineteenth century when she asserted her independence and "masculine" competence as directly relevant to the current plight of women. But Woodhull's arrest under the 1872 Comstock Law could not happen today, nor can her crusade "against the material dependency of women on men" be compared to the expanded economic opportunities today for women, even if access still falls far short of the ideal, especially for the many who lack access to a first-rate education.

When Andrea asks "Is there a way out of the home that does not lead, inevitably and horribly, to the street corner?" she means for us to treat the question as still being accurately descriptive of the either/or options available to women today. But if housewife or whore no longer covers the available range of options, the range for most women remains, especially working-class women, sharply limited. Still, it was probably an overstatement to say (as Andrea does) that "women's work that is not marriage or prostitution is mostly segregated, always underpaid, stagnant, sex-stereotyped." Nor is the ideological commitment of right-wing women sufficiently explained by the formulaic "they do what they have to in order to survive." Many, if not most, could survive even if they did not hate Jews and homosexuals. Similarly, Andrea's flat-out insistence that, as in the past, women today "cannot be responsible for pregnancy, in the sense of acting to prevent it, because women do not control when, where, how, and on what terms they have intercourse" is simply not an accurate accounting of the options currently available.

Fortunately, there is far more insight than hyperbole in *Right-Wing Women*. And the hyperbole itself is sometimes fetching, expressed with a power and certitude that prove captivating even when we blink in disbelief at the actual content. Some of the power of Andrea's prose comes from a free-wheeling mix of the sonorous sentence with in-your-face street talk. A sample: "In sorrow or not, bearing babies is what women can do that men need—really need, no handjob can substitute here . . ." What is so disarming about Andrea the human being is that, with all of her fears and fragilities, she could front on the world like a pugilistic tough guy.

A few years before *Right-Wing Women* was published, Andrea and John had finally been able to leave their rat-infested slum apartment and move to a fourth-floor walkup on Tenth Street in Brooklyn. She'd long wished for more space and a reprieve from the sordid surroundings of their tenement apartment on Second Avenue and 14th Street—the flashing lights, the ambulance sirens, the music blasting through the night, the screams from the street, the junkies blocking their doorway, the piss and shit, the rats. The new setting delighted them—birds, flowers, and just enough cement to forestall Andrea's terror of the countryside. They settled in and nervously awaited the book's critical reception; having been trashed so mercilessly in the past, and misunderstood so often, Andrea was understandably apprehensive. Then came the unexpected blurb from Alice Walker: "Simply brilliant, groundbreaking . . . extraordinary in its passionate lucidity." Andrea knew better than to think she was home free ("Whom the Gods Would Destroy, They First Make Mad with Power" could well have been her talisman).[18]

Then came the news that the Women's Press wanted to publish the book in England. Then came the reviews, many of them positive—a jarring surprise to Andrea, steeled as she'd become to hurtful dismissal. For self-protection (for confirmation that she was doomed to be misunderstood) she latched on to Elaine Markson's report that the *New York Times* had a feminist on staff read the book and she'd reported that it "had no new ideas and wasn't interesting." "The indignity of it," Andrea harrumphed, possibly with relief. Someone else reported that they'd heard Katha Pollitt at *The Nation* describe the book as "kill your husband feminism" and declare she would not be reviewing it. Now that was more like it—familiar territory Andrea knew how to navigate. "I am barely hanging together," she wrote an admirer.

But the Furies refused to run to type. Ann Jones, author of the much-admired *Women Who Kill*, praised *Right-Wing Women* as a "brilliant, compelling analysis." The influential leftwing magazine

In These Times ran a review praising Andrea for confronting a major question for feminists: "Why aren't all women feminists?" The Canadian cultural periodical *FUSE* ran a long review declaring flat out that "if you want to know about sexism and feminism, *Right-Wing Women* is a superb text" and describing Andrea's prose as "crisp and aggressive." And the well-known sociologist Pauline Bart, in a lengthy review in *New Women's Times Feminist Review*, declared *Right-Wing Women* "a brilliant book," not "judicious" and not air-tight in its arguments, but marked by "acute sensitivity."[19]

There were, to be sure, some dissenting reviews, and one suspects that these rang louder in Andrea's ears—confirming as they did her "fate" to be a misunderstood visionary—than their number warranted. At a guess, the unfavorable review that probably hurt the most was Jan Clausen's in *Womannews*. Clausen was an out-lesbian writer much admired for her 1980 book, *Mother, Sister, Daughter, Lover.* Her critique mattered, and it was wide-ranging. She rightly pointed out that Andrea had never paused to define which right-wing women she was analyzing and how they differed from women "who hold less extreme views." In Clausen's view, Andrea was best seen as "a premier rhetorician of female victimization" and thought she *did* "succeed brilliantly in conveying the emotional tone of *some* female experience." But she felt strongly that Andrea's critique of men on the left was over-drawn, and decried as not analytic her vision of "monolithic male power and universal female victimhood."[20]

8

The Ordinance

"A leak from the visiting professorship committee," Kitty
MacKinnon wrote Andrea from the University of Minneso-
ta, "has it that we/you have been awarded it"—that is, a jointly taught
course on pornography. All that was needed was "a letter in hand on
the precise financial terms." It was welcome news. Andrea's reviews
may have markedly improved, but her financial situation remained
precarious; a university salary, even for a single term, would be a
considerable bonanza. By mail the two friends began to plan the
course and debate the merits of whether to assign Henry Miller ("he
is the real pornographer," Kitty thought) or D.H. Lawrence.[1]

Then the plot thickened. Word came down to Kitty that the
Women's Studies faculty wasn't willing to invite Andrea for even a
part-time teaching job. Opposition to the course seemed tenacious,
and the resistance to it ugly—including graffiti scrawled on Kitty's office door. Though still not a tenured professor, Kitty riskily
refused to withdraw the course proposal, and eventually the opposition gave in and the joint course with Andrea was finally approved
for the fall term of 1983.

Yet the ugliness periodically resurfaced. A parody of the course
description began to make the rounds; it may possibly have been

intended as good-humored ribbing, but if so its misogynistic, anti-Semitic overtones fell far short of the mark. It upset Kitty so much that she was "unable to sleep or eat for four days." (When the term was over, a still indignant Kitty resigned from the university and went "back on the academic road"). Andrea, more inured to mockery, agreed to a student newspaper interview, but when the resulting article turned out to be full of misrepresentations, she wrote an angry rejoinder that may not have cleared the air but did state her views with notable clarity:[2]

> I did not say that Professor MacKinnon and I have been working for almost ten years to formulate an argument to make pornography illegal. *Banning* is not in my political vocabulary. . . . It is not *illegal* to seek the aid of government to "suppress" ideas one doesn't like, especially when those ideas amount to a systematic oppression of a group of people because of a condition of birth. . . . People have fought the idea of racism, for instance, by getting the government to outlaw segregation. It was not *illegal* for people to try to do this . . . I am distressed and disgusted by [the student's] . . . need to search out men to tell her that I am wrong on every score. Being an "objective" journalist might consist of getting what someone says right (being accurate), rather than trying to balance a view you don't understand with one that is reassuringly familiar even though staggeringly ignorant.

Then came the Andrea-esque closing line: "You do not have permission to abridge this letter." Period.

While teaching the course together (Andrea taught a second one of her own, on English literature), a citizen's group approached her for assistance in persuading the city of Minneapolis not to rezone their working-class neighborhood to allow for the sale of pornography, fearing they'd be "horrendously affected by it." Andrea consulted with Kitty, who proposed drafting a piece of legislation based on the ideas they'd earlier developed for the aborted Linda ("Lovelace")

Marciano case. The basic concept was that pornography was a sex discriminatory practice that violated women's civil rights through coercion, trafficking, and other sex-based violations. Appearing before the city's zoning and planning committee, Andrea elucidated the likely harms that derived from pornography, and Kitty addressed possible solutions—including a legislative ordinance.[3]

Their presentation was so effective that the Minneapolis City Council retained their services to hold public hearings on pornography and to draft a model ordinance for dealing with it. Avoiding hitherto standard (and contested) words like "prurient" and "obscene," they settled on defining pornography as "the graphic sexually explicit subordination of women" (Andrea sometimes used a shortened form: "the sexualized subordination of women"). She and Kitty viewed pornography (as Andrea had earlier put it) as "where all the nerve endings connected for the sexual abuse of women, and how it got legitimized and turned into a form of entertainment. . . . I thought it was a damn good way to continue to fight against rape and to begin to fight against prostitution."[4]

In ideologically grounding their project on the view that pornography violated women's civil rights, they were adopting a legal strategy that the right wing hadn't previously employed as part of its own assault on "smut." Andrea further distinguished between the two movements: "we are against hierarchy and for equality . . . against the sexual and civil subordination of women . . . that is why we are feminist, not right-wing." Even if pornography is viewed as a symptom rather than the root cause of women's oppression, "the fact that something is a symptom (as Andrea would later put it) does not mean that it's not crucial to the health of the organism"—if you're sick with a 104 temperature, "the first thing you have to do is to get rid of the temperature before you can get better."[5]

Recognizing that the definition of pornography as "graphic sexually explicit subordination of women" was an abstract umbrella term, they itemized the various specific acts it covered, like being "penetrated by objects or animals," or portrayed "as sexual objects who enjoy humiliation or pain," experience sexual pleasure in "rape, incest, or other sexual assaults," or are "presented in scenarios of

degradation, humiliation, injury, or torture." The model legislative
ordinance they drew up added the critical sentence—which opponents of the ordinance rarely acknowledged—that "the use of men,
children, or transsexuals in the place of women is also pornography
for purposes of this law."

Legally, the ordinance made pornography actionable: it allowed
women who'd been its victims, through coercion, force, assault, or
trafficking, to bring a civil suit, and for the first time to do so *not*
under the previously used—and mostly useless—grounds of obscenity or zoning infractions. A civil suit had the additional advantage of
requiring for conviction only a "preponderance of evidence," unlike
a criminal case, where guilt must be proven "beyond a reasonable
doubt." Under the model ordinance the burden of proof, as in all
civil cases, would be on the plaintiff. To bring a successful suit, a
"victim" would have to prove that pornography had harmed her in
a specific way or—in regard to trafficking—had harmed women in
general. After a plaintiff testified to injury, it would be up to the
presiding judge to award damages or issue some other form of relief.

Though cries of "censorship!" immediately arose, the charge
wasn't factually applicable, since no part of the ordinance involved
prior restraint, nor was any reference made in it to obscenity law
(which empowers the state to use criminal law to suppress speech,
in contravention of the spirit of the First Amendment). The ordinance was (in Andrea's words) "a harm-based equality law, which
derives its constitutional claim from the principles underlying the
Fourteenth Amendment, especially the equal protection clause."
Andrea wanted no part in censorship. She abhorred the idea of putting more power in the hands of the state, and Kitty entirely agreed.
Later, Andrea herself would be a victim of censorship: customs officials in New Zealand would ban *Pornography* as obscene, and *all* of
her books would be suppressed in South Africa.[6]

After drafting the ordinance, Andrea and Kitty began pressing
for its implementation. They organized a set of hearings in Minneapolis and drew up a press release to publicize them (as they
were dropping the release in the mail, Andrea laughingly—and
prophetically—turned to Kitty: "We are about to become two of
the most notorious women in America"). The initial hearings in

what would be the first round of a protracted struggle took place before a committee of the Minneapolis City Council and were open to the public.

To substantiate their view that pornography both represented and further encouraged violence against women, they called on a host of both expert witnesses and individual victims to provide testimony. The witnesses included psychologists and therapists, adult individuals who'd suffered sexual abuse, social workers, and academic researchers from various fields of expertise. A string of women came forward to offer testimony about their own experiences, including Carol L., an American Indian who described being gang-raped by men who kept calling her "squaw"; Ruth, who described her husband as using pornography as a kind of textbook in demanding her compliance with his prescribed sexual experiments; and Rita, who recounted a Girl Scout camping trip during which, at age thirteen, she was gang-raped at gunpoint by a group of hunters aroused by a session with porn magazines.

Taken together, the witnesses embodied Andrea's claim that the split in the feminist movement, which would shortly become a chasm, over the issue of pornography was a *class* division. The ordinance, she and Kitty believed, made it possible for the first time for poor women who'd previously had no public voice, to present their grievances and to seek redress for them, even as it alienated the educated, academic elite of feminists already comfortable enough with power and privilege to consider themselves immune from sexual exploitation.

The Minnesota hearings also heard testimony—either cited or given in person—regarding what in 1983 was still an early stage of formal research into the effects of pornography on actual behavior. Much of the early work had been done by psychologists Edward Donnerstein and Neil Malamuth, which—though to some extent inconclusive—had led them to conclude that "violent imagery does change men's attitudes about sexual aggression towards women" (increasing, for example, the number of rape fantasies; Malamuth found that 30 percent of the men he studied who regularly used pornography admitted to "some likelihood" of raping women if they could be assured of not being caught and punished).[7]

A later update, published in 1990, would go still further: acknowledging that some studies more or less exonerated pornography from harmful effects on women, it would nonetheless conclude that "the weight of evidence is accumulating that intensive exposure to *soft*-core pornography desensitizes men's attitude to rape, increases sexual callousness, and shifts their preferences toward hard-core pornography . . . exposure to violent pornography [in turn] increases men's acceptance . . . of violence against women." Not all people, of course, will react the same way, whether seeing a depiction of women being bound and gagged or viewing Monet's water lilies floating serenely in an idyllic summer pond.

The Minnesota hearings were the opening salvo in what would be a long series of presentations, conferences, and debates—a general war of words marked by heated rhetoric and wounding accusations on all sides. In response to the ordinance, a number of prominent "pro-sex" feminists who'd earlier spearheaded the controversial 1982 Barnard Conference formed a new organization, the Feminist Anti-Censorship Taskforce (FACT), to work against the passage and implementation of Kitty and Andrea's model ordinance. Among the leading figures in FACT were Gayle Rubin, Pat Califia, Amber Hollibaugh, Joan Nestle, Dorothy Allison, Carole Vance, Nan Hunter, and Lisa Duggan. Not that they agreed with each other on all particulars. In a long letter to Nan Hunter, for example, Gayle Rubin conceded the need to "include people with a wide range of opinion on pornography itself," but underlined her wariness "of any tendency that includes the 'middle of the road' at the expense of those who have taken more radical positions"—those, for example, who demand open access to sexual materials for minors ("outlandish child porn laws continue to be passed at an appalling rate," Rubin wrote) and who are actively working to destigmatize S/M.[8]

The FACT forces filed an amicus brief in the U.S. Court of Appeals, 7th Circuit, that accused Kitty and Andrea of depicting men as "attack dogs" and women "as incapable of consent." The brief also cogently insisted that the language of the ordinance was "unconstitutionally vague and shifting," that its central terms—like "sexually explicit exploitation"—had no fixed meaning, and that sexually explicit speech "does not cause or incite violence in a manner sufficiently direct to justify its suppression under the First Amendment." It broadly claimed that "women need the freedom and the socially recognized space to appropriate for themselves the robustness of what traditionally has been male language."[9]

The foundational charge of a lack of sufficiently direct evidence particularly irritated Andrea. The empirical evidence that FACT demanded, Andrea argued, meant evidence produced in a laboratory—precisely the kind of causative proof that FACT had to know could never become available. Researchers can find, she argued, "that exposure to certain kinds of pornography will cause men to administer larger doses of and more electric shocks to women in a laboratory setting—[but] you cannot set up an experiment that lets men rape women. So the finding comes out like this: exposure to pornography . . . leads to greater aggression against women; or, pornography increases aggression against women. But there will never be a finding that pornography causes rape."

There *is*, she pointed out, empirical evidence in abundance from clinical psychologists or the police or battered women's shelters, but because such evidence "is based on the story of the woman," it "has the lowest legitimacy." The fact remains, Andrea insisted, that there is more correlational evidence that pornography causes rape than that tobacco causes lung cancer. The only way to produce direct evidence of the effect of tobacco would be to "take 300 kids, lock them in a lab, give some tobacco to smoke, some a placebo, and see which ones develop lung cancer. That is the way research into *causation* has to be modeled."

The various local battles that ensued would be hard fought in a number of separate venues, including Indianapolis, Los Angeles, Boston, Detroit, Des Moines, Omaha, Columbus, St. Louis, Cincinnati, and Madison, with FACT alliances in a number of instances barely winning out over the anti-porn brigades: in Suffolk County, New York, and on the Los Angeles County Board of Supervisors, the model ordinance was twice defeated by a single vote. Proof of injury—the whole question of the causal relationship of pornography to harm—was the most vigorously contested issue. By 1984, the anti-pornography forces were able to cite the research collected in Malamuth and Donnerstein's book, *Pornography and Sexual Aggression*, which reported a wide variety of studies affirming the desensitizing effects of pornography and claiming that men who watched violent pornography were more likely than non-users to hold attitudes about rape that primarily blamed the women involved: "she led him on"; "she got him sexually excited"; "she really wanted it but enjoyed pretending otherwise." Though Kitty and Andrea frequently cited Malamuth and Donnerstein, they were sometimes irritated at the wishy-washy, evasive testimony they gave: "They are holding back even on the results of their own work," Andrea commented to a friend.[10]

For much of the next two years, the ordinance struggle absorbed most of Andrea's time and energy. "I am travelling like a maniac, organizing," she wrote a friend. "We are pushing so damned hard on pornography and we are getting somewhere, though sometimes it isn't clear whether backwards or forwards." To another she wrote, "I am travelling all the time . . . and it makes me more restless, not less." Toward the end of 1984 she—all in the same week—gave a speech before some eight hundred people, testified before a Senate subcommittee, and spent three hours in the ACLU office in Washington, DC, trying to convince its head that she wasn't "a fascist censor." During one stretch she gave two to three speeches a day for eleven days in a row, and unlike her earlier experiences, they were filled less with applause and adulation than with a "quite considerable" increase in "anger and threatened violence."[11]

Judging from both media coverage and personal testimony, Andrea had grown into an extraordinarily charismatic public speaker—direct, authentic, emotionally powerful, thoroughly grounded in the relevant arguments and blessed with singular clarity in conveying them, even drily humorous occasionally, despite her antagonists' portrait of her as a dour curmudgeon. Though in many ways a natural on the platform—her command of language, her quick thinking, the emphatic boldness of her arguments, the potency of her personality—she was nonetheless often dissatisfied with her performance, and throughout the two years of continuous public debate she continued to hone her skills, often feeling shaky and vaguely nauseated before the curtain went up ("I always get very scared before I speak," she wrote a friend at one point, "knees knocking literally, trembling, cold sweats").[12]

After she and Kitty had completed their work drafting a model ordinance, and Andrea had something concrete to work with, she felt more at ease when speaking publicly, especially since she could find comfort in the tumultuous receptions she often got. But there were plenty of brickbats too. She was often denounced to her face as a fascist out to destroy the First Amendment, a prude who hated men *and* sex, a "hysterical dyke," a leftwing turncoat wasting her energy on a trivial issue like pornography instead of what really mattered: poverty or nukes. Through repetition the charges lost some of their sting, and through practice she learned to remain patient and calm in confronting red-faced verbal denunciation. None of it was easy, but most of it became possible—a considerable triumph in the face of what was often gross derision. "The more hostile they are," she advised a friend about to participate in a public event, "the quieter inside you have to be able to get . . . in addition to concentrating on what it is essential to say, one must also concentrate on staying absolutely centered, being able to withstand a host of onslaughts. . . . You have to remember that better people than you and I have been heckled, hurt, beat upon, etc. You have to see it in terms of a long time . . . you are going to have to talk to a hundred years' worth of room-fulls of people to make change."

It would all have been easier if she and Kitty had been able to fall back on institutional support. Fundraising was about as antithetical to Andrea's skill set as yachting, and for much the same reason: having been poor most of her adult life, she also felt "terribly humiliated" when having to solicit rich people for money. The ordinance issue *did* arouse considerable interest and widened access to a broad constituency, but it wasn't a particularly prosperous one. If more funds could somehow become available, Andrea dreamed of a two-person staff that could take on a host of needed tasks: organize training sessions for speakers around the country to argue in favor of an ordinance; set up workshops on the hundred or so legal issues that the pornography question raised; oversee grassroots work in support of the ordinances; set up events; do mailings, handle the press, arrange the thousand details of travel, etc. Andrea was well aware that conflict was an inescapable part of any movement for social change, and she knew "there was no smoother way." Still, she couldn't help longing now and then for some respite from the struggle, for the blessed isolation of reading and writing—her true sources of solace.

They did find an ideally qualified litigator in the person of Anne Simon, who'd been in law school with Kitty, had worked with the NOW Legal and Educational Defense Fund, and was currently working at the Center for Constitutional Rights. Anne became, as Andrea put, "a personal source of infinite information for me about law, which I have needed desperately" (though most of her tutoring came from Kitty: the two spoke on the phone virtually daily, much of the time about legal matters). Though Anne, who believed in the cause, worked pro bono, she had to attend to her full-time job as well and could make herself available for only some ten hours a month.

Coverage of the ordinance battles was widespread in the press, frequently harsh, and sometimes downright ugly. In Minneapolis, the very first site of confrontation, the ordinance passed the city council twice—and Mayor Donald Fraser vetoed it twice. In response, an angry and deeply disappointed Andrea, who'd lobbied Fraser in person several times, wrote him a lengthy letter castigating his decision:

> I understand that you give speeches around the country in which you say that politicians should do something about torture in the world. I understand that you were instrumental in developing the human rights guidelines that affected Federal funding to El Salvador. Yet in our conversations—and in conversations reported to me by other women—you are entirely indifferent to the torture of women in and because of pornography. . . . You offered the Minnesota Twins $400,000 to stay in Minneapolis, and you say you have no money to defend the civil rights bill from . . . threatened litigation. The Twins left. What will happen to the $400,000? Whose rights will it be used to advance? Can it be true that someone of conscience has

money for baseball, but none to stop a trade in torture? I do
not believe this of you. It cannot be possible.[13]

But it was. Mayor Fraser held firm, and the struggle to pass
the ordinance moved on to Indianapolis, where the bill was nar-
rowed to overtly violent pornography—the kind, presumably, that
"everyone" was against. Yet when the ordinance passed the Indianapolis City Council, the ACLU—with whom Andrea had already
tangled—got into the act, filing a brief accusing Kitty and Andrea
of advocating censorship, even though the term technically refers
to government-sponsored control of speech. Andrea also had a particularly nasty give-and-take with the *Village Voice* columnist Nat
Hentoff. The two had tangled before about the sanctity (or not) of
the First Amendment (Hentoff proudly called himself a free speech
"absolutist"—though conceding that libel might not qualify). In
a *Voice* article headlined "Is the First Amendment Dangerous to
Women?" he denounced the ordinance, suggesting it was so broad
that the Bible itself would come under censorship, and labeled Kitty
"the Anthony Comstock of our time."[14]

Despite Hentoff, the procedure outlined in the Indianapolis ordinance for a woman to bring a civil suit was quite specific, though its
implications were broad. If, say, a sexually explicit magazine—such
as the *Hustler* cover photo montage showing a naked woman being
passed through a meat grinder—was used in an assault or attack on
an individual, that individual could file a complaint with the Indianapolis Office of Equal Opportunity, which would then investigate.
If the material met the statutory definition of pornography and the
assault or attack could be proved to be due to it, the case could go to
civil court, which could assess damages. Under the trafficking pro-
vision, a plaintiff was also allowed to sue the publisher and distribu-
tor of the discredited material for damages and for an injunction
forbidding its further dissemination.

According to Hentoff, the MacKinnon/Dworkin ordinance had
"contributed to a moral crusade that is threatening to expand to
other places on a wider scale" (indeed, it was already on the docket
in Detroit, Des Moines, Omaha, Columbus, St. Louis, Cincinnati,
and Madison). He singled out one such place, Suffolk County, New

York, where a right-wing Republican legislator had recently introduced a version of the ordinance that cited pornography as causing sodomy, the "destruction of the family unit," and in general
"crimes inimical to the public good." But what Hentoff failed to
mention was that Andrea and Kitty, on hearing the specifics of the
Suffolk County ordinance, immediately denounced it and successfully worked against its passage.

In a second article, Hentoff used Kitty's own mentor, the distinguished and progressive Yale Law School professor Thomas
Emerson, as a witness against the ordinance. He honorably noted
that Emerson expressed his *agreement* with MacKinnon that "pornography plays a major part in establishing and maintaining male
supremacy in our society," but Emerson also expressed the view that
her solution to the harm done by pornography was "nearly limitless"
in its scope and could theoretically "outlaw a substantial portion of
the world's literature." The ACLU agreed that such an outcome was
not farfetched. In an amicus brief, it argued that since "sexual subordination"—the key operative term in the ordinance—"is inherently vague," it opened up a can of worms. As did other terms in the
ordinance, such as "sexually explicit," "abasement," and "shown as
filthy or inferior."[15]

In "Equal-Opportunity Banning," Hentoff used one of Kitty
and Andrea's own chosen experts, Edward Donnerstein, to testify
against them. It was true, Hentoff argued, that current research
indicated that if men are shown movies containing a good deal
of violence against women, some of their attitudes toward wom-
en become more negative. But what Donnerstein's research did
not conclude, Hentoff argued, was that the *behavior* of those men
changed. He quoted Donnerstein himself to the effect that his
research had been misinterpreted; he had *not* found a connection
between violent pornography and actual violence against women—
nor had any other researcher. But this was, in fact, an instance of
Donnerstein reinterpreting his data—a tendency to obscure the
findings of his own research, about which Kitty and Andrea had
earlier complained.

In this instance, Donnerstein himself, in a letter to the *Voice* that
his co-researcher Daniel Linz also signed, insisted that Hentoff

had misrepresented their findings. "While it is true," they wrote, "that many zealous persons both of feminist and conservative political persuasions have attempted to overstate the conclusions of our research (claiming, for example, that our work demonstrates that exposure to pornography *directly* causes rape), *Dworkin and MacKinnon have not.* [their italics] They have consistently used social psychological research cautiously in their legal documents, and as only one form of evidence, linking violent pornography with violence against women. They have rightly placed the research in its proper perspective, saying only that the research shows that certain forms of pornography promote attitudes of callousness toward victims of violence and cause increases in aggressive behavior in a laboratory setting. . . . [MacKinnon and Dworkin] are the *only* individuals from among the many conservatives and feminists involved with this issue who have taken the time to check with us personally about what conclusions can legitimately be drawn from research in this area."[16]

Also present at the Indianapolis hearings was the young historian Lisa Duggan, who became a member of FACT. She, too, wrote a lengthy account for the *Village Voice* and, unlike Hentoff, spent considerable time interviewing the central figures in the dispute. Though the ordinance had passed the city council and been signed by the mayor, it was not yet in effect: a coalition of publishers, booksellers, and the like, joined by the ACLU, had immediately challenged the statute in federal district court as a violation of the First Amendment.

In her article Duggan took issue with the MacKinnon/Dworkin view, as expressed in the ordinance, that sexually explicit images subordinating women were "singularly dangerous, more dangerous than nonsexual images of gross violence against women, more dangerous than advertising images of housewives as dingbats obsessed with getting men's shirt collars clean." It was a clever thrust, yet not exactly accurate. Kitty and Andrea knew perfectly well that the over-riding culprit was the structural patriarchy, not one of its offshoots like *Hustler* or "snuff" films. They had never argued, as Duggan claimed, "that pornography is at the root of virtually every form of exploitation and discrimination known to woman."

Nor had they been calling for any sort of ban of sexually explicit material, though "ban" was the accusatory word Duggan used
against them. What they advocated was not a ban but rather the
creation of a legal channel whereby women who felt they'd been
harmed by pornography could bring civil suit for damages. They
had not called in the ordinance for prior restraint of any media outlet, nor had they advocated any enlargement of police or prosecu-
torial power; their emphasis was on the exercise of civil rights, not
censorship. Nor—as FACT also charged—had they "allied" with
the right-winger Moral Majority. They found themselves on the
same side of the pornography argument, but not for the same reasons: the Moral Majority was against all non-traditional forms of
sex and promoted traditional family life and gender roles; Kitty and
Andrea were against the abuse and subordination of women and *for*
the rights of sexual minorities and gender non-conformists.[17]

As a result of the widespread publicity generated by the ordinance
hearings, Attorney General William French Smith resurrected on
the federal level the Commission on Obscenity and Pornography, which had been moribund since 1970. Andrea herself testified
before it on January 22, 1986, toward the end of the Commission's
hearings in New York City. By that point, it had already become
the object of a sophisticated, coordinated attack for what was perceived as its growing sympathy for Kitty and Andrea's civil rights
approach. The pro-pornography Media Coalition had hired the
largest public relations firm in Washington, DC, Gray and Company (with known ties to the Reagan White House), to come up
with a strategy that would discredit the Commission. Working with
a million-dollar budget, they organized a campaign that planted a
variety of stories discrediting both committee staff members and
witnesses, as well as debunking as fake any newspaper stories that
reported various scientific studies linking pornography with harm
to women and children.[18]

Andrea began her testimony before the Commission by spelling
out some facts and figures: 65–70 percent of the women who worked
in pornographic media had themselves been victims of incest or
childhood sexual abuse. At least that high a percentage came from
low-income homes, had had limited educational opportunities,

were themselves poor, and had few economic options. The younger ones were frequently runaways who'd been raped, filmed, and
exploited by pimps. The powerlessness of most of the adult women
in pornography made them, out of fear (and with frozen smiles),
involuntarily complicit with the brutality of the scene—including
overt violence.

Having painted the terrain with grim accuracy, Andrea moved on
to examine some of pornography's broader implications. She took
on the free speech issue directly. Precisely whose free speech is at
stake? she asked. Should we consider the presentation of a woman
bound and gagged as speech? "Who is that speech for? We have
women being tortured and we are told that that is somebody's
speech? Whose speech is it? It's the speech of a pimp, it is not the
speech of a woman. The only words we hear in pornography from
women are that women want to be hurt, ask to be hurt, like to be
raped, get sexual pleasure from sexual violence; and even when
a woman is covered in filth, we are supposed to believe that her
speech is that she likes it and she wants more of it."

Besides, Andrea argued, the absolutists righteously rising to
the defense of the First Amendment failed to note that it did *not*
license libel, slander, blackmail, bribery, so-called fighting words
(for instance, walking up to someone on the street and calling him a
fascist), incitement to violence, or—in a recent 9–0 decision by the
Supreme Court—child pornography. The Supreme Court itself had
on occasion refused to interpret the First Amendment as an absolute
bar on government regulation. Along with the well-known rejection of the right to shout "Fire!" in a crowded theater, the Court
had found that speech or action could be so harmful that it could
constitutionally restrict the expression. Similarly, it had found that
the standard remedy of encouraging more speech wasn't always
available or effective; the individual is seen as harmed by the *speech*
itself, not by subsequent or prior acts. And what of the history of the
First Amendment? To Andrea it was "a sick mixture of patriotism
and racism"—as if the Amendment "did not coexist with slavery or
segregation; as if it does not now exist with illiteracy, hunger, and
poverty."[19]

By the time of Andrea's testimony, the Commission members

had already stumbled several times through the thicket of conflicting terms and definitions that characterized obscenity laws and
case decisions. It was a morass of contradiction and confusion. Was
"indecent" the same as "obscene"? Should restrictions exist on the
production and distribution of printed material as well as material
with pictorial content? Where does erotica fit in? Didn't that term
relate solely to literary merit—James Joyce, say, or perhaps Henry
Miller? Did the so-called Hicklin test corrupt those whose minds
are open to such immoral influences? But who did that leave *out*? In
the *Jacobellis* decision in 1964, Justice Potter Stewart had settled for
"community standards" as the best guide in determining obscenity, but opinions in even small communities varied; whose should
get primacy? In 1973, the Supreme Court in *Miller vs. California*
had established a three-tier test for determining what was obscene
rather than merely erotic.[20]

The "Miller test" had invoked terms like "offensive sexual conduct" and "lack of serious value"—but who had the moral confidence (and legitimacy) to define such vague terms? Where did
nudity fit in (was the film *Carnal Knowledge* obscene?)? Beside the
intrinsic definitional problems lay the real-world issue of whether it
was *possible* for a mere individual to win a lawsuit against a big-time
pornographer. Even several corporations had failed in the attempt.
The Pillsbury company had earlier brought suit against Al Gold-
stein and his publication, *Screw*, which had run a series of cartoons
portraying the trademark Pillsbury Doughboy fucking—and had
lost in court, mostly due to the testimony of an ACLU attorney
arguing against any infringement of free speech.

In the whole tangled history of legal approaches to pornography, about the only definition that *hadn't* been suggested was precisely the one Andrea and Kitty introduced: productive of harm
to women and children. As Andrea put it in her testimony before
the Commission, obscenity laws were hopelessly vague; "prurient
interest" (what gave an erection, say, to a male juror) "has nothing
to do with the objective reality of what is happening to women in
pornography"—to them as performers, and to them as the partners
of men influenced by the endemic violence of pornographic depictions of sex. Nor, Andrea argued, was the standard of "community

values" that some state obscenity laws had adopted any more satisfying. What did it even "mean in a society when violence against
women is pandemic, when according to the FBI a woman is battered
every eighteen seconds and it's the most commonly committed violent crime in the country? What would 'community standards' have
meant in the segregated South? What would 'community standards'
have meant during the heyday of Nazi Germany?"[21]

What *women* needed, Andrea told the Commission, is "the equal
protection principle of the Fourteenth Amendment"; the "reality
of pornography" was that it embodied "the subordination of wom-
en. . . . I am here asking the simplest thing. I am saying hurt people
need remedies, not platitudes, not laws that you know already don't
work. . . . People silenced by exploitation and brutality need real
speech, not to be told that when they are hung from meat hooks,
that is their speech . . . the law that Catharine MacKinnon and I
developed applies only to sexually explicit material that subordinates
women in a way that is detrimental to our civil status." (Addressing
an all-male conference in 1983, Andrea made a comparable, if still
more eloquent plea: "Why are you so slow? Why are you so slow
to understand the simplest things? Not the complicated ideological things. You understand those. The simple things! The cliches!
Simply that women are human to precisely the degree and quality
that you are!")[22]

Before the Commission, Andrea's words and manner were powerful to the point where several of the members—their awe of her
performance palpable—thanked her for her contribution. They did
ask for several clarifications, but did so with the utmost respect.
One commissioner posed this question: "If we could find a man and
a woman who totally and freely agree to sadomasochistic activities,
would you think that should be prohibited, even though in itself it
is a very degrading thing to occur to a woman and to a man also?"

Andrea, honorably, made it clear in her response that she
opposed sadomasochism, objected to "the degradation intrinsic to the acts" (though "degradation" would of course not be the
description—certainly not a *sufficient, inclusive* one—that practitioners of S/M would themselves use to depict their acts). She did go
on in her reply to raise the knotty, usually ignored question of the

nature of consent. What in fact did that word mean? "The forms of coercion—including the reality of poverty, the vulnerability of child sexual abuse" make it "very difficult to understand" when something close to true volition is actually present.

Another commissioner followed up: "I take it from your response . . . that you believe it does not occur that a woman voluntarily poses for pictures for *Penthouse* or *Playboy*." No, Andrea responded, "I believe that it does voluntarily occur." But *Playboy* "is the top of the ladder . . . the highest amount of money that a woman gets paid for posing . . . [but] the fact that women sometimes voluntarily are part of pornography should not stop us from doing something about the women who are coerced . . . the fact that most women . . . sixty-five to seventy-five percent . . . who are in pornography are victims of child sexual abuse is probably the most telling point about what the pornography system is all about . . . we have to deal with pornography as a real system of coercion that operates both in terms of physical coercion and economic vulnerability."

Toward the end of her testimony, a question finally came up about men—about whether some men who performed in pornography couldn't also be considered exploited. Andrea's response was a decided "yes"—that is, "for young men, for men who are runaways, for men who are dispossessed in some sense from society; but men who don't die in it get out of it, usually . . . it doesn't become a way of life in the same way that it does for women. It's not a total dead end with no other options ever." In regard to black men, she thought the question had "tremendous implications . . . their constant, constant use as rapists in pornography is very [much] tied to their low civil status." She recalled as well that during the hearings in Minneapolis, "we had a great deal of testimony about the use of all-male pornography in homosexual battery; I believe that that is real . . . that under civil rights legislation, men who are battered in that way must have a right to sue."

It was at precisely that point, April 1985, that *Ms.* magazine entered the fray with a lengthy article, "Is One Woman's Sexuality Another Woman's Pornography?" The title alone hinted at how the article would be tilted, though trying all the while to appear even-handed. Given *Ms.*'s wide circulation and the large chunks of time and information that Kitty and Andrea had given to the article's author, Mary Kay Blakely, they were at first disheartened—and then livid. Andrea described the article to a friend as "a nightmare of malice and misogyny . . . and it hurts like hell. It's our political reality." In terms of incidence and length of quotation, the *Ms.* article featured MacKinnon and Nan Hunter, the ACLU lawyer and FACT member, about equally, with somewhat less space given to the two other leading antagonists, Andrea and Carole Vance. But the tone of authority in the article did rather subtly lean to the FACT side. All four women emerged as smart, committed, and well-informed—but Hunter at a bit greater length came off as a bit more trenchant. In some eyes, that emphasis reflected the comparative worth of the two opposing arguments; in others', the disparity resulted from the greater appeal to *Ms.*'s editors of FACT's arguments.[23]

Carole Vance, without challenge, was allowed to say in the *Ms.* article that "attitudes are very poor predictors of behavior." (But wasn't a rabid anti-Semite *more* likely to *behave* badly toward a Jew?) Kitty, on the other hand, was quoted as acknowledging that "the research can't tell on an individual basis which man will go and rape a woman after having been exposed to a certain amount of pornography," but she also said (which wasn't included) that the research showed "the rate of abuse of women will increase with the consumption of pornography." When *Ms.*, moreover, elaborated on the legal issues in play, opponents of the ordinance were given considerably more space, and filled some of it with dubious accusations—like the suggestion that the anti-porn forces were being hypocritical in objecting to violent sexual images while not protesting the violence in non-sexual war films (as if any movement for social justice has ever taken on all possible issues simultaneously). It was true enough, as another FACT member insisted, that "pornography is a part, but not all of a violent, woman-hating culture," but while awaiting the total renovation of that culture couldn't a bit of credit be granted to those taking on at least one aspect of the assault against women?[24]

Andrea wrote a furious, over-the-top letter to the managing editor of *Ms.*, outlining her and Kitty's grievances. *Ms.*, according to Andrea's indictment, had made "the sexual abuse of pornography invisible"; had "ignored the phenomenally invigorating" effects of the ordinance on women, even though it was not yet a working law anywhere; had made no reference to "the racist hatred in pornography," though she and Kitty had provided "a staggering amount of information" on the subject; had "given us no credit, no honor"—the only moment in her letter that Andrea let her personal hurt show— "for working on this issue in the face of unremitting hostility"; and had inaccurately portrayed the women in FACT, who opposed the ordinance, as "more than 50% of the women's movement, which they are not. You have made their criticism and solipsisms more important than the issue of pornography or the ordinance."[25]

Her summary was vintage Dworkin (when the wound was deep and she breathed fire):

> I don't want anything more to do with *Ms.* ever. Not ever.
> As a feminist courtesy, I have never made public my deep political objections to the way . . . [*Ms.*] trivializes feminism. That period of self-censorship is now over.
> We brought you extraordinary information . . . [and] you turned what we gave you into shit. This letter is not for publication.

———

The attorney general's Commission's final report essentially adopted Kitty and Andrea's civil rights approach, and called for direct relief to the victims of the injuries "so exhaustively documented in our hearings throughout the country." The Commission further concluded that since the harms "are real," "the need for a remedy for those harms is pressing," and it recommended that Congress consider legislation. Various bills did follow, including in 1994 the Violence Against Women Act, which provided for a federal civil remedy for gender-based violence attendant on instances of rape and battering.[26]

The ordinance that Kitty and Andrea had designed, however, did not become law anywhere. It did pass in Minneapolis, without any right-wing support, and by two city councils—though the mayor vetoed it. It also passed in Indianapolis, where the mayor signed it in April 1984. There, however, a media coalition backed by the ACLU sued, and a Reagan-appointed judge declared the ordinance unconstitutional on First Amendment grounds—a ruling initially affirmed in 1985 by a three-judge panel of the Seventh Circuit Court of Appeals and then "summarily affirmed" (that is, without argument) by the Supreme Court. Kitty and Andrea took some comfort from the opinion of one of the judges that "depictions of subordination tend to perpetuate subordination."

At the time, the highly regarded constitutional scholar Laurence Tribe wrote to the Minneapolis City Council in defense of the ordinance (though he later modified his views somewhat): "While many hard questions of conflicting rights will face any court that confronts challenges to the ordinance, as drafted it rests on a rationale that closely parallels many previously accepted exceptions to justly stringent First Amendment guarantees. . . . I urge you not . . . to prevent the courts from adjudicating what may eventually be found to be the first sensible approach to an area which has vexed some of the best legal minds for decades."

After the ordinance was defeated in Cambridge, Massachusetts, 57 percent to 43 percent—it won in the working-class wards, lost in the wards around Harvard—the game seemed played out. Or, to put it perhaps more accurately, for a time nobody seemed to know what route to pursue next, or even what the central issue was that remained in need of solution. Kitty and Andrea remained entirely committed to the broad goal of ending the subservient status of women and, as a part of that, the endemic violence employed against them. But despite all their ingenuity and perseverance, no legal solution seemed available. Arrayed against them was the same coalition of prominent feminists—"the Barnard Conference crowd"—determined to resist any effort that they felt jeopardized the rights of sexual minorities and the uninhibited exercise of free speech.

Legal scholars, down to the present day, continue to debate the interlocking issues intrinsic to the debate over pornography. A number of them still insist—as did Kitty and Andrea—that the right of free speech has never been considered an unencumbered liberty; as the First Amendment scholar Rodney A. Smolla has pointed out,

"Justice [Hugo] Black aside, the absolutist view has never been fully accepted by any member of the Supreme Court . . . absolutism proves to be too brittle and simplistic a methodology, and is simply not viable as a general working approach to free speech." The relationship between speech and harm has constantly shifted, and hard questions remain. To protect women from harm, are curtailments on the right of free speech acceptable? "Speech" has long been constitutionally confined to white males; to attain, or even to approximate, equality for women, is it essential to broaden the restrictions on pornographic materials that cause harm to women?[27]

In point of fact, religious beliefs still find much greater protection in the courts than does the argument for women's equality. Of course in the era of the internet, with mounting billions being spent on pornography, the entire notion of trying to curtail its potential harm becomes something of a fool's errand. What can be done, moreover, about the fact that U.S. jurisprudence continues to privilege the First Amendment's right to freedom of expression over the Fourteenth Amendment's right to equal protection of the law? The former favors those in power, the latter gives prime emphasis to the injuries of women and minorities; it remains true today that the unalloyed free speech of pornographers outweighs the civil rights of women. Allowing for the occasional pro-ordinance legal decision, the bottom line seems still to be that the harm pornography causes does *not* outweigh the harm that might follow from placing restrictions on it. As Andrea put it after the Supreme Court declared the ordinance unconstitutional, "Right now, we have nothing. We have bottomed out. None of us have money left; or time; or heart. We are tired beyond belief."[28]

The prolonged and angry debate took its toll on personal friendships. In Andrea's case, the chief casualty was her relationship with Adrienne Rich (which had never been untroubled). When Adrienne in 1985 signed on to a FACT amicus brief, the feminist publication *off our backs* asked her to write an article for them explaining her decision. Adrienne agreed, and the resulting piece led to a round-robin of recriminations. Earlier, Adrienne had participated in WAP meetings and events, but had grown concerned (as she put it) "that the affirmation of lesbian sexuality was being downplayed in the interests of reaching a wider constituency." She continued to have "no doubt" that "images of victimized women, purveyed as sexual turn-ons, serve both to suggest and to justify acts which are . . . causing extreme suffering and destruction to thousands of women." Adrienne also still had serious doubts about the efficacy of the First Amendment "in a society where the flow of information and access to mass media is controlled by those with access to wealth, over-whelmingly male and white."[29]

She had not been, in other words, a ready or easy recruit to the ranks of FACT; instead, Adrienne still believed that the organiza-tion underestimated "the actual toll taken on women's lives" and too easily dismissed "the coercive conditions which impel women into the pornography industry." Pornography, as she currently saw it, *did* have profound consequences for those women who worked in the industry, and on the men who used pornography as well.

What *had* changed in her position was that she felt "more and more loath to ascribe the subordination of women, the prevalence of male violence, and the stunning asymmetries of material power" between men and women to any one cause. Yet she had come to believe that pornography was *not* central "in creating and main-taining the civil inequality of the sexes." She believed misogyny was deeply embedded in the country's—and most of the world's—institutional structures. She now felt that the anti-pornography ordinance, "like the patriarchal family, offers false protections, at too high a price." In her *off our backs* statement Adrienne took spe-cific issue with one of Andrea's recent articles, "Against the Male Flood: Censorship, Pornography, and Equality"—but centrally misread it as a call for heightening the power of the police to control the pornographers: "I am less sure than Dworkin and MacKinnon that this is a time when further powers of suppression should be turned over to the State."

Neither Andrea nor Kitty had made such a proposal; indeed, it would have been anathema to their unequivocal rejection of police power or the use of "prior restraint" to curtail the effects of por-nography. Both were outraged at Adrienne's misrepresentation, and both wrote responses to *off our backs* that were howls of indignation. "The basic problem, as I see it," Kitty wrote, "is that you took your view of our work from the opposition—meaning your information was minimally one-sided, a lot biased, and some false."[30]

Kitty went on to explicitly state that the ordinance does not involve the police any more than, say, sexual harassment or race discrimination in housing does. "It does not empower prosecutors to initiate suits in the name of the state or to send police to seize materials." Moreover, Kitty added, Adrienne had misstated their argument about causality: "To find something [pornography] 'central' in sex inequality . . . is not to find it exclusively causal, or alone in its centrality. You assume both and we never said either. . . . I can't believe that if the issue were racism . . . you would go on about all the other things that contribute to the problem as a reason to do nothing about a part of it. Eliminating segregation didn't eliminate racism. Did you therefore oppose desegregation? Was it therefore not 'central'? . . . you say the harm of pornography is real to you. Yet you still side with the status quo, with letting it go on, with doing nothing."

If Kitty's response to Adrienne was a thunderstorm, Andrea's was a tornado: "The FACT women are the old S/M crowd," she wrote (in an inflated generalization). "The brief you (Adrienne) signed is woman-hating, antifeminist, racist, intellectually dishonest, and politically reprehensible. And that is kind." The ordinance she and Kitty had been proposing "is in behalf of powerless, poor, mostly women (though some young men, many gay), frequently illiterate, often refugees from incest and prostitution as well as pornography . . . the women who signed the FACT brief are . . . lawyers and academics for the most part . . . [they] don't have anything at stake except their privilege. . . . As you know, access to print is a form of wealth; and the academy is not a street corner. . . . It ends up being exactly this, dear sister: the comfy women, to keep what's theirs, are prepared to let the powerless women be hurt forever . . . most women are silenced through civil inferiority and sexual abuse and thus have no recourse to the protections of the First Amendment . . .

"If this is feminism, it deserves to die. I want nothing ever to do with it. I think, though, that feminism is in the aspirations and courage of those other women I mentioned, the ones I think you have forgotten about (if you ever knew them): the poor, the genuinely powerless. I think that there is a movement based on their experiences, many of which are also my own; and we are determined to change this system. . . . If this FACT brief really represents you, I am happy to sever all political affiliation with you. If the FACT brief does not represent you, you had better do something about the fact that you have signed it."

More than a decade later, Kitty and Andrea edited the hearings and testimony generated during the 1980s in four cities—Minneapolis, Indianapolis, Los Angeles, and Boston—into a thick volume, *In Harm's Way: The Pornography Civil Rights Hearings*. It was their answer, as they had frequently complained during the ten-year period preceding the volume's appearance, to the media reports recounting testimony at the various hearings that had often appeared truncated and inaccurate to them, and in some instances even rewritten by editors to conform more closely with their own subjective views.[31]

Kitty and Andrea wrote separate introductions to *In Harm's Way*, with Kitty elucidating the legal history, and Andrea—always somewhat allergic to theory—summarizing and commenting on the specific human stories (including her own) that illustrated the central issues aired during the hearings. In her piece, Andrea came down hard on the left, accusing its lawyers of buying into the argument—originating in the counter-cultural sixties—that pornography was merely an artifact of "liberated sexuality," no more, no less. They had labeled anti-porn agitators "right-wing collaborators" and described themselves as defenders of free speech (even though in the sixties, the left had flexibly rejected an absolutist adherence to free speech when faced with racist speech that incited violence). Andrea was less persuasive when accusing the left of equating rape with "free sex"—and not at all persuasive when accusing the left of defending rape within marriage. Kitty, in her own introduction to *In Harm's Way*, made it convincingly clear that she and Andrea regarded the right with abhorrence. She fully and persuasively rejected the widespread charge that they actively sanctioned an

anti-pornography coalition between radical feminists and conservative women, pointing out that with only one exception (a Republican woman who supported the ERA) *all* the sponsors of anti-porn
ordinances in all of the cities in which they had been introduced
self-identified as either liberal or radical.

Much still lay ahead, in regard to both the continued sparring
between opposing forces already on the scene, and the later entrance
of third-wave feminists, whose new voices would offer innovative
perspectives on issues that dated back to the 1980s, and in some
instances would introduce related topics (for example, the effects
of various forms of parenting on subsequent patterns of sexuality
and gender presentation) that had been unknown or ignored in the
earlier debate.[32]

There *were* a few voices raised as early as the mid-eighties that
pointed ahead to issues that would prove central to third-wave
feminism. The English media critic Richard Dyer was one. As a
pro-feminist socialist and a gay man who had easy access to porn
and acknowledged the pleasure he took in it, Dyer felt that some
aspects of the porn debate were being ignored or underplayed. The
role of capitalism, for one. Did capitalism provide unusually fallow,
or even unique, grounds for the production of pornography? For
Dyer, the answer was yes, yet at the same time he didn't believe
that "all capitalist cultural production always all the time expresses
capitalist ideology." He was interested in "moments of contradiction, instability and give in our culture"—those points, in other
words, "at which change can be effected." He believed, too, that the
MacKinnon/Dworkin side of the debate on pornography rightly
stressed "the degradation of women that characterizes so much heterosexual porn," and that they were right to emphasize such porn
as "woman-degrading representations of sexuality." Yet he thought
their arguments would have profited from paying more attention
than they did to gay porn.[33]

Kitty and Andrea's critique *had* focused on heterosexual porn
(with a largish sidebar disparaging lesbian S/M), yet in the few
places where Andrea chose to comment on gay male porn, Dyer
thought her characterizations were inaccurate. This was particu-

larly the case, as he saw it, in the way she depicted young, black men as primarily occupying "feminine" roles in gay porn. Her characterization was true enough in regard to scenes involving drag, Dyer conceded, but decidedly not true for those porn depictions of muscular, hyper-masculine black men dominating and penetrating feminine "little white guys" or (less frequently) those shown having sex with equally butch white men. The matter, he felt, was of some political import: though porn in general mostly reinforced "the worst aspects of the social construction of masculinity," the wider range of representations of gay male sexuality suggested a standard narrative that depicted a lifestyle as one combining "a basic romanticism with an easy acceptance of promiscuity." That dominant pattern of gay cultural production, egalitarian and non-familial, had a potentially valuable—and radical—story to tell mainstream viewers.

The media critic B. Ruby Rich is another example of a dissident voice in the mid-eighties that asked questions about some of the basic assumptions and absences that typified that decade's porn debate. Citing the Samois anthology *Coming to Power: Writings and Graphics on Lesbian S/M*, Rich questioned by indirection the unwavering anti-S/M position that Kitty and Andrea had adopted in their anti-porn writings. A more productive debate, Rich suggested, would be "honest enough to confront the continuum of sexual practice that links S/M to a more common experience." Drawing on Jessica Benjamin's essay "Master and Slave: The Fantasy of Erotic Domination"—notable, in Rich's view, as one of the few "to bring psychoanalytic theory to bear upon issues of sexuality"—she stresses in particular Benjamin's view that the erotic attraction of domination/submission scenarios rests on "the need for transcendence"; or, in Benjamin's own words, "the experience of losing the self . . . is increasingly difficult to obtain except in the erotic relationship . . . sexual eroticism has become the heir to religious eroticism." To which Rich adds, "It is indeed peculiar that the debate on sadomasochism should have arisen as a lesbian issue when the practice is so widespread among heterosexuals."[34]

In regard specifically to pornography, Rich points out that the debate remained inconclusively poised "between two inadequate definitions: either a conscious degradation of women, ideologically aligned with misogyny and psychologically linked to actual violence against women; or one of the few expressions of explicit sexuality in a repressive culture lacking in sex education and opposed to the taking of pleasure." In Rich's view, the debate had been severely hampered by the paucity of empirical studies in combination with "the lack of honest testimony" among the debaters—that is, their refusal to explore in depth how their own histories had been instrumental in placing them on one side or the other of the debate.

The example Rich gives is startling and refreshingly unnerving: in Scott MacDonald's article "Confessions of a Feminist Porn Watcher," he suggests (to quote Rich) "that pornography functions as a repetitive reassurance machine for a male psyche far more fragile than generally acknowledged—so tenuous indeed, that it requires a continual assertion of its powerfulness to neutralize incipient physical and spiritual impotence." Pornography's psychological function, in other words, is not—or not simply—to subordinate women, but to comfort men.[35]

Rich's review essay is studded with comparable provocations: "Do women not objectify men as well, albeit in a different manner? In fact, if the male form of objectification is degradation, then perhaps the female form, as demonstrated by the Harlequins, is idealization"; "All sexual relations seem to concern some kind of power disequilibrium, some kernel of psychic domination or surrender, some terror of dependence fighting a wish to depend, a simultaneous desire for—yet horror of—merging"; "The adoption of butch-fem roles or lesbian sadomasochism may well constitute an alternative remedy to the problem of merging identi[ties] . . . [in S/M] women are constructing and insisting upon the *otherness* of the partner."

Rich's intervention in what had become a somewhat claustrophobic debate, the two sides implacably opposed and hostile, is not in itself immune to challenge. But that isn't the point. What her speculations demonstrate—as early as 1986—is that closure is hardly imminent. Not only hasn't the issue of pornography been resolved, but the many side issues into which it opens out (ideologically aligned with misogyny, psychologically linked with the male fragility that secretly feeds it) have barely been explored. Kitty and Andrea had done basic spade work, and in the face of mockery and belittlement, but the soil they tilled may turn out to have additional layers, largely unexplored. A prolonged dig—downright archeological given its potential depth—remains on the calendar. What needs to be added, as the sun beats mercilessly down, is a modicum of compassion for all those sweating to get below the topsoil.

The MacKinnon/Dworkin ordinance stayed in play a while longer, until the Supreme Court in the spring of 1986 affirmed an appeals court decision that had declared it unconstitutional. That decidedly took the air out of the balloon, yet even then, for Kitty and Andrea, not decisively so. Retreat was inescapable, but surrender wasn't in their nature. They continued, though irregularly, to argue that the central issue was not censorship but harm to women. That harm in fact escalated—not only did VCRs and the internet lead to a still further expansion of sexually violent pornography, but some of the local women who'd testified at various ordinance hearings and remained in their communities became the subsequent subject of harassment. Andrea had come to know several of these women rather well and felt personally responsible when one of them actually committed suicide.

She and Kitty remained closely in touch, though they did disagree on the value of trying to redefine obscenity law; Kitty's position was that if a court decides that pornography is not as important as the pornographer's free speech, then you have a precedent that can be used to try and pass the civil rights law. Andrea felt—and so it turned out—that ultimately it's the police who decide what part of an obscenity statute will be enforced and what part won't. As late as 1998, when Susan Brownmiller was interviewing Andrea for a book she was writing (*In Our Time*) and casually said, "So you're out of the ordinance business now? You're back to just writing?," Andrea's response was, "I did get out of it to write" but "my own view is that [eventually] it's going to pass" and probably first in a foreign country, not the United States. "The U.S. is making a lot of money exporting sexual abuse."[36]

9

Writing

Andrea tried to get others active in the anti-porn campaign to take over a portion of her political work, but had only mixed success. In truth, she wasn't replaceable in most instances. A few (including MacKinnon) were equally brilliant, but no one else could match Andrea's oratorical skills, nor the incantatory power of her writing. Yet another drain on her time opened up when she decided that politically she *had* to file a lawsuit against publisher Larry Flynt and *Hustler* magazine; for some time it had been running a series of scatologically mocking cartoons depicting her in what she called "defamatory, vile, and obscene" ways.[1]

One of the cartoons showed two women engaged in a lesbian act of oral sex with the caption, "You remind me so much of Andrea Dworkin, Edna. It's a dog-eat-dog world." Another was a two-page spread of fifteen pictures showing women masturbating and engaging in sex with each other, with a caption that read "While I'm teaching this little *shiksa* the joys of Yiddish, the Andrea Dworkin Fan Club begins some really serious suck-'n-squat." The December 1984 issue of *Hustler* contained a photograph of a woman receiving cunnilingus from a man as he masturbates; the caption read "The woman in the throes of ecstasy is the mother of radical feminist Andrea Dworkin." Taken collectively, Andrea regarded the imagery as "a form of assault and as such an effort to intimidate me into abandoning my rights of free speech, assembly, and petition." Put another way, she was deliberately personalizing the issue at the heart of the anti-porn debate: Flynt's claim of free speech pitted against the personal harm, both psychological and professional, being inflicted on her—an assault, in short, on her civil rights, to "still and chill" *her* ability to exercise her First Amendment rights.

A recent Supreme Court decision had concluded that "an aggrieved party could sue the publisher of libelous materials in any jurisdiction in which the materials were distributed." Andrea's choice of venue was Wyoming—the first state to grant women suffrage, and so the most fitting place to air the case. The well-known lawyer Gerry Spence represented Andrea. He'd recently announced himself a convert to feminism and in 1974 had won the case brought by the family of whistleblower Karen Silkwood following her death. Spence expected Wyoming's courts to reject the case, but then planned to bring suit in a federal court. The *Hustler* legal battle would prove (in Andrea's words) a "hard and long" process.[2]

Another development—this one a *welcome* claim on her time—was the news that an English publisher had finally, after multiple rejection slips in the United States, agreed to publish a paperback edition of her proposed novel, *Ice and Fire*. The terms, though, were stringent: the contract stipulated that Andrea had to complete a chapter each month from May 1, 1985, to July 1986, or the contract would automatically become null and void. Such draconian demands may well have been unprecedented, but the publisher, the distinguished house of Secker & Warburg, felt it was taking a chance on a highly controversial writer whose earlier books had sold poorly. Andrea, for her part, had no other suitor waiting in the wings—though soon after Secker & Warburg's offer on *Ice and Fire*, the Free Press picked up *Intercourse*, her hefty non-fiction work that had been turned down by numerous houses. That left Andrea with a happily dizzying publication schedule, which saw, in the space of six months, English editions of *Ice and Fire* in hardcover (Weidenfeld and Nicholson) and paperback (Secker and Warburg), and the publication of *Intercourse* in both England and the United States.[3]

"It is all quite incredible," Andrea wrote, having marked 1986 her "now-or-never" fortieth birthday. Secker & Warburg proceeded to put icing on the cake by offering to bring her to England for a publicity tour. "I am dropping anything I have to drop to work on my book," Andrea announced in mid-July, 1985. To meet her assorted deadlines, she withdrew as much as possible from human contact into what she called "a kind of shabby solitude, not really real because I have so many political responsibilities that are tied to my relations with other people," including a number of pre-arranged speaking engagements.

As it would turn out, she wasn't able to sequester herself to the extent she would have liked; too many requests for her time seemed worthy and necessary. She felt obligated during her retreat to pass out anti-porn leaflets at the annual NOW convention in New Orleans and lead a march down Bourbon Street, bullhorn in hand: "Hey, hey, ho, ho, pornography has got to go!"; to fly to Wyoming for the opening arguments of the *Hustler* lawsuit (only to have the case postponed at the last minute); to testify before the Presidential Commission on Pornography; to picket a Republican gathering; and to fly over to England for ten days of editorial meetings and public appearances.[4]

Also, the Supreme Court's 1986 negation of the ordinance still lay ahead and it was due to be voted on in two different places that summer of 1985. As Andrea wrote to one friend, "The political pressure is still on—creating a lot of conflict and trouble, when peace and solitude are needed to write; money is awful, not much coming in, actually nothing over the summer at all. . . . I am very worried that the ordinance will fail legally and politically, partly because we are all so resource-less, so unable to mount the campaigns that need to happen." John, as before, became the sole breadwinner. He'd been working as managing editor at *Essence* magazine, but left in May 1985 in order to have enough free time to put together the book that became *Refusing to Be a Man*, as well as to continue working for passage of the ordinance. For roughly six months he subbed for the managing editor of *Working Woman* and then for years thereafter cobbled together various consulting jobs (only some of which provided a full-time-equivalent salary with benefits).[5]

As Andrea battled *Hustler*, John—through *Sex & Justice*, the newsletter he edited for the National Organization for Changing Men—protested the December 1984 issue of *Penthouse*, which had featured pictures of naked Asian women tied up with rough hemp ropes and hanging from trees. "In the ten or so years I've been an activist in the feminist anti-pornography movement," he wrote, "I have learned never to underestimate how much further the pornography industry will go in its sexualization of brutality and contempt."

The most consequential draw on Andrea's time was her appearance before the Attorney General's Commission on Pornography, the so-called Meese Commission—an eleven-member investigatory panel (seven men, four women) chaired not by Meese himself but by Henry Hudson, the commonwealth attorney of Arlington, Virginia, who, notoriously, had shut down every adult bookstore in his jurisdiction. Meese was widely viewed as the leading spokesperson for President Ronald Reagan in his determination to reassert traditional moral values—despite the supposedly sacred Republican tradition of minimizing the interference of the federal government in the lives of the citizenry. In the 1960s and 1970s, it had been the left pushing for government intervention to promote the black civil rights struggle and to end the war in Vietnam. But by the mid-eighties the pendulum had decidedly swung back, as it always had (the free-wheeling twenties, for instance, gave way to the buttoned-up fifties); this time it was the Right calling for the government to step in and regulate morality (or, in Jerry Falwell's deathless words, "to push pornography back to Sleaze Town to live amongst the roaches where it belongs"). In the midst of the ferocious AIDS epidemic, even Jesse Jackson spoke out against "sex without love."[6]

Nearly twenty years earlier, during a far more permissive period, Richard Nixon's presidential commission on pornography had recommended that a massive sex education campaign be initiated, that open discussion and long-term research should be encouraged on issues relating to sexuality, and that legislation "should not seek to interfere with the right of adults who wish to do so to read, obtain, or view explicit sexual materials." (Both Nixon and Congress turned down the permissive report.) By the time the Meese Commission began its hearings in the summer of 1985, the cultural climate had unmistakably shifted, and the Commission's executive director, Alan Sears, prematurely sent out a warning letter of notification to a number of companies that they were "dealing in pornography"; as a direct result, the 7-Eleven chain immediately stopped selling adult magazines in its 7,500 stores. A federal district judge soon ordered the Commission to retract Sears' threatening letter, characterizing it as constituting "prior restraint on speech."[7]

Still, the direction in which the Commission was headed was abundantly clear (prior to their appointment, seven of the eleven members had previously spoken out against pornography), passions on all sides were quickly enflamed, and pre-existing antagonisms within feminism were emphatically underscored. For a time the wounding accusations stayed relatively low key, but when the Meese Commission concluded its investigation and in July 1986 formally released its report—a staggering 1,960 pages—a cloudburst followed.

Of the Commission's multiple conclusions—and ninety-three recommendations!—a few proved particularly inflammatory. The rape of women, the report announced, was a prominent theme in pornography, and some of the women were depicted as *enjoying* the sexual violence done to them ("they say 'no' but really mean 'yes'"); further, the report insisted that violent pornography led directly to violence against women and that even non-violent pornography could be degrading when it depicted, as it often did, women "as existing solely for the sexual satisfaction of others, usually men," or when it showed "people, usually women, in decidedly subordinate roles in their sexual relations with others." Perhaps the Commission's most provocative statement was its flat-out assertion that "none of us believes" that "uncommitted sexuality . . . [is] a good thing," thereby implicitly condemning a considerable segment of gay male subculture that deplored monogamy and celebrated sexual "adventuring."[8]

The Commission recommended stricter obscenity laws but also endorsed the MacKinnon/Dworkin civil rights approach to pornography, characterizing it as "alternative and preferable." Andrea and Kitty applauded the endorsement: "For the first time in history," they wrote, "women have succeeded in convincing a national

governmental body of a truth women have long known: pornography harms women and children." Yet they also deemed the Meese
report flawed in its recommendation to strengthen obscenity laws
and extend their enforcement; they'd long denounced such laws as
dangerously irrelevant and as heightening the discretionary powers
of the police. As Dorchen Leidholdt, the spokesperson for WAP,
added, "Obscenity laws misconceive the harm of pornography as an
affront to sensibilities instead of an injury to women's lives."

Nan Hunter, a prominent figure in FACT, made a point sounded
by many: the conservative commission's true concern was not harm
to women's lives but rather the spread of sexually explicit material,
especially the part that represented sexual minorities; what truly
horrified most of the commissioners, Hunter convincingly insisted,
was homosexuality, abortion, and teenage, premarital, and extra-
marital sex. Nor was FACT alone in its opposition. The ACLU,
where Hunter was a staff member, tried to discredit some of the testimony given to the commission; *Playboy* and *Penthouse* threatened
lawsuits; and a National Coalition Against Censorship (NCAC) was
formed (its ranks filled with celebrities like the novelist Kurt Von-
negut and actress Colleen Dewhurst).

The dissenters all hammered home the view that there was a
direct link between the influence of MacKinnon and Dworkin and
the growing climate of suppression, despite the fact that they had
both frequently made it clear, and publicly, that they opposed any
sort of categorical ban on written or visual material. Their goal—
often repeated, just as often ignored—was to extend the recourse
of the courts to those women who could prove harm from materials (such as depictions of non-consensual S/M) that subordinate
them through words or pictures. If pornography, as the Commission insisted, did represent an assault against women, then why
wasn't it considered just as harmful as anti-black and anti-Semitic
material?

Should legal decisions under their model ordinance go beyond
awarding damages to individuals into a general proscription against
pornography that portrayed women as asking for and receiving
debased treatment, the result, Andrea and Kitty argued, would *not*
amount to an unconstitutional assault on the First Amendment. In
their view, the access of poor and marginalized women to speak (and

be heard) had long been obstructed, and to a more total extent than
anything the ordinance threatened. As Andrea put it, "Pornography has precisely to do with the situation of poor women—which
in my view is why we are getting so much shit thrown at us in the
women's movement. People have no idea how middle-classed and
privileged their liberal First Amendment stuff is—how power and
money determine who can actually speak in this society." Besides,
she argued, the First Amendment did not intend a free pass to any
form of speech; both libel and perjury had never been forms of protected expression.

Perhaps in an imperfect world, Andrea argued, the best that could
be hoped for would be to reach for the very first time something
like a *balance* between the civil rights of pornographers and those of
women; the former would lose some iota of the fullness of their freedom of (murderous) expression, and the latter would no longer have
to remain *entirely* silent. Resistance to such a compromise would
draw heavily for its justification from the uncertainty surrounding
the issue of causality, the weakest link in the theoretical positions of
both the pro- and anti-pornography forces. *Did* violent pornography
increase violent behavior toward women? *Was* the graphic portrayal
of male sexual aggression and female subordination responsible for
(or merely reflective of) the wide gap in power between men and
women—even to the point of some women accepting and *defending* their lesser status? Did depictions of violent sexuality *cause* rape
and battering, or were both merely secondary symptoms of a male
supremacist culture? Who would dare to deny, Andrea asked, that
men ruled and that women were subordinate? Short of defending
such an arrangement—as many did—as an inescapable feature of
biology, what grounds *other than* an attack on pornography could be
enlisted in the struggle to curtail the male propensity to domestic
aggression and global war? Curtailing the contribution that violent
pornography made to maintaining male dominance might be no
more than a start in diluting—and ultimately ending—it, but who
was offering a more substantive or better way?

When Andrea herself testified before the Commission, she spoke
with such moving simplicity that one of the commissioners, Park
Elliott Dietz, director of the Institute of Law, Psychiatry and Public Policy at the University of Virginia, later said that he'd been

brought to tears. ("I am asking you as individuals," Andrea had said, "to have the courage, because I think it's what you will need, to actually be willing yourselves to go and cut that woman down and untie her hands and take the gag out of her mouth, and to do something, for her freedom.")

As it would turn out, most commentators expressed emotions quite distinct from Dietz's—closer to fury than tears. In a long article in the *Village Voice*, Walter Kendrick, a professor of Victorian literature (no less) at Fordham University, singled out Andrea for special excoriation, in his outrage all but condemning her to the witches' pyre. Linking Andrea to Anthony Comstock, who Kendrick saw as her nineteenth-century soulmate, he mocked her as "fat, humorless, and literal-minded." Then, for good measure, he announced that Dietz "would have made an excellent Nazi," which is more than a bit looney given Dietz's admiration rather than denunciation of Dworkin the Jew. Kendrick referred to himself as a feminist even as he insisted that "a woman can choose to make or view pornography" and denounced those who would "infantilize" them by treating them as victims by fiat of gender." To be sure, he loftily concluded, "pleas for reason" such as his, would be drowned "in the shrieks of phony do-gooders and disingenuous rabble-rousers"—people like Andrea Dworkin, who would continue to insist that Linda Lovelace represented many more battered wives and drug-addicted porn stars than did Kendrick's woman, who "can choose," who had a resplendent array of prospects and options from which to pick.[9]

Judging from the rage with which Andrea and Kitty were denounced—including a strenuous attack from the ACLU to the effect that no evidence exists (which wasn't true) for the claim that pornography sparks sexual violence—one might never have guessed that Andrea and Kitty had in fact greeted the Meese Commission's conclusions and recommendations with considerable caution. "The Commission's report is flawed," they stated publicly, "by recommending extension and escalated enforcement of obscenity laws." All that those laws, by their nature, could achieve was a male-dictated definition of what constituted "obscenity" and a male-dictated political decision as to where it should (and *could*) be made available in specifically designed zones.

The FACT feminists denied that pornography was central to the oppression of women—certainly not to the extent that it caused sufficient harm to justify any curtailment of free speech. On the contrary, FACT argued, pornography actually served some useful social functions of benefit to women. It magnified, according to one of FACT's leaders, "the misogyny present in the culture" (but didn't that mean it *did* further oppress women?) and even carried the subliminal message that lifetime monogamous pair-bonding and vanilla sex did not meet the citizenry's sexual needs, that what also needed advocacy was sexual variety, non-marital sex, group sex, homo-sex, public sex, anonymous sex. To all of which Andrea might have said amen, but she would have been quick to add that what poor women of limited education and options had a far greater need for was to be free from beatings, rape, and general subservience to the unpredictable whims of their male masters.

Though pleased with the Meese Commission's acknowledgment that depictions of violent sexuality *did* harm women, Andrea and Kitty decried its lack of certainty about the causal link—the *extent* of the consequences of viewing sexually violent material. The Commission during its hearings relied on some of the same experts that Andrea and Kitty had—in particular, Professors Donnerstein and Malamuth. Andrea had earlier complained about the professors vacillating in laying claim to the findings of their own research, but that irresolution accelerated when testifying before the Commission.

Both Donnerstein and Malamuth issued disclaimers after the Meese report was published, claiming that it misrepresented at least part of their research: they denied the report's assertion that sexually violent materials had increased to such an extent in recent years as to become the most prevalent form of pornography. In fact, they argued, the empirical data was limited and contradictory: depictions of violence seemed to show an increase through the late seventies, but then a decline. Research on films showing women enjoying and becoming aroused at scenes of sexual violence were particularly "tricky to interpret." As for men, they found "no reason to think that exposure to violent pornography is the cause of these [aggressive] predispositions," yet they felt as well that it was counterintuitive to believe that even if not the cause of male sexual violence, these films in all likelihood did reinforce those predisposi-

tions. What remained unclear was whether the violence itself provided the reinforcement, or the violence within a sexual context.[10]

The Meese Commission itself initiated no original research.
However, it did sponsor one weekend workshop, headed by Surgeon
General C. Everett Koop and confined to "recognized authorities"
in the field. At its close, the participants announced consensus in
certain areas; the two most crucial were that "pornography that
portrays sexual aggression as pleasurable for the victim increases the acceptance of the use of coercion in sexual relations," and
that "exposure to violent pornography increases punitive behavior toward women." Koop summarized the evidence as "slim," yet
persuasive enough to conclude that "pornography does present a
clear and present danger to American public health." To which Neil
Malamuth, a participant in the workshop, objected: although he
agreed that films portraying sexual aggression "as pleasurable for
the victim" do increase the amount of coercion in sexual relations,
he did not agree that such pornography was "at the root of much of
the rape that occurs today." He offered no alternative explanation.
And there the matter rested for a time.[11]

Andrea's novel, *Ice and Fire*, and her new non-fiction book, *Intercourse*, were published in England almost simultaneously. In many
ways, *Ice and Fire* is a *tour de force*. In its harrowing theme of living on
the margins, the austere, jagged prose mirrors the horrors it recites,
and the novel achieves the kind of hallucinatory intensity associated with the work of William Burroughs or Hubert Selby: "the
needle just gutted her with pleasure: so afterward, in retrospect, one
inferred that there had been a lack, a need, before the needle: but
in fact she had been complete before and heavy and thick like some
distilled perfume, sweet to the point of sickness, a nauseating sweetness: something transporting and divine: something that translated
into eyelids weighed down and swollen, lips puffed up, the cracks
in them spreading down, the body suddenly soft and pliant, ready
to curl, to billow, to fold: a fragile body, delicate bones suddenly
soft, eyes hiding behind lush eyelids: the hard tension of her hips
dissolved, finally. The way other women look when they've been
fucked hard and long, coming and coming, is how she looked: the

way other women look fucked out, creamy and swollen, is how she looked. The needle gave her that, finally: dissolved."[12]

Using initials ("N.") for the two protagonists in the novel underscores the encompassing abstraction—anonymity, really—that simultaneously lifts the lives recounted to myth-like impersonality even while recording the inescapable individuality of suffering. The driven, relentless quality of the writing is for a considerable portion of the novel mesmerizing, as is the staccato tempo of the corrosively macabre narrative. Ultimately, though, the repetitious rhythm turns irksome, the relentless, unwavering pace tedious, the desolation too unvarying to sustain its grip; we move outside the experience, our nerve endings shut off; we refuse to participate further.

Intercourse is a very different kind of book. It's a work of intricate argument—and easily misinterpreted. If *Ice and Fire* testifies, finally, to the limits of Andrea's imaginative powers, *Intercourse* impressively demonstrates the range of her analytic skill. It is far too complex a work to lend itself to simplistic summary, and Andrea doesn't make it any easier for us by devoting the first half of the book to *approaching* her essential subject through the indirection of literary criticism. Taking on a panoply of male writers as diverse as Tolstoy, James Baldwin, Isaac Bashevis Singer, Kobo Abe, and Tennessee Williams, she ranges from the contestably abstract ("The normal fuck by a normal man is taken to be an act of invasion and ownership undertaken in a mode of predation") to the provocatively epigrammatic ("We are inarticulate about sex, even though we talk about it all the time to say how much we like it").

It's only in the second half of *Intercourse* that a less veiled political agenda emerges, even if, some thirty years later, it sometimes reads as timeworn: "Most women are not distinct, private individuals to most men. . . . Women live inside this reality of being owned and being fucked; are sensate inside it; the body learning to respond to what male dominance offers as touch, as sex, as love." Now and then, Andrea's essential combativeness takes on the elegant contours of aphorism: "The old virginity—with its real potential for freedom and self-determination—is transformed into the new virginity—listless, dissatisfied ennui until awakened by the adventure of male sexual domination: combat on the world's tiniest battlefield."[13]

More typically, defiance is upfront and foremost: "The political meaning of intercourse for women is the fundamental question of feminism and freedom: can an occupied people—physically occupied inside, internally invaded—be free; can those with a metaphysically compromised privacy have self-determination; can those without a biologically based physical integrity have self-respect?" Andrea makes it clear that in her philosophy "there is nothing implicit in intercourse that mandates male dominance in society." The various and "staggering" civil inequalities that characterize the culture are injustices *not* related to "the natural, healthy act of intercourse . . . this book does not say that all men are rapists or that all intercourse is rape"—a clear enough statement, though her critics, then and now, settle for the simplistic dismissal of her position as "a rejection of intercourse."

Relying heavily on the findings of Shere Hite—a personal friend (whose first two books, *The Hite Report* and *The Hite Report on Male Sexuality*, Andrea fully credits)—she proceeds to itemize the *context* in which intercourse generally takes place, a context that both expresses and extends male dominance: intercourse is "frequently performed compulsively," usually requires the female partner "to look a certain way, be a certain type—even conform to preordained behaviors and scripts," and a female who "cannot exist before or during the act as a fully realized, existentially alive individual." But current conditions can, in Andrea's view, be improved—even radically so. The circumstances surrounding intercourse could be made to include "more deference to female sensuality prior to the act; less verbal assault as part of sexual expressiveness toward women . . . less romanticizing of rape . . . strong, self-respecting role models for girls." Should such conditions be met, "intercourse could be experienced in a world of social equality for the sexes."

Not that Andrea was optimistic. She concludes *Intercourse* with the observation that "incestuous rape is becoming a central paradigm for intercourse in our time. Women are supposed to be small and childlike, in looks, in rights; child prostitution keeps increasing in mass and in legitimacy, the children sexually used by a long chain of men—fathers, uncles, grandfathers, brothers, pimps, pornographers, and the good citizens who are the consumers; and men, who are, after all, just family, are supposed to slice us up the middle, leaving us in parts on the bed."

Ice and Fire received handsome blurbs from Kate Millett ("one waits for years to hear a new voice like this!") and Robin Morgan ("a major book") but she wasn't successful—though she always took a personal hand in securing blurbs—with Susan Brownmiller. In response to Andrea's solicitation, Susan wrote back: "I thought you knew that I don't do blurbs anymore. . . . My life has been a lot more pleasant since." Not good enough for Andrea. She wrote again, icily: "I am glad yr life is more pleasant not doing them, but I think for most of us life as feminist writers is harder and harder . . . I think yr decision is wrong." Susan didn't budge.[14]

Both *Ice and Fire* and *Intercourse* received (in Andrea's words) "exceptionally contemptuous" reviews, with *Ice and Fire* getting the somewhat warmer reception.[15] Marilyn French (*The Women's Room*) praised the book in *Ms.* as "a serious novel, a *bildungsroman* that portrays vividly and intensely, with a strong sense of reality, the substructure of male-female relations." In *The Women's Review of Books*, Louise Armstrong hailed *Ice and Fire* as "absolutely first-rate, totally of a piece; it risks everything and triumphs." And Kitty, not quick with compliments, read the novel in manuscript and told Andrea it was "astounding, political, to the end . . . I am gripped and thrilled." Still, on the whole, a number of the reviews were, as Andrea accurately described them, "pretty consistently spiteful and awful."[16]

A number were downright harsh, and the worst were in the most prominent publications. The review by Carol Sternhell, at the time director of the graduate program for journalism at NYU, in the *New York Times* provided ample grounds for Andrea's fear that she was destined to be misunderstood. She (accurately) described Sternhell's review as "unremittingly depressing . . . foul, illiterate." Ordinarily an entirely negative review in the *Times* would have meant—such was the paper's power—that a book was dead in the water. But Andrea's English publisher, Weidenfeld, decided—quite miraculously—to fight back against the Sternhell piece; it took out a full-page ad in the *Times* strongly pushing the novel. That led to an appearance, along with Erica Jong, on the influential Phil Donahue television show, on which Andrea acquitted herself splendidly (as Jong confirmed in a gracious letter to her). The reviews for *Intercourse* were still worse. Sternhell, in the same review for *Ice and Fire*, simply trashed *Intercourse* as a "harangue." In the process, she got certain important matters quite wrong: Andrea did *not* believe in "(unchanging) biological design," nor did she "confuse our sexual organs with our social organizations"—another version of pre-destination.[17]

The Nation paired *Intercourse* with Kitty's new book, *Feminism Unmodified* and—though it should have known better—turned over the assignment to Maureen Mullarkey, a conservative Catholic associated with the Federalist Society. The result, predictably, was a slashing, vituperative attack reminiscent of the edicts of Torquemada. Mullarkey dismissed "Dworkin's lunatic *pensees*" as a "hate-mongering tantrum . . . shackled like an S/M bondage slave to a primitive abhorrence of men." She thought Kitty merely "intellectually sloppy," though bracketed both books as "playing Hitler." Hinting strongly that feminism was a lesbian plot ("Heterosexuality is on trial in a kangaroo court"), Mullarkey either didn't know or didn't care that Kitty was not a lesbian. Perhaps in atonement, *The Nation* subsequently ran a number of letters protesting the savagery of the review, but the damage was done.[18]

"I live in a world," Andrea explained to a recent acquaintance, the English science fiction writer Michael Moorcock (who, with his wife, Linda Steele, would become close and lasting friends), where a *Nation* review "represents the political consensus among intellectuals and so-called radicals. And so I don't know what to do. What is there to do? I keep trying to understand it, and I can't." The review, she added, "was not out of line with the way my work and I are treated here. Usually MacKinnon is treated better"—though only by a hair in the case of Mullarkey—"partly because she is more lady-like in some ways, partly because she is much-credentialed (lawyer, Ph.D., actually earns a living, publishes in academic journals, lots of footnotes). She and I do our best to discuss this all politically and personally, because otherwise there can be such bitterness on my part and such insensitivity on hers, and vice versa."

Even some feminist publications were savage. *Sojourner* headlined its review of *Intercourse*, "A Distorted and Anti-Sex Vision," though "distorted" more accurately applied to the review itself (matched by a nasty, condescending tone); it dismissed the book as "anti-sex" and even claimed that Andrea believed intercourse would always be oppressive to women. It's worth noting, given the dismissal of Andrea as a man-hater, that in a *Sojourner* interview Andrea gave this response to the question "Are there any good men?": "I probably see both the best and worst of men. I think when you deal with pornography, you see the worst of men, and when you deal with social change, you see the best of men." Negative reviews by feminists disheartened Andrea more than any others. To her they were a marker of the movement's decline: radical feminism, dominant in the early seventies and demanding a revolution in attitudes and institutions, had given way to a far more accommodationist attitude—namely, a bigger piece of the pie.

Sojourner, at least, gave Andrea a chance to respond and she seized on it, vigorously correcting the opinions fallaciously ascribed to her: she was not anti-sex, she was not anti-male, she was not anti-intercourse. She also took the opportunity to again point out—citing Shere Hite—that most women (seven out of ten) "just don't like intercourse very much" and do not reach orgasm from intercourse. If intercourse brings so few women pleasure, "the real question," Andrea said, "is why intercourse is the central sex act in our society." The answer, she suspected, is that "men only feel they've had sex when they've had intercourse."[19]

Her publisher, Secker & Warburg, failed to stand by her. Though they'd managed to make a quite handsome paperback sale of *Intercourse* to the Free Press in the United States, they disinvited Andrea from the planned tour in England for the hardcover. The Free Press treated her no better, telling her in essence that even having been on the Donahue show, watched by five million or so viewers—*and*, they acknowledged, having performed "superbly"—they had *still* been unable to sell out the 7,500 first printing (as if that was strictly *her* fault), and were damned if they were going to spend any *more* money on trying to promote the book. Not surprisingly, Andrea began to feel "a lynch mentality around my work" had developed and it was being treated like "deranged garbage."[20]

Andrea was a firm believer in fighting back. She not only wrote a blistering response to Sternhell, but the *Times*, for once, actually printed it. "I despair," she wrote, "of being treated with respect, let alone fairly, in your pages," but the Sternhell review had crossed the line—it was "contemptuous beyond belief," the work of someone "who seems to be functionally illiterate." *Ice and Fire* was a novel, not an autobiography (as Sternhell had called it), and it cannot resonate for anyone who refuses to acknowledge "the intersection of poverty and sexual exploitation. You needed to give a damn about that interconnection before the novel could mean anything to you. It is probably easier to celebrate prostitution as a so-called feminist option for women, the current liberal dogma in this country, than to read *Ice and Fire* and feel the cost of being bought and sold."

In her wounded pride, Andrea may have gone a bit overboard, but "going overboard," she would probably want to claim, was an essential ingredient of her persona. Though *Ice and Fire* wasn't a literal transcription of her own life, it came close enough for a reviewer who called it "autobiographical" to have reason. The book, after all, is written in the first person, doesn't contradict any of the known facts in Andrea's life, and seems at most to embellish them. Curiously, though, in an interview she gave at the time to *New Directions for Women*, Andrea insisted that "if I were writing about myself, I wouldn't want to see all the things that I showed you about this character that I've created." Perhaps, as someone with an inflated view of the sanctity of literature, Andrea was intent on claiming the exalted ground of "novelist" or, more simply, attempting to separate herself from some of the personal ramifications of what she included that were likely to follow. Along these lines, when Kitty dashed off her glowing praise after finishing the manuscript of *Ice and Fire*, she added, with palpable anxiety, a few nervous questions: "Will everyone know that it is literally accurate? Can you survive your portrait of the publisher at Perigee? . . . John has seen it?"[21]

———

Along with a rock-bottom, almost corporeal, commitment to telling the truth as she saw it, sugar-coating nothing, Andrea held a parallel conviction that women "can understand the truth"—can absorb it and fight back against it. Now she wasn't so sure. The double-downed denunciation—two books dismissed simultaneously—was, she wrote a friend, "the most awful publication thing I have ever been through. I am close to devastation most of the time." She told Elaine Markson that the ruinous round of reviews "feels like being gang-raped"; she felt "pretty much at the end of my rope." Hating the feeling of being "paralyzed and passive," she started to badger Secker & Warburg to bring her over to England to defend herself against the "bare-boned misogyny" assailing her. They finally gave in; the books hadn't been selling, and they may have become persuaded that Andrea's oratorical skills could turn the tide. Another boost to her spirits came from Germany. The well-known feminist theoretician, Alice Schwarzer, and the other women who put out the influential journal *Emma*, hearing that Andrea was planning a trip to England, invited her to add Germany to her itinerary. Yet another invitation arrived from Kvinnefronten, the Women's Front of Norway.[22]

That same month of August 1987, there was even a bit of good news on the home front. The novelist Erica Jong, who'd earlier appeared with Andrea on the Phil Donahue TV show and been deeply impressed by her, now let her know that she, Erica, had made a deal with the *Washington Post Magazine* to do a cover story about Andrea as an example of "how badly women writers are treated" and also stressing her own conviction that the women's movement had failed because it had lost its nerve and retreated from its radical origins. "This is all astonishing," Andrea wrote Michael Moorcock and Linda Steele, "and it comes on the back of another astonishing media event": she and Gloria Steinem had just done a 2 a.m. to 4 a.m. network show called *Nightwatch*, and Gloria had unexpectedly come out with a strong endorsement of *Intercourse*.[23]

That was all decidedly cheering. Yet Andrea felt a bit leery too. "It is hard because I don't respect Erica's work, but I do respect her sense of what doing work costs women. She wants her work respect-

ed and feels it is not." It didn't help that Erica had said she wanted
to interview Andrea for a "psycho-history"; this, Andrea humorously commented, "she will not get, but I am pretty terrified of her
because she is smart and I am a bad liar and don't lie and at the same
time want to protect my privacy like I have never wanted anything
in my life. So this is the current dilemma. The current cosmic joke,
on me." Andrea was willing to hold out the hope that Jong's article
"will actually do some good, not just for me but for the movement."

First, the interview had to get published. The *Washington Post*
quickly turned it down, telling Erica that it was self-serving—"and
so it is business as usual in the land of free speech," Andrea wryly
commented. Not that she had held out high hopes for the piece:
"Everything Erica has said to me has made me think she doesn't
know the differences between us, and it is a very peculiar feeling . . .
[Yet] she is . . . very nice and very smart. [Her] kindness is treasured.
It's a little disgusting on my part: the cowering dog . . . her conversation [is] absolutely cliché-ridden. There is no new-age verity
too bland, too dull, or too stupid for her." Yet Erica did mean well,
and did come through: Jong's "Changing My Mind About Andrea
Dworkin" appeared in the June 1988 issue of *Ms.*, was clearly meant
kindly, and despite some unfortunate bits ("Andrea dresses to keep
men and the world at bay; I [dress] not only to attract but also for my
own delight in costume and color"), was not only clearly admiring
but tailored to persuade others that Andrea was an important writer
whose work should be held in serious regard.

Just a week before she was due to leave for England, Andrea got
the news that her case against *Hustler* magazine over the sexually
explicit cartoons they'd published had been thrown out of court
on summary judgment ("there is no genuine issue as to any material fact"). The presiding judge ruled, bizarrely, that Andrea had
failed to show "by clear and convincing evidence" that *Hustler* had
"acted with actual malice" (which he defined as publishing a statement "with knowledge that it was false or with reckless disregard
of whether it was false or not"—implying that he was a devotee of
truth). The judge acknowledged that the likenesses in the cartoons
were unmistakably Andrea and that her own name *had* been used,

but nonetheless ruled that there were no grounds to move forward to trial.[24]

The judge acknowledged that the cartoons were vicious but (here his opinion echoed the intrinsic confusion of libel law) had not been presented as factual in form; they were *fantasy only*—satire and hyperbole—and therefore protected. On the grounds that "vicious and gratuitously personal attacks may well attract support and sympathy for their targets," he ruled further that "Dworkin cannot maintain a separate cause of action for mental and emotional distress." Andrea's translation: "A man's fantasy has legal protection; my life, which is real, doesn't. I mean, shit. I am so fucking angry." Her lawyer emphasized the positive: the judge hadn't punished her for bringing the suit—hadn't required that *she* pay *Hustler*'s legal costs. No, Andrea told him, she did not feel grateful: "I'm not going to lie back and enjoy it." She found it hard to believe that no precedent existed for holding a cartoon libelous. Both Gloria Steinem and Susan Brownmiller agreed to Kitty's request to write amicus briefs, and Bella Abzug also submitted one on Andrea's behalf. With those in hand, she insisted on proceeding with an appeal—though in the upshot to no avail.[25]

The following week, on September 15, Andrea flew to London, to stay only a few days, less than she'd hoped. The *Emma* feminists in Germany had fallen behind schedule in getting out an edition of *Pornography* in time for Andrea's arrival, so that part of the itinerary was put off for a later trip. In the meantime, the group had gone ahead and initiated a (bastardized) version of the model ordinance in West Germany against pornography; the SPD (Socialist Party) had pledged its support, and a political campaign for passage was underway.

The trip to England proved much tougher than anticipated and then, soon after Andrea returned home—and just before Christmas—John lost his job as editor-in-chief of a start-up publication, *Working Woman Weekends*. The magazine had in fact been his idea, and he'd been hired full-time to get it off the ground. The root cause of his firing, Andrea felt, was his active role on behalf of the anti-pornography ordinance. In her opinion, his job became overtly in jeopardy when the disastrous double review of her two books appeared in the *New York Times*: as she reported to Moorcock, "He [John] was made to account for his relationship to me, [and] to show his superior his deposition to *Hustler* about our relationship." All of which John too believed was contributory to his firing, but he felt the decisive reason had been the stock market crash and the decline in ad revenue.

Fortunately, no immediate financial crisis was at hand, thanks to the small amount of savings they'd been managing to put aside. Within a few months John landed another position, initially temporary, at *LEAR'S*, a magazine for women over forty that Frances Lear (ex-wife of Norman) was rather chaotically putting together with her thirty million in alimony. John reported that *LEAR'S* was "a madhouse," full of "knotty problems" in need of solving, but a challenging, creative one (he would stay at *LEAR'S* nearly three years). He also had good news from Elaine Markson about the collection of his speeches and essays that she'd been shopping around. The publisher was a small West Coast one, Beitenbush, but Elaine said they had an excellent reputation and would do well by him; as it would turn out, Meridian, a Penguin Group subsidiary, would reissue the collection in 1990.

On the whole, as Andrea acknowledged to Alice Schwarzer, "I have rare happiness in my personal life." Lately, with John unemployed and usually at home (and their apartment small), "it has been hard, and that takes its toll, which, I think, one cannot help." Yet overall, she added, at a certain point in life, "parts of you go dead, and things you could feel before you can no longer feel, and youth and hope seem further." She gave that sentiment a more humorous twist in a letter to Robin Morgan: "Love is strange (but not as strange as men in cars)."

Andrea was eager to start on a new novel that had been going around in her head for some time; she wanted, she wrote Michael Moorcock, to write about "what it's like being raped over and over and what it means and what it does. Most women are raped more than once and we don't even dare acknowledge it . . . because in this world it suggests the woman is at fault." Entitled *Mercy*, the novel would eventually come out in 1991, but initially Andrea had "great trouble slowing down and having patience after running so hard and so far these last years."[26]

She'd been running hard because she had to, driven by both temperament and political necessity. "I can stand almost anything when I am working," she once wrote. When not working, she was quite incapable of relaxing. At one point, she tried to watch television, but decided "I simply haven't got the discipline"—a curious explanation for someone whose tendency to self-castigation kept her bound to the obligatory grindstone. Her few attempts at a vacation simply confirmed her inability to enjoy one. Persuaded at one point to take a few days off in North Carolina, she drolly reported back that "the beach was beige. So was the apartment . . . I don't know how to rest."

Mostly out of financial necessity she again began, soon after the double publication in 1987 of *Ice and Fire* and *Intercourse*, to accept speaking invitations that kept her intermittently hop-scotching from place to place. Friends in various locales would offer her a bed, a guest room, a whole apartment. But she would rarely "inflict" herself; I'm an "impossible guest," she'd say, with restless tics and disruptive habits: preferring to write at night, she usually slept during the day—that is, when insomnia didn't interfere. "I'm always waiting for the Cossacks to come basically, ready to run, so it's absurd to even try" to relax. Nor did travel hold any appeal, unless connected to promoting a book or fulfilling a political commitment. "I've gotten bug-o-phobic," she reported to Moorcock. "It seems like some kind of metaphysical agoraphobia to me; my small and self-destructive recognition that the earth is not mine to live on in peace."

She would willingly, even eagerly, embrace travel when the need to promote—or more typically to try to *salvage*—one of her books arose. And that was decidedly the case during most of 1988. Her anger alone propelled her from place to place. At age forty-two, with five substantial books behind her, Andrea had become increasingly well known, thanks to a trail of brutal, demeaning reviews, more as a figure of derision than esteem. On one level, she had faith in the originality and acuity of her work and was able to ascribe

some of the belligerent derision which had greeted it to its innovative nature. But no one is *that* immune to persistent mockery;
besides, despite all her public bravado, she'd carried with her from
childhood the constant and torturous aspersions cast on her character by a distraught and ill mother. As she acknowledged to herself
early in the year, "I have never felt so little confidence in myself or
in my chosen way of life. It's gotten to me."

She wasn't desperate now for money, but she *was* feeling desolate—
and perplexed—about her ongoing difficulty in getting published
and, once published, finding an understanding, appreciative audience. She put together a collection of her articles and speeches,
entitling it *Letters from a War Zone*, and wrote introductions to
each piece, but Elaine was unable to rouse any interest at all among
American publishers. Secker & Warburg agreed to publish the collection, and it appeared in England in 1988, but Andrea had long
been unhappy with Secker's off-handed, we're-doing-you-a-big-
favor attitude toward her. At the same time, *Intercourse* had failed
to find a paperback publisher in the United States. To top off the
grim accounting, both *Pornography* and *Right-Wing Women* went
out of print, and *Ice and Fire* was remaindered. Andrea and Elaine
tried resurrecting as *Love Letters* her early, unpublished novel
Ruins, which after more than a decade had taken on the status of an
ancient artifact—but it failed to spark any interest. Andrea summed
up her reaction in two lines: "I am facing an overwhelming number of dead ends here and . . . I am sick of being marginal in every
sense."[27]

An offer eventually came in from a Secker & Warburg subsidiary, Arrow Books, to do a paperback edition of *Intercourse*. They
even offered to bring Andrea over to England to help promote the
book. Unalloyed good news was unthinkable; swift on the heels
of Arrow's offer came the Supreme Court's unanimous, broadly
worded decision extending First Amendment protection to pornographers for parodies—under which *Hustler*'s Dworkin cartoons
obviously qualified. The appeal she'd filed after *Hustler*'s initial victory went straight out the window. Andrea predicted to Robin Morgan, tongue in cheek, that "Pat Robertson is well on his way to being
president" (and Robin thanked her for her "wonderfully mournful

comments"). Andrea added, on a more serious note, that the Court's decision had simply exposed what she and Kitty had been saying all along: that the Right *defends* pornography. Obscenity law had previously served that function, but no longer did, forcing the Supreme Court "to go out in the open to protect the pornographers."[28]

The trip to England in May provided a boost, though a minor one. She did the requisite number of appearances, but was told several times that *Intercourse* was "a bit too radical" for English tastes. Certain English feminists didn't strike her as radical enough; at several dinner parties she met a number of the more prominent figures in the British movement: "Well, he's a fucking man, what do you expect?!" seemed the canned response to all issues relating to their lives. "I couldn't get them to listen to anything specific or anything that had really to do with social policy decisions. . . . I just cannot figure out how their politics don't add up to just being superior human beings. I can't locate where they see change; who changes and how. Anyway, it drives me nuts."

When *Letters from a War Zone* appeared in England, press coverage, though limited, was more positive than usual. The *Irish Times* even gave her a rave: "Dworkin is a passionate essayist, full of wit, morality and an acute sense of justice." The review was apparently enough to catch the ear of the powers-that-be at E.P. Dutton, Andrea's very first publisher, with whom she'd parted on less than cordial terms. Negotiations began for an American edition of *Letters*, which would appear the following year—at which point the *New York Times*, still hot on her trail, would publish yet another damning review ("rage and self-righteous indignation . . . vulgarity and crassness of language," etc.). "It is a very discouraging time for me," Andrea wrote Robin Morgan. "I am truly being buried alive."[29]

Back in 1978, Andrea uncovered, of all things, a knack for real estate. According to John, she had a nose for a bargain, a sense of timing about the market, and the eyes to envision how to remodel a livable home from its present decay. For a long time, financial stringency had made escape seem impossible. But then they had an unexpected windfall. After the fumes from the ground floor restaurant, which had long plagued them, grew unbearable, they went to court to try and force a recalcitrant landlord to take action. The case had dragged on—but then they suddenly found themselves on the winning side of a $30,000 court judgment. With those unheard-of riches in hand, they had begun house hunting, and Andrea's keen eye had spotted the fourth-floor walkup of a co-op on Tenth Street in Brooklyn's Park Slope, near Prospect Park. John was terrified at the prospect of giving up their affordable rental and taking on a mortgage, but Andrea was adamant, and for two or three days (according to John), they came very close to breaking up. Then, talking about his plight to a friend over lunch, John suddenly started sobbing, and realized he couldn't bear the thought of separating from her.[30]

And so, soon after Andrea's return from England in the spring of 1988, they slowly began to pack up their old apartment and begin repairs on the new one. It became a drawn-out process that lingered on through the early fall. But Andrea was cheerful throughout, joking about how she'd always "longed to have a sofa" and, more seriously, how she felt "an overwhelming sense of joy at having figured out how to have a sense of permanence." Though surrounded for months on end with the usual chaos of moving, she managed between chores to do serious work on her new novel. She called it *Mercy* in reference to the passage in Isaiah, 54:7–8. Andrea's exegesis turned the parable on its head: "God turned his head away for a minute in wrath, but when he turns it back you'll get all this mercy. Well . . . the question is, when women are raped is it that he turned his head away or that he's watching. Are we his pornography? It rather feels that way."[31]

There was better literary news as well. In the spring, *Intercourse* was published in a mass market edition in England and—quite a shock to Andrea—was actually on the *London Sunday Times* bestseller list, if only briefly. Her books also began to be translated: *Pornography* came out in Germany, and was both a critical and commercial success; *Ice and Fire* in Sweden, and *Intercourse* in both

Denmark and Norway. Secker & Warburg, moreover, bought *Mercy* on the basis of just three chapters, and for what Andrea called "a decent amount of money."

None of which, in her mind, was a substitute for an American market that continued in large measure to be closed off to her. No American publisher made an offer on *Mercy*. "If I couldn't publish in England," Andrea wrote a friend, "I would cease to exist as a writer." She added, the tone more bitter than humorous, that "virtually nothing of mine on pornography is available to an Amerikan [sic] audience, which is the freedom of speech that makes this country great, as people here tend to say."

Yet on still other fronts, there were positive signs. The antipornography ordinance continued to draw support in Germany; reports came in of its introduction in the Philippines and New Zealand; and Kitty even managed to get a commitment from a legislator (a gay environmentalist) in Tasmania to introduce it as a private members bill (when Andrea heard the news she expressed mock horror at the prospect of having to move to the South Pacific). The ordinance even showed renewed signs of life in the United States. In the small coastal city of Bellingham, Washington, known as something of an arts-oriented enclave, a local group, Civil Rights For Women (CROW), petitioned to put the bill on the ballot.[32]

The state ACLU initially opposed it, citing the now hoary grounds of free speech (though the organization had always defended the ballot as "speech"). That led a group of feminist lawyers to threaten to resign from the organization, and when the ACLU's national board came out in support of the right to put the ordinance on the ballot, the Washington ACLU reversed itself. In the balloting that followed, the ordinance not only garnered two-thirds of the vote, but carried 118 of Bellingham's 120 precincts—a stunning popular victory. Still, it proved a temporary one. Andrea herself went out to Bellingham to join the struggle for four days in October, right in the middle of the move to Park Slope. But when the ACLU again reversed itself and asked a federal district court to find the ordinance unconstitutional, the court complied.

Andrea loved their new home, though of course—those hovering Cossacks again—she managed to squeeze in a sidebar of guilt: "It's troublesome to me to move some place that has such an outward meaning of wealth; I've never done such a thing or had such an experience. . . . I'm not at ease with it at all. . . . I just mean that a house in New York City means wealth." The fact that repair work was still in progress when she and John moved into the apartment served the secondary purpose of easing her guilt: "I've been a captive here and my brain is pretty soggy from lack of sleep and sawdust and plaster dust. It's been a kind of a nightmare." She went off to do a week's lecturing in Michigan, and then, "terribly excited," attended an international conference in Israel, after which she planned to go for a few days' rest in Spain. But while in Israel she became "terribly sick and exhausted"—to her sorrow, she never got to see Vad Vashem—and had to return to the States.[33]

Once recovered, and with construction work on the Park Slope residence finally at an end, Andrea sealed herself off from public events for a number of months, determined on finishing *Mercy*. Now and then she'd let herself be pulled away for some uncommon reason or cause, and one in particular: the notorious, hideous revelation that a criminal defense lawyer named Joel Steinberg had over a period of time beaten to death his adopted daughter, Lisa, age six. Andrea's sometime friend, Susan Brownmiller, publicly blamed Lisa's death on her mother, Hedda Nussbaum, the battered woman who'd lived with Steinberg since 1976. Brownmiller's accusation stunned and horrified Andrea. She began to have flashbacks of her own earlier history as the battered wife of Iwan de Bruin, when no one heard her screams or believed her stories. She decided she had to write something in Nussbaum's defense; she hardly had a choice: flashbacks were worse than memories—"involuntary, outside time, vivid, almost three-dimensional . . . the air is the same—you are there and it is happening." Writing about it was the only way she knew to coax it back into the corner, to regain footing in the present.[34]

"My friend and colleague Susan Brownmiller," Andrea's article began, "does not want Hedda Nussbaum to be 'exonerated'—something no battered woman ever is, even if a child has not died." To those who agreed with Brownmiller that Nussbaum was legally and morally responsible for Lisa's death, Andrea's response was: "I don't think Hedda Nussbaum is 'innocent.' I don't know any innocent adult women; life is harder than that for everyone. But adult women who have been battered are especially not innocent. Battery is a forced descent into hell and you don't get by in hell by moral goodness. You disintegrate. You don't survive as a discrete personality with a sense of right and wrong."

She went on in the article to describe her own experience as a battered woman—the neighbors who hear nothing, the family members who look right through your bruises and injuries, the doctors who diagnose paranoia (or the kind ones who pat you on the head and prescribe tranquillizers). "You lose language, you want to die, you hope the next beating will kill you. You're present when he 'hurts other people'; you don't help them. 'Judge me, Susan.'" Even after escaping the marriage, for years you "wake up screaming in blind terror in the night. You're repelled by the hypocritical sentimentality that mourns the child Lisa but has no sympathy for her adult counterpart, for the battered wife you say 'wants it, she likes it, she chose it'. You conveniently forget that 'the only way to have helped Lisa Steinberg was to have helped Hedda Nussbaum.'"

Newsweek immediately accepted her article, but the magazine's lawyer intervened and halted publication on the grounds that it libeled (as Andrea put it) "the man who had battered me—unless I could prove through medical records or police records it had happened." Which of course Andrea couldn't; that was an essential part of the case at hand: doctors, police, even neighbors and friends, rarely credit a battered woman's story, let alone file formal reports. As Andrea would later write in the Dutton edition of *Letters*, "We learn fast that the system won't protect us—it only endangers us more—so we hide from the man and from the system—the hospitals, the police, the courts—the places where you get the proof. I still hide. It's not easy for a public person, but I do it. I'm a master of it." John vividly remembers that even years after they'd been living together, if he happened to enter Andrea's bedroom when she was asleep, she'd sometimes awaken and yell out in terror, thinking he was Iwan (both men were blonde and tall). Even after she realized it was John, shaken at the flashback, it would take time for her to calm down.

In any case, rather than alter her piece, as *Newsweek* suggested, Andrea withdrew it; the *Los Angeles Times* published it with only minor changes. Short though the article was, it had a powerful impact.

10

Mercy

Facing a March 1990 deadline from Secker & Warburg for *Mercy*, Andrea burrowed in, except for an occasional lecture to make some money. She was buoyed by the news that Dutton planned a print run of 25,000 for the American edition of *Letters from a War Zone*, and on top of that had agreed to publish *Pornography*.

As she worked on *Mercy*, at the forefront of Andrea's mind was her concern that many women who suffer rape are assaulted "more than once, and the way it hurts women—the way it slowly destroys us—isn't understood at all or felt at all." She wanted her novel to somehow succeed in conveying what that process of disintegration was like. It proved a painful book to work on because it brought her back "to some parts of my own life, and it's very hard. I'm sort of understanding that most of what I've experienced in fact isn't common—there's some stability there for most people that I don't have or some continuity or some respite. . . . The last 15 years with John and with my writing have been very different from all my life before that, which was very violent and vagrant."[1]

Yet, as always when consumed with the writing process, Andrea also felt profoundly at peace, in touch with her gifts, confident of making some contribution. In the case of *Mercy*, that peaceful period was brief, abruptly shattered by an attack so vicious that it left her feeling nearly unbalanced.

In the summer of 1989, as if out of nowhere, a book entitled *Burning Desires: Sex in America*, co-authored by Steve Chapple and David Talbot, appeared under the respectable auspices of Doubleday. The contents, though, read more like *Penthouse* magazine. The book—claiming to be drawn from interviews and other primary sources—contained a malign portrait of Andrea as a violent, hypocritical molester. Among the authors' specific charges—based, they claimed, on interviews with the well-known biographer Patricia Bosworth—was that Andrea had physically assaulted her in an attempt at rape. Andrea knew Bosworth, immediately contacted her, and learned that she'd never said such a thing and would gladly provide an affidavit to that effect should Andrea want one. She did— and Bosworth promptly provided it. *Burning Desires* rattled Andrea so badly that for a brief period she wasn't sure *what* she wanted to do, how next to proceed. "I can't talk about it without crying" she wrote to friends. "I am so tired, so upset in so many ways, so nervous, that my mind started getting *weak*, you know, buckling, my back has gone out again, and my periods gone bananas."[2]

But she did recognize that the book's accusations couldn't go unchallenged, and she enlisted both Elaine Markson's and Kitty MacKinnon's help in trying to get to the bottom of the whole awful business. Elaine discovered that the Doubleday editor of *Burning Desires* was Paul Bresnick, who'd previously been an editor at *Penthouse*. With that revelation, the plot began to unravel. Bresnick disclosed to Elaine that the two authors had told him that they'd interviewed Andrea herself—which they hadn't—and had taken careful notes. He further divulged that *Playboy* had paid "a ton of money" for four excerpts from *Burning Desires*, and had already started to run them in the April 1987 issue of the magazine.[3]

After further sleuthing, Andrea was able to discover that an interview she'd given to a woman who'd identified herself as an Israeli journalist—purportedly for a large daily newspaper in Israel—had in fact then been sold to *Penthouse*, where, partly cut and partly invented as an "exclusive"—it appeared in the magazine's April 1987 issue. Along with an introduction to the article that characterized

Andrea's recent novel *Ice and Fire* as pornographic, *Penthouse* printed a sidebar to the interview that set a new high in vilification: Andrea Dworkin, it read, is "a grotesque effigy of intellectual slime and hypocrisy . . . an inflexible, man-hating fanatic who cannot be taken seriously." The body of the "interview" was little better. It even had Andrea attacking feminism: "The problem with the women's movement," she's quoted as saying, "is that it hasn't significantly helped the advancement of women." To challenge her purported statement, *Penthouse* quoted two female professors to the effect that "women in America now enjoy an unparalleled measure of freedom."

Kitty urged Andrea to bring a libel suit against *Burning Desires*, and put her in touch with a San Francisco lawyer Kitty trusted. He—and several other lawyers as well—told Andrea that "as a public figure" she had "to accept any amount of insult, poison, distortion, and stupidity as a proper reward for having entered into the public dialogue." She could persist with a lawsuit, the lawyers told her, but the cost would run between $50,000 to $150,000—and she would lose. Andrea was understandably distraught. Without a verdict of libel to point to, the assorted accusations in *Burning Desires* would stand unchallenged—both her personal and professional lives put in jeopardy. What she needed was a court-mandated retraction and a public apology. Without those, she feared that the charges against her would become part of her biography and be used henceforth to destroy her credibility.

It was a fear she would have to live with. No lawyer would take the case; no legal judgment proved possible. The stalemate put her in touch with "a new aspect of powerlessness as a woman and punishment for having fought back." Short of continuing to butt her head against the wall—and wasting her life in the process—she had no choice but to pull back, had to try "to stay alive as a writer economically while being blacklisted and morally while being defamed and having the defamation being the only mirror and close to a major contaminant of self-consciousness." It all put her in "a rage about money," tormented about who has it and who doesn't: "it's not a new rage but the lawyer question brings it into high relief."

One added indignity now emerged from the wings: a detective story, *The Dog Collar Murders*, published that same year. It contained a fictionalized yet easily recognizable portrait of Andrea, strangled to death in a dog collar during S/M sex while attending an anti-pornography conference. Hearing about it, Andrea counted her blessings: "I don't have a copy, hallelujah!" Then for toppers came word that *Burning Desires* would have a paperback edition, with Doubleday reiterating its confidence in the integrity of the two authors and the paperback publisher, accordingly, announcing its refusal to remove the material about Andrea assaulting Patricia Bosworth. They suggested that if Andrea was upset, she could sue, apparently on the assumption that she'd be unable to afford the cost. Ordinarily they would have been right on both counts, but Elaine had recently succeeded in selling *Pornography* for a decent sum in Japan, and Andrea, feeling that her entire future was at stake, emptied her limited savings account, found a lawyer willing to accept a low fee, and did finally succeed in getting the material deleted from the paperback.[4]

And who was the paperback publisher? New American Library—E.P. Dutton in its new subsidiary guise, the same house that had published Andrea's first book, *Woman Hating*, and was currently publishing the U.S. edition of Andrea's *Letters from a War Zone*. The general mishmash got more disordered still when she received a phone call from her new (third) editor—currently at NAL—asking what she might know about an unexplained second printing of *Letters*. Nothing, Andrea answered. It seemed *someone* at NAL—it was all "a mystery"—had ordered a second printing of 4,300 copies of *Letters*; everyone professed ignorance, and no one knew what to do. "Well," Andrea laconically suggested, "you might try selling them."

Andrea had to lock herself away to finish *Mercy*. "Every bit of molecular energy," she later wrote, "was geared to writing it; I had terrorized all my friends such that no one dared call me for any reason; I had backed up mail and bills and so on for six months." But finally it was done, and she sent the manuscript off to her editor, Lesley Bryce, at Secker & Warburg; publication in England was set for October 1, 1990—just a few days, coincidentally, after Andrea's forty-fourth birthday. Knowing that *Mercy* had as yet been unable

to find an American publisher, and aware as well that the male president of one U.S. house had earlier vetoed a female editor's enthusiasm for publishing *Ice and Fire*, Lesley Bryce took it upon herself to
organize what Andrea called "an entirely female network inside the
company"; they managed to put *Mercy* into production without any
male editor at Secker having read it.[5]

In the meantime, John seemed to be in a good place—not that
he'd ever been demanding of Andrea's time; to the contrary, from
the earliest days of their relationship he'd put himself in service to
what he believed was her genius. But in the last few years he'd been
carving out a career of his own. Long active in the "male feminist"
movement, and speaking often at public events, he'd collected his
speeches in a book, *Refusing to Be a Man*. It was due out at roughly
the same time as *Mercy*. Secker suggested that John and Andrea
join forces in a combined promotional schedule; the underlying
assumption, as Andrea saw it, was that both books were works of
non-fiction anti-pornography, which she further took to imply that
both could be lumped into the over-arching theme of sexism. She
promptly hit the roof, refusing absolutely to join the planned duet.
She and John were distinctive individuals, she told Secker, as were
their two books. John agreed with her, and Secker mumblingly
backed off.[6]

"I don't expect good reviews" for *Mercy*, Andrea wrote Moorcock,
"or for it to be much appreciated," and in fact the book's reception would prove somewhat divided, certainly complex, mostly
negative. Which wasn't surprising: *Mercy* isn't a book one simply
likes or dislikes. It isn't a story, has no coherently laid-out narrative,
and most assuredly is not an entertainment; if anything, the book's
harrowing, imperious, and high-pitched repetitions more closely
resemble an anguished set of prophecies. *Mercy* has no fleshed-out
characters that one either does or doesn't identify with—or rather,
it's one leading character ("Andrea") and its other ("Not Andrea")
are so decisively *not* three-dimensional that one engages with them
(or doesn't) on an abstract rather than emotional level. The various
men who abuse and rape "Andrea"—starting at age nine—have no
identifying features, no explanatory histories or exculpatory psychology, not even names.

Collectively they are MAN, the violent, brutalizing force that condemns "Andrea" to an unending cycle of subordination and terror—molested as a child, abused as a wife, converted into a servant, raped at will, ultimately ignored and abandoned. She has two and only two options: to play out her prescribed social role and become a mute survivor, or to turn into "a body packed with rage," become an unforgiving "citizen of the night," accept no excuses ("he didn't mean it; or he didn't do it, not really, not fully, or not knowing, or not intending; he didn't understand; or he couldn't help it; or he won't again"), become her own judge and jury—and destroy the oppressor. Her piercing cry of pain unfolds into an apocalyptic retaliation that vengefully obliterates her torturers.

It can be argued that *Mercy* has a humanizing underbelly: "It's the Nazism," "Andrea" writes, that "you have to kill, not the Nazis. People die pretty easily, but cruelty doesn't." Simply murdering an abusive male, in other words, does nothing to destroy the structure of male complacency and power: "So you got to find a way," "Andrea" tells us, "to go up against the big thing, the menace; you have to stop it from being necessary—you have to change the world so no one needs it." Or as the real-life friend of Andrea's, Michael Moorcock, put it, she "still believes that most men could be both just and sensitive, that men and women are socialized into their roles and that legal reform and enlightened education together can change society, ridding us of inequality, providing genuine liberation for women and, incidentally, for men."[7]

That benign reading of *Mercy* hasn't persuaded most of its readers, either at the time of publication or since. The nearly uniform denunciations fell within a narrow range: a "mad, bad novel"; a "long, largely unpunctuated scream"; "grossly disgusting"; a "novel-length rape fantasy"; "*Mercy* left me feeling as if I had been carefully and thoroughly pulped with a verbal sledgehammer"; a "vulgar, reckless shout"; "sheer bad writing"; "grossly disgusting"; "Andrea isn't shocking us into truth. She is ranting"—and so on. In a stack of reviews, only two could be called well-disposed. One of the two was by a man, Frederic Lindsay, in the *Sunday Telegraph*, and not incisive: "the hypnotic power of her writing compels an empathetic sense of the vulnerability of women."[8]

Months, even years later, a few essay reviews appeared that were more nuanced and benign, and to some extent more positive. One of the more recent and probably the most incisive of them has been the critique of Martha Nussbaum, the cultural philosopher. In a lengthy analysis, published in 1999, Nussbaum makes clear that she regards *Mercy* as an important work: "it brings to the surface for scrutiny the strict retributive attitude that animates some portions of our moral and legal tradition and allows us to see this attitude as a reasonable response to terrible wrongs." Nussbaum emphasizes her agreement with Andrea's stress on "the pervasiveness of male violence against women," with her refusal "to deny and conceal these wrongs," and with "protesting loudly" against them. But Nussbaum rejects the view of *Mercy*'s narrator in the concluding section of the book when she refuses all sympathy with her tormentors ("None of them's innocent and who cares? I fucking don't care"). Though Nussbaum appears to agree with Andrea that "the social norms of the American heterosexual male are in some ways those of a rapist, and that . . . rape is not abnormal but 'normal' heterosexual intercourse," she nonetheless wants Andrea to acknowledge that there are individual exceptions. Vengeance, Nussbaum insists, is not the only alternative "to cowardly denial and capitulation." There is also the notion of clemency. If we are all products of social conditions that subvert justice and love—and we are—"slow, patient resistance" is the most reliable path to change.[9]

To which—I'm guessing here—Andrea might well have replied, "Thus have you liberals always argued, and with what result?—not the amelioration of injustice, but its steady advance." Anticipating such a response, Nussbaum repositions her argument: "if you really open your imagination and heart to admit the life story of someone else, it becomes far more difficult to finish that person off with a karate kick." The real-life Andrea's friends would argue that in fact she exemplified that humanistic approach—that she possessed precisely those qualities that Nussbaum urges on us all: sensitivity to the nuances of human suffering, calm, centered attention to what the Other is trying to say, a gentle and generous response (ordinarily) to human failings.[10]

Having known Andrea personally, if briefly, it came as no surprise when I read again and again in letters and interviews the often expressed astonishment at how, on a personal level, people found her "open," "quietly receptive," and "generous." One woman who heard her speak in 1993 wrote her to say that "what impressed me even more than the ideas you stated, was the way you put your ideas into practice . . . you responded more respectfully than anyone I had ever seen to women both whose ideas differed 180 degrees from your own and whose voices were filled with anger." Similarly, an interviewer wrote her to say, "Last night during the call-in radio show I was amazed at how patient you are even when a man says something truly ridiculous . . . how [do] you manage to do that? After hearing this shit over and over, year after year, that you don't want to just put your fist through the wall." To which Andrea responded, "Well no, not about that. I really have learned that it's mostly an opportunity . . . that this is my job, this is what I have to do, so I try to find better and better ways to do it."[11]

In her column "Between the Lines" in the *San Francisco Sunday Examiner and Chronicle*, Patricia Holt put it this way: "Andrea Dworkin writes very tough-minded books . . . but there is a sweetness about . . . [her] personality that always seems to light up an interview. She laughs, she listens; she never raises her soft, almost baby voice, never argues, never sounds polemic. She looks at you thoughtfully with wide and sympathetic eyes and explains her ideas with patience, even tenderness. Who can figure." Doubtless a detractor would use such material to describe Andrea as a dissembler, but no—she was simply multi-faceted, a person who saved her empathy for personal encounters and her fiery vehemence for the public platform.[12]

She sometimes *wrote*—especially in *Mercy*—in a "nightmarish and impolite" style, militantly on guard against sentimental sympathy. When she did so, it was in the name of the underdog, of those who, like her own younger self, had been silenced by the world's brutality. To confuse or equate the ferocious, morally problematic, ruthless harridan "Andrea" of *Mercy* with how the real-life Andrea actually treated people in everyday life would be to reduce a generous spirit to a murderous automaton.

Still, something more needs to be said about Andrea's rejection

of Nussbaum's recommended stance of "patient resistance." In her
private life, yes: Andrea would spend many a precious hour explaining to a friend or a neophyte feminist that when she wrote—in
Intercourse, say—that "violation is a synonym for intercourse" she
was *not* saying (though it was often and still is claimed) that she
viewed all sex as rape—she valued reciprocity, not celibacy. Nussbaum's patient resistance may be a plausible tactic for dealing with
moderate mistakes of ignorance and with negotiable adversaries.
But the more massive inequities may require comparable resistance.
Thanks to the recent emergence of the "Me Too" movement, it's
once again understood that male privilege is more likely to yield to
angry confrontation than to polite appeals to conscience. The collective anger of women has—some thirty years after the publication
of *Mercy*—found new license and approbation. And as Rebecca Traister has recently reminded us, rage is not the opposite of rational: it
can be—and in the past often has been—an appropriate response to
appalling injustice; yes, the Jews of the Warsaw Ghetto were right
to have taken up arms; yes, Toussaint L'Ouverture was right to have
violently thrown off his chains.[13]

In the aftermath of finishing *Mercy*, Andrea felt "very detached,
very remote"; she had "no ambivalence, no second thoughts"; "I
don't quarrel with a tree, I don't quarrel with *Mercy*. It has that
self-evidency, that simplicity, to me, now . . . a certain period of
almost not existing at all for me." She felt something of the same
kind of stasis in regard to the feminist movement. By 1990, in
Andrea's view, violence against women and the weakness of the radical feminist movement had in tandem become "much worse." In
part, she blamed the ever-expanding industry of pornography. She
reiterated yet again that she saw no reason to preclude the existence
of erotica, though she continued to feel puzzled as to why two people happy with each other would need it. She worried, too, that what
the debate about the difference between erotica and pornography
had come down to was that "erotica simply means pornography for
intellectuals"—which meant (like so much else) that it was a class
issue. For her, the difference between erotica and pornography was
easy to ascertain: "look at the status of women" in the film, maga-

zine, or book; if they're represented as subordinate, or if the threat of violence is present, then what you're looking at is pornography.

Ideally, Andrea believed that every movement should have a "whole spectrum" of people in it—"mainstream feminists, reformists, people who do different kinds of work and make a variety of contributions." She ascribed the "solid middle" of the feminist movement as having fallen away due to the "very serious and very systematic" campaign against women who protest. She believed that a number of feminists had "cut and run," fallen back on individual lifestyle goals. And she included in that indictment part of the lesbian community. She believed that in 1990 lesbians "are still responsible for a lot of the leadership" of the movement but that on the grassroots level "there is much more hiding and secrecy and duplicity again"—which she found "very frightening." There was also, she felt, an intensification of "male identification" among lesbians, as represented by the heightened prestige of a sadomasochistic lifestyle, which Andrea abhorred, and a kind of "self-referential clubhouse" tone: "we're special, we're different." She put her hopes primarily in the global spread of international feminism.[14]

One sign of the times had been the demise of *Ms.* magazine in 1987 (which Andrea had *not* lamented) and its purchase by an Australian media company. Two years later, concerned about the amount of "Cher-centered" content, a group of American feminists bought back the magazine and hired Robin Morgan as its editor-in-chief. That delighted Andrea. Her friendship with Robin went back some twenty years, and no serious quarrel had ever troubled it. The new male owner of *Ms.*, Dale Lang, guaranteed Robin a free hand for two issues, and in the run-up to her taking over, she and Andrea had several pow-wows about what the magazine's ideal reincarnation would look like, including a discussion of including the piece Andrea had been writing on Israel.

Robin ultimately decided that the new *Ms.* would be a bimonthly, run roughly a hundred pages per issue, carry no advertising or color—and *not* feature any mainstream celebrity on its cover. "A radical journal at last!" Andrea cheered. As the first issue neared publication, she glowingly reported to her London editor that "Robin has done an astonishing job in creating something worth publishing, worth reading." In her enthusiasm, Andrea's glum assessment of the feminist movement's decline went into abrupt reversal: "I think the zeitgeist really has changed . . . and millions of women can't stand it anymore—I'm saying there is a critical mass now in this direction, and I doubt that I'm misjudging it."[15]

Even in one of her rare upbeat states of mind, Andrea soon reverted to emphasizing instead all that remained undone. Her detractors liked to say that her bleak temperament made her incapable of sustaining a hopeful attitude—which has an element of truth to it. But far more intrinsic to Andrea's character was an inability to indulge for long in that chipper all-American boosterism so successful in blocking out reality. She put it bluntly in a 1991 speech to the Canadian Mental Health Association: "Violence against women is a major past-time. It is a mainstream cultural entertainment. And it is real. It is pervasive. It saturates the society. It's very hard to make anyone notice it, because there is so much of it."[16]

Several decisive events combined during 1991 to compound the sense of a passage, of a significant turning point. At the beginning of the year, after multiple medical crises, Andrea's mother, Sylvia, passed away. Andrea had been long estranged from her parents, but they had recently reconciled, preceded by renewed contact first with her brother, Mark, with whom she'd been in at least occasional touch.

But with her mother, Sylvia, the wounds had gone deep. From childhood on she'd hounded—not too strong a word—Andrea with accusations of inadequacy, of pointlessly, imprudently resisting established norms. Being made to feel profoundly deficient had contributed immeasurably to the underlay of masochism and anguish Andrea suffered as an adult. Sylvia, of course, was herself the product of a time when female dutifulness and conformity were standard measures of worth, and her ongoing bouts of serious illness did nothing to soften her wretched outbursts of wrath.[17]

Of late, though, the seventy-five-year-old Sylvia had become, in Andrea's words, "incredibly benign . . . she just seems to have realized (finally) that I am a separate person with a separate life." Sylvia had been going regularly for psychotherapy, and Andrea credited her mother's change with the simple fact of "having someone to talk to. . . . She's of that generation of women so completely isolated and yet responsible for everything the kids do, every failure, every act of non-conformity." The adult Andrea was able to empathize fully with how it had been for her mother: Sylvia had been unable to talk about the poverty of her life without indicting herself (rather than the culture) for its shortcomings, unable to explore impulses and interests considered "improper"—though she'd loved to read as a youngster, she felt she had to do it in secret. For Andrea, the "new" Sylvia came as "a great relief"—she was even able to tell Andrea how sorry she was that her daughter had had "such a hard life"; Andrea reassured her that "she shouldn't worry, because everything's fine, which it is."

Her father, Harry, had deeply loved his sometimes difficult wife, and he was bereft at her death; Andrea and John let him know that they would welcome his coming to live with them in Park Slope, but he decided to remain in Camden. "It seems very important to me," Andrea wrote her brother, Mark, "that in these last years he does what he wants for as long as possible. Whatever he wants."[18]

Soon after Sylvia's passing, her brother Mark revealed that he was about to be operated on for cancer of the esophagus. Though a stoic, it soon became clear that Mark was desperately ill, and on impulse Andrea flew to Vienna, where Mark lived with his wife, Eva, and worked as a scientist. Though at one point they'd been estranged, Andrea and Mark had a strong bond, and she wanted to spend time with him before his condition worsened, which he'd been told would be likely to happen soon, probably within the next few months. At the moment he was responding well to chemotherapy, though the cancer had already spread to his liver. It wasn't long after Andrea's visit that he suddenly took a turn for the worse.

The chemo abruptly stopped working, and the amount of pain markedly increased. Mark finally decided to tell his father that he was dying, and Harry and Andrea at once booked flights to Vienna; before they could arrive, Mark died. They reached Vienna immediately afterward and made arrangements for his burial. It was, according to Andrea, "physically demanding and emotionally deranged." Meeting Mark's friends and colleagues provided some solace, but

Harry was heart-broken. "I can't imagine his grief," Andrea wrote a friend. "My own is almost beyond my imagination. . . . It has been shattering." For a time after returning home, she became "very solitary. Can barely stand to speak to anyone," she wrote Michael Moorcock.[19]

For a while she was literally not earning anything. Then her father, in some unfathomable reaction to his son's death, started to send her substantial checks. They deeply upset her—she felt he was divesting himself of all earthly things, signaling his own imminent departure. "What I hate most," she wrote friends, "is that I need it and so I use it." To make herself less needy, she again started to accept invitations to speak.

Her prowess as a speaker and her prominence as a feminist nearly always guaranteed an overflow crowd and an enthusiastic reception. Gratifying though that was, traveling around the country did nothing to improve her mood. The AIDS crisis was at its height, with thousands dying and no miracle drugs on the horizon. Andrea wrote next to nothing directly on the crisis, in part because she no longer knew many gay men, in part because she saw her battles centered elsewhere. Yet neither she nor John thought they were immune to the HIV scourge. Quite the opposite. Since John enjoyed being anally penetrated and since he and Andrea continued to have occasional sex, they both assumed that they would test positive. When they finally took their courage in hand and got tested, they were astonished to learn they weren't infected.

Yet so much else remained depressing that their mood barely shifted. Yes, the Cold War had ended—the Berlin Wall had come down in 1989, yet Mikhail Gorbachev had been forced from office in 1991. Robert Bork's nomination to the Supreme Court had been defeated, yet the Right wing seemed stronger than ever, and gender discrimination, segregated schools, police brutality, rising global temperatures, and the heightened concentration of wealth continued to remain the dominant, and accelerating, patterns. "The general situation here is so corrupt, so degraded," Andrea wrote a Norwegian friend, "that it is hard to know how to anticipate the next blow, which always falls, followed by another one." Most of what she saw around her was "distressing, painful, or difficult."

Her spirits got something of a boost when she learned that *Mercy* had found translators and publishers in Germany, Japan, and—"can you believe"—Korea. But the United States? Not a nibble—not, that is, until the two young editors who'd recently launched the small house, Four Walls, Eight Windows (4W8W), expressed interest. It would not be a match made in heaven, though it started out well enough, with Andrea deliberately ignoring the obvious: that youthful ardor was usually a poor substitute for adult competence. Mutual antagonism was almost immediate, and was all the more bizarre because it had absolutely nothing to do with Andrea's own book. To cut straight to the end point of a mountainous and excruciatingly extended thicket of controversy, the 4W8W editors solicited a blurb from Andrea for another book they were publishing. She graciously agreed, only to be brought up short by several paragraphs in the manuscript (written by two women) that seemed to suggest that lying about rape or incest was sometimes justified, even advisable, in order to obtain an abortion.

To Andrea, that was shockingly irresponsible. When she contacted various women who worked in rape crisis centers, they concurred: "we do not make false charges of rape" and we "do not knowingly collude with anyone who does lie"—to do so would feed directly into the wrong-headed, popular stereotype that many women lie about having been sexually assaulted. The two female authors promptly accused Andrea of launching a campaign to prevent publication of their book; then an article appeared in the *New York Observer* ridiculing her as a "censor"—and on and on it went. Andrea accused the 4W8W editors of launching a whispering campaign to further discredit her; the ACLU named her Bigot of the Year; and in the agonizing upshot, the 4W8W editors canceled all publicity plans for their recently released paperback edition of *Mercy*. "I've just lost my very marginal publisher," Andrea wrote friends in England, "and am sinking fast."[20]

It soon got worse. After a period of relative inactivity, the "pornography wars" again heated up. One major catalyst was the nationally televised and wrenching 1991 Senate confirmation hearings of Clarence Thomas to the Supreme Court. Anita Hill's brave and damning testimony against her former boss, charging him with insistent sexual harassment, explosively reintroduced the specters of male entitlement and female endangerment. As several male members of the Senate Judiciary Committee—in particular Orrin Hatch, Alan Simpson, and Arlen Specter—piled on ugly innuendos about Hill's "stability," strongly implying that she was simply a spurned lover seeking revenge, many women across the country relived their own toxic memories of workplace harassment—and further conflated male sexuality with dangerous aggression. As for Clarence Thomas himself, Andrea felt utter disgust: she regarded him as "an incredible reactionary . . . setting a new record for judicial sadism. . . . Impeachment or assassination can remedy the appointment, nothing else. Natural death, but God is not on our side."[21]

That same year saw the introduction of a pornography "victim's compensation act" in Congress. The bill was narrowly written: one could only sue for damages if the material said to cause harm involved child pornography or obscene material, neither protected by the First Amendment. Still, criticism of the bill came from various directions, including from two hundred NOW chapters—and from the novelist John Irving. In an essay for the *New York Times* entitled "Pornography and the New Puritans," he expressed concern that if the bill passed—it didn't—"it will be the first piece of legislation to give credence to the unproven theory that sexually explicit material actually causes sexual crimes." He called the bill "a piece of back-door censorship, plain and simple."[22]

That phrasing conjured up porn wars past—and still present, if comparatively dormant. Andrea was among those who sent in letters protesting Irving's piece; uncharacteristically, the *New York Times* printed hers in its entirety. In it, she singled out as her chief concern Irving's blanket declaration that no proof exists for claiming that "sexually explicit material actually causes sexual crimes." Strangely, Andrea didn't cite the Donnerstein and Malamuth studies that she and Kitty had earlier used to back their claim that pornography *can* produce harm of varying sorts. She settled instead for an orphic declaration: pornographers "materially promote rape, battery, maiming and bondage; they make a product that they know dehumanizes, degrades and exploits women; they hurt women to make the pornography, and the consumers use the pornography in assaults both verbal and physical." But a pronouncement is not proof. By 1991 a significant number of confirming studies had already accumulated, and Andrea's failure to cite them in her letter to the *Times* may well have been a gauge of her having grown weary of the repetitive struggle—and her eagerness to shift focus to her new engagement with Israel.[23]

Whatever her wishes may have been, the Canadian Supreme Court's 1992 landmark decision, *Butler v. The Queen*, rekindled the pornography question in concentrated form and again plunged Andrea into the tangle of debate. The Canadian Criminal Code of 1985 had been structured on the principle that one right can be overridden by another right. Citing that principle, the Court in *Butler* voted unanimously to prohibit the production and distribution of obscene materials and defined as obscene any visual or written materials that degraded or dehumanized women, precluding their equality, denying them access to all the rights of citizenship. The Court openly acknowledged in its decision that such restrictions would sometimes abridge freedom of expression, yet defended the curtailment as regrettable but necessary. As precedent, the Court cited the 1983 *Rankine* decision, the first to address pornography "from the point of view of the victims of the sexual abuse, rather than of the sensibilities of the observers," as well as the 1985 *Ramsingh* ruling that women "have a right to demand that some limitation be imposed by government on freedom of pornographic expression." In other words—as Andrea put it in a letter to Erica Jong—the Canadian Supreme Court had weighed "pornography's harms to women against the speech rights of pornographers. They held that women's equality had the higher value."[24]

The Court's underlying assumptions—not previously articulated openly by a prestigious legal body—produced a predictable uproar. On May 7–8, nearly two hundred "anti-censorship" feminists gathered to discuss the issues at a conference in New York entitled "The Sex Panic: Women, Censorship and 'Pornography.'" Leonore Tiefer, president of the International Academy of Sex Research and one of the conference's lead speakers, put the matter bluntly:

legal restrictions on explicit sexual expression, she predicted, "will force erotic experimentation in art, video, books and performances underground, which will deprive most women of access to unconventional inputs to their erotic imagination. . . . Now is the time for more sexual experimentation, not shame-soaked restraint." The witty Texas journalist Molly Ivins had a somewhat different take: "We've all read the studies of pornography and sexual aggression saying yes it does, no it doesn't, yes it does, no it doesn't. You could just shit or go blind trying to figure that one out . . . common goddam sense tells me there probably is some truth to the theory that all those ugly pictures do encourage violence against women." Few of the conference attendees were willing to give even that much credence to their "anti-porn" opponents.[25]

The reasons go deep and range from differing perspectives on sexuality to the legitimacy of social institutions. Without pretending to play philosopher or to be expert in the dozen or so specialties at issue, at least some outline can be made of the underlying assumptions that once again fiercely divided the feminist movement. To focus on Andrea and Kitty, it might be easier to describe the areas in which they did *not* subscribe to the values their opponents commonly attributed to them. Though they did sometimes find themselves—to their own maximum discomfort—on the same side of the pornography debate as right-wingers, they were profoundly at odds with their basic worldview.[26]

Both Andrea and Kitty were—and had long been—committed lefties. Kitty had worked with the Black Panthers and had staunchly opposed the Vietnam War; in 1986 she'd also been co-counsel and the guiding spirit behind a pathbreaking Supreme Court case that established sexual harassment as a legal claim for sex discrimination. Andrea, even as an undergraduate, had been active in left-wing causes, and—unlike those on the Right—had viewed religion, monogamous pair-bonding, and the traditional family as enemies, not exemplars, of the good life. She believed in *lots* of sexual experimentation and, like Kitty, objected to violent pornography because she concluded that it subordinated and harmed women, not because it encouraged lust—which to them was the path not to the devil but to pleasure and human connection.

Nor did Andrea believe, as many of those on the right did, that humankind was intrinsically sinful. As a young woman she held firm to the belief, which some call "utopian"—in the essential goodness and malleability of people, and wholly blamed institutionalized injustice and bigotry for the deformations of human life; faced as an adult with the obstinacy of "imprinting," she gradually (and sadly) modified her faith in utopian notions of progress, yet an intractable and to herself sometimes irritating faith in the possibilities of change remained at the core of her temperament.

She and Kitty *shared* many attitudes and assumptions with pro-pornography feminists—including, primarily, their contempt for patriarchal privilege and sexist assumptions of male superiority. Andrea vehemently agreed with those of her feminist opponents (the majority, probably) who insisted that gender was *not* a biological given; she believed that masculinity and femininity were social constructs, not immutable products of biology. In Andrea's ideal world, the traditional gender binary would be supplanted by androgyny— the view that all human beings are capable of developing all those traits currently parceled out to *either* men *or* to women. But agreement about what men might potentially become elided into *dis*agreement over what men currently *were*.

The pro-pornography camp tended to hold the more positive view of heterosexual men; it saw them, generally speaking, as more negotiable, more emotionally available, more appreciative and considerate of their female companions, and less prone to violence, sexist rigidity, and ruling the roost. As part and parcel of that view, these feminists were less likely to see women as victims, as unwilling or unable to assume active agency (like initiating—or rejecting—sex) on their own behalf. They were more likely to regard sexuality as the *mutual* pursuit of pleasure and an expressive outlet for tenderness rather than as a battleground for asserting control. Neither camp viewed sex, as many on the religious Right did, as the source of sinful temptation or as primarily designed for procreation.[27]

It was, and still is, often claimed by their antagonists that Andrea and Kitty believed all heterosexual sex was rape, though neither did; as Kitty put it in a rather sharp rebuke to a correspondent, "I did not say 'all sex is rape' or anything that amounts to that. Ever. Not here.

Not anywhere. You know it. I know it." Andrea agreed, yet could become heated when a straight woman persisted in describing her male partner as a paragon of gentle tenderness, and she breathed fire when one well-known female writer kept insisting that "when I hear an unqualified narrative of male sexual destructiveness, and do not interrupt it, I feel that I betray my body's deepest friendships."

In that last instance, Andrea let loose with the kind of harangue she currently rarely indulged: "You tell us that there are these millions and millions of men who do not rape or use force or hit or use prostitutes, and that they are the norm. And guess what . . . you made it up. Because the 50 percent of married women who *Time* says are beaten by their husbands are ordinary women beaten by ordinary men. . . . And ordinary men of all kinds from all places in society use prostitutes and revel in their abjectness. And ordinary men of all kinds force sex. Not all men do, no. . . . Study those who don't, commend them, no argument . . . your formulation . . . *demands* a silencing of women: because yr happiness cannot co-exist with so very much that so many women have to say . . . you put yr sexual happiness above her voice, her life, which is yr political choice to make. Nevertheless, we have fought very hard to be able to begin to say these terrible, but very ordinary, things, to articulate these terrible, but very ordinary, experiences. . . . Yr 'agency' shit is pretty pathetic next to this fight. And don't you just wish that I accepted being a victim over agency?"

Andrea in fact had her own doubts about the *Butler v. Queen* decision, though overall she regarded it as "a tremendous victory for women in Western legal systems." Although Kitty had written the legal brief for the Canadian women's group Legal Education and Action Fund (LEAF), Andrea had opposed their attempts at intervention, arguing that no criminal obscenity law—even when reinterpreted to provide greater protection for women—should be actively supported; obscenity laws meant governmental and police intervention, and both agencies were in bed with the pornographers.[28]

Yet overall the *Butler* decision represented a long-sought legal vindication of their insistence that pornography could be harmful. Despite her doubts about the decision, Andrea never voiced them publicly, even after the ruling was later claimed to have had some negative consequences that she and Kitty hadn't foreseen or had dismissed as improbable. They were blamed especially for what their opponents claimed was—as a direct result of the *Butler* decision—a clamp-down by Canadian Customs on material emanating from gay, lesbian, and feminist sources, including the seizure of *Bad Attitude*, a sexually explicit lesbian-feminist magazine.

Andrea and Kitty took the claim with the utmost seriousness and set about trying to pin down the actual extent of the purported censorship. After considerable digging, in which they enlisted the help of various on-the-ground sources, including the progressive Canadian Women's Legal Education and Action Fund, they issued a formal statement summarizing their findings. In it, they pointed out that under *Butler*, it was illegal for Customs to seize materials because they are gay or lesbian, though previously it *had* been legal to do so—and those earlier confiscations had led to "vociferous" complaints from gay and lesbian groups. As Kitty tellingly put it in a letter: "If materials are being seized because they are gay or lesbian, i.e., for moralistic reasons, it is only possible *because* Canada Customs has *not* re-evaluated its standards to conform with *Butler*." She thought "the real problem with *Butler* is lack of enforcement, not excessive enforcement."

Two of Andrea's own books, *Woman Hating* and *Pornography*, were briefly impounded at the U.S.–Canada border on the grounds of their "obscene" content. Her detractors delighted in the "irony," and the *New York Times* printed an op-ed piece, "Censors' Helpers," which gloried in the news. Yet Canadian border seizures had been commonplace long before *Butler*, and no causal relationship has been established between the court decision and the post-*Butler* seizures: Canadian Customs did not, at least not through 1994, officially revise its guidelines to reflect or incorporate the ruling. In fact, as Andrea and Kitty learned, the charge of a crackdown on importing gay and lesbian material had been largely fabricated; according to LEAF, Customs officials "are not using the Butler decision *at all*." Andrea and Kitty believed that the probable source of the false rumor lay with the ongoing and increasingly contentious debate *in the United States* between speech rights guaranteed by the First Amendment and equality rights at the heart of the

Fourteenth Amendment. To date, the U.S. Supreme Court had come down heavily on the side of those declaring that speech rights took precedence. The Canadian Supreme Court's *Butler* decision had taken the opposite position, explicitly adopting the view that "society's interest in sex equality outweighs pornographers' speech rights." As Robin Morgan put it, "having legal recourse to defend one's civil rights is a far cry from censorship."[29]

The week after the *Times* published its mocking op-ed, the latest edition of *Screw* magazine carried the headline "Dworkin/MacKinnon Lesbo Orgy," an editorial entitled "Catherine MacKinnon: Whore for Censorship," and for good measure a doctored photograph with Kitty and Andrea's heads pasted onto other bodies, showing Andrea "fucking" Kitty. The text read, "Sapphic sow Andrea Dworkin has a new battle to fight. Thanks to the efforts of her pussy partner-in-crime, Catherine MacKinnon, some of Dworkin's own books have been banned in Canada because of their violent and sexual content. When will these two book-burning bull dykes learn that the sword of censorship cuts both ways?" Soon after, PBS ran its own version of the story—in the King's English, of course.[30]

11

Prelude to Israel

Back in 1988, at age forty-two, Andrea had decided to go to Israel. In doing so, she was embarking, somewhat to her own surprise, on a double journey: reawakening her childhood as a young Jewish girl and starting on a path of inquiry into the state of Israel and her own relationship to it. For more than a decade the subject of Israel would preoccupy her, leading initially to a 1990 article in *Ms.*, "Israel: Whose Country Is It Anyway?" and eventually her 2000 book *Scapegoat*, arguably her finest—or certainly among them.[1]

The ostensible reason for Andrea's 1988 visit had been the first International Jewish Feminist Conference. Middle-class, male-dominated American Jewish groups (including the powerful American Jewish Congress) had put the conference together, but for Andrea the main goal was to meet with grassroots Israeli feminists who objected to the exclusion of the poor and of Palestinian women from the mainstream conference—women she did manage to meet in Haifa, Tel Aviv, and Jerusalem. In retrospect, she described herself at the time as an innocent, a typical secular American Jew who supported the state of Israel and knew very little about it.[2]

The trip was an eye-opener. She became horrified, above all, by the tales she heard of Israeli soldiers shooting rubber-coated bullets at boys who threw stones at them, and the multiple stories of the troops brutalizing Palestinian women. As for the Orthodox rabbinate, Andrea was appalled at their insistence on the strict observance of ancient Talmudic misogyny that codified male dominance and treated women as an inferior, even unclean, species. She knew that the low status of women in Israel wasn't unique, yet felt "we"—American Jewry—were "uniquely responsible for it."

Andrea's mounting interest in Israel was inescapably linked to a heightened awareness of her own Jewishness, a conscious identity that went back to childhood. She remembered her Hebrew School principal when she was growing up in Camden, New Jersey, who'd told the students that they had the obligation to be first a Jew, second an American, third a human being, a citizen of the world. Andrea, age eleven, had dared to argue with him, had boldly announced that she was primarily a citizen of the world. Enraged, the principal told her that Jews had been killed throughout history precisely because many had felt the way she did. Andrea persisted: if everyone was a human being first, then Jews would be safe. He told her she had the blood of other Jews on her hands and stormed from the room.

Andrea hadn't picked up her views from her own family. Both sets of her grandparents had been immigrants and had refused to talk about the past. To Andrea their attitude represented "an incomprehensible and disquieting amnesia," but that didn't deter her from developing her own set of views early on. She never forgot the time when she was only ten years old that she'd unexpectedly come upon her hysterical, tear-stained aunt, caught up in the midst of a traumatic flashback to the series of concentration camps in which she'd been imprisoned during World War II, and the death march she'd somehow survived. The aunt broke down in front of Andrea only once, but a window had been opened; she'd been profoundly shocked. Many years later, she told an interviewer that the incident had led her in college to sit down in the library with the record of the Nuremberg trials and read it, volume after volume. "I might go through six months," she later wrote, "when I won't read it and a few months when I will and I have been doing that since I was a kid."[3]

In high school she argued that the idea of a Jewish *state* was intrinsically wrong, because "anyone who wasn't Jewish would be second-class by definition," and "we didn't have the right to do to other people what had been done to us." To be a *fair* state, Israel could not be a *Jewish* state. Besides, she insisted, Palestine had not been an *empty* land prior to the establishment of Israel, as the Zionists claimed; "the Palestinians were right," she announced, "when they say the Jews regarded them as nothing." The Jewish state, she declared, was "an imperialist act."

All of this had been moderated in childhood by an awareness that Israel at its inception had declared itself a socialist democracy based on the premise that men and women were equal in all ways, and that "servility was inappropriate for the new Jew, male or female." Israel had even established egalitarian collectives (the *kibbutzim*), where the entire community raised the children and the traditional nuclear family was declared obsolete; children no longer "belonged" to their biological parents. Andrea's disapproval of Zionism had further softened when other issues, relating to race, gender, and the war in Vietnam, had gradually absorbed her attention, and her Jewishness had receded; its conscious influence became dormant.

Andrea in time went off to Bennington College to lead the life of a lusty, literary, non-religious voluptuary. In the decades that followed, she never joined a Jewish group or political organization, nor in her writings ever engaged, except for a passing mention, the many controversies that arose regarding Israel. (The one exception is her 1983 book, *Right-Wing Women*, in which the references are largely scholarly and abstract.) Which isn't to say that as an adult she dismissed her Jewishness or soft-pedaled its importance in forming her character. To the contrary. She told an interviewer in 1980 that "everything I know about human rights goes back in one way or another to what I learned about being a Jew . . . when I began to think about what it means to be a woman, it was that experience that I called on . . . my Jewishness is the background that's most influenced my values."[4]

Her 1988 trip to Israel for the international feminist conference, and writing about her experiences subsequently for *Ms.*, aroused much in her that had been lying dormant. Had her grade school principal after all been right, she now wondered, in telling her that if Jews had no homeland to call their own, then those who disapproved of the creation of the state of Israel—including herself—would "have the blood of Jews on her hands"? The question resonated far more deeply within her when in Israel than it had when sitting as an eleven-year-old in a Camden, New Jersey, classroom.

On one side of the ledger remained her conviction that Israel from its inception had been based on a fundamental betrayal of egalitarianism: it had excluded and stigmatized those who were not Jews. In her view, the starting premise of the state had been implicitly racist. And yet . . . she had now lived long enough to see and understand how profoundly anti-Semitism was rooted—implacably so among Israel's immediate neighbors. The profundity of anti-Jewish hatred in combination with the fact that Israel had been created on the principle of exclusion inescapably meant, as Andrea put it, that "Israel had to become either a fortress or a tomb." She didn't believe that having their own state made Jews any safer, but it did make them different "from the pathetic creatures on the trains, the skeletons in the camps"—and that was "a great relief." Enough of a relief that she resolved not to do or say anything that might "have the blood of Jews on my hands."

And the Arabs? What could one say about the Palestinians whose land—and on this point Andrea remained obdurate—had been appropriated, stolen? As early as the seventies, Andrea had started to read books by and about the Palestinians. Among much else, she'd begun to realize that despite her parents' good intentions, she'd imbibed from them a certain amount of anti-Arab prejudice. They were uncommonly conscientious for their generation in speaking out against racial and religious bigotry, and "went out of their way to say 'some Arabs' when making a negative comment." Yet in truth, as Andrea put it, "my education in the Jewish community made that caveat fairly meaningless."

The more she read, the more convinced she became that the Palestinians were a people wronged, that Israel had violated their basic human rights, even while denying the fact. The land had *not* been empty. The Israeli seizure of Palestinian territory had been, in her view, an imperialist act, and it contradicted "every idea we have about who we are and what being a Jew means . . . we took a country from the people who lived there; we the dispossessed finally did it to someone else." While in Jerusalem in 1988 Andrea joined with some four hundred other women in a vigil against the occupation.

On that particular point, her opinion held firm, but her considerable ambivalence in other areas remained. She reminded herself that in Israel, unlike in the Arab world, men and women were at least officially equal, though in practice a male-dominant structure remained intact. From her perspective, "women were pretty invisible"—and for that she blamed the power of the Orthodox rabbinate in particular. In 1988 there were separate religious courts for Christians, Muslims, Druze, and Jews, and as far as Andrea could see "women from each group are subject to the authority of the most ancient systems of religious misogyny." The husband remained the master, and a "rebellious" wife could easily lose custody of her children and all financial support. And as well, "of course, Israel has all the other good things boys do to girls: rape, incest, prostitution, sexual harassment in public places."

After returning to the States, Andrea wrote up her piece, "Israel: Whose Country Is It Anyway?," for *Ms.* magazine. The article produced a small avalanche of letters to the editor, almost all protesting Andrea's views. She was denounced as an "Israel-basher" bent on attacking the right of "a dispersed people" to have a homeland. One letter dismissed her as "the stereotype of a self-hating Jew," another rejected her opinions as those of a myopic tourist, a third accused her of defaming the Talmud. A few of the letters did thank her for "spreading the word," for "letting the truth be known." Hurt but never deterred for long by criticism, Andrea decided to explore the issues relating to Israel in more depth—and the subject would come to absorb her for nearly a decade. For the time being, though, she felt "far away from writing: it seems like a geographical distance, as if I would have to swim rivers and climb mountains to get anywhere near it. And, while I would like to be there, I don't know how to get there. So nothing seems right."[5]

Yet Andrea felt irresistibly drawn to preparing a full-length work on the subject. Deeply committed to the project, she wrote up what she thought was a persuasive proposal, and Elaine sent it out widely. Only one publisher, the Free Press (which had published *Intercourse*), expressed any interest. Their terms were borderline insulting—very little money coupled to a demand for world rights. To supplement her income she would have to continue the arduous job of traveling around the country giving speeches, leaving her insufficient time and energy to work on the book. She'd also over the years accumulated a multitude of commitments, mostly centered on the ongoing pornography struggle, and she refused to abandon them, though the tug-of-war on her time was often a daily one. Even at the start of her research, she lamented how far away she was from writing the book: "I feel so frightened," she wrote, "because time goes so fast, each day just moves past me, and I have so much to learn, constantly interrupted by whatever, life."

In order to make a living, Andrea traveled widely from 1991 to 1993 giving lectures for more than half of each year. The constant trek upset her natural body rhythms—she wrote at night and slept days—and also kept her from finding enough concentrated time to make significant progress on her book. The brief bursts of free time that were her own were often spent recovering from too little sleep in too many hotel beds, which was more and more difficult as she approached fifty. Late in that year she decided to make yet one more effort—all her previous ones had failed—to persuade a foundation to buy her some release time.[6]

Someone suggested that the Diana Foundation in California might be receptive, and Andrea worked up a provocative proposal that as a secondary benefit helped her to further define the essence of what she hoped to accomplish. Women and Jews, she wrote the foundation, "seem to be nearly universal scapegoats . . . used to represent traits that then are stigmatized and must be extirpated from individuals or nation-states to establish a pure sexual or racial identity." She wanted to explore what the two groups had in common. Though women and Jews have historically repudiated violence, she wrote, "many forms of violence, overt and subtle," have been used against them. Both Jews and women have often been seen as "the carriers of civilizing values," yet each has been maligned "as low, craven, venal—moneygrubbers and sluts respectively." And both groups have managed to find "an affirmative cultural value and identity in the signets of oppression (for instance, for Jews religious learning and ritual, for women, maternity and childrearing)."[7]

Never one to conceal or prettify her views, not even when desperate for money, Andrea audaciously included in her proposal the assertion that "in the fight for statehood, Jews for the first time became associated with violence, and Israel is now widely recognized not only as a military power but as a militarist nation, a warrior nation." For garnish she added this eye-opener: "Inside Israel, Jewish women still have no country, since there is not civil equality for them. . . . Jewish women continue to be scapegoated by Israeli men. How and why? And is there a relationship between the new masculine identity of Israeli men, anchored in a warrior mentality, and the growth of an indigenous Israeli racism: hatred of the Palestinians?"

Miraculously, the Diana Foundation decided to award Andrea a $5,000 grant. It was a huge relief; she was now able for a time to say no to any overnight invitation to speak or to attend yet another conference, to pick and choose based solely on the urgency of the call, how much time would have to be invested, and the importance of the subject. She still cared too much about the issues that affected women's lives to leave the public arena entirely behind; she simply cut back. She basically had a scholar's disposition: a large capacity (and need) for solitude linked to a driven hunger for "getting to the bottom of things," plus a minimal capacity for mere chit-chat. But she scorned scholarship as practiced in academia, with its disdain for "excessive" entanglement with the merely "transient" affairs of everyday life. In one of the speeches on prostitution that Andrea still occasionally gave, she put the issue this way: "Academic life is premised on the notion that there is a tomorrow and a next day . . . or that there is some kind of discourse of ideas and a year of freedom in which you can have disagreements that will not cost you your life. . . . If you have been in prostitution, you do not have tomorrow on your mind. . . . No woman who is prostituted can afford to be that stupid, such that she would actually believe that tomorrow will come." The far more pressing problem for women "is that being hurt is ordinary. It happens every day, all the time. . . . We count ourselves goddamn lucky when whatever happens falls short of rape."[8]

John, at least, seemed to be in a good place. *Refusing to Be a Man* had drawn both good reviews and considerable sales, and he rather easily secured a contract for a second book, and with an advance larger than Andrea had gotten for all of her books combined, making it possible for him to leave his day job in magazine publishing. That second book, *The End of Manhood*—a practical guide for overcoming our "defective conditioning" in masculinity—came out in 1993, and it, too, did well. Its success launched him into a variety of new projects, including a novel, a children's book, and a collaborative effort to write a "rock/rap" opera.[9]

The next stage in Andrea's work on Israel involved two extended visits to the Holocaust Museum in Washington, DC, in September and November of 1993. Each time she spent four days, five hours each day. The experience proved searing; it was "almost unbearable . . . overwhelming." She ended up writing a forty-page article about her visit, though she allowed *Ms.*, given its space limitations, to condense it down to little more than ten pages. The longer piece, fortunately, exists in manuscript form; it gives us far more of Andrea's distinctive voice, and the anguish the experience had cost her. Throughout the eight days she spent at the museum two voices continued to haunt her: the grade school principal shouting his prediction that "the blood of the Jews" would be on her hands; and the terrified, piercing shrieks of her aunt reliving in flashback the horrors of the Auschwitz-Birkenau concentration camp in which she'd once been imprisoned. Andrea would steady herself, needed to steady herself, with the constant reminder that to know more about the Holocaust "would be a victory over it—over the fear it creates, over the hate it incarnates, over the desperate sadness it always evokes."[10]

She took with her to Washington an article Kitty had recently written for *Ms.* on the current rape/death camps in Bosnia, the ethnic cleansing, the hurricane of violence that the Serbs had unleashed against Bosnia's Muslims and Croatians—in Kitty's words "the forced prostitution, the making of a pornography of genocide." Andrea brought the article with her, as she put it, in order to remind her of "the kind of material I needed to find" at the Holocaust Museum. She brought with her, too, many questions, particularly questions about the treatment of women in the camps. In what numbers were they raped? Were some of the camps brothels? Where and how were women used in medical experiments? "What happened to the women? Concretely, the specifics."

She did get some information about the women whose teeth were pulled out and vaginas searched for gold; the women subjected to x-ray and surgical treatment as part of the Nazis' "infertility experiments"; the Polish women whose bones were broken for transplant to German patients; the women sterilized with chemical injections into their wombs. But she would be disappointed in the answers she got.

Andrea had written in advance to the Museum staff, posing some of her questions; they were extremely kind; they presented her with a great deal of material; they guided her to areas that might further inform her particular inquiries. Yet she felt she'd "met a blank wall when I tried to explain that I wanted to know about rape as a genocidal strategy, the sexual destruction of personhood in the brothels (serial rape), the aggression against women's reproductive capacities." She told the "nice" female staff member with whom she'd earlier corresponded "how wrong I thought it was that the Museum, which pays scrupulous attention to the political sensitivities of ethnic groups targeted by the Nazis for slave labor or forced labor or, in the case of the Romani, even for extinction—did not pay any attention to crimes against women." The "nice staff member" revealed that "the women who work at the Museum . . . sort of felt the same way." She gave Andrea the names of seven people to whom she could explain her disappointment in writing. Andrea decided not to: "Critical questions are not really possible; the burden of knowing is too great to ask to know yet more. And who looks *for* the story of women; and if it is missing sees the absence?" The Museum told the story, "brilliantly told" it, "of annihilation, mass murder . . . one emerges sober, sad, knowing more, in grief. . . .

There is a visual eloquence that does not let the mind drift . . . it is an astonishing achievement." It was enough.

But not quite enough, not for Andrea. What about the issue of outside intervention? As word of the Nazi terror gradually leaked out, what was the international reaction? Who tried to intervene? Did anyone try? Andrea turned to the documentary films at the Museum. They told her much: "that Germany was 'morally isolated from the whole world'; that various politicians threatened to sever diplomatic relations; that there was *only* condemnation, no action of any kind; that the U.S. did not want any of the endangered Jews to come here; that labor opposed increases in immigration; that some Jewish groups were afraid more immigrants would mean more anti-Semitism here . . . that the State Department did all it could to keep Jews excluded . . . that F.D.R. never made a move to help; that in 1939 there was an effort to get the U.S. to let in twenty thousand children (the logic being that they would not steal jobs) but the children were not let in; that from 1933–1941 refugees could get out of Germany but could not get in elsewhere. . . . In other words: we knew. We did not like Jews and we kept Jews out."

And then there were the films about the survivors, "straightforward and simple, even though they are narrating horror. They are more like us than not like us, or so it appears. What they have to tell us is substantive and necessary . . . but their other gift to us is in their demeanor, they are generous not to hurt us with their inner world of turmoil, often depression, often terror, often despair. They are calm and reassuring and we can leave believing that they are fine now." Andrea, though, knew better; Andrea had grown up with these people: "I know they are not [fine]. What they are is American now—and Americans like happy endings. Don't accept this part of their gift. Listen to what they say, not how they have learned to say it."

Andrea returned to New York, came back to her home in Brooklyn, knew that for however long it would take she must give priority from now on to years of researching and writing, to preparing her study of how and why outsiders, women and Jews especially, but also others, the Palestinians prominently, had been scapegoated through time—writing subliminally, inescapably, about her own lifelong alienation from "normalcy." Though she wouldn't have predicted it in 1993, the project would consume her until nearly the end of the decade.

She would do her best during much of that time to keep the rest of the world at bay, though now and then it would creep in over her objections. And she did not always object: unrelieved immersion in the historic plight of the downtrodden and the despised would have risked a kind of unbalance, a form of derangement. Besides, there were people she cared about, commitments she valued; in her hermit-like retreat she'd now and then welcome interruption, live voices, needed companionship.

What she mostly got, though, what she had long gotten, were distorted representations of her views; cartoon-like depictions of her as an over-sized, rampaging ogre; dismissive mockery. There was no hiding from all that, though John, with limited success, tried to intercept some of the more scurrilous articles about her. She'd become something of a celebrity, though in the guise of a pariah. In the anti-porn wars, still enflamed, she remained everybody's favorite target, easy to deplore, easy to parody—the unvarying overalls, the lack of make-up, the frizzled hair: the harridan personified.

What was spoken publicly or put in print was, of course, far more mannerly, except for the no-holds-barred gutter treatment of the *Hustler/Penthouse/Screw* crowd. But the professors and the pundits—the "rational" crowd—prided themselves on civility and knew how to hone their urbane vocabulary to a fine edge. Still, there was no mistaking the underlying animus against her *person*, not simply her politics.

Among Andrea's more skillful antagonists was Nadine Strossen, who was president of the ACLU from 1991 to 2008 and author of *Defending Pornography*, the doyenne of sophisticated leftwing dissent and discourse. One could argue that it was an antagonism all but destined to occur. One could even argue that Andrea herself had inaugurated it when, way back in 1981, she wrote a piece (for which she'd been unable to find a publisher) entitled "The ACLU: Bait and Switch" that excoriated the civil rights group for defending the "free speech" of the Nazis in Skokie and the Klan in Alabama. "I am tired of the sophistry of the ACLU," Andrea had written in the article. "It does not even make a distinction between those who have genocidal ambitions and those who do not. The ACLU prides itself on refusing to make these distinctions."[11]

Strossen's 1995 book, *Defending Pornography*, struck back hard, devoting a sizeable chunk of her text to an irate attack on the "MacDworkinites" (as she called them). Though lengthy, the assault was unoriginal, largely repeating the multiple accusations long leveled at Andrea (and often Kitty, too) and fully addressed by them many times over. The two were, Strossen insisted, anti-sex prudes who'd actively sought alliance with the right-wing Moral Majority in an effort to censor offending (pro-sex) material. Yet the Right had favored not the ordinance (if it had, such legislation would have become law under Reagan), but outright censorship of "smut." Andrea and Kitty, oppositely, had made clear on multiple occasions that censorship in the context of the First Amendment involved *state-based* actions of prohibition, which they strenuously opposed.

Nor had they objected to pornography that didn't subordinate *anyone*—not solely women—or in which the performers hadn't been abused and drugged (Strossen saw no reason "to believe that force or violence are endemic to the sex industry," the implication being that Linda Lovelace had been an anomaly—or had lied). Instead, their ordinance allowed individual women to bring civil suits that itemized instances of harm resulting from pornography and the industry surrounding it—changes *they* were required to prove. Yes, Strossen was correct: the right wing *did* indeed oppose any and all sexually explicit material. But Andrea and Kitty did *not*, and had never sought an alliance with the right wing. Nor, for the umpteenth time, had either of them *ever* said that all heterosexual intercourse was rape.

Strossen claimed that she'd carefully reviewed the scientific literature on the harmful effects of pornography and had found it feeble. In a confrontation first on National Public Radio, and then in print, Diana E.H. Russell, professor of sociology and the pioneering author of *Against Pornography*, pointed out to Strossen the gaping holes in her research. As Russell later put it, the scientific discussion in Strossen's book was "a sham." Most of the key researchers on the relationship between pornography and violence against women, Russell charged—"Neil Malamuth, James Check, Dolf Zillman, Bryant Jennings, myself—do not rate a single mention in her book." In reply, Strossen said that she'd relied on what *she* called "the best source on the subject"—which it assuredly wasn't—a short book, *Sex and Sensibility*, by Marcia Pally, a columnist for *Penthouse*. What the scientific evidence *did* show, according to Russell, was that violent pornography predisposed some men to rape and intensified the predisposition in others; that it undermined "some men's *internal* inhibitions" as well as their "*social* inhibitions against acting out their desire to rape." Russell concluded with a show-stopper: Strossen's view that many men who consume porn have never raped a woman, ergo porn doesn't cause rape, is comparable to saying "that because some cigarette smokers don't die of lung disease, there cannot be a causal relationship between smoking and lung cancer."[12]

Russell also took issue with Strossen's charge that anti-porn feminists distorted the evidence by choosing for their educational slide shows "overtly violent, sexist samples." That was analogous, Russell suggested, to "arguing that the horror and devastation of anti-Semitism in Nazi Germany cannot be judged from photographs of the concentration camps, because a lot of Jews weren't incarcerated in them." She made comparable mincemeat of Strossen's assertion that "the more unconventional the sexual expression is, the more revolutionary its social and political implications become." Russell went in for the kill: "I suppose rape doesn't qualify as unconventional sexual expression any more—but would child porn qualify as revolutionary? Or images of sexual mutilation and woman-killing?"

Robin Morgan also weighed in. In a letter to the *New York Times*, she protested its mostly favorable review of Strossen's *Defending Pornography* for having ignored her "vulgar personal invective against women with whom" she disagrees, as well as for mischaracterizing Morgan herself as having repudiated her support of the MacKinnon/Dworkin position. In making that claim, Morgan pointed out, Strossen had used "a manipulated excerpt" from a twenty-five-year-old article: "I have never repudiated my anti-pornography position, knowing as I do how pornography destroys many women's lives and serves as an instrument of social control over all women . . . [but]

I have never supported censorship (nor have Dworkin or Mac-
Kinnon)." Andrea had earlier put the same sentiment in a letter to
Gloria Steinem: "I think it is unbelievable what these women [like
Strossen] do. And get away with, in the name of a movement for
women's honor."[13]

Yet another instance in which Andrea was called away from work on
the Israel book to join in public protest was the 1994 murder of O.J.
Simpson's ex-wife, Nicole Brown Simpson. Flooded with memories of her own battering when married to Iwan, Andrea wrote not
one but three pieces on Nicole, making her story emblematic of
the plight of women whose lives were linked with men determined
to control or kill them. In 1993, Andrea pointed out, there were
300,000 domestic violence calls to the police in New York City
alone. The common reaction to such brutality was the standard,
indignant, question: *"Dammit, why didn't she simply leave?!"* In fact,
Nicole *did* leave: she was killed in *her own* home; besides, more battered women are killed *after* they leave their spouses. And before
Nicole left O.J. she'd tried damned near everything else, including
calling the police multiple times—nine, to be exact. The police had
been incredulous. They were fans; they'd stopped off at Simpson's
house many times for a pat on the back and a beer.[14]

    Five days before Nicole's death, after months of being tracked and
suddenly accosted by O.J., she'd called a battered women's shelter.
She told her mother that she'd reached the end of her rope: "I'm
scared. I go to the gas station, he's there. I go to the Payless Shoe
Store, and he's there. I'm driving, and he's behind me." She wrote
all that in her diary, where she also recorded detailed descriptions
of O.J.'s physical attacks on her. All of which, at O.J.'s trial, was kept
from the jury. The judge dismissed such evidence as "hearsay" or
"inadmissible." He did allow testimony from those who'd witnessed
O.J. hitting Nicole in public—though most battery, of course, takes
place behind closed doors and has no witnesses. "The voice of the
victim," as Andrea put it, "still has no social standing or legal significance. She has no credibility."

    O.J. was acquitted. As Andrea pointed out, the jury was made up
predominantly of women, and polls conducted during the trial con-

firmed that "women were indifferent to the beatings Nicole Simpson endured." Andrea wasn't surprised; *people*, not just men, ignore signs of battering, don't hear the screams, don't see the bruises, assume the woman is exaggerating, or had wanted it. Andrea herself, more than twenty years since she'd laid eyes on Iwan, was still haunted by fears and flashbacks. Andrea's last line in her series of articles on Nicole Brown Simpson says it all: "Everybody's against wife abuse, but who's prepared to stop it?"

It enraged Andrea—and not solely Andrea—that the murder of Nicole Brown Simpson should be so quickly followed by the 1996 Milos Forman film *The People vs. Larry Flynt*. For Andrea, the juxtaposition was classic: in her mind, O.J. Simpson and Larry Flynt were both products of a culture that valorized male brutality while disavowing the value of women. Unlike Hugh Hefner, who'd become elevated in the popular mind to the role of a glamorous sexual liberationist, Larry Flynt had been widely seen as a coarse and gross vulgarian. Then along came Hollywood, waving its magical wand.

Not only did the prestigious Milos Forman direct *The People vs. Larry Flynt*, but the likeable Woody Harrelson played the porn king. *New York Times* critic Frank Rich wrote of the film that what made the movie "so effective is that it doesn't sentimentalize or airbrush Larry Flynt." In an interview, Forman agreed: "I didn't try to cover the ugly side." The two screenwriters made the same point more forcefully: "I don't think anyone will accuse us of whitewashing here . . . we try to be honest." If true, that would mean the real-life Flynt was the authentic voice of plain-talking working-class America, a crusading, passionate defender of the First Amendment, and the faithful, monogamous partner of his beloved wife, Althea. What the movie entirely omits or *merely* downplays is Flynt's unbridled racism, his *five* marriages, his daughter's published accusation of molestation when she was a child, and the repetitive images in *Hustler* magazine of women being tortured and raped.[15]

Thanks to the arrival of Paula Duffy as the new publisher of The Free Press—Andrea described her as "a genuine feminist and extremely down to earth and nice"—she got a contract to compile a third collection of her writings and speeches (after *Our Blood* in

1976 and *Letters from a War Zone* in 1988). Andrea was of two minds about the opportunity: she hated putting *Scapegoat*, her work-in-progress on Israel, aside for a time, but she delighted in the unexpected chance to put her shorter pieces into print. She completed the job in May 1996, and closed her preface to the book with a bold challenge: "I am asking men who come to these pages to walk through the looking glass. And I am asking women to break the mirror. Once we all clean up the broken glass—no easy task—we will have a radical equality of rights and liberty."[16]

The injunction was challenging, and way too optimistic. The book got two wonderful pre-publication blurbs from Simone de Beauvoir's biographer Deirdre Bair ("We should all treat Andrea Dworkin like a national treasure") and the wide-ranging English writer (and Booker Prize winner) John Berger ("She is perhaps the most misrepresented writer in the Western world"). But the good omens went unfulfilled. The book did get published in England, and Andrea went over for a modest publicity tour, but in the United States (as she wrote to Gloria Steinem) *Life and Death* was "a failure"—it got little attention and negligible sales.

That was pretty typical not only for Andrea but also for collections of pre-published short pieces—in her case by someone far better known for her politics than for her writing. Still, "My Life as a Writer," the one new and lengthy piece at the start of the volume, had it been read, might well have brought Andrea some much-wished-for attention *as a writer*. It has none of the oracular, melodramatic provocations that had sometimes marred her earlier work, yet "My Life as a Writer" does have her familiar steely clarity, her eloquent bluntness—as well as a good deal of basic information about her early life that she'd previously avoided or masked in generalities. We were "bad children in adulthood; smart adults in childhood," she tells us at one point about herself and her friends, "precocious; willful; stubborn; not one age or one sex or with one goal easily advanced by a conforming marriage and inevitable motherhood."

And in her brief portraits in the essay of some of the women who'd been of central importance to her survival, Andrea lets her always-present-but-usually-guarded tenderness and generosity emerge. She singles out three women for special gratitude: Grace

Paley, Barbara Deming (yes, despite the furious misadventure of Sugarloaf Key, which Andrea never mentions), and Muriel Rukey-ser. "Each of these women," Andrea tells us, "had faith in me—and I never quite knew why; and each of these women loved me—and I never knew why. It was a lucky orphan who found each of these women and it was a lucky striving writer who found each of these writers. They are all taken more seriously now than they were then; but I had the good sense to know that each was an Amerikan [sic] original, wise with common sense and plain talk, gritty with life; they were great craftswomen, each a citizen and a visionary. I know what I took; I hope I gave enough back."

At the moment she doubted it. "I really do have to find some way or place I can live," she wrote Kitty, "to do whatever still is left to me to do, which I fear is not much. You have a right to know this, I think. I'm simply used up. I feel virtually nothing except sometimes pain."[17]

12

Scapegoat

Despite her lapses into melancholy, which now and then dipped deeper into depression, Andrea was determined to finish *Scapegoat*. Having invested the better part of half a dozen years on the book, and with the end in sight, she managed to hunker down for the final lap. Transitioning from typewriter to computer, she gratefully substituted emails for long-form letters (alas, what she gained in time, history has lost in textured detail). She cut back her commitments on all fronts. With rare exceptions, she turned down invitations to lecture that involved extensive travel or preparation, wrote only a few short pieces, and almost never gave interviews; the one notable exception was an uncommonly long session with Susan Brownmiller, who was preparing her memoir *In Our Time* and needed to talk over the early years of the pornography wars.

Andrea also found irresistible an invitation early in 1998 to speak at the Yale Law School on the twentieth anniversary of Kitty MacKinnon's pathbreaking book, *Sexual Harassment of Working Women*. She took the occasion to outline the additional contributions that she felt feminist jurisprudence might make to social justice issues beyond (or accompanying) those relating to women: the need to intervene in "other social hierarchies . . . I mean white supremacy . . . [and] class inequities, which in this country are becoming worse and worse such that whole parts of our population are being thrown away."[1]

Of the few short pieces she wrote during the late nineties, the one standout, published in England's *The Guardian*, was her reflection on the Monica Lewinsky scandal—it was brief, but fierce. She slammed into Bill Clinton: "We are talking about a man who, in a predatory way, is using women, particularly young women. . . . [His] fixation on oral sex—*non-reciprocal* oral sex—consistently puts women in states of submission to him." And she had no sympathy for Hillary: "She is covering up for a man who has a history of exploiting women. If there is one thing being a feminist has to mean it's that you don't do that." In a stab at humor, Andrea offered "a modest proposal. It will probably bring the FBI to my door, but I think that Hillary should shoot Bill and then President Gore should pardon her." The "deafening" silence from other feminists on the Lewinsky case distressed her.[2]

Andrea was concerned in general at the current state of the feminist movement. She and Kitty had in 1997 published *In Harm's Way: The Pornography Civil Rights Hearings*, a compilation of testimony, mostly from women, that had been given over time at various public hearings on the pornography ordinances—women who then had often become targets for harassment and abuse. Much of the testimony was searing, and Andrea and Kitty hoped that *In Harm's Way* would serve as a future source book for resurrecting the idea of giving those who felt injured by porn the chance to sue for damages. John and a friend of his, Adam Thorburn, made a theater piece out of the material called "Freed Speech"; it had a well-received reading, but hopes of performing it elsewhere, particularly on college campuses, went unrealized.

Waiting in the wings instead was George W. Bush. Within two years of becoming president, he would declare himself "a war president" and would embark on a disastrous conflict in Iraq that condoned the wiretapping of American citizens at home and the torture of prisoners abroad. The Christian Right—the true censors—would seize the reins of power during the Bush administration. *Their* war against pornography (unlike that of Andrea and Kitty) had everything to do with the sanctity of marriage, the importance of maintaining the monogamous, male-dominated family unit, and the "protection" of women in their "natural" roles of wives and mothers.[3]

Andrea, by then, had taken the long view. "What we kept trying to do," she told Susan Brownmiller in 1998, "was to make it clear that we were talking about harm to women" and "civil inequality." Now, with the internet, we'd gone a step further "and things are rapidly getting worse than anyone could have imagined. I'm back to not knowing what to do." She placed some hope in the fact that there did exist "a community of resistance to entrenched male violence that is international, militant, [and] across generations. . . . We are the hard core, the front line, the ones who cannot be bought off or scared off. We will not reconcile with male power. . . . We know we have another three-to-four hundred years of struggle. We are committed for the duration."

Scapegoat, from inception to completion, took nine years. (It was published in 2000.) Hugely ambitious, it's a monumental if sometimes problematic piece of work—monumental in the profundity of its inquiry, the boldness of its argument, the lucidity of its prose, and the sheer scope of its inquiry (though it should be said that its bibliography, containing seventy-eight pages of notes citing some fifteen hundred works of scholarship, has—along with attesting to Andrea's profound engagement with the subject—the uncomfortable secondary effect of suggesting the autodidact's self-conscious fear of not being taken seriously. This is further confirmed by the lengthy multiple quotations in the body of the text).

Scapegoat is something of an anomaly in Andrea's body of work. Her long-standing theme of misogyny shares the stage this time around, and is often crowded off it, by her impassioned discussions of anti-Semitism and the militaristic turn taken by the state of Israel. *Scapegoat* is also the most traditionally academic of Andrea's books (though her insights go deeper and the pulsating intensity of her prose is more riveting than can be said for most academic works); it seems a surprising anomaly for a writer who in earlier books experimented with twisting autobiography into fiction, and

then back again, to end up in *Scapegoat* with all the scholarly apparatus of the professoriate and a prose style all but free of onrushing
proclamation. Singular, too, is the near absence in *Scapegoat* of those
occasional apocalyptic outbursts that previously studded her work.
Aside from the innate drama of the subject matter itself, *Scapegoat*
is notably free of showy theatricality or grandiloquence. The tone
throughout is highly sophisticated, the analysis measured, deliberate, exquisitely cerebral.

The central theme of *Scapegoat* is the analogous dehumanization of Jews and women in Nazi Germany, and Palestinians and
women in the state of Israel. Andrea nowhere suggests any equation between the unmitigated vileness of the German Nazis and the
current behavior of Israeli men. In her view, the link between the
two, though only marginal, is the cultivation in both instances of a
hyper-masculinity reliant for believability and force on the scape-
goating of others. The matter of scale is all-important, as is the
differing cultural context in which the warrior model emerged in
the two countries, and the ways in which it was publicly deployed.

Andrea harshly condemns the Israeli treatment of the Palestinians, and sees its origin—but not its justification—in the Jewish
determination to safeguard the homeland from the enmity of its
Arab neighbors. She stresses the pained consciousness of many
Israelis over their ugly treatment of the Palestinians as far different
from the almost gleeful arrogance of the Nazis as they proceeded
to hunt, torture, rape, and kill millions of Jews, whom they defined
as mere scum, as not human. Andrea avoids any implication that
the Holocaust, murderous and merciless, a lunatic pursuit of racial
purity, is comparable on any level with the Israeli determination to
defend the Jewish state from destruction.

Yet she is exceedingly tough on the Israelis, inviting denunciation
of the new breed of warrior Jews and providing the ammunition for
it. At the very beginning of *Scapegoat*, she outlines her ambivalence:
"The line between self-defense and aggression has been breached
by my particular ethnic group represented by the Israeli government; the line itself is often not self-evident, in that violent acts
sometimes serve to head off enemy attack and are arguably a form
of self-defense. I believe that threatened peoples and individuals

have a right to self-defense. This goes against the pacifism that has been instrumental in my political life."

On her 1988 trip to Israel, Andrea had been able to meet women, both Jewish and Arab, and had been deeply distressed at their stories of widespread prostitution, pornography, rape, and battering. Why, she wondered, should she have expected otherwise? Her answer in *Scapegoat* is simple: "because the Israelis are my guys, a miracle of self-determination and courage." There was no question in her mind that Jewish survival depended on confiscating Palestinian land, and even ten years after her trip to Israel she remained convinced that "they had to." Yet in the course of the armed conflicts that followed, she laments that "brutality has become institutionalized in Israel as expressions of male dominance and state sovereignty—over Jewish/Israeli women as well as over Palestinian men and women." In her view, a radical shift had occurred: the ideal of Jewish manhood that for thousands of years had emphasized the virtues of gentleness, nurturance, and studiousness had given way to the belligerent, macho Israeli male. What had inescapably followed this surge of aggression, Andrea believed, was the increased subservience of Israeli women *and* "the subordination of a racial or ethnic other"; male dominance "needs internal and external scapegoats."[4]

In Andrea's universe, the primary, if not the sole, grounds for hope was that Israeli and Palestinian women, "often motivated by feminist ambitions and feminist ideas," have found each other; "cooperation," she writes, "is the female equivalent of male conflict"—but she stresses that "this is a social, not a biological, point" (though in much of her writing Andrea powerfully argues against any valid biological explanation for gender differences, she herself occasionally slides into what can *sound like* an essentialist vocabulary; for example: "Is it masculinity itself that both causes and motivates violence?").

In several elliptical and passing remarks in *Scapegoat*, Andrea—briefly recapturing her oracular voice—suggests that "women have to be literate in both strategic violence and the violence of self-defense. It is one thing to choose not to kill; it is quite another to be defenseless by virtue of ignorance and socialization. . . . I have become certain of one thing: that women cannot be free of male dominance without challenging the men of one's own ethnic group and destroying their authority. This is a willed betrayal, as any assault on male dominance must be." Andrea can even be read in this passage as suggesting—her old sibylline voice to the fore—that we take the notion of "assault" literally. Meaning an armed gender war? Surely not; the hint is broad enough to allow us to dismiss it as a mere vestige of flamboyance, of Andrea briefly indulging her penchant (and knack) for florid theatrics. The solemn new Andrea of *Scapegoat* would confidently settle for something less apocalyptic, as she does when she proceeds simply to advise women to be on guard.

There are manifold riches to be found in *Scapegoat*: lush yet lucid descriptions ("Muslim women do not have a government that protects them. . . . So women—even though forced—try to prove their loyalty through self-abnegation, covered, often enclosed . . . and the gangs that attack and harass women on the street are the state's voluntary and eager enforcers, self-righteous and swollen with male pride"); epigrammatic insights ("States do not exist in nature; states do have a view of what is natural"); complex summaries of contested material (Israel "could have been an ethical nationalism, a step toward a global family, an obligation of honor to a global community; a first step to making the unit of the state archaic, a nonimperial state with a particular human rights agenda, a state with metaphysical borders rather than military borders, a state beyond the constraints of geography"); highly original and persuasive interpretations that border on the metaphysical ("Even the emancipation of Jews in Europe from the official margins of the ghetto—ciphers in shadows made more monstrous by being nearer—reified hate and created the silencing imperatives of assimilation").

Along with its many distinctions, *Scapegoat* has some less laudable features. Two of its eleven chapters could have used a demanding editor. "Hate Literature/Pornography" takes almost forty pages to make what is essentially a single point. "Religion/Maternity," about human origins ("who are we and how did we get here?") is surprisingly pedestrian, relying almost completely on familiar scholarship, only occasionally relieved by the intervention of Andrea's own unique voice.

An additional disappointment in *Scapegoat* is her glib dismissal of postmodernism: "Deconstructionists . . . learned the mesmerizing tactic of nothing meaning nothing, everything meaning nothing, nothing being both itself and its opposite as well as the absolute unknowable." They are "completely uncompromised by meaning; and non-elite readers and writers, trapped in a false existence (not a false consciousness, Hegel having been taken out by Heidegger), longed for a literate Rabelaisian fart, which would, indeed, signify." That's essentially a cheap shot (if elaborately garbed), not worthy of Andrea's characteristic respect for knowledge she did not have, nor of her usual appetite for learning it.

Andrea had a talent for generalization, only occasionally over-indulged ("The only sheep led to the slaughter in World War II were the Germans"). She raises, succinctly and cogently, questions of profound importance, if perhaps unanswerable ("Can the Jewish state sustain itself without the use of torture on a subject population? Can a secular Jewish morality—which tends to be leftwing and rights-based—withstand the imperatives of militarism?"). Aiming for the sociological summary, she sometimes falls back on the banal, like when her attempted synthesis of "Jew-hate and woman-hate" eventuates in the disappointingly obvious: "both women and Jews were defined as parasites who live off the vitality of the so-called Aryan male."

Though Andrea's passionate eloquence is muted for much of *Scapegoat*, it occasionally resurfaces, and to great effect: "This targeting of Arab civilians . . . has never been part of the Jewish history of Israel. . . . [It] has been ignored in order to maintain, among Jews, a self-conception that repudiates brutality. Arabs commit murder. Jews do not. Arabs terrorize civilians. Jews do not . . . no Jew would have easily believed Arab charges that seem to stain the character of the Jewish people: a morally superior people is a consequence of a history of suffering."

Toward the end of *Scapegoat*, the central theme of all Andrea's books—of her life—re-emerges: the plight of women. "One must ask: if the Holocaust can be denied, how can a woman, raped or tortured or beaten, be believed?" She concludes that "degraded men need to degrade women . . . the struggle to subordinate women becomes a basic struggle for male identity as such; in liberation movements, women get a temporary pass from complete servility, because they can be used and useful in any subversion or underground fighting. Once the liberation struggle is won, the women are re-colonialized." The reversion at the end of *Scapegoat* to her lifelong theme is accompanied by the reappearance of her persistent attempt over a lifetime to come up with a solution for ongoing female degradation. Since none is readily available, she turns back again to a portentous vision: "Women need land and guns or other armament or defense; or women need to organize nonviolently in great masses that grow out of small demonstrations using civil disobedience. The latter is harder than the former but gets fairer results. One needs to target individual men who commit crimes against women and institutions that objectify, demean, and hurt women: using either violence or nonviolence. Indiscriminate violence is never justified; there are always innocents. . . . The harm of objectification and dehumanization must be recognized as prelude to normalized violence."

As if dissatisfied with her own inability to produce "the" answer, Andrea settles for a command: "The past thirty years—1970 to 2000, the time of the so-called second wave of feminism—have been prologue: the question is, To what? Answer the question."

The enormous labor of *Scapegoat* finally behind her—the manuscript completed and the rituals of proofreading and reviews still many months off—Andrea drew a deep breath and, running counter to her nature, tried to relax. Everything seemed to conspire against it. Along with being emotionally drained, she'd developed osteoarthritis in her knees, which caused constant and increasing pain. Her spirits dipped a bit lower still when her editor at The Free Press, after a quick read, gave the *Scapegoat* manuscript what Andrea called a "cold reception."

Her unsettled state ill-prepared her for an incident she might otherwise have taken in stride. Attempting an idle walk one day, she was accosted and threatened by a group of young men who tried to force her into a van. A friend who worked at a local rape crisis center later told her that several women had recently reported being raped inside vans, the rapes videotaped (they never found out who the perpetrators were). Her nerves already taut, her energy depleted, the encounter shook her deeply. She decided it was the ideal time, at age fifty-two, to take a *real* vacation, to treat herself to a wholly uncharacteristic splurge—a first-class flight to Paris, a city she'd always loved, and a week's stay in a five-star hotel. It was a luxury beyond her means, but it felt like a necessity.[5]

Initially all went well. She and John spoke by phone every day, she took long walks, went to several museums and, staying pretty much to herself, rested and read in the hotel's garden. John thought she sounded happy and he felt reassured that her mood had lightened. Then suddenly all that changed. He picked up the phone one day to hear a tearful and jumbled Andrea blurt out the appalling news that she'd blacked out from a drugged drink and been raped. Thinking fast and trying to calm her, John suggested that she locate a gynecologist, call the police, and then take the first flight home. Not speaking French and too rattled to think straight, Andrea simply packed up and left for New York.

Months later, her misery having lessened, she decided to write about what had happened in Paris (writing had always been the most reliable way of understanding her own experience). What came out, though, underscored how incomplete that understanding still was—and would likely remain. John, as always, read Andrea's completed manuscript, "The Day I Was Drugged and Raped," and felt uneasy about it. But he decided that for once he would *not* make any editorial suggestions or give an opinion about whether or not she should go ahead and publish the piece. Ultimately, more than a year after the episode, Andrea did finally decide to submit the article to *The New Statesman*. They published it in early June of 2000 (as *The Guardian* did as well).

According to her article, at the start of the misadventure she'd been sitting in the Paris hotel garden reading a book on French fascism, drinking kir royale. Though she rarely drank, she decided to order a second one, but it tasted peculiar and she didn't finish it.

Then (to quote directly from her own account), "I became sort of sickish or weakish or something, and all I could think about was getting to my bed and not making a fool of myself in public view." She managed to get to her room, where she "conked out." Then suddenly "a boy was in the room" with the dinner she'd earlier ordered, the same boy who'd served her the second drink in the garden. Andrea tried to get up, but couldn't stand; she regained balance only long enough to sign the check. Then she fell back on the bed and again passed out.

Awakening in the dark four or five hours later, she didn't at first know where she was. She became aware of vaginal pain, found blood on her hand and "huge, deep" scratches on her leg, which she cleaned in the bathroom. Hours later—she may have fallen back to sleep—she managed to shower. It was then that she discovered "a big, strange bruise on my left breast, next to the aureole, not a regular bruise, huge, black and blue with solid white skin in the centre, as if someone had sucked it up and chewed it. . . . I thought I had been drugged and raped, but I felt confused. I couldn't stand the thought of making a wrong allegation."

She thought that maybe the bartender had done it since he'd "flirted grandly with me in the hotel garden. . . . I didn't know if the boy had been there or not, but I thought yes." She remembered, before passing out, that when the boy brought her dinner to the room, she'd asked him to report her plight. She remembered, too, that he'd appeared suddenly in her room, though the door had been dead-bolted. "I had literally no memory of what the man and the boy had done. It's like being operated on. You don't feel anything until you feel the pain that comes with a return to consciousness." She'd heard about so-called amnesiac drugs—Rohypnol and GHB—and wondered if one of them had been put in the second drink. Her mind went over and over that day and evening, but could come up with little more. "I had decided long ago," she wrote, "that no-one would ever rape me again; he or they or I would die . . . I was scared. I thought that being forced and being conscious was better, because then you knew; even if no one ever believed you, you knew . . . how can you face what you can't remember?"

In the period immediately after returning to New York from

Paris, Andrea felt weighed down with fear and bewilderment. Then, ten days later, her spirits further wilted: her beloved eighty-four-year-old father, after months of failing health, had broken his knee and been hospitalized; he died in hospital in early December 1999. ("I miss him every day," Andrea wrote. "He's the best person I've ever known.") Three weeks later, she was found wandering the streets in delirium from a high fever and was hospitalized with bronchitis, pneumonia, cellulitis, and blood clots. She remained in the hospital for a month. After being released, still depressed and unable to sleep, she started—for the first time in her life—to see a psychiatrist (she somehow found one "whose specialty is in dealing with people who have been tortured"), and also consulted with a psycho-pharmacologist. She began, on a nightly basis, to take on average twelve pills to sleep—and they only worked now and then. Both specialists told her that she was experiencing "perpetual terror," chronic PTSD that dated back at least to Iwan's battering. At times she blamed herself, as rape victims often do (and as Andrea had been doing for a lifetime). She "couldn't be consoled . . . couldn't talk to anyone," not even John.

Initially, as Andrea would subsequently write in *The New Statesman* article, "John looked for any other explanation than rape. He abandoned me emotionally"—which John later acknowledged had in a sense been true, though Andrea had been unable to accept his explanation: "I desperately did not want her to have been raped again." What also contributed to the misunderstanding was that the more they talked about what had happened in Paris, as they "went around and around about the details of it," she experienced John as remaining skeptical. As she later wrote, "this calamitous experience . . . nearly tore us apart [Andrea actually began making plans to leave him] . . . it was really a tough, rough patch in the relationship." John wasn't alone in his doubts about Paris; several of Andrea's close friends—feminists all—seriously doubted her account, and they worried she might be headed for a breakdown.[6]

It was probably to try and clear the air that Andrea had ultimately decided to write *The New Statesman* piece. Yet the response to it hardly clarified matters or soothed her distress. The ensuing uproar—a mix mostly of scorn and disbelief—caught Andrea by surprise, setting back her still fragile recovery. A torrent of ridicule—yet again—came down on her head, and seems to have triggered a retraumatizing from which many of those close to her, including John, felt she never fully recovered. Longtime friends like Nicki Craft (who managed Andrea's website) immediately rallied to her defense, but the voices of mockery drowned them out. Andrea's article, atypically muddled, in spots contradictory and evasive (what might be called clinical symptoms of trauma), all but invited disbelief—that is, for those already hostile to her and unwilling to accept what now seems obvious: that the Paris experience had reopened multiple wounds from her past—the rape in childhood, her mother's disapproval, the battering by Iwan, the death of her father—leaving her disoriented, her memory dull and scrambled, even her prose uncharacteristically limp.[7]

A number of articles appeared in rebuttal to her own piece, and they were uncommonly mean-spirited. No well-known feminist was part of the posse: indeed, her detractors' lack of reputation in comparison with Andrea's and their possible envy of her may have fueled some of the venom that poured forth. Not that any prominent feminist leapt to her defense either (Nicki Craft was one exception), probably due to the controversy's being pretty much confined to the English press. Had it spread to the United States it seems certain that at the least Gloria Steinem and Robin Morgan—always staunch defenders of Andrea, despite occasional misgivings—would have joined the small chorus of her defenders.

A few of her English critics were civil, even respectful. Catherine Bennett, writing for *The Guardian* on the official day (June 7, 2000) of *Scapegoat*'s publication, used the occasion to point out that although Andrea was "often maddening on paper . . . in real life [is] endearing and seemingly vulnerable." Given "her seniority in both feminism and misery," it seemed to Bennett that "to argue with her would be not just impertinent, but akin to saying: 'I don't give a toss about your tragic life.'" Even the sympathetic Bennett, though, couldn't understand why Andrea hadn't called a doctor "to staunch the bleeding," along with notifying hotel security and the police. She was puzzled that Andrea hadn't behaved *rationally*, apparently unaware that following a rape the victim is often befuddled and terrified; or, sometimes, too busy blaming herself—as Andrea had been trained—for having done something to provoke the rape. Andrea had provided the key explanation long since: "There is always a problem for a woman: being believed."[8]

At the opposite end of the empathy scale, Leah McLaren weighed in with an article that was equal parts malign and ignorant. Using the opportunity of the Paris episode as a starting point, she then moved on to a more general attack, studded with inaccuracies, on Andrea's entire career. Like the far more judicious Bennett, McLaren characterized Andrea's 1999 "nightmare scenario" as "full of inconsistencies and logical gaps." Why hadn't Andrea gone directly to a hospital? Why did she never report the rape to the police? How, if the door to her room had been dead-bolted, did the waiter manage to gain entry? Andrea herself would have loved to be able to answer precisely those questions, and had been unsuccessfully trying to do so over the past year. The only truly pertinent question escaped McLaren's notice: why do some women go out of their way to try and discredit the testimony of a rape victim, while raising no questions at all about the aggressor? Deeply wounded, Andrea told Kitty that "if after all my years of work, I could still be raped and not believed, my life has been worthless."

The reception of *Scapegoat* helped to somewhat dilute Andrea's depression. Though the reviews were far from glowing, they were more benign than she usually got ("While she frequently overstates her case . . . Dworkin makes potent points"). By this point in her life, Andrea was generally regarded as a feminist icon, if of a vaguely disreputable sort; she was assuredly not, like Gloria Steinem, a widely respected household name. She fell more into the semi-lunatic-if-brilliant Shulamith Firestone category, which was a few cuts above Valerie Solanas, the attempted assassin of Andy Warhol and author of the "SCUM Manifesto."

The *New York Times*, weighing in a month after the publication of *Scapegoat*, managed to put a damper—as only the *Times* can—on whatever momentum might have been building for the book. The *Times* usually ignored Andrea; she was not an acceptable *in-house* maverick, not male. *Scapegoat* was a different matter: it had a lot to say about Israel, much of it negative, and had to be addressed. The assignment was given to Richard Bernstein, a *Times* book critic since 1995 and the author of *Dictatorship of Virtue*, an attack on the "excesses" of multiculturalism. He did the needed job expertly, mixing just enough praise ("learned and thought-provoking") into his essential pan to offset any suggestion that he might be an admirer. And most of the criticism he leveled had the patina of considered judgment. He granted that Andrea had "read widely," wrote with "stylistic eloquence," and had distilled "many of her ideas into pithy aphorisms." Yet overall he found *Scapegoat* "more an angry rant than a cogent careful argument . . . troubling in its extremism . . . a kind of agitprop."[9]

By the beginning of 2001, Andrea gradually began to regain her strength. To test her readiness, she took two trial runs—a book review for the London *Times* and an essay for Robin Morgan's planned new anthology, *Sisterhood Is Global*. She completed both pieces, but wasn't at all certain that they were up to par: "I hope I haven't let you down with this," she wrote Robin. "I'm very shaky nonetheless." Still, the successful completion proved a boost, and she felt ready to undertake a larger project. Tired of having other people write about—and often misinterpret—her, Andrea decided to try her hand at writing directly about herself.[10]

In a real sense, as she herself put it, "autobiography is the unseen foundation of my non-fiction work" (one is tempted to add "her fiction as well"), but she now aimed for a succinct, first-person account limited to some of the significant events in her life. Entitled *Heartbreak* and barely over two hundred large-type pages, it appeared in 2002. Andrea's choice of topics for the book seems strangely arbitrary: four pages on Petra Kelly, co-founder of the German Green Party, but the barest mention of Grace Paley, with whom she'd once been so close; a chapter on the conservative group, Young Americans for Freedom, with which she'd never been remotely connected, but not a word about Students for a Democratic Society, which she'd enthusiastically joined. It's almost as if she still needed to distance herself from any topic that carried emotional weight, that might threaten her still unsteady balance.

Spare and episodic, *Heartbreak* has a haphazard, almost random feel to it—more like the skeleton outline for some larger work to come. The prose, too, lacks Andrea's characteristic authority and intensity; it consists mostly of simple declarative sentences, the density and complexity of her earlier work notably absent. It might perhaps be said that *this* is what Andrea currently felt capable of writing, this and no more. And this, with its limited distinction, is nonetheless well worth having for its occasional sagacity.

Heartbreak starts off powerfully: "I have been asked, politely and not so politely, why I am myself. This is an accounting any woman will be called on to give if she asserts her will. In the home the question will be couched in a million cruelties, some subtle, some so egregious they rival the injuries of organized war. . . . So here's the deal as I see it: I am ambitious—God knows, not for money; in most respects but not all I am honorable; and I wear overalls; kill the bitch. But the bitch is not yet ready to die. Brava, she says, alone in a small room."

The impact is startling, the words strong, leading one to expect something of a *tour de force*. Yet it never arrives, or rather does so according to the prescription Andrea shares with us only on the very last page of *Heartbreak*: "A memoir, which this is, says: this is what my memory insists on; this is what my memory will not let go." And like everyone's memory, Andrea's proceeds to retain or repress, highlight or minimize, experiences that when strung together appear puzzlingly random, even specious, especially to those of us who cling to expository notions of logic and ordered causality, ignoring (suppressing) their subordination to the muddled, disordered chaos that actually characterizes our paths through life.

And what, in the end, does Andrea's memory insist upon? What does she find comprehensible in explaining herself to herself? That she was "an exile early on." That she had a cousin who "stuck his penis down the throats of at least two of his children when they were very young." That what she loved about Bessie Smith was that "her detachment equaled her commitment." That her mother's real failure was in telling her "not to lie." That her father had told her that it was "a moral wrong [to] read books of only one view." That what she learned "eventually evolved into my own pedagogy: listen to what adults refuse to say; find the answers they won't give; note the manipulative ways they have of using authority to cut the child or student or teenager off at the knees."

From her father, she remembers learning never to shut down inside, "to defer my own reactions and to consider listening an honor and a holy act." She remembers, too, when starting out as a writer, working four part-time jobs all at once, and every other day—after tithing herself for the Black Panther Party—taking out $7 from her tiny savings account. She remembers—this she could never forget—that Grace Paley, who'd helped her when she got out of the Women's House of Detention, had helped her again— this time to get an apartment in a Lower East Side tenement, for which she bought a desk, a chair, a $12 foam-rubber mattress, one fork, one spoon, one knife, one plate, one bowl; after the disaster of her marriage to Iwan, she "was determined to learn to live without men."

She remembered her anger at pacifists who would not take a stand against violence against women, of feeling "that nonviolence was not possible if the ordinary, violent deaths of women went unremarked, unnoticed." She remembered the years of speaking "in small rooms filled with women," someone passing the hat afterward, sleeping on the floor of whoever had invited her, and eating whatever she was given—"bad tabbouleh stands out in my mind." She remembered that after she became well known, "the more money I was paid, the nicer people were . . . when someone was nasty to me, I just raised my price. It was bad for the karma but good for this life."

It had taken longer for her to learn, after years of "watching rapists and batterers go free almost all the time," that her pacifism "could collapse like a glass tower [and] I began to believe that the bad guy should be executed—not by the state but by the victim, if she desired, one shot to the head." She learned, first from prostituting herself, then from other prostitutes she came to know, that "essential to doing the deed, you had to separate your mind from your body. Your consciousness had to be hovering somewhere near the ceiling behind you or on the far side of the room watching your body." She came to realize that although "most people thought that women prostituted in order to get money for drugs . . . it was the other way around; the prostitution became so vile, so ugly, so hard, that drugs provided the only soft landing, a kind of embrace—and on the literal level they took away the pain, physical and mental."

Though scornful of NOW, finding its "milksop politics" deeply offensive and run on the national level by women "who want to play politics with the big boys in Washington, DC," over the years Andrea spoke at rallies and events organized by local NOW chapters and discovered that on that level the members "were valiant women, often the sole staff for battered women's shelters and rape crisis centers, often the only organized progressive group in a small town or city. I've never met better women or better feminists."

At the end of *Heartbreak*, looking back at age fifty-six on her life, having lived through a cascade of mockery and pain, Andrea saw nothing redemptive in suffering. "Surviving degradation," she wrote, "is an ongoing process that gives you rights, honor, and knowledge because you earn them; but it also takes from you too much tenderness. One needs tenderness to love—not to be loved but to love."

"One is alone," she stoically concluded, "not just at the end but all the time. . . . The orphan is always an orphan." She'd heard "so much heartbreak among us"; she longed "to touch her sisters." Yet she felt, she wrote near the end of *Heartbreak*, that she'd "pretty much done what I can do; I'm empty; there's not much left, not inside me. I think that it's bad to give up, but maybe it's not bad to rest, to sit in silence for a while."

By 2002, Andrea's health had taken a turn for the worse. John blamed the toll on her intense years of work on *Scapegoat*. Andrea blamed the drug-rape in Paris in 1999, though her doctors disagreed. The most significant physical change was the increasing pain in her knees, the loss of mobility. An orthopedic surgeon diagnosed her with severe osteoarthritis, exacerbated by years of obesity, and put her on an anti-inflammatory drug. When it failed to work, he shifted her to Vioxx, which did help—until taken off the market as a dangerous precursor to strokes and heart attacks. The next attempt at relief was a series of painful cortisone shots directly into the knees, which worked only once—a period of blessed relief, though of short duration.[11]

As her mobility decreased, she could no longer travel or give speeches. Six months later, she could walk only a few steps at a time, her knees refusing to bend and the pain excruciating. Back in 1989 she and John had moved to a four-story house in Brooklyn—with a renter in the garden apartment. The kitchen was on the first floor, the toilet on the second and her desk, books, and shower on the third. The only way she could navigate the stairs was to crawl up on her hands and feet and to go down on her butt, one step at a time. As she put it, "my physical world became tiny and pain-racked." By then she'd become almost entirely housebound, leaving only for doctor appointments, and when at home usually confined to bed. The doctors told her that unless she was prepared to live the life of an invalid, she'd have to have surgery. With regard to medical expenses, she and John had decided to marry back in 1998, which meant that Andrea, as his spouse, could receive health insurance benefits.[12]

She soon progressed to painful swelling and burning in her legs, with what was diagnosed as "a life-threatening case of inflammation, with possible blood clot complications"; she very nearly died and had to stay a full four weeks in the hospital. After a period of recovery, she then had bariatric—weight-loss—surgery to reduce the pressure on her heart and her arthritic knees. Following *that* recovery, she then had both knees replaced at the same time. "I was in a nightmare of narcotics and untouchable pain," she later wrote. "The horror is that no-one dies from pain. This means that suffering can be immeasurable, enduring, without respite. So it would be for me for the next two years."[13]

Once able to leave the hospital, she was transferred to an institute for physical rehabilitation. The doctors told her she had only two responsibilities: to take her pain medication and to show up, via a wheelchair, for rehabilitative exercise; the cycle was "hideous." Months later, with the help of a walker, she increased from two steps at a time to three; after several more weeks she graduated to crutches and occupational therapy. She was taught how to stand up, how to water a plant, how to use a "grabber" to pick up something she dropped out of reach, how to shop when disabled.

When finally discharged, she was cautioned against relying on John as her primary care-giver: she needed professional help. The rituals of recovery were divided between a visiting nurse (who turned out to be underpaid and badly trained) and a "social aide" to assist with baths and light housework. Still in considerable agony, Andrea left her bed only to go to a "pain management centre" for basic lessons in movement, and for prescriptions. Fentanyl patches and methadone were added to her armory; they slurred her speech and impaired her memory, but she would need the medications for a full two years. By then the pain finally receded to a more manageable level. She was able to go outside on crutches, and then graduated to a cane. She gave up the pills but had "a nasty withdrawal."

At that point John got a job offer to become managing editor of *AARP The Magazine* in Washington, DC. The salary was good, but a move to DC was a mandatory part of the deal. Andrea had loved their Park Slope home, yet realized that managing the stairs had become too great a hurdle. Fortunately, they found a large, sunny, Art Deco–era condo in Washington on Devonshire Plaza NW, all on one level—meaning no steps—and the move was set in motion for February 2004. It proved, as expected, difficult, yet once settled in, Andrea's pain did dim still further; the mix of medications wrecked her appetite, and she lost a good deal of weight. She now and then began to feel rudimentary optimism.

Then, one day, standing up from the kitchen table, without warning her right knee suddenly gave way. The physical therapist told her that the quadriceps above the knee had simply given out; she was put back on crutches, and a restrictive brace was added to help her avoid the danger of falling. The brace went from beneath her calf to the top of her thigh; Andrea named it Darth Vader—evil incarnate. It took her two months to learn how to position the brace perfectly so that it properly supported the damaged knee; she had to lock the brace when ready to walk and unlock it before sitting. As Andrea described it, her wry humor having somehow revived: "in public, locking it makes me look as if I am masturbating, and unlocking it makes me look as if I am fondling my thigh."

With the help of the brace, she was occasionally able to leave the apartment. At one point she and John went to Christopher Hitchens and Carol Blue's apartment for dinner, joined by the former Bush speechwriter David Frum and his wife, Danielle Crittenden. "Andrea had fun that night," John later recalled; they found common ground talking about how much they all hated Bill Clinton and how they thought he was "a rapist." Once, on a self-dare, Andrea said yes to keynoting a conference in DC on the Holocaust. The organizer, unaware or unthinking, picked Andrea up in a truck; she was unable to climb into it. On another occasion, a party was given in her honor, but she couldn't manage the three flights of stairs; were the hosts even aware, she wondered, that she was disabled? Andrea's political instincts, never dormant for long, kicked in—a sure sign she was getting better. "The low consciousness of the able-bodied," she mused, needed attention: "they don't seem to realize that each disabled person lives always on the threshold of separation, exile, and involuntary otherness," is always seeking a way to "mitigate the loneliness."[14]

She *did* start to write again. She had the idea for a new book, though she didn't want to talk about it yet with John; she thought it might be a mirage and that discussing it would make it vanish. She spent most of her days sitting on a red chair in her bedroom, taking notes on a yellow legal pad. Early in 2005, she finally let John know that she was working on a book of literary criticism combined with—of course—political commentary. She temporarily entitled it *Writing America: How Novelists Invented and Gendered a Nation*, and before long she had accumulated some thirty-five pages. She began to believe that she really did have another book in her; after all, she was only fifty-eight. "I am, I think, healing," she wrote, sounding an optimistic note rarely heard over the past few years. She even had an idea for a second new book: it would be about Lynndie England, the young woman in the photographs from Abu Ghraib; it would have combined (as John put it) "all her themes—pornography, prisons, relationship abuse."[15]

On April 8, 2005, Andrea, retiring for the night, complained of feeling unwell. The next morning, when John went into her bedroom to check on her, she didn't seem to be breathing but was still warm. He tried to rouse her, but she was unresponsive. At some point during the night, as an autopsy would later reveal, Andrea had died of acute myocarditis—heart inflammation. The shock was all the more profound because of late all signs had been pointing upward. John was desolate, unable for months to put his feelings down on paper.

Word of Andrea's unexpected death spread quickly. Encomiums poured in, the obits effusive in praise of her unflinching struggle to challenge the status quo, to protect women from harm, to win them full rights of citizenship. Her efforts when alive had been mostly greeted with cruel derision and mockery. Safely dead, the acclaim consistently denied her during her lifetime was showered on her grave. The irony might have amused her. More likely, the hypocrisy would have made her angry. A few people, those who knew her best, mentioned more than her public accomplishments: they spoke of her essential kindness, her dry, hilarious wit, the sympathetic gentleness that belied her fierce public persona. Robin Morgan had a nickname for her: "Creampuff"—in recognition of her softness, her "fragility."

Months after Andrea's death, when John felt emotionally ready to look through her computer, he found to his astonishment a 24,000-word unpublished manuscript entitled *My Suicide*, dated August 30, 1999. Andrea had apparently designed the piece as an autobiographical summing up, not as a final goodbye; in her six remaining years of life, and despite agonizing debilitation, there's no evidence she actually contemplated suicide. *My Suicide* is more accurately seen as an accounting of the wild, dangerous roller-coaster of a life that she'd led—an account true to the life: no holds barred, scorchingly intense, emotionally raw. And always, the underlay of self-doubt: "I wonder if anything that we've done over these years," she told a reviewer toward the end of her life, "is going to survive in any form. . . . I would hate for another generation of women to have to begin inventing the wheel all over again."[16]

Andrea comes back again and again, in *My Suicide*, to her rape in Paris in 1999: "I take my mind in hand and try to compel it to forget what it can't remember anyway but it won't. In a way it's like a vulture picking at a corpse, tearing the flesh off the bones, it wants to remember what isn't there, to know what happened in the missing hours, it picks and picks at the sopping mess."

And always there is the self-blame—not simply in regard to the rape but for all the bad things that had happened to her and all the good things that *she* had prevented from happening: "I blame me no matter what it takes, no matter how abstract or abstruse I need to be . . . for being someone who insists on everything out of her reach," who "thought moderation was a form of stupidity." In the end she gives Sylvia authoritative control of the narrative: "everything my mother ever said about me pretty much turned out to be true. I feel for myself, not for others. I pretend to care but I don't really. I'm not grateful for what people have done for me. She [her mother] had my number. She'd blame me for the rape. She'd say, I'm sure he knew you were a slut. She'd say, if you dressed like everyone else, it wouldn't have happened to you. She'd say, why were you in such a place, why weren't you home? . . . She'd say, there's no reason for anyone to respect you so what did you expect? . . . She'd say, you deserve it."

In *My Suicide*, Andrea the little girl abjectly replies, "Mother, love me, take care of me, care about me." But mother has her own ill health to contend with, and tells her daughter that "you always want everything for yourself and you don't care about anyone else." But its "the pheromones," little Andrea tearfully says. "I have really bad pheromones . . . huge roaches on New York sidewalks run towards me, I change direction and they do too and keep rushing towards me. The bad men and the bad bugs, or I was a monster in my last life and I'm paying now. I don't want any more lives or any afterlife."

And most of the world for much of Andrea's life had agreed with her brutal self-estimate and had reinforced her self-hate. To this day, her accusers remain multiple; they still denounce her as "sloppy with the truth," a "melodramatic, hysterical crank," an unkempt, fat, hairy, ugly "male-hater," a "feminist Nazi."[17]

Yet remarkably and only recently, the tide seems to be turning, signs of appreciation and admiration have emerged, the naysayers yielding a bit of ground. Detectable at a distant remove is a modicum of acknowledgment of Andrea's insistent bravery, her mesmerizing public voice, her generosity of spirit, even, and often, her flat-out brilliance. The turnabout is welcome and deserved. Though her reputation is still contested, the yeasayers have once more found a voice—if only Andrea had lived long enough to find some solace in the sound.

Acknowledgments

This biography is primarily based on archival materials, most notably the extensive Andrea Dworkin Papers at the Schlesinger Library, Harvard. I'm very grateful to John Stoltenberg for giving me unhampered access to the entire archive, which hasn't previously been available to scholars and which is wonderfully rich and consequential (the correspondence files alone are remarkable, since Andrea was in close touch with many leading figures in second-wave feminism and even kept copies of her own letters to them). I'm grateful to Stoltenberg, as well, for giving me access to the sizeable collection of photographs (most never before published) in his possession.

Additionally, I've utilized the archives of a number of other feminists housed at the Schlesinger Library, especially those of Susan Brownmiller, Charlotte Bunch, Barbara Deming, Catharine A. MacKinnon, and Ellen Willis. The staff at Schlesinger, as I knew from earlier expeditions, is celebrated for the skill and grace with which they assist visiting scholars; their standards, thankfully, are as high as ever, and I'm deeply grateful for their many assists. I'm also thankful to them for putting Jordan Villegas in my path as a research assistant. He proved an ideal one—resourceful, wholly reliable and uncomplaining, and a digital *wunderkind*; I'm much in his debt.

The Rubenstein Library at Duke (cited as RLD in the footnotes) also proved rich in feminist source material. The most relevant collections at RLD for telling Andrea's story have been the papers of Dorothy Allison, Phyllis Chesler, Leah Fritz, Merle Hoffman, Robin Morgan, and Dorothy ("Cookie") Teer. Garrett McKinnon, a graduate student in history at Duke, gave me an invaluable assist in ferreting out relevant materials.

In the hunt for photographs, I had expert help from a number of archivists. At Smith College, I especially want to thank Nicole Calero, Maureen Callahan, and Margaret Jessup; at Schlesinger, Diana Carey and Kathryn Allamong Jacobs. For access to Elsa Dorfman's photographic archive, I owe special thanks to Margot Kempers and Harvey Silverglate. My detailed footnotes on secondary sources fully acknowledge, I hope, my indebtedness to the work of other scholars (and in some cases, my disagreement with their conclusions).

Marcia Gallo, Michael Kimmel, Catharine A. MacKinnon, John Stoltenberg, and my partner Eli Zal, all read the first complete draft of the biography, and I'm profoundly grateful to them for their careful, detailed (and sometimes alarming) commentary. Among the five I deliberately chose two who I knew in advance had polar opposite views of Andrea; they reacted true to form—and I profited greatly from their disagreements. At The New Press, its reigning seer, Ellen Adler, came through with her usual wise supervisory advice; Emily Albarillo handled the production side with an ideal combination of insight and tact. I'm grateful, too, for having had Emily Janakiram as my publicist. The scope of her knowledge about feminism and her insight into the issues involved greatly eased the book's path.

As for my editor Ben Woodward, I can hardly say too much. In today's publishing environment, where accession editors vastly outnumber wordsmiths, Ben restores my faith. His tough-minded scrutiny of every line in the manuscript is not what most writers expect (or get) these days. Ben's sharp eye, keen ear, and acute sensitivity to language are matched by a calm persistence that in *almost* every instance brought me around to seeing things his way.

Notes

1: Beginnings

1. Transcript of Susan Brownmiller interview with Andrea Dworkin (henceforth AD), August 10, 1998, in the Andrea Dworkin Papers at the Schlesinger Library, Harvard (henceforth ADP/SLH).

2. For this and the following paragraph: James Wechsler, "Who Sinned?," *New York Times*, March 8, 11, 1965.

3. AD, "Letter to M.," *WIN*, June 26, 1975.

4. Wechsler, "Who Sinned?"

5. For this and the following two paragraphs: *New York Times*, March 6, 13, 19, 20, 30, April 2, 14, May 4, 1965.

6. AD, *Ruins* (manuscript of unpublished book-length "novel in letters," begun in 1975; turned down by publishers; abandoned in 1979), Part I, chapter 1 ("Once"), ADP/SLH.

7. The chief sources for Dworkin/Spiegel family history are "Draft #7" (ms), date December 7, 1987; AD to Henk Jan Gortzak, March 12, 1984; "Marty" (Spiegel, AD's much-loved aunt) to AD, October 27, December 22, 1981; AD to Suzanne Kappeler, March 2, 1988—all in ADP/SLH; Moorcock/Dworkin, "Fighting Talk," April 21 1995: http://nostatusquo.com/ACLU/dworkin /MoorcockInterview.html; AD, "Feminism, Art, and My Mother Sylvia," first published in *Social Policy*, May/June 1975, and reprinted in AD, *Our Blood: Prophecies and Discourses on Sexual Politics* (New York: Perigee, 1976), chapter 1; AD, "My Life as a Writer," in *Life and Death* (New York: The Free Press, 1997), 3–11; AD, *Heartbreak: The Political Memoir of a Feminist Militant*, especially pages 23–25, 29–30, 53 (New York: Basic Books, 2002); AD to Leah Fritz, Box 20, c.1., Fritz

Papers, Rubenstein Library, Duke (henceforth RLD). Several of Andrea's cousins on her mother's side survived Auschwitz, and their descendants live in Israel (as detailed in "Marty" Spiegel to AD, October 27, 1981, ADP/SLH.

8. AD to "Mother, Dad, Mark," n.d. [1964], ADP/SLH; AD, *Life and Death*, 10.

9. For this and the next four paragraphs: AD's unpublished manuscript *Ruins*, ADP/SLH; a section of it appeared as "First Love" in Karla Jay and Allen Young, eds., *Lavender Culture* (1979), then in Julia Wolf Mazow, ed., *The Woman Who Lost Her Names* (New York: Harper & Row, 1980); AD, "My Life as a Writer."

10. For this and the following paragraph: AD, *Ruins*; AD, "First Love."

11. Sources for this and the following five paragraphs: ten postcards, five undated, five dated: two on September 16, the other three September 21, October 12, and October 14—all 1964; AD to "Mother, Dad, Mark," October 2, 1964 ("deadening"), plus seven other letters with the same salutation but undated [all 1964], ADP/SLH.

12. Leah Fritz interview with AD, n.d., Fritz Papers, Rubenstein Library, Duke (RLD).

13. AD, *Letters from a War Zone* (London: Secker & Warburg, 1988), 49; *Ruins* (Kafka); AD to Michael Moorcock, April 6, 1988, ADP/SLH.

14. http:www.nostatusquo.com/ACLU/dworkin/MoorcockInterview.html

15. AD, "The Rape Atrocity and the Boy Next Door," initially a 1975 lecture, then published in AD's collection of essays, *Our Blood*.

16. For this and the following two paragraphs: AD, *Heartbreak*, 107–12

17. For this and the following two paragraphs: AD to her mother, October 22, 1965, AD/SLH. When still in high school Andrea had written to Judith Malina and Julian Beck of the Living Theater commending them for refusing to participate in the air raid drills then mandatory (Brownmiller 1998 interview with Dworkin, ADP/SLH).

18. AD to parents and Mark, January 21, 1966, ADP/SLH; untitled poem, dated "Iraklion, Crete November 1965," which Andrea published in a 1967 chapbook, *Morning Hair*, in an edition of 120 copies.

19. For this and the next four paragraphs: transcript of Susan Brownmiller interview with AD, August 10, 1998, in ADP/SLH; AD, "The Simple Story of a Lesbian Childhood," *Christopher Street*, November 1977; AD, typescript of unpublished *Ruins*, ADP/SLH.

20. AD to Mark, October 27, 1965, AD/SLH.

21. AD, "Margaret Papandreou: An American Feminist in Greece," originally published in *Ms.*, Vol. XI, No. 8, February 1983, later reprinted in AD, *Letters from a War Zone* (New York: Lawrence Hill Books, 1993), 153–61. A series of far-right military juntas ruled Greece from 1967 to 1974. See Seymour Hersh, *The Price of Power* (Ontario, Canada: Summit Books, 1983) for the links between the Greek fascists and the Nixon administration.

22. For the quotes in this and the political comments in the next few paragraphs: AD to her parents, October 30, November 2, 10, 20, 22, 23, 28, December 5, 17, 1965, AD/SLH; also, AD, "Margaret Papandreou."

23. For this and the following section: the manuscript of her unpublished *Ruins*, ADP/SLH, and a section from it, "First Love" in Mazow, ed., *The Woman Who Lost Her Names*.

24. Two years later, Andrea actually started preparations to return to Crete, but by then civil war had broken out and E wrote her a letter saying that his friends were being tortured and killed, that "I am only bitter," and that Americans were too stupid to understand: "Come if you can bear it, I can't promise you anything." Andrea decided not to return. She blamed herself: "I was so afraid, so afraid of the reality of what had happened/was happening to you. The real guns. The real police. The real torture. The real dying." She was also disheartened that the letter E had sent her had "no image of romantic love . . . to propel me toward you, toward self-sacrifice, toward bravery" (AD, *Ruins*, ADP/SLH).

2: Marriage

1. AD to mother, April 21, 1966, ADP/SLH.

2. AD to family, February 11, March 16, 19, 1966, ADP/SLH.

3. January 31, 1966, plus two letters n.d., ADP/SLH

4. Kathleen Norris, *The Virgin of Bennington* (New York: Riverhead Books, 2001), 14 (Oracle).

5. For this and the next four paragraphs: AD to Mark, April 10, 1967, ADP/SLH.

6. For this and the following six paragraphs: AD to "Mom, Dad, Mark," October 1, 20, 1968, ADP/SLH. The Provo manifesto is printed in Richard Kempton, *PROVO: Amsterdam's Anarchist Revolt* (New York: Autonomedia, 2007), which is the most succinct, reliable account of the movement in English.

7. AD ms., "Whatever Happened to Provo or The Saddest Story Ever Told," ADP/SLH, a short section of which appeared in the *Village Voice*, January 15, 1970. In my account I rely mostly on the manuscript version, which includes excerpted transcriptions of Andrea's interviews with a number of prominent figures in the movement.

8. For this and the following two paragraphs: AD, ms. "The Perfect Social System," ADP/SLH.

9. AD to family, October 1, 1968, ADP/SLH; AD, ms. "Dwarfing the Issues: Kabouters in Amsterdam," ADP/SLH.

10. AD to "Mom, Dad, Mark," October 31, 1968, ADP/SLH.

11. For this and the next three paragraphs: AD, ms. transcript of interview notes for "Whatever Happened to Provo," AD/SLH.

12. AD to "dearest Mom, Dad, Mark," October 31, November 12, 1968, ADP/SLH.

13. AD to "Mom, Dad, Mark," December 2, 10, 21, 1968, ADP/SLH.

14. Ibid.

15. For this and the following paragraph: AD, Ms., "Heroes and Villains: Allen Ginsberg" [1992], ADP/SLH.

16. Their exchange of postcards, n.d., are in ADP/SLH. Andrea became friendly in the early seventies with the photographer Elsa Dorfman, whose longtime companion was the lawyer Harvey Silverglate. When their son Isaac was born, Andrea and Ginsberg became his godparents. Later, when the time came for Isaac's bar mitzvah, both Andrea and Allen traveled to Cambridge, Massachusetts, for the services. In the interim since they'd last seen each other, and on the very day of the bar mitzvah, the Supreme Court announced its unanimous decision that the First Amendment right to free speech did *not* forbid states from passing criminal laws against child pornography. The decision elated Andrea—and infuriated Allen. Out of deference to Elsa and her family, Andrea made the firm decision to avoid Allen and any possible confrontation that might spoil the bar mitzvah. But Allen (as Andrea later described it) "affixed himself to me in a rage over the Supreme Court decision. The Cheshire cat had nothing on me. I ordered Allen into a different car to the synagogue, to no avail. I hip hopped around, the way women do avoiding men, and he tailed me, the way men do refusing to be avoided. It became terrible. Allen shadowed me, even when I directly asked him to leave me alone. . . . He insisted on the rightness of sex with children . . . no child would be hurt [Allen said], because sex is always good. Anyone who would stand in the way of consummation was a tyrant. The right wing, the Supreme Court, wanted to send *him* to jail." At which point, as Andrea tells it, she gave up her vow to hold to "the Trappist discipline" and told him that what he was talking about was rape, and that "rape destroyed people . . . I'd shoot you . . . unless you prefer prison." A stunned Allen said that "of course I prefer prison." Andrea came through with a door-stopper: "Then you should thank the right, though they're a little sentimental for my taste." For a somewhat different version, see AD, *Heartbreak: The Political Memoir of a Feminist Militant* (New York: Basic Books, 2002), 43–47. She later remarked that she still regarded Allen as a "hero . . . a poet standing for freedom," but she now also regarded him as "a sexual predator, a nasty piece of trash. . . . I threatened it but he's the assassin." See: https://drive.google.com/drive/folders /1np_HoNiUzM4uWv5DzKJ2DPpvBaOkLWNV; AD to Sharon Doubiago, December 18, 1990, ADP/SLH; Harvey Silverglate to me, November 6, 2019.

17. From 1968 to 1978, Anne Waldman was the director of the Poetry Project at St. Mark's; during that period she, Ginsberg, and others founded the Jack Kerouac School of Disembodied Poetics at the Naropa Institute. Having first met at Bennington, where both were involved with the undergraduate literary journal *SILO*, Andrea and Waldman stayed in touch for a number of years (e.g., AD to parents, [Sept/Oct] 1965, November 12, 1968). Andrea also met Peter Orlovsky at some unknown point and thought him "so lovely, very kind and gentle" [AD to parents, n.d., 1965?].

18. AD to "Mom, Dad, Mark," January 5, February 3, 1969, ADP/SLH.

19. For this and the following three paragraphs: AD to "Mom, Dad, Mark," January 5, 27, February 3, 11, 19, 1969, ADP/SLH.

20. The wedding and its immediate aftermath: AD to "Mom, Dad, Mark," February 28, March 5, 14, 21, April 7, 16, May 5, 15, 1969, ADP/SLH.

21. AD to "Mom, Dad, Mark," January 5, February 22, March 8, 1969, ADP/SLH. In a letter (September 3, 1970, ADP/SLH) to Mark, Andrea described Grace Paley as "my closest friend."

22. Andrea's advice to her brother is mostly contained in three letters: AD to Mark, November 23, 1965, April 10, 1967, and March 8, 1969, ADP/SLH.

23. AD to Mark, February 13, 1970, ADP/SLH.

24. Andrea to her parents, June 4, 11, 27, July 9, November 7, 14, December 4, 1969, January 14, February 3, 6, 14, March 10, April 8, May 15, June 16, 22, 1970, ADP/SLH.

25. Ricki even trusted Andrea to intervene in an angry dispute she was having with her mother, Gladyce Abrams Axelrod, over her involvement with Thatcher Clark. Andrea wrote Ricki's mother an acrimonious letter denouncing her interference (Gladyce and Sylvia merging into a common enemy). The entire three-way correspondence during the spring of 1970, somewhat hair-raising, is in ADP/SLH.

26. For this and the following paragraph: AD to "Mom, Dad, Mark," June 3, 1970.

27. For this and the following paragraph: AD, "The Third Rape," *Los Angeles Times*, April 28, 1991, and "My Life as a Writer, *Contemporary Authors* (Farmington Hills, MI: Gale, 1995)—both essays reprinted in AD, *Life and Death* (New York: The Free Press, 1991); AD to parents, August 17, 1970, ADP/SLH; AD, ms., "A Survivor's Birthday," in the Leah Fritz Papers, Rubenstein Library, Duke (RLD).

28. For this and the following five paragraphs: AD to Mark, September 3, 1970, ADP/SLH; AD to parents, June 3, October 11, 1970, February 20, 1971, April 1, May 5, 1971, ADP/SLH; AD, "A Battered Wife Survives" (first published as "The Bruise That Doesn't Heal" in *Mother Jones*, Vol. III, No. VI, July 1978), reprinted in AD, *Letters from a War Zone* (New York: Lawrence Hill Books, 1993); AD, ms., "A Survivor's Birthday," Leah Fritz Papers, RLD.

29. For this and the following paragraph: AD to parents, March 13, June 9, 1971, AD to Mark, June 9, 1971, ADP/SLH.

30. For this and the following four paragraphs: AD, *Ice and Fire* (London: Secker & Warburg, 1986), 82–83; conversation with John Stoltenberg, February 18, 2019; AD, unpublished manuscript *Ruins*; AD, "A Survivor's Birthday," Leah Fritz Papers, RLD; AD, "A Battered Wife Survives"; AD, "What Battery Really Is" (about the notorious 1987 Joel Steinberg case, in which he beat to death his adopted daughter Lisa)—a shorter, somewhat more personal version was initially published in the *Los Angeles Times*, March 12, 1989. The two "battery" articles are reprinted in AD, *Letters from a War Zone*. Andrea subsequently wrote as well about the Lorena Bobbitt and Nicole Simpson cases ("Trapped In a Pattern of Pain Where No One Can Help"), *Los Angeles Times*, June 26, 1994.

31. For this and the following paragraph: AD, "A Battered Wife Survives," 101.

32. At the risk of dissolving Andrea's personal experience into a categorical one—and thereby robbing it of its non-repeatable individuality—the trauma specialist Bessel Van Der Kolk (in *The Body Keeps the Score: Brain, Mind, and Body in the Healing of Trauma* (New York: Penguin, 2014) emphasizes certain features of trauma that do seem to apply to Andrea's situation: "The mere opportunity to escape," Van Der Kolk points out, "does not necessarily make traumatized . . .

people, take the road to freedom. . . . Rather than risk experimenting with new options they stay stuck in the fear they know . . . the continued secretion of stress hormones is expressed as agitation and panic and in the long term, wreaks havoc with their health" (p. 30). Van Der Kolk is also suggestive in separating "remembering" from "reenacting"; the former, often as a result of psychotherapy, can be a path to recovery, the latter a panicky lifelong repetition of profound anxiety (p. 184). Andrea *did* write about her history, though whether she remembered it fully or accurately must remain an open question; consciously or not, *writing* about the past can be seen as a self-treating form of psychotherapy (rather than taking the form of consultation with specialists). See also Judith Lewis Herman's classic, *Trauma and Recovery* (New York: Basic Books, 1992). In regard specifically to wife battering, the problem has today reached epidemic proportions: half of all murdered women in the United States are killed by a current or former partner, and domestic violence cuts across all lines of class, race, and religion. Awareness of the issue, moreover, is relatively new: until the 1990s the United States had more animal shelters than women's shelters (for more about the issue, see Rachel Louise Snyder's excellent book, *No Visible Bruises* (London: Bloomsbury, 2019). Finally, it needs to be remembered that at this point in time there were virtually no shelters for battered women. The first one in the United States opened in 1974 in St. Paul, Minnesota; by the early eighties, thanks to the women's movement, there were more than three hundred (see Larissa MacFarquhar's "A House of Their Own," *The New Yorker*, August 19, 2019, 36–49).

33. AD to parents, July 30, September 10, 1971, ADP/SLH.

34. AD, transcript of "A Survivor's Birthday," Leah Fritz Papers, RLD.

3: Joining the Fray

1. AD, "First Love," reprinted in Julia Wolf Mazow, ed., *The Woman Who Lost Her Names* (New York: Harper & Row, 1980). In my view, the most compelling discussion of the early years of the feminist movement remains, despite effective challenges to some of its analysis, Alice Echols, *Daring to Be Bad: Radical Feminism in America 1967–1975* (Minneapolis: University of Minnesota Press, 1989).

2. For this and the following two paragraphs: AD to parents, April 28, July 2, 8, November 20, 30, December 10, 1971; also a two-page untitled, undated [October 1972] "preface" designed, but not used, as an introduction to the second section of *Woman Hating*, ADP/SLH.

3. For this and the following paragraph, AD to parents, December 10, 1971, January 24, February 25, August 26, 1972, ADP/SLH.

4. AD to parents, April 25, June 24, 1972, ADP/SLH.

5. For this and the following paragraph: AD to parents, December 10, 1971, September 15, plus one undated letter, ADP/SLH.

6. Jim Hougan to Andrea, March 8, 1996, four pages; AD, "My Suicide," as excerpted in the script for "Aftermath"—both items courtesy John Stoltenberg. Andrea *had* heard earlier rumors that Iwan had been charged with attempted murder.

7. For this and the following two paragraphs: AD to parents, April 28, June 15, 22, October 10 (five-page untitled "statement"), 19, 29, 1972.

8. For this and the following paragraph: AD to parents, December 13, 1972, ADP/SLH; AD, "Living in Terror, Pain: Being a Battered Wife" (heroin), *Los Angeles Times*, March 12, 1989, reprinted in AD, *Life and Death* (New York: The Free Press, 1997). Her later partner, John Stoltenberg, would subsequently manage to persuade Andrea to pay her back taxes; as he puts it, "I wanted our life together to be as safe from charges of illegality as possible. . . . For the same reason we had no drugs in the house" (Stoltenberg to me, June 16, 2019).

9. For this and the following paragraph: AD, *Heartbreak: The Political Memoir of a Feminist Militant* (New York: Basic Books, 2002), 107, 123–24; AD to parents, December 17, 1972, January 22, February 16, March 12, 1973, ADP/SLH; AD, "On Returning to These States," *Village Voice*, August 2, 1973.

10. AD to parents, January 12, March 12, 1973, plus one undated, ADP/SLH.

11. AD, *Heartbreak*, 123; Stoltenberg to me, June 16, 2019. In a piece published in *Vice* after her death, Andrea described the overwhelming anguish she felt after once having hit Velvet (https://www.vice.com/en_us/article/bnd834/velvet -v13n12). Andrea subsequently acquired a cat, George.

12. For this and the following paragraph: AD to parents, January 12, 22, 1973, plus one undated letter [February 1973]; AD to Mark and Carol (Mark had recently married), March 12, 1973. It was through REDRESS that Andrea and I for a time became good friends, though by 1975 we'd drifted apart. Andrea's recollections of REDRESS in her 2002 memoir, *Heartbreak* (127–28) are a good deal harsher than mine; the group certainly did have its prima donnas, and any number of its members were annoyingly self-important. Yet REDRESS also had a number of committed and even self-effacing members—Noam Chomsky and Benjamin Spock are two that come to mind. Nor do I think Andrea is fair when (on page 128 of *Heartbreak*) she writes, "I would be cut in two for putting an idea forward"; that never happened in any meeting I attended, and I was at most of them. For more on my own take on REDRESS, see Duberman, *Cures: A Gay Man's Odyssey* (Boston: Dutton, 1991), which mentions Andrea a number of times, including her brief involvement with the Gay Academic Union, to which I'd introduced her. According to Stoltenberg, he and Andrea first met Joe Chaikin when Joe invited them both to a GAU meeting in my apartment (Stoltenberg to me, June 16, 2019).

13. I knew Joe better than I knew Andrea in these years, but never spent time with both of them together and so don't feel possessed of any special insight (or bias) about their relationship. For this and the following three paragraphs: AD to "J" [Chaikin], September 15, October 28, November 5, 1974, May 16, 1975; Chaikin to AD, five letters n.d. [October/November 1973], ADP/SLH.

14. Andrea's original title for *Woman Hating* was *Last Days at Hot Slit*; Johanna Fateman and Amy Scholder have used *Last Days . . .* as the title for their anthology of Andrea's writing (Los Angeles: Semiotext(e), 2019). In my 1973 diary I note that Andrea asked both me and Muriel Rukeyser to read the manuscript of *Woman Hating*. She'd already described it to me over dinner with (says my diary) "so much clarity and force" that I felt the book would be "a major event." Yet when

I read the manuscript I felt somewhat disappointed—parts of it seemed (as I wrote at the time) "too summary, un-argued, abstract." Muriel, on the other hand (so Andrea reported to her parents) told her "'it's one of the most important books of our time'—wow!" (AD to parents, April 3, 1973, ADP/SLH).

I still believed in Andrea's gift, and it was then—*subsequent* to reading the manuscript—that I sent her to Hal Scharlatt. He encouraged her, but she complained to me about his "heavy vibes." I told her that I thought she was off the mark about him, that along with being a brilliant editor, he was a gentle, generous man. Hal did end up giving Andrea a contract, though while still in the process of editing the book, he died suddenly of a heart attack at age thirty-eight.

While researching Andrea's biography, I came across a letter to her friend Jackie Lapidus (October 9, 1976, ADP/SLH) in which she writes that, following publication, Jack Macrae, the head of Dutton, "expresses just simple contempt for WOMAN HATING," and that "the person who has most purposefully stood in WH's way [is] Dutton's sales manager, [who] hates the book and just sabotaged it outright—this is intelligence that comes to me from within the company."

As for Hal, Andrea goes on to write Lapidus, he "misunderstood the nature of the book—I think he thought it would be sensationalistic in a way that men would be aroused somehow . . . as if the gynocide would continue to be, in its covers, what is in life for men—exciting." That doesn't sound to me at all like the feminist-conscious Hal. "Many things happened when the book was finished," Andrea continues, "to change his mind—he read it for one thing. For another thing, Martin Duberman who was his close friend and confidant, who had told him to read it in ms. to begin with, didn't like it and called Hal to say so."

Reading that in Andrea's 1976 letter proved a shock. I have no memory of saying such a thing to Hal nor of ever discussing *Woman Hating* with him after making the initial introduction. Nor do I believe I would have tried to sabotage a friend's work, especially after recommending it. But as no one needs reminding, memory is tricky, and I felt the need to reveal here Andrea's take on the situation. If nothing else, it may well help to explain why we grew apart as friends.

15. Huey Newton to AD, May 17, 1974 (with enclosures), ADP/SLH; *The Black Panther*, June 22, 1974 (the review is mostly a summary but the tone positive); AD, *Heartbreak*, 123 (Huey). The second review by the leftwing playwright Karen Malpede was also favorable. As was the writer Leah Fritz's in *Sojourner* (October 1976): she predicted that "Dworkin may prove to be an authentic prophet of feminism." An excerpt of the book appeared in *VIVA* (July 1974), though Andrea had to threaten to withdraw if "crucial political material" wasn't restored; it was. She was equally adamant in denying the charge that in *Woman Hating* she advocated incest; no, she insisted, she was instead pointing out that the frequency of father-daughter rape already broke the taboo (AD to Ellen Bass, August 18, 1981, AD to Dick McLeester, August 20, 1980, ADP/SLH).

16. "w.e.a.n.ed: on women writing," *off our backs*, January 1975; "Towards Androgyny," *Berkeley Barb*, January 17–23, 1975.

17. AD to parents, January 25, 1975; Sandra Parke to AD, August 23, 1975; Reesa Vaughter to AD, n.d.; Sandra Liebenstein[?], September 11, 1975; Kate Millett to Elaine Markson, n.d. [1974]; the programs include "A Feminist Lecture Series"

at the Woodstock Women's Center, the Community Church of Boston, and the Pratt/Phoenix Center, ADP/SLH.

18. "An Open Letter to Rennie Davis," six-page ms., ADP/SLH.

19. Dell Williams to AD, September 16, 1974, ADP/SLH; AD, "Renouncing Sexual 'Equality,'" *WIN*, October 17, 1974.

20. For a fuller discussion of all these points, see AD, *Woman Hating*, "Part Four: Androgyny" (New York: Plume, 1976).

21. AD, *Woman Hating*, 184 (pansexual); the remaining quotations in this and the following three paragraphs derive from an entry I made in my diary.

22. John Stoltenberg shared AD's concern that GAU was disinterested in a serious discussion of sexism within the organization (JS to GAU conference planning committee, October 12, 1974, ADP/SLH. For Andrea's discomfort, see Duberman, *Cures*, 276–77 (New York, Plume, 1997).

23. *OUT*, August 1973; Andrea's article, in typescript, is in ADP/SLH. See also AD, "Lesbian Pride," a speech delivered in Central Park for Lesbian Pride Week (June 28, 1975) and reprinted in AD, *Our Blood* (New York: Perigee, 1976), 73–75.

The second (and last) issue of *OUT* printed a letter from the writer Dotson Rader, a friend of Mailer's, protesting Andrea's piece. Mailer himself, who I knew slightly, sent me—on the assumption that I was the editor of *OUT*—a sharp note denouncing the "attack" on him. I responded in kind, and we went at it for several more rounds. Quotes from the correspondence are in Duberman, *Cures*, 289–90; the letters themselves are in the Berg Collection of the New York Public Library.

24. The chief source for the description of the early period of John and Andrea's relationship derives from John's manuscript, "My Life with Andrea Dworkin," courtesy Stoltenberg (henceforth, "My Life"). Additional information is in John Stoltenberg, "Living with Andrea Dworkin," *Lambda Book Report*, May/June 1994; Stoltenberg's speech, "Refusing to Be a Man," delivered at NOW in NYC, May 19, 1974. I have no memory of it, but John tells me that he and Andrea initially met at a GAU meeting in my apartment.

25. AD interview with Leah Fritz, n.d. (partner), Fritz Papers, RLD. In regard to friends' disapproval of their living together, Barbara Deming wrote Andrea, "It pains me very much to know that you have to brace yourself against challenges from one sister after another—about your living with John. I know that you can understand why so many sisters doubt. They just can't imagine such a relation. But how exhausting for you. Please don't let it make you bitter" (Deming to AD, November 12, 1974, ADP/SLH). John, diplomatically, wrote Andrea's parents that "she is the most important person to me in the world" (Stoltenberg to the Dworkins, July 17, 1974, ADP/SLH).

26. JS, "Toward Gender Justice" (November 29, 1974), typescript in ADP/SLH. See also JS, "Refusing to Be a Man," first delivered at the June 19, 1974, meeting of the NYC chapter of NOW, then published in *WIN*, July 1, 1974 (though John protested their change of "ejaculate" to "ejaculation" and drew a clear distinction between them (JS to "People" [*WIN*], July 6, 1974).

27. Stoltenberg, "My Life," courtesy Stoltenberg.

28. Adrienne to Andrea, December 31, 1975, Barbara Deming Papers, SLH. Barbara was quick to reassure Andrea that Adrienne "is blindly compelled (I do think blindly) to establish with you her *Authority*. . . . That compulsion even prevents her from reading you with complete attention apparently . . . [she's] unable in spite of herself not to have to try and keep one in one's lesser place . . . [though] Adrienne clearly values you" (Deming to AD, July 26, 1976, January 29, 1977, ADP/SLH).

29. AD, "A Letter to M.," *WIN*, June 26, 1975. Andrea had first fallen in love and had sex with another girl when both were fourteen ("though we didn't speak one honest word to each other").

30. For more on Deming's history and political views, see Martin Duberman, *A Saving Remnant: The Radical Lives of Barbara Deming and David McReynolds* (New York: The New Press, 2011), quotation on page 165.

31. For this and the following paragraph: Deming to "friends" [*Liberation*], November 10, 1974, ADP/SLH. To underscore her respect for Andrea's work, Deming gave her a $500 grant from the "mini-foundation" she'd set up with the $20,000 settlement she'd received following a severe automobile accident (Deming to Andrea, November 12, 1974, ADP/SLH).

32. Gwenda [Blair] to Andrea, December 12, 1974, ADP/SLH. For this and the following paragraph: Maris Cakars to AD, December 30, 1974; AD to Gwenda, December 27, 1974, January 21, 23, 1975; Pam Black to AD, December 31, 1974, January 4, 1975; AD to Cakars, January 3, 11, 1975, ADP/SLH; Leah Claire Allen, "The Pleasures of Dangerous Criticism" (intersectionality), *SIGNS*, Vol. 42, No. 1 (2016).

33. AD to Susan Cakars, June 30, 1975; AD to *WIN* collective, July 6, 1975; AD to *WIN* editorial board, November 30, 1975. "Redefining Nonviolence," originally a speech (April 5, 1975, Boston College; "We must not accept, even for a moment, male notions of what nonviolence is. . . . The men who hold those notions have never renounced the male behaviors, privileges, values, and conceits which are in and of themselves acts of violence against us"). Andrea reprinted the speech in *Our Blood*, 66–72.

34. AD to Maris Cakars, January 3, 1975, ADP/SLH. It was particularly galling to Barbara Deming (and doubtless Andrea as well) when *Liberation* published an unusually lengthy article by Gina Blumenfell attacking Andrea's work (in words that echoed Adrienne Rich's earlier critique) as failing to understand that "sexual domination must be understood in the larger context of domination per se," and assailing the women's movement in general as "unreflective" and "anti-intellectual" (Deming to the *Liberation* collective, March 12, 1975; the Blumenfell typescript is in ADP/SLH).

35. As Andrea summed it up: "Believe me, the problems were not resolvable— no effort was spared to try to resolve them" (AD to Paul Rayman, April 29, 1976, ADP/SLH). For the serious problems that subsequently erupted between Barbara and Andrea, see Duberman, *A Saving Remnant*, 189–93. In *Remnant*, I let most of the blame for their disagreements fall on Andrea, but I was then focused on Barbara's story and entirely smitten by her generosity of spirit. Now that I'm

deeply engaged with Andrea and sympathetic to *her* history, I'm less certain of the emphasis I then placed.

36. Mary Daly to AD, May 21, 1975; AD to Daly, May 26, 1975. In her letter, the notoriously testy Daly described *Woman Hating* as showing "great potential" despite its "sloppy" and "weak" fourth section (the one on androgyny).

37. Dean Smith to Lawrence Pitkethly (for the search committee), June 2, 1975, ADP/SLH.

38. For this and the following two paragraphs: AD to Phyllis Chesler, n.d. [1975] ("de-escalate" crisis), ADP/SLH. A copy of the Redstockings press release, dated May 9, 1975, is in ADP/SLH. An earlier piece in the *New York Times*, "C.I.A. Subsidized Festival Trips," February 21, 1967, had originated the controversy.

39. For this and the following three paragraphs: AD to Gloria Steinem, June 18, 1975, ADP/SLH.

40. AD to *off our backs*, May 2, 1980 (twice); AD to Steinem, May 3, 1980, ADP/SLH; Echols, *Daring to Be Bad*, 265–69 (Sarachild). Though the controversy died down, it was no thanks to Betty Friedan, who in her 1976 book, *It Changed My Life*, reiterated, if obliquely, the charges against Steinem, apparently annoyed at her rise to prominence.

4: The Mid-Seventies

1. Anonymous, *off our backs*, September–October 1975.

2. For this and the following two paragraphs: AD, preface to *Our Blood: Prophecies and Discourses on Sexual Politics* (New York: Perigee, 1976).

3. *New York Post*, October 1, 1975. My discussion of *Snuff* has been especially informed by Linda Williams, *Hard Core: Power, Pleasure, and the "Frenzy of the Visible"* (Berkeley: University of California Press, 1989), 189–95; Susan Brownmiller, *In Our Time* (New York: Dial Press, 1999), 297–302; Whitney Strub, *Perversion for Profit: The Politics of Pornography and the Rise of the New Right* (New York: Columbia University Press, 2010), 230–36.

4. AD to Susan Yankowitz, February 11, 1976; Yankowitz to AD, February 19, 1976; AD, two-page typed release dated February 24, 1976, ADP/SLH.

5. For this section on *Snuff*, see the following: Nat Hentoff, "Look Who's Snuffing the First Amendment," *Village Voice*, March 15, 1976; AD to *New York Times*, November 12, 1982, ADP/SLH; Leah Fritz, "Why We Had to Picket 'Snuff,'" *Village Voice*, April 12, 1976; John Leonard, "'Snuff,' Built on Rumor, Lacking in Credit," *New York Times*, February 27, 1976 (genocide); Don Morrison, "'Snuff's' Moral Is Don't See It," *Minneapolis Star*, February 26, 1976; press release re: Dworkin and Karla Jay meeting with the Manhattan District Attorney's Office, March 8, 1976; *Gay Community News*, March 25, 1978. I was also among the signers of Andrea's petition.

6. See, for example, AD, "Feminism: An Agenda" and "For Men, Freedom of Speech; For Women, Silence Please," both reprinted in AD, *Letters from a War Zone* (New York: Lawrence Hill Books, 1993).

302 NOTES TO PAGES 94–103

7. For this and the following three paragraphs: AD, *Our Blood, passim*. For samples of Andrea's resort to press agentry: AD to Kate Millett, June 15, 1976; AD to Gloria Steinem, June 15, 1976. In discussing the book's contents, I draw especially from two of the nine essays: "The Root Cause" and "Renouncing Sexual 'Equality.'"

8. For this and the following paragraph: AD to Marleen Le Febvre, June 13; AD to Barbara and Jane, July 5; AD to Kitty Benedict, January 6; AD to Mander and Rush, October 17—all 1976; Markson to AD, January 6, 1977, ADP/SLH.

9. AD to Yankowitz, July 23, 1976; AD to Kathy Norris, July 27, 1976, ADP/SLH.

10. AD to Marleen Le Febvre, October 2, 1976, ADP/SLH.

11. For this and the following two paragraphs: AD to Eleanor Johnson, October 4; Karla Jay, October 6 (killing), 16; AD to Yankowitz, October 17; AD to Eleanor Johnson, October 17; AD to Markson, October 18; AD to Leah Fritz, October 24; AD to London and Romero, November 12—all 1976, ADP/SLH.

12. For this and the following four paragraphs: Karla Jay to "Strange Her" (AD), October 2, 16; AD to Wendy Stevens, October 4; AD to Robyn Newhouse, October 10; AD to Leah Fritz, October 10; AD to Yankowitz, October 17 (muscled); AD to Eleanor Johnson, October 17 (prisoner); AD to Markson, October 18; AD to Karla Jay, November 3; AD to London and Romero, November 12—all 1976; AD to Deming, March 14, 1977 (taxes), ADP/SLH.

13. AD to Karla Jay, November 3 (Sylvia), 1976; AD to Jackie Lapidus, December 19; AD to Yankowitz, February 16, 1977; AD to June Duffy Dongel, March 14, 1977, ADP/SLH.

14. For this and the following five paragraphs: AD to Yankowitz, November 11; AD to Karla Jay, November 17 (*Ms.*; crazy), 25; AD to Kathy Norris, to Jackie Lapidus, December 19 (whoring), December 20, 1976 (Barbara); AD to Leah Fritz, November 22; AD to Eleanor Johnson, November 22, ADP/SLH. Barbara's extensive notes, written between October 8 and December 25, 1976, are in the Barbara Deming Papers, SLH. Barbara later persisted in trying to restore the friendship: "I still don't understand it—how you and I could have hurt each other (and yes, angered each other) as we somehow did. This is just to say how deeply sorry I am that I hurt *you*. I love you very much; and I respect you very deeply" (Barbara to AD, January 29, 1977, ADP/SLH). By 1979, not having had a response from Andrea, Barbara temporarily gave up trying to save the friendship (though ultimately considerable cordiality was restored). I've described Barbara and Jane's reaction in more detail in Martin Duberman, *A Saving Remnant: The Radical Lives of Barbara Deming and David McReynolds* (New York: The New Press, 2011), 190–92. Some limited contact by letter resumed in 1979, but on Andrea's side was not immediately friendly, though she did recommend a publisher to Deming (AD to Michalowski, January 13; Deming to AD, March 31, 15, July 2; AD to Deming, April 10—all 1979), ADP/SLH.

15. For this and the following paragraph: AD to Eleanor Johnson, November 22 (Chaikin); AD to Jackie Lapidus, December 19; AD to Kathy Norris, December 20—all 1976 (Chaikin), ADP/SLH.

16. For the section on June Arnold: AD to Karla Jay, November 25, 1976; AD to

Johnson and Kataloni, February 27; June Arnold to AD, April 13; AD to Arnold, April 26, May 20; Steinem to Andrea, May 16; AD to Lapidus, May 18—all 1977, ADP/SLH.

17. The individual involved has asked me to use a pseudonym for her real name. For this and the following two paragraphs: AD to Allen Young, August 22, 1977; AD to "Joanne Kastor," August 22, 1977, May 20, 1978; Kastor to AD, August 24, 1977, ADP/SLH; AD to Anne McCallister, September 27, 1980, Leah Fritz Papers, RLD; Kastor to me, March 27, April 30, 2019. In Andrea's unpublished *My Suicide* (1999 MS, courtesy Stoltenberg), written during a despondent period and found after her death, she wrote these lines: ". . . I want women. I have a flat-out appetite now. But I'm not touching anyone . . . touching is even harder than talking and I'm buried alive."

18. AD to Leah Fritz, February 10, 1977, ADP/SLH. Abbie Hoffman, Alice Hoffman, Grace Paley, and Tillie Olsen were among Elaine Markson's other clients, and Hoffman described her as "a fierce and loving protector." It was probably Grace Paley who introduced Andrea to her. Markson died in May 2018.

19. For this and the following two paragraphs: AD to Leah Fritz, February 10, March 13, 1977; AD to Lapidus, April 25, 1977; AD to Martha Shelley, May 2, 1977, ADP/SLH.

20. Andrea and John only later learned that their actions while at Cummington had more impact than they knew at the time. The women on the community's Board of Trustees organized a Women's Caucus "to act against sexism at Cummington," and passed a resolution thanking Andrea and John for their work on the library (AD to Leah Fritz, September 17, 1977, ADP/SLH).

5: The Gathering Storm

1. For this and the following two paragraphs, AD to Jackie Lapidus, April 25, May 18; AD to Eleanor Johnson, April 25; AD to Elsa Dorfman, May 6; AD to Gloria Steinem, May 16; AD to Ellen Frankfort, May 18; AD to Leah Fritz, May 18—all 1977, ADP/SLH.

2. AD to Steinem, June 12, 1977; AD to Karla Jay, June 28, 1977, ADP/SLH.

3. For this and the following paragraph: "WOMEN FOR THE ABOLITION OF PORNOGRAPHY," three-page statement of purpose, n.d.; "Dear Sisters of the Women's Anti-Defamation League," June 11, 1977; AD to Neil Miller, June 12, 1977 (*GCN* editor); *Gay Community News*, June 25, 1977, ADP/SLH.

4. For this and the following two paragraphs: AD to Martha Shelley, June 17; AD to Susan Brownmiller, June 14, 1977; AD to Karla Jay, June 28; Adrienne Rich to "Sisters," June 28; AD to Rich, June 29; Shere Hite to "Dear Women," n.d. (challenging use of the word "abolish" in regard to pornography—she was for consciousness-raising, not legal action); AD to Lois Gould, July 1; Karla Jay to *Times*, July 1; Leah Fritz to AD, July 1, 7 (a further critique of Brownmiller); AD to Fritz, July 6; AD to Robin Morgan, July 7; AD to Janet Sternberg, July 30; Steinem to AD, September 7—all 1977, all ADP/SLH.

5. For this and the following two paragraphs: Gould, *Times*, June 30; Fritz

to "Dear Sisters," July 1; Fritz to AD, July 1; AD to *Times*, June 30; AD to Jane Alpert, November 6; "Another Memo," September 23—all 1977, all ADP/SLH; AD to Brownmiller, June 14; transcript of Brownmiller interview with AD, August 10, 1998, Brownmiller Papers, SLH.

6. AD to Susan Yankowitz, July 9, 1977, ADP/SLH. It was at just this time that the *Soho Weekly News* unexpectedly reprinted in its August 4, 1977, issue Andrea's "Why So-Called Radical Men Love and Need Pornography" (under the title "Fathers, Sons and the Lust for Porn"). *Soho* paid her a munificent $10.

7. Andrea's most detailed and cogent argument against biological determinism is found in her earlier piece, "An Open Letter to Leah Fritz," *WIN*, November 21, 1974.

8. AD to Shelley, June 17; AD to Fritz, August 8 (hissed), 17 (ghetto); AD to Allen Young, August 22 (GAU); AD to Yankowitz, August 26; AD to Steinem, September 21 (hurt)—all 1977; AD to Laura Lederer, July 19; AD to Robin Morgan, July 19; AD to "Robin, Susan, Lois, and Gloria," August 7—all 1979, ADP/SLH. Andrea laid out her complaints against gay male attitudes in *Gay Community News*, June 12, 1977 (ERA), and in "The Lesbian/Gay Movement," *Gay Community News*, June 25, 1977. Wayne Dynes, the conservative gay art historian answered her in his "The New Victorianism," *GCN*, August 20, 1977, in which he managed to demonstrate precisely the disdain about which Andrea had complained.

9. "The Power of Words" was first published in the *Massachusetts Daily Occupied Collegian*, May 8, 1978. It's included in AD's collection, *Letters from a War Zone* (New York: Lawrence Hill Books, 1993), 27–30.

10. AD to Mark, March 3, 1978; AD to Fritz, May 17, 1978 (NYC), ADP/SLH. Shortly before leaving Northampton, Andrea did participate somewhat more in local activism (*Collegian*, April 10, 15, 1978). She also spoke at the Women's Week Conference at Smith: "Look, Dick, Look. See Jane Blow It," reprinted in AD, *Letters from a War Zone*, 126–32. Because the documentation of AD's lecture dates is voluminous and repetitive, I've decided against detailed citations regarding contracts and so forth

11. For this and the following two paragraphs: AD to Steinem, September 21, 1977, March 30, 1978; Steinem to AD, May 9, 1978, ADP/SLH; AD to Corona Machemer, August 19, 1978, Leah Fritz Papers, RLD.

12. For this and the following two paragraphs: Steinem to AD, January 31, 1981, plus three undated notes, ADP/SLH; AD to Robin Morgan, February 14, 18, 1981; AD to Steinem, February 14, 1981, Robin Morgan Papers, RLD.

13. AD to Paula Rayman, April 29, 1976, ADP/SLH.

14. For this and the following paragraph: AD to Fritz, May 17, 1978; AD to Hite, June 27, 1978, ADP/SLH. AD's defense of Hite is in *off our backs*, May 1978. Hite did an interview with Andrea (June 21, n.y., ADP/SLH); the six-page typed transcript is in ADP/SLH. Andrea subsequently had trouble with her *Mother Jones* article: after "the third revised abridged version of my essay . . . they are being nasty as hell" (AD to Lederer, July 19, 1979; AD to Robin Morgan, July 19, 1979, ADP/SLH). The only part of Hite's book that disappointed Catharine MacKinnon was "the same old humanism" of the chapter on pornography (MacKinnon to AD, January 3, 1982, ADP/SLH).

15. For this and the following two paragraphs: Shere Hite interview with AD, June 21, n.y. [1978?]; AD to Leah Fritz, May 6, 17 (*Mother Jones*); AD to Phyllis Chesler, May 18, 24, June 11; Chesler to AD, June 7; AD to parents, June 15—all 1978, ADP/SLH; Leah Fritz to *Mother Jones*, June 7, 1978, Fritz Papers, RLD.

16. AD to Mark, May 22, 1979, December 26, 1980, ADP/SLH.

17. For this and the following three paragraphs: AD to Phyllis Chesler, January 20, 1977, May 18, 24, June 11, 1978; Chesler to AD, June 7, 14; AD to Leah Fritz, February 10, 1977, May 6, 1978; Chesler to Vincent Virga, May 12, 1978—all in ADP/SLH. Andrea may have had the dispute with Chesler in mind when, in her unpublished article "Sororicide" (ms. is in the Leah Fritz Papers, RLD), she lamented that women "are socialized to despise and distrust each other."

18. In 2018, more than a dozen years after Andrea's death, Phyllis published *A Politically Incorrect Feminist* (New York: St. Martin's Press, 2018). In it (pp. 131, 192), she calls Andrea "a genius" but more than compensates for the compliment with an assortment of negative comments about her—"a fanatic, a terribly wounded one . . . who accused practically everyone of high crimes, never mere misdemeanors"—that perhaps tells us as much about Chesler's capacity for hyperbole as Andrea's for outsized accusation.

In an earlier work, *The Death of Feminism* (London: Palgrave MacMillan, 2005, 68), Chesler had been far more generous toward Andrea, calling her "visionary, both in literary and intellectual terms," and deploring Katha Pollitt's article in *The Nation* (April 9, 2005), in which she'd mocked Andrea as "she of the denim overalls and the wild hair and wilder pronouncements," summarizing her as "an oversimplifier and a demagogue."

19. AD to Robyn Newhouse, July 21, 1978; AD to Yankowitz, July 19, 1978, ADP/SLH.

6: Pornography

1. The literature on the pornography issue is vast. Some good starting points on the debate are Andrea Dworkin and Catharine A. MacKinnon, *In Harm's Way* (Cambridge, MA: Harvard University Press, 1997); Lisa Duggan and Nan D. Hunter, *Sex Wars* (New York: Routledge, 2006); and Whitney Strub, *Perversion for Profit: The Politics of Pornography and the Rise of the New Right* (New York: Columbia University Press, 2010), chapter seven; Caroline Bronstein, *Battling Pornography* (Cambridge, UK: Cambridge University Press, 2011).

2. Transcript of Elisabeth Warren interview with AD, n.d. [October 1981], ADP/SLH. See also, Wilson to AD, November 4, March 6; AD to Wilson, April 10—all 1981, all ADP/SLH. See pages 12–14 for more on Andrea's literary education.

3. For this and the following three paragraphs: Both AD's 1977 speech, "Pornography: The New Terrorism," and her 1978 speech in San Francisco, "Pornography and Grief," are reprinted in AD, *Letters from a War Zone*. *New York Times*, December 4, 1978. It's worth noting that in her San Francisco speech Andrea included gay men in what she called the male need to "despise" women: "This same motif also operates among male homosexuals, where force and/or convention designate some males as female or feminized. The plethora of leather

and chains among male homosexuals . . . are testimony to the fixedness of the male compulsion to dominate and destroy that is the source of sexual pleasure for men" (*Letters*, 22). Andrea's words make it sound as if S/M was (and is) endemic in the gay male world; I believe it's a good deal less than that. Some would argue that a milder form of dominance/submission is inherent in all sexual coupling.

4. See Paul Chevigny, "Pornography and Cognition," *Duke Law Journal*, Vol. 1989, No. 2 (April 1989).

5. Barbara Mehrhof and Lucille Iverrson, "When Does Free Speech Go Too Far?: https://google.com/drive/folders/1qimgo1YBgjRjsFv8gz46ZSYEWhzlJ239; Women Against Pornography pamphlet: https://drive.google.com/drive/foldrs/1mo34KMB88MG3SelTO5adJ51HizZiH4-0.

6. Susan Brownmiller, "Let's Put Pornography Back in the Closet," July 17, 1979, *Newsday*.

7. For this and the following paragraph: AD, "Pornography and the New Terrorism?," *The Body Politic*, August 1978; AD, "For Men, Freedom of Speech; For Women, Silence Please," *Letters from a War Zone*, 222–25. On the inception of WAP: Bronstein, *Battling Pornography*, chapter 6.

8. Brownmiller interview with AD, August 10, 1998, transcript in Brownmiller Papers, SLH; Brownmiller, *In Our Time*, 308–10. Andrea's difficulties with WAP included (according to one of her fans) "silencing" her at a press conference because she didn't fit with their "carefully cultivated public image. . . . I guess you don't project a 'nice girl' image enough to publicly represent WAP," she wrote Andrea. "WAP is too afraid of freaking people out by using lesbianism as both an alternative kind of sexual relating and a model for eroticism in general." (Julie Melrose to AD, September 24, 1979, ADP/SLH). Yet in regard to lesbianism WAP, as part of its formal literature ("Lesbian Feminist Concerns in the Feminist Anti-Pornography Movement") specifically states that "Women Against Pornography upholds the right of every woman to the self-determination of her sexual and affectional preferences" (copy in ADP/SLH).

9. A copy of Wendy Kaminer's position paper, "Where We Stand on the First Amendment," is in ADP/SLH.

10. For this and the following three paragraphs, the most detailed coverage of the September conference is in *off our backs*, November 1979; see also, Leslie Bennetts, "Conference Examines Pornography as a Feminist Issue," *New York Times*, September 17, 1979 (Abzug).

11. Most of Ed Donnerstein and Neil Malamuth's work lay in the future, and will be evaluated, along with research done by others, at a later point in this book. Of the early work, Malamuth's "Rape Proclivity Among Males," *Journal of Social Issues*, 1981, No. 4, is probably the most significant.

12. For this and the following four paragraphs: Ellen Willis, "Feminism, Moralism, and Pornography," *Village Voice*, October and November 1979, reprinted in Nona Willis Aronowitz, *The Essential Ellen Willis* (University of Minnesota Press, 2014), 94–100. In the Ellen Willis Papers at the Schlesinger Library, Harvard, there are a few dozen pages of undated, handwritten notes apparently representing EW's preliminary thoughts, some of which contain additional reflections on the anti-porn movement. For example, in one set of notes (based on internal evidence, they probably date from the mid–late eighties) Willis writes: "Anti-porn

movement: preocc. w. violence—porn causes violence & is violent. porn=rape. rape loses its status as an act & comes to mean something like 'the assault of this male-oriented sexual culture on female sensibilities' + this assault is to be fought by crusading against porn. What can be the aim/effect of such a movement? 1) eliminate porn. Mostly, anti-porn movement denies they want to do this. Just 'raise consciousness.' In fact their denial doesn't hold up. . . . They are reinforcing right's attempts to censor & right just co-opts their arguments."

13. For this and the following paragraph: AD, "For Men, Freedom of Speech; For Women, Silence Please," as reprinted in AD, *Letters from a War Zone*, 222–25.

14. The transcript of AD's "Rally Address," October 20, 1979, is in ADP/SLH.

15. For this and the following paragraph: AD to Susan Hester, May 22, 1979; AD to Elsa Dorfman, May 22, 1979; AD to Laura Lederer, June 8, 1979; AD to MacKinnon, March 31, August 5, 1978; MacKinnon to AD, August 11, 1979, ADP/SLH; Fred Strebeigh, "Defining Law on the Feminist Frontier," *New York Times*, October 6, 1991; AD to Charlotte Bunch, December 12, 1980 (Doubleday), Bunch Papers, SLH.

16. AD to MacKinnon, March 31, 1978, ADP/SLH.

17. MacKinnon to AD, October 16, 1980; AD to MacKinnon, December 2, 1981, ADP/SLH.

18. AD to Amy Hoffman, December 24, 1979, ADP/SLH.

19. For this and the following two paragraphs: AD to Kathy Norris, July 27, December 20, 1976, AD to Robin Morgan, January 5, 1977, June 26, 1979. It may be—though this is purely speculative—that the antagonism between the two was largely ideological: Andrea strongly resisted the notion of biological determinism in regard to gender, whereas Adrienne found "cultural" feminism—the view that men and women are *innately* different—mostly congenial.

20. AD to MacKinnon, January 3, 1980; AD to Marge Piercy, January 10, 1980, ADP/SLH.

21. Leah Fritz to AD, January 3, 1980, Leah Fritz Papers, RLD (nearly a year later, Fritz itemized her discomfort: "I felt several of the stories . . . corroborated the myth of female masochism & the Marxist notion that the enemy is the 'bourgeois' woman" (Fritz to AD, October 1, 1980, ADP/SLH). See also AD to Gloria Steinem, March 17, 1980, ADP/SLH; AD to Alix Kates Shulman, January 31, March 21, 1980, Shulman Papers, RLD; AD to Letty Cottin Pogrebin, January 18, 1980; AD to Vivian Gornick, February 25, 1980, ADP/SLH. Frog in the Well, not Andrea, sent the manuscript to Rita Mae Brown, who did respond with a favorable blurb: "A remarkable collection of short stories that challenge existing definitions of feminist literature. Andrea Dworkin's passion confounds and frightens the patriarchs. It's pure joy for the rest of us" (Rita Mae Brown to Frog in the Well, April 14, 1980, ADP/SLH); Andrea, in turn, wrote favorably about Brown's *Six of One* ("the book is original and beautiful")—the ms. is in ADP/SLH. Andrea's friend, the poet Jacqueline ("Jackie") Lapidus, also loved the book and reported that Kate Millett had agreed with her that "it was an original, outrageous, beautiful, terrifying and gut-wrenching piece of work" (Lapidus to AD, May 9, 1980, ADP/SLH). The *New Women's Times* (July/August 1980) also carried a favorable review.

22. AD to Robin Morgan, March 17, 1980, Robin Morgan Papers, RLD; AD to Deirdre English, March 10, 1980; English to AD, June 18, 1980, ADP/SLH.

23. AD to "Letter to the Editor," *Mother Jones*, March 10, 1980, ADP/SLH.

24. AD to Vicki Smith, April 2, May 30, ADP/SLH; Grace Hardgrove to AD, June 12, 1980.

25. For this and the following two paragraphs: AD to Loretta Barrett, August 4; AD to Steinem, May 3, August 3, 5; AD to Adrienne Rich, August 5; AD to Jan Raymond and Pat Hynes, August 18—all 1980, ADP/SLH; AD to Charlotte Bunch, December 12, 1980, Bunch Papers, SLH.

26. AD to Wendy Goldwyn, September 1, 1980, ADP/SLH.

27. For this and the following paragraph: AD to Adrienne Rich, September 27, 1980; Karla Jay to Eleanor Rawson, September 3, 1980, ADP/SLH.

28. AD, *Ice and Fire* (London: Secker & Warburg, 1986), 100–2.

29. AD to Steinem, September 28, 1980; AD to Lapidus, December 9, 1980, ADP/SLH.

30. AD to Robin Morgan, February 3, 1981, Morgan Papers, RLD.

31. AD to Letty Pogrebin, November 30, 1980, ADP/SLH.

32. For this and the following paragraph: AD, *Pornography* (New York: Perigee, 1981), 167–78; see also, AD, ms. "The Pornographic View: Women in Private—Harlots and Sadists"; AD to Michael Moorcock, April 22, 1988 (Sontag), ADP/SLH. The Sontag essay, "The Pornographic Imagination," is in her *Styles of Radical Will* (London: Secker & Warburg, 1969).

33. AD, *Pornography*, 81–100.

34. MacKinnon to AD, October 16, 1980, ADP/SLH.

35. *Sojourner*, July 1981; AD to Dorothy Allison, August 4, 1981, Allison Papers, Duke; AD to Ellen Frankfort, July 27, 1981, ADP/SLH. In the all-important *New York Times* (July 12, 1981), Ellen Willis denounced *Pornography* as "a booklength sermon with a rhetorical flourish and a singleminded intensity that meet somewhere between poetry and rant. . . . *Pornography*'s relentless outrage . . . is less a call to arms than a counsel of despair."

36. Leah Fritz, "Dworkin Review," n.d., 8 pp., Leah Fritz Papers, RLD.

37. Willis, "Nature's Revenge," *New York Times*, July 12, 1981.

7: Lovelace; Trans; and Right-Wing Women

1. AD to Leonard Lopate, February 15, 1981, ADP/SLH.

2. Ellen Willis, *New York Times*, July 12, 1981; Barbara Deming to AD, July 22?, 1981, Deming Papers, SLH; AD, *Pornography* (New York: Perigee, 1981), 51.

3. AD's unpublished letter to the *New York Times*, November 18, 1979, ADP/SLH.

4. Julie Bindel, What Andrea Dworkin, the Feminist I Knew, Can Teach Young Women," *The Guardian*, March 30, 2015. See also: Christine Stark, "Andrea Dworkin and Me," *Feminist Studies*, Vol. 34, No. 3 (kind and soft). Asked

by me to characterize what Andrea was like in person, John Stoltenberg replied, "So sweet and funny" (Stoltenberg to me, June 16, 2019).

5. Articles by Pat Harrison and Catherine London in *Sojourner*, July 1981.

6. AD, a *new woman's broken heart* (Frog in the Well, 1980).

7. The chronology of events in this and the following two paragraphs is based on Brownmiller's interview with AD, August 10, 1998, transcript in Brownmiller Papers, SLH; MacKinnon to me, May 29, 2019; phone conversation with Mac-Kinnon, July 25, 2019.

8. There's considerable documentation relating to the case in both the Dworkin and MacKinnon Papers at SLH, but since it did not go forward, I've refrained from further detailing. Some of the key letters are: AD to Steinem, May 18, 1980; AD, "Statement," May 31, 1980; MacKinnon to Marchiano, April 27, July 2, July 14, July 15, 1981, February 21, 1982; MacKinnon to AD, October 26 (cheering), 1981; MacKinnon to Gloria, et al., October 28, 1981, ADP/SLH; Susan Brownmiller interview with AD, August 10, 1998, Brownmiller Papers, RLD. There are many admirable qualities to Whitney Strub's *Perversion for Profit* (New York: Columbia University Press, 2010), but his treatment of Linda "Lovelace" Marciano isn't one of them. Of the *Deep Throat* shoot, he mockingly quotes her as saying "I hated to see it end" (p. 246), and portrays her "victimhood" as Andrea and Kitty's invention—which is wretchedly off the mark. See MacKinnon, *Feminism Unmodified* (Cambridge, MA: Harvard University Press, 1987), 127–33.

9. For this and the following paragraph: MacKinnon to AD, November 22, December 11, 26, 1981; AD to MacKinnon, November 27, December 2, 22, 1981, ADP/SLH; AD to Susanne Kappeler, July 31, 1993, ADP/SLH; see also AD to Moorcock and Steele, June 21, 1993, ADP/SLH; MacKinnon to me, May 29, 2019.

10. For this and the following paragraph: AD to Jane Meyerling, July 12, 1982; AD to Jan Raymond, July 12, 1982; AD to Letty Pogrebin, May 4, 1982, ADP/SLH; John Stoltenberg, "What Is the Meaning of S&M?," *Gay Community News*, February 23, 1980.

11. AD, *Woman Hating* (New York: Plume, 1974), chapter 9.

12. AD to Jan Raymond, January 15, 1978; MacKinnon to AD, December 11, 1981, ADP/SLH. Down to the present day Andrea is sometimes still accused of having been transphobic; John Stoltenberg has written a persuasive reply to the charge: https://web.archive.org/web/20160317032310/http:/www.feministtimes .com/%e2%80%8egenderweek-andrea-was-not-transphobic/.

13. For this and the following two paragraphs: transcript of Kim Fullerton interview with AD, April 16, 1982, ADP/SLH; Michael Kimmel, "Who Are the Real Male Bashers?," in *Misframing Men* (New Brunswick, NJ: Rutgers University Press, 2010).

14. The Barnard Conference has produced a substantial amount of commentary and controversy, though the lack of reflection on it in AD's papers is an index of her detachment from the event—though not from the issues it raised. As a result of her non-participation, I've held my discussion of the conference to a minimum. My own understanding of it, however, has been enriched by the extended commentary in *off our backs* (usually regarded as the feminist newspaper of record), and particularly the several articles in its June 1982 issue—especially Claudette

Charbonneau's unsympathetic and highly controversial one; Gayle Rubin's important letter to *oob*, June 8, 1982; and *New Directions for Women*, July/August 1982. See also: Carole S. Vance, *Pleasure and Danger: Exploring Female Sexuality* (containing the revised proceedings of the conference), especially the Epilogue, pp. 431–39 (Abingdon, UK: Routledge & Kegan Paul, 1984); The Steering Committee of WAP's eleven-page protest letter, December 30, 1983, to *Feminist Studies* (a copy is in ADP/SLH); "Diary of a Conference" (*GLQ* 17:1); Gayle Rubin's important, even essential corrective to WAP's various distortions, "Blood Under the Bridge," in *GLQ: A Journal of Lesbian and Gay Studies*, Vol. 127, No. 1, 2011, Duke University Press; and the June 14, 1982, list of grievances against the conference disrupters signed by ("a partial list") more than 150 women, Dorothy Allison Papers, RLD. A particularly cogent discussion of the conference and its aftermath is in Carolyn Bronstein, *Battling Pornography* (Cambridge, UK: Cambridge University Press, 2011), 297–307.

15. AD to Katherine Thomas, September 21, 1986, ADP/SLH.

16. For more on cultural feminism, see Alice Echols, *Daring to Be Bad*, as well as the central texts of adherents of biological determinism frequently cited, including Mary Daly, *Gyn-Ecology* (Boston: Beacon, 1978); Adrienne Rich, *Of Woman Born* (New York: Norton, 1976); and Susan Griffin, *Pornography and Silence* (New York: Harper & Row, 1981).

17. Laura Cottingham, "Strangers Bed Partners," *Village Voice*, September 27, 1985. Alice Echols quotes one (unidentified) "brilliant but conflicted writer" admitting to sympathy with a conference attendee "who berated academics for 'debating the niceties of leather and shit'" while ignoring the 'real, material struggles of women'" (Echols, "Retrospective: Tangled Up in Pleasure and Danger," *Signs*, Vol. 42, No. 1 [2016]).

18. For this and the following paragraph: Alice Walker to AD, February 4, 1983; AD to Steinem, March 21, 1983; AD to Ann Jones, April 25, 1983, ADP/SLH.

19. *In These Times*, April 27–May 3, 1983; *FUSE*, September/October 1983; *The New Women's Times Feminist Review*, November/December 1983.

20. *Womannews*, May 1983; several responses to the review are in the issue of June 1983.

8: The Ordinance

1. For this and the following paragraph: Kitty MacKinnon to AD, February 8, April 19, 1983, ADP/SLH; phone conversation with MacKinnon, July 25, 2019.

2. MacKinnon to AD, n.d. [October? 1983]; AD to "The Editor," October 31, 1983, ADP/SLH. See also, Dworkin and MacKinnon, *In Harm's Way: The Pornography Civil Rights Hearings* (Harvard, 1997), which in an appendix prints the Ordinances drawn up for several cities.

3. Catharine A. MacKinnon, "Testimony on Pornography, Minneapolis," *Butterfly Politics: Changing the World for Women* (Cambridge, MA: Harvard Univ. Press, 2019), 96.

4. See Dworkin, *Pornography* (New York: Perigee, 1981), *passim*.

5. For this and the following two paragraphs: MacKinnon, "An Open Letter

to Adrienne Rich," July 4, 1985, APD/SLH; AD to Editor, *Wall Street Journal*, February 2, 1984; transcript of Brownmiller interview with AD, August 10, 1998, ADP/SLH. "An Excerpt from Model Antipornography Civil Rights Ordinance" was published in Dworkin and MacKinnon, *Pornography Civil Rights Hearings*, 138–42.

6. For this and the following three paragraphs see: phone conversation with MacKinnon, July 25, 2019; "An Open Letter on Pornography," *off our backs*, August/September 1985. For the issue of "proof of harm," see MacKinnon, "Pornography," in *Civil Rights & Civil Liberties Review*, Vol. 2, No. 1 (1985); Carol Anne Douglas, "A House Divided?," *off our backs*, June 1985; AD ms. of the February 1984 Toronto conference on pornography, Pauline Bart Papers, RLD; AD to Dorothy ("Cookie") Teer, April 24, 1985, Teer Papers, RLD.

7. For this and the following paragraph: James E.P. Check and Neil Malamuth, "An Empirical Assessment of Some Feminist Hypotheses About Rape," *Journal of Women's Studies* (1984, 8); Edward Donnerstein, "December 12, 1983 testimony in Minneapolis Hearings," and January 10, 1984 "Interview," both in *In Harm's Way: The Pornography Civil Rights Hearings* (Cambridge, UK: Harvard University Press, 1997), 44–60; Neil Malamuth and Ed Donnerstein, eds., *Pornography and Sexual Aggression* (Academic Press, 1984).

Later studies: Mike Baxter, "Flesh and Blood," *New Scientists*, May 5, 1990; Mike Allen et al., "A Meta-Analysis Summarizing the Effects of Pornography," *Human Communication Research*, December 1995; Catherine Itzin, ed., *Pornography: Women, Violence and Civil Liberties* (Oxford, UK: Oxford University Press, 1992); Diana E.H. Russell, *Making Violence Sexy: Feminist Views on Pornography* (Hoboken, NJ: Blackwell, 1993); Elizabeth Oddone-Paolucci et al., "A Meta-Analysis of the Published Research on the Effects of Pornography," in *The Changing Family and Child Development*, Claudio Violato et al., eds. (Abingdon, UK: Routledge, 2000). For a fuller citation of the research to date into pornography's harm, see Catharine MacKinnon, *Sex Equality*, Third Ed., Foundation Press, 2015), 1716–49. See also *off our backs*: Catharine MacKinnon, "Pornography Left and Right," in *Harvard Civil Rights-Civil Liberties Law Review*, Winter 1995, 143–45 for a persuasive denial of ever having said (or believed) that "all sex is rape." She sued over the misquotation many times over, and consistently won, forcing even the *New York Times* to print a retraction.

8. Gayle Rubin to Nan Hunter, June 5, 1985, Dorothy Allison Papers, RLD. For a detailed and cogent analysis of the issues at stake, see Lisa Duggan and Nan D. Hunter, *Sex Wars: Sexual Dissent and Political Culture*, 10th anniversary ed. (London: Taylor & Francis Group, 2006).

9. For this and the next two paragraphs, see: "An Open Letter on Pornography," *off our backs*, August/September 1985. For the issue of "proof of harm," see MacKinnon, "Pornography, Civil Rights & Civil Liberties Review," Vol. 2, no. 1, 1985; Carol Anne Douglas, "A House Divided?," *off our backs*, June 1985; AD ms. of the February 1984 Toronto Conference on Pornography, Pauline Bart Papers, RLD; AD to Dorothy ("Cookie") Teer, April 24, 1985, Teer Papers, RLD.

10. Malamuth and Donnerstein, eds., *Pornography and Sexual Aggression*, Academic Press, 1984. See also Donnerstein, "Erotica and Human Aggression," in Green and Donnerstein eds., *Aggression: Theoretical and Empirical Reviews*

(Academic Press, 1983); and Malamuth and Donnerstein, "The Effects of Aggressive Pornographic Mass Media Stimuli," in Berkowitz, ed., *Advances in Experimental Social Psychology* (Academic Press, 1982).

11. AD to Henk Jan, September 20, 1984; AD to Gale O'Brien Green, June 12, 1984; AD to Joyce Keener, June 12, 1984; AD to Jalna Hammer, May 8, 1984—all ADP/SLH.

12. For this and the following three paragraphs: AD to Priscilla Moree, August 14, 1985 (trembling); AD to Dorothy ("Cookie") Teer, April 24, 1985, Teer Papers, RLD.

13. AD to Fraser, July 5, 1984, a copy is in the MacKinnon Papers, SLH.

14. For this and the following two paragraphs: AD to Johanna Markson, March 26, 1990; *Village Voice*, August 21, 1978, October 16, 23, 1984; MacKinnon to *Voice*, December 26, 1984, ADP/SLH. For Andrea's earlier run-in with the ACLU, see her 1981 piece, "The ACLU: Bait and Switch," in *Letters from a War Zone* (New York: Lawrence Hill Books, 1993), 210–13, in which she deplores the confusion of bondage photographs and movies with "free speech."

15. Emerson's article, "Pornography and the First Amendment: A Reply to Professor MacKinnon," appeared in the *Yale Law & Policy Review*, Vol. 3, No. 1 (Fall 1984); Nat Hentoff, "Equal-Opportunity Banning," *Village Voice*, October 30, 1984.

16. For this and the following two paragraphs: Lisa Duggan, "Censorship in the Name of Feminism," *Village Voice*, October 16, 1984; Donnerstein, Daniel Linz, and Steve Penrod, *The Question of Pornography*, 1987: PsycINFO_Database Record © 2012 APA; MacKinnon, *Feminism Unmodified* (Cambridge, MA: Harvard University Press, 1987). Both the lower and appeals courts, presided over by conservative judges, agreed that violent pornography harmed women, but struck down the ordinance on First Amendment grounds (transcript of Dworkin interview, December 7, 1987, ADP/SLH).

17. Lisa Duggan, "Censorship in the Name of Feminism," *The Village Voice*, Oct. 16, 1984.

18. Dorchen Leidholdt to Alan Sears (E.D. of Commission), April 30, 1985; AD to "Friends," n. d. (Media Coalition), ADP/SLH. Andrea's testimony was transcribed, and she reprinted it in her book, *Letters from a War Zone*, 276–307. The discussion of Andrea's testimony that follows relies on the account in *Letters*.

19. The literature on the relationship between pornography and the First Amendment is vast. I list here only those articles and books that have most influenced my judgments: Mary Kate McGowan, "On Pornography: MacKinnon, Speech Acts, and 'False' Construction," *Hypatia*, Summer, 2005; Nick Cowen, "Millian Liberalism and Extreme Pornography," *American Journal of Political Science*, April 2016; Rebecca Whisnant, "Pornography and Pop Culture," *off our backs*, Vol. 37, No. 1 (2007); Danny Scoccia, "Can Liberals Support a Ban on Violent Pornography?," *Ethics*, July 1996; Catharine A. MacKinnon, *Only Words* (Harvard, 1993); Laura J. Lederer and Richard Delgado, *The Price We Pay* (Hill and Wang, 1995); Thomas I. Emerson, "Pornography and the First Amendment: A Reply to Professor Mackinnon," *Yale Law & Policy Review*, Fall, 1984; Pauline B. Bart and Margaret Jozsa, "Dirty Books, Dirty Films, and Dirty Data," in Lederer

and Delgado, *The Price We Pay*; Rosemarie Tong, "Pornography and Censorship," *Social Theory and Practice*, Spring 1982; Anti-Pornography Laws and First Amendment Values," *Harvard Law Review*, December 1984.

20. The 1868 "Hicklin test" in England offered a comprehensive definition of "obscenity" that was avoided when the United States in 1933 declared James Joyce's *Ulysses* not "obscene." In 1957 in *Roth v. U.S.*, the Supreme Court, discarding Hicklin, defined "obscenity" according to "whether to the average person, applying contemporary community standards, the dominant theme of the material taken as a whole appeals to prurient interest." The vague terminology of "community standards" and "prurient interest" continue to defy exactitude down to the present day.

21. In a speech, "Not a Moral Issue," at the University of Minnesota Law School in April 1985 (transcript in ADP/SLH), MacKinnon summarized the insufficiency of current standards: "liberalism has never understood that the free speech of men silences the free speech of women. . . . The first amendment says, 'Congress shall not abridge *the freedom of speech*' . . . [the assumption is] that which if unconstrained by government, *is* free. This tends to assume that some people are not systematically silenced *socially*, prior to government action."

22. Transcript of AD's speech to Upper Midwest Men's Conference, October 15, 1983, ADP/SLH.

23. AD to Dorothy ("Cookie") Teer, Teer Papers, RLD.

24. In the same month of April 1985, *Newsweek* (in the issue of March 18), ran its own feature article on "The War Against Pornography." It revealed a recent Gallup poll that showed "nearly two-thirds of those surveyed supported a ban on magazines, movies and video cassettes that feature sexual violence" and that roughly three-quarters of those surveyed agreed with the anti-porn feminists that sexually explicit material denigrates women and leads some people to sexual violence." But the poll also revealed that by a wide margin, non-violent porn had become accepted in American life, and with the advent of VCRs home porn proliferated. *Newsweek* also reported on the recent research findings of psychologists Edward Donnerstein and Neil Malamuth that "young men shown sexually violent films and then asked to judge a simulated rape trial are less likely to vote for conviction than those who haven't seen the films." They also found that male college students "who briefly watch porn report that 30 percent of the women they know would 'enjoy aggressively forced sex'"; as many as 57 percent indicated "some likelihood that they would commit a rape" if they knew they would not be caught. *Newsweek* also recounted a number of reputable recent studies documenting that 10–40 percent of men who watched violent porn subsequently attempted to re-enact it forcibly on their partners. For a slew of more recent studies further confirming the link between porn consumption and violence against women, see Gail Dines, *Pornland* (Boston: Beacon Press, 2010), especially pp. 87–88, 95–98, 117–18, 181–82.

25. AD to Suzanne Levine, March 9, 1985, ADP/SLH.

26. For this and the following three paragraphs: *In Harm's Way*, 13–17; AD to Valerie Harper, June 12, July 6, August 14, 1984; AD to Steinem, June 28, 1984; AD to Mikulski, July 5, 1984—all in ADP/SLH; various issues of *Sex & Justice*

(the newsletter of the Anti-pornography Task Group (which John Stoltenberg co-chaired) of the National Organization for Changing Men, especially Issues #1/June 1984 and #2/October 1984); MacKinnon, *Butterfly Politics*, 96–102, 360–4. Harkening back to the controversial 1982 Barnard Conference, Kitty denounced as false Carole Vance's claim (in "Negotiating Sex and Gender in the Attorney General's Commission on Pornography," in *Sex Exposed*, Lynne Segal and Mary McIntosh eds., [London: Virago Press, 1992]) that the Commission "decisively rejected their [anti-porn] remedies."

27. Both Andrea and Kitty predicted early on (1983) that if the pornography industry wasn't legally contained, it would massively expand, and that's precisely what has happened; it became "more visible and legitimate, hence less visible as pornography" (MacKinnon, *Butterfly Politics*, 206, 415–16; Dworkin, "Why Pornography Matters to Feminists," in *Letters from a War Zone*, 206; Rodney A. Smolla, *The First Amendment* (Carolina Academic Press, 1999); Smolla & Nimmer on Freedom of Speech Vol. 2, No. 10 (2009); Cheryl B. Preston, "The Misunderstood First Amendment and Our Lives Online," *Brigham Young University Studies*, Vol. 49, No. 1 (2010); Danny Scoccia, "Can Liberals Support a Ban on Violent Pornography," *Ethics*, Vol. 106, No. 4 (July 1996); Max Waltman, "Rethinking Democracy," *Political Research Quarterly*, Vol. 63, No. 1 (March 2010); Mary Kate McGowan, "On Pornography: MacKinnon, Speech Acts, and 'False' Construction," *Hypatia*, Vol. 20, No. 3 (Summer 2005); AD to Cathy Itzin, April 19, 1990; AD to Ann-Claire Anderson, August 31, 1990—copies in MacKinnon Papers, SLH; Catharine MacKinnon, *Only Words*, Harvard Univ. Press, 1996. For a book-length account generally unsympathetic to the Dworkin/MacKinnon position, see Donald Alexander Downs, *The New Politics of Pornography* (Chicago: University of Chicago Press, 1989).

28. Until the internet made pornography in all its varying forms widely available to the general public, a number of scholars had continued to contend with issues related to the subject. Part of the difficulty in attempting any coherent summary of the ongoing debate is not only its breadth and complexity but also the fact that the disputants, in stating their own positions, often ignore the counter-arguments already put forward by others involved in the argument. As a non-specialist, I can do little more here than give voice to at least some of issues I've encountered that from my limited perspective have not been satisfactorily addressed, let alone "answered." I think, for example, that the apparently varying effects of violent, nonviolent, and "nonviolent but degrading" pornography on male viewers remains ill-defined and murky (see, for example, Lynne Segal, "Pornography and Violence: What the 'Experts' Really Say," *Feminist Review*, No. 36, Autumn, 1990). Similarly, I'd like to see the feminist "anti-censorship" forces explain (rather than merely state) what they refer to as the "chilling effect," especially for sexual minorities, of a civil rights ordinance (see Frances Ferguson, "Pornography: The Theory," *Critical Inquiry*, Vol. 21, No. 3, Spring, 1995). We would also profit, I believe, from a detailed discussion of how to measure—or whether it is possible to measure with any confident precision—when a sexual exchange can be said to have achieved an acceptably "mutual," "equal," "consensual" level of tenderness, intimacy, trust, and pleasure. When we applaud the presence of certain ingredients (tenderness, mutuality, et al.) in a relationship, are we mistakenly conflating love with sex? (as the mainstream culture insistently has through time). If so, does

it not riskily follow that casual, sexual "hook-ups" become implicitly castigated, with lifetime monogamy, in contrast, being elevated as superior morality?

In regard to the *industry* of pornography, we need to know more than we currently do about what percentage of the industry is devoted, say, to "mutually pleasurable" rather than "degrading" imagery and what gestures or acts are or are not constitutive of female subordination. I understand that pornography (or art, or books) are among of the building blocks in creating social reality, but so are poverty and racism, and how or why do we prioritize our concerns? (see Cynthia A. Stark, "Is Pornography an Action? The Causal vs. the Conceptual View of Pornography's Harm," *Social Theory and Practice*, Vol. 23, No. 2 [Summer, 1997]). Perhaps the overarching question in need of further explication is the causal relationship between the representation of an action and the action itself, with particular reference (if possible) to *which* individuals are more likely than others to move, swiftly or otherwise, from viewing an image to carrying out an action.

I think we also need to introduce more than we have into the debate over pornography the scholarly strategies and findings from the discipline of media studies. As Gail Dines has put it, "Media scholars accept that images have some effect in the real world"—that images do, overtly and subliminally, shape how we view ourselves and others, and how we judge the morality of certain actions. Dines usefully employs the analogy of the imagery connected to the history of racism. She points out that "the Stepin Fetchit images didn't change the views of the average white person so much as they delivered to the white population ideas that were floating around in the culture"—namely, that blacks are lazy, shiftless, sex-crazed, and violence-prone—"in a form that was compelling, easy to understand—and even easier to get away with." We need to deal more than we have with Dines' compelling question: "If racist porn images can have a detrimental effect on people of color in general, then why can't images of women—black, white, Asian, Latina—being choked and ejaculated on while being called cunts have a negative effect on women of all colors?" (Dines, *Pornland*, Beacon, 2010, 81–2, 87–8).

Finally, it seems to me critical that we further clarify the relationship between the First and the Fourteenth Constitutional Amendments. As Shannon Gilreath has succinctly put the issue (in *The End of Straight Supremacy* [Cambridge, UK: Cambridge University Press, 2011]), the two amendments are sometimes complementary and sometimes competing. He points out that for a very long time, public signs adorned the American landscape announcing NO BLACKS SERVED HERE and WHITES ONLY. Those "speech acts," clearly discriminatory, are now outside the legal pale. "The courts," Gilreath writes (pp. 126–28), "have weighed the competing rights of the speaker [the First Amendment] with those of the people affected by such speech and have held that equality rights [the Fourteenth Amendment] "were more important than the right to unfettered speech." Gilreath concludes—persuasively, in my view—that when the constitutional commitments both to speech and equality collide, "equality should prevail as the subsequent and preeminent principle of liberty." Ideas contrary to equality—Kill the Nigger! Kill the Jew!—can still be expressed, but they become within the bounds of Constitutional challenge and regulation.

29. For this and the following two paragraphs: AD to Laurence Tribe, May 1, 1985; AD to Moorcock, April 9, 1987 (Cambridge), ADP/SLH; Rich, "We Don't

Have to Come Apart Over Pornography: A Statement by Adrienne Rich," *off our backs*, July 1985. Andrea's article "Against the Male Flood" is collected in her *Letters from a War Zone*, 253–75.

30. For this and the following three paragraphs: MacKinnon, "An Open Letter to Adrienne Rich," *off our backs*, Vol. 15, No. 9 (October 1985) (a draft dated July 4, 1985 is in ADP/SLH); transcript of AD's untitled, undated letter to Adrienne, ADP/SLH. Also relevant, though I've not excerpted it here, is MacKinnon, "Coming Apart: Feminists and the Conflict Over Pornography," *off our backs*, Vol. 15, No. 6, June 1985. If Adrienne responded to Andrea, we can't now know: their correspondence (part of the Adrienne Rich Papers at SLH) is closed until 2025.

31. MacKinnon and Dworkin, *In Harm's Way: The Pornography Civil Rights Hearings* (Harvard Univ. Press, 1997) (henceforth cited as *Harm's Way*).

32. See, for example, Jessa Crispin, *Why I Am Not a Feminist* (Melville House, 2017); Ariel Levy, *Female Chauvinist Pigs* (New York: Free Press, 2005); Jane Gerhard, *Desiring Revolution* (New York: Columbia University Press, 2001); Andi Zeisler, *We Were Feminists Once* (New York: Public Affairs, 2016); Anne G. Sabo, *After Pornified* (Zero Books, 2012); Robert Jensen, *Pornography and the End of Masculinity* (South End Press, 2007); Robert Jensen, *The End of Patriarchy* (Spinifex, 2017); Gail Dines, *Pornland* (Boston: Beacon Press, 2010); Rebecca Traister, *Good and Mad* (New York: Simon & Shuster, 2018); and Christopher N. Kendall's brilliant *Gay Male Pornography* (UBC Press, 2004). Michael Kimmel has provocatively suggested that "both FACT and WAP each had it half right: feminism was about [both] protecting women who were harmed [i.e., Dworkin and MacKinnon] and freeing women to explore their own lusts [i.e., FACT]. They always talked past one another, as they do today in the conversations about 'sex work' and 'prostitution' and 'trafficking'" (Kimmel to me, May 9, 2019).

33. For this and the following paragraph: Richard Dyer, "Male Gay Porn: Coming To Terms," *Jump Cut: A Review of Contemporary Media*, No. 30, March 1985, 27–9. Another gay male critic, Tom Waugh, also expressed his "solidarity in words and actions with women's rightful denunciation of pornography as an instrument of antifeminist backlash." Waugh insisted that "anti-patriarchal gay men still have an important contribution to make" to the feminist debate on sexuality (Waugh, "Men's Pornography, Gay vs. Straight," *Jump Cut*, No. 30, March 1985). If so, gay male porn may not be the best vehicle—as Christopher N. Kendall has recently, and powerfully, argued in *Gay Male Pornography* (UBC Press, 2004): "Gay male pornography . . . works to maintain gender roles by encouraging gay men to adopt an identity that valorizes male dominance . . . hence [it is] anti-woman and does . . . a great deal to ensure the survival of a system of gender inequality that is degrading and dehumanizing and that reinforces, by sexualizing, the power dynamics that ensure systematic inequality" (p. 129).

34. B. Ruby Rich's remarkable review essay "Feminism and Sexuality in the 1980s" is in *Feminist Studies* Vol. 12, No. 3 (Fall 1986), 525–61; the Samois anthology was published by Alyson, 1982; *Against Sadomasochism*, edited by Robin Ruth Linden, et al., was published by Frog in the Well Press, 1982.

35. Reading Rich and MacDonald, I was reminded of the study I came across long ago (and may not remember with entire accuracy) that during the Blitz over England during World War II, far more men had nervous breakdowns than

did women; Scott MacDonald, "Confessions of a Feminist Porn Watcher," *Film Quarterly* 36 (Spring 1983); see also Philip Weiss, "Forbidden Pleasures: A Taste for Porn in a City of Women," *Harper's Magazine*, March 1986, 68–72.

36. AD to Jalna Hammer, March 5, 1986, ADP/SLH; *Sex & Justice*, March 1986; AD to Moorcock, June 7, 1987; transcript of Brownmiller interview with AD, August 10, 1998, ADP/SLH.

9: Writing

1. For this and following paragraph: Julie Melrose to Judy Klemsrud, September 4, 1985 (still and chill), "Andrea Dworkin Fights Back," *New Directions for Women*, Nov/Dec 1985.

2. AD to Charlee Hoyt, July 17, 1985, ADP/SLH.

3. For this and the following paragraph: AD to Linda Zlotnick, February 28, September 21, 1986; AD to Therese Stanton, August 14, 1985; AD to Valerie Harper, May 28, June 12, 1985, August 14, 19, 1986; AD to Gerry Spence, April 4, 1986, ADP/SLH; *The Philadelphia Inquirer*, July 21, 1985.

4. For Bourbon Street: https://chieforganizer.org/2019/06/13/the-story -behind-the-iconic-andrea-dworkin-bullhorn-picture/?fbclid=IwARODODEX OnoDSdhB6cQrQlkgQxcpzMXLq51JjnV4_clXz21QMpuvPpDUMoc. Andrea told the *New York Times* reporter, Judy Klemsrud, that "The National Organization for Women is incredibly cowardly and timid on the issue [of pornography] because they don't want to alienate their liberal supporters." She added a still more encompassing denunciation of liberals: "When the so-called liberals who claim to care about torture in prison in right-wing countries bring themselves to understand that a woman being tortured for entertainment is also a violation of women's rights, I'll be very grateful" ("Joining Hands in the Fight Against Pornography," *New York Times*, August 26, 1985). Klemsrud told Andrea and John that the *Times* refused to let her say that they were lesbian and gay (Stoltenberg to me, June 21, 2019). Andrea characterized the Wyoming postponement as "bizarre. . . . No new date has been set yet and even the place of the trial is uncertain. . . . Meanwhile *Screw* has taken over where *Hustler* left off; and what they are doing to me is vile beyond any imagining" (AD to Susanne Kappeler, August 16, 1986, ADP/SLH).

5. For this and the following paragraph: AD to Gerry Spence, August 30, 1985; AD to Charlee Hoyt, July 17, 1985; AD to Gale O'Brien, August 14, 1985—all in ADP/SLH; *Sojourner*, December 1985; Stoltenberg editorial, Issue #4/March 1986, *Sex & Justice*.

6. "Sex Busters," *TIME* magazine's cover story, July 21, 1986; *New York Times*, April 15, 1986.

7. For this and the following paragraph: FACT "Briefing," [n.d., 1985], Dorothy Allison Papers, RLD; David M. Edwards, "Politics and Pornography," http: //home.earthlink.net/-durangeodave/html/writing/Censorship.htm. See especially Whitney Strub's persuasive argument in his *Perversion for Profit* (198–206) that the Commission's hearings were stacked "toward anti-porn witnesses"—a charge weakened by his determined mockery (see, for example, p. 203) of female witnesses who felt they'd been personally harmed through pornography. Though

Strub's research is admirably comprehensive and his insight rich, I believe he's mistaken in describing the willingness of "anti-porn feminism . . . to call on the power of the state in the name of suppression" (Strub, *Perversion for Profit*, 214); certainly that mischaracterizes the MacKinnon/Dworkin position. Nor is he accurate in implying (215) that Andrea muted her criticism of capitalism—which she never did—to appease her "conservative allies." Strub's further characterization of Andrea's "publishing profile" as with "mass-market imprints and prestigious academic publishers (p. 247) is strangely at odds with her actual struggle to get published *at all*.

8. For this and the following discussion of the Commission's report: Carol Anne Douglas, "Pornography: The Meese Report," in *off our backs*, Vol. 16, No. 8, August/September 1986; AD to Theresa Funiociello, June 12, 1985, ADP/SLH; Barbara Ehrenreich, "The Story of Ed," *Mother Jones*, October 1986; *Time* magazine, June 21, 1986. Two of the four women on the eleven-member panel—Judith Becker, professor of clinical psychology at Columbia and Ellen Levine, editor of *Woman's Day* magazine—dissented from the report. They disagreed with the conclusion that a clear-cut causal link between violent pornography and violence against women had been found and further argued that "no self-respecting investigator would accept conclusions" from a commission that had done no original research.

9. Walter Kendrick, *The Secret Museum* (Berkeley: University of California Press, 1987).

10. David M. Edwards, *Politics and Pornography*.

11. Edward Donnerstein, the other expert whose testimony both sides in the debate would cite, later made a similar point: he stressed "that his studies showed the effects of violent images on attitudes, not the effects of sexually explicit materials on behavior" (as quoted in Lisa Duggan, "Censorship in the Name of Feminism," *Village Voice*, October 16, 1984).

12. *Ice and Fire* (London: Secker & Warburg, 1986), 47–48.

13. For this and the following three paragraphs: AD, *Intercourse* (New York: Basic Books, 1987), 83, 135, 156–60, 230, 246–7.

14. Susan Brownmiller to AD, n.d. [October 1986], ADP/SLH; AD to Brownmiller, October 16, 1986, Brownmiller Papers. Perhaps contributing was Brownmiller's negative reaction to the ordinance campaign. In regard to the Minneapolis ordinance, as she wrote to me years later, "I thought it was terrible and unconstitutional, and told her [Andrea] that I would not support it." Brownmiller to me, December 9, 2019.

15. AD to Leah Fritz, April 21, 1987; AD to Michael Moorcock, March 19, April 9, 1987, ADP/SLH.

16. AD to Gerry Spence, May 3, 1986, ADP/SLH; Marilyn French, "A Lyrical Novel of Violence and Exploitation," *Ms.*, April 1987; Louise Armstrong, "Publish and Be Damned," *Women's Review of Books*, May 1986; Kitty MacKinnon to AD, August 4, 1983, ADP/SLH.

17. For this and the following paragraph: *New York Times*, May 3, 24, 1987. MacKinnon wrote a letter to the *Times* protesting the Sternhell review

(MacKinnon to Iacovelli, May 6, 1987, MacKinnon Papers, SLH).

18. For this and the following two paragraphs: *The Nation*, May 30, August 1/18, 1987; AD to Erica Jong, June 8, 1987; AD to Jan Raymond, June 12, 1987; AD to Linda Steele, June 16, 1987; Steele to AD, June 22, 1987, ADP/SLH.

19. AD to Raymond, June 12, 1987; AD to Moorcock and Steele, July 28, 1987; AD to Elaine Markson, July 23, 1987, ADP/SLH.

20. AD to Moorcock, April 9, June 12, 1987; AD to Sarah LeFanu, June 12, 1987 (garbage), ADP/SLH. *New Directions for Women*, July/Aug 1987; *Reader* (Chicago), October 9, 1987; Paul Seidman to AD, July 1, 1987; AD to Seidman, July 8, 1987, ADP/SLH; *Sojourner*, July, September, December, 1987.

21. The review by Roy Porter in the *London Review of Books* (June 25, 1987) was even more venomous than that in the *New York Times*; Porter called her "a sick lady" who writes "offensive, abominable crap." Lynn Rosen interview with AD, *New Directions for Women*, July/August 1987; MacKinnon to AD, August 4, 1983, ADP/SLH.

22. AD to Alice Schwarzer, July 28, August 2, August 10, 1987; Anne Soyland to AD, August 7, 1987; AD to Agnete Strom, August 18, 1987, ADP/SLH.

23. For this and the following two paragraphs: AD to Linda Steele, August 3, 24, 1987, ADP/SLH. Steinem wasn't the only political friend from earlier times that Andrea still saw. She and Robin Morgan tended to have dinner together roughly once a month and, Andrea wrote, "it always brings me up" (AD to Moorcock, August 10, 1987, ADP/SLH). She also—"at the instigation of Phyllis Chesler"— saw Kate Millett now and then, which she did not enjoy. She described one such evening in a letter to Linda Steele, August 24, 1987, ADP/SLH): "I venerate Kate for all she has taught me; but she has retreated into an almost mindless leftism, it's like autism isn't it? Kate [had] signed the FACT brief even though she didn't *read* it—say 'anti-censorship' and she signs. Her friends have tried to get her to understand what she's done wrong. Kitty has spent much time with her. I haven't the heart."

Subsequently, Andrea and Erica Jong tangled briefly over a misunderstanding that they patched up rather quickly, but Erica did make it clear that she opposed the ordinance route. She did not believe, she wrote Andrea, that it was "depictions of violence against women that *creates* violence against women, because the deep sexism of our culture needs many broader & more far-reaching remedies. . . . We need equal pay for equal work. We need the end of sexual stereotyping in the media. We need health care for women & children." (Erica Jong to AD, April 4, 1993; AD to Jong, April 13, May 25, 1993, ADP/SLH).

24. AD to Rosemary McIntosh, September 7, 1987; AD to Moorcock and Steele, September 4, 1987; AD to Gerry Spence, September 7, 1987, ADP/SLH; *Dworkin v. Hustler Magazine, Inc.*, 668 F. Supp. 1408 (C.D. Cal. 1987).

25. For this and the following four paragraphs: AD to Moorcock, November 15, December 10, 1987; AD to Cathy Itzin, December 15, 21, 1987; AD to Alice Schwarzer, August 2, 1987; AD to Mark and Eva Dworkin, January 25, 1988; AD to Linda Steele, August 24, 1987; AD to Kathy Norris, February 8, 1988; —all in ADP/SLH; AD to Robin Morgan, March 2, 1988, Robin Morgan Papers, RLD;

AD to Cookie Teer, December 3, 1986 (England), Teer Papers, RLD.

26. For this and the following three paragraphs: AD to Sarah LeFanu, November 16, 1987; AD to Moorcock, March 19, 1987, December 23, 1987, January 21, March 20, 1988, ADP/SLH.

27. AD to Moorcock, June 12, 1987, February 26, March 20, 1988; AD to Suzanne Kappeler, December 29, 1987, ADP/SLH.

28. For this and the following paragraph: AD to Moorcock, February 26, 1988, ADP/SLH; AD to Robin Morgan, March 2, 1988, Morgan to AD, n.d., Morgan Papers, RLD.

29. AD to Morgan, March 2, 1988; AD to Moorcock, April 6, 1988; AD to Linda Steele, May 8, 1988, ADP/SLH.

30. Conversation with John Stoltenberg, February 18, 2019. See Andrea's vivid description of life in the East Village in *Ice and Fire*, 106–9.

31. For this and the following two paragraphs: AD to Valerie Harper, August 20, 1988; AD to Kathy Norris, August 20, 1988; AD to Suzanne Kappeler, August 30, 1988, ADP/SLH.

32. For this and the following paragraph: AD to Valerie Harper, August 20, 1988; AD to Cathy Itzin, September 26, 1988; AD to Moorcock and Steele, September 6, 1988—all in ADP/SLH.

33. AD to Lesley Bryce, November 9, 1988; AD to Alice Shalvi, December 10, 1988; AD to Cathy Itzin, December 29, 1988, ADP/SLH.

34. For this and the following four paragraphs: conversation with John Stoltenberg, February 18, 2019; AD to Sarah LeFanu, November 16, 1987; AD to Jane Wood, May 1, 1989, ADP/SLH; AD, "What Battery Really Is," reprinted as the last piece in the American edition of *Letters from a War Zone* (New York: Dutton, 1989), 329–34.

10: Mercy

1. AD to Sharon Doubiago, July 17, 1989; AD to Moorcock and Steele, July 17, 1989, ADP/SLH.

2. AD to Kathy Norris and David Dwyer, August 21, 1989; AD to Moorcock and Steele, August 28, December 4, 27; AD to Charles Morgan, July 28, 1989, ADP/SLH. Bosworth's affidavit is in ADP/SLH.

3. For this and the following three paragraphs: AD to Charles Morgan, July 28, 1989; AD to Moorcock and Steele, August 28, 1989; AD to Norris and Dwyer, August 21, 1989, ADP/SLH; *Penthouse*, April 1987.

4. For this and the following paragraph: AD to Moorcock and Steele, December 4, 1989, April 17, May 21, 1990; AD to Susanne Kappeler, May 29, 1990, ADP/SLH. A copy of the settlement agreement, dated May 17, 1990, is in ADP/SLH.

5. AD to Kappeler, May 29, 1990, ADP/SLH. Similarly, when John Herman, the Houghton Mifflin editor, wanted to do *Mercy* in the United States, the publisher "on principle" refused (AD to Moorcock and Steele, March 8, 1990, ADP/SLH).

6. AD to Moorcock and Steele, May 21, 1990, ADP/SLH. A sample of the divergent reviews: *Publishers Weekly*, July 25, 1991 (*Mercy* "brilliantly captures the narrator's mental and physical degradation") vs. the *Tribune*, October 5, 1990 (" . . . breathless . . . sometimes clumsy"). For two of the more considered, yet ultimately negative reviews, see Wendy Steiner, "Declaring War on Men," *New York Times*, September 15, 1991; and Roz Kaveney, "*Mercy* by Andrea Dworkin," *Feminist Review*, No. 38 (Summer, 1991), who accused Andrea of "messianic fantasies," thinking of herself as "Everywoman," and claiming superior moral insight.

7. The "humanizing" argument derives from Marisa Anne Pagnattaro, "The Importance of Andrea Dworkin's 'Mercy': Mitigating Circumstances and Narrative Jurisprudence," *Frontiers: A Journal of Women Studies*, Vol. 19, No. 1; Michael Moorcock, "Political Gets Too Personal," *New Statesman*, May 27, 1988.

8. For a sampling of the reviews: *Independent*, October 13, 1990; *Literary Review*, October 1990; *Tribune*, October 5, 1990; *Sunday Correspondent*, October 7, 1990; *Sunday Times*, October 14, 1990. See also, AD, five-page typescript, "The Reviews of *Mercy* in the United Kingdom: I Answer," ADP/SLH.

9. Martha C. Nussbaum, *Sex and Social Justice* (especially ch. 9: "Rage and Reason") (Oxford, UK: Oxford University Press, 1999). Nussbaum had separately reviewed *Mercy* in the *Boston Review of Books*, and Andrea had sent her a scorching letter in response: "You don't need to like my work to write about it in a way that is not thoroughly and absolutely insulting" (AD to Nussbaum, March 14, 1994, copy in MacKinnon Papers, SLH).

10. For two additional sympathetic readings of Andrea, see Rosa A. Eberly, *Citizen Critics: Literary Public Spheres* (especially ch. 5: "Andrea Dworkin's *Mercy*: Pain and Silence in the 'War Zone'"); and Cindy Jenefsky with Ann Russo, *Without Apology: Andrea Dworkin's Art and Politics* (Westview Press, 1998).

11. https://drive.google.com/drive/folders/11KL14jhWQjjuWz4Gptlvpj5lnrw7uQ_z

12. Walter Kendrick, *The Secret Museum* (Berkeley: University of California Press, 1987).

13. For this and the following paragraph: Rebecca Traister, *Good and Mad: The Revolutionary Power of Women's Anger* (New York: Simon & Schuster, 2018). See also Soraya Chemaly, *Rage Becomes Her: The Power of Women's Anger* (New York: Atria, 2018).

14. For this and the following paragraph: AD to Linda Steele, August 17, 1990, ADP/SLH; "Andrea Dworkin Interview," *off our backs*, January 1990; AD to Robin Morgan, February 8, 1990, Morgan Papers, RDL. In regard to her own self-identification as "lesbian," as early as 1978 when an interviewer (Andrea herself) remarked, "There are a lot of rumors about your lesbianism. No one quite seems to know what you do with whom," Andrea's response was "Good" ("Nervous Interview," in AD, *Letters from a War Zone*, 59). Many years later, Ariel Levy provocatively quoted one of Andrea's "closest friends" as saying, "In 30-plus years of knowing her, I've never heard of a single romance with a woman—not one." Levy herself comments that in Andrea's writings, "there are too many smoldering descriptions of heterosexual sex to count, but the mentions of lesbianism are either bloodless . . . or funny" (http://nymag.com/nymetro/news/people/features/11907/index4.html#print). *Behaviorally*, we have plenty of evidence of Andrea's sexual experiences up through the late seventies, but thereafter, aside from a very

few hints, there's almost no evidence of a lesbian romance or sexual encounter. It may be that Andrea's steady increase in weight in the later years of her life was related, as is often the case, to the earlier sexual trauma with Iwan; as the old chestnut has it: "the overweight girl is the overlooked girl." But we need to be cautious about equating *behavior* with *feelings*. If Andrea at some point stopped having sexual *feelings* for other women—or indeed sexual feelings in general—she never said so.

15. AD to Moorcock, December 27, 1989; AD to Jane Wood, January 1, 1990; AD to Florence King, February 16, 1990, ADP/SLH.

16. AD, "Terror, Torture, and Resistance," keynote speech in May 1991 to the Canadian Mental Health Conference on "Women and Mental Health"; first published in *Canadian Woman Studies; Les Cahiers de la Femme*, fall 1991, Vol. 12, No. 1.

17. For this and the following paragraph: AD to Mark and Eva Dworkin, January 25, 1988; AD to Moorcock and Steele, December 4, 1989, ADP/SLH.

18. For this and the following paragraph: AD to Harry Dworkin, January 10; AD to Joyce Keener, March 19; AD to Linda Steele, November 18; AD to Mark Dworkin, November 23, December 16, 23—all 1991, all ADP/SLH; AD to Moorcock, February 1, 28, March 4, May 10; AD to Florence King, May 13—all 1992, all ADP/SLH; AD to Leah Fritz, December 28, 1992, Leah Fritz Papers, RLD.

19. For this and the following four paragraphs: AD to Moorcock and Steele, September 1, 1992; AD to Agnete Stromn, September 15, 1992; AD to Scheerer and Reemtsma, December 22, 1992, ADP/SLH.

20. The key documents detailing the dispute are AD to Markson, September 17, 18, 30, 1992; Judith Herman to Simon, September 29, 1992; AD to Moorcock and Steele, October 1, 1992; Melissa Farley to Downer, October 19, 1992; AD to Susan Hunter, October 25, 1992; Chalker/Downer/Hekert to "Dear Friends," November 16, 1992; Wendy Smith to AD, January 25, 1993; Barbara Ehrenreich to AD, March 5, 1993; Chalker and Downer to Gloria Steinem, September 15, 1993; Chalker and Downer to AD, February 27, 1994; AD to Chalker and Downer, November 5, 1993, March 24, 1994—all in ADP/SLH; *New York Observer*, October 26, 1992.

21. AD to Moorcock, February 28, 1992, ADP/SLH.

22. John Irving, "Pornography and the New Puritans," *New York Times*, March 29, 1992.

23. AD, "Pornography and the New Puritans: Letters From Andrea Dworkin and Others," *New York Times*, May 3, 1992; Gail Dines, *Pornland: How Porn Has Hijacked Our Sexuality* (Boston: Beacon Press, 2010), especially chapter five. Dines also points out, importantly, that contrary to critics who characterize the Dworkin/MacKinnon position as "watching pornography leads men to rape women," neither of them ever "saw porn in such simplistic terms. Rather, both argued that porn has a complicated and multilayered effect on male sexuality, and that rape, rather than simply being caused by porn, is a cultural practice that has been woven into the fabric of a male-dominated society" (page 85). For a discussion of the research up to 1993 linking porn consumption and violence against women, see Catherine Itzin in *New Statesman & Society*, January 31, 1993, ADP/SLH. For

the post-1993 period, Dines primarily cites the following studies: Neil Mala-muth, Tamara Addison, and Mary Koss, "Pornography and Sexual Aggression: Are There Reliable Effects and Can We Understand them?" *Annual Review of Sex Research* Vol. 11 (2000); Pamela Paul, *Pornified: How Pornography Is Transforming Our Lives, Our Relationships, and Our Families* (New York: Time Books, 2005); and Dolf Zillman, "Effects of Prolonged Consumption of Pornography," in *Pornography: Research Advances and Policy Considerations*, Zillman and Jennings Bryant eds. (Erlbaum, 1989). Additionally, there is Max Waltman's notable summation of the data in "Rethinking Democracy: Legal Challenges to Pornography and Sex Inequality in Canada and the United States, *Political Research Quarterly*, Vol. 63, No. 1 (March 2010)—henceforth "Waltman, 'Rethinking Democracy.'" For an invaluable discussion of the roots of the ideological division between pro- and anti-pornography feminists, see Ronald J. Berger, Patricia Searles, and Charles E. Cottle, "Ideological Contours of the Contemporary Pornography Debate: Divisions and Alliances," *Frontiers: A Journal of Women Studies*, Vol. 11, No. 2/3 (1990).

24. AD to Erica Jong, March 26, 1993, ADP/SLH; Waltman, "Rethinking Democracy," 231. For more detail, see Carolyn Bronstein, *Battling Pornography: The American Feminist Anti-Pornography Movement, 1976–1986* (Cambridge, UK: Cambridge University Press, 2011), and Brenda Cossman et al., *Bad Attitudes on Trial: Pornography, Feminism and the Butler Decision* (Toronto: University of Toronto Press, 1997). For a more negative assessment of the effects of the *Butler* decision, see Cossman, Bell, Gotell, Ross, *Bad Attitude/s on Trial: Pornography, Feminism, and the Butler Decision* (Univ. of Toronto Press, 1997). In her brilliant article, "A Sensible Anti-porn Feminism" (*Ethics*, July 2007, 674–715), A.W. Eaton has dissected the points of similarity and difference between pro- and anti-porn feminists with illuminating skill.

25. A copy of the conference report, *The Sex Panic*, with highlights from the proceedings, is in the Ellen Willis Papers, SLH.

26. For further distinctions along these lines, see Alexandra G. Bennett, "Theory to Practice: Catharine MacKinnon, Pornography, and Canadian Law," *Modern Language Studies*, Vol. 27, No. 3/4 (Autumn/Winter, 1997); Berger, Searles, and Cottle, "Ideological Contours of the Contemporary Pornography Debate: Divisions and Alliances," *Frontiers: A Journal of Women Studies*, Vol. 11, No. 2/3 (1990); and, in particular, Nancy Whittier's incisive article, "Rethinking Coalitions: Anti-Pornography Feminists, Conservatives, and Relationships between Collaborative Adversarial Movements," *Social Problems*, Vol. 61, No. 2 (May 2014).

27. For this and next two paragraphs: MacKinnon to Jennifer Brown, January 7; AD to "Naomi," September 28; AD to Michele Landsberg, December 6; AD to Steinem, December 6; AD to Kathleen Mahoney, December 6 (twice); MacKinnon to AD, December 6, 16; AD to MacKinnon, December 7—all 1993 ADP/SLH; MacKinnon to Michael Levitas, January 1, 1994 (gay/lesbian), ADP/SLH; AD keynote speech at October 28–30, 1992, Austin, Texas conference, ADP/SLH; *New York Times*, December 4, 1993.

28. For this and the following two paragraphs: AD to Erin Shaw (LEAF staff lawyer), April 29, 1991, Susan Brownmiller Papers, RLD. For some of the tensions that developed between Andrea and Kitty over the *Butler* decision, see AD

NOTES TO PAGES 248–256

to Kitty, May 8, 25, August 7, 14, 1994; Kitty to AD, May 23, August 13, 14, 1994, ADP/SLH.

29. STATEMENT BY CATHARINE A. MACKINNON AND ANDREA DWORKIN REGARDING CANADIAN CUSTOMS AND LEGAL APPROACHES TO PRONOGRAPHY, six-page typescript, ADP/SLH. See also Michele Landsberg, "Supreme Court Porn Ruling Is Ignored," *Toronto Star*, December 14, 1993; Robin Morgan to *New York Times*, February 2, 1995, Morgan Papers, RLD. There is also considerable correspondence in ADP/SLH between Andrea and Kitty, especially between May and August 1994, discussing the issues at stake and the wording of the statement.

30. AD to Michael Levitas (*Times*), December 27, 1993, ADP/SLH.

11: Prelude to Israel

1. AD, *Heartbreak: The Political Memoir of a Feminist Militant* (New York: Basic Books, 2002); "Israel: Whose Country Is It Anyway?," originally published in *Ms.*, September/October 1990, and reprinted in *Life and Death: Unapologetic Writings on the Continuing War Against Women* (New York: The Free Press, 1997), 217–39.

2. For this and the following two paragraphs: AD, transcript of nine-page "The Sexual Mythology of Anti-Semitism," ADP/SLH; AD, "Israel: Whose Country Is It Anyway?"; AD to Mark Dworkin, December 23, 1991, ADP/SLH.

3. For this and the following two paragraphs: "Take No Prisoners," *The Guardian*, May 12, 2000.

4. For this and the following five paragraphs: Jil Clark interview with AD, *Gay Community News*, Vol. 8, No.1 (July 19, 1980).

5. AD to Moorcock and Steele, July 19, 1993, ADP/SLH.

6. AD to Moorcock and Steele, June 21, 1993; AD, "Aftermath" (ms.), ADP/SLH.

7. For this and the following paragraph: AD's proposal to the Diana Foundation, and the correspondence surrounding the grant are in the Merle Hoffman papers, RLD.

8. AD, "Prostitution and Male Supremacy" (ms.), and "Pornography Happens to Women" (ms.) 1993/4, ADP/SLH. Both are reprinted in AD, *Life and Death*.

9. John Stoltenberg letter to "Dear Friends," May 1994, ADP/SLH. John had long been part of the Task Force on Pornography of the National Organization for Men Against Sexism (as of 1990 known as NOMAS, the National Organization for Changing Men); he had also been active on behalf of local efforts to pass the ordinance (http://nomas.org/history/).

10. For the next section: AD, "The Real Pornography of a Brutal War Against Women," *Los Angeles Times*, September 5, 1993; "The U.S. Holocaust Memorial Museum: Is Memory Male?, published in *Ms.*, November/December 1994; and the forty-page manuscript version ("Pictures at an Exhibition: The United States Holocaust Museum") in ADP/SLH. All quotes, unless otherwise indicated, are from the manuscript version.

11. Andrea was finally able to print "The ACLU: Bait and Switch" in her 1993 collection, *Letters from a War Zone* (New York: Lawrence Hill Books, 1993).

12. For this and the following paragraph: Diana E.H. Russell, "Nadine Strossen: The Pornography Industry's Wet Dream," *On the Issues*, summer 1995. For another insightful anti-Strossen review, see Mark Hussey writing separately in the same issue (summer, 1995) of *On the Issues*. Hussey particularly emphasized a point Andrea had long stressed about the class dimension—who did or did not have access—of the free speech issue: "the abstract principle of absolute freedom of speech will tend to work to the advantage of those whose speech is already privileged by the gendered social relations that exist."

13. Robin Morgan to the *New York Times*, February 2, 1995, Morgan Papers, RLD; AD to Steinem, December 6, 1993, ADP/SLH. In an interview with Vance Lehakuhl (*Z*, May 1995) and in an article for *USA Today* (January 12, 1995), Strossen reiterates most of the same views, though in a still less nuanced way. For example: "a causal connection has *never* been established" between porn and violence toward women"; the MacDworkinites' view is "that *all* sex is inherently degrading to women"; "it is more important than ever for the public to understand the link between the pro-censorship feminists and the right wing." And yet again, this time in *USA Today*: "Anti-pornography feminists believe sex itself is degrading to women"; the MacDworkinites "are a reincarnation of puritanical, Victorian notions that feminists have long tried to consign to the dust"; "the pro-censorship feminists have tried to distance themselves from traditional conservatives like Jesse Helms . . . but both groups are united by their common hatred of sexual expression and a fondness for censorship."

14. For this and the following two paragraphs: AD, "Trapped in a Pattern of Pain Where No One Can Help," "In Nicole Brown Simpson's Words," and "Domestic Violence: Trying to Flee" appeared consecutively in the June 26, 1994, January 29, 1995, and October 8, 1995, issues of the *Los Angeles Times*. Andrea reprinted them in *Life and Death*, The Free Press, 1997, 41–50.

15. Hanna Rosin, "The Larry Flynt Revival," *The New Republic*, January 5 & 12, 1997; Gloria Steinem, "Hollywood Cleans Up Hustler," op-ed *New York Times*, January 7, 1997; AD to Susan Brownmiller, January 9, 1997, Brownmiller Papers, RLD.

16. AD to Steinem, October 15, 1997 (Duffy), ADP/SLH; Preface to *Life and Death*, xvii.

17. AD to MacKinnon, March 5, 1995, MacKinnon Papers, SLH.

12: Scapegoat

1. AD, "What Feminist Jurisprudence Means to Me" (ms.), February 27, 1998, ADP/SLH.

2. AD, "Dear Bill and Hillary," *Guardian of London*, January 29, 1998.

3. For this and the following paragraph: John Stoltenberg to "Dear Friends," September 1998; AD, "the meaning of feminism to me now" (ms.), ADP/SLH;

transcript of Brownmiller interview with AD, August 10, 1998 (internet), ADP/SLH.

4. Curiously, in her vast bibliography Andrea never mentions the important 1997 book, *Unheroic Conduct*, by Daniel Boyarin, a towering figure in Talmudic Studies, whose basic findings agree with her views on the shifting ideal of Jewish manhood. It's hard to avoid the sense, deeply touching, that Andrea's zealous scholarship is somehow a reflection of and compensation for her father's thwarted ambition to complete his doctorate; her book can be incidentally seen as a way of fulfilling his dream—awarding him full accreditation.

5. AD to Cookie Teer, April 18, 1999 (cold), ADP/SLH; John Stoltenberg, *Aftermath: Andrea Dworkin's Last Rape*, http://archive.feministtimes.com/andrea-dworkins-last-rape/.

6. The account combines Beth Ribet's "First Year: An Interview with John Stoltenberg," March 11, 2006 (http://www.andreadworkin.net/memorial/stoltinterview.html) with Stoltenberg, "My Life with Andrea Dworkin," courtesy Stoltenberg; Stoltenberg, *Aftermath*, http://archive.feministtimes.com/andrea-dworkins-last-rape/. See also, Ariel Levy, "The Prisoner of Sex," *New York*: http://nymag.com/nymetro/news/people/features/11907/index4.html#print.

7. For this and the following paragraph: *The Guardian*, June 2, 2000; *The New Statesman*, June 5, 2000.

8. Catherine Bennett, "Doubts About Dworkin," *The Guardian*, June 7, 2000.

9. Richard Bernstein, "Confronting the Barbarity of Hatred," *New York Times*, July 13, 2000.

10. *The Times*, March 2, 2001; AD, thirteen-page ms. "Landscape of the Ordinary: Violence Against Women"; Robin Morgan to AD, April 9, 2001; Morgan notation May 7, 2001; Morgan to AD, June 17, 2002; Morgan to Stoltenberg, July 9, 2002—all in Robin Morgan Papers, RLD.

11. Ariel Levy, "The Prisoner of Sex," http://nymag.com/mymetro/news/people/features/11907. For the account that follows, the essential source is: AD, "Through the Pain Barrier," https://www.theguardian.com/books/2005/apr23/features.weekend

12. In November 1999, John got a position as managing editor of *Golf Digest Woman*, and the benefits took effect just in time to cover Andrea's hospitalization costs (Stoltenberg to me, June 21, 2019).

13. Beth Ribet, "First Year: An Interview with John Stoltenberg," March 11, 2006, http://www.andreadworkin.net/memorial/stoltinterview.html.

14. David Frum had a more mixed reaction to the evening: "I can't say I was charmed. But despite myself, I was impressed. Dworkin was a woman of deep and broad reading . . . her mind ranged free . . . I'll just say that although I would never, ever have expected to think so: She'll be missed" (*New York Times*, "Week in Review," April 17, 2005).

15. Beth Ribet interview with Stoltenberg, March 11, 2006: http://andreadworkin.net/memorial/stoltinterview.html; Stoltenberg to me, June 28, 2019.

16. The manuscript is not in SLH; my copy, courtesy of John Stoltenberg, is John's excerpted version, which he retitled *Aftermath* and (as I've mentioned earlier) had been edited for the stage by Adam Thorburn. The staged reading was performed seven times in New York City in 2014, and nine times in Montreal in 2015 (https://howlround.com/directing-andrea-dworkins-aftermath). "My Suicide" has also been excerpted in Johanna Fateman and Amy Scholder, *Last Days at Hot Slit* (Semiotext(e), 2019), 375–93.

17. For one of the more egregious recent examples of the ongoing mockery and misinterpretation, see Erica West, "The Pitfalls of Radical Feminism" (https://jacobinmag.com/2017/radical-feminism-second-wave-class), in which she characterizes Dworkin and MacKinnon as "relying on the state for censorship"— a total misreading of the model ordinance—and being "noticeably silent on the question of racism" (a claim easily disproven by even a cursory reading of Andrea's essays). Moreover, a prominent thread of "third-wave feminism"— exemplified in the work of Katie Roiphe, *The Morning After* (New York: Little Brown, 1993) and Rene Denfield, *The New Victorians* (New York: Warner, 1995)—has also continued to single out Dworkin, MacKinnon, and Robin Morgan as representative of "victim feminists" with an anti-sex agenda, in contrast to their own focus on expanding sexual possibilities for women and treating sexual pleasure as a positive good. Their analysis manages simultaneously to seriously misinterpret Dworkin/MacKinnon/Morgan and to ignore such decidedly pro-sex feminists of the second wave as Susie Bright and Gayle Rubin. For an antidote to Roiphe/Denfield, see Astrid Henry's astute analysis in *Not My Mother's Sister: Generational Conflict and Third-Wave Feminism* (Bloomington: Indiana University Press, 2004); as well as Andi Zeisler's tart, insightful *We Were Feminists Once* (New York: Public Affairs, 2016) for its reminder to the third wave "that while feminist movements seek to change systems, marketplace feminism prioritizes individuals." Alice Echols, in turn, has emphasized an additional concern: "Those of us who teach college are witnessing a sea change on our campuses as students mobilize for greater protection from all manner of danger, sometimes including our own dangerous ideas. Feminists are not the only students insisting on a less discomfiting curriculum, one that comes with trigger warnings and safe rooms, but they have sometimes played an outsized role in such efforts" (Echols, "Retrospective: Tangled Up in Pleasure and Danger," *Signs*, Vol. 42, No. 1 (2016).

Recently, some generous (and prominent) assessments of Andrea's role in the feminist movement have been appearing, beginning with Gail Dines, *Pornland* (Boston: Beacon Press, 2010), and then—primarily in response to the appearance of Johanna Fateman and Amy Scholder's anthology of Andrea's writing, *Last Days at Hot Slit* (semiotext(e), 2019)—Lauren Oyler, "Sex Ed: How to Read Andrea Dworkin," *The New Yorker*, April 1, 2019; Michelle Goldberg, "Not the Fun Kind of Feminism," *New York Times*, February 24, 2019; Moira Donegan, "Sex During Wartime: The Return of Andrea Dworkin's Radical Vision," *BOOKFORUM*, February/March 2019; Jennifer Szalai, "A New Light for a Feminist and Her Work," *New York Times*, March 13, 2019; Julie Bindel, "Why Andrea Dworkin Is the Radical, Visionary Feminist We Need in Our Terrible Times," April 16, 2019;

Jeremy Lybarger, "Finally Seeing Andrea," *Boston Review*, February 23, 2019; Maryse Meijer, "How to Fuck Your Neighbor," *Los Angeles Times*, April 23, 2019; Elaine Blair, "Fighting for Her Life," *New York Review of Books*, June 27, 2019; and Charlotte Shane, "What Men Want," *Dissent*, Spring 2019.

Yet even some of these respectful appreciations continue to repeat some dated misrepresentations. For example, Moira Donegan in *BOOKFORUM* claims that Andrea and Kitty "partnered with religious and social conservatives . . . working together to try to get" the ordinance passed. They *never* worked together. Nor did Andrea (as Donegan has it) try "to wield the power of the state against pornography." The precise opposite is true: she and Kitty designed the ordinance to allow for *civil* (not criminal) cases, thereby deliberately circumventing any prospect of involving or augmenting governmental power.

Index

The abbreviation AD refers to Andrea Dworkin.

AD's relationship with, 35–39, 40, 41–42, 106
AD's separation from, 58–59, 61
de Bruin, Cornelius Dirk (Iwan)
criminal charges against, 61, 296n6
hiding U.S. military deserters, 64
as Provo movement member, 36–37, 41
remarriage of, 61
de Bruin, Martin, 41
Deep Throat (film), 156, 157, 309n8
Dellinger, Dave, 91
Deming, Barbara
AD on television show of, 5
AD's *Our Blood* dedicated to, 96
AD's relationship with, 77–78, 79, 80, 81, 83, 96, 98–100, 265, 300–301n35, 300nn31, 34, 302n14
on AD's relationship with John Stoltenberg, 299n25
on AD's *Woman Hating*, 69, 77, 78
pamphlets written by, 140
Prison Notes, 5, 78
on Adrienne Rich, 300n28
on *Snuff*, 91
and Ellen Willis, 154
on Women's Anti-Defamation League statement, 112
Women's Fund of, 99–100
Democratic Organizing Socialist Committee, 120
Democratic Party, 152
democratic socialism, 120
Denfield, Rene, 327n17
Denmark, 224
Dershowitz, Alan, 155–56
Dewhurst, Colleen, 205
Diana Foundation, 254–55
Diehl, Digby, 95
Dietz, Park Elliott, 206–7
Dines, Gail, 315n28, 322n23, 327n17
Divine Light, 70
Dodson, Betty, 70
Doe v. Commonwealth (1976), 87
The Dog Collar Murders (detective story), 230–31
Donahue, Phil, 213, 214, 216
Donegan, Moira, 328n17
Donnerstein, Edward, 133, 175, 178,

182, 208, 242, 306n11, 313n24, 318n11
Dorfman, Elsa, 109, 155, 294n16
Doubleday, 138, 142, 229, 231
Duberman, Martin
on AD's androgynous view of gender, 72–73
AD's friendship with, 66, 68, 101, 109, 234–35, 297nn12, 13, 298n14
on AD's *Woman Hating*, 297–98n14
and Norman Mailer, 299n23
Duffy, Paula, 263
Duggan, Lisa, 176, 183–84
Dutton, 68, 222, 226, 228, 231, 298n14
Dworkin, Andrea
death of, 285–86
family background of, 6, 7, 9, 137, 250
personal characteristics of, 10, 74, 98, 155, 178, 233–34, 259, 264–65, 277, 280, 286, 287, 305n18, 309n4
pets of, 55, 59, 61, 66, 75, 297n11
as secular American Jew, 6–7, 8, 137, 249, 250, 251
sense of privacy, 9, 21, 27, 30, 60
temperament of, 35, 50, 165, 220–21, 238, 245, 266
—CAREER AS WRITER
AD's identity as feminist writer, 80–81
on Amerikan ignorance, 16
in Amsterdam, 33–35, 36, 39, 42–43, 57–60, 293n7
on battered women, 122–23, 225–27, 262–63
Phyllis Chesler's accusation of plagiarism, 123–24
contract that works could not be changed, 101
critiques on AD's work, 220–21, 259, 287, 300n34, 327n17
on feminism, 80–81
finances of, 60, 65, 66, 77, 87, 89, 96, 99–100, 102, 109–11, 117, 125, 132, 138, 141–43, 145, 158, 159–60, 171, 179, 202, 220, 222–23, 225, 230, 240, 254, 274, 281
in Greece, 18, 20–22, 26

About the Author

Martin Duberman is Distinguished Professor of History Emeritus at City University of New York, where he founded and directed the Center for Lesbian and Gay Studies. He is the author of numerous histories, biographies, memoirs, essays, plays, and novels, which include *Cures: A Gay Man's Odyssey*, *Paul Robeson*, *Stonewall*, *Black Mountain: An Exploration in Community*, *The Worlds of Lincoln Kirstein*, *Saving Remnant*, *Hold Tight Gently*, and more than a dozen others. He is the recipient of the Bancroft Prize, multiple Lambda Literary Awards, and the Lifetime Achievement Award from the American Historical Association, and he has been a finalist for the Pulitzer Prize and the National Book Award. In 2012, Duberman received an honorary Doctor of Humane Letters from Amherst College and in 2017 an honorary Doctor of Letters from Columbia University.

Publishing in the Public Interest

Thank you for reading this book published by The New Press. The New Press is a nonprofit, public interest publisher. New Press books and authors play a crucial role in sparking conversations about the key political and social issues of our day.

We hope you enjoyed this book and that you will stay in touch with The New Press. Here are a few ways to stay up to date with our books, events, and the issues we cover:

- Sign up at www.thenewpress.com/subscribe to receive updates on New Press authors and issues and to be notified about local events
- Like us on Facebook: www.facebook.com/newpressbooks
- Follow us on Twitter: www.twitter.com/thenewpress

Please consider buying New Press books for yourself; for friends and family; or to donate to schools, libraries, community centers, prison libraries, and other organizations involved with the issues our authors write about.

The New Press is a 501(c)(3) nonprofit organization. You can also support our work with a tax-deductible gift by visiting www.thenewpress.com/donate.